WHY JACQUES, JOHANN AND JAN CAN READ

WHY JACQUES, JOHANN AND JAN CAN READ

(August 15, 1979, Revised September 8, 2004)

By
Geraldine E. Rodgers

"Why Jacques, Johann and Jan CAN Read," by Geraldine E. Rodgers. ISBN 978-1-60264-179-2.

Published 2008 by Virtualbookworm.com Publishing Inc., P.O. Box 9949, College Station, TX 77842, US. ©2008, Geraldine E. Rodgers. All rights reserved. No part of this publication may be reproduced, stored in a retrieval system, or transmitted in any form or by any means, electronic, mechanical, recording or otherwise, without the prior written permission of Geraldine E. Rodgers.

Manufactured in the United States of America.

Table of Contents

FOREWORD i
CHAPTER 1 The Problem and Its Background 1
CHAPTER 2 On the Definition of Reading and on Prior Oral Reading Research 7
CHAPTER 3 On the Nature of the Test That Was Used 25
CHAPTER 4 Anecdotal Log on European School Visits 33
    Luxembourg 33
    Brussels 40
    Amsterdam 47
    Stockholm 71
    Hamburg 89
    Innsbruck 98
    Paris 102
    Quimper 108
    Avignon 115
CHAPTER 5 Anecdotal Log on American School Visits 130
Phonic Groups:
    Lippincott 130
    Open Court 138
    Economy 146
    Alpha One Letter People 149
    Initial Teaching Alphabet 151
Sight-Word Groups:
    Houghton, Mifflin 154
    Scott, Foresman 171
CHAPTER 6 On the Methods Used in This Research 183
    Some Tests Which Demonstrate How Misleading an Average Can Be 188
CHAPTER 7 On the Results 193
    Concerning The Total Scores 193
    Concerning Certain Individual Scores 194
    The Pattern of Scores Was the Result of the Teaching Method Used 197
    Concerning the Speed of Reading 198

On Outside Factors Which Can Affect Achievement 200

CHAPTER 8 The Test Results Show Not Just One Kind of Reader, But Two Different and Opposite Kinds, or Mixtures of Those Kinds 202

CHAPTER 9 The Data Suggests That Black Children Become the Best Readers When They Are Taught by Phonics 217

CHAPTER 10 On the Superior Reading of Phonics-Taught Swedish and Dutch Sixth-Grade Students 223

CHAPTER 11 Further Supporting Data Confirming the Existence of Different and Opposite Kinds of Readers 229

CHAPTER 12 *Conclusion* 235

APPENDIX 1 *American Sight-Word Programs Have Been Exported Around the World Because W. S. Gray Seeded UNESCO With His Errors* 237

APPENDIX 2 *French Language Primers - Belgium and France* 243

APPENDIX 3 250

FOREWORD

The original text of this book was rushed to completion in 1979, even though it badly needed editing and revision. The reason for the rush was that I wished to put my 1977-1978 research data on the oral reading accuracy of children in America and Europe on the record before others did so, since others would surely realize the need for such data. The rush was certainly not warranted because, so far as I know, in the intervening 25 years, no one has attempted to do anything like it.

The original, badly organized version of this book was submitted to an editor at Harper & Row in the late summer of 1979, the same editor who had handled the works of Dr. Rudolf Flesch who wrote the blockbuster 1955 book, Why Johnny Can't Read. My travel-agent sister had arranged the appointment through an old client of hers, an officer of Harper & Row. That editor rejected my text - most emphatically, but partly because my typewriter ribbon had been faint and he had just had (old-style!) cataract surgery. Yet a new ribbon would not have helped, I feel sure.

In November, 1979, I sent a short review of my research to Dr. Rudolf Flesch and he found the content of that paper of interest. We started a correspondence, and, about January or so of 1980, Dr. Flesch spoke to the president of Prentice-Hall and asked him to have his company review my book, of which Dr. Flesch had seen only excerpts. (Those excerpts had resulted in Dr. Flesch's comment to me that I couldn't write, and should meekly acquiesce to any editing suggestions I should receive.) The president agreed to Dr. Flesch's request to have his company consider the book, and so, off went the book again, to the Prentice-Hall editor whose name I had been given. A month or so later, back the book came again, as unacceptable. I do not blame Prentice-Hall. The book did most desperately need editing and revision.

In the intervening 25 years I have written many papers and books based on later exceedingly heavy library research, but I have regretted that my massive sabbatical oral reading research has remained unpublished. The basic finding of my 1977-1978 oral reading accuracy research was that two different and opposite kinds of readers (or mixtures of those kinds) result from the methods used to teach first-grade reading: sight-word, global "meaning" or phonic (or syllabic) "sound." Those research results are as valid today - and will be as valid in a hundred years - as they were 25 years ago. Therefore, I still want my research data on the record, and so have finally done the badly needed editing and revision of my original text and I am now finally publishing it.

Because the text and the data are a kind of "snapshot" in time for the years of 1977, 1978, and 1979, I do not want to do anything to alter that time frame. As a result, very few comments have been added to my original text from information that I developed later. That later information can be found in my papers and books written after 1979. One of the most recent is my 2003 book, The Born Yesterday World of the Reading Experts, A Critique of Recent Research on Reading and the Brain. That 2003 book discusses the brain-based origin for the two different and opposite conditioned reading reflexes (or mixtures of those reflexes), the discovery of which was the major finding of my 1977-1978 sabbatical research.

It should be mentioned that the 1977-1978, truly phonic, ITA, Lippincott and Open Court American materials are no more. It is true that a present-day, very weak phonic program carries the Open Court name, but it is in no sense comparable to the 1977-1978 Open Court program, and even gives some sight words to rank beginners.

One further comment is in order, and it concerns the title of this work, <u>Why Jacques, Johann and Jan CAN Read.</u> My European research data from the late fall of 1977 showed that European students could, indeed, read back then, when they were taught dominantly by phonic or syllabic "sound". Yet my friend in Paris, John McNulty, has told me that, unlike the Jacques of 1979, the Jacques of 2004 often CANNOT read. That is because most beginners in France are now being taught to read by the sight-word, global "meaning" of print, instead of by its "sound". It is my hope that my "snapshots" from the French first-grades in the late fall of 1977, when beginners were being taught successfully by the "sound" of print, may possibly be of some help in changing that exceedingly regrettable situation.

It is encouraging that an excellent Parisian website, <u>lire-ecrire.org</u>, is currently reporting on the literacy problem that has arisen in France as a result of following the advice of education "experts." Presumably, the reason the French schools switched to the sight-word, global "meaning" method (though, curiously, they deny it IS the global method) was because such "experts" counseled them, in effect, to do so. Yet schools, and the public in general, should take great care to avoid being duped by the Myth of Competence, which is to assume, without hard evidence, that the "experts" in ANY field know what they are doing.

CHAPTER 1
The Problem and Its Background

"Eeny, meeny, miney, mo," chanted by children today is burned into our cultural consciousness. Perhaps the story is true that it is because that chant was used by the Celtic Druid priests, of the oak tree and the holly, in selecting their victims from assembled young adults. Those victims reportedly sometimes died of fright on the way to the human sacrifices. Whether the particular legend is true or not, it is certain from other reports that the Celts of two thousand years ago were a very grim lot.

A later, and also disturbing, group in history were the Vikings. Longfellow has his Baltic Viking speak in the poem, <u>Skeleton in Armor</u>:

> But, when I older grew,
> Joining a corsair's crew,
> O'er the dark sea I flew,
> With the marauders.
>
> Wild was the life we led,
> Many the souls that sped,
> Many the hearts that bled,
> By our stern orders.

Yet now, over a thousand years later, in 1977, I was sitting in a beautifully appointed living room in Sweden, far removed from the Celts and Vikings of past, dead ages. The lovely furnishings included some old family pieces polished so that the wood gleamed. I was having tea in the presence of my highly educated, cosmopolitan hosts. But they were descendants of such Vikings, and I was an American descendent of Irish Celts. It was true that they, like the Viking of Longfellow, could say, truthfully, "O'er the dark sea we flew," but they had done it on a liner like the Queen Elizabeth II where they had dressed formally for dinner while on their way to America to visit and study American schools.

Their grown son showed us something from his collections, a replica of a Viking helmet. He put it on and, standing right in front of me, was an exact reproduction of a Viking of old - blond, tall, and handsome, but not fierce, just friendly. It struck me that in the frames of these people were virtually the identical genes of the old Vikings from over a thousand years ago, of whom Christian Europe used to pray, "From the fury of the Norsemen, O, Lord, deliver us!" In my body were the genes of the old Celts of some two thousand years ago, with their often loathsome practices. What was the difference between us and these grim ancestors of ours, since we had their same physical inheritance? The difference was culture, and only culture! We were now all members of Western Civilization, with its Judeo-Christian heritage.

But this culture of ours is a living thing. It was born, and it can die. Konrad Lorenz made this point when he differentiated between human culture and animal behavior. Animals pass on the behavior patterns necessary for their survival either through instinct or direct imitation of parents. But the complexities of our Western Civilization could never survive from one generation to another by any process so simple. We now depend on the written word.

If Einstein had been denied access to our written cultural heritage, there could have been no relativity theory. Denied even a spoken access to our cultural heritage, he would have been just a Tarzan of the apes.

Human culture, then, unlike animal behavior, is a living, growing thing, generated by a civilization. It is passed on through training. If we remove the training, the culture obviously dies. The fabric of our Western civilization - all its inherited knowledge and culture - is dependent on transmission from one generation to another to survive, but, as our civilization has become more and more complex, more and more of our culture has had to be passed on, not just by the spoken word, but by the written word. The written word has therefore become the critical factor on which the survival and progress of our Western civilization depends.

The uniformity of this living Western culture of ours is impressive, considering the vast area it covers. Something else that is striking is that all of us in our 20th Century Western civilization are closer to each other, despite our national differences, than we are to our own ancestors. We are embedded in our own age which has its own particular stage in culture. Our real relatives are our age-mates in this time and culture, not our long-ago ancestors.

We tend to forget that "family" is something that is not just limited in space but also in time. Mathematically, our ancestors of 200 years ago are very distant relatives, since eight generations back produce 256 common ancestors in that generation. Obviously, every generation further back doubles our ancestors, and the effect of doubling is notorious. Actually, our ancestors of 500 or 600 years ago have to be looked at simply as a common gene pool, and not as relatives at all. Twenty-four generations back, or 600 years ago, produces 16,777,216 common ancestors in that generation! For small countries like Sweden or Ireland, it would be possible for a present-day descendant to say he is related to everyone who lived in that country in the 1300's, when the population was probably less than a million, at least SIXTEEN TIMES!

The important thing to remember, therefore, is that it was each of these generations <u>as a whole</u> which inherited and slightly altered the common cultural heritage before passing it on to the next, as a ball can be passed over the heads of a crowd but altered in the process. It is now our turn, collectively, to pass this ball of culture on to the next generation. Since, at its present stage of development, our culture is now desperately dependent on literacy for transmission, and since literacy in the United States is below acceptable standards, we in America are in danger of mortally wounding our cultural heritage. By the ripple effect, any problems in the United States should ultimately affect other Western nations.

Concerning our further progress (and survival!), it is almost self-evident that our exploding population is aimed at the stars. Isaac Asimov has written much fiction on the prospect of populating deep space, including the use of propelled asteroids hollowed out for habitation - New Earths, of a kind. The prospect of space colonies is no longer just conjecture. Gerard O'Neill of Princeton, with others, is working on a solid, pilot program envisioning practical colonies in space. But no such stage in our Western Civilization can possibly be achieved except with a SUPER-literate society! We can no longer be content just to maintain our literacy level, and we certainly cannot permit it to backslide, since our survival may well depend on increasing it.

It is highly civilized and technically-advanced countries which will produce the "thrust" to populate and successfully to manage something like Gerard O'Neill's projected "space colonies" which eventually will have a universe in which to expand. From such pressing future demands of an increasingly technological society come the terrible urgencies facing our schools, which are how best to transmit our culture and how best to increase learning opportunities. However, if the educational process is short-circuited by border-line literacy, we may instead kill our culture. Our culture's survival, therefore, now depends on basic literacy.

Yet the record shows that basic literacy has declined - and the readability levels of children's books is one of the indications. Some of the best selling books of all time, which appeared in the late nineteenth and early twentieth centuries, were the Horatio Alger novels. They all have the same theme. A deserving boy succeeds against all odds by hard work and virtue. The Store Boy, or the Fortunes of Ben Barclay, was published by Alger in New York in 1874. By today's Fry readability guide, it has a Fry estimated readability level, based on the six samples I took, of 8th grade. One hundred years ago, when the book was published, the average educational level in the United States was considerably below 8th grade. Yet Horatio Alger was an author of best-selling books to adolescent children, many of 8th grade age, who paid for the books, in all probability, with money they earned themselves, since most of them had to leave school long before 8th grade.

Besides the fact that by today's standards the "readability" is high on Alger's books, which "readability" only reflects sentence length plus multi-syllable words, the multisyllable words tended to be uncommon ones. They were real vocabulary stretchers for adolescents, such as "vociferously," "accession," "imprudent," and even "verdancy". I had to look that last one up myself to be sure it had something to do with "verdant." It did - means greenness, or immaturity. Yet the armies of boys and girls who never went as far as eighth grade years ago read these books with gusto - at what reading specialists now would call their "independent," not "instructional" level of reading.

Among the poor boys who read them, most of them were unsung, but they built a magnificently solid United States where the railroads and the subways and the post offices and the cars and the appliances WORKED when you used them, and you were not cheated half out of your wits when you were not looking. Some of the poor boys, however, were later not so "unsung." According to the notes on the above edition, some of those "boys" were Henry Ford, Thomas Edison, David Sarnoff, James A. Farley, George Eastman, John D. Rockefeller, General Goethals and many, many others. In S. N. Behrman's delightful introduction to Strive and Succeed, (Holt, Rinehard and Winston, New York, 1967), which reprinted two Alger novels, The Store Boy being one, Behrman referred to the concept which he believed Horatio Alger had added to the composition of the American image:

> "The Algerian concept of the infinite possibility in this country for the enterprising, and, if you take Alger's word for it, the virtuous, is persistent and inescapable, either for panegyric or disparagement."

Also, he said:

> "Alger believed in the basic moral axioms; he insisted constantly upon their truth and observance. Those who, in his books, violate them come to a bad end."

Behrman also states the indisputable fact, "Alger's books were written for juveniles."

Three years ago, I took a college course in literature for adolescents. During the course, I learned that today there is a good market for books written specifically for adolescents, but the nature of a great many of these books was a revelation to me. First, concerning readability, from samples I took from six such books at the time, using the Fogg readability formula, these books which were written for adolescents of perhaps 13 to 16 years old had readability levels sometimes as low as the 4th grade, averaging 6th, compared to Alger's 7th to 11th grade, averaging the 8th

grade level, using the Fry formula. Not only has the readability level dropped, but so have the "basic moral axioms." It is called "realism" because we are not supposed to "shield" adolescents. Behrman stated he had read practically all of Horatio Alger's books before he was 14 (simultaneously independently reading Shakespeare!), but running across them today was like "taking a shower bath in innocence." They form quite a contrast to much of the raunchy material that passes as adolescent literature today. Some of the content of today's adolescent books is so out of line with normally spoken conversation that I find it unsuitable to refer to here.

These books, however, although they sell, are not "best sellers." No adolescent books today are "best sellers." But Alger's were - and to a market of boys and girls, most of whom had left school by 6th grade! Certainly his books were more objectively appealing than much of the dreary tripe sold to adolescents today, much of which has had good "reviews" and is "technically" good. No one seems to worry much about its being seedy or so tiresomely lugubrious. Laughter seems to have gone out of style, and everything is in deadly - oh, so deadly! - earnest. But it is not just a question of Alger's having produced a better product. He was dealing with a different market. His market could really READ!

In 1955, Rudolph Flesch was the first one to shout out, concerning reading, that there was a fox in with the chickens. He wrote the landmark book, Why Johnny Can't Read. His thesis was simple. Children taught by a sight- word approach may be crippled readers or non-readers. Instead, children should be taught to read by phonics or letter sounds, not whole words. His book was greatly derided by the reading "experts." He was characterized in the reading instruction literature as an outsider in their field of reading instruction. Actually, he never had any connection with primary reading except for teaching his own children to read, but he had fathered one of the earliest and most prestigious "readability" formulas used to determine the grade level of books. His 1955 book, Why Johnny Can't Read, remains one of the most readable and informative in the literature.

The sight-word approach opposed by Flesch was later modified somewhat by the addition of more phony phonics after his 1955 book was published, (and as a result of the uproar that followed the publication of his book) so there was some slight improvement.

However, the pre-1955 use had left fossilized tracks in the statistics of the 1952 New Iowa Spelling Scale. The scale had been arrived at by testing 30,000 American children. Listed below are some of the test words at the third grade and fourth grade levels. Most are phonically regular and most can be spelled correctly by most phonically taught first graders before the end of first grade. After each word is indicated the percentage of U. S. children in 1952 at 3_{rd} and 4th grade levels who were able to spell each word. What is appalling is that each figure implies the number of children who could NOT spell each word.

	Percentage of Children Who Could Spell Words	
	Beginning Third Grade	Beginning Fourth Grade
tan	53	73
lift	26	55
pin	33	68
pine	40	66
stood	24	49
picture	10	40
spot	50	68
straight	1	12
such	21	58
steps	33	46

spell (!)	48	70
number	25	62
dish	34	70
garden	30	62
strange	7	42

The highest percentage of correct responses on this list came on the spelling of the word, "tan," a phonically regular word, yet the percentage of children who could spell it was still dismally low -only 73% at fourth grade! That means that, after three years of reading "instruction," at beginning 4th grade, 27% of the thousands of American children taking this fourth grade level test, could not spell even this simplest of words. Yet virtually all of my first-graders could spell such simple words correctly by Halloween in the first grade year. The 4th grade results given above are appalling.

A slight increase in phonics instruction appeared in programs after Flesch's block-buster book was published in 1955, but the reverse is now happening. Now a highly vocal anti-phonics propaganda movement is under way.

It has been called by Dr. Patrick Groff of San Diego State University "The New Anti-Phonics." There are two principal proponents. One is Kenneth Goodman, a psycholinguist, and the other is the psycholinguist, Frank Smith, of Ontario. Smith made the startling statement:

> "Fluent readers rarely read word for word, even when reading aloud. Professional speakers and news readers make frequent 'errors' at the word level, but these misreadings are unimportant because meaning is retained.... Usually only actors, singers and poetry readers attempt word-perfect reading, and such an accomplishment always demands rehearsal."

This quotation occurs in Smith's 1978 book, <u>Psycholinguistics and Reading.</u> I do not doubt at all that what Smith says about oral reading with "frequent" errors is true of some of his age-mates and himself, who were all raised with the sight-word method and are therefore disabled readers. But Smith should speak only for himself. It is not true for me nor most of the generations preceding me. People in my age-group do not like it at all when someone of Smith's age gets up to read aloud while we are following silently. Their jarring errors very much interfere with our concentration.

Dr. Patrick Groff of San Diego University stated in his article, "The New Anti-Phonics", which appeared in The <u>Elementary School Journal,</u> March, 1977, page 236:

> "This group is spearheaded by Frank Smith, whose book on reading provides the theory and the rationale for this new anti-phonics movement, and by Kenneth Goodman, who censures phonics in most of his writings about the techniques of reading instruction. In Smith's two books on reading, he makes clear his belief that phonics is the 'great fallacy' of beginning reading instruction. One of his 'Twelve Easy Ways to Make Learning to Read Difficult,' is to 'ensure that phonics skills are learned and used.' Goodman agrees that 'phonics in any form in reading instruction is at best a peripheral concern.' Obviously, the new anti-phonics evaluates the usefulness of phonics in a way fundamentally different than its traditional opponents. The latter opposed only the teaching of phonics early and intensively in the reading program. The new anti-phonics movement would ban phonics instruction

entirely from any level of the teaching of reading."

Of course, neither Smith nor Goodman have been first-grade teachers, or teachers at any elementary school level, where reading is actually taught, and not just "discussed." That seems to be the norm for such "experts." I suppose it is akin to Gilbert and Sullivan's Pinafore ditty: "Stick close to your desks and never go to sea, and you can be the ruler of the Queen's Na - vy!"

Dr. Groff presented explicit objections to the Smith and Goodman approaches and concluded that research contradicts them.

Despite Frank Smith's apparent conclusion that oral reading is rather pointless, it is my conviction that, if you want to know how well a child reads, you ask him to sit down and read aloud to you. But this has not been the conclusion of those who test children in reading. Oral tests, except to uncover types of errors, have been in relative disrepute for many, many years. "Experts" conclude, if you want to test a group's reading ability, you give standardized tests, and sit a city of children down with printed test papers and pencils, and the children mark little black dots on the papers, which you feed into a computer, and the computer then tells how well they all read.

Standardized tests and academic disputes on reading theory are not, however, the point of view from which I have been viewing reading instruction over the years. Here is where I am in a position completely different from that of theorists like Frank Smith and Kenneth Goodman, who deliver papers at conferences, which everyone present discusses later over cocktails and dinner.

Instead of dealing with "theory" about sight words and phonics, I have been dealing with the effects of one or the other on little children. Indisputably, the worth of one little child outweighs all the arguments. Children of school age care terribly when they cannot read. Their sense of worth suffers dreadfully. If you ask a child what "to read" means, he will not have a bit of the trouble that the "experts" like Goodman and Smith have with the definition. He will answer you very simply. To him, to read means to be able to say the words on the page in front of him. If he cannot say the words, he KNOWS he cannot read!

Our American prisons tell a sorry tale. The bulk of the offenders are only semi-literate. It has been a truism for years that many boys who are reading problems become behavior problems. They are hurting. But the small percentage (perhaps ten?) of boys who become behavior problems because of reading problems are dismissed by some reading "experts" as breakage is dismissed in a china factory. After all, nothing is perfect. It is we teachers who have to deal with these unfortunate children whom we remember with great clarity. They are never just "statistics" to us. "Experts," however, are concerned with large numbers and "significant differences."

However, it was significant enough, I felt, that in 1978, a very long 23 years after Flesch published his 1955 blockbuster best-selling book calling for reading reform, that there were angry columns in the <u>New York Post</u> about high school students who still could not read.

I decided to see for myself what was going on in the teaching of other first grades in this country and in Europe. To test the second graders in these same schools, I would need a simple oral test - certainly not a silent one. Then I could compare the results from the different approaches - those toward the sight-word/global end of the scale to those towards the phonics end. Then, if the hard statistical data favored phonics, as I believed it would, such proof might help to motivate schools and teachers finally to discard the sight-word approach which I felt had crippled so many children and which I was convinced was the primary cause of our literacy problem.

But, first, before deciding on my oral test form, I had to find out what kind of oral reading research had been done before me, and this concerned also the definition of reading. I set myself to a review of the literature on these last two points.

CHAPTER 2
On the Definition of Reading and on Prior Oral Reading Research

"A man received a letter in a foreign language that he spoke fluently but could not read. He had a friend who could make the sounds indicated by the writing, but who understood nary a word. (This, incidentally, is not strange to those who have learned the ritual use of Hebrew or Latin.) The man who received the letter took it to his friend who said the words that gave joy to the recipient of the missive. Which one was reading?"

Harry Levin recounted this anecdote in Reading Research - What, Why and For Whom (1966). Obviously, it concerns the highly disputed question, "What IS the definition of reading?"

It is from the definition of reading that most of the disagreements about teaching beginning reading have arisen and from which oral reading tests fell into relative disrepute. In order to understand why there are so few oral tests in research in former years comparing the phonics method to the sight-word method, it is necessary to examine these varying definitions of reading.

Harris and Sipay wrote on page 5 of their teacher-college text, "Most reading specialists regard reading as a synthesis of recognizing and comprehending, in which the absence of either makes true reading impossible."

But, if this definition is true, then neither man "read" anything in Levin's anecdote, which is obviously ridiculous.

Albert J. Harris and Edward R. Sipay co-authored the sixth edition of the teacher-college text, How to Increase Reading Ability, David McKay Company, Inc., New York, 1975. The first edition was in 1940. Harris is also the senior author on the Macmillan reading series which teaches sight words and what can be called "incidental" phonics. That means the blending of parts of known sight words to decode new words, with the aid of the meaning of the context in which the unknown word occurs.

Concerning decoding print (which Harris and Sipay call "recognizing") and comprehension, how easy is it to "read" this: "$2 + 4 = 6$"? Now, how easy is it to "read" this "$E = MC^2$" (with the two elevated in the "squared" position)? Both can be "read" in the simple decoding sense by any first grader. (Belgian first-graders who work with the Cuisenaire rods would even be able to read the elevated "2" as "squared".) First-graders can "read" both in the decoding sense but can only understand the former. Even the vast majority of adults are unable truly to comprehend the latter equation. Though some know in a general sense that it means that the energy in matter is equal to its mass times the speed of light squared, most of them feel very uncomfortable with the whole thing, particularly with its pat and incomprehensible neatness. They know better than to ask, "All right, WHY does E=MC2?", as the first-grader might much more confidently ask, "Why does $2 + 4 = 6$?" Does that mean that we adults cannot "read" "$E = MC2$"? Does it mean that our "reading" comprehension is less than Einstein's, who fathered this little statement with its booby-trap simplicity? What is lacking is not our "reading" comprehension, but solely our comprehension!

Arrogant reading theorists have defined "reading" as something that includes every complex operation of the human mind. Yet the human mind existed for untold ages before the "reading" of print became possible, and the human mind managed, without the reading of print, to produce the wheel and the use of fire and myths and world trade and a considerable body of other accomplishments. We have no record of a written language at Stonehenge, but we can see now from the stone monuments that a people lived there once who had an extraordinary understanding of astronomy. The same can be said of the Mayans

Printed matter is not something esoteric. It is no more and nor less than speech recorded in ink. To "read" it, we must decode the speech. To UNDERSTAND speech, however, is something vastly different from decoding it, whether the speech we decode is spoken or written! In comprehension of speech, we draw on our prior knowledge, our judgment, our intuitions, and even more. But we do this in comprehending ANYTHING, not just speech: the stone monuments at Stonehenge, the pattern of the waves on the sand, the motions of the stars, the expressions on our friends' faces, and rumbling in the sky - to distinguish among thunder, jet planes, or guns.

"Reading" comprehension is nothing more nor less than "comprehension." It is built on prior experiences, knowledge, and vocabulary. It is the very purpose of the school to expand on these. If a child is truly educated in history, geography, science, mathematics, art, music, and - most of all - literature, his so-called "reading comprehension" had to grow because his over-all comprehension has grown.

Yet, when listening to speech, if a hearer's attention is not on what is being said, his comprehension will be almost nil. If a person reads with such wandering attention, his so-called "reading comprehension" will also be almost nil. The critical factor of paying attention - or not paying attention - is never mentioned in materials pretending to teach so-called "reading comprehension."

Rudolph Flesch wrote, "I once surprised a native of Prague by reading aloud from a Czech newspaper. 'Oh, you know Czech?' he asked. 'No, I don't understand a word of it,' I answered. 'I can only read it.'" (This was on page 23, Why Johnny Can't Read, 1955, and was cited by Harris and Sipay on page 5 of their text).

Harris and Sipay's reaction to this, from the standpoint of the definition of reading they gave, was that Flesch was "making noises, not reading" (Harris and Sipay, page 5).

Some linguists, however, are on Flesch's side. David W. Reed said, "Anyone who has learned to read can read many sentences whose meanings are almost completely unknown to him" ("A Theory of Language, Speech and Writing," Elementary English, December, 1965, page 847, cited by Harris and Sipay on page 5 of their text).

Kenneth Goodman, the psycholinguist, and one of the authors on the Scott, Foresman sight-word reading series, said, "Reading is a selective process. It involves partial use of available minimal language cues selected from perceptual input on the basis of the reader's expectation. As this partial information is processed, tentative decisions are made to be confirmed, rejected, or refined as reading progresses." (Reading, A Psycholinguistic Guessing Game, 1967, page 126).

Goodman is apparently saying that reading is principally the use of context to arrive at comprehension. Presumably, "available minimal language cues selected from perceptual input" means paying some attention to the print while engaging in the "Psycholinguistic Guessing Game," as Goodman puts it. Reading to Goodman, therefore, appears to be primarily guessing from context.

I am baffled by all this emphasis on context in reading, as if using context is peculiar to reading. Context is brought into play in almost every human experience. Sherlock Holmes' great achievements were just exercises in seeing details in a meaningful context. Of course, we use context all the time to understand spoken language. Quoting a sentence "out of context" is a notorious way to misrepresent someone's whole thought. Also, if someone slurs a word in speaking, we can very often infer it correctly from the context and the partially heard sounds. People who are going gradually deaf depend on the context of the flow of speech to decode the words they are continually hearing imperfectly. As they grow progressively deafer, however, the form of the word and the context itself becomes weaker and weaker. Then they miss so much of the meaning that communication breaks down.

Context is used to check word accuracy and to alter it where necessary in speech - and in print, as well, because, to beat a poor, dead horse, print is nothing BUT speech. If, in reading, a child decodes to a non-word, he knows he has to alter part of the sound - usually the vowel - to arrive at a word which fits the context. Of course, if he has been rendered partially "deaf" to print by sight-word methods, he is in the position of the deaf adult who is beset with many puzzling words and who must constantly strain agonizingly with the use of the context to decode the partly heard words.

Sight-word programs, like Goodman's, have crippled children in their decoding skills, claiming they are instead teaching "reading for meaning." We are aghast at deliberately "soring" Tennessee walking horses so that they have a pretty gait. Should we not be a great deal more aghast at reading programs which deliberately make little children partially "deaf" to print?

I never could fully appreciate myself what this sight-word dependency on context was like until I came to need reading glasses. Without my glasses now, print is rather blurry, and I find myself when trying to read without glasses making for the first time, at middle age, the kinds of reading errors that sight-word trained children do.

But, according to Goodman, reading is a guessing game. We guess what words are coming next from the words that came before.

Levin added the following to his anecdote about the letter:

> "I suggest that, as a first approximation, reading may be broken into two broad sub-skills. The first is the skill of decoding the writing system to its associated language...."
>
> "The second rubric of component skills in reading concerns... the many uses to which reading may be put.... comprehension, reading for different levels of meaning, reading for pleasure, and so forth. By dividing the process of reading into these two very broad categories, I am not implying that one is more important than the other or that emphasizing one skill excludes the other. I am frankly at a loss to understand the furor that this essentially bland statement arouses. To say that reading is really comprehension is like saying that ice skating is really performing figure eights." (Levin, ibid, 1966, p. 139-140.)

The only fault I have to find with Levin's conclusion is that he, too, seems to make reading into a set which includes the subset of comprehension, although he seems to say that first comes decoding and then comprehension. But, as said before, comprehension is common to all mental efforts, not just to reading. I do not see how words that reach the brain from translating printed symbols to sound (which is to say, from "reading") should be processed any differently in the brain from words that reach it directly from sound (which is to say, from "spoken language" without symbols as intermediaries). The fundamental nature of both is "sound". (Of course, this does not apply to the unfortunate readers who have been taught to read print like some deaf-mutes, as soundless, meaning-bearing "sight words").

People who strain at a definition of reading are trying to make reading into some sort of esoteric process. Did the brain develop new cells when writing was invented? Words which reach the brain through decoding print or through decoding heard sounds should be processed in thought in the same way. However, here, indeed, is the difficult field. To answer the question, "What is thought and how does it work?" has probably puzzled mankind since the beginning of time and probably will continue to puzzle mankind to the end of time, despite the enormous labors of linguists, psychologists, psycholinguists, philosophers and hosts of others. But, for reading specialists to make the definition of reading to include formally, as a subset OF ITSELF, the complex area of thought is insufferable arrogance.

It is self-evident that we should encourage children to use their powers of comprehension when they read, as in all activities, and certainly direct instruction is essential in forming proper habits of attention to what is read. Nevertheless, what we label "reading" is neither more nor less than decoding print into words, which should then be processed in thought in the same manner that spoken words are processed.

But, to those who saw reading as comprehension, decoding became an ugly stepchild. This, of course, occurred as the sight-word, or reading-for-meaning, approach took over from phonics, beginning in earnest about 1920, but not making a clean sweep till after 1930. The sight-word proponents buttressed their position, of course, by "proving" it with "research," which proof has been rather systematically discounted by Dr. Jeanne Chall in her 1967 book, Learning to Read: The Great Debate. To test for oral accuracy alone was considered largely a waste of time. During the ascendancy of pure sight-word programs in this country, before Dr. Rudolf Flesch wrote Why Johnny Can't Read in 1955, not only was little research of any kind done to test phonic vs. sight-word programs, but almost none of it included research on oral reading accuracy. Much derision was directed at children who were "word-callers" and who "barked at print." Silent reading selections, followed by comprehension questions, were the make-up of the test tools with status. Volumes and volumes of such tests have been completed, but very little even of these silent tests concerned the comparison of phonics programs to sight-word programs.

Concerning oral reading accuracy comparisons between phonics programs and sight word programs, no researcher ever had an easier time than I did in fulfilling the mandate, "Cite all pertinent previous research."

From 1912 to 1976, I could find in the literature in English only eleven such oral reading accuracy studies comparing sight-word programs to phonic programs. Although libraries are filled with volumes of other reading research, which is now completed at an estimated rate of a thousand a year, according to Dr. Jeanne Chall of Harvard, there are only a small number of oral reading accuracy studies of any kind. Yet only eleven of those oral reading accuracy studies are known to have compared phonics programs to sight-word programs. This is despite the fact that the two leading "authorities" in reading instruction from about 1917 to about 1960, William Scott Gray and Arthur Irving Gates, had been authors of oral reading accuracy tests long BEFORE they published their famous sight-word basal readers in 1930-1931, Gray's Scott, Foresman and Gates' Macmillan.

In his book, Why Johnny Can't Read (1955), Dr. Rudolph Flesch referred to the very few known studies before 1955 which compared phonics programs to sight-word programs, but only on some of them is it clear that they tested oral reading accuracy. Those studies are among the eleven to be reviewed later. However, on most of the rest of the small number of studies Flesch cited, he did not specifically state whether or not oral reading accuracy had not been tested. It appears unlikely that it was, but, in order to be thorough, those other studies Dr. Flesch mentioned are reviewed below very briefly.

One is a famous and often-cited study which was reported in December, 1916, in the Elementary School Journal (with a follow-up in 1923) by Lillian Beatrice Currier and Olive C. Duguid of Franklin, New Hampshire. These two women (apparently educators) listened to the oral reading of first- and second-grade children in Tilton, New Hampshire, some of whom had been taught by phonics, and some of whom had not been taught by phonics. Yet Currier and Duguid produced no statistics of any kind from their study and simply concluded that the non-phonics children read orally with more expression and interest, but the phonically-taught were more accurate. The vague nature of this "study" which is so mystifyingly famous disqualifies it as serious research.

Elmer K. Sexton and John S. Herron published an article entitled "The Newark Phonics Experiment" in Elementary School Journal, May, 1928. Their results, which may or may not have tested oral reading accuracy, favored instruction in phonics.

A study by Raymond M. Mosher and Sidney M. Newhall entitled "Phonic vs. Look-and-Say Training in Beginning Reading" was published in Journal of Education Psychology in October, 1930. Eight of their ten tests favored phonics.

An article in New York State Education, October, 1930, was written by Miss Helen R. Braem, Head Teacher at Letchworth Village, a state institution for mental defectives. For one year, she taught reading to boys with IQ's from 30 to 75, teaching some with sight-words and teaching others with phonics. At the end of the year, those with the sight- word approach had reportedly made three times as many mistakes and took three times as long to read. She then taught that sight-word group with phonics and they then achieved the accuracy of the phonic group. Whether the "accuracy" was tested with a silent written test or an oral test was not specified.

In the June, 1937 issue of Elementary School Journal, a study by Harry L. Tate was published under the title, "The Influence of Phonics on Silent Reading in Grade 1." Tate wrote, "Phonetic instruction and drill... is far superior to the look-and-say method in developing the ability to recognize words." As a "silent" test, oral reading accuracy should not have been covered.

In December, 1943, Dr. David H. Russell reported in Journal of Educational Research on a study of first and second-grade children, some taught phonics and the others little or none. Twelve different tests of reading and spelling were given. Russell concluded, "The table...clearly reveals that the early and rather direct type of instruction in the phonics group has a favorable influence on achievement in spelling and reading." Flesch commented on the inexplicable fact that Russell later became the senior author on the widely-used Ginn sight-word series. However, whether Russell gave oral reading accuracy tests in 1943 is unknown.

William Scott Gray had prepared his first standardized oral reading paragraphs for his master's thesis in 1914, directly under E. L. Thorndike at Columbia Teachers College. His tests were reviewed in the Teachers College Record in September, 1914, by Edward L. Thorndike in his article, "The Measurement of Ability in Reading." which also reviewed Thorndike's first silent reading comprehension tests. Gray published his revised oral reading paragraphs and his later statistical test results in his doctoral thesis at the University of Chicago in 1917 under Charles Hubbard Judd. Gates published his own oral reading accuracy tests and the results he obtained from them in a 1924 article in the Teachers College Record, Columbia Teachers College, "A Test of the Ability in the Pronunciation of Words." However, these very interesting oral reading accuracy test reports of Gates (in 1924) and Gray (in 1917) made no mention of comparing the sight-word approach to the phonics approach (although it is almost self-evident that Gray and Gates must have made such a comparison informally). However, a different report Gray made in 1917 did make such a comparison and that report is discussed later, and a 1927 report by Gates, discussed later, also attempted to do so.

By discounting the value of oral reading accuracy and inflating the value of what they called "silent reading comprehension," the post-1914 researchers largely cut off oral reading accuracy research between different teaching methods. Oral testing is used now largely to study types of reading errors, in something called "cloze" tests. A reader guesses at blacked-out words in a selection and is graded on the quality of his guesses. Good guessers equal good readers, according to this point of view.

My 1977-1978 study concerned the comparison of the oral reading accuracy of phonics-taught children to sightword-taught children, so it was necessary, for comparison, to search the literature for any similar studies that had been done previously. While it is possible that one or two of the few studies just mentioned may have included such an oral reading accuracy comparison between phonics and sight word teaching, the only way to find out would be to unearth the original research reports, but that has not been feasible. Therefore, aside from those very few possible comparisons, <u>only eleven studies which clearly compared the oral reading accuracy of phonics-trained children to sight-word trained children can be found in the literature before 1977-1978.</u>

It will not take long to summarize these eleven previous oral reading accuracy studies, most of which concluded that teaching reading by phonics is superior to teaching reading by sight-words. Those studies, of course, received little attention since the consensus has been that oral reading accuracy, by itself, means little or nothing.

The <u>first</u> such oral reading accuracy comparison between phonics-taught children and sight-word-taught children was made in 1917 by William Scott Gray. Gray discussed his testing years later on page 207 of his 1956 UNESCO book, <u>The Teaching of Reading and Writing.</u> In Cleveland, Ohio, in 1917, Gray had given oral tests on rate and accuracy in grades 1, 2, and 3. He did not report on the number of pupils tested in each grade, nor what he meant by his descriptions of the programs, nor did he produce (anywhere that I could find them) the statistics on his tests. However, it is probably safe to conclude that Gray did have some kind of firm statistics, unlike Currier and Duguid. Gray reported in his 1956 book:

> "26 schools used the Aldine Method, in which the reading of stories for meaning was emphasized."
>
> "17 schools used the Ward Method, in which phonics and word recognition were stressed, and one school used a method of its own."

Gray did not say that the widely used Aldine method did not also teach supplementary phonics, which it probably did since supplementary phonics was in heavy use in first grades in 1917. The widely used Ward method, however, did teach phonics directly in its texts. Gray said that both methods produced high-ranking schools and low-ranking schools and that "individual and class scores using the same method varied a great deal."

Yet, besides Gray's inadequate description of the programs, Gray showed no scores by which a comparison could be made by others to check his conclusions. The words, "varied a great deal" in the absence of his supporting data are largely meaningless. In his 1956 book, Gray cited, as his previously published reference to this 1917 research, pages 127-128 of "Studies of Elementary Reading Through Standardized Tests," <u>Supplementary Educational Monographs, No. 1,</u> Department of Education, University of Chicago, 1917. However, it is probable that Gray could not have given very precise data in that short 1917 reference, either, since it covered only two pages or less. It would have been very difficult to cite the oral accuracy statistics for 132 classes (three classes in 44 schools) and then to critique them adequately in no more than two pages, and probably less than two full pages. Gray's conclusions, therefore, are not specific and his definition of the programs tested is inadequate.

The <u>second</u> such study was reported by Dr. Jean Chall in her 1967 book, <u>Learning to Read: The Great Debate.</u> Dr. Jean Chall stated that in 1927 Arthur I. Gates did a study comparing the results from synthetic phonics to the results from intrinsic phonics. However, Gates later told Chall, as also reported in her 1967 book, <u>Learning to Read: The Great Debate,</u> that the intrinsic phonics programs were extremely well programmed, teaching the alphabet along with the words. Chall therefore felt that both groups had probably received similar amounts of decoding practice.

In April and May of first grade, Gates had found that both groups performed equally on a test of oral reading. However, Chall's reference to Gates' study also omitted concrete statistics.

The third study on oral reading which compared phonics programs to sight word programs, but the first with real statistics, was performed by W. H. Winch of England. It was reported in 1925 in Teaching Beginners to Read in England: Its Methods, Results and Psychological Bases, Journal of Educational Research Monographs, No. 8, Public School Publishing Company, Bloomington, Illinois. Winch compared English children under six who had been taught by look-say, phonics, and a special phonic system using diacritical marks on letters, called Hayes Phonoscript. The children who had been taught by the phonics systems read more accurately, and, if accuracy of words were considered, faster than the children with look-say. If the accuracy of words were not considered, the look-say children said more words in the time given than the phonics children, but they were not the words on the page. According to Chall, however, Winch's look-say was closer to our present linguistic programs. The children who had been taught by Phonoscript phonics did score better than those who had been taught by ordinary phonics.

The fourth study to be considered was done by S. C. Garrison and Miss Minnie Taylor Heard in 1931, reported as "An Experimental Study of the Value of Phonetics," Peabody Journal of Education, Vol. 9, pp. 9-14. Garrison and Heard gave oral tests, among other tests, to first-grade children in May and June. One group had been given 15 minutes a day of phonics and the other had received 15 minutes a day of Gates' intrinsic method. They reported that the intrinsic phonics group read better orally, but that the systematic phonics children did better on other parts of the testing. To "read better orally" may have only concerned reading with "expression". It may not have concerned oral reading accuracy. However, Dr. Rudolf Flesch reported on page 63 of Why Johnny Can't Read that the series of tests which included second grade as well as first had a total score, and that the phonics group's total score was 58.5 and the other group's total score was 55.5. Dr. Flesch also reported that Garrison and Heard said the phonics group did considerably better than the other in spelling.

The fifth oral reading research which compared systematic phonics to intrinsic phonics was completed in 1939, and it was the last such research in the literature until 1958. In 1939, Donald C. Agnew wrote his doctoral dissertation at Duke University in Durham, North Carolina (originally unpublished), titled The Effect of Varied Amounts of Phonetic Training on Primary Reading. He compared third-grade children in Raleigh, North Carolina, which had a sight-word program with intrinsic phonics to third-grade children in Durham, North Carolina, which had a systematic phonics program. Agnew gave the Gray Oral Reading Check Test, Set II and Set III. On Set II, the Durham phonics children made on the average 2.35 errors, but the sight-word Raleigh group made 8.79. On Set III, the Durham phonics children made 7.02 errors, and the Raleigh sight-word children 17.50. There was a marked advantage for the systematic phonics group. The scores for rate on these tests gave the phonics-trained Durham children a little over a minute to read each set, while the Raleigh sight-word group took considerably less than a minute. As Flesch put it, "... the little Raleigh word guessers took considerably less than one minute to make two to four times as many errors."

Agnew stated, "Should phonetic methods be employed in the teaching of primary reading? The answer to this question can be given only when the purposes for teaching primary reading have been agreed upon. If the basic purpose in the teaching of primary reading is the establishment of skills measured in this study (namely: independence in word recognition, ability to work out the sounds of new words, efficiency in word pronunciation, accuracy in oral reading, certain abilities in silent reading, and the ability to recognize a large vocabulary of written words, the investigations would support a policy of large amounts of phonic training. If on the other hand, the purposes of teaching primary reading are concerned with 'joy in reading,' 'social experience,' 'the pursuit of interests,' etc., the investigations reported offer no data as to the usefulness of phonetic training." (Published reference: Agnew, D. C., The Effect of Varied Amounts of Phonetic Training on Primary Reading, Duke University, Research Studies in Education, No. 5, Durham, North Carolina: Duke University Press, 1939).

Flesch's comment on the above in Why Johnny Can't Read was:

> "I can fully understand Mr. Agnew's outburst of sarcasm, since I worked my way through the same literature. It's exactly as he says: if you want to teach children how to read, you need phonics; if you just want to make them feel good, you don't."

Besides scoring better on oral reading accuracy, Agnew's phonics group scored better on vocabulary and on reading comprehension questions.

The sixth of these ten studies did not appear until 1958, almost twenty years after Agnew's 1939 report. Dr. Donald D. Durrell of Boston University, who is now the author of a first-grade supplemental phonics program, ran a large-scale cooperative study on beginning reading in general with the language arts staff of his school. Various students undertook separate aspects of the study. Durrell's student, Linehan, compared the reading achievement of children who had been given early instruction in letter names and sounds in grade 1 with children who had such instruction only incidentally during the year. Linehan gave both silent and oral tests in May or June of first grade. Her test on oral reading, pertinent to this research review, showed, as did all her other tests, that the children who had been trained in heavier phonics were superior, ("Early Instruction in Letter Names and Sounds as Related to Success in Beginning Reading", Journal of Education, Boston University, Vol. 140, pp. 44-48, 1958).

The seventh such study was done by R. D. Elder in 1966, A Comparison of the Oral Reading of Groups of Scottish and American Children. This was Elder's unpublished doctoral dissertation at the University of Michigan. Elder had compared the oral reading performance of Scottish third-grade children with two American samples of the same age and a year older. The Scottish children had been given more analytic training (heavier phonics) than the American children. Apparently, Elder's main purpose was to compare the differences in the KINDS of oral reading errors made by both groups, judging from the account of his work as reported in an article in Reading Research Quarterly. However, it was also stated that the Scottish phonically-trained children read more accurately orally, which is pertinent to this research review, compared to those their same age but second graders in this country. American third graders, a year older than Scottish, showed "no significant differences on the Gray Oral Paragraphs." However, the scores were reported as "mean achievement" and not ranked, and, as will be shown in the conclusion to this book, that can obscure very sharp differences. It should be mentioned that Dr. Dykstra's account of this study in the text, Teaching Reading, referred to elsewhere, is far clearer than the account in Reading Research Quarterly.

Concerning types of errors, it was evident that the American children were using the context to arrive at unknown words because their mistakes altered the meaning of the sentences less often. The Scottish children's errors changed the meaning of the sentences more often, and so it would seem apparent that they were concentrating on the form of the unknown word rather than guessing it from those around it.

It was implied however, in the Reading Research Quarterly summary used as a primary source for the information given above, that the American children's guesswork was more desirable behavior. Yet it was the Scottish children who had not abandoned the code in front of them, the printed word in question, to engage in creative guessing! As a teacher, I have frequently been appalled by something I have observed in children who had sight-word training. When they miss a word in reading, instead of studying it on the page, they will often gaze off into the distance to decide what the word might be. They are, of course, guessing from the context. It boils down to the old argument between sight-word vs. phonic camps about which of the following errors is more acceptable:

Two children have to read the sentence. "My father was in a battle." Neither one knows the word, "battle," and both read it incorrectly. The sight-word-trained child, remembering the part of the story which had been read before that word was encountered, reads the sentence as, "My father was in a war." The child who had been trained in phonics reads the sentence as, "My father was in a bottle." The sight-word-trained child who picked "war" is praised to the skies by the sight-word camp because he got the meaning. But the child who read "bottle" KNOWS he made a mistake. Before anyone can correct a mistake, he has to know that he made it, The sight-word-trained child, however, is not worried about the mistake but will grow to adulthood doing that same kind of thing over and over. If you doubt that, listen to some Americans who learned by the sight-word method as children, when they read aloud as adults.

The <u>eighth</u> study I picked up, not from my library research, or from the computerized search in the famous ERIC files for which I paid, but from a newspaper magazine advertisement! Bremner-Davis advertised their home-study course in phonics, which used phonograph records. They cited research to back their claims, so I sent for their data. The <u>Journal of Educational Psychology,</u> Vol. 49, No. 1, in 1958, had printed an article on page 28 by Carolyn Luser, Eileen Stanton and Charles I. Doyle of Loyola University, Chicago. These researchers had divided a sample of 214 third and fourth graders in an under-privileged area into two groups. The experimental group received 43 drill sessions in Bremner Davis phonics over a period of 15 weeks. The experimental group showed "significant" gains over the control group on <u>Gray's Oral Reading Paragraphs</u> and on tests of spelling, paragraph meaning, and a paper and pencil IQ test.

WHY WAS THIS RESEARCH NOT IN THE READING COMMUNITY'S LITERATURE AND READILY AVAILABLE? It is totally respectable on academic grounds. Why did I have to get it from a newspaper advertisement?

The <u>ninth</u> study was the U. S. Office of Education survey of first-grade reading programs in 1967, which was continued with some programs into second grade the following year.

The first-grade study was reported in "The Cooperative Research Program in First-Grade Reading Instruction," <u>Reading Research Quarterly,</u> Summer, 1967, International Reading Association, Newark, Delaware. The report was prepared by Dr. Guy L. Bond, Director of the Coordinating Center for the First-Grade Reading Studies, and Dr. Robert Dykstra, both of the University of Minnesota.

The later second-grade study was reported in "Summary of the Second-Grade Phase of the Cooperative Research Program in Primary Reading Instruction," by Dr. Robert Dykstra, Director of the Coordinating Center for the Follow- up of Studies in the USOE-Supported Cooperative Research Program in First-Grade Reading, Fall, 1968, <u>Reading Research Quarterly,</u> International Reading Association, Newark, Delaware. This second-grade report, however, contained no results on oral reading accuracy tests, which had been reported in the first-grade report.*

---

* About May of 1980 or 1981, I called Dr. Dykstra at his office in the University of Minnesota to ask if it would be possible to locate the second-grade oral reading accuracy data. Dr. Dykstra told me that it was not available. All of the final USOE test data had to be "treated" to adjust it for readiness of pupils, etc., but, someone had accidentally pushed the wrong button on the computer and wiped out all the "treated"second-grade USOE oral reading accuracy tests. The remarks given here concern only the first grade "treated" USOE data.

The original survey included 27 projects, each of which paired classes receiving a particular beginning instructional method in reading against classes receiving the standard basal reader approach. Some projects paired heavy phonics classes (such as Lippincott) against basal readers such as Scott, Foreman. Others paired the Initial Teaching Alphabet (ITA) classes against basal readers. Some paired what was called "basal plus phonics" against standard basals. Some paired linguistic methods against basals. Some paired what is called "language experience" (in which the children learn from stories written by them with teacher help) against standard basals.

Of all 27 projects, only six can be considered truly phonic: the three Lippincott, and only three of the five Initial Teaching Alphabet (ITA) projects. These three ITA programs used the ITA expanded-alphabet Early to Read series by Mazurkiewicz which presents phonic material in very much the same order as Lippincott. Two ITA programs were not heavily phonic. One was Hahn's, using the English Downing ITA readers which are very much like any sight-word basal approach despite the use of the expanded ITA alphabet. The second ITA program which was not heavily phonic began with experience charts before it introduced the ITA Early to Read series. Furthermore, it used the Downing readers for weaker students.

The 1967 USOE first-grade studies were almost totally dependent on scores from silent-reading tests. However, they did produce some data on oral reading accuracy, although its usefulness is limited by the fact that the tests were given at grade level 1.7, or March, only 140 days into the first-grade school year. The Lippincott program moves very slowly in the introduction of phonic elements, not all of them being taught to the top two-thirds of the class until June (almost grade level 2.0, not 1.7), and some of them not taught to the bottom one-third of the class until well into its second-grade year. The Lippincott children were therefore being tested on "reading" long before they had been taught how to read standard texts which have all the English phonemes. Furthermore, the ITA-trained children, at grade level 1.7, would only have read material printed in the expanded ITA alphabet and would not yet have been asked to read standard print.

Nevertheless, despite such enormous drawbacks, most of the Lippincott and Mazurkiewicz ITA grade 1.7 classes sharply outscored all the other approaches on oral reading accuracy.

At the Reading Reform Foundation's 16th Annual Conference in Cincinnati, Ohio, in August, 1977, Dr. Dykstra commented that, while heavy phonics programs definitely outscored the basal classes on almost all oral tests and on many of the silent tests, the data from silent comprwerpoehension tests given to second graders showed even greater differences among various school systems than between the basal and phonics programs within each system. Dr. Dykstra obviously thinks that such "silent reading comprehension tests" are valid.

The fallacy of the "silent reading comprehension test" as an index to reading ability will be discussed again in the conclusions at the end of this study. However, briefly, there are major problems with so-called "reading comprehension tests". They are not really testing "reading" beyond the ability to recognize the 300 highest frequency words which compose about 75% of most texts.

Appreciably more than 50% of most texts are composed of the 250 most commonly used words in English, according to The Ladybird Key Words Reading Scheme brochure, citing as its source for that statistic Key Words to Literacy, The Schoolmaster Publishing Co., Ltd., London, England, published apparently about 1965. (The Ladybird program is a sight word program built on such high frequency words). However, far earlier, in 1915, Leonard Porter Ayres published A Measuring Scale for Ability in Spelling, Russell Sage Foundation, New York, New York, which publication was even more informative concerning the huge proportion of most texts occupied by a relatively small number of the highest frequency words. From statistics Ayres compiled on written materials which contained a total of 368,000 running words (two-thirds of the materials from personal and business letters), Ayres found that only 300 of the highest frequency words accounted for 3/4, or 75%, of the total 368,000 running words.

If a reader can recognize at least those 300 highest frequency words, he may be able to guess the meaning of a selection from the 75% containing those known words, and from the initial consonants of the unknown words. What is really being tested, therefore, in "silent reading comprehension tests" is not the degree of word-decoding competence, but is instead the test-taker's intelligence, his knowledge of the language and his knowledge of the subject being discussed, and his degree of attention to the text he is reading.

The present study, however, unlike the so-called "silent reading comprehension tests", is concerned with the ability to decode print, so the only pertinent data from the USOE study is that concerned with the decoding of print. The USOE studies showed (both in raw data and in data "treated" to allow for differences between classes) that the phonics programs were sharply superior in their ability to read print aloud correctly.

Three oral reading accuracy tests were given in the USOE projects. Two were on word lists. One was the Fry word list of phonically regular words, which put the sight-word basal groups at a disadvantage. As expected, the phonics group did overwhelmingly better on this test. The other word list was the Gates list of high frequency words, on which children trained in basal reader programs should have done better (but did not). The third test was the Gilmore Oral Reading Test of connected oral reading which included high frequency words taught in sight-word programs. The Gilmore test provided the guessing "boost" that results from reading meaningful context, instead of disconnected word lists. Therefore, on the Gilmore, the basal groups certainly should have done better, but, again, they did not.

On the Fry oral reading accuracy test of phonically regular words, 18 paired programs took the test (for a total of 36 groups). Six of those 18 pairs compared phonics approaches to the standard basal sight-word approach. (Three of the phonics program were Lippincott phonic, and three were ITA phonic). All six of the phonics groups scored in the top 11 scores in the field of 36, sharply out-performing the great majority of non-phonic programs.

On the USOE first-grade Gates word list test, when the 36 scores are ranked from top to bottom, four of the top five scores were made by phonics programs (two Lippincott, two ITA, and the fifth the Murphy-Durrell Speech to Print Phonics, a basal-plus-phonics program being compared to a standard basal approach). An ITA phonic program placed 12th of 36, but its basal sight-word mate placed 21st. A Lippincott phonic program placed 13 of 36, but its basal sight-word mate placed 35th of 36.

So ALL of the six phonics programs of the total 36 programs placed in about the top third, on the Gates word list test, which means, of course, that ALL phonics programs were better than about two-thirds of the whole sample on this test of high frequency words.

On the Gilmore test of connected oral reading, four of the five top scoring programs were phonics programs, and the 10th in the total of 36 was also a phonics program, which left only one phonic program scoring lower. It was, surprisingly, the Tanyzer Lippincott which had scored third in the field of 36 on the raw scores but which dropped to 25th place in the field after treatment. Since the Tanyzer ITA had kept its place rating after treatment, and since the Tanyzer Lippincott sample was not greatly different from the Tanyzer ITA on the pretest scores on IQ, phoneme and letter knowledge, etc., for the whole group, it seems probable that either the small samples (20 to 50 students) randomly chosen for the oral tests were statistically peculiar for the retest scores in the Tanyzer Lippincott group, or there was an error made. The latter seems more probable. It is evident, however, that the phonic programs generally markedly outscored the non-phonic programs on the Gilmore test of connected oral reading.

Despite the handicap of too-early testing of Lippincott and ITA classes in March of first grade, the phonics classes still markedly outstripped the basal sight-word groups on oral reading accuracy. On all three oral tests, the Gates, the Gilmore and the Fry, the six phonic programs appeared generally in about the top one third of the 36 program sample.

In the college text, Teaching Reading, by Charles Walcutt (and others), Macmillan and Company, 1975, Dr. Dykstra made the following comment on the total USOE test results:

> "The evidence clearly demonstrates that children who receive early intensive instruction in phonics develop superior word recognition skills in the early stages of reading and tend to maintain their superiority at least through the third grade... We can summarize the results of sixty years of research dealing with beginning reading instruction by stating that early systematic instruction in phonics provides the child with the skills necessary to become an independent reader at an earlier age than is likely if phonics instruction is delayed and less systematic. As a consequence of his early success in 'learning to read,' the child can more quickly go about the job of 'reading to learn'."

A "closed shop" protecting the sight-word method is certainly operative in the reading instruction community, so that information on phonics vs. sight word achievement almost has to be bootlegged. That is why it is not surprising that I had spent TWO YEARS on this reading research project (not to mention 16 years of teaching reading and reading educational journals) before I heard of this next phonics vs. sight-word oral reading study.

This tenth study was done by Mary Johnson, a housewife from Winnipeg, Canada. She discovered to her horror in 1956 that her own children were not learning to read, and she decided to do something about it. Her book, Programmed Illiteracy in Our Schools, recounts her Alice-in-Wonderland odyssey through the worlds of the bureaucrats and the reading "experts" in her attempt to bring about change. Her book has to be read to be appreciated, and I cannot do it justice here.

Among other tests, Mrs. Johnson devised what she labeled Johnson Test No. 5 - Oral Reading, consisting of 18 sentences. Three of the sentences were taken unaltered from the Scott, Foresman 1946 sight-word series. The other 15 sentences were composed of phonic elements presented by Scott, Foresman in Grades 1 and 2, most words of one syllable. Mrs. Johnson felt this followed what Scott, Foresman was attempting to teach, because the authors of the Dick and Jane materials had promised that mastery of the so-called substitution method of reading new words would be developed in Grade 1. She quoted from Professor William Scott Gray's Guidebook for the Basic Primer, Fun with Dick and Jane, published by Scott, Foresman & Co., Chicago, Illinois, 1946, page 17:

> "The substitution of one phonetic element for another is one of the simplest ways of applying knowledge of phonetic elements. Let us assume, for example, that the child knows the printed words jump and bump but has not yet met the word lump in his reading. To recognize the word lump he may merely note that it looks like bump except for the first letter. He then mentally substitutes the sound of l for the sound of b in the word and checks the meaning with the context.
>
> "Mastery of this substitution technique is developed at Book One Level in the Basic Reading Program."

Mrs. Johnson used this test to test the oral reading of children on Winnipeg playgrounds in the summer, and provided this test and others of her devising for testing throughout the English-speaking world to teachers in interested schools. The performance on these tests from 1958 to 1967 are reported in her book very precisely, and can only be viewed as absolutely appalling. The cover of her book has exact quotations taken from tape-recorded oral reading in Winnipeg playgrounds in July and August of 1967 by children who had completed first grade. Their reading of the sentence from her Test No. 11, "Mike hid a jar of gum drops in the shed," ran from "Make (blank) a jar of guns (blank) in the shelt" to "Mike did a jar of cough drops in the shell" to "John hided (blank, blank, blank) plums (blank) in the shed." Very few were correct.

However, only on Test No. 5 does Mrs. Johnson have results which compare children learning with sight-word programs to children learning with heavy phonics programs (for the obvious reason that so few schools when she tested were using phonics programs.)

To obtain results for children who were taught to read by a phonics program, Mrs. Johnson wrote to Superintendent Wingo of Argo, Illinois, who was a co author of the program, Reading with Phonics, by Hay-Wingo-Hletko. Wingo is quoted in Rudolf Flesch's 1955 book, Why Johnny Can't Read, and it was Miss Hletko's first-grade class which astonished Flesch with their reading ability. Argo was described by Flesch on page 96 of his book as an industrial suburb of Chicago, with working-class people and a sizable black community.

Superintendent Wingo agreed to test some children in Wingo with Mrs. Johnson's material. In September, 1958, Superintendent Wingo gave Mrs. Johnson's Test No. 5 to 12 Wingo children and recorded their oral reading. In the previous June, 4 of the 12 children had finished first grade, 4 had finished second grade, and 4 had finished third grade. For each grade, 2 of the 4 were from the upper level and 2 from the lower level. The tape-recorded results were then sent to Mrs. Johnson who scored the results. This table shows the percentages of Argo children who were able to read each section of the test with less than four errors.

Sentences			Completed	Number. of	Average
1-3	4-9	10-18	Grade	Children	Age
100%	100%	100%	1	4	7
100%	100%	25%	2	4	8
100%	100%	75%	3	4	9

Mrs. Johnson said that three of the children who had been in Grade 2 had below average IQ's, even though one was in the upper level of the class. Yet even they read the first nine sentences with excellent accuracy and with expression. She said the only noticeable difference between the pupils who had finished Grade 1 (and who were in Grade 2 in September) and those who had finished Grade 3 (so were in Grade 4 in September) was that the older pupils read more rapidly.

In August of 1958 she had tape-recorded 84 primary-age children's reading of Test 5 on Winnipeg public park playgrounds. She said the test was unavoidably biased in favor of the superior readers since some children would not even try the test because they said they could not read at all. Her table showing the percentages of Winnipeg children at each grade level who read each section with less than four mistakes provides an appalling contrast to Argo's results:

	Sentences		Completed	Number. of	Average
1-3	4-9	10-18	Grade	Children	Age
34%	10%	0%	1	21	7
59%	27%	2%	2	34	8
82%	42%	17%	3	29	9

In Argo, 100% of all grade levels could read sentences 4 to 9 satisfactorily, but in Winnipeg only 10% of first-graders, 27% of second-graders, and 42% of third-graders could read them satisfactorily.

This tenth oral reading accuracy study, comparing phonics to sight-words is the next to the last one that I could find.

There was one more, the eleventh, which I found by consulting the ERIC computer files on research. It was by Dr. Kay Wedel McKnab and compared Distar phonics to the Holt sight-word basal. It purported to show no statistically significant difference in the test results. I am saving this till Chapter 6 of this book, to show how reality can be distorted by the wrong kind of statistical treatment. Yet Dr. McKnab's misleading test conclusions were easily obtained simply by applying to ERIC, the computer files on research. ERIC dutifully printed out her results which purported to prove that Distar is not better than a sight-word basal reader on oral reading accuracy. In Chapter 6, I will demonstrate from Dr. McKnab's test figures that her conclusion, when properly analyzed, is wrong.

But the tenth oral reading accuracy study, with Mrs. Johnson's amazing results, I did not find in the literature. I could only find it in an out-of-the-mainstream way, which is perhaps the most damning indictment of the whole sight- word juggernaut. Yet, from even a cursory examination of all of the other research data that I have cited, it is obvious that Mrs. Johnson's results are extremely significant, since there are no other studies like hers.

Yet her material certainly should not have been obscure and essentially buried when I checked the general literature in 1978 and 1979. After all, her testing dates from 1958, and Mrs. Johnson played her tapes from Argo on a Winnipeg CBWT television panel discussion on reading on October 30, 1958. The panel was composed of Mrs. Johnson, a local reading specialist, and a local school administrator. The latter two were defending sight-word basal readers, stating that silent reading tests were all that counted. Yet this was after they had shown, unwittingly, their amazement at the high quality of the Argo reading.

Mrs. Johnson's tapes hardly went unnoticed even earlier, since her Winnipeg, Canada, recordings of the oral reading of Winnipeg children had made the front page of the Winnipeg Free Press. An instructress at the Manitoba Teachers College was annoyed, and said, "We have enough trouble in education without letting this irresponsible stuff make the front page."

The tapes were later used on TV and radio by many broadcasters, and Mary Johnson's phonics crusade was reported favorably and often by Manitoba newspapers for some time. She has been corresponding and working with people all over the English-speaking world ever since, running further oral tests reported in her book. Yet, strangely, Mary Johnson and her crusade, dating back to the 1950's are nowhere to be found in the index to such books as Bond's Reading Difficulties: Their Diagnosis and Correction, or Harris and Sipay's How to Increase Reading Ability, or in any other sources whatsoever that I checked in my library work on reading instruction. Harris and Sipay's book was revised and enlarged in 1970 and Bond's book dates from 1973, ample time for 1958 results to have reached them. The simple fact is that Mary Johnson's extensive tests are apparently not to be found anywhere in the reading instruction literature.

I found them only as a result of a phone conversation with Mrs. Bettina Rubicam, President of Reading Reform Foundation in Scottsdale, Arizona. When I told her that I had done a review of the previous research and (at that time) had found only eight oral reading accuracy studies since 1912, she asked if I had heard of Mrs. Johnson's work, and I had not. She sent me Mrs. Johnson's address and I ordered her book.

Mrs. Johnson's research is, surprisingly, not even cited in Jeanne Chall's book, Learning to Read, The Great Debate. Although Mrs. Johnson is a lay person and not a reading "authority," she had tape recordings of children's reading, taken at random, chance samplings, to substantiate her data. I believe, had Jeanne Chall been aware of this research, she would at least have cited it. But Orwell's 1984 "unthink" had been at work. Any data which made the sight-word establishment uncomfortable was automatically ignored, altered in its interpretation, or dropped. Since Mrs.

Johnson's data was not available to me through library research, it raises the specter of how much other "unthink" has operated through the past sixty or seventy years, ignoring or in effect erasing the meaning of any data not popular with the sight-word reading establishment. I find it extremely difficult to believe that only eleven oral reading accuracy studies, in addition to mine, have been done in the last sixty or seventy years, particularly since many thousands of other kinds of reading instruction studies have been done during that time.

In obtaining data for my research, I ordered a fair number of texts on reading instruction from the International Reading Association, because the titles suggested that the contents might be pertinent. Yet I found little of value to me except a collection of papers by foreign reading experts and a review of research papers given during the 1975 IRA Annual Meeting. The IRA president, Dr. Constance McCullough, had asked Dr. S. Jay Samuels to invite the participants, and his speakers represented a broad spectrum of opinion on reading. This useful book was published with the cooperation of both Dr. McCullough and Dr. Samuels.

In talking by phone with someone connected with the reading "establishment," I had been told that the Reading Reform's The Reading Informer was "just a little newspaper." (I was also told that my instructor "wouldn't like it" if I cited The Reading Informer in my graduate courses in reading.) Yet, from this newspaper, in contrast to the generally useless material I had ordered from IRA, I had found some 18 pertinent citations for my research!

The eleven studies were all the American research that I could locate up to 1979 which compared the oral reading accuracy of phonics-taught children to the oral reading accuracy of sight-word-taught children. I had turned up an astonishingly small total, but it had favored phonics overwhelmingly.

This had largely been American research, but most research from other areas was not available to me. However, John Downing published Comparative Reading, a collection of essays from people in various countries. One particularly useful essay was by Berta Perelstein de Braslavsky, Universidad Nacional de la Plata, Argentina, and another was by Franz Biglmaier of Germany. Developments elsewhere in reading instruction, such as in Argentina and Germany, paralleled very closely the development of reading instruction in the United States. Yet each area often produced "experts" not quoted in the literature of other areas. For instance, Decroly was quoted in the Argentine article as important in European theory, but he is scarcely mentioned in the United States. William Scott Gray wrote The Teaching of Reading and Writing in 1956 which concerned other countries, and Gray did mention both Decroly and Freinet of Europe. Other than in Gray's text, I have never seen either man mentioned in American texts. Yet, so important do they seem to be to European pedagogy that, in a casual five-minute talk with a teaching specialist in an Amsterdam school, he mentioned both names as very influential in the history of reading, and appeared to be dumbfounded that I had never heard of them.

The European Freinet's ideas appear to resemble the Americans, Francis Parker and John Dewey, in the attempt to bring nature into the classroom, and to use materials such as printing presses for children to write texts based on their own experiences. The ideas of the Belgian Decroly resemble those of the Americans, Arthur Irving Gates, William Scott Gray, et al. Decroly was influential at about the same time, the 1920's. Decroly published an article, Le role de phenomene de globalisation dans l'enseignment in the Annuel Bulletin of the Royal Society of Natural and Medical Science, Brussels, 1927 (p. 65-70), in which he said:

> "...as psychologists have demonstrated... children recognize things and ideas as wholes more or less vaguely at first, proceeding gradually to the recognition of details.

It is interesting, however, that in 1977, when I went into a Brussels, Belgium, textbook store and asked for primary reading texts, I was given only phonics texts (four publishers). If the clerk understood me properly and these were the only reading texts, this could indicate that Decroly's influence in his native country has waned.

Franz Biglmaier of Pedagogische Hochschule, Berlin, Germany, contributed an article to Comparative Reading. He referred to the headlines that could be read in the mid-1960's in German newspapers and magazines such as the following: "Stupid Children or Stupid Methods?" - "The Downgraded Global Method" - "The Thalidomide Case of Education" - "Attack Against Global Method." He closed his article, after referring to conflicting research studies for and against the global (sight word) method, which he said were still being fiercely discussed, by restating:

> "...the basic question... What is reading? Is reading only a decoding process, is it a thinking process, or is it both?"

Biglmaier opted for the complex process:

> "...including perceptive, apperceptive, assimilative, associative and intellectual processes."

If you want to know where a persons stands on phonics vs. sight words, just ask him what his definition of reading is. If he says, "Turning print back into words," he is a phonics man. If he gives you a paragraph of something else like the foregoing, he is a sight-word man.

Biglmaier cited Reinhard's Stage I (the Preanalytic Stage of Primitive Global Reading), Stage II (the Analytic Stage where the child sees details of words), and Stage III (the Synthetic Stage with building of new words). Some 80 different words might be learned in the pre-analytic Stage I, then varied and used in different order in new sentences. In Stage II, words are analyzed to learn the alphabet and sounds of letters. In Stage III, new words are learned by substitution of letters, or by rhyming families of phonograms (meaning a vowel plus letters, as the "at" in mat, fat, hat, sat, etc.), with different beginning letters. This work is "always done in a meaningful situation, with no drill on isolated letters or letter combinations." New words are introduced in the context of well-known words. Finally, with this method, he said that all normal children should be able to read texts with many new words by the end of second grade. Yet, according to the headlines in the German papers, children were NOT able to read with this global method!

Besides Downing's useful book, another helpful study was by Taylor, Frankenpohl and Pettee. Children are given sight words because it is assumed that children perceive words as "wholes" before focusing on their parts. Yet the research by Taylor, Frankenpohl and Pettee contradicts that assumption. Their data on eye movements showed that first-grade children can only see on the average 0.45 of a word with each separate eye fixation, so the children obviously find it impossible to take in a whole word at a glance. It is not until the 11th grade that the span of recognition exceeds a word, 1.04. At college level, on the average, the span of recognition is still only 1.11. My reference source on this study did not specify the length of the words. (Research Information Bulletin No. 3, Huntington, N. Y., Educational Development Laboratories, Inc., a division of McGraw-Hill Book Company, 1960, p. 12, table 13, "Eye Movement Norms," cited in Harris and Sipay's How to Increase Reading Ability, 1970).

The beginning reader, therefore, who is taught by the "whole word" method never sees whole words in one glance but only in two or more parts, which he processes as whole words only afterwards in his mind. Should he be having problems with left-to-right progression, I conclude that he could process one half left to right, and the other half right to left, which might account for part of the higher levels of reversals observed in some whole word programs, where the child is not almost forced by the decoding process itself to move in left to right progression. These data, however, that prove conclusively that beginning readers do not truly see whole words at a glance, disproves the claim that beginning readers can take in sight words as "wholes."

Another claim of whole-word advocates is that teaching phonics to children in supplementary drill does not transfer to the actual reading of connected texts. Arthur I. Gates of Columbia Teachers College, New York, wrote in 1927, as cited by Jean Chall on page 165 of her book, Learning to Read, the Great Debate:

> "In the light of the theory which considers all learning to be the establishment of definite reactions to specific situations and in the light of established facts concerning the transfer of training, the validity of phonetics and other supplementary devices may well be questioned. Their probable weakness lies precisely in the fact that they are supplementary and not intrinsic. They depend upon the transfer of training which probably occurs in small degree, if at all."

E. L. Thorndike of Columbia Teachers College published his Teachers Word Book of the 10,000 commonest words in 1921 (later expanded) presumably to aid teachers to avoid the "problem" caused by the supposed lack of transfer in phonics teaching, so that children could learn high-frequency words directly. Gates of Columbia Teachers College proposed, for backward readers, training in decoding which was not separate from the "process of reading." First came the teaching of whole words, followed by analysis of sound-letter correspondence from words learned as wholes, and no direct learning of sound values of letters or blending of letter sounds. William Scott Gray outlined this basic program, like that of Gates, in his 1948 book, On Their Own in Reading, which ideas Chall said were incorporated into other conventional basal series since then. "Above all," she said, "Gray followed through on Gates's suggestion about 'not teaching analysis in isolation,'" presumably because of the "problem" with transfer of training.

Our reading instruction intellectuals took these theories and applied them to the teaching of reading to justify the teaching of sight words.

Although Thorndike's ideas prove false when applied to phonics-taught children, they strangely do receive support when applied to children who have been taught to read by the sight word method if they are reading connected texts with unknown words instead of columns of unknown words. Something different happens to children when they have been taught to read by sight-words instead of by phonics. If teachers try to graft phonics skills on to such children's reading at second grade or above, the teachers find that the sight-word-trained children are unable to apply these new- learned phonic skills on unknown words if they are reading the unknown words in connected contexts, instead of in columns of new words. The new phonic skills do not "transfer" to the reading of new words whenever they are in texts instead of on word lists. Yet such readers can remember as "sight words" any words they learn from studying them phonically on word lists.

My research, as discussed in Chapter 8, demonstrated that two kinds of readers result from the two kinds of initial teaching, by the "meaning" of print or by its "sound". The reader who has been taught to decode by "meaning" will always decode connected texts by "meaning." The reader who has been taught to decode by "sound" will always decode connected texts by "sound".

Concerning the present state of reading research in America, one of its greatest handicaps is that it is now being done by and on people who learned to read with the Gates - Gray et al sight-word method. The sad but untestable premise is that many of these people are crippled readers and have no way of knowing how an uncrippled reader would perform. After all, the majority of American children today learned by a sight emphasis in the first half of first grade and the most of them, as a result, are unable to decode words properly.

The marvel is that so many children and adults in English-speaking countries cannot read properly, since the symbol- to-sound association is almost self-evident after a little training. The reason is because they have been systematically drilled in psycholinguistic guessing, and later, any attempt to superimpose another association - symbol to sound, just does not "take." They have an irreversible mind-set to read that way. For 13 years, I taught third grade reading to children who had been through the old-fashioned Scott, Foresman and Ginn sight-word readers. Attempting to give them word-attack skills, which most of them totally lacked, I taught them Martin Brennan (J. F. Kennedy School Principal, Wayne, N. J.) and George Ameer's brilliant Reading in a Nutshell drill phonics. The children could all learn these skills, although it was sometimes difficult because so many of the common words used to drill on at this third-grade level had been learned as sight words, so it was hard to know if the children were merely "word calling" with these words or actually applying phonic rules.

The real problem, though, came in getting the children to use these skills on unknown words when reading connected texts. It was made evident to me over and over again until I was sickened by it that the children's only approach to "decode" an unknown word when in a reading context was to guess from the meaning of the known sight words in the context, and the initial consonant of the unknown word. Yet, what else could be expected? In the previous two years, they had been systematically drilled in the Scott, Foresman and Ginn readers to context-guess and had been told that they were reading when they were only guessing. Now I wanted the children to sound out the words instead of to guess, but their brains could not change gears. They had become largely immune to applying phonics when actually reading texts.

In other countries, as in America, there has been opposition to the sight-word global method for over twenty years. There was strong opposition in France in the 1950's. A Latin American Seminar on Dyslexia took place in 1963 and recommended the phonics method instead of the global method. In Germany, in the 1960s, a great outburst appeared, covered in their daily papers, against the global sight-word method. These reactions, occurring at approximately the same time, between about 1955 and 1967, appear to be largely independent, unconnected developments. It would be tempting to wonder if the match that lit them all in 1955 could have been Rudolf Flesch's Why Johnny Can't Read. However, a year before Flesch's book appeared in America, Hunter Diack, who had written a phonic series in England, wrote an article for the London Times Educational Supplement on May 7, 1954 (No. 2036, p. 441), entitled "First Steps in Reading: Phonics the Key," so there has been widespread but spontaneous dissatisfaction with failures in reading from the global sight-word method for a very long time.

Yet, in America, in 1977, 22 years after Flesch's landmark book and 10 years after Chall's call for teaching decoding skills in the first half of first grade, most American schools still taught sight words during that period, despite the addition of some foot-dragging phonics to many basal programs, and new anti-phonics attacks were gaining momentum.

In 1977, I wondered about the current state of the teaching of beginning reading in the schools in Europe in comparison to American schools. I wondered about the comparative results between American schools and European schools. I decided to find out.

CHAPTER 3
On the Nature of the Test That Was Used

I had determined my purpose. It was to observe reading programs in the critical first half of first grade, rating them on a scale from extreme sight-word emphasis to extreme phonics emphasis, and then to test children from these programs in second grade on an oral reading test to determine the relative success of the programs. Therefore, I needed a rating instrument for these observations in first grade and a test for oral reading in second grade.

Before I could construct a scale on which to rate first-grade programs as sight-word or phonics oriented, I had to define these and other related terms.

To define the terms, it is necessary to go back some 5,000 years to when the alphabet began to develop. Its roots came from someone in Egypt. The Egyptians had their hieroglyphs, of course, but a syllable form of writing also developed, as it did elsewhere in the world. Words are really just combinations of syllables, and smart men have figured out how to write the syllables down. But this Egyptian, who wanted more than just plain picture writing, was apparently too lazy to write down all the Egyptian syllables. So, instead, he just wrote one sign for all similar-sounding syllables, as "b" for ba, be, bi, bo, and bu. The idea of a true alphabet with vowels, however, and not a syllabary, apparently never occurred to him. The Semites borrowed his idea and still thought of the symbols as abbreviated syllables, but named them with the names of real objects in their life, as, for instance, "h" might be called "house" because house starts with the sound of all syllables beginning with "h."

The Greeks borrowed the bulk of their alphabet from the Semitic Phoenicians, although scholars argue that there were separate borrowings. But I will go along with old Herodotus, the ancient Greek who was far nearer to the scene, who claimed that the alphabet was borrowed from the Phoenicians all at once. I like to think of its being borrowed by a smart Greek, who can be called Anonymous I.

In the confusing Phoenician shorthand syllable system which lacked vowels, the phrase, "The cow jumped over the moon," would have to be written like this "THCWJMPDVRTHMN." Anonymous I thought this was very confusing, so he invented the vowels to complete those abbreviated syllables, which would make the notation pronounceable: THECOWJUMPEDOVERTHEMOON.

The Greek invention of the vowels is one of the greatest landmarks in human thought. An abbreviated syllable system had been replaced with a complete syllable system, but, unlike other syllable systems, it was astonishingly compact and easy to use. With the addition of the Greek vowels to complete the abbreviated Phoenician syllables, the new alphabet presented an accuracy and efficiency in writing which had never existed before. It was no longer necessary to invent a different symbol for each spoken syllable, because, with only 26 or so symbols, it had become possible to write down all the syllables in speech. With only those 26 or so symbols, it had become possible to write down ANYTHING that ANYONE could say for ALL TIME and to teach even simple minded people to do so!

Anonymous I and his cosmopolitan Greek friends, probably seafaring merchants, probably had no trouble with the names of the letters that they had borrowed from the Phoenicians because they probably spoke Phoenician as well as Greek. The Phoenicians had named their letters by Phoenician words that began with those letters' sounds, and those Greeks would probably have known the Phoenician words. What the Phoenicians had done in naming their letters is what the Alpha One phonics program in America does. So that children will know the sound of "b", for instance, it is called Mr. Beautiful Buttons, and "m" is called Mr. Munching Mouth, and so on. The names of the letters demonstrate the sounds of the letters.

But the ancient Greeks then made a bad decision. They kept the Phoenician names for the letters which were meaningless for anyone not knowing Phoenician, instead of choosing Greek equivalents which would have far more clearly demonstrated letter sounds for beginning readers. Beginning readers had to memorize the newly invented alphabetic syllabary - ba, be, bi, bo, bu - ab, eb, ib, ob, ub, etc., but in doing so had to recite the names of each letter with their cumbersome letter names: beta, alpha - ba, beta, epsilon - be, etc. Reciting the letter names of each syllable was supposed to help in remembering the sound of each syllable.

Memorizing the sounds of the syllabary, and doing so while reciting letter names which did little to demonstrate letter sounds (see-aye-tee, cat), is where the teaching of beginning reading remained until the seventeenth century. That is when Blaise Pascal invented synthetic phonics, in which letters were named by their actual sounds (cuh-ah-tuh, cat). With Pascal phonics, the syllabary no longer had to be memorized, but only the sounds of the letters, because it was then possible to work out the sounds, not just of all the syllables in the syllabary, but of all words.

Despite the difficult Phoenician letter names, Anonymous I had greatly improved things with the invention of the vowels. The world could now read, instead of "THCWJMPDVRTHMN", the far clearer "THECOWJUMPEDOVERTHEMOON."

According to Claire Thomas, Vice President of The Reading Reform Foundation, in her article, "Our Beautiful English Language," September, 1975, The Reading Informer, it was not until the English scholar, Alcuin, who lived from about 735 to 804 A. D., that this method of writing changed. Alcuin had accepted Charlemagne's invitation to teach in France and lived there for many years. Mrs. Thomas said:

> "[Alcuin's] lasting gift to us is lower case letters, punctuation, and the division of paragraphs into sentences and words. Every time we pick up a book to read, it is easier for us to do so because of a dedicated teacher who lived 1,200 years ago."

So, it was not until the 700's A. D. that spaces were shown between words, that lower case letters arrived, and that texts were divided into sentences. It had finally become possible to write "THECOWJUMPEDOVERTHEMOON" as "The cow jumped over the moon."

The fact that the division of words in texts was not normally done until the 8th century is amusing when reading of some research that has been done lately. That research uncovered the not-at-all surprising fact that first-graders have no real concept of what is meant by "words" but perceive spoken language as an uninterrupted flow of sound. Yet nothing else should have been expected since the whole literate world, including, presumably, minds like St. Augustine's and Plato's and all of brilliant Rome perceived spoken language as an uninterrupted flow of sound - and so did all of the literate Western World until Alcuin's day, halfway through the Middle Ages! Before Alcuin's improvement, written texts had been separated for beginners into syllables, not words, so the beginners were obviously being taught to read whole syllables, not whole words.

Amazingly, a teacher's scroll dating from the third century B. C., for teaching beginning reading in Greek, was found just before World War II in the sands of north Africa. This Greek scroll was miraculously preserved in those dry sands of Egypt on what had apparently been a garbage heap where school trash baskets had been emptied. It dates from a Hellenistic school of approximately 217-200 B. C. This teacher's copy shows that, after the children were taught the names of the letters of the alphabet, they were given two letter syllables, such as ba, be, bi, bo, bu, in every possible combination, systematically, and then three-letter syllables, such as bab, beb, bib, bob, bub, the same way. Eventually they were given multisyllable words which were generally names.

H. I. Marrou told of this scroll in his book, A History of Education in Antiquity, (Sheed and Ward, New York, 1956, translated from the original book published by Editions du Seuil, Paris). The document was referred to as the Papyrus Gueraud Jouquet, and the original account was given by O. Gueraud and P. Jouquet in their article, "Un livre d'ecolier du IIIe siecle avant Jesus Christ," Publications de la Societe Royal Egyptienne de Papyrologie, Textes et Documents, II, Cairo, 1938.

According to Marrou, Greek-speaking children in the third century B. C. spelled each syllable before they read it, as beta, alpha - ba, etc. The whole words they were eventually given, however, were printed with the syllables separated. This is clear proof that the children were reading by syllables. The first connected reading matter was also separated into syllables, NOT words, until the adult form was introduced in which no separations at all were made between letters. Obviously, from Marrou's account, the children were NOT taught words, but syllables.

Marrou said, "There was nothing comparable to our reading by wholes," and he mentioned children's psychological problems, which implies a widespread penetration of Decroly's global ideas to the intellectual French community at the period when Marrou wrote this (1948) and a reflection of the possible general acceptance of the global method in France at that time, although this method was later greatly opposed there.

But, to go back to that brilliant Greek, Anonymous I, who added the vowels to complete the alphabet - what he produced was a totally phonetic system of encoding and decoding speech. Sight-word or global concepts had nothing whatever to do with it. There was only a stream of sounds to translate mentally into speech, just like a tape recorder, today.

The history, therefore, had provided my needed scale.

Teaching by isolated letter sound at one end of the scale is Code 10 on the scale which runs from 1 to 10. Programs which move the teaching of reading in the critical first half of first grade all the way down the scale to meaning-bearing hieroglyphs are labeled Code 1.

At Code 1 (the pure Chinese character type of reading) and Code 10 (alphabetic reading), or simultaneously at Code 1 and 10 as in Japanese reading which employs both picture characters and syllable sound characters, it should be possible to read automatically, since both characters and sounds can be memorized. However, between these extremes, from Code 2 to Code 9, reading is done by using a mixture of visual information and phonic information on the SAME symbol at the SAME time, as a word is partially decoded by its meaning and partially decoded by only some of its phonic elements. Context is then used to check the choice, and the use of context demands conscious attention. Therefore, completely automatic reading is, by definition, impossible from Code 2 through Code 9, since readers must use consciousness to deal with contextual meaning. However, the closer that reading approaches Code 10, the closer it approaches automaticity.

Furthermore, the mind may have great difficulty using TWO sensory processing systems, both letter sound and visual meaning, on the exact same stimulus at the exact same time. The resultant conflict from trying to employ these two opposing systems simultaneously on the same object may contribute additionally to the use of conscious attention in decoding.

Terms mentioned in Chapter 2 are covered by this scale. For instance, the term, "intrinsic phonics" refers to programs towards the sight-word end of the scale (towards Code 1) and "systematic phonics" to programs towards the phonics end of the scale (towards Code 10). The actual numerical code I eventually gave when I observed classroom programs was dependent on the degree of "sound" or "meaning" emphasis in decoding.

However, phonic methods and sight words methods can both be used either analytically or synthetically, so the use of the terms, "analytic" and "synthetic" to distinguish between programs has only clouded the history of reading. Also, as Mitford Mathews pointed out in his history of reading, the term "word method" can also be very misleading. It has been used to describe both sight-word and analytic phonics programs. As used originally in Germany, it was a heavy analytic phonics method, which Horace Mann saw in Germany but did not understand. A schoolmaster taught the word "haus," illustrated it, and then broke it down into its sounds (h - au - s). This was a highly phonic approach. Mathews coined the phrase, "words to print" to describe it, but this is very inadequate. On my scale, it is Code 10 - analytic. Mathews called the use of global, or sight words, "words to meaning," when a child learns a word by its meaning, not its sound. On my scale, that is Code 1.

The linguist, Leonard Bloomfield, endorsed his "linguistic" method of teaching reading. It rates Code 5, using syllable "sounds" to read whole word "meanings". Bloomfield had great contempt for "sounding out" of isolated letters (which would be Code 10).

Children taught by the linguistic method are aware, of course, that letters, when written in linguistic phonograms, represent encoded sound. It just is harder for them to encode or decode phonograms without having the isolated sounds of the letters as keys. Therefore, the "linguistic" approach, or any other approach also doing a half-way job in decoding, for ANY reason, is considered to be at the mid-point (Code 5), between heavy letter-sound emphasis (Code 10) and whole word "meaning" emphasis (Code 1).

The pure sight-word "meaning" method at the opposite end of the scale from the pure phonics "sound" method is a complete jettisoning of the alphabetic principle and a return to writing by meaning-bearing hieroglyphics. Each new idea in a hieroglyphic system needs a new symbol which has to be committed to memory with all its peculiar markings intact. This has to be done for thousands and thousands of such shapes which represent ideas. Obviously, such a system can only be used effectively by people with astonishingly good visual memories. However, the alphabetic principle can be used by anyone who is able to memorize only 26 shapes, not thousands, and who can already speak a language, which means it can be used by children with I. Q. levels even below 70. I have personally taught 8-yearold children with I. Q.'s in the low 70's to read, with the use of phonics.

Horace Mann, Colonel Parker, Huey, Dewey and all their followers like Gates and Gray almost totally jettisoned the alphabetic principle and returned to the hieroglyphic principle for the first year or two of school. Now, the American Goodman and the Canadian Smith want to throw the alphabetic principle out the window altogether at all levels, relying essentially on context plus some syntactic language clues and sight words. I saw Goodman's Scott, Foresman program in use in some schools and rated it Code 2, because it did have, as I will describe, some minimal use of letter sounds.

Concerning my ratings of Code 1 to Code 10 as I eventually gave them to programs I observed, in most cases published texts are available to confirm my judgment in labeling. The exceptions were one American school, when a teacher adapted a sight-word basal program to her highly phonic approach, the Swedish schools using the LTG method predominantly, and the French schools which used teacher-prepared materials. In the American school in which the teacher used her own phonic approach, the phonics rating I gave is justified by the teacher's direct statements to me on how she had run her first-grade program. The French and Swedish ratings are corroborated by my observational notes on these schools.

Obviously, there are many differences in first-grade classrooms besides the degree of emphasis on phonics or sight-words. Such differences, or variables, may affect the achievement of the classes and mask the effect of more or less phonics or sight-word teaching. However, since all schools were chosen by chance, both here and in Europe, this chance selection might tend to cancel out the effect of other variables than phonic or sight-word emphasis. More importantly, I dealt with a large sample of children, over 900. If taking large samplings by chance did not tend to cancel out such variables, there would be little point to such surveys as Roper's or the Gallup polls.

My only request was to observe reading programs, not any particular kind of program. As a result, I saw and tested largely standard programs in standard schools. I could reasonably hope for a cancellation of these other variables by chance, thus revealing instead how the groups differed on the one factor being tested: phonic vs. sight-word emphasis.

Having determined how to observe and rate first-grade programs, my next step was to devise an oral reading test for second-grade classes. It would have to use very, very high-frequency words (the sight-word approach) instead of phonically difficult words, and would have to be at "grade level" by sight-word standards. Otherwise, it would be impossible to test sight-word children as most are unable to decode new, lower frequency words unless they can guess those words from a context. To make any comparison between phonic and sight-word programs, therefore, which would not immediately be dismissed by sight-word proponents as inappropriate, I had to use a sight-word instrument. However, since phonics-trained children do not drill on high frequency words but instead on phonically regular words, such a test results in a large handicap in favor of the sight-word group.

The source I finally chose for my reading test was Booklet 3J, Reading Speed Test, a portion of the International Educational Achievement Study, from which I used the first five of its 40 items. This material had been copyrighted in 1969 by IEA (International Association for the Evaluation of Educational Achievement), Stockholm, Sweden. Permission to print results from the use of this test portion was requested from IEA and permission was granted, with the provision that I acknowledge IEA in any written material resulting from my research and that, wherever possible, a copy of such material be sent to IEA International in Stockholm.

IEA had been the sponsor of international studies in educational achievement in six curriculum areas, including reading. The original IEA reading test included three sections: comprehension, speed and word meaning. A part of the IEA speed test was used in this present research as a second-grade oral reading test.

The IEA speed test had originally been given to ten and fourteen year olds as a four minute, 40-item silent-reading test, and had been graded on two grounds, number of items completed and number correct on the first page. It had been considered appropriate as a speed test for these ages because of its very simple vocabulary.

It is the simple vocabulary of the first 5 of the 40 items which made it appropriate as an oral reading accuracy and reading comprehension test for second graders. (The items on the IEA test became progressively more difficult, the easiest being the first five.) My oral reading test, which consisted of those first five items from the original 40 items, totaled in English 144 words and used 64 different words. It was suitable for second graders in sight-word programs, not as a speed test, but as a test of accuracy in oral reading, since 40 of those 64 different words are among the 250 most commonly used words in English, according to The Ladybird Key Words Reading Scheme, as reported in Key Words to Literacy, The Schoolmaster Publishing Co., Ltd., London, England. (As previously mentioned, the Ladybird program is a sight word program built on high frequency words).

Most of the rest of the words on the test are among the 500 most commonly used words listed in the section Original Thorndike Words 1 to 500 of The Teacher's Word Book of 30,000 Words (Thorndike and Lorge, Columbia University, New York, 1944). This original list is considered more suitable for children than later lists. Only 11 words of the 64 different words on this test are above the 500 frequency. Six of them are on the list from 500 to 1,000 (brown, catch, dog, gray, leg and spot). Five are above the 1,000 frequency (Peter, trick, fed, hind and puppy). It is obvious that even the words above the 1,000 frequency are simple. Some words have simple suffixes and are not counted as new words when this occurs.

Children from sight-word programs should have been able to decode by the "skill" of consonant substitution, since it is commonly taught in sight-word programs. Knowing the sight-word "find" should have made it possible to decode the word, "hind." It did not. This was one of the most frequently missed words by sight-word taught children.

Since a child was told the correct word if he missed it, and since sight-word taught children rely heavily on context, they should not have missed any word more than the first time it occurred, since they were told a word if they missed it. With only 64 different words, on a test totaling 144 total words, some words were repeated many times. Yet some sight-word-taught children missed the same word multiple times, even though they had been told it the first time and any subsequent times that they missed it.

The readability of the five selections also appears to be appropriate for the first half of second grade. The Harris-Jacobsen Readability Formula 1 (accepted by sight-word standards) was applied and yielded a grade level of low second grade (about November).

Because most European languages are derived from a common Indo-European root language, it was assumed that high frequency words in English are high frequency words in German, Dutch, Icelandic, Swedish and French. The test, which is exceedingly simple and straightforward in content, is assumed to haves translated well into French, German, Icelandic, Swedish and Dutch. I had the test translated by a commercial translating firm, Berlitz. The content of the test should have been common to the experiences of most of the children (except in Reykjavik, where dogs are not permitted by city ordinance).

Each of the five items is followed by three words, one of which completes the meaning of the selection, and this obviously provides a check on comprehension. This makes it possible to get a reading comprehension score as well as an oral reading accuracy score.

All European teachers spoke English and communicated easily with me in English, except in France, where I usually tried to use my French instead of speaking English.

Even though the test was explained to the children in European classes by their teachers, since I did not speak their languages (except for French), I assumed that I had to explain by voice inflection that a child had to pick the correct word from the three words at the end of each selection. On the European testing, I used the first of the five questions to demonstrate to children that they had to pick a "right answer." The first of the five items was, "Peter's dog was mostly - black, brown gray." The correct word to complete the selection which the child had just read was "black." After the first selection was read aloud, if a child did not immediately pick "black" from the three words under the selection as the correct answer (as many did), I would reread orally the incomplete sentence printed in their own language, and then read with a questioning tone all three of the possible answers in their own language for the words: black? Brown? Gray? I then emphatically pointed to the translation for "black" and repeated in their own language from the printed sheet, "Peter's dog was mostly black." Even if a child had picked the correct answer, which I would indicate was correct by a smile and a nod of the head and "okay," which seems to be in the "universal" language, and by pointing to the answer on his test paper, I would ask him to read aloud the other two words, as they were computed in the accuracy score. This I could do merely by pointing at them.

My repeating of the sample item, and using a questioning tone on the three possible choices, had one amusing effect in one school outside of Stockholm. A Swedish teacher told me she said to a child when he returned to his classroom after reading the test for me, "Do you know that American lady does not speak any Swedish?" He answered, "Oh, no! She speaks VERY GOOD Swedish!" Yet, outside of the Peter and his dog opus, I speak absolutely NO Swedish!

On the European scores, I computed comprehension by using, therefore, only the last four of the five questions, since I had given the answer to the first. On American scores, because I could explain fully in English that the task was to pick one of the three words as the correct completion for the item, and so I did not have to give the answer to the first, I computed comprehension scores on all five questions. The European comprehension scores, however, are lower than the American because there were always a very few children who never did understand that they were to pick a correct answer. These few children obviously lowered the overall scores. Since they were present, however, in all programs, they did not affect the comparisons between global and phonic programs on comprehension.

The testing situation was uniform, because all tests were given by the same person and in the same manner. Children from second grades were tested in Europe in the last half of October and November, usually in the afternoon, since I observed in first grades in the morning. In the United States in September and the first half of October, I observed in first grades in the morning and tested in second grades in the afternoon. However, after returning from Europe, I tested American children in January. In some of these January schools, I observed in first grades in the morning, but in others I had observed their programs in October so just tested additional second grades in January in both the morning and the afternoon. During testing, I usually arranged to sit in the hall, with two chairs, reading with one child from the class at a time for a period of about five minutes.

For most classes, it was possible to test all children present, as class sheets show. In some, time did not permit this. In these cases, scores were computed on the chance sample actually tested. Children were usually chosen from each class by seating arrangements, starting with rows or tables near the door or near the windows and continuing as far as time permitted, or until all were tested. The last child being tested, if time did not permit his finishing, had his score computed on the portion he had read. However, if a child, by the end of the first or second of the five examples, had already made more than the total 15 errors which produce a failing score if all five examples have been read, he obviously was failing very badly. Therefore, testing was stopped at the end of example one or two, and his percentage of errors was computed on the portion he had read of examples one, or one and two together.

The actual errors which I heard children make are recorded on each child's original test sheet in my files. Many of the errors, of course, were errors of omission where the child did not attempt to read the unknown word. It would be unwieldy to record all errors on the class sheets in the appendix to this book. I have, however, recorded in the appendix on the European class sheets all errors which involved the reversals of syllables or in some cases where letters were reversed, as when "b" was read as "d", etc. My purpose in giving this oral test was to test decoding only as I did not record as "errors" hesitation, misplaced accent or omission of punctuation, as is done on other oral tests.

For 18 years I was a secretary for a chemical affiliate of Exxon, and have taken and transcribed great quantities of dictation of chemical terms completely foreign to me, simply by their sounds.

This experience assisted me greatly in being able to "hear" reading accuracy in a language unknown to me and to recognize when errors were made.

It seemed very desirable to have a sampling also of the oral reading accuracy of upper grade children, to compare it to commonly observed adult reading in this country and to standardized oral reading test norms in America. The Bible seemed the natural choice for a book which I could obtain in the United States in German, Dutch, Swedish, French, and Icelandic translations. The American Bible Society in New York very kindly sent to me at my request photocopies of verses 10 to 18 of the 1 04th Psalm, which I picked since it is my favorite. I obtained the English translation from my own Bible (the 103rd in my Catholic Bible), and had 100 copies made of each translation. I intended to attempt to read with sixth-grade children whenever there was time and opportunity to do so. As it developed, it was only possible to do so in Holland and Sweden.

Arranging appointments to observe and test in schools in New Jersey was not too difficult though perhaps only two-thirds of the districts I approached granted permission. Obviously, at the time I made my request, I stated that all scores would be anonymous.

It was not at all difficult to obtain permission to observe and test in European schools.

Only one city refused permission, Munich, Germany. In Europe, also, scores were to be anonymous. What was difficult to find, from this side of the ocean, was the proper person to whom to address my letters in Europe. Eventually, the itinerary was arranged, and I was ready to begin observing and testing.

In the United States, in suburban New Jersey schools, this covered a period from September to October 14, 1977, and the month of January, 1978. In Europe, my visits were from Monday, October 17, 1977, to Friday, November 25, 1977, originally scheduled for the countries of Iceland, Holland, Sweden, Germany, Austria and France. I chose these countries because of their languages' relationship to the English language. English grew from a Germanic root language (as did those in those countries other than France), and English had French "grafted" onto it after the Norman Conquest. I will report on those European visits first, and then on the American schools, combining both fall and January visitations.

I have generally been a vacation-only tourist for all my life, but I was to learn on this trip that the BEST way to visit a country and really to appreciate its color is to visit the schools to which its people entrust what is most important to them, their children!

CHAPTER 4
Anecdotal Log on European School Visits

Luxembourg

My first stop was to have been Reykjavik, Iceland, and then Akureyri, Iceland, to observe and test in schools the week of October 17, 1977. I had seen a consolidated Icelandic school on an earlier camping trip in Iceland and had been impressed by its attractive furnishings and large, modern building. Also, a primary-grades teacher in Iceland (the cook on that commercial camping trip that summer) had told me that normally her Icelandic school had no reading failures by third grade, although some few children received special instruction because they read slowly.

Of course, the high rate of literacy in Iceland has been a byword for generations. Nevertheless, in such a small country (with about 200,000 population), with its own ancient language (from the same root as Norwegian and English but with a slightly different alphabet), it was astonishing to visit bookstores in Reykjavik and Akureyri and to see shelves stocked with a variety of Icelandic books in numbers that could rival New York book stores. Each Icelandic book had to be printed in the special Icelandic letters and language, and therefore had a maximum potential sale of probably far, far under 200,000. (Of course, so many Icelanders speak English that a market certainly exists for English language books as well.)

I still covet a beautiful, but expensive, botany manual I saw in Akureyri which I resisted buying, which had exquisite drawings of hundreds of obscure (to Americans) Icelandic glacial-age plants, and explanations in beautifully printed Icelandic. Separated as Iceland is from Europe and America, many glacial-age plants which died out from the competition of other plants on either side of the Atlantic Ocean reportedly managed to survive in mid-ocean Iceland.

It would have been fascinating to visit the schools that produced the highly literate Icelandic population that was buying such books as the beautiful botany manual, but chance ruled otherwise. The visits I had planned to Icelandic schools the week of October 17, 1977, had to be canceled because of an unprecedented strike by government workers in Iceland, and the Reykjavik airport was closed to all flights.

So, instead of landing in Reykjavik as planned on Sunday, October 16, 1977, my flight terminated in charming Luxembourg, the last stop on Icelandic Airways trans-Atlantic flights. A quick call to the Ecoles Primaires de la Ville de Luxembourg on Monday resulted in an appointment that day with a gracious and helpful official who very kindly gave me permission to visit any school in Luxembourg during the week (after I had managed to find his offices on winding, old-world streets). He told me that the first grades had hours from 8 to 10 a. m. and from 2 to 3 p. m. on Wednesday and Friday (I believe on Monday, also) but no afternoon hours on Tuesday and Thursday. I therefore decided to wait until Wednesday for my school visit.

He also told me that the official language of Luxembourg is French, but the language spoken by most citizens in their homes is German. When the little ones come to first grade, they are taught to read in German, but switch to French in the second grade. This information helped me to understand a little better something I had noticed in his offices while waiting for my interview. A very attractive young woman answered a telephone across from where I was sitting, and, in the course of a few minutes' conversation, switched back and forth from French to German perhaps ten or twelve times. I had seldom before heard anyone speaking in this fashion and was intrigued by it. In the next few days, I learned it is standard practice for most native Luxembourgians, as I listened to them on the streets, in restaurants, in coffee shops, on buses - and even in the schools! It is not that the two languages are mixed and used together. When they are speaking French, they are speaking only French. I understand enough French to be able to follow that. But when they switched to German, all I heard was German. What the cue is that causes the conversation to switch from one language to another would be fascinating to learn.

My visit to a Luxembourg school turned out to be, in some ways, the best of all my school visits. I was able to choose, all by myself, which school to visit. There was therefore almost no chance at all that it was an atypical demonstration school. On the contrary, the school I picked near the downtown business center was in what was perhaps the poorest residential area of Luxembourg. Perhaps four-fifths of the students were children of poor immigrants, and spoke neither German nor French at home. The teachers in this school were faced with the appalling task of teaching first-graders to speak German so that they could teach them to read in German, and then teaching the same children in second grade to speak French so that they could follow the instruction which is given in French in second grade.

On the face of it, this is a ludicrously impossible task. It seems apparent that it cannot be done. Yet it might be said that these Luxembourg teachers have something in common with bumblebees. It has been said that, according to aerodynamic theory, bumblebees should not be able to fly. But no one has told that to the bumblebees, and so they go ahead and fly anyway. According to general teaching wisdom, it is very difficult to teach in a bi-lingual situation. But, teaching in a tri-lingual situation in the primary grades (foreign language plus German plus French) should be manifestly impossible. But apparently no one has told that to the Luxembourg teachers I saw, so they just went ahead, like the bumblebees, and did it anyway, with astonishingly good results.

When I arrived at the Luxembourg school which I had chosen, shortly after 8 a. m., I found it was divided into two separate old buildings, with separate entrances. Until about 1961, classes here were reportedly separated by sex, so perhaps one-half of the school was used then for girls and the other half for boys. The school was surrounded by a playground which the children in this city neighborhood could use all day, and by a high iron picket fence. Inside, the building was very pleasant, with nicely tiled halls. I showed my letter of introduction to the first member of the staff I met when entering the building. I expected to be sent to a central office, but instead was sent upstairs to a first- and second- grade classroom, and asked to wait until the class returned from religious instruction, which they were receiving from a visiting nun with another class in a straight second-grade classroom.

While waiting for the first- and second-grade class to return, I spoke with a third-grade teacher in another room across the hall. She was a middle-aged woman, relaxed, gentle and warm. There was affectionate badinage going on between the class and her, as they worked on a written assignment from the board. The room was full of sunshine, and it was not all coming in the windows. Having taught third grade for 13 years myself, I was impressed with the work she was requiring from them in this second month of school. (In Luxembourg, school began on September 12.) She had taught many years, she said, but never third grade until this year. She had a class of 16 which she had taught in second grade the year before. She would have had to retain five children at the end of second grade, but did not want to do it, so instead she moved ahead with the class to third grade.

It was a very happy room. The children were working, relaxed, at their desks, which faced the board. She said that instructional methods were very traditional. The children were drawing three basic triangles from directions in writing at the board. The teacher said, deprecatingly, "They cannot give the actual names of the triangles. I just want them to understand."

I saw their notebooks in French which she had opened and stacked in a pile on her desk, and I remarked on the neatness of the mathematics work in the books and the paragraphs written in French. She appeared honestly startled, and said, "These?!!! THESE aren't very good."

The teacher was doing a fantastic teaching job but did not seem to know it.

She pointed to a girl whom she said was a "victim of the global method." The girl could read anything once she had read it once, but could not read new material and "could not write from dictation."

Only about five children in the class were native Luxembourgians, which she said was a large proportion for this area, and the rest were Yugoslavs, Portuguese, Germans, Italians, etc. It was only recently that they had so many foreign children. For the Yugoslavs, Portuguese, Italians, etc., French was commonly the second language of the parents. They did not know German. Therefore, in kindergarten, the foreign children from different backgrounds began communicating among themselves in French, not German.

The religion class across the hall finished and the little first- and second-graders returned to their own room with their teacher at 9 o'clock. The teacher was a very pleasant and friendly young man. I followed his class into their classroom.

In his vertically-grouped class were ten first-graders and six second-graders. The second-graders talked quietly while doing extremely neat arithmetic work on cross-hatched paper, as the teacher taught the first-graders. (All the work I saw in this school was surprisingly neat.) During the teacher's lesson with the first-graders, which he gave in German, he spoke briefly to a second-grader but it was in French. The second-grade child then turned and talked in German to a classmate.

The children had double desks with a tray under each for their belongings. They also all had very large, important- looking book-bags which they put on racks at the sides of their desks. This certainly served to bolster the amusing self- importance of first-graders! What on earth could they have had to put in those enormous bags? The children went home at noon, so they could not even carry lunch!

In the front of the room was a flannelboard, on which had been placed adhering cards with pictures of children, trees and other things, and cards with printed words. A great many other flannelboard materials were stored on a rear table. Also in the front of the room was a large, movable blackboard and a screen in back of it. Also visible were Cuisenaire rods, "Nombres En Couleurs," from Calozen, Brussels. (When I first arrived, I had been told that the second-grade class across the hall would have a mathematics lesson with the rods after religion.) A portable clockface was on a shelf for telling-time practice, with a 12-hour dial and 24-hour dial. (Unlike the United States, most Europeans seem to use the 24-hour clock. It never seems to be 3 p. m. there anymore, but 15:00 hours.) The room had what looked like two pieces of audio-visual equipment on a cart. Although there did not seem to be a great deal of teaching equipment in the room, everything that was visible was good and really counted from an instructional standpoint.

The young teacher said it was his first year teaching. Today, he would begin with a reading lesson for the first- graders, and then work later with the second-graders. (If I understood correctly, the first-graders would leave at 10 but the second-graders stayed till ll:30.) School, he said, had begun on September 12, 1977, and today was October 19, 1977. He said the children were taught by a global method, being given 50 sight words before the first sounds were introduced. (The other first-grade teacher whose class I visited later referred to the program as a mixed method, with analytic phonics.)

Yet, after only a month in school, the children were learning the sounds of consonants and vowels, and the critical skill of how to blend them. In a month or less, they had already covered the 50 sight words and had started on synthetic phonics - quite a contrast to Chall's comment that in 1965 it was mid-first grade before children in America had 150 sight words and began to learn the sounds of the alphabet. Also, in those American programs, blending of sounds was absolutely forbidden!

The children in this room, after only one month in first grade, had learned the sounds of two consonants (m and l) and two vowels (a and i). In the other first-grade room I visited later that day, they had learned one consonant (m) and two vowels (a and i) and were beginning study of "l". In this room, and in the first-grade I visited later, the first-grade children were systematically studying the blending of these known consonants and vowels. In this room, I saw blending being done synthetically, but in the first grade I visited later, the particular lesson was on the analysis of blends.

The fact that the children had been exposed to 50 sight words in the first four weeks of first grade did not alter the fact that in practice the reading program in this school was a heavily phonic program. The Luxembourg mixed global method, as I actually observed it being taught, was far closer to an American synthetic phonics series like Lippincott than to any American eclectic sight-word-plus-phonics program. From what I have observed, the use of the words, "global," or "phonics," without definition is nearly meaningless. To avoid the use of those largely meaningless "global" and "phonics" labels, the first-grade programs I observed on my sabbatical were coded, as discussed previously, from Code 1 for a straight sight-word ("meaning") program to Code 10 for a straight phonics ("sound") program, with mixed approaches falling in between, from 2 to 9. I coded the Luxembourg program on this instructional scale at Code 8, which the notes that I took and the text which I later saw justify.

My use of Code 8 was confirmed when I received an actual copy of the children's text. I had written the school administration in Luxembourg after I returned to the United States, requesting information on where I could buy a copy, and instead received a complimentary copy! It was more of the wonderful courtesy I met throughout my project!

This text, Toni, Bim, Karin, Leo, Ann - Witta Wir Lesen Fibe fur das este schuljahr, is a compulsory book for beginning first graders in Luxembourg. It introduces sight words on the first twelve pages, with charming illustrations. The first vowel isolated from sight words is on page 13, "au" from lauf, but apparently it is not studied but just given a passing analytic approach. The first real study of a letter is "M" in Mama and Mimi (analytic study of "M") on page 14. Page 15 has a string of upper and lower case M's and a charming picture scene (presumably to use to identify "M" words in auditory discrimination of "M"). Page 17 introduces "i" and has "i" and "m" written in isolation and in syllables (synthetic blending - pure phonics). Page 18 has a little story and page 19 introduces "a" and more synthetic phonics blending with "m" and "a".

This page was where the other class I visited later in the morning must have been working, as the page had picture sentences beginning "Mama im" and "Mimi am" which sentences ended with pictures. Page 21 introduced "l" in syllables, which confirmed my notes taken in the two first grades, that they had covered "m", "a" and "i" and had begun "l". Each succeeding two pages then followed the same pattern: a little story on the even numbered page and a new letter introduced on the odd-numbered page with synthetic blending into syllables.

This first book, which became quite complex in reading matter by the last page (66), introduced letters in this sequence: m, i, a, l, o, p, e, ei, u, d, s, w, au, r, t, h, sch, n, g, v, o with an umlaut over it, k, p, b, r. Christmas pictures are on page 49, so the last page (66) is probably reached about the end of January.

The second book introduced the few remaining letters of the alphabet and special vowels and blends. By the end of the second book (59 pages) the stories were quite complex. To judge by the book alone, this is a heavily phonics program, at least Code 8, and my observations made before I saw the book gave me the same impression.

In the first- and second-grade classroom that I visited first, some of the initial 50 sight words were written on the board when we came in. They were (if I transcribed the German spellings correctly): die, musik, kommt, schule, laufen, lauf, wo ist da ist singen kommt. A child had an envelope with about 50 sight words in it. The teacher began the lesson, which proceeded from board practice on phonics (blending m plus a and i) to workbook practice involving cutting out letters, then dictation of words using those letters, and then auditory discrimination on a new sound, "l", using the workbook again.

First, the teacher put "am" and "im" over each other on the board and had them sound it, then "mi." Then he wrote "Mi" with a capital letter. He wrote and had them sound "am, ma ma, mi mi." Perhaps one-third knew "ma" when he first called for answers. Then "mi - im." He put colored chalk on the "i's" and then colored chalk on the "a's". He had them sound "a". He then wrote these on the board and had the children read them: Ma, mi, im, am, mimi, mama, mami, with colored chalk under i and a. He said the use of colored chalk was his addition to the program.

The teacher proceeded from board practice to the workbook. The workbook pages had large and small m's, a's, and i's. The children cut out the letters, m, a, and i, and put them on pictures in their books (presumably pictures of words with these same sounds, m, a, and i, for auditory discrimination). This page had a cartoon figure saying "Hallo," and pictures in circles and some words on the bottom. He told the children to hold up "m" and they showed it. (This part of the lesson - auditory and visual discrimination of m, is not unlike the first lesson in the American phonics program, Alpha Time, with Mr. Munching Mouth (m) involving the same skills, auditory and visual discrimination, but at this point these children were proceeding from a small known sight word, such as mama and mimi, to its parts, consonant and vowel (analytic approach) while Alpha proceeds from a known consonant (m) and later known vowel (a) to blend a new word (am, etc.), a synthetic approach.

The teacher asked the children to show the large and small a. Then he proceeded to dictation, a synthetic approach now, the children building words on their desks as he said them. He said, "mim" and they built it with letters and showed him for approval.

At this point, while they were building words on their desks, I became conscious of the little-boy problems of a youngster in front of me. (His soul brothers sit in every classroom on earth!) He had two "i's" in front of him, which he had not separated from the workbook page they were cutting, as he was supposed to do. The little girl next to him corrected him. He then immediately dropped half of his letters on the floor and left them there. Another little girl disapprovingly told him to pick them up. He finally did.

The teacher proceeded to work on auditory discrimination of what appeared to be a new letter, "l". The children were apparently following the work by marking pictures on a new workbook page. What is interesting is that he did not just practice the discrimination in the beginning position of the word, as is common in most American beginning programs, but also in the medial and terminal positions. He asked, in German, "Does 'liter' start with an 'l'? The children then marked the picture of a liter on the workbook page. Then, in German, "Do you hear 'l' in the words... (luma, hammeg, finzel, schlussel, schule, cater)".

At least, these were some of the "words" he seemed to be dictating, as heard by my non-German-language ears. The only "German" words that I felt completely comfortable with were the words in the German translation that Berlitz had made for me of the "Peter has a little dog..." oral reading test that I was carrying, which was 144 words long in the original English version. I was to use the German translation of the "Peter..." test later in the day to test the second graders in another classroom in this Luxembourg school.

Most of the children appeared to have good auditory discrimination, far more than my first-graders at the beginning of October.

The teacher continued, in German, "Locomotive, do you hear 'l'? He continued auditory discrimination on "l" for more than ten minutes. After this, the little ones had their snacks. (I wonder how much of the book-bags they filled?) While they had their snacks, the first-graders colored the pictures in their workbooks under which they had just finished putting marks.

The workbook was entitled, "ABC, Eine After... Editions des Instituteurs Reunis, Luxembourg, 1975." It had the alphabet at the beginning of the book and then pages of heavy phonics. This workbook was not mandatory, but the reading text, Toni, Bim, Karin, Leo, Ann, was mandatory. The 50 sight-words were associated with this text.

When the first graders had been working, the room had been relaxed. There had been no enforcement of silence, as the repartee between the little boy who had dropped his letters, and his disparaging female classmates, showed. There was, however, the natural silence that resulted from concentrated work. I was to learn later that the common American classroom dictum, "Talking is forbidden," was almost nowhere to be found in the European schools I visited (nor in the English open-classroom schools I had toured for two weeks in 1971 in company with fellow American teachers). When seeing a demonstration lesson on Cuisenaire rods in Brussels later, the little first-graders did not talk, but, since I was accompanied by an official of the school system, it was an unusual situation and may not have been the normal practice.

Not much time was left in the short first-grade morning, so I went quickly to the other first grade in the other half of the building. This first-grade class had 22 children, all but six of them with Portuguese parents. The tables were arranged in two L forms, one nested inside the other, with two and six children seated at the first L, and six and eight children seated at the larger L. In the front of the room was another movable blackboard as in the previous room, and a hanging flannelboard with sight words grouped in a fashion which suggested that the teacher was using them to concentrate on the "l" sound as I had seen in the previous room. The children were talking quietly here as elsewhere while they worked. The children's drawings were displayed around the classroom, and some seemed very far advanced, using the scale from the Draw-A-Man IQ test as a standard. I had been told that perhaps as many as one-third of the children in this particular school had to be retained in first grade because of the severe language problem for children of immigrants, so perhaps this apparent superiority in drawings simply reflected the older ages of some of the children.

This man teacher (also very friendly and helpful, and extremely witty) told me later after the children had gone home for lunch that he had begun teaching 16 years ago with 50 children in first grade, all boys. He said the present text had far too many sight words for duller children. He said it was a mixed method, global, with analytic phonics, and two volumes were covered in the course of the first year. He said in this system there was less instructional freedom for the teacher. In the older method, starting with one letter, he said he could make a story for one week using it. The children, he believed, had more fun. Also, there was less of a problem in the older method with dictation.

This teacher might have been appalled if he had seen some of the sight-word texts used for American children in the 1950's and before, where dictation for first-grade children would have been out of the question, as the children were taught no vowel sounds at all. The Iowa spelling norms from the 1950's illustrate how impossible dictation would have been for second-graders as well.

This instructor said that the newer global approach for the Luxembourg schools had been in use less than ten years, and he felt the newer teachers could not be in the position that he was to be able to compare both methods, since newer teachers had never taught with the older method.

As mentioned previously, the compulsory book for beginning first-graders is named Toni, Bim, Karin, Leo, Ann. It begins, as mentioned, with the sight-word vocabulary of 50 words, and is called a mixed method with analytic phonics.

At this point, a child read a sight-word page correctly in a notebook (not the text) while I watched, beginning, "Mimi is in der schule. Mimi matt eine maus." The first page of the book itself read, "Ada ist Bim. Bim ruft. wo ist Anni? wo ist Leo? wo ist Karen? wo ist Toni?" Page 4 had, "halt, halt. Bim ruft. Halt, halt, da kommt ein auto."

I was to find two of these beginning words recurring in another German language beginning program that I saw in Hamburg, Germany, "Mimi" and "ruft." However, only this Luxembourg program had an initial sight-word load. The word, "Mimi" showed up later in the Belgian and French programs as well, probably because it lends itself so well to sounding-and-blending, and both languages use the Latin syllable-ending- "i" sound heard in "do, re, MI, fa, sol, la, TI, do."

Since I had arrived in this second room later in the morning, I could only see the completion of the reading lesson. At this point, the teacher was giving dictation. It was evident that this was synthetic phonic practice, using "m" and "i" to spell two words, "Mimi im." As he dictated they wrote on slates, cross-hatched like the paper I had seen, and with the alphabet on the top and bottom. He dictated, "Mimi im auto," and the children wrote "Mimi im" and drew a picture of an auto. He said, "Mimi im haus," and they wrote "Mimi im" and drew a picture of a house. They were writing very painstakingly.

He lapsed momentarily into French from German. Since most of these children had Portuguese parents, and the official language of Luxembourg is French, it was unlikely that these first-grade children could have understood very much of the German he was mandated to speak when teaching first-graders. However, as mentioned elsewhere, the non-German-language children in kindergarten in this multi-language school began to communicate in French on the playground, so the teacher's use of French at this point, instead of the mandated German for first-graders, was apparently necessary if he wanted to teach these particular first-graders any fine points. Therefore, in French, he directed the first-grade children on how to form the letters exactly, and showed a child how to use the graph to aid in proportioning letters. The teacher then lapsed back into German, and dictated, "Mimi im garten," and guided the pencil of a child as she wrote "Mimi im" and she then attempted to draw a picture of a garden.

From this exercise which I observed, it was evident that, despite the 50 sight words, in this second month of school, the children had learned the sound of a consonant and vowel, and how to blend them in the position with the vowel before the consonant, "im," and after the consonant, "Mimi." When children have, by only the second month of first grade, already learned to associate sound with letters, and have learned how to blend the letters into words, the program is heavily phonic, whether it considers itself to be "global" or not.

The bell rang and the class was dismissed, after which I was able to talk with the instructor.

In summary, in this school, although the compulsory text was labeled a mixed global method with analytic phonics, in actual practice, only a month after the start of school, the children in both first-grade rooms had been introduced to letter sounds and blending. In the first room, letters covered had been m, i, and a, and they were beginning l. In this second room, they may also have covered the same work, but, since I came in later in the morning, I only saw the section of work on dictation. This covered the letters m and i, but from flannelboard materials arranged in the front of the room, it appeared they also were beginning the study of "l", using the sight-word base of 50 words. Despite the sight-word base, such heavy emphasis on analytic and synthetic blending in both rooms made it seem appropriate to assign a Code 8 to this program, based solely on the class work I observed. The book itself, however, as mentioned, rated Code 8 also. As I actually saw it practiced, the Luxembourg program was very much based on "sound," not "meaning".

When school reconvened at 2 p. m., I tested a second-grade class, asking the teacher if I could start with the rows farthest from the window, which self-chosen sampling increased the probability of testing by "chance," instead of by ability grouping. In the part of the hour that was available until school dismissed at 3 p. m., after arranging for the testing in the hall, I managed to test 12 of the 18 pupils in that second grade. The teacher said that those I did not have time to test were neither brighter nor duller than the rest, so my self-chosen sample was probably an average one.

Considering the problems faced by the teachers in this school, with its severe language barriers, the results of the tests were extraordinary. Of the second-graders tested, 92% scored at or above the instructional level on oral reading, and ALL above the frustrational level. On comprehension, despite the language barrier between the children and me in explaining how to answer the questions, and despite the obvious language barrier because these children did not speak German at home (most of them), 30% passed the comprehension test. (For comparison, in January in the United States, the average number passing, where there was no language barrier, ran from 44% to 83%). Four of the 12 children read slowly, and none fast, although one, or 8% read fairly fast. One of the 12 children, 8%, made reversals. Exact class scores for Luxembourg are given in the appendix.

I took a taxi (which was hair-raisingly fast on the modern highway) back to my hotel at the airport outside of town.

After my flight to Iceland had ended unexpectedly in Luxembourg instead of Iceland, I had stayed at that airport hotel. I had been told when I got to Kennedy Airport in New York before I took the plane that I could not get off my flight at Iceland because of the general strike, so I had decided to go anyway and to stay on for Luxembourg which was the last stop on the scheduled flight. I had called my travel agent sister before leaving New York, who made a trans-Atlantic phone call immediately and reserved space at that airport hotel in Luxembourg. It was super-modern, and very luxurious, with a golf course attached (of no use to me, unfortunately).

It was there that I first saw something that I later saw all through Europe - the acceptance by public establishments of pets as family members! I had my dinner one evening in the Luxembourg airport hotel coffee shop. Two women were sitting at an adjacent table, and had their dog sitting under it. However, the dog disapproved of this beautiful establishment totally, being very unimpressed with its elegance, and was saying so in periodic yelps that sounded as if he were getting his tail caught in a door. No one - neither the coffee shop personnel nor the other guests - paid the slightest attention to these ear-splitting yelps, once they knew they were coming from a dog which had no other problem except that he was having a temper tantrum.

Being so close to Belgium, the home of the Cuisenaire rods for math instruction which I regarded so highly, and, with no further appointments for the week, I decided to try to get an appointment in a Belgian school which used the Cuisenaire rods.

Brussels

After telephoning Brussels in Belgium from Luxembourg, I received the address of the appropriate office to contact on Thursday afternoon, after my arrival in Brussels. I checked out of my Luxembourg hotel on Thursday morning, early, to take the train for Brussels, dragging my abominable luggage after me from the taxi into the railroad station. Station porters are almost as extinct as dinosaurs, and the inadequate little baggage carrier with wheels that I had brought with me accomplished little more than to bruise my fingers and to ruin my already frayed disposition. I had so many pieces of luggage because I had to carry hundreds of copies of blank test papers in five languages, since I had no way to know how many I would need, and I also had to carry reference books as well. I felt like a bookmobile without wheels.

On the train, after stuffing my luggage under seats and in racks, I found myself seated in a compartment opposite a courtly old German man who later said he was 70 (although he did not look that old). He was on his way to visit his son in Brussels, where his son worked for the

European Common Market. We communicated with my fractured French. When the snack cart came by, I bought a cup of coffee, the container strangely arranged in tiers. Unknown to me, it was a fancy new gadget - a disposable drip coffee pot. When I removed the top section too soon, half the coffee dripped out on my dress, and the kindly man opposite me immediately handed me his paper to save my clothes from the deluge!

The train traveled through long stretches of woods - probably, I assumed, lumber lots - but I was fascinated by the drabness of the fall colors. Some fall coloration, to be sure, was on the leaves, but it was very dingy. I tried to tell my companion in the compartment that, in America, our fall leaves are brighter, but through the fog of my French and his European pride, he answered, "Yes, our European leaves are very much nicer." I let the misunderstanding slide - it seemed only courteous - and started to wonder why there is a difference.

From out of the natural history books, I remembered something called Gloger's Rule, that animals nearer the equator have heavier pigmentation. (They do, unless it is canceled out by protective coloration, as occurs in desert animals, or as occurs in the marine iguanas of the Galapagos. Their colors, black with white spots, are a startling example of protective coloration. They fit them to live on their black lava rocks jutting into the sea, which are splattered with white from cormorant bird droppings!)

However, the rule generally holds true. For instance, tropical seashells are much more desirable to collect than seashells from our temperate regions, because they are so much more beautifully colored when they are closer to the equator.

Gloger's Rule apparently works with plants, as well, since tropical flowers are normally more brilliant than northern flowers. The yellows we see in our North American deciduous leaves in the fall are colors that were really there all summer but masked by green chlorophyll. When the chlorophyll dies in the fall, the colors are revealed, as is the red that develops during cool fall nights. When the chlorophyll dies in European leaves, however, it reveals far fainter yellows, and the developing reds are weaker., A glance at the latitude is all that is needed to tie the difference in with Gloger's rule. Europe is steamheated by the Gulf Stream, and most of Europe where there are deciduous trees lies above the 50th meridian (about Land's End, England), where at this latitude in North America, since it is colder, there is instead the Canadian evergreen forest. American deciduous trees lie largely below the 45th meridian (about the Canadian border at Vermont), so Gloger's Rule should have produced the different, fainter pigments in the leaves that I observed. I was to see children display these fainter European leaves with pride, however, in elementary schools all over north Europe.

When I arrived in Brussels on Thursday, I was not able to contact anyone at the address I had been given, but left a note requesting visits at schools the following day. Hoping to visit a school that day, Thursday, also, if possible, to observe reading as well as the rods, I spoke with an administrator at a large elementary school nearby. He received me in a large and graciously furnished office, explaining that it would be impossible at this late hour (about 2:30 p. m.) to set up such a visit, since approval had to be given by a central office. He mentioned a parents-teachers meeting at 4:15 for parents of the three first grades, which he said I could attend without prior arrangements, but I declined. However, he gave me a good deal of his time to discuss reading methods in first grade, which discussion was very interesting.

Some 25 years ago, this man had taught first grade, using the analytic phonic method, but he said he preferred a global method which had been in use in a school where he had formerly been an administrator. He proceeded to describe the method, and succeeded in giving an exact description of what in America is called the language experience or experience chart method. The teacher and class, working together, compose a story about some common experience which the teacher immediately writes down, as it is being composed, on a large chart in the front of the room. The "experience chart" is used for later study. He said:

> "The teacher is the program. She gives the sounds when the children are ready. In September, they begin with four-sentence experience charts, and the stories get longer as the year goes by. By Christmas, they know more letters and sounds. The sounds come by syllables in February. Most children know the alphabet by Easter, and are reading by the end of the year."

Much more phonic emphasis is used in the European experience chart versions than in American versions. This administrator also made no mention of memorizing whole words, although the children were obviously working with whole words. The method begins very much the same as it is practiced in America, but its ultimate use can be very different.

The administrator's reason for preferring this global method was, "It is much more enjoyable." Yet this was the same reason I was given by an experienced Luxembourg man teacher who preferred the older phonic method, beginning with only one letter: "It is much more fun." (This man had made up stories about the letter, which stories lasted for a week per letter). Each man seemed to favor a different program, but for the same reason. I think what they really liked was the common element they themselves had injected into each program. They adapted the curriculum and improvised on it to meet the interests of the children.

In Sweden I was to find that the experience chart method was becoming very popular (called LTG there, and incorporating a mix of sight-word/global and phonic approaches). All through France, I found the experience chart method being used very successfully, but it was usually employed to teach very heavy phonics, a very different thing from its use for decades in the United States.

The history of reading, as written by Mitford Matthews, interestingly enough places the origin of something like the experience chart method, not in the United States, but in Germany in the early nineteenth century, where the normal words method was witnessed by Horace Mann,. The true experience chart method was used in Colonel Parker's famous school in Chicago in the late nineteenth century. One of Parker's most highly regarded teachers, Miss Flora J. Cooke, a third-grade teacher there, who is mentioned rather often in Mitford Mathews <u>Teaching Reading, Historically Considered,</u> (1966) had one of the school's experience charts reproduced in E. B. Huey's 1908 book, <u>The Psychology and Pedagogy of Reading</u> (page 198).

> "October 2, 1897. We went to visit a farm.
> It was a beautiful day.
> There was a deep blue sky above us, with not a cloud in it, and cool, fresh air around us. We had bright sunshine all day long.
> 'The nicest day of all the year!' said Fritz.
> The farm we visited is 15 miles from our school.
> It is on Halsted Street.
> We might have gone all the way in wagons, but that was too slow for us.
> It only took us 42 minutes to go on the train.
> Then we were only one mile and a half from the farm.
> Big hay-wagons were waiting for us at the station." (etc.)

It is highly likely that European visitors to Parker's famous school during the Chicago world's fair in 1893 observed the experience chart approach as used by the teachers there, and brought it back with them again to Europe.

The experience chart method to teach beginning reading began to be used in the early twentieth century by the famous Belgian medical doctor, Ovide Decroly, who initially used it with retarded children (but with heavy phonics). It was later used - but without the heavy phonics - by the equally famous (more properly infamous?) Celestin Freinet of France, who wrote enormously dreary and boring tomes through some of which I later waded.

At the end of my interesting discussion with this Brussels school administrator, since it was by no means certain that the woman for whom I had left a note would see it in time to arrange an appointment for me on Friday, he also gave me the name of the official at the town hall through whose office such visits are arranged.

After leaving his office, I found the town hall (Hotel de la Ville) and became instantly a tourist again. Our town hall in little Lyndhurst, New Jersey, was built in 1924, but the huge Brussels town hall appears to have been built about 1294. It is a fascinating, architectural treasure. I went up marble stairways from the first floor to a huge central hall on the second floor, complete with enormous paintings, twelve-foot-high tapestries, ancient furniture, and suits of armor. Stately doors led off this incredible central hall in all directions, and I felt suddenly gauche, not knowing what to do with the piece of paper in my hand with the name of an official written on it. From out of nowhere appeared two men in tuxedos (I never did find out why they were wearing such formal dress at 4 p. m.). They sent me down a winding corridor which suddenly left the Middle Ages and became carpeted, hushed and modern-office-building-like. I felt much more at home.

The tuxedoed two men had directed me to the office of a young man, not the official whose name was on my paper, but who could handle my question. He listened courteously as I made my request, made some telephone calls, and told me that I had a ten a. m. appointment on Friday to observe Cuisenaire rods in use in first and second grade. I would be accompanied by a school administrator.

The extraordinary courtesy and helpfulness I found in Luxembourg had been duplicated here in Brussels! I was to find to my delight that this kind of helpfulness and cooperation was the norm almost everywhere I went in Europe, except in one unfortunate initial contact that I made in Paris. Upon arrival in Paris from Innsbruck, when I telephoned the official whose name had been on the letter I had received in answer to my request for appointments, which letter had stated that school visits could be arranged, the man simply snorted and banged down his telephone receiver. The probability is that he was a self-important department head, who had his important name routinely added to every letter leaving his department, while the real authors of those letters remained anonymous, unless the receivers knew how to decode the authors' initials somewhere on the bottom of the paper. This self-important man probably never expected to be contacted directly by anybody getting such department letters, such people as myself. It probably would have taken Sherlock Holmes to find the courteous man who had actually acknowledged my letter from the United States, and who undoubtedly WOULD have been helpful to me if I could have gotten through to him.

After the self-important official slammed down the phone in my ear on Monday morning shortly after nine a. m., I realized I would have to find the Parisian schools' central office, and present my curiously useless letter to see if I could be directed to someone who could handle it. I eventually did find a courteous young man who called a local school and made an appointment for me for the following day, Tuesday. Unknown to me, Parisian schools were routinely closed on Wednesday. The Tuesday appointment was with a school principal who was delightful and warm, and who arranged for me to observe in a first grade and test in second grade. I therefore managed to salvage at least one day's observation and testing out of the three days I had scheduled for Paris, before leaving for Quimper and Avignon, where, again, as elsewhere in Europe, the courtesy and cooperation once again surpassed all my expectations, and where specific appointments had been made for me ahead of time, in answer to my letters requesting those appointments. However, my unpleasant initial experience in Paris only served to make me even more thankful for the cooperation and help that I received elsewhere in Europe, such as in Luxembourg and Brussels, which I believed then and still believe was absolutely astonishing.

I returned to my hotel, the Brussels-Hilton, the only one I could get into on such short notice. Near the town hall was a charming old hotel I would have preferred, but hotel space was very difficult to get that week. The Hilton, however, had a delightful semi-outdoor dining room, done in green and white stripes, potted palms and awnings, and wonderful greenhouse-like windows. While having dinner there, I studied the smartly dressed and coiffed Brussels women. I assume they were having their meal-for-the-week, because I am convinced that is the only way that middle-aged women can stay so smartly thin - but their clothing was fabulous! No matter how simple, their garments had flair and personality.

The next morning at ten, I met the Brussels school administrator who was to bring me to the Cuisenaire demonstration lessons. For the school administrator to give me a complete morning of his time was wonderfully courteous! We walked to a building which was only a short distance from his office and rang the bell of that fairly narrow building which did not look at all like a school. I learned that the blocks in Brussels are very, very deep so that a very large school stretched out behind this narrow entrance.

After we were met at the school door and crossed a large entry hall, we were taken to a beautifully furnished office, where we waited for the principal. I made no notes, but my impression was of a richly carpeted room, with Louis XIV chairs upholstered in velvet, a delicate, polished wooden desk and a lovely old fireplace. In the days when this old building was constructed, it was often customary to make very large rooms, very tall ceilings, fireplaces, and elaborate plaster-sculptured borders around the ceilings. In so many ways, our 20th century "progress" is really regression.

The woman principal arrived and, after receiving us very graciously, led us through the high-ceilinged halls on the way to the first classroom I was to visit. I could see from materials hanging in the hallways that the school used the Hungarian Kodaly method in music. I was told that a woman head teacher had visited Hungary and studied it there, and that all Brussels schools used it. (The music teachers in my school in New Jersey used it also.)

The principal led us through the children's dining room. I cannot call a room with curtains, sideboards, tablecloths, and place settings on each table, as I saw there, a cafeteria. Eventually we arrived at a first-grade room. It was furnished traditionally, with the desks facing front. The little girls wore smocks, for a kind of Alice-in-Wonderland look. The school administrator spoke pleasantly to the classroom teacher, and she said she was just beginning the mathematics lesson.

The room was very attractive. On the walls were pretty pictures and the children's work, of high quality. I saw as class equipment a large thermometer, a clock with movable hands, and a display showing the months of the year. Each child had his own set of Cuisenaire rods on his desk. My attention was focused on the Cuisenaire-rods lesson after this and I noticed nothing else.

We sat in the back of the room, and the school official explained to me the sequence of the curriculum. School began on September 1. The first-graders would do qualitative work with the rods until November 15, and quantitative work after that. Doing qualitative work before November 15 meant that they would study the rods only in relation to their colors and relative lengths. No numbers would be used in the study, and it would be separate from their work on sets of actual numbers. It would only be after November 15 that they would apply numbers to the rods, which they had been referring to by color name only until now.

This was a very different approach from the American Cuisenaire programs, which often keep qualitative work with the rods through the primary grades, so that there may be little carry-over from the rods to the regular arithmetic work with actual numbers that the class is studying. In these American qualitative programs after beginning first grade, the rods often have very little meaning either to children or teachers, and teachers therefore avoid them.

The rods were invented by a brilliant Belgian school principal, Georges Cuisenaire, sometime during the 1930's. It was only in the 1950's that their use became widespread in other schools.

Cuisenaire took a white cubic centimeter in wood, and used that as his primary unit. The next wood rod was two cubic centimeters long and painted red, a rod of three cubic centimeters in length was light green, four was purple (rose in Belgium), five was yellow, six was dark green, seven was black, eight was brown, nine was blue, and the final rod, an orange rod, was ten cubic centimeters in length. If the two centimeter (red) rod and the three centimeter (light green) rod are lined up end to end (called a "train") they are naturally exactly as long as the five centimeter (yellow) rod, when it is placed parallel to the "train.".

It is possible to demonstrate to a child who is having trouble understanding the meaning of arithmetic operations not only that 2 + 3 = 5 (red plus green equals yellow), but the meaning of subtraction, division, multiplication, fractions and bases.

The brilliant invention of the Cuisenaire rods shares something of the utter simplicity of the brilliant inventions of our decimal system of numbers and our alphabetic system of writing. The Cuisenaire rods are so utterly simple that it is puzzling to understand why it took so long for someone to conceive of them, and so utterly simple that they can be understood by little children, just as the alphabetic principal can be understood by them.

In studying the rods in this Brussels classroom, the class had started with white (1) and then red (2) but without using numbers, only color names (which names in French are blanc and rouge). The class started with the concepts of addition and subtraction while they were working with only three rods and two colors. For example, red minus white equals white (2 - 1 = 1). The teacher wrote this on the board as r - b = b (rouge - blanc = blanc). The beginning first- grade children therefore were being taught to read and to understand mathematical notation such as plus, minus and equals, and mathematical relationships, before they dealt with actual numbers in the use of the rods.

Later in the day, I visited the Cuisenaire bookstore and bought the text this teacher was using, and the text I later saw the second grade teacher using. The books were entitled <u>A La Decouverte de la Mathematique et Les Reglettes Cuisenaire, Book I</u> and <u>Book II,</u> by Louis Jeronnez and Isabelle Lejeune, teachers in Waterloo, Belgium. The texts were published by Editions Calozet, 40, Rue des Chartreux, Brussels, but are not available in English. Calozet also published many other materials for use in primary school mathematics.

From the notes I took, the first-grade teacher was using pages 70 and 71 of the teacher's guide for this lesson, which means she had covered a considerable amount of material to date. On this date, October 19, 1977, she was introducing the orange and last rod (later to be called 10). The children placed the rods in front of them on their desks, and she asked them to make as many equivalences as they could to match the orange rod. That meant the children would put together as many different combinations of rods as they could to equal the length of the orange rod. She asked the children to tell her the different ways they had been able to make combinations the same length as the orange rods. They dictated the color names of the combinations they had made and she wrote those combinations on the board, but with the letter abbreviations for the colors of the rods, not the whole color names.

To understand the teacher's board notations which are reported below, it is necessary to list the French names for the colors of the rods:

> blanc (b) for the white 1 rod
> rouge (r) for the red 2 rod,
> vert clair (v) for the light green 3 rod,
> rose (R) for the 4 rod (which is purple in America),
> jaune (j) for the yellow 5 rod,
> vert fonce (V) for the dark green 6 rod,
> noir (n) for the black 7 rod,

marron (m) for the brown 8 rod,
blue (B) for the blue 9 rod,
orange (O) for the orange 10 rod.

As a child dictated that orange is two yellows, the teacher wrote on the board, "O = 2j." A child dictated that orange is light green and dark green and blue, and the teacher wrote on the board, "O = v + V + B."

The teacher had the children dictate such equations to her for some time, and she wrote them all on the blackboard. Then she changed her approach. Instead of the children's dictating to her what they had built with the rods on their desks, and having her write from their dictation, she now wrote equations on the board with the letter abbreviations for the colors, but with the "answers" missing and asked the children to solve the equations using the rod equivalents at their desks.

The teacher wrote the following on the board and read each equation to the children, (probably because some of the children did not yet know how to read all the letters!) The children were able to solve the equations from her dictation, with very little additional help, as I could see for myself, since I was sitting next to some of the children's desks. The relationships and mathematical notation which the children had been able to absorb at this early date in first grade, October 19, was astonishing.

b + r + n =	b + __ = O	r + (2xr) =
r + V + b =	V + __ = O	R + (3xr) =
v + V =	O - (2xr) =	O - V =
O - m =	O - (3xr) =	O - R =
O - B =	O - (4xr) =	v + __ = O

To use the rods at this point in first grade assumes, of course, that the children had to have already been taught at least the particular letters used with the Cuisenaire rods (which in the French rod notation is six in the lower case and four in the upper case, plus the x used in multiplication examples).

The sureness of the little ones in working with the rods was demonstrated by an amusing little happening. The school official who brought me to the school was sitting next to the desk of a little girl and reached over to borrow some of her rods to demonstrate to me what the teacher had dictated. He paused momentarily in picking one of the rods dictated, and the little girl self-importantly shoved the correct rod across her desk to him, looking very disapproving because he had not picked up the rod as quickly as she did.

We adults are handicapped in using the rods and cannot fully appreciate what they mean to little children. We think of equations in numbers and then, in using the rods, have to translate each number to a color. This little girl who corrected the adult school official did not yet, in all probability, understand the meaning of numbers to 10. Yet she could already think concretely in terms of sets, using only colors. I taught first grade and know that, while beginning first-graders can often count numbers happily for their parents, perhaps to 100, they still do not really understand sets to ten. When they are asked to make piles of things - buttons, perhaps - with 1 in the first pile, 2 in the second pile, and so on to 10 in the last pile, they often break down at about 6 or 7. This, of course, is at the very beginning of first grade, but not later in the year, since the understanding comes quickly once it starts.

This little girl, who was able to think concretely in terms of sets, using only colors, had been given the "mental furniture" of dealing with pure relationships independently of fixed numbers. This is what made possible the amazing achievements I saw in the second-grade class I visited next.

When we entered the second grade room, the children had no rods at all on the desks in front of them, and, using nothing but what was in their heads (these Cuisenaire color relationships), they answered the teacher's questions with ease on factors of 12 and 21 and prime numbers to 21. Later, when I compared my notes taken during the lesson to the second grade text, I found that the teacher had already reached pages 106, 107 and 108 of the second-grade book, and the children were handling the concepts with ease. This lesson concerned the decomposition of 12 into its prime factors (2 x 2 x 3 = 12), which they later worked with the rods. They were working also breaking certain numbers (11, 13, 17, and 19) down into their prime numbers and addend remainders, such as (9 x 2) + 1 = 19. She later handed out the written material. The children completed the table with the rods, determined what the unknown fact was in each example, and then decided whether the statement that was printed was true or false (vrai ou faux). The material in the second table the children were apparently required to complete after I left, but its content was discussed also.

This helpful official, in making a point about the second-grade lesson, drew a number line to illustrate. In American primary mathematics texts, such number lines are always straight lines, marked off with numbers, just as on a ruler. I was amused by his more creative and actually more reasonable version of a number line, which was a curved line like the lines in a paisley print, and the numbers were affixed to the curve. After all, why should a number line be straight? I am ashamed to say I do not know the significance of his curved line, but I am sure it had significance!

These second-grade children completed this very difficult work for beginning second graders with apparent enjoyment and ease. The Cuisenaire rods are not just a better way to teach mathematics; they are a different way.

Cuisenaire rods (and such materials as Diene's base blocks which are an extension of the Cuisenaire concept) are to the teaching of mathematics what heavy phonics is to the teaching of reading. They are a "match" to the very essence of the systems themselves. As sight word teaching methods turn our writing system into a hieroglyphic writing system and destroy the brilliant alphabetic principle of writing by sound, the teaching of mathematics in our decimal system by rote memorization alone (important as memorization is in the proper place!) makes children fail to understand much of the meaning of arithmetic operations. By contrast, with the Cuisenaire rods, children are given a set of mathematical relationships which are mutually dependent, and they have these relationships with which to think ever afterwards.

The child psychologist, Piaget, stated that one of the first operations in which children can "conserve" quantity (really understand it) is in length, not counting. Teaching little children "counting" operations before they can "conserve" or understand quantity can be a waste of time. Since little children "conserve" or understand length relationships before quantity, the Cuisenaire rods are a natural method to use in beginning mathematics instruction in first grade and provide more of a "match" to the child's mental development. However, as the text for this program makes clear, counting exercises are also employed for beginners, although the "counting" aspect does not combine with the "rods" aspect until November 15.

Amsterdam

On Sunday, October 23, 1977, I left Brussels, Belgium, for Amsterdam, Holland, for school visits which, unlike those at Brussels and Luxembourg, had been arranged long before. The courtesy that was shown to me in Amsterdam exceeded anything I could have expected. A member of the school administration staff met me and brought me personally to the first two schools I visited in Amsterdam, showing me how to manage on Amsterdam's fantastically efficient trolley system, and introducing me to the administrators at the schools. On Thursday of that week, the schools were closed so that teachers could attend a city-wide seminar. The school administrator volunteered to take me to the meeting, and explained and translated the content of a lecture concerning a new phonic method in Dutch. This woman was one of the most delightful people it has been my good fortune to meet on my travels, but Amsterdam does rank high in producing kind and generous people.

I was to see three reading systems in use in Amsterdam. One was the Caesar method, one was Dijkstra's Leesfeest, and the third was Kooreman's Letter Village. I heard Professor Kooreman lecture on this method at the Seminar the following Thursday. However, the school which was using his method in first grade had used the Caesar method the previous year, so my final Amsterdam test results did not include the Kooreman method, but were instead on three classes which had used Caesar and one which had used Leesfeest.

The only one of these three Dutch programs which requires an extensive description in order to understand its use is the Caesar program, which was by far the weakest of the three Dutch reading programs which I observed in use. In contrast, the Dutch reading programs, Leesfeest and Kooreman's Letter Village, were excellent and their methods are easily understood. Therefore, before discussing the first Amsterdam school visit, since it used the Caesar materials, the following extensive background, including the history of similar American sight-word materials, is given in order to make the use that is made of the Caesar materials more understandable.

The Caesar materials are discussed in their 40-page brochure, of which I had 14 pages translated later for reference. Also, I bought copies of the first three Caesar readers, the workpad, and the first two Caesar workbooks. The workpad was available in two types of print. The "werkblok a" version which I did not see was in "lichtheilend schrift". The "werkblok b" version, which I bought, was in "blokletters," which were large, lower-case printed letters, which appeared to be handprinted.

F. B. Caesar, who is the author of the Caesar series, referred in another booklet, Zo Veilig Leren Lezen, Kort Overzicht (no date), to previous reading methods. One was supposedly the spelling method of the 19th century, when a Dutch child learned to read "zit" by spelling zet, ie, tee. Another was the "Klankmethode" which differed from the spelling method in that the child had the sounds of the letters. Both methods were synthetic. Caesar claimed these were followed by the analytic-synthetic method in the beginning of the 20th century, with "normal" words (some 20 to 30) which provided the sounds of the letters analytically, and from which sounds new words could then be spelled synthetically (hence the name analytic/synthetic). This "normal words" method was obviously the "haus" method seen in Germany by Horace Mann in 1843, when the instructor pulled the word "haus" apart to its phonemes, h -au -s, and then put it together again. Cesar mentioned the Dutch analytic-synthetic methods of Hoogeveen and Reynders-Doumen.

Caesar claimed the global (sight-word) method appeared in Holland about 1930, and that it was attributed there to Gestalt psychology. Yet the date he gave of 1930 for the introduction of sight words is of great interest, because 1930 was also the publication date of the first deaf-mute-method sight-word readers for mass use in American schools. Those 1930 deaf-mute sight-word materials were William Scott Gray's Scott Foresman series, and the primers of the Arthur I. Gates' Macmillan series. (The bulk of Gates' Macmillan readers appeared later.) Both Gray and Gates used the method by which many little six-year-old deaf mutes were then being taught to read.

A supply of sight-words were taught to the deaf-mute children first, by "meaning," with the use of pictures and the context of "stories." Then, new words were slowly introduced, the meaning of which the deaf children could guess from the story's context. The deaf children then compared these new words to old words to see like and different parts, so that they could silently tell them apart the next time they saw them. This silent, visual comparison, usually with the help of a story's context to assist in guessing, is exactly what Gray and Gates used in their American readers for hearing children. Yet Gates and Gray called this essentially silent, visual exercise by the name "intrinsic phonics," even though it was dependent principally on the meaning and visual appearance of words. Gates' "intrinsic phonics" was actually an exercise that had originated in classes for poorly-taught deaf- mutes, who were not taught lip-reading first and so could not use that knowledge to learn to read by phonics. The tragedy is that the lip-reading-first method for the deaf has been known for over 200 years to produce far, far better results than sign-language and sight-words.

There is no doubt whatsoever that Gates knew the nature of the reading method he used for hearing children in his 1930 readers. That is because, in his 1930 text for teachers, Interest and Ability in Reading, Gates obliquely admitted the deaf-mute-method connection, telling of sight-word work with deaf-mute children which had apparently been carried out at Columbia Teachers College where Gates was a professor. The identical materials were then used to teach beginning reading to children with normal hearing but of "dull" intelligence. In a footnote on page 17, Gates listed "Helen Thompson. An Experimental Study of the Beginning Reading of Deaf Mutes. Teachers College Contributions to Education, No. 254, 1927. Gates wrote on page 17:

> "These materials were originally arranged for the instruction of deaf-mute children entering school between the ages of 5 and 7. The first edition is described in a monograph by Dr. Helen Thompson. The revised form, used in most of the groups to be described shortly, and consisting of 1040 pages of materials, is available for inspection in the Teachers College Library.... The first studies were made to determine whether these materials would be suitable for dull children otherwise normal.... This material has been tried with thirteen different dull children, individually, by eight different teachers. A few of these case studies will be briefly summarized...."

From Gates' description of those materials, they were arranged in the same fashion as his "work and play" 1930 Macmillan readers, and they used the same general approach as the W. S. Gray "Dick and Jane" Scott, Foresman materials. (Note Gates' insensitivity in his use of the term, "dull."

W. S. Gray had been the graduate student and close assistant of the psychologist, E. L. Thorndike, in 1913-1914. That was the same academic year that Thorndike composed his first silent reading comprehension tests, and Gray composed, under Thorndike's direction, his original oral reading tests, for which he received his master's degree at Columbia Teachers College, before returning to the University of Chicago. Gates received his doctorate at Columbia in 1917 with help from Thorndike and Cattell (as he stated in his thesis) and Gates later worked closely with Thorndike at Columbia all through the 1920's and into the 1930's. Gates had lived with the Cattell family briefly in 1917 and lost his draft exemption at that time because of Cattell's notoriety in 1917, which resulted from the socialist Cattell's, opposition to the draft in wartime. Thorndike, who worked on Army IQ tests in 1917, got Gates' draft exemption reinstated.

The controversial psychologist, James McKeen Cattell, is best remembered today for his sight-word experiments in 1883, under G. Stanley Hall, who had been the psychologist William James' graduate student at Harvard in 1878. The psychologist Thorndike had been James' graduate student and friend in 1895, and Thorndike was Cattell's graduate student and later friend at Columbia in 1897. The psychologist Hall's 1883 graduate class at Johns Hopkins University included, besides Cattell, the psychologist John Dewey and other later well-known men. Cattell's 1883 sight-word experiments at Johns Hopkins falsely purported to support the "need" to teach by sight words.

Many years later, in September, 1929, Cattell was the President of the ninth International Congress of Psychology at Yale University. The 1929 International Congress of Psychology was attended by some 900 people from many countries, including Pavlov and other luminaries. Starting about 1930, the year after that congress of world psychologists, the "global" sight-word method was widely promoted in Europe (but not the Soviet Union) as being psychologically correct. Certainly it is no coincidence that it was in 1930, the year following that 1929 Yale congress, that beginning reading books using the global "sight-word" method appeared both in America and Holland. Gray's and Gates' materials appeared in print in America in 1930. It should be noted that Caesar said it was in 1930 that the first text on the global method appeared in the Netherlands. It was entitled, <u>Echt Lezen</u> of M. C. Versteeg, and was attributed to so-called "Gestalt" psychology, a concern with the "whole," or "global" aspect of things. Nor is it any coincidence that the early 1930's marked the massive introduction of the global method in other European countries and in South American countries, to which countries many of those 900 psychologists or associates of psychologists had returned after attending the International Congress of Psychology in September, 1929.

The massive use of the global method in Europe after 1930 should not be confused with the widespread adoption of "progressive" methods long before 1930 by certain "intellectuals" there. So-called progressive methods had roots going back to the eighteenth century, to Rousseau in France and to Johann Bernhard Basedow's Philanthropinum school in Germany, in the early nineteenth century to Pestalozzi, and to other Europeans throughout the nineteenth century. Progressive methods were retreaded and highly publicized, of course by Colonel Francis W. Parker in America starting in 1875, after Parker's European study tour.

The most well-known proponent of "progressive" methods in America was John Dewey, and Dewey openly credited Parker as the source for Dewey's methods. In the Soviet Union in the 1920's, Lenin's widow, Krupskaya, who had great influence on Soviet schools until the late 1920's, was entranced with Dewey's ideas. When Cattell visited the Soviet Union in 1928, at their specific invitation, he was joined by John Dewey. The Manuscript Files at the Library of Congress contain Cattell's remarks at a May 17, 1933, Aristogenic Club dinner in honor of John Dewey, which took place at the University Club. Cattell's remarks made it clear how highly Dewey was regarded in the Soviet Union at the time of their 1928 visit. Cattell said:

> "At the invitation of the Soviet Government, I was asked to organize and lead a party to visit that modern purgatory, halfway between heaven and hell. When I got there, I was no where for St. John [meaning John Dewey] was worshipped everywhere."

The radical socialist elementary school teacher, Celestin Freinet of France is correctly regarded as one of the major proponents of the global (sight-word) method, but his highly publicized arguments for the global method came after 1930. It is true that, when Freinet started to teach in a little country school in France in 1920, he almost immediately began to use "progressive" methods. Those methods just happened to include Dewey's "interest" ideas in teaching beginning reading so that Freinet set up a classroom printing press for printing what amounted to "experience charts." Then, in 1925, Freinet accompanied the first group of European teachers to visit the U. S. S. R. Elise Freinet (apparently Freinet's wife) reported on pages 46-47 of her 1949 book, <u>Naissance d'une pedagogie populaire,</u> that Lenin's widow, Krupskaya, received that group at the Kremlin, where they:

> "...all ate apples offered with simplicity..."

Freinet and Krupskaya may have discussed how "wonderful" John Dewey's ideas were, since they shared a common interest in his ideas. However, many years later, Celestin Freinet had become a major sight-word proponent in Europe and wrote dreary, interminable works, not about Dewey's "progressive" ideas in general, but instead specifically endorsing the global sight-word method. Freinet's pro-global books apparently did not appear until long after the 1920's. Krupskaya lost her power over Soviet education when Stalin took over, and Stalin then threw out progressive education and put Soviet schools back on "basics". The 1974 Great Soviet Encyclopedia claimed that the switch from the whole-word method to phonics took place in the Soviet Union in 1932, but evidence exists that it took place earlier. In her December, 1959, article in The Reading Teacher, "How Russian Children Learn to Read," Gertrude Hildreth told of seeing a 1930 edition of a Russian primer in which the syllables in words were separated by blank spaces. When syllables are emphasized in that manner, no doubt can reasonably exist that the method being used is based on "sound" phonics.

Ever since, the Soviet Union - and every single country in the Communist world - has taught beginning reading by phonic "sound," not sight-word "meaning" and their psychologists have written convincingly concerning the value of properly taught phonics! For instance, see D. B. Elkonin's article, "The Psychology of Mastering the Elements of Reading", in Educational Psychology in the U. S. S. R., edited by Brian Simon and Joan Simon, Stanford University Press, 1963, page 165 and following. Elkonin said:

> "In the present paper we start from the proposition that reading is a reconstitution of the sound forms of a word on the basis of its graphic representation. Understanding, which is often considered as the basic content of the process of reading, arises as a result of correct recreation of the sound forms of words. He who, independently of the level of understanding of words, can correctly recreate their sound forms, is able to read."

In Eastern Germany, when still under Communist control, only phonics was in use in the 1970's. Yet, in Western Germany, according to Franz Biglmaier in John Downing's Comparative Reading, (Macmillan: 1973), 74 per cent of the German primers in 1964 used the global method, and Biglmaier himself wrote a largely global primer. The endorsement of the global method was largely limited to such "experts," not teachers, when I visited Hamburg in 1977, because seven of the eight teachers that I met endorsed the heavily phonic text, Bunte Fibel, which will be described later.

The curious Communist endorsement of heavy phonics was no where more strange than in China, shortly after the Communists took over in 1949. One of their very first actions was to institute the study of Pinyin, which is a sound- bearing alphabet, in beginning reading classes. Only later are Chinese children gradually introduced to Chinese meaning- bearing characters.

Downing's Comparative Reading also included an article by Berta Perelstein de Braslavsky of Argentina. She wrote:

> "When the 'global,' 'ideovisual,' or 'natural' method was at its zenith in
> Europe in the 1930's, one of the most orthodox variations of its 'pure' form
> was elaborated in Argentina....
> This method was anything but a success. An increasing number of children
> showed signs of difficulty in reading, writing and spelling, both in primary
> school and, even worse, in alarming numbers in secondary school."

The Argentinian, De Braslavsky, therefore, confirmed Caesar's comment that the "global" sight-word method only really arrived in the 1930's, despite the fact that the method had often been attached, almost as an afterthought, to the progressive method of the 1920's. When the global method finally did explode in earnest all over Europe in the 1930's, the rationale behind its adoption was not progressive education, but gestalt psychology.

By 1977, "Gestalt" psychology itself had been discarded by psychologists, but the "global" method, based on its errors, lived on in Europe to a large degree in programs like Caesar's. The "global" sight-word method still showed up in the initial stages of many other European programs, even though they later heavily emphasized phonics, such programs as the Luxembourg program that I saw, the <u>Remi et Colette</u> texts in France, and the so-called LTG program in Sweden.

In the critical first half of the year, Caesar's program is like the American phony-phonics sight-word method, in which sight-words are learned and then later pulled apart and put together in new combinations, like the pieces of a jigsaw puzzle. However, the program does eventually depend more on isolated letter sounds and eventually seems to analyze all the letters in words. Caesar's program, called the structuuremethod, is meant to be a combination of the analytic-synthetic and global methods, with the emphasis on the structure of words. Yet it is only by December, to judge from the first-grade books and workbooks, that anything like real phonic study begins (four long months after school starts in mid-August). However, the Caesar classes ultimately do make a real study of all the parts of words, grouping like-sounding words together, which is certainly not the case with American sight-word programs, where the so-called phonics is usually almost worthless.

The critical fact, and the most grievous failing, of the Caesar program is the fact that introduction to heavy phonic analysis for beginning readers is delayed for about four months, until Christmas (equivalent to about January in American schools). However, since the program eventually does cover heavy phonic analysis, I found it necessary to code it at Code 6, on the instructional scale where Code 1 is pure sight-words and Code 10 is pure sound.

A table on pages 8 and 9 of the publisher's descriptive booklet on the series, <u>Zo/Veilig Leren Lezen</u> (Uitgeverij Zwijsen bv, Tilburg, The Netherlands), gives the outline of the reading materials for the first year. Basically, they consist of ten little booklets. At each booklet's level, supplemental materials are to be used. The first reading book is used with a box of sight words and a workpad. Filmstrips accompany this first book, and the stories told by the pictures (with some few words) are apparently told more completely by the teacher with the use of these filmstrips.

The first story is a picture story, "Little Elizabeth," through page 5. Elizabeth is fairy-sized, and sits in roses and consorts with little elves and a motherly looking mouse in a housedress and kerchief. The purpose of these attractive little drawings (and presumably the filmstrip story) is to teach the accompanying first six sight words which are printed on one page and immediately shown on the next page with their terminal consonants missing and replaced with spider webs, so the children can presumably concentrate on the terminal letters, m, r, and s, in these known words. The children are gradually taught the sounds of letters analytically from whole sight words in the first two books, but in a way that parallels American sight-word basal readers, focusing in the beginning only on one letter in each whole word.

After the first little picture story, "Little Elizabeth," pages 6 and 7 apparently cover the picture story in the second film strip, "The Dream of Miep" (Maria). Miep and Kees (Cornelius) are with the elves at their school when a huge wolf appears at a window. The pictures in the story are labeled with sight words: bell, book, window, bird, school, Miep and Kees (their names all in lower case letters). This is followed by a page of analysis of terminal consonants in these words, and the lining up of the words with terminal m's with the words with initial m's (boom, pim and raam over mus and miep). The letters l, s, and m are studied in this way as terminal or beginning consonants through page 14, and pages 10 through 14 are concerned with sight words, the 12 introduced so far and six more.

On pages 14 and 15, p and t are studied as terminal consonant sounds. Page 16 practices sight words (attached to pictures). Page 17 asks for recall of the other letters in pictured sight words which have only beginning or ending consonants shown. Possibly this is where the sight-word cards given to each child are to be placed in the book. Under a picture of a bell (bel) is a place for two words ending with l, and under a picture of a fish (vis) is a place for two words beginning with a v, and so on. This is the first time attention is focused on the letters r, v and b from known words (making this total of letters analyzed so far: l, s, m, p, t, r, v, and b).

Page 18 practices sight words, some attached to pictures, and introduces the article, de (the). Page 19 analyzes beginning and ending consonants by lining up words with similar sounds, one on top of the other. The next filmstrip story, "In the Zoo" is apparently geared to pages 20 and 21, which show the little boy and girl at the zoo with an adult man, "oom" (uncle) and the first connected reading of sentences appears, using known sight words (but still no capital letters).

Page 22 and 23 introduce eight new sight words, and focuses again on terminal consonants, including the letters g and k. With the 8 letters already studied that way, that brings the total of letters actively studied to 10. Whether the children are asked to name the letters, or whether they have already learned the alphabet before beginning this book, is unknown. However, it seems unlikely that they had learned the alphabet first since it appears no where in the materials I was sent from the publisher (at my request and for which I paid) for the first half of the year, reading books 1, 2, 3, the workpad, and workbooks 1 and 2.

Pictures, phrases and sight words are on the next two pages, 24 and 25, and short sentences and phrases on pages 26 and 27. Work with sight words and some attention to terminal consonants is on pages 28 and 29, which have blank spaces apparently for placing sight-word cards. Pages 30 and 31 have a few sentences, the past tense ending "t" is added to known words, and the book ends on page 32 with a review of 29 words that have been taught.

Both first-grade classes that I visited in Holland who were using the Caesar program during the school week of October 24, 1977, had not progressed much beyond book 1. From board work I saw, one class had reached at least the third page of book two, where the sight word, "is", is introduced, and were working on a workpad page geared to the last page in book one. The other first-grade class, to judge from written work on the board, had possibly reached either page 23 or 30 of this first book, so they were also finishing book 1.

The emphasis in book one, despite teaching letter sounds analytically from sight words, was nevertheless greatly on sight words and, except for attention to beginning and terminal consonants, very little attention was given to phonics. The workpad was effectively more explicit on phonic analysis of sight words than the text, although much of it at the beginning consisted simply of copying known sight words, with no analysis involved.

Book two which began with "Snow White" and some more appealing elves (covered after late October in both classes, or two and a half months after school had started in mid-August) would introduce the rest of the letters analytically except for q, x, and y, but the emphasis in this book continued also on meaning and sight words, instead of phonics. There was no indication in this text of sounding and blending phonics, and only a minor part of it concerned analysis of sounds from known sight words.

The workpad on page 22, had an analytic puzzle of pictures of known sight words, with only their vowels shown under them. Yet those vowel sounds had not yet been studied analytically. The children were to pick one set of letters from paired letters at the side of the page to fill in the missing beginning and ending letters so as to spell the pictured word. For instance, under one of those pictures, a picture of a window, were the isolated vowels aa. The children were to select the paired letters at the side to use to complete the spelling of the pictured word, which paired letters were r - m, to produce raam (window). The children had previously studied the sight word raam so this was only visual analysis based on a known sight word and was not sounding and blending phonics from a known phoneme, aa. The other isolated vowels under the other pictures on page

22, in this sight-word exercise, had never been studied, so far as I could tell from the workpad or the texts. Nor were the vowels ever really studied after it through book 3 and workbook 2 (which means to mid-term), except very casually and in passing, by occasionally grouping sight-words with the same vowel sound in those later books.

School one was about at workpad page 39 on Monday, October 24, 1977, when I visited that class, to judge from the board work, and in school two, I saw the children were working on page 49 of the workpad. Page 39, on which school one was working, was a color-and-cut puzzle of pictures and sight words. The children were to cut up the pictures and letters, and, presumably, reassemble the words, matching them to the pictures. This was obviously a straight visual memory exercise. Page 49 on which school two was working was essentially a handwriting exercise, in which children copied two sentences whose sight words had already been learned, with lines underneath for copying the sentences, and with pictures of the sentence's meaning attached. Again, obviously, this was only visual memory practice on sight words, so far as reading instruction was concerned.

Book 2 began about November 1, apparently for both classes, and it would have the additional workbook 1, besides the workpad which was already being used and which would continue to be used. However, book 2 did finally have a very little bit of analytic and synthetic phonic emphasis, actually focusing on vowels. However, it was too little, too confused, and too late. The emphasis remained on pure sight words and the pulling apart of those sight-words to make new words. Workbook 1, introduced about November 1, would continue after book 3 was started about the feast day of Saint Nicholas (December 6), to judge from the first picture in the book. It was only halfway through this new workbook (or about the time book 3 would start about December 6) that there was any real use of vowels to build new words, but it was very little and without emphasis. No attention is ever drawn - through the first three books, the workpad, or the first two workbooks, to the fact that there are two kinds of letters, consonants and vowels, and that vowels are a DIFFERENT KIND of letter than consonants. When whole words are pulled apart in this program, the emphasis may be on a consonant part, or on a vowel part of the pulled-apart word, but the overwhelming number of exercises are on the consonant parts! Even the workbook is heavily oriented to sight words, and to the jig-saw puzzle approach of pulling sight words apart. In no sense are such jig-saw puzzle exercises real phonics, since they can, almost as easily, be done by deaf-mute children.

When children using the Caesar program begin book 3, about the beginning of December to judge from the St. Nicholas pictures, they are given a box of letters, and the workbook exercises then concern synthesizing and analyzing words from word parts. After this, the program appears to have much heavier phonic emphasis, at least in the workbook. However, the reading book 3 continues to be overwhelmingly concerned with sight words, story line, and, presumably, story meaning. Yet the teacher has, from the beginning of the year, "structure cards" which permit her to demonstrate by folding of the word cards the initial and terminal consonants in known sight words, and their vowels. At the time book 3 begins, synthesis cards are also available which show words altered by substitution, as "dag, dak, dam, das," and on the opposite side of these cards each word is used in a meaningful sentence. While the children are working on book 3, the second workbook (not workpad) is to begin, and it is finished when the children read book 4. Book 3 is apparently to be finished by Christmas, since the final picture is of a Christmas tree, and the other seven books in the first grade series are handled from January on.

These Dutch children began school in the middle of August, so it would not be until Book 3, the beginning of December, that any stronger phonic emphasis would begin, which is comparable to American classes beginning phonic emphasis in January. In effect, then, this program is not following Jeanne Chall's recommendation for heavy decoding emphasis in the first half of first grade, despite the fact that it eventually does teach heavy phonics with the substitution technique (dag, dak, dam, das - mentioned before, which they call synthesis). The Luxembourg school, it is true, had 50 sight words, but only a month after the beginning of school had begun true sounding and blending, or synthetic phonics. The Caesar program also has only about the same number of sight words as the Luxembourg program, but the difference in the speed of introducing any kind of phonics to make new words, and in the textbook readers, is very marked. These Caesar readers emphasize sight words and story line far more than phonics, which was not at all true of the Luxembourg books, and the Caesar program delays actual heavy phonic work until much later in the year than was true in Luxembourg. I coded the Caesar program Code 6, although, if the phonic emphasis had continued at the low level evident in the first two books, it would have required a much lower code. Eventually, Caesar's program becomes a heavier phonic-emphasis program, so the overall effect, despite the delayed introduction of heavy phonics, called for a higher code than 3 or 4. which is why I rated it Code 6.

The publisher's brochure describing this program, portions of which I had translated (Zo/Veilig leren lezen door F. B. Caesar, Overzicht van de leer - en hulpmiddelen, copyright 1976 by Uitgeverij Zwijsen b.v. Tilburg) said that in 1977 the handbook would have its 9th revised edition (indicating the series had been in use for some time). It would include the addition of a chapter on auditory exercises, a test for the evaluation of children's knowledge of graphemes and phonemes, and an explanation for the use of the synthesis cards and other material. (I do not know if earlier editions had earlier versions of these items.) It is interesting that the test for phoneme-grapheme knowledge occurred at the end of the second book, to see if the student could connect letter signs to letter sounds, since they said in the third textbook the greatest part of the attention was on the process of synthesis (which I consider only substitution whole- word phony phonics in this series - dog to log, for instance, and not sounding and blending: d + o + g). However, while I do not think that in book 3 the greatest part of the attention was on synthesis, by which most people would mean phonics, I do think that book 3 had relatively more than books 1 and 2.

The teacher's guide suggested the test be taken before the third book so that special help could be given to children with trouble identifying letters and sounds, and again after the third book to be sure all knew letter-sound correspondences. It is evident that the first two books are to be used with little real attention to letter sounds. Any real building of words by sounds from known sight words is apparently held off until the third textbook, apparently begun about the beginning of December. Therefore, this notation from the publisher's brochure largely confirmed what I had concluded from examining the first three reading books of the series, the workpad and workbooks one and two.

The Caesar program was the heaviest sight-word/global program I tested in Europe, although I saw a far heavier one in a Hamburg first grade (Code 2 or 3) but no second grade class which had the program in first grade was available for testing. What is interesting about the Caesar program, however, is that the overall effect is nevertheless much heavier in phonic emphasis than that of any eclectic sight-word basal reader series published in America, to the best of my knowledge. After the phonic emphasis is eventually begun in Caesar, the focus then is on analysis of the TOTAL word in all its phonic elements. Workbook 2 shows words broken down into their individual phonemes, and the use of the letter box (so children can build letters into words) is the best testimonial to the difference. The children are held responsible to reproduce the structure of the entire underlined word. By contrast, the American Houghton, Mifflin program, Reading for Meaning, in its teacher's guide, asks children in the last half of first grade to distinguish between the words "evening" and "everything" by the CONTEXT of the sentence, instead of holding the children responsible to see and hear the internal sounds in these words! This American purportedly phonic program is far, far down the scale from Caesar. (I rate it Code 3).

In making my study of the Caesar program, it was quite simple to follow the children's primers without knowledge of the language, but with just a little Dutch-English dictionary. This is another testimonial to the common roots of English and the north European languages, since words in children's first readers are frequently high frequency words (fish-vis, boek-book, bell-bel, rose-roos, etc.). For more detailed information on Caesar teaching techniques, I depended on translation of 14 pages by a commercial translating firm from the 40-page brochure of the publisher's which advertises this reading program. I believe, with these translations, it has been possible for me to understand the rationale of this program reasonably well.

It is meaningful, however, that I did not feel it necessary to have any translations to understand the rationale of the far more phonic Dutch <u>Leesfeest</u> and <u>Kooreman</u> methods, the Swedish <u>Nu laser</u> primer, or the highly phonic German <u>Bunte Welt</u> and <u>Bunte Fibel,</u> or the Austrian highly phonic <u>Kommt, Wir Wollen Lesen und Schreiben.</u> Correspondingly, in America, explaining (and understanding) the rationale behind Lippincott's or Open Court's or Alpha's phonic series is extremely easy, but to follow what Houghton, Mifflin <u>Reading for Meaning</u> is doing, or what Scott, Foresman or its earlier editions, are doing is a work - literally - of years. When I had to use the Scott, Foresman and Ginn series years ago in third grade, I have to admit it was difficult to understand what they were driving at with their bits and pieces of analytic phonics splintered through the third grade guide, with no easily understandable sequence. The fall and spring third-grade guides for these old readers, if put together, compete with <u>Gone with the Wind</u> in length - but compete badly on interest! This Caesar series is far superior to any of the American basal readers, unsatisfactory as it is, but, with its emphasis on sight words and reading for meaning, it shares with them a complexity which makes its curriculum more difficult to follow, which is not true at all of the European phonics series.

The Caesar materials are highly unsatisfactory because of their major emphasis on word "meaning" instead of syllable "sound." In the critical first six months of beginning reading instruction, the Caesar materials almost ignore the vowels. In ancient times and until the eighteenth century, vowels were emphasized immediately after the whole alphabet was taught, as can easily be seen by looking at a picture of an old hornbook. The alphabet was written first, and then the vowels in isolation. Children were then taught how to decode the sound of print by themselves, syllable by syllable, by learning how to combine the sounds of consonants with the sounds of the vowels (ba, be, bi, bo, bu - ab, eb, ib, ob, ub, etc.). Yet the Caesar program not only does not emphasize or possibly even teach the whole alphabet - except analytically in passing - it focuses absolutely no attention whatsoever in the first half of the year on vowels or on the fact that they are something very different in the structure of words than consonants. The failure to deal properly with vowels means the failure to teach children how to read syllables independently, apart from those in already memorized sight words.

As already mentioned, the Caesar program had been used in first grade in three of the four second-grade classes that I tested in Holland. The fourth second-grade had used <u>Leesfeest</u> in first, which will be discussed later. In one school in which the second-grade class had been taught by Caesar in first grade, the current first-grade class was using Dr. Kooreman's method, which will be described later. However, the first school I visited in Holland had Caesar in first grade and a second-grade class which had been taught by Caesar, and I visited that school on Monday, October 24, 1977, after my Sunday arrival in Amsterdam from Brussels.

On October 24, after a Dutch buffet-style breakfast at my hotel of multitudinous kinds of wonderful breads, rolls and cheese with coffee, I met, in the lobby of the hotel, the delightful member of the Amsterdam school staff who was to accompany me, and to whom I will be forever grateful for all her courtesies that week. We went together by trolley to a school on the outskirts of the city, in an all-new apartment area. It was an almost brand-new school, very beautiful, with carpeted halls in radiating wings, off which classrooms opened and which had central large assembly halls in wings.

Walking through the halls of the school, it was immediately evident that the school was operated in a fashion which in America would be called "open classroom," but I found no evidence of such labeling of curriculum approaches there or elsewhere in Europe.

At 9 a. m., the principal talked to the whole school in an assembly and discussed the vacation the previous week, which had been a fall holiday. The school met in one of the central areas off which classrooms opened, and the children sat on the floor. I could see on the windows of some classrooms nearby fascinating yarn spider webs, and made a mental note to try that art project at home. The principal then read a story, very spiritedly, to the assembled group.

I studied the faces of these children from first to sixth grades, sitting on the floor in front of me. I could see Chinese faces, faces from India, and black faces mixed in with Dutch boys and girls. One of the little faces was indisputably American Indian. I learned later that there were a few children from Argentina, Brazil and Chile. No where in this whole beautiful city, in this school or elsewhere, did I hear or see anything that could be called discrimination.

I had asked a question before the assembly began, when I had talked to the principal, about the dominant reading methods in Amsterdam. I was told that the global method had been in use perhaps 12 years, but that there was no uniformity of methods of instruction in Holland. On the contrary, many new methods were being tried, and there was much experimenting.

After the assembly ended, I joined a first-grade class. Seventeen children were present, at least seven of whom were obviously not European. The teacher was a charming young woman. She had arranged the children's chairs in a circle for a kindergarten and first-grade activity that in America we call "show and tell." She insisted that I pull up a chair and become part of the circle, and she then introduced me. Most of the children had brought in fall leaves to show with pride, which had the same poor faint colors by American standards that I had seen from the train window on my way from Luxembourg to Brussels. One child brought bark from a fir tree and a chestnut. The teacher listened to all their ideas with great courtesy. This was obviously an activity geared to oral language development. Language development is an essential primary activity with all children, but particularly so with a group like this, where it was evident that many of the children came from a non-Dutch background and would experience language problems.

I glanced around me. It was a lovely classroom, with brick walls, a glass wall opening on a courtyard, and plants in boxes. The children were very well behaved. One of their projects was on a table - boxes covered in tissue paper, making a town, and tubes from paper rolls to form trees.

During the class meeting-in-the-round, a boy tossed a book in the air, and caught it. He was spoken to quietly, and he put the book under his chair. I looked back again at the surroundings. A long piece of paper had been colored by the children in their own way to represent some scene, and then hung. It was obviously not teacher-directed, as the objective "quality" of the work was poor, but instead its originality was high. This was not a room with cut-and-paste teacher productions on the walls to impress visitors, but instead was a room where the activities were obviously conducted for the children's intellectual growth.

A hyperactive boy sitting next to me was moving back and forth, and the teacher asked him to sit next to her. Her control was very gentle but very good. One little child had nothing to offer, so the teacher kept talking to her about something and smiling. Finally, the child responded - obviously a foreign child.

Finally, the children sang a song and moved to it, indicating by their motion falling leaves. The teacher then handed out paper, in six-by-six-inch squares, and explained about the drawing session. She had the children hold up their leaves and discuss the colors.

I saw some sight words on the board, in which the t was marked with orange chalk.

    "Kees op de wip. Ik wip. Miep wipt."

In the story which followed on the board were 21 more words. Two more t's were marked. After the story were questions, with the question marks in orange chalk.

The board in the back of the room had pictures with words under them, and the vowels outlined in different colors. Not at that point having any familiarity with the Caesar system, I said to the teacher that this seemed to indicate that the children must be learning sounds, but she said, "Not now, but later." She said, "They don't pull words apart in the beginning of the first year, only beginning and terminal consonant letters to be identified in context. Later they get the vowels."

Yet, in looking through books 1, 2, and 3, the workpad and workbooks 1 and 2, essentially the first half-year's work, I found only glancing and occasional material on the vowels. The "later" to which the teacher referred had to come in the last half of the year. However, I question whether such a program as Caesar ever got around to dealing with the vowels adequately.

The letter "t" is introduced on pages 14 and 15 of book 1 in the new words "pet" and "eet" and the ending "t" sound studied again on page 17 where the two words are to be given in blank spaces ending "t", under a picture of "pet" (cap). "Ik" (I) and "wip" (see-saw) are introduced on page 22. "Op de wip" (on the see-saw) is on page 23. Making verbs into the past tense form by adding "t" is shown on page 30 (translation: row: I row and Uncle rowed) - "vaar, ik vaar, oom vaart," and "loop, ik loop, kees loopt." The class then was probably either on about 23 (new words: see-saw, etc.) or more likely on page 30 (using the ending "t" to form the past tense of a verb).

I learned that in this school reading is taught by groups, and the school also groups for mathematics instruction in the first and upper grades, where classes change on schedule. I did not learn if the first-grade reading groups were simply within a class as in the United States, or if the children changed on schedule for reading also, as for mathematics. However, the fact that the teacher had painstakingly written a "story" from the reading book before class began, and then marked parts with orange chalk, certainly suggested that all her first-grade children, at least, were being taught as a group, even if her class might have been split up later for particular instruction geared to ability levels. It is very improbable that a teacher could find time painstakingly to write three separate "stories" on the board, and then to mark certain letters with orange chalk, in the same day, so as to instruct three separate reading groups, each of whose sessions would probably last less than an hour. I therefore concluded that her class, as a whole, had probably reached page 30 in book 1 of the Caesar series.

The first grade had some fascinating math materials (Niveaucursus Rekenen, Handleiding Niveau 1B, Malmberg den Busch, Stichting Reprorecht, Herengracht 257, Amsterdam). Boxes were coded with letters and numbers to indicate where in the series they occurred (A to 13, B to 4, etc.) and carried the name Aanvankelyke Rekenspelljes. Each puzzle-like activity within the boxes was approximately six by six inches, with 16 squares in each of small tiles. The activities with these puzzle-like materials covered such things as counting, one-to-one correspondence, materials which were either the same or different, and the concepts of larger-smaller. The child could check his work by turning the puzzle over. If he had placed the 16 pieces correctly, the other side showed a correctly formed picture. Similar materials are available in the U. S. from Flip-Chex Perceptual Development Kits and Durorama Sets, for instance.

The teacher said that in their mathematics first-grade program, they deal first with terms such as "greater than", "less than," and sets and then move up to numbers.

After I left that first grade room, evident in the halls in lovely cabinets were visual discrimination materials, and a profusion of kindergarten-like materials stored, which looked highly expensive, for the teachers "to share." Some of these were on carts with wheels, and the carts also looked very expensive. In this new school, however, the grounds had not yet been landscaped, but the open courtyards had real possibilities.

While I was there, a mother brought a Dalmatian dog on a leash into a kindergarten. No one paid any particular attention to the presence of the dog, but the woman's daughter ran up and nuzzled her face in the dog's back. I was amused and delighted by the total acceptance of the importance of pets, here as in Luxembourg.

I saw children in stocking feet on the carpeted floors, and piles of shoes under the coat racks, even including some of the famous wooden ones, so the school staff is obviously very interested in keeping the lovely carpets clean.

While there, I visited upper-grade rooms and saw much evidence of children's using colored ink felt pens, as popular there as in the United States. In some third-grade rooms, children were working on individual book reports. The library books I saw were very attractive.

I visited an upper class room, which was either a straight sixth or a vertically grouped fifth-sixth grade, where I was to give my sixth-grade test, which had been arranged ahead of time. The fifth and sixth grade classes apparently were grouped for instruction in mathematics, reading and spelling by achievement levels, and not by grade levels. The classes left their homerooms for these groups, but I am not sure if homeroom groups were mixed fifth- and sixth-graders as well. This class was handled by a charming and helpful Black teacher from Curacao. Her room had a beautiful construction paper city built in the middle of the rug - very imaginatively done art work. This teacher had the same gentle approach I had seen in the first grade. She called the children together for a meeting, and they grouped their chairs together in a circle in the center of the room. Afterwards, when the children were seated, she gently tapped on the carpet with a ruler for attention and the class became silent.

She suggested I wait to test her homeroom class until after they had returned from their grouped lessons in other rooms. I waited till they returned, and tested them using the Dutch version of the 1 04th Psalm in the Protestant Bible (103rd in the Catholic), 1 0th to 18th verses. At my request, the American Bible Society had very kindly sent me (at no charge!) copies of these verses in Icelandic, Dutch, Swedish, German and French. It was another example of the astonishing cooperation I had been given all through my sabbatical research, which research could never have been completed without such cooperation. I then had about 200 copies made of each of these language versions, so that I would have enough sheets in each of those languages to record immediately each student's performance on a separate sheet at the exact time that the student was reading from a test sheet. Unfortunately, I was not able to test in Iceland at all, nor was I able to test sixth graders in Germany or France because of insufficient time. I was, however, successful in testing sixth graders in Holland and Sweden.

This first sixth-grade class in Holland did extraordinarily well at oral reading, scoring at 9 8.4% accuracy on the average. Of the 22 pupils tested, 86% scored 98 or above. Below 98% accuracy were only three of the 22 scores. One was 94, one was 93, and the last was 91. Ten of the 22 children read at 100% accuracy with no errors at all. Most of the children read rapidly. The actual scores are shown in the Appendix.

I had no data on the reading method used by these children in first grade. Since the Caesar structure method (Code 6) had been in use 12 years, and this was said to be the most common in Amsterdam, perhaps many had Caesar, but they may also have had one of the other programs.

In the afternoon, I tested a second grade in this new school, as many as time permitted. The reading specialist came to pick up one of the children I had read with, who was doing poorly and who was on her remediation schedule. This young woman was very interesting and we discussed reading problems, While I read the test with individual second graders, their regular teacher was doing a lesson drilling on words ending with the consonants, pt.

I had time to test 10 children from this Caesar second-grade class, (Amsterdam 1, Code 6), taken at random. Of the 10, 7 or 70% read above 90% accuracy, and 3 (or 30%) below 90% accuracy, at 89%, 87% and 64%. Nine of the ten were included in the comprehension score. One child, who read at 99% accuracy, was omitted from the comprehension scores since he read so slowly I did not feel I had time to let him complete the test, as time was at a premium. Two of those who failed the test on accuracy also did not complete the test, but their reading was so poor that I felt it reasonable that they would have failed the comprehension test if they had been given a chance to read the whole test. My notes next to these three children's scores on the test summary sheet are as follows:

> 87% accuracy, Incomplete (Read ex. 1 and 2 of 5 ex.) Took about five minutes to read this much, word by word, incredibly.

> 64% Accuracy, Incomplete (Read ex. 1 and 2 of 5 ex.) Exceedingly slow. Reversals: bruin does not equal druin, iets does not equal iest.

> 99% Incomplete (Read ex. 1 and 2 of 5 ex.) Very slow. Waited 20 seconds for him to read "plek." 20 seconds for "vooral," 10 seconds for "dan." Bell rang. Too slow to ask to finish later, when class resumed.

Using the nine pupils (not the last one mentioned), 33% passed the comprehension test. Using all ten, 60% read slowly and none read quickly. Reversals were made by 20% of the pupils.

The child who was receiving help from the reading specialist did complete the test, though he also read very slowly. His comprehension score was 75% and his accuracy 89%. He also made reversal errors.

Complete scores for this class are listed in the appendix.

This Amsterdam school was the only school I visited in Europe where I met or heard that a reading specialist was employed at second grade, although I assume others might have had reading specialists. Also, this Amsterdam school is one of two where I saw first-grade phonics being taught in second grade, the other being a Swedish school using the LTG method. Of course, it is also possible that phonics was taught in other second grades I visited. Nevertheless, it was in this school which had a greater emphasis on sight-word learning in the first half of first grade that I first encountered the American sight-word norms: a reading specialist dealing with failing readers, and second-grade teachers finding it necessary to teach first-grade phonics.

I took the subway back, and then the tram. There was much merriment on the train, because two of the young sixth-grade girls sat opposite me, on their way into central Amsterdam for dancing lessons. They obviously enjoyed being able to talk to "the American teacher" in their budding English. The prettier of the two said to me, out of the blue, "Do you believe in God? I don't." I answered, "Yes, of course!" It was a strange, sad part of the conversation.

At the end of the week, I observed the Caesar method being taught in one other first grade in Amsterdam. That visit took place on Friday, October 28, 1977. (The other first grades which I observed on Tuesday and Wednesday of that week used Leesfeest and Dr. Kooreman's materials, and will be discussed later.) That other Caesar first grade was in a school near the center of Amsterdam, in a poorer city neighborhood, in which much urban renewal was going on. Very large apartment houses, which did not appear from the outside to be in terribly poor shape, were being completely gutted and rebuilt into beautiful new buildings.

Apparently, a larger foreign population lived in this area, but the Amsterdam schools had materials to deal with the resultant language problems. In another school, I had been shown a manual used to teach foreign children to understand Dutch. It consisted of 21 lessons, including experiences children would find in Amsterdam, at the table, watching television, traveling by tram, and so on. It was said that after approximately four months of these lessons, the average child could speak understandable Dutch.

This school in the center of Amsterdam did not look like a school from the outside, just as the school in Brussels did not. I rang a bell, and a boy answered, taking me through clean but rambling high old halls. I waited outside the principal's office for a while as he completed a phone call, after which he received me and cordially offered me coffee. (People in the Amsterdam schools drink much coffee, just as people do in the schools in the United States!) The principal brought me to a first-grade class, where the reading lesson was already under way. I was to see the Caesar method in use in this school by a thoroughly competent teacher who knew exactly how to handle her materials and her class, even though I understood it was her first year in the school.

A list of words was on the chalkboard as I came in. The teacher told me that at first the children learned about 30 words, then a few sentences, and then the letters. In the sight words that I saw, all the vowels were printed in red letters. (This obviously was a sharp deviation from the Caesar philosophy and should have produced sharply better results than the results from comparable classes using Caesar!) School had begun on August 18, and, by three weeks later, the teacher had the children working with letters, starting first with s, m, b and r. After perhaps a month, she gave them simple vowels, and by now, October 28, 1977, she had given them most of the consonants. However, she said that not all the children were able to recognize them.

With this teacher's obviously phonic "sound" deviation from the Caesar "meaning" emphasis at the very beginning of the year, her final results could be anticipated to be much better than the Caesar norm for similar first-grades.

I saw the children working on work sheets with pictures of a boy whistling and walking, and a monkey in an easy chair smoking, and words under them (which turned out to be page 49 of the workpad when I obtained it.) Another work sheet had pictures of objects and words beneath. Another work sheet had children copying words in boxes, "je, wip, een" The class had sight word cards like Bingo with pictures of objects. The children picked words out of their boxes and placed them under the pictures. The teacher said the class had much trouble with the "connecting words" (words that are not nouns) and she always gave them in the same order, listed on the board, from top to bottom: de, het, en, een, op, naar, is." I saw sight words written around the room, over the window, cabinets, wall, etc. Concerning the connecting words, the children arranged the words from the boxes in the same pattern as on the board, and on the word cards. Another exercise concerned a card with 27 sight words, and "connecting" words to be put on the side of the card. Most of the children could place the words on the card as required, as far as I could see. That is, they had a word under each picture, and the children's cards agreed with each other, visually. The teacher said this was only the third time that they had done this.

The teacher then dictated, "de boom en de ruiis," and the children reached for the words and placed them in front of them. She dictated "un" (means een) and they picked it out of the list, then vis, then op, then de. The exercise ended with the phrase, "Een vis op de kar."

One little child there was Turkish; another was South American. They talked to me. I asked the teacher to tell them I could not understand Dutch, but she said they could hardly understand her yet!

The South American child had made the last phrase correctly from the sight word cards, but the Turkish child had not, as she had been talking to me instead of listening to the teacher. The teacher then dictated a phrase, "Ik loop naar het raam," and the children reached for the words. The Turkish girl did this phrase correctly. On these sight word cards, the nouns were on green cards and the "connecting" words were all white. The word cards, I felt, were too small for fumbling little fingers to control, not like those I saw in another reading program in Amsterdam at another school. As a result, some of these cards were dropped on the floor.

The South American boy had a word missing in his phrase. After the teacher patiently explained to him which one was missing. "het," he put it out of order in the phrase, after "raam." The Turkish girl kept dropping her words on the floor. These words were kept in little plastic boxes, three by four inches. In addition, each child had a word folder in his or her desk.

It was evident that this was a very carefully run, well-managed classroom, and the teacher was thoroughly competent, with good but gentle discipline. Silence was not enforced in the room, which contained 23 children, and seven children appeared foreign.

I glanced around the room and saw evidence of manipulative materials with which the children could work. A Franklin-type stove was on the side of the room. I understood that this school was about 50 years old, but that a new replacement school was under construction. The Amsterdam school I had visited on Monday had also been a brand-new one, and presumably was also a replacement for an old one.

The teacher had phrases written in colored chalk on the boards which were very neatly done. Pictures were drawn in chalk of trees, one with an elves' door, and a man being carried aloft by balloons, with birds acting surprised to see him. She had labeled the trees on the board with the word "blad" next to a leaf, and "eikel" next to an acorn. She had written these phrases in chalk: "Oom en de kar. De kar naar de boom. Oo, oo, de boom. De boom in de kar. Miep en de kar. Kees en de kar. De kar naar het vuur. De boom in het vuur." These translate roughly as, "Uncle and the cart. The cart to the tree. Oh, oh, the tree. The tree against the cart. Mary and the cart. Keith and the cart. The cart to the fire. The tree in the fire."

After the children read the phrases together, the teacher called on one child to read them alone, and the child could. Then the teacher pointed to isolated words in the phrases and asked the children to raise their hands to identify them.

The desks in the room were arranged in clusters of three or four on a wooden floor. The blackboard was movable, hinged on either side, but attached to the wall. The folding board, when closed, had graph marks on the back.

Then came the next portion of the lesson. This teacher was fantastically well-prepared and kept the children's interest high. She demonstrated a piece of paper divided into six pieces, numbered out of sequence - 3, 1, 4, 6, 2, 5 for the words on the chalk board, which had pictures attached to the words. She dictated fish (vis) and the children wrote it in the first box numbered three, and drew three fish. In the next box, numbered 1, the children wrote "boom" and drew one tree. (The little Turkish girl drew only one fish in the first box, obviously not able to understand the instructions.) On the chalkboard, previously, the teacher had demonstrated how to draw a fish and an acorn, in simple line drawings. It was obvious that one other foreign child in the room did not understand at all. This class was, indeed, a heavy teaching load for any teacher.

I was puzzled when I later bought the Caesar books 1, 2 and 3 by ordering them after I returned to the United States. (Book 3 was apparently covered by about Christmas.) I did not find in the books "eikel" (acorn) but on page 15 of book 2 is the word, "nut, (and a picture of a walnut). Yet this class had apparently reached only the beginning of book 2. The teacher's use of "blad" (leaf) and "eikel" (acorn) were sight word additions to the regular program, apparently.

On October 28, 1977, this class had covered book 1. This meant that they could have officially covered about 33 sight words and 10 consonants in this book. The box of sight words for use with the workpad contained 52 words, 26 apparently nouns and the rest articles, prepositions, "and" and "I". On the children's workbook were words from the last two pages of book 1 (loop and zit) and the word "is" introduced in page 3 of the second book, apparently which they had reached on this date.

While the children left the room for recess, a young man teacher, apparently a specialist, came in and talked to me. He looked at the Caesar book which I had and said he did not care for it. He extolled the views of Celestin Freinet, originally a village teacher in France after World War I and into the 1 920s (who was later, as discussed, a leading European global sight-word proponent). The young man praised Freinet for trying to arouse children's interest by bringing nature into his class. The young man also referred approvingly to the Belgian, Decroly, after whom some 13 schools are named, according to him. It seems reasonably certain that the deceased Freinet and the deceased Decroly are neatly packaged and presented to students in the teacher-training colleges of Europe, even though they are unknown in America.

I went next to a sixth-grade class, and spoke with the very helpful man teacher. He said he operated his class on a "theme" basis. Each child picked a theme and worked on it. He had individualized the instruction in arithmetic, with each child operating on his own. He said he preferred this system because he could help the children personally, correcting the errors and giving directions at the same moment.

As at the first Dutch school, I had the sixth-grade children read a Dutch version of Psalm 103, (Psalm 104 in the Catholic Bible) verses 10 to 18, and here, as at the first school, most read at 98% or above (90% of the group of 19). One read at 97% accuracy, and the last at 96% accuracy. Three of the group, or about 16%, read at a fast rate.

This sixth-grade teacher told me that there were broken homes in the area, as well as many foreign children, so that the government made sure the classes were small. One child in his class was Turkish, in the Netherlands six years. One was South American, in the country also six years. Another Turkish boy had been in the Netherlands since he was two months old. A Spanish boy had been in the country for six years. The Spanish boy and one of the Turkish children spoke only their native languages at home. Another child in the class had an Italian father but a Dutch mother and spoke Dutch at home. Two of the children were absent, so the class totaled 21 normally.

At lunch time, since there were no restaurants in this poorer area, I stopped at a little bakery for Dutch pastry, a nut spice bar and cheese crescent, and went to a nearby little park to eat. Everywhere in this beautiful city were little parks. This one was perhaps two acres, with trees and benches, and people exercising their fat, happy dogs on leashes. Behind the bench where I sat was a fuchsia-colored wiegelia bush still blooming, and slightly bedraggled white roses in bloom on this late date in the year of October 28, 1977. I found that surprising, considering Holland's latitude.

I ran into the first-grade teacher on the street during lunch time, and chatted with her. Her remarks revealed a basic difference in viewpoint from that of most American primary teachers. Her remarks in the morning had indicated that she had covered letter sounds to a far greater degree than called for in her Caesar sight-word program, but all the work I had actually seen being done in her room concerned whole-word identification. Yet, when I told her that the older American global sight-word texts did not introduce the special vowel sounds to children until third grade, and no vowels until second grade, she exclaimed, "But HOW can they ever be independent readers if they do not have the sounds?"

It was evident that she valued phonics for first graders and must have given it emphasis, despite the sight-word program I happened to see her use. It was also evident that her class could not have been getting the straight Caesar program, but a variation of her own devising that was far more phonic oriented! It may be over-simplification, but I think it can be said fairly accurately that most American teachers teach phonics so that children can remember their sight-words, but most European teachers, like this Amsterdam teacher, teach sight words so that children can learn their phonics!

In the afternoon, I went back to give my oral reading test to the second grades. The first-grade teacher had mentioned that perhaps two or three had been held back at first grade. The second-grade class was having gym, girls first and then boys. I started reading first with the boys in the hall, again with real helpfulness having been shown to me by the classroom teacher. When the girls returned from gym, I read with them, and the scores are recorded in the appendix. This second-grade Caesar class, Amsterdam 4, was rated Code 6 like the previous second-grade Caesar class, since the phonic-stressing first grade teacher had not been here last year and had not taught it. The class scored with 67% passing at 95 or better, and 86% passing at 90 or better. Forty-three per cent read slowly, and none read fast. There were 5% reversals, and 37% passed comprehension. The total number of children tested was 21. One child, I understood, was receiving remedial reading instruction. One who failed the test had been classified as subnormal in intelligence and was enrolled in a special program.

On Tuesday, October 25, 1977, I tested at one other school in Amsterdam, Amsterdam 2, in which the second- grade class had been taught by the Caesar method (although the first-grade class in that school was currently being taught by the Kooreman method.). That was a school in a higher income area. Of the 15 tested, one child was omitted from the scores as he had been there only two weeks and was failing. The scores were as follows: 86% read at 95 or above, and 93 at 90 or above. On comprehension, 71% passed. On relative speed, 29% read slowly and 7 per cent read at a fast rate, and there were 14% reversals.

As mentioned, this last school, which I visited on October 25, 1977, was no longer using Caesar in its first-grade class, but the Kooreman method, the method I heard discussed at a teacher's seminar on the following Thursday, October 27, to which the Amsterdam school representative kindly brought me. She quietly translated his remarks to me as his talk was being given - more astonishing kindness! Before reporting on my observations on this first-grade Kooreman class, a summary of the lecture follows. It was given by Dr. H. J Kooreman of Pedagogisch Centtrum Enschede on his program, the <u>Letterstad</u> reading method. The other information on the program which follows I received from the school principal and first-grade teacher in the school which was using the Kooreman materials.

Kooreman modeled his method after a Russian reading program which he translated and adapted for Dutch schools. Kooreman's belief is that difficulties in initial reading arise from three sources: inability to scan from left to right, lack of knowledge of letters, or inability to synthesize letters. His multisensory program was meant to deal with these problems, and to involve each child actively in the lessons. To teach letter knowledge, his "Letter Village," a bulletinboard-like display for the classroom, has "streets" on which letters "live." (This is apparently a way to separate the letters into consonants, single vowels, double vowels, etc.) The children must demonstrate the small letters and large letters in class, and physically bring each letter to the "street where it lives." Each letter apparently has its own little song, which the children recite and sing as they work with it, taking it out of their individual boxes of letters. Scanning from left to right is handled by little boxes on each child's desk, in which the children place the letters from left to right as words are being built, with a compartment for each letter. Synthesizing is handled by the children's physically moving their arms in a swinging motion from left to right as a word is synthesized orally from its letters' sounds.

In the letter village is a "sign thief," who sometimes steals letters from words, an interesting way to teach little children irregular spellings. Dr. Kooreman's program is concerned with spelling, which is apparently far more difficult to learn in Dutch than reading, because of complex spelling patterns in Dutch. At the lecture, Kooreman discussed how to teach divisions of words into syllables, and accented syllables. His program uses a "sound foot" to "walk" a word, the children using their hands to show the motion of the "foot," moving from left to right. They show accent by thinking of high or low notes, raising a hand high for a "high" note to accent it, and dropping the hand for an unaccented syllable. A word can be marked as well to show the accent.

I was to see only first-grade materials at the school which I visited, but upper grade texts exist. The program uses stories at the second and third year levels to teach spelling rules and exceptions.

On Thursday, the school representative and I had found our way to the lecture room in which Dr. Kooreman was to speak, after working our way through lobbies with commercial materials on display, reminding me of the convention hall in Atlantic City used for the annual New Jersey Teacher's Convention. This convention hall was brand new.

Dr. Kooreman's lecture was very heavily attended. He appeared very young to have accomplished studies in Russia and then to have written this complex language arts program adapted from a Russian model.

After the lecture, the Amsterdam school representative asked if I would like to attempt to speak to Dr. Kooreman, who was answering questions at the back of the hall. I did so briefly, and I mentioned to him a program in use in the United States, Alpha One, which stresses the learning of letter sounds and synthetic blending, while it delights the children with its imaginative treatment of letters as people.

At the school I visited which was using Kooreman materials, I was told that his method had been in use for seven years in the eastern part of the Netherlands. This school was in a different sort of suburb than the other Amsterdam school I had visited earlier, not high-rise apartments, but small, one-family brick homes, surrounded by small, well-kept gardens in which the roses were still blooming in late October. Lovely, lace curtains were in big picture windows, and a pleasant aura of prosperity and stability was all around. It was obviously a housing development, but very different from American counterparts. Later, at lunch time, I walked a short distance from the school to a shopping center. It had red brick buildings around a sort of square, with small hardware and clothing stores and a wonderful delicatessen in which to have lunch.

At 8 a. m. on the morning of Tuesday, October 25, 1977, at this second Amsterdam school that I visited, the principal received the Amsterdam school representative and me in his office. We had coffee while we discussed the program for the day. In our discussion, he referred to the Hoogeveen method which I believe he said was a synthetic method, no longer in use. I was told that there was a kindergarten preparatory program for the Kooreman method, the Sound Village, which came before the Letter Village. The multi-modal first-grade program involved singing, rhyming, physical movement and the use of manipulative materials. This school was said to be one of the first schools in Amsterdam using the Kooreman materials, as an experiment. I was somewhat puzzled when the principal referred to this program as a synthetic/global method, as I was to see it as a totally synthetic method, Code 10. This demonstrates again the uselessness of "labels," and the necessity for some standard scale to use in referring to reading programs.

It was interesting, however that the principal implied disapproval of the Hoogeveen, apparently old, phonics method which in all probability he had never actually seen in use. It was like the specialist in another Amsterdam school who had spoken so approvingly of Celestine Freinet, who promoted the global method. Their opinions on the matter of course, would have been formed in their courses in the teachers' colleges, as neither man had any necessary connection with beginning reading. Brain-washing in favor of the global method, therefore, apparently takes place in European universities, just as brain-washing in favor of the sight-word method takes place in American teachers' colleges. I am still reeling from the discovery that William Paterson College in Wayne, New Jersey, as of 1978, did not even have Rudolf Flesch's book, Why Johnny Can't Read, in its card catalog. I then called Montclair State Teachers College and found that it, also, did not have the book! I heard a very intelligent and wonderful American first-grade teacher say that she had never even heard of Why Johnny Can't Read! She stressed far more phonics than most teachers, but it certainly was not because of the preparation her teachers' college courses had given her!

After our meeting with the principal, when he outlined the reading program, he brought us next door, where the teachers were gathered in the teachers' room for morning coffee just as in America! We joined them, many of whom also spoke English, including a young student teacher.

The Amsterdam schools' representative left, and I went to the first-grade classroom, whose teacher, a black woman, was wearing a superb dress. When I complimented her on it, she said it was a very popular style now in the stores - a paisley print, something like a Hawaiian mumu, with large sleeves. She gave me the teacher's guide to follow while she did the reading lesson. Even though the guide was in Dutch, it was possible from the tables and sequence to see that she was following it quite completely.

In appearance, this school was traditional. No rugs were on the floors, and the desks were arranged in tables. The classroom had no free talk while I was present, and the lesson was a whole class activity. Eighteen children were in the classroom, including two who had been held back the previous year and who were doing other work.

The lesson was principally on the sound, "eu," occurring in the word nose, "neus." The teacher drew a profile with a large nose on the board and put the letters "eu" on the nose. Each child had a sturdy plastic box with sturdy white plastic letter cards. Each child had a small chart in front of him with three letter-sized panels in which to place those cards. The teacher held up a card with the letters "eu" on it, and they sang a song with the sound. She paused to correct them, because they did not make exactly the right sound. She held her nose and demonstrated the sound. The alphabet in this program is recited by sounds, and not by letter names. (It is interesting that the principal said, "The parents do not understand." It is said so often in American schools, and I heard it said elsewhere in Europe.)

On the chart board in the front of the room were nine words with pictures. It was obvious that these words also had previously been built letter by letter. The children built the word "neus" on their word charts from the letters in their boxes. The teacher had the children say "n - eu - s" while they waved their arms from one side to the other. Then the children recited a song, picked up the letter "n" and put it back in their boxes. The teacher then had the children pick another letter, "r", which they found in their boxes. They sang a song for "r" and placed it on their word charts in place of "n", waving their arms from left to right and saying the separate sounds of the new word, "r - eu - s" This activity was certainly a variation of the analytic/synthetic approach. A word which had already been built (neus) was rebuilt with "r" in the initial position, but with a continued emphasis on all the other parts of the word.

The uninitiated might see a resemblance in this analytic/synthetic activity to the jig-saw puzzle so-called phonics in American sight-word basal readers, but the resemblance is only illusory. The American sight-words readers might use a memorized whole-word like "bat," and another memorized whole word like "cake," and then pull off the beginning sound of the whole word, "bat", to substitute it for the beginning sound of the whole word, "cake," to produce "bake" That jig-saw puzzle activity is certainly not real phonics. American children are taught to do such harmful exercises when they have no knowledge at all of vowels in isolation, such as the short "a" in bat and the long "a" in cake, or any other isolated vowel. Yet these little first-grade Dutch children, only two months into the first-grade year, were being carefully drilled on the vowel sound, "eu." which was used in this lesson. The major emphasis in this entire lesson was that vowel sound, "eu."

In the Kooreman teacher's guidebook, I could see the picture of the nose that the teacher had drawn on the board. On the next page, I could see the list of words from which she was to write on the board for initial consonant substitution on the word "neus" and finally terminal consonant substitution, where the "s" would become "k". Eventually, the teacher substituted "k" for 's" and the children sang a song in Dutch, which rhymed in that language: "One, two, three, four, the letter "k" is here." Further building of words went on, with the children saying the separate sounds for each phoneme and then waving their arms from left to right as they blended the phonemes together into words. As they picked up each letter to put it back in its box, they sang a little song about its name. The children seemed to be absorbed in the work. The principal said they were very pleased with the results of this program.

I could see on the display board words the children had built by collage from little pieces of colored paper on white paper.

The teacher then held up letters in the front of the room which the children connected to the idea of the Letter Village, going to the chalk board to identify letters by symbols that meant their "street" in the Letter Village.

After this drill on synthesis of words and letter identification, the children got notebooks out of their desks. The teacher held up a copy of this workbook pad to show the children that they were to circle all words on that page that contained the sound they had been studying, "eu".

Following this, a drill took place relating letters again to their sounds and to their places in the Letter Village. The children picked up individual letters, showed them to the class, said the letter sounds and then went to the Village and placed the letters in the right streets. Following this, the children sang a song, the purpose of which I missed. They pointed to one another in the song and laughed, saying, "Where is my ear?", then apparently, "Where is your ear?" Next, "Where is my nose?" The "eu" sound in nose (neus) may have been the reason for the activity. Then the children clapped the song, not saying it. Following that, one child sang while the others clapped.

The Kooreman heavily phonic program, new in this school, was a highly structured program, but one of its stated purposes was to involve each child actively in the lessons. Hence, it included the heavy use of letter tiles, singing and pointing. The program certainly met supremely well that stated purpose of involving each child actively. It also rated a phonic Code 10 on the sight-word "meaning" to phonic "sound" scale. However, I regret that it was not possible for me to test a second-grade class which had the Kooreman program in first-grade.

After lunch at a little delicatessen in the shopping center, I returned to test the second-grade children who had the Caesar method, which fact I confirmed by telephone later. The second-grade test results on this school's Caesar- taught second grade were reported previously.

The last reading program I saw used in Amsterdam was <u>Leesfeest,</u> published by Dijkstra Uitgeverij, Zeist N.V. After returning to the United States, I contacted this company, asking for their price list on their first-grade books, and received instead copies of the two books in first grade, without charge! This was more of the wonderful Dutch courtesy!

On Wednesday, October 26, 1977, I went to the school using the <u>Leesfeest</u> readers, again by one of the efficient Amsterdam trolleys, but without the help of the delightful representative from the Dutch schools. I had left the hotel probably later than I should have, and then managed to get lost by getting off at the wrong place and wandering a while, despite the very careful directions I had been given. I got back on a trolley, and eventually found the right stop in the suburban outskirts of Amsterdam, in a section of very attractive homes, landscaped parks, and some large apartment buildings.

The school was a new, large, rambling, two-story building, with many wings, nicely landscaped, and with an impressive, very large brass rooster in the courtyard. It is possible that the rooster had some cultural connection with the picture of a rooster to be found at the beginning of European Protestant ABC books in the 17th and 18 centuries. Andrew W. Tuer discussed the ABC rooster in his <u>History of the Horn-Book</u> (1897, 1979) and included an excellent illustration of one.

In Amsterdam, as in England, a small percentage (perhaps one per cent) of building cost is spent on such an art object as that rooster. On my June, 1971, two-weeks' tour of English open-classroom schools with fellow teachers from Wayne, New Jersey, we saw quite a few of such interesting art works at English schools.

This two-story school building was in an area which was obviously a higher economic one. The principal met me courteously, and I apologized for arriving late. He brought me to a first-grade class to observe the reading lesson which was obviously well under way by the late time I arrived. When I came in, the children were working orally with synthetic blending of words from letter sounds. The teacher later stated that school had started August 15, 1977, and that the children had covered three consonants by the fourth day (page 3 of <u>Leesfeest</u> book 1). By the second week, the children had reached the tenth page, on which the first vowel sound was introduced (oo). The teacher said the first book was finished after seven or eight weeks, and an extra week was taken for additional practice on the first book. The second book had been started about a week ago, and it was now October 26. From the texts I received later from the publisher, and from the notes I took on the teacher's lesson, the children were then on page 22 of book 2. Class practice, she said, was geared to word synthesis from letter sounds. She stated that only ten schools in Amsterdam used this method, and the others mostly used Caesar. In her opinion, Caesar had far too many things in one lesson for the children to handle.

The first two Leesfeest books were brightly illustrated with the doings of a little boy and girl and their naughty pet cat. The cat's antics would amuse any little first-grader. For instance, the cat leered at a goldfish for a while but then managed to get his paw nipped when he used it to fish in the bowl, because that Dutch goldfish surprisingly had teeth!

In the first book, from the schedule the classroom teacher told me she had followed, it apparently took from one to two days to cover each page. Most pages had a "story" text and picture, and then six to fourteen isolated words to use to study phonic elements. Following is the material on the first twelve pages of book 1, which means the material for about the first three weeks of first grade. Delightful pictures were on each page, also.

Page	Story Section	Phonics Study - Letters Studied Being Printed in Red
1	Three sight words which were names.	
2	14-word story, using first three sight words and one more (Total: 4)	
3	18-word story, using one more sight word (Total: 5 sight words)	
4	13-word story, using 3 more sight words (Total: 8 sight words)	Three words isolated to teach the letter s
5	13-word story from known words	Isolated words shown to teach letters p, s, t in terminal position
6	25-word story from previously taught sight words with two new words (Total: 10 sight words)	Isolated sight words to study beginning p and t, ending p and t, and letters t and p alone outside words
7	23-word story told with 3 new sight words (Total: 13 sight words)	Two of the three new words are written in isolation and used in the phonics lesson on terminal p
8	25-word story using one new sight word (Total: 14 sight words)	Isolated sight words using terminal p and s, initial b, and letters p, b, s written alone
9	16-word story using known sight words	Phonics study on isolated sight words on terminal p and k and initial b. Letters p, k and b printed by themselves.
10	22-word story from sight words and 3 new words (Total: 17 sight words)	Isolated sight words to teach initial t, b, j. Vowel of "oo" and b and s isolated and written as separate letters. New word

		boos is arrived at from b of bas, oo isolated from toos and ook. All parts of new word boos printed as separate letters at bottom of page. This is pure analytic/synthetic phonics.
11	22-word story with 2 new sight words introduced (Total: 19 sight words)	Isolated sight words to teach new vowel, "ee" from nee and word "mee" from this vowel. Isolated sight words written to study terminal t, p, s, and vowel oo
12	29 words in sight-word story, One new word given. (Total: 20 sight words)	Phonics study on isolated sight words on a, aa, oo, oe, initial p, terminal s. The new word, "baas" from page 11 is related to the new vowel aa and the known words bas and boos. The new vowel oe is related to the known words poes and joep. (Total letters of the alphabet studied by page 12 are 6 consonants and five vowel forms: oo, ee, oe, a, aa)

The 20 sight words had been introduced in this order: bas, toos, poes, en, de, ik, heet, joep, nee, ben, wip, op, ook, zit, is, boos, niet, mee, bas, van.

The sight-word base by page 12 (only the third week of first grade) was therefore 20, but five of these had been introduced only to demonstrate new letters, and the others had been used shortly after introduction to teach letters. At the end of this three-week period, on a sight-word base of 20 words, a total of 6 consonants and three vowels (building five vowel sounds) had already been studied. The sight words demonstrated to the child the proper sound to bqe given to each consonant and vowel form. In addition, the children had already done a complete phonic analysis of a word, "boos," by the second week of school!

This was a highly phonic program, beyond a doubt. From looking solely at the child's text, as abstracted above, it might appear that it was an analytic phonics program, but I was to find from the class lesson that in practice it was very much a synthetic phonics program. In any event, synthetic or analytic, it was very heavily phonic and should be rated at least a Code 8.

By the end of book 1 (about October 1 in this class), 18 letters are introduced. On October 26, 1977, this class was on book 2, page 22. All letters had been introduced except those rare in Dutch (c, q, x, and y) and some special Dutch vowels had not been covered. According to the first-grade teacher, most of the Dutch vowels are covered by the ninth or tenth week.

Book 2 of the first-grade Leesfeest program had covered the terminal blend, "pt" on page 14, which blend I had seen also being studied in a Caesar school at the second-grade level (although the "pt" blend had been covered previously in the Caesar first-grade program on page 32 of book

3, by Christmas of first grade). The fact that the blend, "pt" had to receive class study again at second grade in the Caesar program, which program had such a heavy emphasis on sight words in beginning first grade, certainly suggests the "pt" sound had not been taught adequately by the first-grade Caesar materials. The first-grade Leesfeest heavily phonic program could reasonably be anticipated to have greater success teaching letter sounds.

In the Leesfeest program, initial blends such as "st" were to be covered on page 44 of book 2. No work would be done in book 2 on two-syllable words, but, since book 2 was half finished, that should only have meant that two- syllable words were not be studied up to about the middle of November. They may or may not have been studied soon after that.

The first-grade teacher, who said she had been teaching 13 or 14 years, was working with the class when I came in, on blending the new vowel introduced in page 22, "ui" (pronounced in English, "ou"). She called on each child, had each child name the vowel, and then name other letter sounds, and blend those sounds together after naming them. For instance, a child said the "r" sound and the "ui" sound, and then, "reu," then the "l" sound, and "ui" sound, and then "lui."

The blending exercise which they were doing was printed on the bottom of page 22, with the new vowels, "ui", printed in red in the child's book:

h ui s	b ui	ui t	sui s
m ui s	l ui	ui l	r ui s
ui	ui	ui	ui

h ui l - m ui l - k ui l - r ui l

Neither in this book nor book 2 were any capital letters used, which made the memory load on the little rank beginners much lighter: only 26 lower-case letter shapes to memorize, and not an additional very different 26 upper- case letter shapes to memorize as well. It is surprising how few people realize how unnecessary it is to teach uppercase letters to rank beginners, and that the study of those letters can be held off until the children have learned the basics of decoding the sounds of words. After all, even adult texts are printed overwhelmingly in lower case letters. Yet, in almost all commercial materials sold to parents for the use of their children, such as rugs for the nursery, or wallpaper for children's bedrooms, or bedspreads for children, it is the relatively useless (for learning to read!) capital letters which are used to decorate such items.

The organization of the classes in the school appeared to be traditional, rather than interest-centered. However, it was apparent that much money had been spent on instructional materials. Among other materials which were visible, I saw Unifix cubes for mathematics, but I understand that they did not use Cuisenaire rods. I did not make a note at the time, but believe the children left at this moment for recess, and that it was then that I was able to talk with the teacher. In our conversation, she mentioned that this had been a high economic area but was beginning to change because of the apartments.

In the second-grade class, it was necessary to work rather quickly because this was an early dismissal day. The teacher of the second grade, as of the first, was charming and helpful. Thirty children were in the room, and I tested 19 of the 30, taking them in rows, and testing in the little cloakroom attached. The teacher's husband arrived to take pictures of her class, and snapped me as I was testing in the little cloakroom attached. When the time was up, the teacher said I had missed reading with three of her best students, but had read with the worst. Few foreign children were in this class, though one child was apparently Indonesian. I understand two children had been retained from the previous year, but the principal said normally the retention rate was only 2% to 3% (not 6%

as this would indicate). In the last two Dutch schools, however, I had been told of two or three children retained in each first grade. In the first Dutch school I visited, I have no note to confirm it, but do have a memory that the reading specialist said they did not hold back children in first grade in that school.

These second-grade children, Amsterdam 3, who had been taught to read with the Dijkstra Leesfeest Code 8 program tested very well, indeed, particularly since my scores included all the worst and missed three of the best, according to the second-grade teacher. Ninety-five per cent of the class passed at the instructional level, 95%, and 100% were above the frustrational level, meaning they scored at 90% or higher. Twenty-one per cent of the children read slowly and 11% read quickly, and 11% showed reversals. In comprehension, 42% passed the test. In the five schools I had tested so far in Europe, this was the most heavily phonic program and the best score! The second-best score came from another heavy phonic program in Luxembourg, but, to counter the possible charge that Dijkstra's scores were high because the school was in a higher economic area, Luxembourg's score came from a school in one of the poorest areas of Luxembourg!

Amsterdam is one of the world's most charming cities, with its wonderful canals in the center of the city, its fantastic department stores which are more artistic in their window decorations and merchandise selection than any stores I have ever seen, except in Italy (more innate artistic ability, perhaps?) and its wonderful, winding little streets full of small shops. The museums are a joy. One entire modern one is devoted to the works of their native Van Gogh. The Reichmuseum is a monument to centuries of culture and high standards. Besides the galleries of Rembrandts and Vermeers, etc., there are also galleries of home furnishings of Amsterdam two and three centuries ago. The workmanship, originality and artistry are a physical testimonial to Dutch culture, which was achieved, as we all know, in an atmosphere of human dignity and dedication to freedom. Many, many more people than the American pilgrims sought refuge in Holland and received it, and that tradition survives there today. I saw this in the schools, where the greatest consideration and attention were given to the non-Dutch immigrants, Turks, South Americans, Blacks, Spanish and so on.

I enjoyed hearing concerts at the Concertgebouw - the Amsterdam hall built in 1907 - with its gilt, its crystal chandeliers, and its red plush. The first evening I attended, an orchestra and choir performed an all-Beethoven program, including the Beethoven Missa Solemnis. The performance was magnificent, but the 84-year-old conductor was dissatisfied with the women's part of the choir at one point, and banged on the podium for the chorus to stop and start again. It was old-fashioned dedication to excellence.

I sat with a lovely English couple from Chester, England, who were staying at my hotel. We walked back together across the park to our hotel, and I learned the English woman was a school teacher, working with first-year children. She explained with great pleasure about the success of her heavy phonics program to teach the little ones to read, and the great strides they were making. She was particularly delighted with the progress of a little Chinese girl in her class, only four years old. That Chester teacher's opinion of the sight-word approach, however, was very low!

The English couple had a very amusing story about their stay at our small hotel. In the little downstairs bar, they had met a Chinese tourist. After speaking with them a little while, he complimented them both on how very GOOD their English was!

Stockholm

It was a long train trip from Amsterdam in Holland to Stockholm in Sweden, so the journey was broken by an overnight stay in Copenhagen, Denmark, an obviously prosperous city. The prosperity I saw everywhere I went on this trip was remarkable. Not a trace of poverty or slum conditions were to be seen anywhere I traveled. My overall impression was at that point, and continued to be, that northern Europe is more prosperous than America in terms of actual physical wealth, leaving the economists' tables and charts out of the discussion.

On Sunday, I continued by train from Copenhagen to Stockholm. The entire train was placed on a ferry for part of the trip, and the passengers climbed out of the train, went upstairs on the ferry, and had coffee or whatever in a lovely glassed-in dining room which looked out over the water. The water trip, however, was brief. The rest of the overland journey to Stockholm was through miles and miles of northern forest, largely evergreen, and glacial terrain strewn with rocks dropped by the long-gone receding ice. Occasionally, we would see habitation, but, judging from the impression from the train window, beautiful Sweden is under-inhabited.

I had an immediate positive emotional reaction to this terrain. It reminded me of Lake Bonaparte in Lewis County in northwestern New York State, where the Canadian climate zone reaches down into the United States. Lake Bonaparte is relatively close to the Canadian border. I spent portions of summers there as a child, and, getting out of "subway stations" in suburban Stockholm later, I would see evergreens under which were lichen-covered glacial rocks, just like those I played on as a child next to the white-sand shore of the lake.

To while away the time on the long trip, I walked back to the cafeteria car, not just for dinner, but also for coffee later. It was a beautiful train - new cars with shining paneling and American "coach" type seats, not compartments as on most European trains. On the doors between cars were placed the Swedish equivalent words for the English words, push and pull, so easy for English-speaking people to understand because of the common ancient root for English and Swedish. For instance, pull was drag, easily understood by any English-speaking person.

Not only are so many Swedish words similar to English words, but I was startled to have a preconception shattered. I had expected to find the majority of Swedish people to be tall and blond, but, instead, they were, for the most part, not exceptionally tall and not overwhelmingly blond. Physically, I thought that they, as well as their language, strongly resembled the English. Of course, because of the influence of French on the English language, and because of the enormous passage of time, the syntax of English is very different from that of Swedish.

Nevertheless, the great similarity in many of the common words in English and Swedish might be explained by remembering the eddying movements of migrating Germanic tribes in northern Europe some two thousand years ago. Jutland, in Denmark, across from Sweden, is presumably named after one of the three tribes (the Angles, Saxons and Jutes) which settled, in part, in England. Perhaps the tribes which settled in England about 400 A. D. were more closely related to the tribes which settled in Sweden than to the other Germanic tribes at the time.

My little 144-word oral reading test in English was a portion of a longer silent-reading IEA test which I used with the permission of IEA (International Association for the Evaluation of Educational Achievement). I had the beginning portion of the IEA silent test translated into Dutch, German, Swedish, and Icelandic, as well as French. The test itself was another reminder of the relatively recent, common origin of the Germanic North European languages. French is instead, of course, one of the Latin group of languages, although it is also a major root, along with the Germanic languages, of modern English.

The Germanic and Latin languages are themselves only part of the ancient and massive Indo-European family of languages, but the ancient root from which all the Indo-European languages arose disappeared eons ago. In contrast, the northern European Germanic languages, such as Dutch, German, Swedish, Icelandic and English, split apart from a common root far more recently. Even though English is heavily indebted to the French language, even for its syntax, it is surprising that it is on the highest-frequency words that the Germanic root influence shows up most clearly, as can be seen from the following table.

Almost all of the 64 different words on my very simple 144-word-long oral test in English are high-frequency words in any language. The highest-frequency words apparently alter surprisingly little, even over millenia, to judge from the following table showing 13 of those 64 high frequency words in English, Dutch, Swedish, German and Icelandic. As is self-evident, those high-frequency words are very closely related across all of those languages.

English	Dutch	Swedish	German	Icelandic
has	heeft	har	hat	a
dog (synonym is hound)	hond	hund	hund	hund
black (synonym is swarthy)	zwart	svart	schwarz	svartur
white	witte	vit	weissen	hvitan
learned	geleerd	lart	gelernt	laert
named	noemt	kallar (Eng. call?)	namen	heiter (no similarity)
ear	oor	ora	ohr	eyranu
ball	bal	boll	ball	bolta
back (close in meaning to rug)	rug	rygg	rucken	bakinu
day	dag	dagen	tag	dag
now	nu	nu	jetzt (like yet?)	nu
years	jaren (pronounced yar-en)	ar	jahre (pro- (pronounced yar-uh)	ara
is	is	ar (like Eng. are?)	ist	er (like English are?)

Many more isolated words on this test in each of these languages were similar to English words or to their synonyms. However, on the 13 words just given out of the 64 different words, the similarities held in general across all five related languages. On the English translation of this reading test, 63% of the 64 different words were among the 250 commonest words in English (as shown by the Ladybird research), but on these words which were similar in all five languages, 85% were on the 250 commonest English list, and none above Thorndike's 1,000 commonest words. It would appear that high-frequency words in a language are more resistant to change with the passage of long periods of time than are those used less frequently.

When I arrived at my small hotel in Stockholm about 10 p. m. Sunday night, October 30, 1977, I found a comprehensive schedule and explanatory material awaiting me at the hotel desk - even with the train times to outlying suburbs listed! I marveled at the efficiency and courtesy of the Swedish Institute.

My fifth-floor room was small but very pleasant, with a new colored television. Television, I was told, was fairly new in Sweden. The programs included local Swedish productions, but many were foreign - English, French and American. In Sweden, as in the Netherlands, the majority of younger people appear to be multi-lingual, so many do not apparently need the subtitles which were sometimes given to foreign programs. I enjoyed tremendously seeing the American TV series, Bonanza (with Swedish subtitles), and Ben Cartwright riding out on the Ponderosa there in Sweden! In another program, I tried to follow, with my fractured French, a filmed study on the doings of a French Communist family living in Paris, as they were on their daily rounds and at their dining table

My suggested departure time to my first school was very early on Monday morning, October 31, 1977, so breakfast in my room had also been early - lovely Swedish breads, cheese and coffee. I found my way to the subway, studied the beautiful tile designs on the station wall in the oh-so-clean station, and then changed later at the central railroad station to take my suburban train. On my way, I saw no litter on the subway or anywhere else, and learned later that no litter was to be found almost anywhere in the Stockholm area, but instead just wonderful, civilized prosperity. The debate over the Swedish socialist system is argued there and here, but I wonder if people should not consider that the Swedes did not just have a socialist system. They had a SWEDISH socialist system. Perhaps it is the wonderful reliability of their people, demonstrated in one way by that absence of litter, which made it work as well as it did.

When I left the suburban train which I had taken at the central railroad station, it was easy to find the recommended bus. However, when I got off that bus and tried to find the school, I was lost. An elderly Swedish woman came to my assistance, read my paper with the directions, and indicated by sign language (she did not speak English) that I was to follow her. We smiled, but could not communicate on a five-minute walk through pleasant, suburban streets. I said "Thank you!" profusely when we arrived at the very large school. It was then that another preconception was shattered, the idea received from the media that Swedish people are cool and reserved. This lovely woman, who apparently was feeling motherly, gave me in answer to my "Thank you!" a big smile and a hug. My conviction grew even stronger that the Swedish are wonderful people!

At this school which I visited on October 31, 1977, I was to learn that the arrangement of the primary grades is different in Sweden (and, as I was to learn later, in Hamburg) from that in most places. One teacher keeps the same group of children through first, second and third grades. I would be testing in second grades and observing in first grades, but, unlike in many other places, the second graders I tested would not have been taught to read by the first- grade teachers I observed. However, with an examination of the textbooks in use and by questioning the staff, it was possible to arrive at a reasonably firm conclusion concerning the teaching approach that had been used in first grade for those second grade classes. The notes which follow will make that clear.

While waiting to speak to the rector of the enormous, centralized school, I met one of the women administrators. She was interested in my project, and told me that a large minority, perhaps one in four, of Swedish primary teachers were presently using a reading method called LTG (which I believe are the initials for the Swedish words for reading, speaking and writing).

The administrator said that the use of this method had not originated with the Swedish School Board and that there were no courses dealing with it. Instead, she claimed it was coming absolutely voluntarily from the teachers, as far as she had read in the Swedish teachers' journals. She said the teachers had been astonished at what the pupils could do by themselves with this method.

This woman administrator's revealing that such information had been obtained from teachers' journals I found to be particularly interesting and particularly ominous. The question was whether the journals were reporting on a trend and its results, or actually initiating a practice and making a value judgment on its probable results. Our American teachers' journals have managed to obscure for years the realities concerning the teaching of primary reading. No reason existed to believe that those Swedish education journals were any different, or that the Swedish teachers' unions publishing those journals would be any more receptive to the true opinions of their rank-and-file teachers.

I eventually learned, as will be discussed, that the so-called LTG method was only an application of the faulty experience chart method that was used by Colonel Parker in Chicago in the 1890's, and by Celestin Freinet and Ovide Decroly in France and Belgium in the 1920's and later. The Swedish education journals, like the American education journals, were apparently praising what they should have condemned. I believe that the expression which my mother heard from her parents as long ago as about 1890, and which she passed on to us, is never more appropriate than when used concerning journals published by teachers' unions: "Paper never refuses ink."

The administrator gave me the name of a woman neighbor of hers who had studied the LTG method and who could give me detailed information on it, as well as the names of others who were familiar with the method.

On Monday evening, October 31, 1977, I spoke by phone with the woman whose name the administrator had given me earlier that day. I received a very thorough explanation of LTG philosophy. It is quoted below, very largely as expressed by her, since I took her remarks down in shorthand. Possibly there are some transcription errors.

> "Originally in Sweden, there were special books and the teacher began to teach the class at the same time - "a", then "o", then "s". When they knew a few sounds, the children put them together into words. Later, they read in the books, but they were all in the same books, and some already knew how to read. With LTG, it is different. They do not use this kind of book. The children do not all learn the sounds at the same time. They make their own books. The teacher and the group, after talking of an experience, put it in writing. The teacher writes what the class tells her. At the same time that she writes, she sounds out the words. She writes the story on a big piece of paper so that all the children can see what she does. Then, on another day, the teacher picks out certain things in this piece of writing. Perhaps some children look for "a's". Taking a word and cutting it into pieces, she asks what sound can you hear in the beginning, and how many sounds. In this method, the text is the children's story. Then the teacher types this text on a special typewriter with big type, and every child gets his piece of paper with the text they have written themselves. They have read it many times and they read it once again, on their own, perhaps. Some can read; some can't. The teacher reads with children so that the children read the text, and when they can't read it, she gives the word.
>
> "They begin to illustrate the text so that they are occupied with this. During that time, the teacher can go around to others. The child and teacher read together, and the teacher helps when necessary. Then the child and teacher pick out certain words in the text that the child ought to work with afterwards. At the beginning, they pick words that are not too difficult and not too easy. First the teacher picks the word, but later the child picks it himself. Then, when the teacher has gone to another child, the child starts to work with these words. He has a small box with a lot of cards in it, sight-word cards, in alphabetical order. If the child had "cat", he writes it on white paper, and on the back of the paper the child draws a cat.
>
> "Later, there is another lesson for the child, and the teacher takes all the cards from the past lesson, and the child has to read for the teacher, or, if clever, to spell the word. When the teacher thinks that the child can read, and perhaps spell, the word, the child can file it. By the time the child has a lot of words in alphabetic order, he can make things with these words. Perhaps he will put all words beginning with "c" in alphabetic order. This method is good because the child can write his own stories.
>
> "Another thing in this method is to draw on his own experiences, and to write down things that have happened to the child and of which he is thinking. The teacher writes the child's dictated story slowly, sounding out the words the

whole time. Afterwards, the child traces over the words with a colored pencil. The main thing is for the child to use his fantasy and to want to use the language to communicate with other people. It is not so important that everything be correct but to use the child's own language. It is important for the child to increase his vocabulary and they can help each other by talking together.

"In learning letters in this method, there is a program so that the children can choose when they want to learn a letter, in what order, and how quickly. In the classroom, there are several papers for every letter for practice. On the paper are directions on how to form the letter with his finger, and he follows the marks. After that, he knows how to go on. He goes to the blackboard, writing in chalk and brushing with a wet brush. Last of all, he writes with a pencil. Eventually, he knows them all."

Although I did not see this LTG method in use in the class in this school which I visited, I was to see it in use in other schools or to hear comments on its relative efficacy. However, wherever I saw it, the teachers were also using to some degree the required primer, Nu laser, which is highly phonic and which I rate Code 9, if used alone. The pure LTG, if used alone, would rate below Code 3.

The first "experience charts" in the LTG method are obviously to be composed before a class has even learned the alphabet. Therefore, the utility of "sounding out" words when a class knows nothing about letters is obviously highly questionable. Also self-evident is the enormous waste of teaching time and the totally confused sequence of skills – and the omission of skills - in this approach. I was to hear later from some experienced Swedish primary teachers that they rejected the LTG method. Almost the only praise I heard for the LTG method came from administrators, who were not actually using the method themselves but who were undoubtedly reading those teachers' journals!

However, it was exceedingly helpful to receive such a complete explanation by phone of the LTG method from this kind woman, and I very much appreciate the time she gave me. Because of her help, I was better able to evaluate the LTG program as I saw it in use in Swedish schools.

Before calling her, I had attempted to call another woman who, I was told, was involved with this method. I was informed when I called that she was visiting in Austria. I received the impression that her visit there was to discuss the use of the LTG method in Austria. If the LTG method had been a good thing, such sharing of methods would have been a good thing, but since the LTG method is not a good thing, the results would not be good. In Innsbruck, I was to test children who would receive some of the best-over-all scores in Europe. They had been taught with a straight synthetic/ analytic phonics primer, Code 10. In Sweden, I was to find that the class which I had reason to believe made the least use of the LTG approach made the highest scores, and the class which made the most use of the LTG method made the lowest scores (although very high compared to American sight-word programs, since even in that class the use of the phonic Nu laser texts was mandatory). Despite its seeming emphasis on "sounding out," the LTG method was a straight language experience method, with heavy emphasis on sight words. According to the description, children would be given many sight words to work with before they knew all their phonic elements. The sight-word load would be increased by almost daily experience stories which did not relate to any particular phonic element being studied.

Despite the report of glowing success stories in Swedish teachers journals, I was to hear the method criticized by several Swedish teachers whose points of view were apparently not reflected in the journals. One, who was working on an individualized reading program with heavy emphasis on phonics, said she did not use the LTG method because it was not good for teaching reading. In another first grade, the teacher, who said she had been teaching 15 years, said she felt confident to blend methods. She was using the Nu laser book and LTG experience charts. She said she analyzed words and gave the sounds, but even the child who remembered the whole word was given the sounds. A second-grade teacher whose class I tested in this same school as this last teacher said the LTG method helped with the children's language development, but if they did not "catch on" to reading right away, it was necessary to give them phonic training. She said the method did not provide for that. Another second-grade teacher said concerning LTG, "I do not like it at all. I do not use LTG."

However, another second-grade teacher did use the method and said she used the text "sometimes," but I saw her doing heavy phonic work with children in her second-grade class. That certainly suggested her class had not properly learned phonics in the first grade when she was using the LTG method heavily with them in the first grade. In the last first-grade class I visited, LTG was in heavy use, and the children were only on page 11 of the Nu laser reader, compared to the first class, where I saw no evidence of LTG in use and they had been on page 27 four days earlier. In this last school (excellent in all other respects except for the unfortunate use of LTG) the rector confirmed that the second grade which I tested had also used the LTG method in first grade. This class scored the lowest on accuracy of the five classes I tested in Sweden. The second grade in the school where I saw no evidence of LTG in use and whose profile of scores appeared to confirm that a phonics approach had been used in first grade (which profile I will explain later) scored the highest on accuracy in Sweden.

Not having spoken directly to the two second-grade teachers whose classes I had tested on oral reading, concerning their possible use of LTG in first grade, I wrote to the rectors of their schools for confirmation on its use or absence. In the school in which I saw LTG in heaviest use in first grade, the rector wrote:

> "The teacher whose children took your oral test has used the same reading method as the first-grade teacher, 'Nu laser vi' and the LTG"

The rector of the school where I saw no use of LTG in first grade wrote:

> "The teacher in 2nd grade whose children last fall took your oral test have had LTG as a complement to their textbook, 'Nu laser vi,' in the first grade."

The reference to Nu laser as a "complement" would indicate less use. But there also was a difference in the "profile" of the scores comparing the heavy LTG class to the latter one, despite the reference to the use of LTG as a "complement" in the latter class. I postulate that this profile showed a heavier emphasis on phonic instruction in the latter class. This will be explained fully in my chapter on final conclusions, since I feel that the discovery of such comparative "profiles" on oral reading scores to be the most important outcome of my research. When comparing the oral reading scores of two groups on accuracy, speed, reversals and comprehension, it is usually possible to show, by that characteristic statistical "profile" which appears, which of the two groups emphasized phonics more in the first half of first grade.

My information on the LTG method did not come until after my visit to the first Swedish school on October 31, 1977. After speaking with the administrator who told me of the method and gave me the names of those whom I could call by phone to get its details, she brought me to the rector of the school. He also was wonderfully cordial and took me through extensive halls, past upper-class locker rooms, past carpeted offices outside which were some lighted threefoot-long aquariums with tropical fish, and through courtyards where students were playing, to the primary wing, a school in itself. I saw some Black children on the playgrounds on the way over. The rector said they had very high status with the other children, which pleased me very much, needless to say.

The first-grade room I visited was cheerful, sunny and relaxed, with a smiling, low-key teacher. The room had the children's desks arranged in tables, with curtains at the windows, and plants. I saw a play stage in the back, a TV, many books and a projector. A pocket chart was visible with alphabet letters. One child in the room was foreign (Scottish) and the teacher said the child did not remember any English. She said the children in the room had been born in 1970 and most had gone to kindergarten for two years. They started school about August 21, at about 7 years of age, a year older than in America. School ended on June 10, but she would be expected to keep this class through second and third grades. Another teacher would have the class for fourth, fifth and sixth.

For two to three weeks after the beginning of first grade, she said the children just listened to sounding and sound analyzing, as well as working on duplicated worksheets with visual discrimination and left-to-right progression. She began to introduce a few letters while the children were still on the sound analysis. The first dictated spelling test included the words "sol, ros, ram, mor" which was given perhaps by September 30. I was visiting this class a month later, on October 31.

Class size in the primary grades in Sweden is limited to 25 pupils, according to E. Malmquist's talk at the 6th International Reading Association World Congress in Singapore in 1976. The primary school week is 20 hours, but the class is divided in halves for 10 of the 20 hours so that teachers have no more than 13 in each half, and often no more than 8 to 10.

The classes, therefore, were small, about 20. Half arrived for about the first hour, all stayed for the greater part of the day, and the other half stayed for about the last hour, after 12:10 until first and second grades were dismissed at 1:20. This method was followed because it permitted more individualized attention. The class was of mixed ability, as I was told grouping by ability level is forbidden in Sweden.

I was told later, in America, by the mother of a Swedish student in my class, that first-graders, however, only spend 16 hours a week in school, although the teacher's day is considerably longer, because of the half-class schedules. She said first-graders spend three hours in school four days a week, and four hours on one day a week.

The first reading book on which they were working was to be completed about February 1. On this date, October 31, they had reached page 27 of the required text, <u>Nu laser vi A,</u> by Borrman Matthis Salminen Wigforss, A. W. Laromedel, Stockholm. The class work as I observed it was in the following pattern.

The few sight words on page 27 were read in chorus first, but the emphasis was all on phonic blending. The teacher said that the children had studied eight letters already, and were building words from the eight letters they knew in upper and lower case: o, s, l, a, r, m, e, and n. However, the basic sight word list of six words printed in upper- and lower-case letters included letters they had not studied yet (jag, du, vi, mamma, hej, pappa). For instance, they could not yet sound out "hej" as they had not learned h or j yet.

In the front of the room were pictures next to each of the letters that had been studied so far to remind children of their sounds (as a rose for R).

The class worked on page 26 of the reader. Before the little story were words at the top containing the letters already taught, apparently for synthetic blending exercises as I saw them done. The teacher said she had taught them blending by starting with O and S. She had a picture of a boat with O on its sail going to the S which was on a bridge. She had told them, "You must sound the O till it comes to the S bridge."

Today's lesson in the book had a colorful illustration of a mother and father and three children playing in the fall leaves. The text read:

"Vi ser pappa. Hej sa pappa. Vi ser mamma. Hej sa mamma. Du ser pappa. Hej sa du. Hej sa du. Hej du sa pappa."

The teacher was apparently having the class blending more words than those on the top of page 26. She had the children reach in the pocket charts and pick up letters to spell the words she dictated, such as "ros, mal, sol." The consonant letters were printed in black, and the vowels in red.

The teacher emphasized to the children that they must blend the sounds, and not say them in isolation. The children blended the words and said them. The teacher said a word, "ros" (rose) and put a picture next to its spelling. Then she had the children speak a whole sentence using the word so that she was sure they were using it with understanding. As the children said each word, the teacher put the matching flannel-board picture next to it and had them use each word in a sentence. She then handed the children worksheets with simple pictures. She told the children they must listen to what they were saying when they spoke a word so they would start to spell words. She said that when she dictated a word to them, she asked, "What letter to do you hear first? What do you hear after?" This of course, is in marked contrast to standard American sight-word texts, where only the first letter - or sometimes the last letter - is ever emphasized for beginning readers.

The program in this school with the Nu laser reader, despite its small sight word content, was obviously a heavily synthetic phonics program, and I coded it Code 9.

The Nu laser book is delightful. The cheerful, colorful illustrations reflect modern Sweden: shopping centers, school room, grandparents, pets and barbecues, and apparently it even included some folk tales and a few pages on children in other lands. It is interesting that, in this northern vegetation zone, many of the plant illustrations in the book are of mosses, ferns and evergreen trees. After the small sight-word (six) load at the beginning, each few pages introduce a new letter and have sample illustrations to show the use of that letter in beginning, middle and ending positions in words. From the beginning, when "O" and "S" are introduced on facing pages, there are illustrations and words underneath them which show blending. The introduction of each new letter is followed by word lists to be used, apparently, for the blending exercises that I saw in the class on this day. The introduction of new letters is interspersed with short little stories using the few sight words and the new phonically decoded words. At the end, the stories become fairly long so that, by February 1, when this book is to be completed, it looks more difficult than American texts in most American programs on February 1.

I was asked to join the rector for lunch in the modern cafeteria and enjoyed talking with him very much. Afterwards, I went to the teachers' room adjacent to the primary-grade classes to wait for the classes to return after lunch. Directly upstairs from the first-grade class I had observed, next to the teachers' room, was the second-grade class I tested. Unfortunately, there was little time to test, since classes dismissed at 1:20, but the second-gr ade class scored amazingly well. Not only did 100% read at 90% accuracy, but 100% read at 95% accuracy, equaled by only one other class in Europe, and by none in the United States. On comprehension, 43% passed, NONE of the class showed reversals, and, while 29% of the sample read slowly, 71% read quickly! Rapid reading, in combination with high accuracy, can indicate the presence of automaticity.

Since only half of the already small Swedish class was present in the afternoon, my sample was concerned with this afternoon half, and I was able to test seven of the 9 children present before it was time for the class to be dismissed at 1:20, the children again being chosen at random. This was, admittedly, a small sample, but so were all the Swedish samples but one. However, I was to find 100% accuracy scores at the 90% level in the majority of European phonics programs (8 of 13) which tended to confirm this high score, but only one of the six European global sight-word programs I tested had 100% at that level. This one program was a Swedish LTG program which also had been mandated to use Nu laser, admittedly a phonics series. Furthermore, in that one Swedish second grade, I personally observed heavy phonics being taught. Therefore, my having coded that second-grade as having been taught with a "global" program can certainly be subject to some question.

I spoke to the second-grade teacher of this first Swedish class, Stockholm 1, that I tested in the afternoon of October 31. However, since I did not receive any real information about the LTG program until my telephone conversation that evening, I did not raise the subject of the LTG program, nor, meaningfully, did the second-grade teacher. She had had the class I just finished testing, of course, in first grade. I did mention the Nu laser text lesson which I had seen in the morning and she showed me a copy of that book she had from the previous year. We discussed that text. In retrospect, I feel that if she had placed much emphasis on LTG the previous year, she would at least have mentioned using it. Since she did not mention LTG, I coded her class which I had tested at Code 9, the same as the first grade I had observed in that school.

I then tested a sixth-grade class in the school on verses 10 to 18 of the 103rd Psalm in the Swedish Protestant Bible. The sixth-grade teacher said she felt the class were very good readers compared to her previous classes, but they scored very much the same as most other Swedish sixth grades that I tested later. All scored above 97% and averaged 99% oral reading accuracy. Four of the eight that I had time to test before the upper grades dismissed at 2:30 scored 100% accuracy in the oral reading of verses 10 to 18 of that Psalm.

The next day, Tuesday, November 1, 1977, I went to another suburban school on the outskirts of Stockholm, and was to marvel again at the incredible European courtesy shown to an ordinary first-grade teacher coming without any special credentials except her interest in studying reading. The Swedish Institute had, of course, made the appointment. The rector, however, had made a formal schedule and program for my visit, including a copy of the school plan. I was met with the greatest courtesy in his very attractive carpeted office. Attractive administrative offices were the norm in the schools I was visiting. I was then escorted to a separate building in which was a first-grade class, next to which was the second-grade class I would test in the afternoon. The school was very large, and the building in which the rector had his offices had a huge central hall, with a marble floor, and corridors opening off it.

The first-grade class was a pleasant room with a charming teacher, who had apparently been teaching for some years. I found the children working with little sticks in which they placed letters, like the sticks used in the English Breakthrough reading program (also marketed in the United States). The children used these sticks to spell words. Breakthrough, of course, is intended to be used as a sight-word program, with such spelling coming later, but it can be used as a spelling phonics program, with the spelling work coming first. This Swedish material is named MinBokstabsvok, Astrid Iverus, Esselta Stadium, and on the cover of its folder is a picture of a boat. I would surmise it is meant to be used for blending as I saw blending used the day before, where the children "sound the boat's sounds till it reaches the bridge". The children had previously had a story read to them, and a few words had been printed on the board to copy and to practice the letter "a" with two dots over it. While this approach had some of the "language experience" elements to it, the phonics study was teacher-chosen and tied directly to the story which had been used - so it was phonic-oriented.

The children were talking normally among themselves as they worked and as the teacher went around to help each in turn. Apparently, they were being asked to add something of their own to the story on the board, and the teacher was helping them to use the letter sticks to sound out the words they needed (synthesis). Their handwriting was very good. In addition to the writing activity, they had a folder in which to keep their new spelling words. I watched the teacher working with the children as she helped them individually to sound the words, asking, "What is the "r" sound?" and reaching for the letter. I asked this teacher if she were using the LTG method, and she said, "No," that it was not good for teaching reading. What is important is that I saw her working with children on sounding and blending letters at this critical point in first grade, and not on sight words.

The children were relaxed, seated in rows facing front, but the attitude of the room was "open classroom." I could see a Black child in the room. Visible on the shelves where the children put the folders for the letters were games and film strip projectors. There was an overhead projector also in the room. The room was curtained and had the alphabet on the side wall. The letters formally introduced so far were in the front of the room, as well as a flannelboard from which I assumed the teacher must do the sort of work that I saw the teacher do the day before with the <u>Nu laser</u> book. I saw one child drawing a picture of an apple and the letter "a". Since I saw children doing far more difficult work than that, I assumed the child was less able than the others and that the teacher was providing for different levels of ability. The handwriting on that was only fair. For the most part, the handwriting, as mentioned, in the children's notebooks was marvelous, although I saw one child who had the proportion of the letters wrong.

I had lunch with the teachers, who eat with the children, and enjoyed the experience very much. Afterwards, in the teachers' room, I was honored by being introduced to some of the faculty, with coffee and a festive cake!

When I went to the second-grade class in the afternoon, the teacher told me that she had been a secretary once, as I had been, and she took shorthand. She was a very beautiful woman, and chic, and I found it unbelievable that she had been 27 years teaching, as it seemed impossible. Her room was also curtained and had many lovely pictures in the front, and geraniums. I was pleased to see her poster, "Don't abandon cats," having found it a tragic and prevalent abuse in the United States, although it is technically against the law in most places. (I am tempted from time to time, however, to abandon a 14-pound white cat of mine who insists on curling up in the wastebasket next to my typewriter while I work, since I prefer not to throw waste paper either on the floor or on his head!)

The teacher had many books and filmstrip materials in her room. I was intrigued with her math table, which had weighing materials, place-value charts plus sticks, and cubes with holes on three sides, so that they could form three dimensional structures. Some materials like the English (and American-used) Unifix, perhaps the same, from Gleerups of Lund, Sweden, were to be used like the American materials, Chip Trading, I understood. I took notes that some of the material was labeled Byggmatte Rahmsboktryckeri AB Lund (1970).

The teacher told me she had informed the parents that they would have a visitor, so it was possible for me to test the whole class, Stockholm 2, Code 8, the seven children from the morning group and the eight children from the afternoon group. On accuracy at 95, 87% passed, and, at 90, 100% passed. On comprehension, 80% passed. Before the testing began, the children sang for me, while she played on the class organ. I saw a Psalm written on the board. Religion is taught in the school. The children sang hymns, but the last song was not a hymn. It was delightful, and the children whistled it for me! I carried away happy memories from this teacher's room, and from that of her companion next door. Children are privileged to sit in their rooms.

Since, in Sweden, the children are kept by the same teacher for three years, it was not possible to observe the actual reading method for the second-grade class being tested, but only to infer it from methods observed elsewhere and the teacher's comments. Since the second-grade teacher's first-grade companion had a program which I would rate Code 8, and since her remarks in a later telephone conversation confirmed that she had used the same methods (she said none of the children could read when they entered first grade) I coded her class also at Code 8. Concerning LTG, she said, "I do not like it at all. I do not use LTG."

I then went to a sixth-grade class where I tested as many as I could before the bell rang at 2:30, choosing them by chance because they were near the door. The teacher said I had an average mix of children. All of the nine I tested scored at 99% accuracy or above on the 103rd Psalm in the

Swedish Protestant Bible, verses 10 to 18. Six of the nine scored at 100% accuracy. Sixty-seven per cent read fast.

My third Swedish school was far out in the country, outside Upsala. An apartment complex was nearby, but the school housed only about 300 children - much less than previous schools. It seemed new. The first-grade room I visited first was extremely cheerful, with the walls painted Dutch blue, with crimson curtains at the windows, desks tops yellow, orange chairs, and Dutch blue linoleum. A large green blackboard, hinged like those I had seen elsewhere, was in the room. When I arrived, the children were doing what appeared to be a social studies lesson together, and there was another visitor, a young student from the teachers' college. The teacher passed out magazines for the children to cut out pictures, and showed them a picture of soup in one magazine. She also distributed large white paper, perhaps 18 inches by 24 inches. She told me after the children had started working that this was a social studies assignment about food. She said this morning they had written the experience chart story I saw displayed prominently, "Om Musikem." She said they had discussed it jointly and then gone back to their seats and each studied a letter. She said it might have been the one they reached in the book, Nu laser, but not necessarily so. She said she felt confident to blend the LTG method and the Nu laser book because she was drawing on her 15 years experience as a teacher. She said, however, that she always gave the sounds. Even the child who remembered the whole word was given the sounds.

The alphabet was mounted on the wall. Below each letter was a plastic envelope of sample letters for the children to take. Also on the wall in magic marker ink were directions for the children using the letters (presumably like those mentioned to me in my phone conversation on the method). Obviously, children who could not yet read could not read those directions, so they must have previously been read to the children and discussed with them.

The children were talking freely while they worked but were very orderly. I saw pillows in the corner for children to sit on, presumably during independent reading or other work. The Nu laser text has a picture of a classroom with such pillows, and the children and teachers gathered together in a discussion group, with the children using the pillows. Nineteen children were in this classroom. The room was well fitted with materials. I saw a flannelboard as in the other Swedish classes, and a phone on the wall. The chalkboard was elaborate, complex and hinged. Part of the board was marked with evenly spaced dots arranged in lines. Drawing instruments were available for the teacher's use, triangles and compasses. Available in shelves along the wall were manipulative materials for the children, including interesting materials with the brand AKTIV by Lagybrikn. These were activity boards with pieces for each, in which children matched pictures of sets, shapes like triangles, letters and words to pictures, etc.

After speaking with the first-grade teacher, I left the room to visit the second grade and to read orally with sixth graders. The halls outside the classroom also were beautiful. They were furnished with light green tables with benches on either side like breakfast table benches with tall backs, and these benches were yellow and upholstered in a cheerful green plaid. Along the walls were yellow cabinets for books and other fascinating looking materials. The walls were in pebbled cinder block, painted orange. The rector said the children loved their school and destroyed nothing. This was indeed a physically very beautiful and colorful building.

The teacher of the sixth-grade class with whom I read said that she had what we would call an open classroom program, the children working on projects. Some few had just come back from a factory visit that morning. The sixth graders all read the Swedish selection from the 1 03rd Psalm in the Swedish Protestant Bible with great speed and ease, although one child from Finland did not do so well as the others. (Finnish is a language related to Hungarian, and their common root is buried in mystery, being unrelated to most other existing European languages. Therefore, presumably, it would be very difficult for a child from Finland to learn to function in Swedish.) These sixth graders all passed this test above the 90% accuracy level. The Finnish boy read at

91%, another child read at 94% whom I marked "slow, uncertain," and all others read at 97% or better. Five read at 99% accuracy and three at 100% accuracy out of the total sample of 16 students (which I believe was the whole class). The teacher said she believed the children had synthetic phonics in first grade in another school, as far as she knew.

At lunch, I joined this teacher in the cafeteria, going afterwards to the teacher's room to talk. In Sweden, the lunch program is state-supported, and I believe the children do not have to pay any fees.

I waited outside the second-grade room for the children to return from their gym period. (Lunch times were staggered there as they often are in America.) The desks in the room I could see were arranged in rows facing front, and I could see the unit values for the Cuisenaire rods mounted on the wall. In the corridors outside this room were lovely round yellow tables with chairs, and also the upholstered benches and tables. While waiting for the class to return, I walked through some other wings in the building. I saw a teacher giving an oral lesson, while seated outside in the hall were three children recopying compositions.

After the second grade returned which I was to test, Class Stockholm 3, I had an opportunity to talk to its teacher, who appeared to be very organized and to be doing a very good job. She said she had two children who were reading in the first-grade book, but successfully. She said the rest of the children could not read independently yet, so she was limited in the amount of individualized work she could give them. (Her later scores for these other children were remarkably high, so her idea of reading "independently" must also have been very high.) Her total class numbered 19, and in this afternoon session which I would be testing she had nine. In her opinion, the LTG method helped with the children's language development, but if they did not "catch on" to reading right away, it was necessary to give them phonic training, as the method did not provide for that.

She had, among the nine I was to test in the afternoon session, one brain-damaged child. He had already repeated one grade. All the time that I was with him, he sucked on his fingers, and he also drooled constantly. He refused to sit next to me, but went to the other side of the table. He gave the impression that he was a severely disabled child. The teacher explained to me that the Swedish schools were trying to "mainstream" such children, giving them the individual help they need with a special teacher and so on, but keeping them with the group. This child read with me after the others, having come back from individualized teaching with his tutor. He did demonstrate that he had some knowledge of phonics rules by being able to decode some words, but he read extraordinarily slowly, and below 90% accuracy, scoring 72% and reading so very slowly that I had him complete only the first selection (27 words in Swedish out of the total Swedish test of 128 words).

One other child in this group of nine had also been out for individualized teaching, but I was not told if he also had some disability. He scored 84% accuracy on the first two selections (55 words out of 128) and read slowly, with obvious "sounding out." I did not have him complete the oral test since he was so obviously failing. Yet the other seven children in this class all read very well, five of them "fast."

One was a Black girl who had learned to read in Russia and could speak no Swedish, according to her teacher, when she arrived in second grade this year. She must have learned to read in Russia in the Western, and not the Russian alphabet, though it is possible she was exposed to both. However, it was amazing to hear her read the Swedish selection, obviously in the Western alphabet, at 100% accuracy, and with ease, considering the difference in language. She could not, obviously, take the comprehension portion of the test since she did not yet understand Swedish.

Of the remaining six Swedish children out of the afternoon group of nine, one read at 98% accuracy, two read at 99% accuracy, and three read at 100% accuracy. Five of the six passed the comprehension test.

Because a severely brain-damaged child would not be included in scores from other countries, I omitted this child from the class averages for Stockholm 3. Using the eight other children, the class had 88% pass at the 95% level and 88% at the 90% level (because one of the eight had failed the test). On the comprehension scores, I had to omit the girl who spoke no Swedish, so, on the remaining 7, 71% passed the comprehension test. Scores were computed on the eight children for reversals, at 0%, and for speed: 22% read slowly (one child) and 63% read quickly (five of the eight). The other 2 read at a normal rate. From the teacher's comments to me, it was obvious that she favored the phonic approach of <u>Nu laser</u> (required in all Swedish schools) and not the LTG emphasis. I therefore gave this second-grade class which she had taught in first grade a Code 9.

Despite this teacher's small class by the standards of other countries (nineteen), it was large by Swedish standards. She also had one non-Swedish speaking child, one obviously brain-damaged child, one severe reading problem, and one boy who, I strongly suspected, was emotionally disturbed. This was an extraordinarily heavy teaching load for one teacher, and I had only seen half of her class. She may have had other children with severe problems in the morning half. To have achieved such fine results with such a difficult group (she had taught them in first grade) was quite a testimonial to her competence as a teacher. Also, this was the only class in Europe outside Belgium where I saw the number values for the Cuisenaire rods in use, although I may possibly have missed that elsewhere. The fact that the number values for the rods were actually displayed certainly indicated that the Cuisenaire rods were being used.

The weather remained surprisingly warm for early November on the morning that I went to my fourth Swedish school, far outside Stockholm. As on the other days, I did not need a coat, and some roses were still blooming. I was told that sometimes they had snow by this date, Thursday, November 3, 1977. The rector of the school, again with extraordinary European courtesy, met me at the station with his car. He was a taller, rangier version of the English movie actor of the 1930's and 1940's, Leslie Howard. I had been complimenting myself that my quiet wool jacket dress looked very Swedish, and my Irish face has been mistaken for Swedish more than once at home in America, but the rector said that he knew, as soon as he saw me, that I was an American!

It was a small school, and everyone was very friendly. Before visiting the classrooms, the rector and I discussed reading programs in his office, again with the oh-so-welcome cup of coffee! In our discussion, the rector referred to the work of Gustav Johnson, who had written a book, <u>Jet Sociala Arvet,</u> meaning the social inheritance. He said Johnson had a village for children who were mentally retarded, or perhaps from broken homes, etc. Reading failures, Johnson felt, might stem from children's lack of belief in themselves, and their lack of confidence and fear of many new things, such as, for instance, what is coming after a particular lesson. In teaching such children reading, Johnson was reported to have felt we must give them more belief in themselves, and, in teaching, we must always remember the triangle that has its points in the home, the school and the child.

In this school, I did not visit a first grade, but saw instead the second-grade teacher as she handled reading with her class, and then tested that class in the afternoon. This was particularly helpful, because of course, she would have been the teacher who initially had taught this class to read last year, since Swedish teachers keep the same class for first through third grades.

She was using an individual teaching approach when I was there, encouraging responsibility, but she stressed that the children needed to have permission for many activities. The children were talking quietly while they worked. Half the class was here in the early part of the morning when I arrived, nine children, including one Chinese girl, and the rest of the class would arrive shortly.

The room was cheerful and pleasant, furnished with materials in general like those I had seen in other Swedish primary rooms. The teacher was very friendly, and, as was obvious from her manner and comments, a truly dedicated teacher. She told me she was using the LTG method, although she used the text "sometimes." I saw posted a phonics lesson derived possibly from an earlier experience chart, dealing extensively with short vowels and the "nk" consonant blend (hink vinka, bank, planka, stanka, ec.) The vowels were also posted in the room in several places. What appeared to be a large class experience chart was on display. I had the "experience chart" commercially translated when I came home, and it turned out to be a science lesson, instead, and a fine one! It read:

> "The sun warms the garden. The water evaporates and turns into clouds. The clouds become heavier and heavier until it rains. The rain falls down onto the garden.
>
> "The sun shines and everything starts all over again. This is called moving in a cycle."

I had the "phonics lesson" words commercially translated also. They obviously were meant to study the "nk" blend as well as short vowels, but it is amusing to see again how closely aligned English and Swedish are sometimes in words and meanings:

hink	bucket
vinka	to wave
bank	bank, embankment
bank (with dots over the a)	bench
planka	plank, crib
tank	tank
frank	frank
stanka	stench, to stink
panka	broken
stinka	stink
tanka	to fill up
ankar	anchor
anka	to anchor

Children's paintings were also posted in the room, and under each a child's story.

When I arrived, the teacher was working individually with the children at their reading. One little boy with whom she was working had a little booklet bound with colored woolen cord and illustrated with pictures. He read this story aloud to his teacher from the booklet that he had made, and she had him sound out words. A little girl then read her story to the teacher. Another boy was reading from a published book, not his own experience story.

After visiting the second grade, I went to two sixth grade classes so that these children could read aloud to me, individually, the Swedish Protestant Bible version of the 103rd Psalm. Again, in this school as in the others, the performance of the Swedish sixth was startlingly good! I tested six children in one class of 26, picking those in the front rows. Five of the six read at 100% accuracy, and one at 99%. One third read fast. In the second classroom, I tested seven pupils. Four read at 100% accuracy, one at 99%, one at 98%, and one at 97%. One of the seven, or 14%, read fast.

After lunch, I returned to the second-grade class, Stockholm 4, Code 6, for oral testing. At 95% oral reading accuracy, 80% passed, and, at 90% accuracy, 100% passed. On speed, 30% read slowly and 20% read quickly, and 30% made reversals. The children certainly did well, but particularly on reading comprehension, 80% passing. This wonderful teacher was anxious to hear this score, as she said she had put such a great emphasis on teaching reading comprehension in her individualized program.

However as will be discussed later, when high so-called "reading comprehension" scores are made on tests in the elementary grades by children who are known to be excellent decoders as this class was, and for whom decoding has become automatic, the so-called "reading comprehension" scores only demonstrate whether or not the children were paying attention ("listening") to what they were reading. The children in this class had been encouraged to pay such attention, and so they scored high. Yet they were not "taught" so-called "reading comprehension" because there is no such thing. Properly taught "reading" is a conditioned reflex, and proceeds automatically in the part of the brain which handles automatic, learned behaviors. Yet comprehension takes place in that part of the brain where consciousness resides, and which does not store automatic, learned behaviors. So-called "reading comprehension", therefore, may be the ultimate oxymoron.

It was difficult to find a code to assign to this program, since I saw such heavy teaching of phonics at the second- grade level, and might presume this teacher gave such emphasis also at the first-grade beginning level. Also, she had made some use of the Nu laser text. Nevertheless, since she said she had used the LTG method, I coded her class with Code 6, lower than for Nu laser alone.

The rector of the school was not there when I left, but had made arrangements for the custodian to drive me to the station. He was an interesting man, and had traveled and worked all over the world before coming home to Sweden to stay. While waiting for him after the classes were over, I spoke with one of the men upper-grade teachers whose class I had tested. He was fascinated with a word on the archaic Swedish version of the 1 03rd Psalm in the Protestant Bible which I had received from the American Bible Society, along with the Dutch, German, Icelandic, and French versions. At my request, the American Bible Society had very kindly sent me a portion of the 103rd Psalm in all these languages. However, the probability is that the American Bible Society had sent translations of the Bible made in the same general period of time as the King James version, roughly the seventeenth century. The King James version is still in wide use in English speaking countries, and is still very familiar. However, a newer version must have been the norm in present- day Sweden, or this older version would not have occasioned the puzzlement that it did.

The word that had so puzzled the Swedish upper-grade teacher was, I believe "klippdassarnas," and he and some others had scoured the school to find an unabridged Swedish dictionary, where it finally turned up! It had been amusing in giving this text to the Swedish children that the teachers often reported to me the reaction of the sixth graders in coming back to the classroom: "What was THAT all about?" They could not understand it, because of the archaic language, but they read it with rapidity and ease, and the majority at 100% accuracy. They were living proof that Frank Smith was wrong when he said, "Fluent readers rarely read word for word, even when reading aloud."

The last Swedish school I visited on Friday, November 4, 1977, was also far outside Stockholm. Again, I was given the real honor of having the rector meet me at the railroad station, and he was a most gracious, friendly man. The rector said that the school was in a mixed economic area, with not so many high income homes as in the last school district I had visited. Some of the children came from housing which was paid for by the government, but some also came from rich homes and some from average.

The school was enormous, and the grounds were landscaped, with many very tall, very lovely evergreens. Outcroppings of granite rock showed in places, as we climbed to the building I was to visit first, again reminding me of northern New York's post-glacial landscape. The rector introduced me to a woman who, I understood, was a supervisor. She brought me to a very cozy teachers' room, with a couch, coffee table, chairs and some few teachers assembled for coffee and Danish pastry, while the children were at recess. I, too, was offered lovely Danish, and, again, the welcome coffee, and enjoyed very much being made a member of their group. I understood that the school was so very large that it was necessary to have several teachers' rooms in different parts of the complex. After recess, a very pleasant first-grade teacher brought me back to her room to see the work in progress in reading. She had eight children present, one half of the class, the others to come in later. The room had pillows in the corner, as in some other Swedish schools. The walls were lined with cabinets, which I presume stocked many of the materials I saw elsewhere. There was also an organ. On the back board was an interesting display. A very large picture of a globe had been cut out and mounted, and children's drawings of people from different countries were standing at the appropriate places on the globe, their heads sticking out towards space, making the globe seem like a round pincushion with the pins facing straight out. It made me think of the SAS slogan, "Navigators of the World - Since It Was Flat!" There is no danger that this class of little Scandinavians will ever think the world is flat!

In mathematics, the class was using books doing work on identifying sets and numbers. This teacher used Cuisenaire rods, too, but said she used number values with the rods from the first.

Reading was being handled with the LTG method, although the book, <u>Nu laser,</u> was also in use. However, it was apparent that the latter was only a part of the reading program, as the class had only reached page 11, while the class I saw on Monday. October 31, which was using it apparently exclusively, had reached page 27.

A large experience chart was on the chartholder in the room. Each child had his own word box with alphabetical dividers, with his words filed in alphabetical order. The children also each had boxes of upper and lower case letters. The children took words from their word boxes and then used letters to spell the words. The teacher ran her finger under words with individual children and sounded them out. I recorded the words with which I saw some children working:

    Child 1: Annette, om, vi (letters a, e, i, n, m, t, v o, total 8)
    Child 2: fin, pa (letters a, f, n, i, p, total 5)
    Child 3: Molly, ek, orre (letters e, k, l, o, m, i, r, y, total 7)
    Child 4: rok, pillar (letters a, i, l, k, o, p, r, total 7

In addition, children picked letters they wished to study from the letter folders in the front of the room.

In the words I had recorded from four children, which words were being studied at that moment, there were a total of 14 different letters, out of the 26 letters of the alphabet, but no single letter of the 14 was being studied by all children simultaneously. The 14 letters were: a, e, f, i, k, l, m, n. o. p, r, t, v, y.

Each child had his own note book. If a child were, for instance, working with "a", he might indicate in his notebook where in a word he heard the "a" - at the beginning, middle or end of a word - by drawing a series of three boxes and checking the beginning, middle, or end box. In this program, the children were obviously not limited to working with just initial consonant sounds as in so many American sight-word programs at this point in first grade.

Since the teacher ran her finger under words and sounded them out with individual children, real blending was being done. Nevertheless, children were working with sight words when it was evident they could not have learned all the letters in those sight words that they were handling and filing as "whole words." Furthermore, the experience-chart story was not focused on any particular phonic element, even though children later chose certain words in that story and would concentrate on some phonic element in that word.

The work in this classroom on letters in words was obviously using an analytic phonics approach. However, it was critically different from the work I saw in Stockholm 2 because of the lack of teacher choice in the words being analyzed. In that classroom, words to be studied were written on the board and work was concentrated, by the whole class, on the sound of the Swedish "a" which has two dots over it. The purpose of the story she had given was to teach every child in the class, on that particular day, the sound of that particular letter, as used in words in that story. Undoubtedly, that teacher had a thorough list of phonic skills to be taught sequentially later. The purpose of her stories at that point in first grade was to teach every child in the class the sounds of the letters in the alphabet. That approach was thorough and systematic.

Yet, with the LTG approach, it would be very difficult to learn whether every child had properly studied and learned every letter, since letter study was totally "individualized," with no whole-class, teacher-directed lessons on the letters. The only whole class activity that was actually "taught" by the teacher was the writing of the experience chart, and the emphasis with the experience chart was on its whole sight words, not on its letter sounds. At the very least, the waste of teaching time and the enormous "testing" and "reteaching" load on a teacher in the hit-and-miss LTG approach is self-evident. For a teacher to go up and down a room, helping children here and there to sound out random words, worth while as it is, is nevertheless not a teaching activity. Properly used, it can only be a follow-up activity on material that has been already taught, but by its very nature it is hit-and-miss.

This beautifully run classroom required a great deal of teacher effort to keep it functioning, and it was functioning wonderfully, but, because of the nature of the LTG program, it had to be coded lower on the phonic/sight-word scale than the class using only Nu laser, Yet the Nu laser program was a great deal less work for a teacher than this individualized approach. I gave this class a Code 6 - which was perhaps even higher than I should have, because it was very well organized. The far easier total Nu laser program of Stockholm 1 was given a Code 9, but it might also have rated Code 10 except for the few beginning sight words.

I learned that the second-grade teacher in this school, Stockholm 5, had used the same method as the first-grade teacher, Nu laser and LTG, and so I coded the test results for her class at Code 6 also. It was possible for me to test both halves of the second-grade class, Sixty-seven per cent of the class read at 95% or better, and 86% at 90% or better. On comprehension, 62% passed. On speed, 38% were slow and 29% were fast, and 33% made reversals.

During lunch time, I went with the second-grade teacher and her class to the cafeteria, a long walk on these big grounds. The children's cafeteria to which she brought her class also was very large, but then we joined the teachers for lunch in their smaller private dining room.

Before leaving, I had time to read orally with a chance selection of ten sixth graders. Again, as elsewhere, the reading of these sixth-graders was marvelous. Two read the 103rd Psalm selection in the Swedish Protestant Bible at 94% accuracy, three at 99% accuracy, and five at 100% accuracy. One of the 10 read at a "fast" rate. Here was more confirmation that there is no necessity whatsoever to accept in America inaccurate reading from adults as the "norm."

To my delight, at the end of the day, the rector asked me if I would join his wife and him at their home for tea. He said he thought it would be a good experience to visit a Swedish home while I was there, and he was so right! Their house was very modern but inside was beautifully and lovingly furnished in a traditional fashion. I was shown some wonderful old pieces that had been in the family for years, and fascinating things they had picked up on their travels. I also met their handsome young son while I was there. I learned that they had spent several months in the United States studying educational methods (his wife was also in the field of education) and they had jointly prepared a paper on their return.

Not content with having extended such wonderful courtesy to me, they also drove me almost all the way back to Stockholm! They came with me to a subway station close to the center of the city. Coming through the waiting room, which was a little run down and with a trace of litter, he exclaimed about its "terrible" condition! I winced inwardly a little. I have seen far, far worse in New York. One of my last memories of Sweden is seeing those two delightful people, waving good-by to me from the platform as I returned on the train to central Stockholm.

When I got to the Stockholm railroad station on Saturday, I wanted to ship ahead to Hamburg one of my abominable bags full of test papers, books, etc., because I was almost unable to carry all of the material that I had with me. Since I was afraid the bag might not get to Hamburg to meet me there on time, I needed to ask the baggage man whether or not the bag could get to Hamburg at least by Monday. I found then to my surprise that, even with my virtually nonexistent Swedish, I could communicate with the Swedish baggage man who did not speak English, because of my little oral reading test in Swedish, the "Peter and His Dog Epic." The baggage man had not understood my question in English, "How long to Hamburg? How many days?" But he DID understand when I raised my voice in a questioning tone and put together just two little words from the Peter story. All I had to say was "Tva dag?" and he smiled and nodded in agreement. I knew then I could pick up my shipped bag in Hamburg in no more than two days!

Hamburg

It was a long train trip to Hamburg in Western Germany. On Saturday night, I took a sleeping car out of Stockholm, which terminated in Copenhagen, and then I took a connecting train from Copenhagen to Hamburg, arriving in the middle of Sunday afternoon.

To me, there is something very thrilling about traveling in a darkened sleeping car and rushing through towns at night with their street lights sailing past the window like shooting stars. European railroads have not been permitted to deteriorate, and traveling on them is like traveling in the United States on crack trains a generation ago, on solid-wellmaintained road beds. Carl Sandburg's famous poem about the immigrant railroad laborer, "Child of the Romans," speaks of the laborer's going back to the "second half of a ten-hour day's work" after "eating a noon meal of bread and bologna",

> "Keeping the road-bed so the roses and jonquils
> Shake hardly at all in the cut glass vases
> Standing slender on the tables in the dining cars...."
> ...when the train "whirls by."

Thankfully, now in 1979, there are few ten-hour days in America and few badly underpaid workers as this poor laborer may have been back about 1916 when Sandburg published this poem. Yet this worker and others kept the railroad beds so smooth that a dining car's roses would hardly shake when a train moved at a high speed. Now, in 1979, American railroads are largely abandoned for other means of passenger travel, and the road beds show it.

There is a sameness about big, modern cities. Hamburg seemed prosperous and enormous. Certainly its railroad station is enormous! It was easy, however, to be able to transfer to my hotel, but it was not so easy finding the school the next day. In order not to be late, I went by taxi.

I arrived at a beautiful, modern school in a suburban area. It was arranged in wings, three stories high, with covered walkways outdoors connecting the wings. The walkways were brick and went through landscaped courtyards. The building was predominantly red brick, but part of the structure was a lovely blue tile.

I was directed to the rector's office. The rector met me most cordially and introduced me to a young man first- grade teacher. On this particular day, this very creative young man had arranged for mothers of some of the children to come in to lead small groups in craft activities. In his classroom, I saw eight children and two mothers cutting up many vegetables to prepare what was apparently going to be soup. Much fine cooking equipment was visible. Off his room, as in all the classrooms, was a very large cloakroom. Here were two mothers and a group of eight working with materials. Some were using pipe cleaners to make little men, covering them with pieces of yarn, and putting on little plastic heads on which they colored in the features with magic markers, and put on hair. Some made animals with spiral tails, and pasted on paper mouths and features. Another group of eight children and two mothers were working with clay. Another group of eight and two mothers were working with peas, corn, and beans, making lovely mosaics with paper spirals on cardboard coasters. This young man teacher said he believed it was a good experience for the mothers to work with the children, and it motivated the children to work very freely on these projects. However, it was self-evident that all this happy, productive activity only resulted because of extensive planning the teacher had done ahead of time to arrange such groups.

This instructor told me had worked with the children in the pre-first grade. Apparently, at present in 1977 in Hamburg, there is conflict between the nursery school levels and the primary grades about which level of school should teach the pre-first (kindergarten in the United States).

This first-grade teacher's classroom had 31 children. He said there were not very many foreign children in this school. He had one, a Yugoslav, last year in 1976, but he said that near the harbor area in Hamburg the enrollment was 40 per cent non-German. The children had started school the end of September, and it was now Monday, November 7, 1977. This teacher was using a different reading method from the other first grades in the building, which were using <u>Bunte Fibel,</u> the 1976 new reader of the Hermann Schroedel Verlag KG concern of Hannover, Berlin, Darmstadt and Dortmund. This company's older reader, <u>Bunte Welt</u> (1971) had been used by the classes now in second grade. These readers will be described later.

The young man teacher had been using <u>Leselehrgang des Padagogischen Zentrums - Materialien fur den ErstLeseunterricht,</u> which was published by Verlag Julius Beltz, Weinhein, Berlin, Basel.

This teacher said his reading method came from the Kennedy School in Berlin (I believe that was its name). He used it for the first time five years ago, and it originally was a tremendous amount of work, as he had to make the materials to use with it himself. The workbook began with visual discrimination, and then practiced initial consonant sounds, and then the first words. (This, of course, is very like the sequence of most American sight-word basal readers.) He said with this system, however, it was not necessary to follow from the beginning to the end, but it was possible to group and omit the simpler lessons for the bright children. He said he had begun with a few words, and his second group of words would come next week. With these words, the children could make their own sentences. The workbooks have words to cut out, and then pictures. Children match the pictures to sentences with the words.

Each child had a looseleaf notebook with his name on it. A child had cut out r's's and k's and pictures of things with those sounds. Very few letters were in this notebook. The instructor said there was a trend away from the whole-word method five years ago (1972) but he felt now, in 1977, there was a trend back. He felt that it was necessary to work both with words and distinguishing words which begin with the same sound. I am not sure if he was expressing his own opinion or that of "Reinhard," to be mentioned later, but he referred to him in this connection.

He said that, for a certain number of children, he felt it is difficult to do sounding, and that they have to take words as wholes. After Christmas, his class would begin to learn more new words and to learn "to hear and to look in the word." From the publisher's brochure which he so very thoughtfully gave me, I assume this would be the third sight- word list, Word Group III. His children had already had Word Group I (auto, flugzeug, geld, rad, schiff, uhr) which translate as car, plane, gold, wheel, ship, and clock. The children would receive the next twelve-word list next week, and the next 30 word list after Christmas. The remainder of the 155 words would be given in three further Word Groups. It was only on the third list - after Christmas - that real study of letter sounds would begin.

It was obvious from the brochure that this was an analytic phonics program, but with extremely heavy emphasis on sight words and on reading for meaning until halfway through first grade. The 155 sight words would later be used to study the sounds of the letters in all positions in the words, however, not just in the beginning positions as was being done now.

While his class was obviously working on the sounds of initial consonants when they were just beginning Word Group II, the brochure showed that work with the sounds of initial consonants was not to be touched until the end of Group II. The workbook before the first group of sight words did not practice initial consonant sounds, but was obviously meant to prepare for that work later. The workbook dealt only with the recognition of visual differences in letters (visual discrimination) and with the identification of spoken words that began with the same sound (auditory discrimination). This auditory and visual discrimination work was in preparation for the work that were to come.

This program was a very good "match" to many American basal reading programs, and I would code it Code 2 for the first half of first grade, though in the last half of the year the phonic emphasis became more pronounced, as shown by the brochure and as the brochure described in Reinhard's "Stages".

The kind of sight-word exercises at Word Group II level, to begin the second week in November, were shown by an illustration in the brochure (from page 34) where a little girl played a sight-word identification game with the class, and by an illustration from page 35 where children drew pictures to illustrate sight-word sentences. That was pure sight-word work for about the third month of first grade.

However, this young man teacher was the only one using this program in this school, and he had not had a second- grade last year. As in Sweden, Hamburg teachers kept their classes from grade 1 to grade 3, and, since no second- grade teacher in the school had used this program in first grade, it was not possible to test it at second grade.

This very competent young man teacher had a beautiful classroom, "open-classroom-like" in appearance, and wonderfully supplied with teaching materials, including even "hula hoops", which is a nice addition for gym class activities.

I visited another first-grade room, where a mathematics lesson was in progress with what are called "logic blocks" or attribute blocks in America and England. The text that the teacher was using was <u>Mathematik Im Schuljahr - Nehansgable</u> from Friche Besuchen. The teachers in this school have a free choice between four or five available texts. This could be the best possible way to put sight-word basal readers out of the schools. Give teachers a choice between truly phonics readers or sight-word readers, and let some time pass. The superiority of the phonics readers will show up, and the teachers will voluntarily - because they are convinced - select the phonics series. All publishers then will HAVE to produce a product to please the teachers or go out of business. Something like this happened in New Castle, Pennsylvania, when the teachers voted to adopt the Lippincott phonics series.

When I came in, the children were sitting at tables, working in groups. Each pair of children shared a set of logic blocks, a not inconsiderable expense for the school budget if they are priced comparably to those in America. From the beginning of the school year, September 20, until about now - November 7, the children had only been playing games with these logic blocks. This may have meant something like the games American primary school children play with these blocks, such as the "Train of One Difference." If a child puts down a large thick red triangle, the next child must put down a piece which differs only in one attribute - size, thickness, color or shape. The second child could put down, for instance, a large thick red circle (differing only in shape), but not a small thin green square (differing in size, thickness, color and shape). To be able to make such distinctions, however, probably requires that a child has reached what is called the Piaget concrete operations mental stage, which assumes a development age of about 7.

At this point, on Monday, November 7, 1977, the children were beginning the actual mathematics book which dealt formally with logic and sets. When I arrived, the teacher was demonstrating the lesson on a flannel board, using plastic logic blocks, on the back of which she had pasted sandpaper so that the blocks would adhere to the flannelboard as she used them. I could see work on the board with the word "Fu", and learned that it was from the reading text <u>Bunte Fibel.</u> I later learned that the text used heavy synthetic/analytic phonics, and I later gave it a Code 10.

The room had many large displays of children's work mounted on the walls, and interesting collages done by each child. The general atmosphere of the room, despite this formal lesson, was informal. There was no enforcement of silence, and the children conversed naturally except during the demonstration lesson.

At lunch time, I was taken to a beautifully furnished school library, where a buffet had been set out with frankly fabulous ham and other salads, and breads and coffee. The teachers in this school apparently mark their own birthdays by bringing in a lovely buffet! It is possible that I misunderstood, and others bring it in, but I think not. It was rather amusing, because in the school in America in which I taught, teachers "treat" the rest of the staff to cakes or doughnuts, etc., on their own birthdays.

I then went to visit the third first-grade room. Children were working on "r" in the <u>Bunte Fibel</u> (1976) text, with the phrase, "Uta ruft." on page 10. Each child had been supplied with an envelope of cards about 12 by 12 inches, from which to punch out cardboard letters, upper and lower case, and other reading practice material. Later cards concerned blending games or exercises for making words, still later cards contained word phrases to put together to make sentences, and the final cards concerned pictures and sentences to arrange in story sequences. The cards were sturdy and a good size for little fingers, but did not look as if they should have taken too much of the school budget, as plastic ones might have done.

The <u>Bunte Fibel</u> text book was colorful and delightful. A group of nine first-graders were on the cover, seated in a laughing group, while one held up the ridiculous but appealing stocking puppet given the name Fu. The very good reason for the name is that Fu's picture and name started the book.

Pages 2 and 3 were a non-verbal illustration of a small group of first graders making stocking puppets with old stockings, yarn and felt (apparently all to become "Fu's in their own right). The next page had another small group of smiling first graders, saying, with comic strip balloons above their heads, "Fu," while one had his finger nibbled harmlessly by the not very fierce looking stocking puppet. Underneath was printed "Fu," and then - hosannah! - immediate phonic analysis of this very first word into its phonic elements - F and u. I was set to like this program from the start, and everything I saw only confirmed my view that it was very, very good! The facing page had the letters F and u - in whole and in parts, to show how the strokes are made in writing them - but they were shown in photographs of F made with pretty pebbles, F made with pretty seeds, and u and F made with seeds and shiny buttons. The partial letters were made out of clay. These activities shown in pictures with pebbles, buttons and clay were to be done in the classroom by the children, so that besides phonic analysis and spelling from the beginning, the students had "writing" from the beginning, and could learn to write with the greatest of pleasure. The "work" of childhood is play, and textbook publishers seldom remember it, but the Schroedel group must have known it when they chose to publish this book.

The next page added the letters r and t as the children played with Fu, and showed the children cutting t's and r's and f's out of newspapers and magazines, while sitting in stocking feet on the carpeted classroom floor. Page 3 had the first "story", "Uta ruft," all made with the letters given so far. On page 10, the little girl Uta was in the back of her father's car at a quaintly drawn city intersection, and this printed "story" was shown: "Uta ruft: '...rot! '" ("Uta cried, '...red'" - the traffic light). Every word had been built synthetically, and the following page had letters on dice for synthesis of more new words - presumably such dice being available in the classroom. The dice were also illustrated, for children's individual use, on the little punch-out cards in each child's envelope.

On this date, November 7, the children had been in school a little less than seven weeks, school having started on September 20, and the children had covered preparatory work before entering this reader. The preparatory work would presumably have covered auditory and visual discrimination as in most reading programs, phonic or global/ sight-word. Yet the children had not been confused by being given sight words as wholes, so that they might unwittingly read them from the end back to the beginning, and possibly have reversal problems ever afterwards. They had not been confused on what print was all about. To these children, print was very plainly something to turn into sound! These lucky little first-graders had been permanently vaccinated against the "sight-word basal reader disease." Wherever they went, even if they left this school at the end of first-grade, for the rest of their lives they would know what real reading is!

In addition to the text and the envelope of punch-out cards, each child had a reading workbook matching the text, with perforated pages to be removed when marked.

I was to learn later when I tested the second-grade children who had learned with this company's earlier synthetic/ analytic phonic reader, Bunte Welt (not so attractive, and without "Fu," but a straight Code 10 phonic rating) that these German children scored remarkably high. More than just the phonic emphasis might have been involved, though. In most of the American phonic first-grade programs I saw before October 15, before leaving for Europe, which will be discussed later, many letters had already been covered. In particular, the Economy program moved far too fast. The Alpha One American program, however, moves astonishingly slowly by American standards, and six weeks into the first-grade term has not covered more than four letters, just as this German program also had not done. The Alpha program also had children doing collage work with beans and buttons to build letters, and hosts of other art projects, just as did the Bunte Fibel program. Phonics programs might eventually be compared to see if those which move slowly at the beginning are more successful for the whole class at the end of first grade than those that move more quickly at the beginning. My suspicion is that the slower ones will be more successful, with fewer children falling behind.

According to the psychology of learning almost anything, initially the rate of increase in learning is very, very slow. After a very long practice and initiation period, however, the curve for rate of learning begins to rise very sharply. Therefore, professionals in any area can absorb large amounts of new data easily, but amateurs cannot do so. This German program and the American Alpha One program seem to make a better "match" to the learning curve of beginning readers.

I visited a second-grade class, and the teacher had a lovely manner, very low-key.

The teachers in this school have the option to operate half-classes, as I saw in Sweden. The first-half comes in the morning, the whole class in the middle of the school day, and the last half stays at the end. This second-grade teacher had elected to follow this pattern. She said that her afternoon class was slower than her morning group and came from a poorer part of town. At the time I came in, they were doing a formal arithmetic lesson with numbers, putting sets together. She said that the previous year she had taught this class with the Bunte Welt synthetic-analytic text, a different reader from Bunte Fibel, but published by the same company and which I also rated a Code 10. As in Sweden, this second-grade teacher would keep the class, which she had since first grade, until the end of the third grade.

One of her students was a new boy. She made to me another of the many negative remarks I would hear in German language schools about the global sight-word method. She said the boy had "learned" to read by the global method in first grade, so she had to teach him to read this year in second grade! Most German schools, she said, used the synthetic method, and not the global. This comment also was in conflict with what I have read, but, I suspect from my experience may be true at present.

I tested the afternoon half of her class, Hamburg 1, Code 10, as many of the children as I could get to of the fifteen present. Testing was done in the very large cloakroom next to the classroom. In this teacher's class, as in the others in this school, silence was not enforced and the children talked freely except during the formal lesson. This room, like the others in the school, was beautifully supplied with materials. On the shelves in the large cloakroom were some games, three being the electric battery type where a child plugs in a peg next to an answer, and it lights up if the answer is correct. A Scrabble-like game was visible. Lovely art work done by the children was hung up in the room, including a two-foot by three-foot crayon overwash, where crayon designs were painted over with black paint, and then the paint was removed in stencil-like shapes (a flower, in this case) so that the effect was of colored flowers on a black background. The room had many lovely plants in the windows. The desks in this informal style classroom were also arranged in cluster groups, as I had seen elsewhere.

The children here, as in the other German language schools, scored well and the results are shown for Hamburg 1 in the appendix. The child who was new to the class was not included in the scores. He scored 75% incomplete. One child scored 85%, incomplete and slow, and another 86% and incomplete and slow (below frustrational). The others scored 97% or better, above instructional, and at the level I call possible automatic decoding. Because of the two failing pupils, only 78% passed at the 90% level, but, because of the high scores of the remaining children, 78% also passed at the 95% instructional level. On comprehension, 44% of the children passed. Twenty-two per cent read slowly (the ones who failed) but 44% read quickly (another indication of possible automaticity). On reversals, only one child made any - again a child who read slowly and failed. Of course, these two failing children may have joined her first-grade late in the year, which might explain their sharply lower scores than the scores of their classmates.

It should be noted, however, that for 7 of the 9 children to score 97% or better, and for four of those seven to read fast, suggests that the two failing children were not representative of the part of the class which I could not test.

The half of her class I was testing, she had told me, was lower than the other half. If these two failing children had been computed with the whole class average (about 30), it might have reduced the failing class per cent to about 7% instead of 22%, but my statistical rationale is that by taking such chance samplings, unrepresentative low scores in one class should cancel out unrepresentative high scores in another class because of a large enough sampling.

At the end of my study, when I averaged all European <u>phonics pupils</u> (not classes) and compared the results to the average for all European <u>global pupils</u> (not classes), I got almost the same score as I did by averaging <u>phonics classes</u> and comparing them to the average for <u>global classes.</u> That proved my point, because the numbers of pupils in the classes being averaged varied greatly from class to class, so the averages from total phonic pupils and total global pupils might have produced very different scores from the averages for classes. Yet they did not produce very different results. That is because what was being compared with both methods were two simple constants: phonic or global, so that the size of the groups being compared which had used those constants mattered very little. These scores are given in the appendix.

I had misunderstood concerning my Hamburg school appointments and found that I had only the first appointment for the three days I was to be in Hamburg. All that was necessary for me to do at this late date, however, was to place a call to the office of the school official who had made my arrangements, and I was instantly fixed up with appointments for the next two days. I had received the same wonderful courtesy in Hamburg as I had elsewhere!

The next day, Tuesday, November 8, 1977, I visited a school near the harbor area, which had a large foreign enrollment. It also was beautiful and modern, but it seemed smaller than the first school. I was told school started at 8 a. m. and finished at 12:35 or 1:35 p. m., with some children starting at 8:45 a. m., the same staggered school day I saw in Sweden. I was directed from the nurse's office to the principal's office, which was beautifully carpeted and which had window curtains. As I remember it, the room had a round coffee table with flowers on it. It was here that I was told that school in Hamburg started on September 20.

The school was close to a beautiful old church near the harbor, and harbor buildings were opposite it. The school was, I understand, 20 years old. It was arranged in two stories, motel-like, and very pretty. It angled around central grounds which were planted with flowers and trees. Marigolds were still in bloom. When I arrived, children were at play in playgrounds with soft sand, school not yet having started. The children were very lively, but most did not look foreign, although I had been told there was a large foreign enrollment, but I did see one oriental child.

The principal and I talked briefly, and she brought me to a first-grade room, whose middle-aged teacher was very warm and friendly. She had been teaching sixth-grade last year, a class she had kept with her since first grade, and she was now starting with another first grade. She said she was attending teachers' courses once a week for two hours, I believe on the new reading book, Bunte Fibel, which had been published the year previously, 1976.

On each child's desk were delightful little name tags with pictures, perhaps two inches by two inches, and covered with plastic film. The teacher said she had the upper-graders make them for her little ones. In her room, as elsewhere, the desks were double desks, but they were also arranged in clusters. The desks were of a fine quality, with fine wood. I could see, displayed on the board, work concerning logic blocks, which I had seen used in the Hamburg school I visited the day before. The room was very attractive, partially paneled and with brick walls. Fall leaves were mounted and displayed. It was early, and half the class, sixteen children, were here for this reading lesson. The other half would have the same lesson tomorrow morning, learning "toll" which is apparently page 13 of the primer.

The teacher also seemed to have been doing pages 17 and 18 of the workbook, which apparently reviewed previous work. When I came in, they were practicing the "r" sound. Then she put on the board "r" plus "o" plus "ll." She had a child make the "r" sound. Then children clapped their hands, apparently as they blended the letters. Having studied the word, "toll," they were making the new word, "roll." She marked the vowels on the board in orange chalk. As she worked, I noticed that one of the little children appeared possibly to be foreign - perhaps Turkish.

Then she discussed with them what appeared to be workbook page 18. This page had reading comprehension questions on the bottom of one side of the paper, matching sentences made of words they had worked out phonically on earlier pages to pictures. Page 17 (the other side of page 18) was on matching letters of the alphabet (visual discrimination).

The teacher circulated among the children while they worked. During this lesson, her lovely, warm manner was very evident. She had the children stop at one point and sing a cheerful little song with her before going back to work. The song, in all probability, related to the study.

The room had a large flannelboard, with wooden strips across it to support letters, like that shown on page 15 of the text, Bunte Fibel. The teacher then used this to do analytic phonic work with the word, "ruft," removing the "t" and having the children say the remaining sound. They worked at this board a while, with the children building words from letters, and sentences from these words, holding them up for the class to see as they put them on the board, purely synthetic phonics work.

Although the class was in perfect order, talk was permitted here as elsewhere in Europe if it did not interfere with the lesson.

Leaving the first-grade classroom, I saw photocopy machines in use, as I saw in European schools elsewhere, as in Holland. They were not cheap copy machines but machines that produced Xerox-like copies.

The woman rector then brought me to a second-grade classroom in which one-half of the class had left, and I would read with the remaining half of the class. I did the testing in a small cloakroom in the rear of the class, and the woman rector stayed with me while I tested the first five or six children in the class. (The scores for the whole class are labeled Hamburg 2, in the appendix).

The woman rector said the children in this class had a program last year like the one I had just seen. That was almost certainly the earlier edition, <u>Bunte Welt,</u> of the first-grade text currently in use in this school, <u>Bunte Fibel.</u> I had been told in the Hamburg school I visited the day before, which was using the 1979 text, <u>Bunte Fibel</u> except in one first grade, that the second grades in the school had used the earlier edition, <u>Bunte Welt,</u> in first grade, and the second grade I tested at another Hamburg school the next day had used <u>Bunte Welt</u> in first grade.

Of the 14 children tested in this school, Hamburg 2, 93% read above the 95% level, and all above the 90% level, so 100% passed on oral reading accuracy. On comprehension, 50% of the children passed. None of the children read slowly, and 29% read fast! The Code 10 program used in this school at first grade, which was almost certainly <u>Bunte Welt,</u> had achieved marvelous results, particularly since this was a school in one of the poorer residential sections of Hamburg.

This was largely a business area, and delightful for a tourist walk, after class dismissed, despite the drizzling rain. Near the school and the harbor area was what appeared to be a financial district, like New York's Wall Street. My lunch was a German speciality, wiener schnitzel, in a pleasant businessman's restaurant, and nearby was a large gift store which was already, this early in November, stocked up with Christmas toys and decorations. It was a real pleasure to shop for Christmas tree ornaments where their manufacture has been a specialty for generations. For my college-age niece, I bought a foot-high red wooden soldier nutcracker, though I really do not know what she is going to do with it now that she has it! It is fun to look at, though, and perhaps she can use it for a Christmas table centerpiece in the years to come.

The next day, Wednesday, November 9, 1977, I visited the third Hamburg school. It was the largest elementary school I have ever seen. I understand the enrollment was between two and three thousand. The lobby was like the lobby of a huge hospital - with a guard and switchboard. The guard was very helpful and brought me to a woman who, I presume, was rector or vice-rector, and she gave me a great deal of her time, discussing reading and the project in which I was engaged.

The buildings were brick, and obviously older than the other two Hamburg schools I had visited. The classrooms were arranged on open courts, with the walkway outside each room roofed over. When I arrived, workmen were planting many new shrubs throughout the huge school grounds. The school had courtyards opening on all wings. The woman administrator, who was very helpful and kind, received me in a beautifully appointed upper floor office in another wing from the classroom which I later visited. Since it was a short day that day, there was not enough time to observe in first grade and to test in second.

I was told, however, that this school was also using the <u>Bunte Fibel</u> 1976 edition this year in first grade, and the second-grade class which I would test had used the previous edition, <u>Bunte Welt,</u> when they were in first grade. This class had learned with printed letters in first grade and not manuscript letters as in the copy of the <u>Bunte Welt</u> edition I received.

The second-grade classroom was very attractive. One side of the room had a wall of windows opening on greenery, but it had high windows on the wall facing the courtyard and the roofed over-walkway. I could see logic blocks arranged on the blackboard, which I understood were from a demonstration lesson that the student teacher in this class had done for her college supervisor. Double desks were here, as elsewhere in Hamburg, arranged in clusters. Much of the children's art work was displayed on the wall. As mentioned, the class had a student teacher present, and the regular classroom teacher smilingly told me that the girl was relieved because her college supervisor had just made her final visitation.

A recess period came up shortly after I arrived. Unfortunately, that left very little time for testing the class. Only the last half returned to the classroom after the recess period, and, furthermore, this was to be a short day. Hoping to test all in the last half of the class in the very little time that was left, I made a tactical error. On ten of the sixteen tested, I therefore only gave a portion of this test, but this made the Hamburg 3 sample not comparable to other classes, where the whole test was given to all children tested except to those who were obviously failing and who would be counted as failures, or to the last child being tested when time ran out and the class had to leave. When this had happened with other classes, I computed the last child's score based on the portion he had read, but that was very different from using ten incomplete scores for a class. As a result, I am reporting this class alone at the end of the European Phonics Programs Table, as Hamburg 3, but I am not including the results in the statistical averages.

Based on testing these 16 children for an average of two examples on ten children and 5 examples on 6 children, the class scored with 63% at the 95% level, and 94% at the 90% level. It was not possible to compute comprehension scores because most children read only two examples. On speed, 44% read slowly and none read fast. Reversals were 31%.

On the American testing in the fall, I had a sight-word (global) class, U. S. 3, to which I could only give the first part of the test, and this class also was not included in the averages, but just reported, so this phonics class, incomplete, can be considered to be balanced by a global/sight-word class, incomplete.

However, I made a subjective conclusion about the scores, although they were respectable enough on accuracy. What I found to be very unsatisfactory were the scores on relative reading speeds and on reversals. The fact that 44% of the class read slowly but that none had read fast, and that 31% made reversals, was in sharp contrast to the kinds of scores made by the two other Hamburg classes tested which had apparently used the same first-grade text, <u>Bunte Welt</u>.

The children in this second-grade class, Hamburg 3, had obviously been taught how to decode correctly in first grade, since they scored satisfactorily on accuracy (although far lower than the other two Hamburg classes and far lower than the class I tested later in German in Innsbruck) but something was definitely lacking. Either the class had not had enough reading practice, which could account for the slow reading speeds and possibly even for the reversals, or the class had an unusual number of students with learning problems, which might account for the extremely high number of reversals, 31%.

Yet, even when testing a class in German in Luxembourg, which class had not had such a strong phonics program as <u>Bunte,</u> and which had many foreign students with grave language problems in first grade, the scores were better on speed and reversals. In Luxembourg, 33 % had read slowly, not 44% as in Hamburg 3, and only 8% made reversals, not 31% as in Hamburg 3. My subjective conclusion, therefore, was that Hamburg 3 had not received enough reading practice on the phonic skills that they had obviously been taught.

On November 9, 1977, I mailed home from Hamburg all my completed tests up to that point, and the first-grade reading books that I had purchased in Belgium, and all the other printed materials that I had picked up on my trip. The collected materials had begun to weigh far too much. Mailing part of the material home lightened my luggage considerably. The Hamburg postal clerk joked about how long I would have to wait to get the mailed package back to me at my home. It was now November, so I jokingly asked, "By Easter?" He answered, "Yes!" Trans-Atlantic mail is certainly not very reliable. Sometimes, letters I wrote to Europe on my project never got there.

I had a long wait in the massive Hamburg railway station for my later evening sleeper to Munich, where I would change the next day for a train to Innsbruck. I brought my luggage to the platform and sat on a bench reading for several hours, watching the trains come and go. I was fascinated by the fact that freight trains were frequently sent through this passenger terminal, and I saw here the first of the endless freight cars carrying Spanish oranges that I would see all through my trip. I had always liked to watch freight trains go by at home in America and to read the names on the cars. Nickel Plate, Santa Fe, Erie Lackawanna, New York Central and so on. It was rather fun here to read very different labels!

After hours of waiting, a train came in ten minutes before my departure time with sleeping cars, and the signs on the cars read variously, "Innsbruck," and "Munich." I staggered on with the luggage I still had left after having just shipped some of it home, but I still had to make two trips of it. Then the steward smilingly told me that I had the wrong train, just as the doors were closed and the platforms were raised. I frantically ran to the car's vestibule, carrying as much of my luggage as I could but leaving a suitcase behind, and a helpful someone opened the vestibule platform and door so that I could get off the train, after which a very helpful German woman handed my last suitcase, that I had left behind me, out the window of the car to me. Just then, another sleeping car train pulled in on the opposite track, with signs in the windows also reading "Innsbruck" and "Munich," and I got on that. It was a great relief. Without all the help that I had been given by total strangers, I would have had to sit up on my luggage all night, while my empty berth sped on its way to Munich in a train behind me.

Innsbruck

My hotel in Innsbruck, Austria, was in the center of town, and very, very old, having been an inn for hundreds of years. The charm of Innsbruck is deservedly world famous, and it was a tremendous pleasure later to stroll through its lovely, almost medieval streets. As soon as I reached my hotel on Thursday, November 10, 1977, I immediately telephoned the official who had written to me concerning possible school visits. I do not, however, speak German, so the young man at the hotel desk placed the call for me. Imagine my astonishment at the fact that the official to whom he spoke went to the trouble to send to the university for a young woman student who could act as translator, so that I could meet with him later in the day!

It was more of the unbelievable courtesy I had met with all through my European trip.

The Innsbruck office building in which we met had a modern convenience, however, which scared me out of my wits, since I am not at all physically adventurous. Beautiful, large marble stairs led to the upper stories, but there was as well a sort of elevator-door opening in the wall, but not for ordinary elevators. Instead, it was a kind of dumb-waiter arrangement, where successive platforms slowly reached ground level and then proceeded to upper levels. I saw people stepping on the platforms, and hopefully stepping off as easily at the upper stories. I am going to have to take it on faith that they did so, because I headed straight for the huge marble stairs and found the official's office upstairs.

Through the young woman interpreter who was there when I arrived, I explained my project. This kind man seemed honestly interested. He pulled a book out of his bottom desk drawer. Even though it was in German, it was evident from the title before the girl translated it that it dealt with the subject of dyslexia. The official asked me through the interpreter what, in my personal opinion, should be the percentages of true dyslexics - those not hampered in learning to read by poor instructional methods but who are innately crippled in the abilities it takes to learn to read. I told him that my instinctive guess would be something in the nature of one to two per cent. He smiled but made no comment. I do not know if I am correct, but my feeling is that he agreed with me! He cited what some authorities claim is the incidence of dyslexia - all the way to twenty per cent, but I said I felt sure this was the result of poor teaching methods.

Something that occurs all through teaching courses concerning learning theory is a graph called the bell curve. Any measurable human trait in a population, if graphed for the population, will show a curve of distribution which is bell shaped. For instance, take shoe sizes for women. Some very few have very tiny feet, more have small feet, most have average feet, fewer have large feet, and very few have very large feet. If this incidence is graphed, it forms a bell shaped curve, with the highest part of the curve being for the majority, those with average feet.

This curve occurs for any measurable trait in a population, from I.Q.s to other qualities. The vast majority will approach the average measurement, and there will be a tapering off to a few individuals at either end, having extraordinarily little of what is being measured, or an extraordinary lot of it.

Statisticians tell us that when a population shows a skewed or non-bell-shaped curve, it indicates that some force was usually acting to produce that result. For instance, a school-age population which was drilled on a particular skill (perhaps times tables) will show a piling up of scores towards the extreme end of high accuracy.

The distribution of such human faculties as vision and hearing should follow the bell curve, so that disabilities in these faculties, like color blindness or deafness would be at the extreme end and constitute a small percentage of the total, normally endowed population. The European schools I had tested before Innsbruck had demonstrated that the vast majority of children could learn to read well. This was to be expected, as it might have been anticipated that a failing such as innate dyslexia - a grave difficulty in the ability to translate print to speech - should occur in the same small percentages as other human defects like color blindness or tone deafness. In schools where dyslexia does not constitute such a small percentage, I believe it indicates another force is acting to produce that skewed curve, and that force in usually incompetent teaching methods.

This was the only time in my life I had ever talked through an interpreter, but I must say I enjoyed the conversation with this charming man! He made an appointment for me for the next day at a school in the suburbs, and I then left his office in company with the pretty young college graduate student. We talked for a while as we walked through the business district. She told me she was working in languages and was very interested in linguistics. She mentioned the American linguist, Leonard Bloomfield, (who is known in America also for the Bloomfield linguistic program to teach beginning reading). She said that Bloomfield had been credited with some linguistic theories which actually were European. I found this interesting, but did not have the background to carry on what probably would have been a very interesting conversation. As has been said, in order to ask an intelligent question about anything, you already have to know nine-tenths of the answer. Unfortunately, the study of the structure of languages is not my field. She had to get back to her college, so I thanked her for all her help, and we parted.

I went on to a lovely afternoon window shopping in the fine shops stocked with garnet jewelry and other lovely things, and bought a long, faceted, garnet necklace as a gift for my sisters. As in Hamburg, I stopped for wiener schnitzel and white wine, but in a 20th century version of a Tyrolean inn, hushed with carpets, and amber lamps, polished peasant-like furniture, and lovely table linens. The restaurant had an elaborate salad bar like those at home in America, but here the waitress served the customers, instead of the customers serving themselves. It is a far more sanitary practice!

On Friday morning, November 11, 1977, I took a taxi out to the school I was scheduled to visit, as I was afraid of being lost taking the busses. The school was in an attractive residential area, with some private homes and some large apartment buildings, spaced very far from one another on extensive grounds. The area was surrounded by the wonderful Austrian mountains.

The school building was in the shape of a capital E with the long bottom wing, the older one, three stories high, and the long wing like the top of the E, the newer one, two stories high. The upright stick of the capital E connecting those two wings was a hall, and off the center of that hall was the third, middle, short wing, like the center line of a capital E. That shorter, center wing was a small dining room.

The hall connecting all three wings of the E was a glass-walled corridor with stainless steel, and it was divided into three sections. The corridor floors were covered with square marble tiles, and two women were mopping the central marble floor as I arrived. Either they or someone else suggested that I wait for the man whose name I had been given. They indicated a waiting room up the stairs at the end of the third section of this long corridor, which waiting room was perhaps 40 feet by 25 feet. It was furnished with attractive redwood chairs and tables. Behind me was a display case in beautifully polished wood. Stairs led to the second story of the new wing from this waiting room, and the railings were solid milk glass from top to bottom, framed in polished walnut. The doors connecting the three sections of this corridor were of heavy stainless steel and glass. Besides the stairs from this waiting room going up to the next floor was a corridor leading into the first floor of the new wing, off which were perhaps seven doors leading to other rooms. In this corridor hall were two or three planters, perhaps two feet by two feet, with rubber plants and others.

The door of a classroom in the new wing opened as I sat in the waiting room in the main corridor next to the new wing. I saw a room beautifully carpeted in brown with yellow and brown print curtains closed at the windows because of the sun. The children streaming out seemed to be about second graders. As they bustled out of the classroom, they were holding hands in pairs and some talked busily. The teacher did not try to enforce silence here, any more than I had seen elsewhere in Europe. In the classroom behind the children, I could see the same double desks I saw in Germany, but arranged facing front.

In a room in the distance, I could hear some children chanting a lesson in unison. Later, I saw some children in what seemed to be a second grade reading from a reader in unison. This amused me later, when I tested a second grade here and got some of the highest scores in Europe. There is so much nonsense in teaching theories. So much of it is just repeated prejudice. It is supposed to be "true" according to most of what I have read in our teachers' journals and books that for classes to practice something in chorus is not desirable. If it is so undesirable, then why did these children in this Innsbruck school later score so well?

I looked through the glass doors to the central part of the long corridor, near the little cafeteria-like room. Two tables were outside it, in that part of the corridor, and chairs upholstered in bright fabric. Very tall floor-to-ceiling partly curtained windows faced those magnificent mountains. The window sills were covered with tropical plants. The grounds around the school were beautifully landscaped. This was a very, very beautiful, expensively constructed school! Today, in America, our elementary schools are largely one-story structures of cinder block which is painted on the inside and faced on the outside with brick - the cheapest form of construction. Yet the old school buildings, in which I went to school years ago, were solidly built, and strong as Gibralter. One such old eight-classroom school, whose third story is an auditorium, stands opposite my home - built in 1906. It has a potential hundred years or so still in it, and two beautiful fifty-foot oaks in front of it on its wide lawn. In Austria, apparently, they are still building schools like that.

I decided that there might have been a misunderstanding about my appointment, and that I should actively look for the person whose name was on the paper I had been given. I walked through the halls, and I saw a teacher in what might have been a second grade, in a charming sunny room, and the children facing front in the formal manner. She was demonstrating sets in a lesson to the class. My memory is that it may have been intersecting sets, but it may have been simple addition of sets. She had the sets written on the chalk board in different colors of chalk. I passed rooms where musical instruments were being played, and I passed a gymnasium. I was eventually directed to the second-grade teacher who was waiting for me.

School would dismiss at 11 a. m. that morning, and I was more than a little nervous about having time to test the children. After a pleasant conversation, when I explained the purpose of my work, she let me use the rather large cloakroom in the rear of the room to test her class. She had taught the class in first grade, and showed me the book which they had used, <u>Kommt, Wir Wollen Lesen und Schreiben,</u> published by Verlag Leitner & Co., Wels, Vienna, and written by Hans Eiter, Adolf Luchner, and Hermann Gritsch.

It was a delight of a book, from a child's standpoint, I should think. I also found it delightful, as it was pure synthetic phonics, from my point of view, and a straight Code 10. It went from a few pages obviously meant to practice visual and auditory discrimination and language development into a study of the vowels in the order of i, o, and a. Then the consonant m was introduced, and all letters had delightful illustrations which lent themselves to class discussion. Following this was a brightly illustrated story, with tiny print indicating it was to be read by the teacher, and then a page of large printed m's, i's and a's in various blended positions. The next page, 25, had almost the identical lesson I had seen in Luxembourg, "Mimi im...." followed by different pictures. Mimi, in this case, was a cat. The next page blended m with a for "Mama." Two pages later were blended words, "Mama, Oma, Mia, Mimi", - all characters who were illustrated next to their names. On page 32, the next letter was introduced, followed with more blending practice with the letters introduced so far (i, o, a, m, and r) to produce the names Irma and Maria. The next page, page 34, introduced another vowel, u. Page 36 introduced s. Page 38 introduced t and the blend au. By page 42, the children were able to have a "reading for meaning" story which should have satisfied the sight-word people, except that EVERY WORD IN IT HAD BEEN ARRIVED AT BY PHONIC BLENDING OF KNOWN LETTERS!

The "story" read, "Ist Tasso im Auto? Ist Rosi im Auto? Rita saust ums Auto. Artur saust mit. Maria ist mit Otto am Tor. Maria, Otto, tut mit!" and so on. Where the word "haus" was used, because "h" had not been introduced, the book had a drawing of a house followed by the known sounds, "aus."

On the early pages of the book, a child had to show in pencil the syllables in words, as An-a-nas and Tas-sen, except that instead of dashes, a half-circle was drawn under each syllable. I later saw this half-circle marking under each syllable in French schools.

The Austrian beginning book continued in this fashion, adding new letters and building more and more complicated stories from the sounds already introduced, but with nary a sight word in the lot! In addition, the book was wonderfully pleasing to the eye, and should interest any child. This was the teaching of reading the way it is meant to be! It was a straight Code 10 text, with synthetic phonics.

Curtains were at the window of the pleasant rubber-tiled cloakroom in which I tested, and it had attractive benches. The children came in, one at a time, to take the oral test While the testing was going on, I was delighted to hear what passed for "bells" in this school. They were not bells at all, but a sort of very pleasant chime. While I was testing, I realized that a recess period must have occurred after one of the chimes, because I could hear the children in the classroom outside the cloakroom immediately began to talk very freely. After the recess period ended, the children in the classroom went back to work, and I could hear at one point the whole class singing, very charmingly and very loud.

The teacher told me that, while she had no foreign children in her class, Turks and Yugoslavs were in other classes. She said that the children were drawn from this area which was either middle income or poor. She estimated their intelligence as probably average. She told me, during our conversation, that she had recently made a tour of the United States!

The area around the school was interesting in its spaciousness. It is true that there were many apartment buildings, but they were spread out widely, so there was no sense of crowding.

What was most noticeable about these children was the speed with which they read, which is one of S. J. Samuels' tests for automatic decoding. I tested 28 pupils, and 14 of them read at a fast rate, or 50% of the group. Only one of the pupils, or 4%, read slowly. This was the best speed rate for second graders anywhere. Remarkably, 93% of the pupils read at the instructional level (95%) and NONE at the frustrational level (below 90%).

Concerning the significance of the speed rate, Perfetti and Lesgold have demonstrated a connection between decoding speed and comprehension. However, I believe that phonically-trained children, whose attention is free, also need specific drill exercises in "paying attention" to what they are reading or they may let their free attention wander, when they are reading materials in which they have no interest, and so fail to demonstrate the comprehension abilities which they possess.

Perfetti and Lesgold also state that general evidence exists that practice produces an increase in speed for simple verbal learning tasks. They suggest verbal coding practice, or as an alternative, practice in everyday text reading, or reading games. Perfetti and Lesgold suggest three levels in verbal coding ability (as in oral reading): inaccurate performance, slow, accurate performance, and automated performance, as mentioned by Samuels. They state it is the middle level that may most benefit from practice. A student who performs inaccurately needs to be taught, not drilled. Their suggestion of three levels of skill facility is interesting, when applied to this Innsbruck class. It could be said that the half of this class which read like the wind had reached the "automated performance" level. Yet this implied that they had passed through the middle level where they benefitted from practice. The class in this Austrian school which was reading a text in chorus was certainly performing such a drill. Despite the tendency of some to discount the chorus approach, it certainly does give the drill which Perfetti and Lesgold postulate is necessary to achieve the "automated" level.

However, the degree of practice is something which my research project made no attempt to determine. It would appear probable that, given the same methods, a class which had more appropriate practice would reach the automated performance level earlier than classes which had less practice. The concepts of levels of skill facility, when applied to the three classes that I tested in Hamburg which had the same reading program, suggest that the first two Hamburg classes, which read so much faster than the third class, must have had more reading practice than the third class

That night, the Innsbruck opera house had Gluck's <u>Ipheginia im Aulis,</u> I heard this lovely work in the red-velvet furnished, beautifully decorated modern opera house, after walking the short distance from my hotel, through the charming, almost medieval streets. It was a delightful end to a delightful Innsbruck visit.

Paris

On Saturday morning, November 12, 1977, I took the train from Innsbruck, Austria, to Strasbourg, France, and was startled at the change in the weather. I had been having Indian Summer all through Europe, scarcely needing a light coat. This morning, frost was on the farmlands as we climbed higher in the mountains. I was to learn it was not just the altitude. Summer had left Europe.

I had to change trains at Basle, Switzerland, before going to Strasbourg. I went through

French customs at Basle, and, dragging all my luggage behind me, took the train for Strasbourg, where I arrived in the pouring rain.

At dinner that evening in a hotel near the railway terminal, I really felt that I had arrived in France. The lovely dining room had a fireplace with a roaring fire, much attention was paid by both guests and personnel to wine lists, the linens were a faint pink with matching napkins, and all the appointments of the table were lovely, including long-stemmed water goblets and silver knickknacks. I did not take notes, but remember lovely tapestries and dark wood paneling in the beautiful dining room.

The next day, Sunday, November, 13, 1977, I took the fast train from Strasbourg to Paris and was ready Monday morning, November 14, for school visits. Shortly after 9 a. m., I called the man whose name had been on the letter sent to me in answer to my request for appointments. I inquired about my school visits. After listening to me briefly, he slammed the receiver down with a snort instead of replying to my inquiry. I then went to the central administration office that morning and learned that no record could be found of any appointments arranged for me. Paris was the only place in Europe where no record of my correspondence seemed to exist.

After my visit to the administration office, and an interview with an official there, an impromptu visit was arranged for me the next day, on Tuesday. However, no mention had been made in the letter which I had received from Paris that Parisian schools were closed on Wednesday. Since I was scheduled to leave for Quimper Wednesday night, that left only one day, Tuesday, for a visit to a Parisian school, instead of the three days for visits that I had hoped would be available.

On Tuesday morning, I arrived at the Parisian school at which I had the impromptu appointment. It was located in Paris proper, and not in the suburbs. In the lobbies were plants and cages of singing canaries. The woman concierge brought me through the first wing, the nursery school area, back through a large courtyard which was a children's playground, to the office of the woman director, which was in an older wing. Across another courtyard on the other side of this was a newer wing. Long, veranda-like porches were on the side of her building, facing the newer one.

I had been delayed in arriving because, along with two French women, I had found an injured, large hound near the Madeleine. He already had a cast on his leg, so obviously he had an owner, and also he had a tattoo. As an animal lover, I was enchanted by the importance that this slightly injured but lost and frightened dog had to all around on this busy street a block away from central Paris. A taxi driver discussed taking the dog to a pound, and there were other suggestions. I was wearing a belt on my dress, so we made a leash of it and walked the dog to the nearest police station. There, also, the dog had great importance. The police said they could locate the owner through the tattoo the dog had.

In the meantime, the dog went behind the counter, where the plain-clothes men petted and fussed with him. The dog then escaped out a door but was caught in time on the stairs. Eventually, the police managed to pen the dog behind the counter by closing all doors, and the work of the Paris Police Department continued while the dog strolled around their office. The two French women, obviously late for work, and I then left. I explained the reason for my delay to the woman director of the school, and she gave me a radiant smile! Apparently, in Paris, helping a lost dog is an excuse par excellence!

The corridors of the building were painted royal blue on the lower four feet and oyster white on the top, a nice effect. The director took me to the first of two first grades. After I had observed in one, I could go to the one connecting by a door in the wall.

I understood the school year in France started the middle of September. Classes in France generally dismissed at 4:30 p. m. on Monday, Tuesday, Thursday and Friday, and, since there was a half-day session on Saturday morning, in Avignon, I presume there was a half-day session on

Saturday elsewhere in France.

This teacher was using a method adapted from the teacher next door, who had made experience chart materials to teach heavy synthetic phonics. I was to find that creativity in teaching beginning reading was the apparent norm in every school I visited in France, rather than the exception, and the teachers that I saw did not use published primers. I do have notes on a published French primer which used analytic/synthetic phonics on a small sight-word base, which I coded 7 on the scale, but I never actually saw the book in use, although I tested one class, Avignon 3, which had used it the previous year. This book, Remi et Colette, is described elsewhere, along with the descriptions of Belgian primers I purchased in Brussels in a textbook store, all of which were phonic materials, at least Code 9.

It is interesting that one of those primers, De La Syllabe a La Phrase Pensee, published by Wesmael-Charlier, Namur, began with the word, "Mimi," also used in beginning phonics in the Luxembourg and Innsbruck primers! In the Belgian book, too, Mimi was a cat, but she was a Belgian cat this time, and not an Austrian one. Latin vowel pronunciations, as in "do, re, mi, fa, sol, la, ti, do" are apparently in use across languages on the Continent, but not in English.

Posted on the wall of the first Paris grade one that I visited were phonics charts: li-la-lu-lo-lau-l'eau-le (this one with a circumflex accent), le (this one with a grave accent), lait, and le (this one with an acute accent). Also posted were little paper houses with vowels that made the same sound "living" in them, as "au, eau, haut, aux, eaux" for the sound that is long "o" in English, and "y and ie" in another, and "est, ait,e (circumflex), e (grave) in another. I was suddenly stricken with a great sense of relief that it was not I who was faced with the appalling task of teaching all the various French vowel spellings to little six-year-olds. It became exceedingly clear to me that the teaching of beginning reading in France, because of the incredible French orthography, is a nightmarish task!

Each child in the first Parisian school room I visited had a little dittoed "Livret de Lecture No. 1" which had apparently been written by the teacher herself, using the children's names and experiences. On the first page, with an "a" shown in the corner, was a little one-sentence story to demonstrate its use, "Sonia has a spider." ("Sonia a une araignee.") Then the word "Sonia" was repeated with the "a" circled and "a" was repeated four more times. On page 2 was a little drawing of a spider which had been colored and labeled "une araignee" and a little drawing of Sonia which was labeled and which had been colored, and, I believe, "a" was repeated four times. Page 3 concentrated in the same fashion on "e" with the sentence, "Alice has made a mistake." ("Alice a fait une betise.") Page 4 concerned i with the words Sonia, Alice and betise with the i's circled. Then came the word, "Review", with the letters a, e, and i repeated, and then a little story: "Sophia and Bruno have brought some fossils."("Sophia et Bruno ont apporte des fossiles.") Then, "Bruno has some fossils. Sophia has some fossils. Alice and Sonia brought some fossils." ("Bruno a des fossiles. Sophia a des fossiles. Alice et Sonia ont apporte des fossiles.")

On this page were pictures of Bruno and Sophia drawn and labeled. The next page concerned "o" with words from the experience story on the previous page used to demonstrate the "o"

This was heavy phonics, of the analytic type, and rated at least a Code 8, since the only apparent purpose of these stories was to introduce the sound and form of the vowels a, e, i, and no apparent emphasis was being placed on "learning" as sight words the words being used to demonstrate the vowel sounds. This work, of course, had been done earlier in the year, before my visit which took place on November 15, and the school had been in session about two months.

Glancing through the little notebook from the page where "o" had been introduced, I could see that the notebook continued in the same fashion to the present, introducing new letters with short little stories using the new letters.

I did not count the children, but there appeared to be about 25 in the class. This room and the room next door were very happy places. The children communicated freely with the teachers and with each other. The teachers wore smocks to avoid getting the board chalk on their clothing. That is something I should try at home, since I frequently lean against the blackboard and have the lesson imprinted in reverse on my clothing, but such a careless thing is not for Parisian women!

When I walked into the room next door, the children were singing about boats and swaying back and forth from side to side. The class was arranged in rows from one side to the other, not front to back, and each row was identified by a picture next to it of an animal, which apparently the children in each row had selected themselves as the name for their row. The song that was underway was using sounds for which the teacher was asking.

In the front of the room was a large, fanciful paper castle, whose towers were made of green paper that had been rolled and trimmed on the top with orange paper fringes. On the wall, instead of houses for the variant vowel spellings,
this teacher had displayed a train, with an engine pulling cars, each car having one vowel sound and the many ways to spell it. In the front of the room was a very large handmade book, perhaps two and one-half feet by one and one-half feet. The children's pictures were mounted in the book, and experience chart materials were on each opposing page. The very first sentence in the book, I believe, concerned the sound for "e," for a boy's name, Emmanuel. An experience chart was visible and the letters of the vowels being studied were shown in ink. The absolutely synthetic phonics nature of the program in the room at present, despite the experience chart approach which in America is geared to sight words, was shown by the work on the board. The class were studying the blending of the consonant "p" with vowels. The date was written: Mardi 15 Novembre. Then were written these words, with each "p" shown in colored chalk:

"Grand papa, poupee, apporte, un pot, un peu, la peau,
la paix, la pipe, papi, papa, poupee, une epee, un pas".

After this was:
"Ecriture" (writing): pu
papa
peu"

The directions in which a child should move his pencil in the forming of "p" in both printed form and cursive form were shown on the board, by arrows. Then:

"Dictee" (dictation): pi
pe
papi
poupee".

The fact that synthetic blending was being done (or at least that a portion of the syllable table was being shown) appeared probable from a tabulation on the blackboard, in which arrows went from each of two "p"'s to a series of vowels opposite each "p". The tabulation is reproduced on the following page.

The experience chart method was in use in this class, but, obviously, it was used to teach heavy phonics. This was the first time in my life I had ever heard of the experience chart method being used to teach heavy phonics! Yet, perhaps, because of the nightmarish problem faced by French teachers in teaching variant vowel spellings, and because of the seas of silent consonants in French spellings, the experience chart method may be a very satisfactory solution to those appalling problems. In any event, I coded this Parisian program Code 8, for its heavy phonic emphasis.

After lunch, I returned to test a second grade. These children would have had a new teacher in second grade, as the primary grade teachers in France do not move with their classes as in Sweden, Germany and Austria. Therefore, most of these children should have spent first grade last year in this school where the first-grade program rated a Code 8.

Unfortunately, Parisian schools were closed the next day and I had to leave that night for my Quimper appointment. It was impossible for me to test the next day. The second grade that I tested represented no more than two-thirds of the enrolled second graders in the school, at least one-third being next door in a vertically grouped first and second-grade room, and I could not test them the next day.

The directrice of the school had told me that the second-grade class I tested was not the top class. The superior students were in the vertically grouped first-and-second grade group, and I was therefore testing the bottom portion of the second-grade. I doubted that I understood her correctly, so she wrote on my test paper, to confirm that the class I did not test was a mixed-grade class, "c. Elementaire 1 e annee + c. elementaire 2e annee."

The first-grade classes that I saw appeared to have under 25 students each, but the total first-grade enrollment in the school included part of the vertically grouped first and second grade room as well as these two rooms. The second- grade room that I tested had 28 students present, and I understood some students were absent. Therefore, the second-grade enrollment was part of the vertically-grouped second-grade plus these 28 students, and those from that bottom class who, I had been told, were absent. These numbers suggest that more than one-third of the second- graders had to be in the vertically grouped superior class, if the second-grade enrollment were close to the first-grade enrollment.

My scores for the bottom half of a second-grade class alone could not be averaged in with the rest of the European scores, but I did not want to discard them. Therefore I counted the bottom students as 2/3 of the second grade (though they could not have been that large a group) and the top students that I did not test as 1/3 of the second grade (though they must have constituted a larger portion.) Since 79% of the bottom two-thirds of the class had passed at the instructional level of 95% oral reading accuracy, I had to assume (which is almost self-evident, anyway) that the top one-third of the class which I did not have time to test would also have passed at the 95% oral reading accuracy level. Most probably, they would have scored much higher than that level and closer to or at 100% accuracy, since they had been acknowledged to be the top students by the directrice of the school.

Therefore, I adjusted the scores for the Paris school to include estimated scores for the top group. Since 79% of the bottom two-thirds had passed at the instructional level of 95% oral reading accuracy, it was only reasonable to assume that 100% of the top third which I did not have time to test would have passed at that level. That resulted in an estimated score of 86% of the second grades in this Paris school passing at the 95% oral reading accuracy instructional level. That adjusted score for the Paris phonically-taught second grades of 86% was almost identical to the scores for similar phonics programs I tested later elsewhere in France, which were 86%, 90% and 85% at the instructional level of 95% accuracy. This tends to confirm the accuracy of my estimated score for the Paris school, although it is almost certainly on the low side.

At the oral reading accuracy level of 90%, which is above the frustrational level, the bottom two-thirds scored at 89% passing, When this score was adjusted to include the top portion of the class, 100% of which would have passed at the 90% oral reading accuracy level, it resulted in an adjusted score of 95% pass. This also is probably too low, but it compares reasonably to other French schools with phonics programs who later scored with 95%, 97% and 93% passing above the frustrational level.

I had free time in Paris on Wednesday, November 16, 1977, since the schools were closed, and visited department stores with their pret-a-porter (ready to wear) designer clothes. The blouson dresses that showed up in New York a year later in numbers were everywhere to be seen in

Pascal-like Synthetic Phonics Table
Blending a Consonant with French Vowels
Or Less Probably
A Shorthand Rendering of the "P" Portion of a French Syllable Table
Seen on a Blackboard in a Parisian Public School
On November 15, 1977

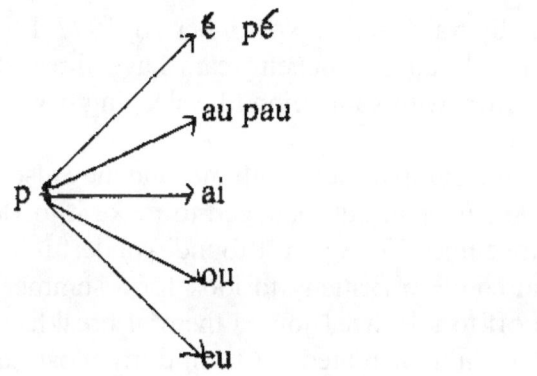 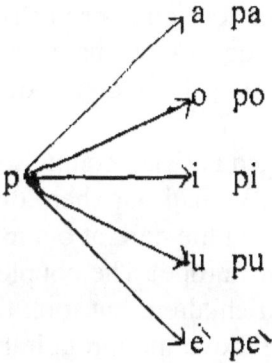

France that year, and I bought one for my niece, who was then at college, for Christmas. It was wonderfully made in sheer wool and looked as if it would last easily into the 21st century, long, long after it has gone out of style! But styles still originate in Paris. I had been there the previous summer (1976) in the middle of the worst heat wave and drought in years, quite unprecedented. Temperatures had been in the 90's Fahrenheit for weeks on end. At my otherwise wonderful hotel (but not air-conditioned) I could have taken an oath in court that my bed pillow was steam heated! All the Parisian women needed cool clothes, and they suddenly appeared - a rash of American-pioneer-women-like gingham prints in tiny geometric figures, usually in reds and whites or blues and whites, with airy, full skirts, round necks and short sleeves. Sure enough, a year later, this "new" summer look in dresses showed up in New York, the same tiny-print American-pioneer-type dresses, but the Paris heat wave that had started the style was long forgotten!

Quimper

Leaving Paris for Quimper in Brittany by train late on November 16, 1977, I took a couchette - something we do not yet have on our railroads. Couchette cars have three shelves in each compartment, arranged one on top of the other, with something like sleeping bags and a camping-out atmosphere.

A middle-aged Parisian couple shared the compartment with me, and they also had never seen anything like it. We had our share of laughs over it, but managed to make it to Brittany without incident, arriving in the dark at 6 a m., November 17. Again, I found wonderful helpfulness from total strangers in Europe! The couple had come to Brittany to look for a summer place to share with their grown children, but took time off to see that I joined them at breakfast in the railway station, and then drove me through the dark in their rented car to find my most unfindable hotel, tucked away in the hills somewhere. It is very hard to find words to thank people like that. I only hope I can return the favor to them or to someone belonging to them some time!

Brittany was an old home of the Celts, and when I checked into what turned out to be a charming modern hotel, I thought of the Celts, as I saw the woods around it filled with oak and holly and ivy.

My appointment at the normal school resulted in arrangements to visit another normal school on the other side of the city. A young student was asked to drive me, so I did not even have to bother with a taxi. I was received most cordially by the normal school director, and we discussed reading methods. He told me I could observe and test in the school which was attached to the normal school. These classes used the program, <u>Pas a pas sur les chemins d'un "savoir -lire"</u> by Rose Foucaud and Bernard Aumont, a linguistic program. I later obtained a copy of this text, and some of its practices and points of view are summarized briefly in the following paragraphs.

As will be seen from the following summary and from the notes taken in a first grade using the program, the program has six-year-old children focusing conscious attention on the syntax and meaning of a language which they already know how to speak. From my point of view, I do not think this kind of "linguistic" approach results in learning (except for language-disabled children). I therefore believe this "linguistic" approach is erroneous and results in an enormous waste of time. In the beginning first-grade program, the work on phonics is meant to be limited to pulling apart and putting together whole words that have been learned in sentences only by their meaning, with no reference at all to their letters. The letters of the alphabet are not even taught to beginners.

Yet, curiously, in actual practice in the classroom in which I observed, and despite the philosophy of the program which I consider to be very faulty, the children were learning isolated letter sounds and were learning how to blend them, even though actual letter names were not used and even though the letters were always shown to them only in whole words. The children managed to learn analytic phonics, and to learn it well, despite what was, in my opinion, an enormous and boring waste of time with taking words out of sentences and substituting other words for those words, and similar "linguistic" activities. What was most meaningful is that, even though the children were given sight-word experience stories as a class activity, they were not given lists of sight words to file, to study, or to use in stories, as in other sight-word programs, so the sight-word effect was greatly lessened.

The philosophy of the program, as outlined in the text I purchased, I have attempted to summarize further below. The great number of points which are similar to American sight word programs will be evident to the reader, particularly the requirement that children read texts silently before reading them orally

The program considers that reading has two levels: the first articulation, which is the organization of a statement by analysis into words, and the second articulation, which is the organization of words by analysis into their letters and sounds. The emphasis at both levels is on the word, "analysis."

At the nursery school level, not only are stories told to the children as in any program but the children are led informally to vary the stories by substituting different nouns or verbs or adjectives, in the course of which the program states that children must unconsciously analyze the structure of statements. This work is done informally without any reference to parts of speech.

At the beginning reading level, word substitution is more formal. Given the sentences, "The gardener picks some flowers," and "I cut an apple," written on the blackboard, the child is asked to put parts together to make a new sentence, such as "The gardener picked an apple," or "I cut some flowers." The program states that, if a child is able to copy the words, he should be encouraged to copy them. If not, the work is only oral. This program states that the child is not expected to memorize these as sight words at this point, because the work is always written on the board for him to see. Obviously, this lessens the sight-word load.

At the beginning of first grade, according to the textbook guide to this program, seven lessons are written on the blackboard, the "seven statements," practicing such work as mentioned already and leading from analysis of sentence structure (the first articulation) to analysis of word structure (the second articulation). The words from these "statements" are to be used as sight-word reference points in the future to work out new words as they are supposed to contain all the phonemes necessary for decoding work. For instance, a child can write "flou" if he knows the vowel "ou" from "coup" and the consonant blend "fl" from "fleur." Obviously, this was a variation of the nineteenth century German "normal words" method.

Such analysis of sounds in words is only briefly covered on page 73 of the text, at the end of the lesson, "The seventh statement." But, as I saw it actually practiced in a first grade room on Thursday afternoon, November 17, 1977, and Friday morning, November 18, 1977, it was analysis of known sight words into their phonemes, and synthesis of these phonemes into new words. The teacher was not using these "seven statements," so far as I could see, but was using experience chart stories for the work she was doing on phonics. The alphabet, so far as I could see, had not yet been identified by name.

The teacher was dictating to children syllables containing the vowel "oi." She wrote on the blackboard: "moi, poire, and feu," and then she said, "Write foi," and the children were to join the phoneme "f" from "feu" to the phoneme "oi" from moi" and "poire."

She wrote "ramasse" on the board and then said, "Write roi," again joining the "r" sound from the known word to the vowel sound, "oi." She continued in this fashion:

    deux - write doi
    cheminee - write choi

    joue - write joi
    frere - write froi
    vu - write voi
    porcherie - write poi
    trouver - write troi
    tue - write toi

Then she said to the children, "Hands in your desk. Look at the board." She had listed, as the result of this blending work, the following:

    boi
    doi
    foi
    joi
    loi
    moi
    poi
    roi
    soi
    toi
    voi
    troi
    froi
    choi

    As can be seen from this listing, these syllables are in alphabetical order, not in the order in which she dictated them, and cover 11 of 21 consonants in the alphabet and three consonant blends. It is meaningful that both "c" and "g" are missing, as those two more difficult consonants can have the "hard" sound (cat, got) or "soft" sound (cent, gem) in French, as in English. These more difficult letters are usually covered later in most heavily phonic programs. Most of the other missing consonants,(h, k, n, q, w, x, y, z) are less common or pose problems (n in French can be part of a nasalized vowel sound). This sequence of introduction of consonants and blending with vowel sounds is the normal progression in any heavily phonic program, and this program was following that normal phonic progression, despite the fact the letters were never sounded in isolation in this program.

    The children then individually took turns reading the syllables that had been written on the board, but as they read each syllable they had to give another word which began with the first sound of the syllable on the board, as "with maman - moi, with tue - toi," and so on. This was obviously auditory discrimination drill.

    The teacher showed me papers the children had done on this work and said, at this point of time, about half the children had it right on the papers. She said it was very difficult. Yet it would not have been so difficult in a heavily phonic program where children learn the letters of the alphabet and the sounds of isolated letters, not just the sound of letters in whole words. The reason that it was so difficult became apparent the following morning. The children were being drilled far more heavily in recognizing sight words than in recognizing the phonemes in those sight words.

    This lesson on "oi" blends had been on Thursday afternoon. I visited the class again Friday morning, and the teacher had a little experience chart story on the board. She asked the children to read the first part silently. It was self evident that they could not have done so if they had not already been taught how to read most of the words, either in that experience story or in other contexts. The story read:

"Stephane jou avec son velo. Le matin Stephane boit son chocolat ou son cafe au lait. Il va dans le jardin ou il voit son petit velo rouge."

("Stephane plays with his bike. This morning Stephane drinks his chocolate or his coffee with milk. He goes in the garden where he sees his little red bike.")

Six hands were raised to read this section. Of course, that suggested that others in the class (about ten others) could not read it. One boy read it. The teacher then kept pointing to the words, as the class all read them. The teacher began analysis of words into their phonetic elements. She pointed to "matin", showed "maman" on the side and covered the "man" ending. Then she showed jardin, covering all but the "in." Then "tue" covering all but the "t". Then she put the "t" from "tue" with the "in" from "jardin" to get "tin". Then she put the "tin" with the "ma" from "maman" to get "matin." This apparently was a new word with its parts being analyzed, and this procedure was very like that of the Macmillan readers at the second-grade level in America, but this was analysis of the whole word, not just parts of the new word, and it was being done at beginning first-grade level, which certainly would not have been the case in any American sight-word basal reader series. This was still a sight-word, global approach to phonics, but it certainly was complete, and particularly this early in first grade. It almost deserved to be called a "syllable' method, except that it was treating some phonemes, in effect, separately, and not as parts of whole syllables.

The story continued:

"Il n'ira pas sur la route car les voitures roulent trop vite" ("He will not go on the street because the cars go too fast.")

The teacher then began to ask questions about the content of the story. When did the boy drink, and what did he drink? The children pointed to the words in answer. The story continued,

"Dans le jardin les allees seront ses routes. It mont sur son velo et il pedale vite. Tu, Tu, Tu, une pomme roule dans l'allee."

("In the garden, the paths will be his roads. He climbs on his bike and he pedals fast. Tu, Tu, Tu, an apple rolls in the path.")

She analyzed "route" as she had "matin," putting on the board, "ramasse, loup" and I believe a "t" word, but without underlining phonic elements as shown here. The teacher worked this way with other words. Then she had the children read this last new sentence, one child at a time. She continued to question about the story, such as, "What color is his bike?" Then came more of the story:

"Tire toi de ma route, joli petit pomme, dit Stephane.

("Get out of my road, pretty little apple, says Stephane.")

"Stephane file mais il a mal aux jambes. Il rentre et sa maman lui fait des crepes au sucre, au chocolat et a la poire.

("Stephane went on but he hurt his legs. He returned and his mother made him crepes with sugar, with chocolate and with pear.")

As a child read a sentence, the teacher asked questions about its structure. If a child could not remember a word, she reminded him of a similar one with part of its structure.

Yesterday afternoon, she had done similar work, besides the phonic blending already reported, but with shorter sentences. The sentences were written on the board in painstaking script. The following sentence was on the board, among others:

"Vincent a mange des crepes au sucre et a la poire.

("Vincent has eaten some crepes with sugar and with pear.")

The teacher called a boy up to the board, where there was a wooden stick with a three inch by four inch flat board at its end. He covered the word, "Vincent," and said "maman" in its place in the sentence. The child then wrote maman on the board. The teacher said it was necessary to hide the word when he changed the sentence. The children discussed which other words to hide. A child changed one of the words then to butter (beurre). She then had them open their notebooks. The children talked quietly while they were working, rewriting the sentence with another word. She said the day before they had almost the same sentence, but it was:

"Papa mange des crepes.

("Papa eats some crepes.")

The children copied that day's sentence into their notebooks with great care. Then they wrote something to change the sentence.

Before Thursday's work on the sentence just given, the teacher had carried on a drill on sentences on the board which were apparently for review. There were ten sentences, but it is possible that some were among the "seven statements" with which this program started, since this appeared to be old work. The teacher had the children read the sentences, and then pointed to words in isolation, asking what they were. The sentences in this drill were:

"Nous avons fait un feu dans le jardin."

("We have made a fire in the garden.")

She asked, "Where is the fire?"

"Les enfants ont plante des oignons."

("The children have planted some onions.")

"Hier j 'ai joue au loup dans la porcheries."

("Yesterday I played wolf in the pig sty.")

"Stephane a tue deux canards."

("Stephane has killed two ducks.")

The last was a surprisingly insensitive and unfortunate sentence, as was the one about trying to frighten caged pigs by playing at being a wolf. In the experience chart story on Friday, Stephane had been a little boy, so these sentences, in effect, represented such cruel little-boy behavior as acceptable to a class of impressionable little children. Both of these sentences may have only been variants on two of the given seven sentences in the program, the "seven statements." If that is so, then those "seven statements" may very well have been unacceptable in content for impressionable beginners.

"Karine a vu un gros bateau."

("Karine has seen a big boat.")

"Mon grand frere distribute les lettres."

("My big brother distributes letters.")

"Anna a ramasse des chataignes."

("Anna has gathered some chestnuts.")

The teacher had a little Black girl pointing to the words as she asked them, and the child could do it with ease. I learned later that this little girl had come from French-speaking Martinique just the previous summer. Despite the difference in dialects between colonial French and Continental French, she was doing very well indeed. Yet her sister, a year older in the second grade, and very possibly just as able, I found was having real trouble because she had not been taught to read well in Martinique.

The sentences continued:

"Olivier a construit une cabine."

("Olivier has built a cabin.")

"Dimanche Houbert a visite une citadelle."

("Sunday, Houbert has visited a citadel.")

"Pres de chez moi, j 'ai trouve des belles feuilles."

("Near my house, I have found some pretty leaves.")

On the sentence, "Vincent has eaten crepes with sugar and pear," the teacher had the children erase words one at a time, deciding how it altered the meaning of the sentence. The children removed the words one by one and then put them back from memory.

It was evident that this program had much in common with straight sight-word programs. I had been told it was neither global nor phonic but something different. This, of course, is true if taken as a whole, but it has global elements, phonic elements, and language experience elements.

On page 75 of the teacher's guide, the end of reading is defined as comprehension. On the surface, this statement is self-evident and necessary, but it is also the very battle-cry for all the sight word programs and the reason they give in varying degrees for their failure to teach phonics adequately. The text for this program also cautions against having children read orally first, urging silent reading. Also, just as in the pre-Flesch American sight-word programs, there is apparently no training in the learning of letter names as such, or letters in isolation. The children also begin by reading sight words, and even writing them, if possible, from the very beginning of reading instruction. They were drilled, as I saw, from the board in remembering sight words. All of these qualify as sight word teaching. Yet, despite all of this, in actual practice the program was teaching very, very heavy analytic phonics

Therefore, the overall effect of the program was something very different from a sight-word/global program, as I saw it in actual practice in the class, as great stress was laid on the what they called the "second articulation," or decoding, at a very early point in first grade. Analytic/synthetic decoding was practiced repeatedly in heavy drill with new words in the experience stories. According to the text, the children had already been given at the beginning of the year in the "seven statements" all the phonemes in written French that were needed to decode printed words.

Although it was to some degree the kind of phonics decoding handled at levels above first grade in global/sightword programs, where the work was always done only with whole words, it differed in that it focused on all phonemes in whole words, and did so very early in first grade. Furthermore, sight-word programs in America only practice phonics in lessons apart from the actual reading selections, and there is frequently no carry-over to reading selections. Yet here it was the reading material itself that was used for the phonic drill so phonic carry-over for future reading selections was almost certain.

Also, and most importantly, on the lesson blending the vowel "oi" with consonants, it was possible on the date of November 17, after only two months in first grade, for half the class to be able to read back to the teacher "oi" syllables beginning with eleven consonants and two consonant blends (tr, fr) and a consonant digraph (ch) arranged, and the syllables were arranged, significantly, in alphabetical order. That means that half the class had reasonably mastered 11 of 21 consonants and how to blend them with vowels at a point when straight phonic programs (such as the American Alpha One and the German programs I saw) had covered far fewer consonants sound with blending. This indicates a program that in practice, despite the enormous word changing activities, had a very, very heavy phonic load.

Calling on children in the room to reread a story which had already been read, where the meaning of a word could therefore easily be obtained through context, is not the same as I saw in heavier global programs in Amsterdam and Stockholm, and later in a school in Avignon, where first-grade children copied or had copies of straight sight words and dealt with them at their desks, filing them and memorizing them in isolation. These Quimper children were not being drilled individually on sight words, despite identifying them for the teacher at the board in a story by the story's context. The effect of the program, therefore, despite the large number of sight words, was not too different from the analytic/ synthetic programs in Germany on phonics because the Quimper children were actually being drilled heavily on phonics and blending, even though letters were not named. They were not being held individually responsible to learn sight words, but only to respond in class, orally.

Therefore, despite the global content and because of the heavy phonic content, I identified this program overall as Code 7.

After the reading lesson, the teacher held a demonstration lesson on sets in arithmetic, dealing with addition and subtraction of numbers to 6, and using real lemons and apples to make her points. Eleven normal school students and their instructor were in the back of the room to witness this very competently run lesson. The teacher was very pleasant and nice, and the children responded well to her. However, it is to be hoped that the enormous time-wasting activities of this Pas a pas... reading program, which drills endlessly on language structure with children who are already speaking their own language automatically, was not being exported to the rest of France by student teachers witnessing the complicated, time-wasting exercises.

This teacher had a reading corner with books and a table with a tablecloth. It was a very old school, but cheerful, with royal blue curtains and pale blue walls. The floors were well polished old hardwood, with three inch planks. The classroom had modern lighting and many plants. In the back of the room, children's drawings were mounted on a collage perhaps four feet long, and it was very nice. Children talked quietly in this classroom, except when the teacher asked them not to.

On Thursday afternoon, I tested a second grade in an older portion of the school, across the central courtyard. I was seated in a delightful, 19th century hallway, outside the second grade classroom. I made a sketch of the hall while I waited for children to come out. Some Van Gogh reproductions decorated the walls. The director of the elementary school stayed with me part of the time I was testing, and I enjoyed talking with him.

This mixed linguistic program was neither purely sight-word nor purely phonic. Yet, because of its heavy phonic emphasis as I saw it in actual use, I placed it at 7 on the scale. The children in second grade, who had this program in first grade, scored very well on this test. They were one of four European classes who showed no reversals, a probable result, I should think, of their decoding method. All those who had been in the school last year passed my test at the instructional level of 95% oral reading accuracy, which was equaled by only one other European program, a phonic one.

However, of the 13 programs which I labeled Code 7 or higher in Europe. this Quimper Code 7 program was one of the three which had no children reading at a speed I could rate "fast". My belief is that more direct instruction in letter names and sounds, rather than teaching the sounds only within words, and less concentration on context, would be beneficial, despite the remarkable score of 16 of 16 pupils reading at 95% accuracy or above. (The little second-grade girl from the French-speaking colony, the seventeenth pupil, was not included, as she did not learn to read in Europe.)

In Quimper, so close to the ocean, the weather was constantly changing from lowering skies to pouring rain to brilliant sun, and sometimes the sun was out while it was raining. It was very cool, and unfortunately I had worn only a light raincoat, expecting Quimper to be mild, but I was disappointed. The flowers were still in bloom in the yards surrounded by five-foot walls that I passed, coming down the steep hill from the school, but winter had come. I stopped at a little restaurant in the business section for some of the crepes I had heard the children reading about, and found they are indeed something very special in Quimper. Sitting across from me was an older woman who studied me with level, intelligent eyes, and who was wearing a very proper hat as she managed her crepes. Apparently there are a lot of the old Celts' genes still around in Quimper, because she reminded me of my very special and dear Aunt Julia, and looked just as competent. I always felt that, if my very ladylike aunt had been born a man, she would have been the kind who could have run a battleship without any effort, and there would have been no back talk from the crew, either!

I took a cab back to my hotel, and was momentarily startled. The smiling young driver was a close approximation of my cousin, Ed Branagan, some thirty years ago. No wonder Brittany is famed as a Celtic stronghold yet!

Avignon

Saturday morning, November 19, I left Quimper for Avignon, a very, very long two-days' train trip. Most of the time, I traveled in an empty compartment, but at one point two very young men, both good looking, got on. Something was different about them, but I could not place it. Shortly after this, an affable middle-aged woman came into the compartment. She solved the mystery. She said, instantly, "Oh, you are cadets!" (from the French army academy). What seemed so indefinably strange was that they had army regulation-style 1950's haircuts!

They were amusing, charming young men. I had been reading a French translation of an Isaac Asimov science fiction novel (I forget the title) and one of the young men seemed to be interested in it. I finished it on the train and asked him if he would like it, since I could not carry it with me because I already had too much luggage. Shortly after this, an elderly man got on. The conversation got very spirited and good humored and so fast I could not follow it. It was evident from the laughter and the little that I could follow that they were insulting one another's native cities with near abandon, though the young men were obviously more restrained in their comments because of the other man's age. The older man was telling one of the young ones that the young man's town was famous for very little. But, since the young man got off at Bordeaux, that was hard to believe! One last, funny little comment was made for my benefit. One of the young men said, "I'm getting off at BorDUCKS." I said, "Now, that's not very nice! You're making fun of American accents! His answer was, "Well, that's what they all SAY!"

I stayed overnight in Toulouse and went on to Avignon the next day. However, the train which had left Quimper at 10:42 a. m. did not arrive in Toulouse until 9:05 p. m. Saturday night, so I had to check into my hotel very late. Since my train to Avignon left just before noon the next day, I saw very little of Toulouse. I finally arrived in Avignon after 4 p. m. on Sunday afternoon, November 20, 1977.

I learned what the Mistral meant during my week in Avignon. That chill winter wind coming up the river valley from the distant Mediterranean seldom stopped blowing while I was there, and, with the trees stripped of their leaves, Avignon was not quite the pretty tourist city of the summer, although it has charm, naturally, at any time of the year. I went to see the restored pope's castle on the hill, which was medieval and fascinating, but I think I know one of the reasons the popes went back to Rome. They must have almost frozen to death in those endless stone halls during the winter!

My first visit in Avignon on Monday, November 21, 1977, was to a first-grade class in a suburb. The teacher had 26 children in her class, and the desks were arranged in clusters. It had been raining, and the teacher had previously had her class put six little buckets and dishes out in the court yard to catch and measure the rain, but it stopped raining after I came. In a nearby classroom, I could hear the children practicing French Christmas songs, which was not surprising on November 21, only a little more than a month before Christmas.

Shortly after I came, during a recess period, the teacher explained her reading method to me. During the first month of first grade, which started about the middle of September, she gave children experience stories about the room's turtles and birds, which she ran off on dittoes so that they could keep copies in their notebooks. After about a month, she began the study of phonics, perhaps identifying all the a's that could be heard in one story. Later she identified other letters. She said she was using a synthetic method, and I saw phonics charts on the walls summarizing the work covered to date.

Nevertheless, the actual activities that I saw for children on this day, November 21, more than two months after the beginning of first grade, were sight-word or global in nature. The teacher had handed out dittoes with pictures on which the children had to indicate a story sequence, and dittoes with sentences on them in which the children had to read the sentences and check "yes" or "no." These were "reading comprehension" questions on what were apparently sight-words.

What made me give her and the program in this school Code 6, lower on the phonics scale than others and more towards the global/sight-word end, despite her very real phonics, was the fact that she had these beginning readers keep whole words from their experience stories, cut out, in little envelopes in their desks. It did not seem possible that the children could have studied all the phonemes in those sight words this early in the term, so they must have been true sight words, to be read by their remembered "meaning" and not by their letter "sound." Handling whole sight words that are written on cards is, of course, normal in American sight-word programs. However, except in one Amsterdam school, in one Hamburg first-grade with a Code 3 sight-word program, and in one Stockholm school, I had seen it no where else in Europe.

Later, I tested a second grade in this school on another floor. The director of this school also joined me for part of the testing session. He was naturally interested in the children's performance, and I found his conversation very interesting. In this school, as elsewhere, some of the children did not understand that they were to pick a correct answer for each of the questions on my test sheet which they were reading orally. It was not just that with my poor French I was not explaining adequately. Even when the Director of the school, explained the task to the children, the same children had trouble. Yet other children automatically knew what they were to do, without explanation.

There was a reason why, in America, I found very little of this problem. Our American reading exercises are organized more in the fashion of my little oral reading test. In the omnipresent and expensive "silent reading workbooks," which are drearily issued to each unfortunate American student from grade 1 through grade 6, a student must pick a correct word to end a sentence from a list of perhaps three words, or do some other kind of "reading comprehension" activity" on each page of the thick manuals (and normally, two such manuals are issued in each school year). Therefore, American children, even by second grade, have had a great deal of practice with this kind of task and with other "reading comprehension" tasks. Yet children in these other countries apparently had never seen this kind of exercise. While the bright children figured out instantly what to do, the slower children did not. This "readiness" factor has to be considered when reading the scores on the comprehension portion of the test for the European schools.

The second grade children in this school, Avignon 1, Code 6, scored with 76% at the instructional level and 84% above the frustrational level. On comprehension, 56% passed. On speed, 24% read slowly and 12% read quickly. One child of the 25 in the class made reversals, which was 4% of the group.

On Tuesday, November 22, 1977, I visited a second Avignon school. The second Avignon school that I visited was also in the suburbs. In consisted of two buildings, with two separate court yards, surrounded by walls. In the newer building was a first-grade class in which a demonstration lesson was under way when I arrived. A woman from the university was there with perhaps eight graduate teachers observing this lesson. I was to meet this charming woman at the next school, and was more than a little disappointed when she was not also at the last school I visited!

On the board in this suburb of Avignon was the world-famous song, "Sur le Pont d'Avignon," serving as the "experience chart". The children were singing the delightful song as their teacher kept time with a drum. Then the children clapped their hands to it, and then stamped their feet. After this spirited beginning, the phonetic work began. The sound being studied today was "on", a nasalized vowel sound in French. The children would later write in their carefully kept notebooks the word, "ronde," from the "Sur le Pont" song, as their sample word with the "on" sound. In the meantime, the teacher had written on the board in script:

> "on
> mon
> son
> ton
> lon
> ron,"

As she pointed to each, she asked the children to say in what word of the song they heard that sound. Then the children went to the board and pointed at the words which they said had those sounds, and they then read the words. Since the children could recite the entire song from memory, their memory of the sung words obviously aided them in finding the particular printed word with the "on" sound.

The syllables in the words on the board were marked with curved lines under them. Dots were also under letters in the word, (or underlining sometimes under two or three letters), to indicate the separate phonemes in the word. The final "e," as in dan-se, was not silent as in northern France (and as it usually is in the English language). Therefore final "e" was also marked for pronunciation since it is pronounced in Avignon.

The children then took out their slates. Here, as in Quimper and Luxembourg, each child had his own slate. The teacher brought the first group of children to the board, where she had written:

> l
> s
> m
> r
> t

The children identified those letters by sound, so they obviously had been taught to them previously by sound. Then, underneath, where the teacher had written the following sounds with "on", the children read orally:

> "lon
> mon
> ron
> son
> ton"

Of course, these are the same syllables that had been written previously, but now they were in alphabetical order. In all probability, her rearranging the syllables was a safeguard against children's reading them only by memory from the previous list.

The teacher now asked this small group for all the words in the song on the board that had "on," and they gave each word.

The professor from the college, who was so very nice, explained to me that the teacher was working with groups of different ability when she had them come up front to blend the sounds. The children who were at their desks in the meantime were working on their notebooks. In their notebooks were pictures of animals that they had drawn previously. I was startled by the fine quality of some of this work. Their exercise now was apparently to decide which animals' names had the sound of "on."

In the second-grade class later, the teacher scolded a child for a careless notebook page. Yet, I have seen much worse. Apparently, untidy written work is very uncommon in European schools, and not only in Europe. When my travel-agent sister visited an elementary school in Uganda in 1967, before all the terrible upheaval there from wars and Aids, she spoke to a highly intelligent teacher in a dirt-floored one-room school, who was apparently teaching his fourth-grade class the geography of the United States (or possibly the major rivers of the world). He very hesitatingly asked my sister if he had been correct in his assumption that the Missouri River fed into the Mississippi. His map of the United States was so poor that it was unreadable in places, so he had been left to decide by himself whether the Missouri River flowed east, and not west, and whether or not it ended up in the Mississippi.

Of course he was correct in his assumption that the Missouri fed into the Mississippi, and those little Ugandan fourth-graders were learning the geography of a foreign country, the United

States, or possibly the major rivers of the world, under this competent teacher. Yet our American "experts" think that plain, unadorned United States geography (or anything so esoteric as the major rivers of the world) is too demanding for fourth graders, unless it turns up in bits and pieces in that John Dewey-inspired catch-all and confusing subject, Social Studies! However, concerning beautiful written work by children in primary school, my sister also saw the first-grade work in this highly competent man teacher's dirt-floored Ugandan school. She came home to tell me with disapproval that Ugandan first-grade written papers were so much more carefully done than the third-grade American papers she saw me marking for hours at home every night.

So Uganda joined Luxembourg and Avignon in producing little first graders with beautifully done written work. I think the reason that American children's written work is usually far less neat is that American children have to do so very much more written work than children in these other countries. Not only do European children appear to do less written work, but often they practice on their slates first, so, when they move to the written paper, they think of it as something special and very important. American primary schools devote far, far too much of the day to written exercises. The time would be far better spent, from a teaching standpoint, in other activities.

My mother, who had been an elementary school teacher from 1906 until 1918 in country schools, suburban schools and city schools, used to find fault with the endless hours I spent at night, marking third-grade papers. She told me I was just wasting my time, and that all the children would do would be to look at the mark before they threw the paper away. She felt the children would learn more if less time were spent in writing and more time on meaningful lessons. I now share her viewpoint completely.

Concerning learning by reading as opposed to writing, it is pertinent to cite Leslie, of the Gregg shorthand method. As a young man, he had a shorthand dictation credit for 80 words a minute, far lower than normal speaking speed. He knew shorthand forms, however, perfectly, and was given a job proofreading shorthand publications for the Gregg shorthand publishing company. His only writing was on necessary corrections of the proofs. At the end of a year of reading proofs and not writing shorthand, he took a dictation test at 80 words a minute to check his speed. To his astonishment, the test was far too easy. He tested at higher speeds and found to his amazement that he could pass the test at the 200 words per minute level, which is the very demanding level required for courtroom reporting.

Leslie's experience resulted in a new teaching method in shorthand. After graduating from high school in June, 1942, I enrolled in the Washington Secretarial School in Newark, New Jersey, for a year's course in typing and shorthand, and the school used the Leslie shorthand method. In the first six weeks of the year's course, the class wrote nothing in shorthand, but only read shorthand. It was only later that writing to dictation began, when it became evident that the unusual beginning had worked very well.

While it is evident that children have to practice writing to perfect writing (and with a script like Chinese, it is necessary to practice the intricate forms of the characters), we should realize that writing does not perfect reading or other study skills and should not be overwhelmingly used for those purposes, as is done now in most American schools, where children are actually writing something down on paper for some assignment or other for a good part of the school day.

However, at the very beginning level, it is very useful to give dictation of letters to avoid reversals, so the Spalding beginning reading method has this to recommend it, since it emphasizes writing of phonemes to dictation. Of course, writing to dictation is certainly not a "silent reading activity" like most written assignments in elementary schools. However, Spalding reportedly does slow down the acquisition of phonics skills by spending too much time on such dictation.

I looked at the notebook of a child in this first-grade class in Avignon, while the child was at the board with the teacher. The notebook was labeled "Course Preparatoire - Notre Journal de Classe 1977 - 1978." The child had written words in script on one of the first pages, with syllable curves underneath and the dots I had seen on the blackboard in this classroom. I was told that the curves indicated separate syllables and the dots under letters separate sounds. The children had to indicate these in their notebooks, and the teacher graded their work. A few words on this page were:

> "pomme de Reinette (apple of Reinette)
> pomme d'api (lady-apple)
> petit tapis gris (little gray carpet)"

Also shown were separate letters, and the sentence:

> "Nos mots avec le son (i),"
> ("Our words with the (i) sound.")

Shortly after this page was an experience chart story with about 20 words and a picture. Another page had, "Our sentences with the sound (y)." Some pages had review of sounds. Blending was evident in the exercises.

The book proceeded in this fashion: first, for instance, a page on "Words with the Sound "M", and then a page with "Sentences for the Sound "M". The child drew pictures on each page. On the sentences, they drew pictures showing story sequence in three boxes on the page, and it was marked.

Today, the class was obviously also working on the "L" sound, because written on the blackboard were lower case l's, written as "l ll l," followed by:

> "la co_e,
> _ete,
> _ami ,
> la sa_ade,
> la ma_e,
> _eau,
> pau_"

These were given to the class for insertion of the single or double l's so as to form words. Possibly this was review from yesterday.

The children also had a notebook besides the one just described, with certain words written in it for each day, and, since today's special sound was "on," the word was "ronde" from the song, Sur Le Pont d'Avignon, which was doubling as an experience story.

The woman from the university said she felt this approach was better since the children were not always getting "methods, methods, methods," and the teachers with her seemed to agree. She approved of it because it used speaking, hearing seeing, and writing.

Whole words had been used in the experience stories in this first-grade class, but, since they were used only to teach phonics, this was a phonic program. I coded this program, Avignon 2, at Code 8. I wrote in my notes at the time:

> "No one in his right mind can minimize the difficulty of teaching children to read in French after he knows the spelling of the language and has seen the problems it causes in the beginning classrooms."

With the great problems posed by spellings in French, the use of experience stories to teach phonics as was done in this program is a way out of the dilemma, so long as the children are not obliged to memorize the words used in those stories as "wholes," but only to focus on the phonemes under study in those words.

Something else makes such PHONIC use of experience charts, as I saw it practiced in France, eminently practical for learning to read French. The French children in this class already knew the correct pronunciation for all the words in the song, Sur le Pont d'Avignon, and they also had obviously already been taught a considerable number of consonant and vowel sounds. The children had been taught the sound of the letter "t", and the letter "t" appears at the end of the word "pont" (bridge). Yet the children read that word correctly, omitting the "t" sound," even though it was right in front of their eyes at the end of the word. That is because they already knew that the word, "pont" (bridge) did not end with the sound of a "t" so they were learning, in the most practical way, that there are such things as silent letters. Their knowledge of their own language was automatically teaching them that sometimes printed letters are silent. Exposure to French spellings in such experience charts must also help to fix in their minds exactly where these peculiarly silent French letters appear in printed words.

Very early exposure to correct spellings seems to be important, even in the English language. When the ITA phonetic, expanded alphabet was used in the nineteenth and twentieth centuries in England and America, children who learned to read from ITA print reportedly sometimes had trouble later with spelling words correctly. The incorrect spellings appeared to have become fixed in their minds.

When the teacher of the Avignon 2 first-grade class was done working with the groups, she joined the visitors in the conversation. The children talked freely when she was done with the lesson. Some read, and some walked around, but the class was well controlled.

I was told later that the school week is 24 hours long, presumably elsewhere in France as well, and not just in Avignon. The children in this room had double desks as I had seen in Austria and Germany. The windows had green curtains, pulled now because of the sun. In the back of the room was a puppet stage, and four hula hoops were in the front. Many library books were evident. Painting materials were on the back table for the children's use, and a long table against the wall with enough room for four children to paint at once. On a shelf were paint pots. Also in the back of the room was an ink pad and roller, presumably for printing. The classroom had a tile floor, but in the hall the floors were terra cotta. Outside was the courtyard where the children could play.

I then went to the second-grade room to test, and passed through a door in the courtyard wall into the other courtyard and the older school. It was a very pleasant sunny afternoon on this date of November 22. A lovely tree was in the center of the courtyard outside the second-grade classroom in the very old building. The classroom had a Franklin stove in the back, with a fence around it.

The second-grade teacher said she worked jointly with the first-grade teacher, and she very much liked the "synthetic method" they were using. She said the common thing in French first grades was a book she showed me, called "Mixte Method" in its description. (It may have been Remi et Colette which I saw later.) She said it had sight words on the first page, and by the sixth page or so a list of perhaps 20 sight words. The vowel sounds were introduced from the first page, but she said it was a syllable method, not a phonetic method. She said, if I understood her correctly, that the children several years later sometimes did not know those sight words from the first book. She joined the ranks, therefore, of most of the European teachers who gave me their opinion of sight words. Wherever an opinion was volunteered to me, except in one case, the teachers were all opposed to sight words! The exception was the young man teacher in Hamburg.

When I tested the class of 23 pupils, which were labeled Avignon 2, Code 8, 86% passed at the instructional level and 96% passed above the frustrational level. On comprehension, 30% passed, and in speed, 30% read slowly and none read fast. There were 4% reversals (one child).

Schools in Avignon as in Paris were closed on Wednesdays. Therefore, it was Thursday, November 24, when I visited the third Avignon school. It was very far on the outskirts, in a lovely suburban town. It was, I believe, a newer school than the others, and very large. I was told that the class in this school which I termed Avignon 3 used a linguistic and structural method at the beginning, but used content immediately to teach the sounds of letters and the blends. To date, Thursday, November 24, they had covered all single vowels plus "e" with the acute and grave accent, and "ou". They had also covered ten consonants.

The teacher and pupils used gestures and voice stress to emphasize letters. There was no evidence of memorization of sight words, even though whole words were sometimes used which had phonic elements that had not been taught. I was later told that this "linguistic and structural method" was not considered a "phonic" method, which shows how badly such labels can translate. By American standards, the phonic element in this program was exceedingly heavy, and I would rate it at least Code 7, despite the use of some sight words.

When I came in the Avignon 3 first-grade room, the same college professor was visiting with a group of experienced teachers, who were obviously doing some graduate work. The children were seated in double desks in rows facing front. Each desk had a grill in the front so that it was possible to see inside it. That is a good safeguard against some of the Collier-brothers-type desks that can develop in classrooms if a teacher cannot see what is being stuffed into them each day. It is astonishing how much junk little children can stuff into schoolroom desks, often including such items as half-eaten sandwiches all set to mold. Of course, that is also where many of a teacher's carefully graded papers end up, wadded in balls stuffed in the back, unless the teacher hands the papers to the children at the door as the children are on their way home. Quite a few of these even get lost on the street. I know, because I live across from an elementary school, and the dropped papers are sometimes a kind of bulletin on the current work being handled over there.

This was a class of about 24 children. Plants were in the room, and windows on the far wall, which wall began not very far above the floor and then went up close to the ceiling, resulting in a fine view outside. Yet the windows facing the corridor were far above eye level. Through the windows facing the courtyard could be seen trees. A stove was in the back of this room, also, surrounded by a fence. The teacher was wearing a smock as in the Parisian school and was working from a hinged blackboard with panels like pages, which meant she did not have to erase. The children were working with little notebooks as in the other school, but these books had fewer pages in them.

The letter being studied for today was "v" and each child had a copy of the notebook page.

When I came into the room, one of the blackboard "pages" was open to these five sentences.

"La moto roule vite.
Le velo ne va pas vite.
Le pneu est creve.
Il est a plat.
Le velo de Marie n'a pas de petites roues".

("The motor cycle rolls quickly.
The bike does not go quickly.
The tire is punctured.
It is a flat.
Marie's bike does not have little wheels.")

A child was reading at the board for the teacher. Then the teacher went over the first sentence with the child, indicating each syllable and grossly accenting the sounds as the other children spread their hands out. The child in front was saying what seemed to be syllables, with great exaggeration of the consonant sounds, with gestures. The teacher pounded the board when the periods were reached. She held her nose on the "n" sound.

Above this board, the teacher had mounted pictures for each consonant letter introduced to date, before the introduction of today's "v," and printed a sample word using each letter in script and in print:

> "l - le lit (bed)
> n - le nid (nest)
> t - des pattes (feet)
> r - le rat (rat)
> c - le coq (cock)
> m - le mot (word)
> p - un loup (wolf)
> d - le domino (domino)
> s - la tasse (cup)"

Also, on the side wall, were sentences with the vowel sounds covered to date. Today, the children were studying the new letter, "v", in two syllables, "ve" in velo and "vi" in vite. The teacher went over the sentences that were on the blackboard, and told the children to write on their papers, "le velo."

As the children said, "le velo," after writing, they clapped the syllables. The teacher had the children hold their hands up to snap fingers, and they put their hands behind their shoulder on "le," on one side for "ve" and the other side for "lo." She then wrote the syllables on the board. Then she gave the word, "vite," and had the children write it, say it, and clap it, with more exaggerated waving back and forth as they clapped.

The teacher told the children to write the syllables for "vite" and, if they had trouble, she went from desk to desk and had the children clap it. The children talked quietly as they worked. As the child said, "te" from "vite," the teacher drew her hand out from her mouth.

The children wrote in the circle provided on the duplicated workbook page the syllable which was the new syllable - "ve." After they finished this, the teacher had the children put their papers in their desks, and had them read again from the board what had been on their papers. She had a boy erase the "e" from the syllable "ve" on the blackboard, and the boy said, "I erase the "e" and leave "v." Then the class repeated it. The teacher added "v" to the chart on the wall of letters that had been covered, bringing the total to:

> l, n, p, t, r, c, m, d, s, v.

Going back to the board, she had a child erase the "i" from the other new syllable, "vi", saying, "I erase the 'i' and leave 'v'".

Then the teacher went to the side chart and demonstrated how the children should write "v" in their books. In the front of the room was a chart with the children's names. She now had the class look for v's on this list. She traced over "v" in Veronique. Then she had the children shout, "V, V, we are saying Veronique's name!" Then, "V, V, we are saying Sylvie's name."

This is interesting because, like the sample words for the consonants covered to date, the letter being studied was shown, not just in the initial position as in American programs at this point in first grade, but in a middle position in "Sylvie".

After this, the teacher had the children clap the two syllables of vite again.

I understood from the college teacher that, with this gesture method, it is possible to tell the differences between difficult consonants, when used in such words as tapi and tati. A child uses a different gesture for each of the difficult consonants to distinguish b, p, t, and d. Not knowing the meaning of these gestures, I had not been able to get more than a general idea of their significance.

The professor said that, at the beginning of this class in September, the teacher had read phrases such as the following, which I saw on the board in addition to the sentences just given.

> "A midi, Maman prepare la salade dans un saladier.
> Maman prepare de la soupe dans une casserole."
>
> ("At noon Mama prepares salad in a salad bowl.
> Mama prepares soup in a casserole.")

I was told that the reason for this practice was to give children, from the beginning, a knowledge of structure and phrases as they actually exist. Reportedly, it was because of the use of such material that the program was called both a linguistic and structural method. The professor said it was not a phonic method (by their standards, that is).

At the end of the teacher's lesson, the graduate group discussed the work. One objected to the fact that the children were being taught to read the word, "vite" as two syllables, "vi - te" (vee-teh) apparently the Avignon accent, while the formal French usage is only one syllable "vit" (veet). The professor answered, "Why argue with six-year-olds the rules of the linguist?" I thought that was a very good point. In my opinion, anyway, too many linguists stirring the "casserole" are spoiling the first-grade "soup."

I made copies of one of the children's notebooks in this class. The first page practiced "l" in a little experience story labeled, "to read". In it, the children had darkened every "l" and underneath it practiced writing the five simple vowels, a, e, i, o and u. The story was:

> "Remi has a bed (lit).
> He has a bed.
> Colette has a bed.
> She (elle) has a bed.
> The bed (le lit) of Remi,"

The next page practiced blending "n" with vowels to make syllables, and a few words:

> "Aline a un nid.
> ("Aline has a nest.")
>
> la lune
> (the moon)
>
> un ane
> (a donkey)"

Opposite was a page with syllables and pictures, and the directions to make the "gestures" in reading, and to color the designs.

The directions that had been given to the parents before the All Saints Day vacation is of interest. Page 13's ditto read,

> "Vacation of the Toussaint, from 29 October to Thursday, 3 November.
> Reread all these texts collected in the notebook. Dictate syllables. (Your child should repeat many times the syllable before writing it.)"

During my trip, I learned that All Saints Day, November 1, followed by All Souls Day, November 2, is a still a very important holiday in many places in Europe. From the little Avignon notebook, it could be seen that it was marked by an entire week's holiday from school. Yet, in America, major public attention is only given to Halloween (All Hallows' Eve, or All Saints' Eve). Nevertheless, there is little or no awareness, even by those going to church services on All Saints Day, that the Halloween holiday has anything to do with All Saints Day.

The last comment that the teacher made on this page was of real interest. This French teacher obviously recognized that writing only assists the learning of reading, and is not the principal route to learning to read for normal children, or her request would have been reversed, to read, "Your child should write the syllable many times before repeating it"!

The syllables given for dictation at home over the "Toussaint" holiday were:

>   u- ne (a, or one)
>   cre- pe (a crepe)
>   un tri-cot (a sweater)
>   u-ne e-co-le (a school)
>   un ca-nard (a duck)
>   un ca-na-ri (a canary)

Listed were 11 more syllables like the above, with the instructions "To read often." I made photocopies of this whole little booklet before returning it, but it was just one "ordinary" booklet from a first-grade class, because all the children in that first-grade class had booklets just like it.

It is evident that these little Avignon youngsters were mastering basic reading since they could take such "dictation".

Because of the very heavy emphasis in this program on phonics, despite its use of some sight words, I coded it Code 7. However, the second-grade class in this school which I tested later had not had this program the previous year. Instead, they had the text <u>Remi et Collete</u> which I also coded at "7" after examining a copy. It was a mixed global method with synthetic/analytic phonics, but heavy on the phonics.

I understood from the director of the school that the ability level in this second-grade class could be considered average for France. This second grade class, I was told, had also had different teachers in first grade, but all had used the <u>Remi</u> book. When I tested them, they did very well indeed. At the instructional level, 90% of the class passed, and 97% passed above the frustrational level. On comprehension, 33% passed, and on speed, 13% were slow and 13% were fast, and no children made reversals.

My last Avignon school, which I visited on Friday, November 25, 1977, was fairly close to the center of Avignon. When I arrived, a young woman university student teacher was present who knew the kind woman who had made my wonderful appointments for me at the Avignon schools. Time did not permit me to look up this official, so I asked this young woman if she would say how very much I was enjoying my visits, and I asked her if she would also give the official a copy of my preliminary testing proposal, which outlined in detail the background for my project and the extent of my testing.

This last Avignon school was in two very old buildings, and it was architecturally very interesting. One building had covered verandas two stories high along the side, and I tried to sketch it, but time and my limited ability did not permit me to do so. Carrying a camera on this trip, along with the incredible papers and books I needed to have, had been out of the question.

Again, there was a high wall around this courtyard, which had trees inside it. The courtyard lay between the two separate buildings on each side. The first grade was in the smaller building of the two.

The first-grade room in this old building, however, was very cheerful. It had many plants, and pink checked gingham curtains on the windows, matched by pink checked ruffles on the shelves. Leaf paintings were displayed, and pretty cut-outs. In the front of the room was another of the folding blackboards I had seen before. Displayed in the front of the room also were the characters in the experience stories used by this gentle and warm teacher. She was a small-framed, pretty woman.

Illustrated in the front of the room were a family of mice, their names under them, and a painted picture of the mice leaving their home. Their names were Mole, Reta, Rati, Loli, Mato and La Maman Souri (the mother mouse). A big, painted pumpkin was also in the front of the room.

Today the teacher was covering the "hard" sounds of c and g, using an experience story on the board:

"Maman est sortie. Elle ferme la porte du jardin. Puis elle appelle, Sunny, regarde. Nicolas, regarde. La famille des escargots est a la table. Le papa, le maman, les bebes se regalent. Ils devorent le belle tarte de Nicolas. Le plus petit escargot s'est glisse a cote du papa et il deguste la plus grosse miette."

("Mama has gone out. She closes the door of the garden. Then she calls, "Sunny, look. Nicolas, look. The family of snails is at the table. The papa, the mamma, the babies are feasting. They devour Nicholas's beautiful tart. The smallest snail has crept to the side of his father and he tastes the biggest bit.")

She also had on the board selected words using the hard sounds of "c" and "g", such as "un escargot," ("a snail,") "la grosse salade" ("the big salad").

This was the last visit of my six-weeks' European trip, and I was late, having missed the earlier parts of the lesson. The teacher was having the children go to the board to search for the c's and g's in the story she gave them. She dictated "ca" and "ga" and the children wrote that on their slates, and she checked their work. Then she asked the children to give words in which they could hear the sound of "ga," and received in answer, "gateau, galant, gant, garage" ("cake, gallant, glove, garage"). Now she dictated "gu," which the children wrote, to which she responded, "C'est bon!" ("That's good!") as they all held up their slates with the correct answers. She dictated "deguste" and they all wrote "gu", the syllable they heard in this word. She then wrote the word on the board and asked a child to find it in the story. It took him a while, but he did. She asked again for samples of words with "g" but this time wanted words in which "g" was in the internal position. A child volunteered incorrectly, "coiffeur," and she corrected him.

There could be no question that this was a heavy, heavy phonic program. The experience story, obviously, was only meant to provide samples of the sounds in actual use in words, and the internal position of letters was being emphasized here as in other French programs.

The teacher continued dictating hard "c" and "g" followed by either the sound of "a" or "u", and most of the children had little trouble writing these syllables correctly on their slates.

I looked at a child's notebook for work done earlier in the year. On September 29, the duplicated story was:

"Maman souri a mis sa rati petites a l'ecole des souris."

("Mother Mouse has put her little mice to the school for mice.")

This was followed by "mi, ri, ti, mi, ri, mi," printed underneath on the duplicated sheet. The "mi"'s had been circled, so obviously the string of syllables had been meant as a task to determine whether or not a child could pick out the syllable "mi" from among other syllables. Underneath this little exercise, the child had written "mi" five times and "i" six times. Obviously, "m", "i", and the blend, "mi" had been the task on September 19.

On September 20, the sentence story was, "The little mouse is at the school." Underneath the duplicated story were duplicated syllables: "ma, la, ma, a, la," apparently to work with the new letter, "a".

On September 22, the sentence story was:

"La classe est joli, dit Rati a ses amis Rita, Moli, Mato, Loli."

("The class is nice, said Rati to his friends, Rita, Moli, Mato and Loli.")

Under this was written one line of "a," one line of "o," one line of "mo" and one line of "lo," and the names Rita, Moli, Mati, Loli. The letters studied to September 22 were apparently, m, i, a, l, o, r, and t.

Each succeeding day had a little sentence story about the mice people and usually introduced a new letter. September 23 had "u, mu, du". September 26 had "c, co, mo." September 27 covered "m, me, mme, comme" and, here, again, was the famous European Mimi, but apparently the French Mimi, unlike the others, was a mouse:

"Mimi est joli comme Rita."

("Mimi is nice like Rita.")

September 29 had "ne, ni, na". September 30 had "le, li, lu". October 3 had "di, de, dodo". October 4 had "milene, nado". October 6 had "pe, pi, papa, capi". October 7 had 'pe" with a grave accent on the "e", and October 10 had "s" and blends.

It was evident from this child's notebook that the teacher had been introducing a consonant at a time and then immediately showing it in combination with vowels. This might be called a syllable method, but the emphasis was on blending, as when she dictated "gu" and "ga." Though she used experience stories, there was absolutely no sign that the children were to be held responsible for remembering these words as sight words. They were only used as examples of the phonic element under study and as a medium with which to arouse the children's interest in the study.

It was enchanting to see the children work with this teacher's little story of the snails. Her little mice stories, when seen in combination with their pictures, were beguiling. It was notable that, at the beginning of the year, she had kept the number of words in her experience stories to a bare minimum. This was obviously a heavy phonics program, despite the apparent use of syllables, and I coded it Code 9 on the scale. From September 19 to October 4, a period of two and a half weeks, she had covered the phonic study of 9 consonants (m, r, t, l, c, n, d, p, s) and all simple vowels plus e grave.

Later, I tested a second grade across the courtyard in the larger building. Most of the class, Avignon 4, Code 9, had been in this lovely woman's class in first grade and read very well indeed. The class averaged 85% passing at the instructional level and 93% passing above the frustrational level, with 30% passing comprehension, 11% scoring slow, 26% scoring fast in reading, and only 4% reversals (one child of the 27 tested).

However, one girl in the second-grade class had not been in the first grade in this school the previous year, and she had already repeated two years. She received a score of 80%, almost the lowest in France. It was evident from the manner in which she read that she had a severe problem, since her reading consisted of great amounts of pure guesswork. One other very weak child in this class, a boy, scored 70%, I regret that I neglected to ask the teacher if he had been in the school the previous year, or, in fact, if the girl who had been retained twice had been in the school in first grade. Therefore, I had to include these two failing scores in with the other 25 in the second grade, which lowered what could have been a very high score. If this boy's score had been excluded, and the score also excluded of the girl who had been retained twice and so who obviously had not been with the second-grade class in first grade, the rest of this class of 25 children would have scored with 92% at the instructional level and <u>none</u> below the frustrational level. The entire class would have passed the oral reading accuracy test.

It was obvious that the method used to teach beginning reading in first grade the previous year had been highly successful for the most of the class, which suggests that the boy had a problem the rest of the children did not, unless he had not been in this school in first grade, which is possible. Since he had the lowest oral reading accuracy score that I found in Europe, 70%, he might be considered a true dyslexic. His low score represented only 0.5% of the total European phonics tests.

The attitude of French teachers, however, to children who score far below the passing score of 90%, scoring as low as 80% or 70%, is different from American teachers. In all the 237 phonics children I tested in Europe, only 6 read below 85%, which means that only 2 1/2 % scored that low. Furthermore, only one - this boy - read below 80% oral accuracy. In the sight-word programs that I tested in America in January, 1978, 15% of the second-grade pupils scored below 85% accuracy, and many in that failing group scored far below 80% Yet, I never heard the remark in the American sight-word classes that this second grade teacher made, concerning the two failing children. She said:

"They can only read a word here and there."

As mentioned in my comments on my Austrian visit, the bell curve should apply to the distribution of any attribute, including the ability to process print. Therefore, true dyslexia should occur only in very tiny percentages, like the 0.4% of the total European phonic group which this boy represented.

The next day, Saturday, November 26, 1977, I took the train north to Paris, a long trip even on an express train. I arrived very late in the evening, having had dinner on the train. For the first time in my life, I was homesick. I had never been away from home as long as six weeks before, and all the pleasures of Paris no longer interested me. The next morning, Sunday, November 27, when I felt the plane's wheels leave the ground at Orly Airport on the way to New York, so that I knew I was finally airborne, I let out a quiet, involuntary "Yippee!"

The middle-aged man seated next to me, a native of Buffalo but working elsewhere in the United States for Eastman Kodak, probably thought I was a madwoman, but perhaps he understood. I just wanted to get home. When we came over Long Island hours later, he laughed and pointed down, saying, "That's the United States down there!" I looked out the window to see a Long Island marsh, and a garbage dump, and said, from the bottom of my heart, "It's BEAUTIFUL!"

But I retained a melange of delightful memories of Europe and its schools.

I remembered the lift I got from being the recipient of a Swedish sixth-grade class's chorused greeting, "Good afternoon, Miss Rodgers!" as they leapt to their feet at a signal from their teacher, bursting with good health and good spirits and their eyes dancing with merriment! I imagine it would be a handful to keep that lively bunch in good order, as I saw her do. But presidents can keep their 21 gun salutes. I'll take a greeting like that from Swedish sixth graders any time!

I remembered standing on the platform in Hamburg's massive central railroad station and seeing freight cars going through with endless cars of Spanish oranges, oranges, oranges, and then seeing freight cars of Spanish oranges thundering through for the last time as I waited in Avignon for the train back to Paris and plane back home.

I shall always remember the smocks in the Belgian first-grade class, the little girls looking like a group of Alices in Wonderland, so appropriate while using the Cuisenaire rods of which mathematician Lewis Carrroll would certainly have approved.

Then there were the Innsbruck children who burst out of their sun-filled and brightly-curtained classroom in pairs, holding hands with their partners, and buzzing with all the important conversations of seven year olds, on their way to music or gym class or whatever.

Then there were the little ones in Avignon working on a delightful experience chart lesson dealing with - of all things- "Sur Le Pont d'Avignon." The old bridge is actually still there on the river.

I shall remember the famous crepes of Brittany, the subject of experience charts in the Quimper school concerning crepes au sucre and crepes au poire, which the little ones there accept as nonchalantly as American children accept peanut butter and jelly.

I shall remember being included as a member of the class "meeting in the round" in a first-grade class in Amsterdam, as the little ones proudly talked about their beautiful fall leaves.

Then there were the huge book-bags in the Luxembourg first grades. They were a witness to the fact that the little ones were being treated by their parents as having earned the badge of the academic world - a book-bag, while their teachers were giving them the only key to that world's door - true literacy.

To taste the real flavor of a country, it is necessary to visit its schools. Unfortunately, the disruption that would cause makes such visits unworkable except for a lucky few. I count myself to be so very, very fortunate to have been one of them.

CHAPTER 5
Anecdotal Log on American School Visits

Phonic Groups:

Lippincott

The American phonics programs (Code 7 to Code 10) will sound very much like the European phonics programs, except that none will have an initial load of a few sight words before the phonics study is begun. I will report on the American phonics programs first, because, with this background, the reader will understand better the hopeless inadequacy of the two American sight-word basal reader programs when I report on them. Yet both basal reader publishers claim they are using phonics! In the make-up of the materials, and in their claim to use phonics, these two basal sight-word programs are representative of most such basal sight-word programs in use at first grade level in 1977 and 1978.

My visits to American schools took place in September and October, 1977, and in January, 1978, and I saw and tested both sight word and phonic programs. I will report first on the phonic programs, and the first phonic program will be Lippincott's.

The Lippincott Code 10 material, which the publisher calls phonic-linguistic, was in use in two American schools which I visited. I tested four second-grade classes in each of these schools, two in October and two in January.

The Lippincott Grade One program consists of four books, Books A, B, C, and D. In "A Message to the Teacher from the Authors," in Book E of the Teacher's Edition of Lippincott's Basic Reading, Philadelphia, 1970, written by Glenn McCracken and Charles C. Walcutt, they state:

> "...the fundamental strength of BASIC READING is in the synthetic development of word analysis skills. The lists of Basic Phonemes and Phoneme-Grapheme Relationships which appear at the end of the Grade One readers illustrate the comprehensive manner in which major English sound-spellings are presented. Each lesson in the Grade One books presents a new linguistic element followed by poems or stories in which the linguistic element appears. Rigid control of the introduction of these linguistic elements is practiced. The pupil is therefore able to attack successfully new words containing previously taught linguistic elements. As the pupil progresses, he meets minor sound-spelling patterns and irregular sound-spellings."

Book E - the first of the two second-grade books, reviews the sounds, and Book F is finished with teaching reading (decoding) and is simply a collection of worthwhile, interesting stories and poems with a heavy vocabulary, exposing the children to the meaning of new words not yet in their spoken vocabulary. People sometimes say, "I am not sure if I pronounced that word correctly, because I have only read it and have never heard it spoken." It is through such reading that most vocabulary growth takes place.

Yet the vocabularies in the American sight-word basal readers, and even in other American school books, are rigidly controlled, and have been so controlled since about 1930. In contrast, the first-grade Lippincott program introduces more than 2,000 words at the first-grade level, compared to sight-word basal readers, some of which introduce as few as 325 words in first grade. Furthermore, at second grade and above, new words are introduced in the Lippincott readers at a rate far in excess of the introduction of new words in the sight word basal readers at second grade and above. Children learn the pronunciation of these new words from their phonic skills, and the meaning of the new words just as they do in conversation - from the context of the material. The gap between Lippincott students and sight-word students, therefore, in vocabulary growth - in real vocabulary growth, which means learning the meaning of new words, and not just the ability to pronounce printed words already in a child's vocabulary - becomes enormous before those students reach high school.

It is exceedingly unfortunate that most American students since 1930 have been taught by the sight-word method, not the phonic method as used by the Lippincott readers, and so most American students have never reached the vocabulary level of which they had been potentially capable. By suppressing such vocabulary growth in American children, the sight word method has effectively lowered the nation's functioning verbal intelligence, because test scores on vocabulary knowledge and test scores on intelligence correlate so closely that the two are essentially equivalent.

The Lippincott program can be very effective, although I think it should be covered more slowly than is usually done in first-grade rooms. Also, I am convinced that its recommendation to use analytic instead of synthetic phonics should be totally disregarded. However, if more time were spent on auditory and visual discrimination on new letters and the introduction of new letters were spaced farther apart in time at the beginning of the program, the already high success of Lippincott would, I believe, increase, particularly with the slower pupils. Many teachers told me that the slower pupils could not handle the program because they had not learned the sounds of the letters, since the program was too fast for them. Most teachers who use this program, however, like it very much. One first-grade teacher said, of the Lippincott children, "They have it for all their lives!"

Yet, despite the reference to "synthetic development" in the "Message to the Teacher" quoted previously, the Lippincott program does not endorse the use of sounding-and-blending phonics (synthetic phonics), but only phonic analysis. This could weaken its effectiveness, but it is probable that few teachers follow the "official" Lippincott advice and use only analytic phonics in teaching it. At a Reading Reform Foundation Annual Meeting, held in Princeton in the summer of 1979, I was present at a workshop under the direction of the late Dr. Charles Child Walcutt, who was, with Glenn McCracken, an author of the Lippincott series. Dr. Walcutt told the small audience at his workshop that he did not endorse sounding-and-blending phonics. That small audience was composed largely of teachers using his program and they reacted vehemently and negatively to his statement. They said that they used sounding-and-blending phonics, and would continue to do so. Their reaction obviously displeased Dr. Walcutt. However, since all phonemes are pronounced in isolation when they are initially taught in Walcutt's Lippincott program, and since almost no words are introduced unless their phonemes have been taught, the Lippincott program adapts perfectly to the sounding-andblending approach which these teachers were using, despite the program's official disapproval of sounding and blending.

The Teacher's Edition for Book E of Lippincott's Basic Reading, pages xi to xiv, contains a discussion, "Sound and Sense: Basic Letter Knowledge with No 'Sounding Out.'" In my opinion, this section of the teacher's guide is replete with errors and should be disregarded by teachers. Walcutt was not himself a teacher, and, as a result, did not really understand the teaching of beginning reading. However, despite that fact, he and McCracken managed to write a phonics series which adapts well to the teaching of beginning reading by Code 10 sounding and blending.

Yet sounding and blending phonics was the invention, curiously, of another man who did not himself teach beginning reading: Blaise Pascal, the famed French mathematician/ scientist. Pascal had proposed its use to his sister, Jacqueline, when she was teaching in the Port Royal school in France. That Blaise Pascal did so is confirmed by an extant letter of Jacqueline Pascal to her brother, Blaise, dated October 25, 1655, and by another extant letter of January 31, 1636, from Antoine Arnauld to Blaise Pascal. (These two letters are cited in the articles "Pascal, Blaise" and "Pascal, Jacqueline" in the Dictionnaire de Pedagogie et d'Instruction Primaire, edited by F. Buisson and published by Librarie Hachette et Cie. in Paris, France, in 1887.)

When children are first learning the consonant sounds in the Lippincott program, they are asked to say the consonants in isolation without adding a sounded vowel. Yet the very word, "consonant," means "together with" and most consonants have to have a vowel sound or they cannot be pronounced at all. Therefore, to recommend that children say the
consonant sound without a vowel is to recommend the impossible.

Pascal's suggestion was that syllables be "spelled" by sound, by saying the consonants with a quickly added indistinguishable vowel sound, what we now call a "schwa" (something like c = cuh). Then, instead of spelling by letter names but by letter sounds (cuh - ah - tuh), the sounds in sequence would suggest the blended syllable or word (cuh - ah - tuh = cat). Spelling by letter names (see - aye - tee) cannot suggest a syllable or word, so Pascal wanted lettername-spelling replaced by his letter-sound-spelling. However, it seems probable that neither Walcutt nor McCracken had any understanding of Pascal's sounding-and-blending, and even more probable that they had never even heard of it.

Obviously, spelling "cuh-ah-tuh" can only suggest the word, "cat." It is objectively impossible to "blend" those three sounds, each with its own vowel, to produce the one sound, "cat" which has only one vowel. Two of the vowel sounds (the two schwas following "c" and "t") cannot simply disappear. Therefore, "sounding-and-blending" cannot actually blend multiple sounds into one sound, nor did Pascal intend it to do so. It was intended only to suggest such blending. However, such suggested sound blendings do, indeed, work in teaching beginning reading, as I can confirm most vehemently myself since I have used the sounding-and-blending approach with great success.

Book A, in the 1970 edition, begins by introducing the vowel sounds in isolation, one at a time, and then moves to the letter "m" in isolation, and "n". Putting the vowels and those consonants together into words begins almost immediately, producing the first words: am, an. By pages 8 and 9 of the text (or page 23 of the workbook, level a codebook), the children are reading such words as "man, Nan, ran, ram," and "rim" from the phonemes they have studied. With this total phonic approach in the first half of first grade, it is obvious that Lippincott is a Code 10 program, whether taught analytically or synthetically.

The 1975 edition of Book A introduces the letters in a different order than the 1970 edition. The short vowels are not all introduced first before any consonants but instead are introduced slowly along with consonants.

Class U. S. 7 used the Lippincott program. It was in a school building more than 50 years old, which was in good repair, and, like so many old buildings, was very cheerful. Much of the attractiveness was the result of the principal's and teachers' effort to make the rooms attractive and warm. The first-grade teacher had the cooperation of this very professional principal who had managed to turn up an artificial fireplace somewhere for the first-grade room, in front of which was a rug and two chairs. The principal said, with obvious satisfaction, "The children sit on the rug and read to each other."

The room was painted a clear, lemon yellow. It had a large classroom library and a television. On the window sill were plants, and paper art work was displayed on the windows. Halloween was coming, so cat and pumpkin paper art work was hung on strings across the room. The seatwork corner had a fair selection of academically oriented games. Some concerned visual discrimination such as picture lotto. Quiet talk was permitted during recess when children got games and had their snacks. Obviously, also, talk was permitted when the children read to each other in the back of the room.

The class had 21 children. The teacher, who had been teaching eleven years, seemed to be a very fine teacher. She had been the first in the school to use Lippincott about six years ago. Eventually, other grades followed. Last year, however, one first-grade in the school still had Harcourt Brace books. The principal said they had, in previous years, run Harcourt Brace and Lippincott in separate classes to determine which was more successful.

I later tested the presumably "Harcourt Brace" taught first-grade class, now in second grade, but learned that it had not been taught beginning reading the previous year in first grade by the Harcourt Brace materials. Instead, its highly competent teacher had used her own totally phonic method and had not followed the Harcourt Brace guide recommendations at all, She gave no sight word drill and had the children in her class sound ALL WORDS from the VERY BEGINNING OF FIRST GRADE! She said the children had all letter sounds before she gave them any words. In sounding the words, she worked from the sounds to the word, true synthetic phonics, and not analytic, from whole words. I therefore coded her first-grade program at Code 10. Since I obviously could not consider it a Harcourt Brace class, I labeled it a "teacher's phonics" class. However, since the comparison between Lippincott and Harcourt Brace had been started six years previously in this school building, it is probable that in earlier years the Harcourt Brace program (geared more heavily to sight-words) may have been used to teach beginning reading for some of the first grades in those earlier years.

In arithmetic, the Lippincott first-grade teacher said she was using the Silver Burdett book by Morton, Gray, Rosskopf and Traxton, which had pictured explanations on the pages. I could not see from glancing at it that it made much use of manipulative materials at this beginning level. The teacher volunteered the comment, "I don't like this book."

On a bulletin board on the side of the room was a large tree made of paper, with a paper squirrel and next to it separate paper acorns on each of which were either capital letters or small letters. This very appealing board was a discrimination game, in which the children took turns going up to the board to match the small letter acorns to the big letter acorns. As a fellow teacher, I know what it cost this teacher in personal time to make and cut all those acorns and the beautiful large paper oak tree and squirrel, plus all the other paper fittings of this game. Since construction paper such as used for this game fades fast, it was exceedingly unlikely that all of this work could be used next year. I wonder how many parents appreciate such extra, unrequired work that teachers put in for the good of their students.

(This was written originally in 1978 or 1979. About 1992 or so, I happened to meet this teacher again, who was using at that later date the Scribner version of the original Lippincott program. The Scribner revision moved the emphasis from "sound" at Code 10 far, far closer to "meaning" at Code 5 or less. Enormous teacher time was wasted teaching so-called "reading comprehension," while the phonic strand was greatly weakened, de-emphasized and badly taught. As evident from my earlier visit, this was a dedicated teacher. Yet she found no fault with the Scribner revision, even though Scribner had moved most of the original Lippincott program from "sound" to "meaning." I was astonished to learn that the teacher could not see that the program had been changed from a good one to a bad one, and that she actually liked the new materials better! Yet the teacher in the same school in 1977-1978, who had refused to use Harcourt Brace materials for her beginning readers the year before in first grade, and who therefore made up her own phonic program, certainly would have understood the nature of the change!)

While I was there, the teacher gave a reading group five minutes of flash card drill on words that had already been sounded out phonically. A child said proudly that they had 65 words already. The words included those with consonant blends like stump, rust and punt. Most of the children seemed to know them, and I could hear them audibly blending the sounds and even see them sounding out visually by their mouth movements. The only word the children had trouble with was the article, "a". This is not surprising, as the article sound is really "uh" and these children were reading sounds, not "sight words". When "a" is sounded like "uh", it is a true sight word.

This program drills on recognition of sight words once the children have decoded them.

Yet, personally, I do not think there is any such thing as a true sight word for people who read phonically, even though they retain visual memories of how words are spelled. Yet they prompt these memories by internal pronunciations, "phonics". They always go from "sound" to "meaning," even though they do it rapidly and automatically. I can read Samuel Pepy's 17th Century diary with ease despite all his variant spellings of the so-called "sight" words. If I were reading pure "sight words," I would stumble over Pepy's variant spellings instead of reading them fluently. Rapid flash card drill as endorsed by the Lippincott program may help to bring decoding skills to the automatic level for some very few children, but it is extremely hazardous and probably harmful for most children because it promotes guessing and reading by "whole words" instead of by sounds.

In Book A, the Lippincott program unfortunately (and unnecessarily) introduces five irregular sight words: "a, the, to, put, for". Yet the last, "for," is not irregular once the children know the vowel, "r-controlled o", so it certainly should not have been introduced until they knew that vowel.

In this Lippincott class, during flash card drill of these 65 words, the children were very successfully, audibly and visibly, sounding out the words. However, very meaningfully, they missed only ONE word, the irregular non-phonic sound for "a", which is "uh." That certainly demonstrates the harmfulness of teaching such sight words to beginners! Sight words cannot get any shorter than "a." I even saw a third-grade child spell it in his composition exactly as it sounds, "u"!

In general, however, despite these obvious failings, the Lippincott materials are extremely effective and attractive. It is interesting that the first workbook page uses rebuses, or pictures, for some words, just as does Houghton, Mifflin, and the Austrian reader!

The teacher was working with one group on Lippincott Basic Reading Book A, the pre-primer. She had the children read orally, using markers to keep their places. From her comments, she was obviously having them read for "comprehension." The children turned to page 22, and she said that, after they read it, she wanted someone to "read the whole story to me." The "story" ran:

> "Stop, Pat, stop!
> Tim is a tot.
> Tim sits on Pat.
> Pat runs and runs.
> Stop, Pat, stop!

The teacher had made a ditto sheet of some of the words the children had been practicing, and the children were cutting them out to make word cards. This was not straight sight-word drill, as all these words had been decoded in all their phonic elements previously, and, as I saw in the word drill, they were still sounded out by the children, with conscious effort on each phonic element. This work, however, must have been the source of the child's comment to me, "We have 65 words already!"

Another assignment was a sheet of paper folded in 8 boxes, on which children were to copy 8 upper and lower case letters from the board, and illustrate with something beginning with the sound of each letter. This, of course, was visual and auditory discrimination of letter sounds. Other board work was to copy the story

> "Nan ran.
> Run, Nan, run.
> Run on.
> Run on, Nan."

This was presumably for the whole class, and not for just one reading group. This reading group was also assigned workbook page 59, which was a review of the alphabet introduced to date.

I understood that later the children would have a class game, "We have to feed Sherlock," which game was a drill on letter sounds. The rules of the game were not clear to me, but it was obviously a candy-coated practice session on the phonic sounds and letters covered to date. The lovely construction paper oak tree on the bulletin board had a squirrel next to it, and perhaps the drill was to feed the letter acorns to the squirrel named, I would assume, Sherlock!

At least one group in the room had covered to page 22 of the text, which means, if they were in the 1970 edition, they had studied the letters a, e, i, o, u (only casually) and d, m, n, short o, p, r, s, and t. If they were in the 1975 edition, they would have covered short a, n, r, d, short u, m, p, short i, s, short o, and t. The board work covered letters introduced to page 22 also. Those who had the alphabet page in the workbook had apparently covered also e, hard c and g, and h and f, which would indicate they were at the end of Book A in the 1975 edition.

When I tested other Lippincott classes in January, they scored comparably to the European phonic programs in November. The second-grade Lippincott class in this school, however, U. S. Class 7, I tested early in October, and this early score was comparably lower, as were all the early fall U. S. scores. Nevertheless, it was very good compared to other classes I tested in early October. At the 95 level, 57% passed, and at the 90 level, 76%. On comprehension, 48% passed. Even at this early point in second grade, only 14% read slowly and 14% read quickly. Reversals were made by 10%. It is remarkable that, in this Lippincott second grade in October, only one child scored below 85, or 5% of the class, which was comparable to the later European scores, when European phonics groups had 2.2% below and European global groups (modified with heavy phonics) 3.3% below. However, in the sight-word American classes I tested as late as January, 1978, 15% of the sample scored below 85%, three times as many as this Lippincott class three months earlier.

In January, I returned to this school to test the other second-grade class which had used the Harcourt Brace textbook the previous year, but whose teacher told me she never used the guide but taught straight synthetic phonics of her own devising from the beginning. This teacher had a delightful room this year, with the same kind of atmosphere I had seen in the first-grade room in the fall. It was obvious that she must have been a wonderful first-grade teacher the previous year.

Her former first-grade Code 10 class did wonderfully well in second grade. They had a different teacher this year, as in American schools classes are not normally handled by the same teacher two years in a row. In January, her former first-grade class, U. S. Class 17, scored with 80% at the 95 level (instructional) and 100 percent above the 90 level (frustrational). It was obvious that her home-grown phonics had worked. Of these second graders, 20% read at a fast rate and none at a slow rate. There were no reversals. In addition, 80% passed the comprehension test. This, I think, in fairness, can be attributed to the Harcourt Brace workbook pages, as well as to teacher efforts to promote good habits of attention to material being read. Reading workbooks drill on so-called "reading comprehension," which drill really results instead in good habits of attention to the text as it is being read. When teaching the primary grades, I found the Houghton-Mifflin workbook pages to be excellent if used to drill for attention habits, not phonics skills.

The other Lippincott school which I visited in October, 1977, and January, 1978, was a very, very old, large building in a lovely suburban town. As I came in through the back door from the parking lot and opened it to go up the back stairs, I noted that its latest layer of clean white paint was probably the fortieth or fiftieth on the old door. Peeling undercoats had been painted over for decades. I realized that there must have been little children who had passed through this door as first-graders 70 or 80 years ago, who had grown up, lived full lives, and were now in their graves. I got the same unsettled feeling that I had on a cruise which stopped at the Isle of Crete, where we saw the king's apartments from about 1900 B. C. As the tour group was herded from one room into another, we passed over a stone threshold. The guide pointed to the scratch marks on the stone, made by the swinging door which had swung back and forth innumerable times, and then stopped swinging forever some 3,800 years ago, to leave there this mute reminder of other humans who had stepped over the threshold and literally gone before us.

It could have been a huge, gloomy old school inside, but instead it was the very model of cheerfulness, not just the result of cheerful paint but of teachers' dedicated decorating of the rooms. The first-grade class I visited first was running an individualized program, and the children were sitting at attractive round tables. The room had a plentiful supply of materials such as tape recorders and filmstrip projectors. Also available were attractive library books, and art work was prominently displayed. The children did not have permanent desks but changed to different work areas at a signal from the teacher, with so long in the math area, and so on. The teacher had five reading groups in the room and had covered six units to date with the low middle reading group: a, n, r, d, u, and m. She was working with this group on page 12 of Book A, reading a sentence for the children to follow, and asking, "What does it mean?"

I saw much emphasis on meaning in her work. Furthermore, in this Lippincott program, in which children are to decode words for themselves, she should not have read the sentence first for the children to follow, which is an approach used in sight-word programs.

After the work in the reading book, the teacher did drill on sight words, but the same sounding-out approach was used as I saw in the earlier Lippincott class. However, she gave the children a word with "f", although this letter was not to be introduced until the end of Book A. That showed that she was not completely following the phonic approach. Her lack of faith in the method was shown by her comment, "If they don't know the sounds of the letters, they are lost. We must drill on sounds."

She said she did not care for the Lippincott program. This same attitude was shown later by the other experienced first-grade teacher, and by the second-grade teachers in this school who used Scott, Foresman books for the slower children, instead of the Book E required by Lippincott. The other first-grade teacher who disliked the program actually gave sight words to slower children.

When I tested the three second-grade classes in this school, I found the effect from the failure to follow the Lippincott program properly. The October class which I tested had 18% below 85, compared to only 5% in the October Lippincott class in another town where the children were drilled by the teacher on letter sounds with the game, "We have to feed Sherlock." In January, when other American phonic programs I tested scored very high, the Lippincott program in this school scored the lowest of any of the American phonics programs I tested, although they were very high compared to the American sight-word programs. That part of the Lippincott program which they did have to follow (the vocabulary introduced in the books follows a phonic progression) was the obvious explanation for their higher scores in comparison to sight-word programs.

The principal also did not like the program, and said they felt it "necessary" to supplement Lippincott with other materials at higher levels because of so-called "reading comprehension" problems. Some day people will finally realize that so-called "reading comprehension" is only an oxymoron. The fact that it is so will be discussed in my research summary.

The last first-grade book, Book D, is often not reached by the slower children, but the phonemes missed can be taught in the second grade in Book E, which reviews all the material from first grade. However, in this school, the slower children presumably never had either book, since they probably never reached Book D in first grade and were given Scott, Foresman in second grade, instead of Lippincott. Therefore, the slower children in this school were probably never taught the complete Lippincott phonic program. Nevertheless, I had to report their scores in with the phonics scores for the rest of this school's second-graders, but their non-phonic scores obviously diluted the total phonic score for the school, since the school had an unusual number of poor readers. (If those slower children had been properly taught instead of being given sight-word materials, the probability is that there would not have been such a high number of those poor readers.)

The classrooms, teachers and principal in this school, however, were delightful, no matter how much I disagreed with their reading views. The second room I visited was another fairyland of creative art work and interesting children's centers. I could write pages describing this and the other attractive rooms, but, to show the emphasis, I will say that I saw a child having a fine time using modeling clay, bright red, to mold and shape on paper the letters she was trying to commit to memory. She was having a fine time, and, in my opinion, that is the best way to learn.

The teacher in this second room made individual ditto work packets, which she shared with the other two first grades, plus taped lessons, with assignments that were stimulating and enjoyable. Along with everything else I saw in her room, it represented a tremendous input of teacher time, but she said she felt a teacher makes the program. These lovely rooms had teachers "making" the program. The child doing the clay work was free when done with that to pick from other assignments in the room. In this room, also, the children changed areas on a signal.

However, this was the teacher who said she gave sight words for the slower children if they did not get the sounds, because she said otherwise they would stay on the sounds "forever." The problem, of course, is with the definition of "forever." If teachers are pressured by parents and the school to have children reading words by October or so, then a month constitutes "forever." Yet, if the teacher is not pressured, almost all children, even the slowest, can master letter sounds and shapes in three months (by December), and that is not "forever." Some programs do follow that slower pace. For instance, the Alpha One program spends three months drilling on auditory and visual discrimination so that almost all slow children do learn letter sounds and shapes. Many European programs, which were reported earlier, also take a slow pace. When the necessary time is taken to teach almost all children the sounds and shapes of the letters, and the time is taken to teach blending, then almost any child can learn to read.

This teacher was drilling the three children in her bottom group on an alphabet song. Another group she had working with an oaktag game, where words were written with the vowels missing, and the child had to insert the proper oaktag vowel in each word.

The third first-grade room was working on pages 9 and 10 of Book A with the low middle group, and using the same ditto pack that I saw in the other rooms. This pleasant teacher was a first-year teacher, and she also was stressing meaning in her work with the children. The words studied on the ditto included mud, mad, man, am, ram, and drum, indicating all classes had the low middle group on the first six lessons.

The Lippincott series could be a very attractive and satisfactory one if only teachers moved much more slowly in the beginning of the year. No where on earth should haste be made more slowly than in the first half of the first-grade year. If necessary, teachers should spend weeks, and in some cases, months, to be sure that the children can distinguish among the sounds of phonemes and the letter shapes which represent those phonemes. Most children could cover the whole Lippincott program, including Book D, in the first grade year, if only the pace of the program were much, much slower at the beginning of first grade.

In October, one of the three second grades, U. S. Class 9, was tested. At the 95 level, 55% of the children passed. At the 90 level, 73% passed. Below 85 and 80 were 18%, and below 70, 9%. In that class, 23% read slowly and 18% quickly. On comprehension, 55% passed.

In January, another of the three second grades in this school was tested. That class, U. S. Class 15, had 74% at 95, and 91% at 90. Nine per cent read slowly and 52% fast. On comprehension, 83% passed.

In January, the last of the three second grades in this school was tested, U. S. Class 16. In U. S. Class 16, 61% read at the 95 level, and 87% at 90. On comprehension, 55% passed. On speed, 17% read slowly and 30% read quickly.

What was notable in both second-grade classes in January, however, was the large number of very low scores. Such low scores were not found in any of the other phonic classes I tested, either in this country or Europe. (Large numbers of very low second-grade scores were, of course, present in sight-word classes I tested in this country. Of course, a very small number of very low scores can be anticipated in any program because of disabilities in hearing, vision, etc.) Both classes in this Lippincott school had an astonishing 9% of the pupils reading, not just below the cutoff point of 90% accuracy, but below 80% accuracy!

As discussed earlier, only 300 high-frequency words account for more than three-quarters (75%) of the different words used on almost any page of print. By scoring below 80% accuracy on this very simple test form, these children demonstrated that they could only read, at best, about 300 words after a year and a half of school, and they were very probably guessing many of those 300 words from the context of the reading selection. It is therefore very evident that, by reading below 80% accuracy, nine per cent of the children in this school were still virtually illiterate by mid-second grade.

The failure of these slower pupils to learn how to read was not just because of the fact that their first-grade teachers did not teach the Lippincott program properly, which program teaches over 2,000 words in first grade, not 300. These slower pupils were still failing by mid-second grade because both second-grade teachers had been using Scott, Foresman for the slower children instead of going back and covering the Lippincott program again. The slower children in this school had paid dearly for their second-grade teachers' decision to use Scott, Foresman for those slower children instead of Lippincott.

Open Court

The Open Court Code 10 program, like Lippincott, was one of the most widely used phonics programs in America in 1977-1978. Although Open Court started with heavy phonics like Lippincott, in its later choice of reading selections, it stressed recognized literature to a greater extent.

September 29, 1977, was the date of my first visit to an Open Court school. The school was located in an attractive suburban town and was more than fifty years old. Its first-grade room was very pleasant, with desks arranged in four rows to form a square. A strongly directed lesson was under way, and the children appeared involved and relaxed. Most responded as if they understood.

The letters introduced to date were m, long e, s, t, h, and w. They were covered in the first three of 24 lessons in the first book. Three such books, or pre-primers, were used in the first half-year, titled <u>Learning to Read and Write, Reading and Writing,</u> and <u>Word Line Book.</u>

The text for the second half of the first-grade year was <u>Reading Is Fun,</u> a very difficult book for children in sight- word programs. In my third-grade class in an upper-middle class New York suburb some years earlier, more than a few of the third-grade children could not read the book at all.

The first of the three pre-primers, <u>Learning to Read and Write,</u> presents all but five letters of the alphabet. It also covers the long vowel sounds and th, sh, and the special vowels er, ir, and ur. The second preprimer covers the remaining five letters and special sounds such as ng, ou, ph, etc. This makes the rate of learning very, very fast, since, with four first-grade books, and the last one with very heavy true reading, no more than about two and a half months are available to spend on this first book which teaches the bulk of the alphabet and the principle of synthetic word blending, along with practice on the material.

On September 29, after only three weeks in school, the children in this class had covered five letters and the principle of blending. These sounds were also being used to practice writing and spelling. But, in Germany, for instance, after seven weeks in school, the children had covered only 4 to 7 letters. In Sweden, after 10 weeks in school, and with children a year older since children start school a year later there, in a school which was using the heavily phonic Nu <u>Laser</u> text and not the weak LTG experience charts, the children had covered only 8 letters and blending. Nevertheless, this same Swedish school scored the highest at second grade on my European testing. The wisdom of moving slowly and starting school later seems to be confirmed further by the fact that Swedish 10-year-olds scored the highest in the 16-country reading comprehension test run by IEA in the 1960s.

However, our phonics first-grade programs are running in competion with the sight-word programs. Children from sight-word classes go home a few weeks after school begins with whole words on their papers, not just letters, and this impresses their parents. Because of this pressure, our phonics programs push children through the alphabet, and rush them through blending, and then are grateful to have so few failures in relation to sight-word programs. Yet our phonics programs have unnecessary failures caused by rushing the program to impress parents and to avoid odious comparisons to sight-word programs. There is, of course, no reason why the Open Court program and the Lippincott program could not be handled more slowly in the beginning. The choice is the teacher's and the school's.

I understood that the teachers in this first Open Court school that I visited had been told to take the Open Court program but had preferred another. That might very well account for their negative responses to the Open Court program. The following day, I visited another Open Court school, whose first-grade teacher had attended an Open Court workshop before using the program. She loved the Open Court program, and, frankly, her class was very much better.

In this first school using Open Court, a very effective, attractive young woman ran a lesson which was complex and demanding. It moved smoothly, and the children seemed to enjoy it, but the pace seemed far too rapid for even average children to be able to absorb the concepts covered. Also, I understood that the IQ average in this school had dropped, and they now had more children below average, which made the pace even more inappropriate. The next day, in an Open Court school with a reportedly higher-than-average IQ, the pace was far slower! Yet it was this second, slower-moving school that had the highest-scoring program on my fall United States scores.

When I visited this first Open Court school again the following January, some comments made by second-grade teachers were negative. They felt that some of the vocabulary in workbooks and readers was so difficult that children had to look up the words, but, even then, the children could not understand the definitions in the Open Court dictionaries. Yet their second-graders could, they said, understand the definitions in the Thorndike Barnhard beginning dictionary.

I sympathize with their dictionary problem, but also know that the Thorndike Barnhard beginning dictionary was hopelessly too difficult for my THIRD GRADE Scott, Foresman- and Ginn- taught classes for the 13 years that I taught third grade, until at least the middle of the year, after I had taught my third-graders the sounding-and-blending phonics that they should have been given in first grade. Yet, even after the middle of the third-grade year, and after I had finally taught the third-grade children how to read instead of how to guess from sight words and the context, these dictionaries were too difficult for at least a third of the class.

One second-grade teacher spoke with approval of the boxed Open Court reading games (which cost about $75 for a dozen games in 1977).

Another second-grade teacher in this school whose class I tested in January was emphatic about her belief in phonics, and said she stressed it. It is interesting that her top readers (above 96%)accuracy) also did very well on "comprehension" and better than the two other Open Court classes in the building. She had a very interesting classroom, and permitted quiet talk. Her class was coded U. S. 14. In her class was one of the only two children I met in American schools who, I felt, were probably real dyslexics. This boy in her class unquestionably knew phonics rules and sound values. He demonstrated that fact in sounding out words. Yet he read exceedingly slowly, and made most errors on words where he had a problem with the direction of letters. He read without difficulty words like "color" and "mostly" where reversals were less likely to be a problem.

I had him stop at the end of the second section, after only 62 words of the 144 word total, because he read so slowly and agonizingly. He missed six words of the 62 words that he read, "Peter" (twice), "than" (once), "dog" (twice), and "back." The first time that he misread "dog," he began by making the "b" sound. The second time he just stared at it and could not decide it it were "b" or "d," apparently. On the word, "back" he started to make a "d" sound. When I corrected him with the "b" sound, he immediately said, "back."

Technically, his sample test accuracy score was 90 per cent, just above the frustration level, and so passing. However, I feel that if I had made him finish the total 144-word test, his score would have dropped. Therefore, I gave him a score of 89 per cent incomplete. Reading for that boy was obviously a torture. His teacher said that he appeared intelligent, but was also having severe problems with the simplest arithmetic. She said the school was arranging to have him given psychological tests.

I tested three second-grade classes in this first Open Court school, and they are reported at the end of this text. The September second-grade class, U. S. Class 5, scored comparably on accuracy to other fall phonics classes, but somewhat lower (which it is my subjective judgment was the result of teacher resistance to this new program). The two January classes, U. S. Class 12 and U. S. Class 14, scored comparably on accuracy to other January phonic classes, but considerably above the January sight-word classes. On comprehension;, the results were mixed, which is discussed later.

On September 30, 1977, I visited the second Open Court school, mentioned briefly previously. The first-grade classroom was in a beautifully appointed room in an old school, and it had a cheerful, open-classroom atmosphere. Talking was permitted. The teacher was delightful, warm with the children, and competent. She said she had used the Macmillan program previously but had been asked to try the Open Court program. She said she had liked it after attending a one-week workshop. She said, if she could take a first-grade to March with Open Court phonics, "I don't care what happens after it is done."

This teacher's faith in the program was obvious. I gathered that she was following the Open Court methods exactly. While I was there, she was doing work on oral blending and reviewing sounds. As she wrote in the air, the children followed, each writing on his own individualized rug with his finger, and sounding orally while he wrote. Then the children switched and wrote the letters with their fingers on each other's backs. This was obviously a lesson on dictation, but with the kinesthetic, or feeling, approach. A child then wrote on the board as the others wrote with their fingers on the rugs when the teacher made the sound concerned. Then she said, "Proofread," and wrote "ee" on the board and they compared the previous board work to her sample. Next, she said, "What can we do better?"

Another approach was to say, "Don't erase - circle."

She then gave dictation to all the children - four lines of writing. In this work, she was making use of many "modes" of learning: auditory, visual, and kinesthetic (feeling) and using both reading and writing, as well as proofreading, all Open Court approaches to reading.

Possibly, since the class work was working on "ee", they were still on the last half of the first lesson, page 3, so they would have covered "m," terminal long "e" (as in "me"), and long "ee" (as in "see"). If so, they were moving much slower than the class I had seen the day before, September 29, which had finished apparently page 22 and Lesson3, for a total of five letters and blending. Also, the Open Court lesson I saw in this second school had a more physical approach, was more individualized, and had real child involvement. It is, of course, entirely possible that the other school did similar lessons which I just did not happen to see.

The first-grade teacher in this second Open Court school said the Open Court approach was to "slide" initial consonants and vowels, a real blending approach. Also, she said their theme was "I see it, I say it, I write it."

When I tested her class from the previous year, U. S. Class 4, by that time in second grade, they did very well indeed for so early in the year, only September 30, even for a class in which the intelligence was reported to be somewhat above average. Seventy per cent scored at 95% accuracy or above, and 100 per cent at 90% accuracy or above. None were slow, and 26% were fast. This was an extraordinary score for only September 30 of second grade. It was the best American fall score, and, even in January, of the 18 American classes I tested, it was exceeded by only two, and not by very much in those (one 78 per cent at 95% accuracy or above, and one 80 per cent at 95% accuracy or above). This September 30 Open Court score was comparable to the best European phonic scores.

Comments made to me by the second-grade teacher and the reading specialist in this school are interesting, however, to demonstrate how American teachers have been brainwashed into believing in the sight-word approach. These second-grade Open Court children that I tested on September 30 were far, far above any sight-word class I had ever received at third grade in the thirteen years that I taught third-grade in an upper-middle income suburban school. My third-grade children had been trained in the first and second grades in standard sight-word texts (largely Scott, Foresman and Ginn). I once had a top-ability homogeneously grouped third grade class. Yet they were not so good at the beginning of third grade as this September 30 second grade class, having been given the typical sight-word basal reader approach before reaching third grade. Most could not decode even simple words if they did not already "know" them as sight words. Yet this second-grade, Open Court teacher was not at all impressed with her fantastically high-scoring class! Instead, she said she saw a "need" in this group for sight- words, and that children who were "bottom" in this second grade class "were just lost for another year."

Yet none of the children in her class had failed the oral accuracy test, and so would have been far above the "bottom" in any other second grade class in America! She said she approved of the phonic section in the first six months of Open Court, but said there was a "need" for "sight."

Her remarks reflected increased expectations. For all their wonderful achievement, these children were still only beginning readers, and, as a group, should not have been expected to read like upper graders. The children who were in the "bottom" portion of this high-scoring group would appear very weak compared to the children who were in the "top" of this high-scoring group.

What this second-grade teacher could not see was that these "bottom" children were actually the "average" children in other classes. As all teachers know, it is the "bottom" children who take the lion's share of a teacher's effort in any program. Raising the achievement level of any group does not automatically remove the "bottom" or difficult-toteach layer, however. Not one of her "bottom" children in this class of 23 children failed this test after only three weeks and two days of second grade, but, as is discussed later, in January almost half-way through second-grade, 25% of the 177 sight-word pupils that I tested failed the test, scoring below 90%, and 15% even scored below 85%!

A below-90%-fail on a context test of high-frequency-words, where "omissions" are read by the examiner to the child which helps him to guess the following words, really MEANS fail. Such children might score as low as 20% on a straight word list at the same grade level, where there is no context to help them guess words. That means, however, that three months later, one out of every four sight-word-trained second-grade children failed this test which NONE of this phonically-trained second grade class failed. Yet its second-grade teacher said she saw a "need" for sight words!

Another second-grade class in this same building, U. S. Class 23, presumably also with higher intelligence if the school as a whole was somewhat above average, was tested by me in January. They had the Houghton Mifflin program in first grade. This Houghton Mifflin second-grade class was almost next door to the Open Court second grade class, but the Open Court second grade teacher was unaware that the Houghton Mifflin class had a decoding problem which her class did not, which decoding problem showed up on the January testing.

In her manner and in her tone, the second-grade Houghton Mifflin teacher showed her low opinion of Open Court, just as the Open Court second-grade teacher had done. The Houghton Mifflin second-grade teacher appeared very content with the Houghton Mifflin program, but she certainly should not have been. That can be demonstrated by the following anecdote, as well as by her January second-grade Houghton Mifflin oral reading accuracy scores which were far lower than the September second-grade Open Court oral reading accuracy scores.

One of the Houghton-Mifflin-trained girls in her second grade class taking the high-frequency-word oral test scored at 99 per cent on oral reading accuracy and 80% on comprehension. To the uninitiated, such scores might reflect well on the sight-word plus context-guessing and jig-saw-puzzle-phonics Houghton Mifflin program. I rated Houghton Mifflin Code 3, instead of Code 10 like the Open Court phonics program. Yet the uninitiated do not understand about high-frequency sight words and context-guessing, which makes it possible for most sight-word trained children to pass the easy oral test I was using. The high-frequency-sight-word, context-guessing approach can produce students who are actually illiterate, in the true meaning of the word, "illiterate," and yet they give the illusion of "reading" when they are reading materials composed mostly of sight-words they have "learned."

That same little sight-word-trained girl, who had such "high" scores, was wearing a shirt when I tested her which had a "fun" design, a word printed over and over on it in different positions. I asked that little second-grader to read the word that had been printed, over and over, on her very own shirt, which shirt she had been wearing all day long, and which she probably had worn on many other days as well. She told me the word was "Australia." It was not. The word was, "outrageous."

That high-scoring Houghton Mifflin student was "illiterate," in the true meaning of the word, "illiterate," which means without a functioning knowledge of the letters. Her letter ignorance made her incapable of reading even the beginning syllable, "out" of "outrageous", because she had not, <u>even by mid-second-grade,</u> been taught the very commonly occurring vowel letter sounds, "ou" of "out" and "au" of Australia.

The Open Court second-grade teacher in this school made a comment like those I had heard in the first Open Court school, that the readability of the books was far above the abilities of some children. She also felt the program had a certain amount of "snob" appeal, since the editorial advisory board included well-known names like Professor Jacques Barzun and Clifton Fadiman.

The learning disabilities specialist, who had joined in our conversation, complained that two fifth graders in the school, who had learned by Open Court, were word-by-word readers. In this school, with two fifth grades containing probably over 50 children, the fact that two of those 50 fifth-graders read in a less-than-perfect, staccato fashion, is not surprising. In the learning of anything, not ALL will achieve perfection. In contrast to the Open Court program, it is a statistical fact that sight-word programs produce a very large proportion of fifth graders who cannot read anywhere near grade level. At least these two bottom-achieving Open Court fifth-grade children could READ all the words, while the far larger bottom portion of sight-word fifth-grade classes cannot!

What I found particularly interesting from these conversations, however, was that neither woman could deny that the Open Court phonics program in the first six months of first grade was very successful.

Here are some excerpts from the Open Court teacher's guide on the program's philosophy in this six-month period:

> "The basic approach during the first semester of the first grade is multisensory. As each new sound is introduced, the child says, sees and writes it. As these activities reinforce each other, the child becomes aware of a dramatic increase in his ability.... He is not asked to learn and apply dozens of rules but discovers inductively the basic relationships of his language.... (The child has) blending (and) 43 main sounds by midyear. Near the end, a number of irregular spelling patterns are introduced as preparation for (the next book) 1:2.... This has a systematic dictation (and) 12 review sessions...."

The third school I saw using Open Court had two second grades in which I tested, but I observed in only one first- grade. The first-grade class was organized in straight rows. The room was in marked contrast to the "open-class" atmosphere of the last Open Court first-grade I had visited. Although many plants were on the window sill, which was a pleasant touch, there was no sign of any materials for children to use for individual work. On the blackboard was the following:

> "It is a cloudy day. It is October 12. It is Wednesday."

The sentences were followed by a smile-face drawing. These sentences, with complex phonetic elements after only a month in school, were apparently meant for the children to copy. The use of such sentences, either for reading or copying, certainly did not fit Open Court philosophy of not using any letters until their sounds have been taught. These sentences had phonetic elements that had not been covered by their program to date.

An Open Court chart was on the wall of the room, and a bedspread was on the back table, probably for the group tactile work, the tracing of letters that I had seen in the second Open Court school. The bulletin boards were attractive, but it is my personal bias that attractive classroom bulletin boards, so loved by school administrators, receive very little attention or interest from the students for whom they are presumably designed.

Taken as a whole, this room had very much of the formal atmosphere of the room in which I started first grade back in September, 1931. As I sat in the back of the room, I saw that the children had very little in their desks, such as individual sets of Cuisenaire rods, paper-cutting scissors, etc. My own preference is for a totally different teaching style than that followed in this bare room, but I know that all teaching styles can work if they are handled properly. At least this teacher did have the Open Court phonics program to give to the children, and I found later when I tested the second grades that it was all that was necessary to get them to learn decoding skills, as they scored very well indeed.

This teacher did have a very nice manner. She began reading a story, as part of the Open Court training in listening skills. While she was reading, nothing was on the children's desks.

The teacher had apparently covered lesson 7 of 24 lessons in the first book, which means the class was probably working on lesson 8, page 29, of the 24 lessons in this book of 97 pages. If so, she had introduced m, long e, s, ee, t, ea, h, w, f, th, l, d, r, z, s, long i and long y.

The teacher went through a game with the children during the reading, and it was evident that the children were enjoying themselves very much. The story the teacher was reading concerned activities in a sequence. A child took his bath, used his towel, etc. The story was read completely once, and then reread multiple times with various omissions or additions. The children were to listen to find if something had been left out or added in each retelling, The children did this whole-class listening activity very well. They seemed to enjoy each altered retelling of the story. She then asked questions, such as:

"What would happen then?"

That question concerned a retelling of the story when the child got into the tub without having taken off his pajamas. The children had to make judgments on the effects of the various omissions. The teacher was doing a good job getting responses from the children, and they seemed contented and interested.

After the story-telling, the teacher reviewed at the board the rules for "a" and "i", and the "i" sound for "y." She wrote the following on the board, which was part of lesson 8, the vowel pattern "i_e." The children were to build words by adding missing letters: "wi__e," etc. On that one, she started with "w," blended with "wi," added "fc" making "wife," and asked, "What is a wife? Use it in a sentence."

Then, "wi" again, adding "de" for "wide." The class did the blending aloud. Then "wi" plus "se" for "wise." She said, "Is this s pronounced 'ss' or 'zz'?"

The children decided on the "zz" sound. She asked someone to use it in a sentence, and the child said, "My father is very wise."

Then, pointing to the three words written on the board (wife, wide, wise), she said, "Someone read that whole line for us."

The teacher then started with a new initial blend, "si_e." The class inserted "z" for size. She ran her hand under the word as a child read "size." She asked the children to use the word in a sentence.

The teacher then asked a boy to sound out a new word, "smile." It was done slowly, "sss," "sm," "smi," "smile." The teacher then asked to have it used in a sentence.

Most of the children seemed to understand this phonics lesson right away. One child, however, was having great difficulty with language. He seemed to have no idea of the structure of language. In using a sentence for smiles, he gave a sentence structure which had no meaning, and he had been having obvious trouble before this. This pointed up again the need for much more readiness work at the beginning of first grade than is provided by programs, good as they are, like Open Court and Lippincott.

Children need great training in auditory discrimination and language development before they formally start reading instruction. A little overlearning on the part of the faster children in the areas of auditory discrimination and language development in the first few months of first grade will not hurt them, but underlearning on the part of the slower children is disastrous. If this child had been given greater opportunity in class to listen to tapes of nursery rhymes and little stories, as in Moffett's Interaction Level l, and to use flannelboard figures to construct and tell stories to his classmates as are available with Breakthrough and other programs, and if there were much class discussion and sharing of experiences as in Pas a Pas sur le Chemin a Lire, the Quimper program, where a child's ideas are listened to, more improvement might have been made in his language skills, at least enough so that he would realize how to use a given word in a meaningful context.

I remember a little boy in one of my first grade classes who came from a family in which verbal development was very much below average, as I knew from having taught two older children in the family. I was reasonably certain, from my contact with the mother, that this was a family in which bedtime stories and nursery rhymes were not part of the background. Yet, in first grade, he had the opportunity to listen to the Moffett tapes alone if he chose them as part of his "work." He consistently chose the nursery rhymes, and I can still see his face light up with pleasure as he listened and as he subconsciously absorbed the structure of our language, the whole purpose of the Moffett tapes. Brighter children were not held back by this approach. They could choose more difficult tapes as part of their "work" and did so.

On the board in this Open Court classroom was an assignment for the children, possibly to copy.

1. We ride.
2. He rides.
3. He hides the meat.
4. Hide these seeds.
5. He rides three miles.
6. Lee sees the sea weed.
7. I feel the heat.

Page 32 in the Open Court book used many of the words in today's lesson.

The first real story in the Open Court book occurred on page 51, lesson 14, not long after this. The final story in the book, page 95, showed that real stories can be written with a phonics method like Open Court very early in first grade.

Lippincott introduces 2,000 words in its first-grade program, in sharp contrast to sight-word basal reader first- grade programs, some of which introduce as little as 325 words in the first grade. But, more importantly, the sight-word basal readers do not prepare children to decode words other than the bare 325 or so. Yet Lippincott and Open Court prepare children to decode virtually any word in the language - or in any language written with the alphabet, for that matter!

This first-grade teacher said she liked the Open Court program. She said the children had trouble catching on at first, but then "it comes." The ability level of her group was, she felt, perhaps a little above average. It was her first year teaching first grade, but she felt she had gotten good results. She had 22 children in her first-grade class.

After lunch, I tested one of the second-grade classes, U. S. Class 6, and in January I tested the other second grade, U. S. Class 13. The two former first grades had been shuffled together before being set up as two second-grade classes. I was told that these present second-graders had their teachers leave in the middle of the year when they were in first grade, one first-grade teacher leaving in January and the other about April. I had been told this had affected the classes' achievement. Of course, this normally might well have been the case. Yet I could not tell it from the tests. I have been told that the Open Court program teaches the phonetic part of its program almost completely by Christmas, and these former first-grade teachers had not left until January. Apparently, the classes had learned to read very well by January when the first of their teachers left, since both classes scored very high on accuracy compared to sight-word programs, as shown by their scores in the appendix, identified as U.S. 6 and U. S. 13.

It is interesting that in this school they had considered eight or nine retentions the previous year in these classes, but made only one from both classes. These possible "retentions" and one who was repeating second grade scored very well on my test, since only three failed in October, which was very early in the year, and none failed in January.

The upper classes in this school seemed far more informal, and many were engaged in class discussions. At the second-grade level, however, as at the first, the classes seemed to be very formally run and talking was apparently not permitted.

Economy

U. S. 2 was a classroom using the Economy program, Keys to Reading. Economy claims to be an analytic phonics program, but makes heavy use of sight words as well, for which reason I rate it lower at Code 7. Economy states, "Rather than delay attention to the critical discrimination skills until a sizable group of sight words has been memorized, as many other basal reading series do, or delay attention to reading for meaning, as some linguistic programs do, Keys to Reading employees a meaning discrimination approach."

Economy considers that decoding and reading for meaning are interrelated skills. Experience chart stories are given at the first-grade level, but their use is only meant to help children to associate meaning with printed symbols. No effort is made to teach sight words at this beginning stage. This is then followed by the first preprimer, which begins with the study of the long and then the short vowels, illustrated in words. Yet, again, the word is not to be remembered but only used to demonstrate the sound. The text stated:

> "Pupils typically have their greatest difficulty in mastering vowel sounds in reading programs in which consonant sounds are taught first and specific attention to vowel sounds is delayed."

To this, I say, "Amen!" If children are not taught vowels in first grade, I have found it is exceedingly difficult ever to teach them properly at the higher grades.

This first preprimer, Pug, covers the long and short vowels first, and then all the letters of the alphabet, in which the sound of the letter is shown in isolation. The children learn the sound of the letter from the whole word. The text also covers "qu," "th," and the blends, "st," "fr," and "pl." It also includes, however, some irregularly spelled words as sight words, which practice would be better delayed until later, and even then these irregular words should be taught by focusing on the phonic elements in them which are regular, and consciously noting to what degree they differ from the sound of the word when it is spoken.

The Economy preprimer is followed by two more preprimers, and then a primer and first book, which means six books are to be covered in first grade.

The Economy first-grade in school U. S. 2 had a fine, organized teacher. She had spent much of her own time accumulating interesting materials for her classroom, asking for any that were in storage and unused which she could adapt for her class. She had also, I gathered, gone out herself and gotten the Economy primers to replace the Scott, Foresman series with which she had been dissatisfied. Economy, of course, is very, very much more phonically oriented than Scott,

Foresman, despite it use of some sight words. Its emphasis on "reading for meaning" does not really separate it completely from programs such as Open Court and Lippincott, because they also "read for meaning" from the first, as I believe my notes show.

Last year, this teacher's class had had Scott, Foresman, however, through December. The bottom one-third, whom she considered unable to succeed in Scott, Foresman, she started with Economy in January. The rest of the class she had do the Economy program in April, after they finished Scott, Foresman. This means that the whole class had exposure to the Economy decoding approach, although the scores are very much diluted by the 2/3 who had Scott, Foresman for most of the year. However, it is the bottom 1/3 which produces failing scores in every program, so I felt it was possible to include this program under the phonics category since it was the critical bottom 1/3 which had learned to read with Economy (and the other 2/3 had the decoding skills of Economy taught to them as well, although later).

This teacher had 28 children in her classroom this year, and showed a very easy manner with the children, as well as being extremely competent and organized. She permitted the children to talk quietly. Much use was made of tapes for reading stories. She had a program, I believe named Spoken Arts, which was used with head phones. She said, "I do not care what they do as long as it deals with words and letters."

This Economy teacher had the children read an experience chart from the board and reminded them, "Remember, today is Tuesday and not Monday."

Monday had been the official observance of Columbus Day. On the blackboard was written, "October 11. John's baby brother Michael came on Sunday. He was 9 pounds."

The children copied this on a paper. She said to them, "What are you going to do after the chart?"

Five children decided to use the blackboard to write words from Pug. Others decided to use tapes, the record player, or books. She said, "You make up your mind what you are going to do - and do it well."

I thought to myself, "Nice!" This was a wonderful classroom. She said, concerning the materials from which the children could select their tasks, that she would put more things out for them to choose from later. The class was arranged in desks facing front, but it was still more of an Open Classroom atmosphere with its pupil selection of tasks from a list of possibilities.

The middle group was working on page 10 of Pug, the first preprimer, which concerned short "o" words. This would be the 9th instructional plan for the teacher in this book, and the children in this middle group had covered five long vowels, plus the double "o" sound in food, and one short vowel. The teacher read a story to this group and then worked with short "o" words such as "clock," "sock," "box". The children gave examples of short "o" words, and used them in sentences. This was obviously auditory discrimination of the short "o" sound.

The top group in the room had reached page 45, covering 18 letters of 26 in the alphabet. On the section entitled, "We Work With Words," they could sound them out fairly well. They knew the short vowel sounds. On the section, "Word Analysis - Do You Know the Words?", I did not see any real application of rules, just "Do you see the long sound?"

The children simply repeated these words after the teacher. Then they read the 14-word story on page 47 together with her, out loud. By October 11, this top group, after 5 weeks in school, had 18 of the 26 letters. This compared to Germany's Bunte Fibel which, after 7 weeks, had covered only 4 to 7 letters (for the whole class), and Sweden, where the best-scoring school had covered only eight letters and blending in the Nu Laser book after 10 weeks in school. Furthermore, the Swedish children are a year older in first grade than American children. This, of course, was also for the whole class, while the Economy group only had the top children covering 18 letters, and the middle group still on the five vowels. Nevertheless, the Economy program shared the greater speed of the Lippincott and Open Court programs, differing from some of the European programs which are slower. In my judgment, the slower pacer of the European programs is far better, since far fewer of the weaker children fall behind when the pace is slower, and nothing at all is lost by taking more time. Does it really matter if children learn to read by June of first grade, instead of by December, or by February?

When I tested the second-grade class which had Economy last year (and the top two-thirds who had also had Scott, Foresman), they did very well indeed. Their second-grade teacher said the group was also bright in other areas as well, such as math. They scored very well for October, and very well in relation to other phonics classes. Their scores are reported in the Appendix.

I visited one other school, U. S. 10, where Economy was being used in first grade in four classes. The staff were very pleased with the program. Previously, they had Scott, Foresman. However, this school had a very recent and very large foreign population, accounting for almost one-third of the first and second-grade enrollment. When I gave my test to a second-grade, there was no way I could separate the non-English speaking children from the group. I realized how bad the language problem was only after I was giving the test, although I had been warned that it existed. One child, who scored only 26% accuracy on the test, was one of those who could not tell me what the word "spot" meant when I asked (and the word is in the oral test). I asked him what "color" meant. He could not answer. I said, "Show me a color," and he just stared. I said, "Can you find a color here" and I pointed to the print on my dress. He continued to stare. It was evident the boy could not understand English.

In a German language school like the first grades in Luxembourg, it is possible for a child not speaking German to learn to read it, because German is so phonetically written. Yet English, unlike German, has many non-phonetic elements in its highest frequency, constantly recurring words. Therefore, children who do not have at least a fair understanding of English will have great difficulty learning to read English. Because of the large number of non-English speaking first-graders in this school, I omitted its scores from my tabulations because they reflected a language problem, not a decoding problem.

Nevertheless, this was a very interesting school. It was in a very old building, immaculate as a battleship, and was run just as efficiently. As soon as I came in the front door, I could almost hear all the wheels turning on their well oiled axles.

The children in the first class I visited sat up straight, proud to be important first graders and proud to be in the class. The reason for the obviously high morale became evident when I talked to the class's very interesting teacher. She said she had been a principal and was not a young woman, but said she had missed the classroom and had chosen to return to it. She had this class "in the palm of her hand." The room had very little on the bulletin boards. This teacher/ ex-principal said she could not be bothered with that kind of thing early in the year, as she was too busy working with the children. It made sense to me!

She had the children giving examples of short vowel words, with initial letters from the children's own names. Then she drilled on the words as sight words, but only after working them out phonetically. Each child had at his desk little boxes, one a "number builder" and the other a "word builder," nice, concrete materials with which to work. The teacher/ex-principal said she had a free-play period later in the day, at which time the children could write on the board and play games. These were lucky children to have this exceptional woman as a teacher!

The other first grades in the building were also very well run, but, since I am not including the test scores for this building, I will not report on their programs, except to say that they were following the Economy program. One teacher, however, who was experienced and competent, said, "Not every child can learn phonically." Yet, according to the psychiatrist/medical doctor/reading authority, Hilde Mosse, the only children who cannot learn to read phonically are aphasic children whose disability is in Broca's area, the sound-processing area of the brain. Since such disabled children are unable to deal with "sound" at all, they are therefore forced to learn by picture meaning. Yet even deaf children, if they have no such Broca's area disability, learn to read best by phonics!

The teacher who was convinced that "Not every child can learn phonically," had the only first-grade room in the building where I saw any work on sight words. She was drilling the children on the names for the colors with a straight sight-word approach, as the children came to the board and cupped the words with their hands. She said, for instance, "Make a picture frame around brown."

This otherwise highly competent teacher had probably spent many hours reading educational journals and did not know - and would be highly insulted if it were said to her - that she had been brainwashed by such journals and by her teacher training courses.

Alpha One Letter People

The Alpha One Letter People phonics program, Code 10, which I also tested, differed from the other American programs in one important aspect. It was much, much slower in its introduction of phonic elements, in its introduction of blending, and in the beginning of actual context reading.

The Alpha One program was written by Elaine Reiss and Rita Friedman, who had both been teachers in Westchester County, New York. In 1979, the Alpha One program was published by Arista Corporation, Concord, California, but publishers of the program have changed several times. (The Alpha One reading workbook, Chatterbook, which had been an excellent Code 10 workbook originally, deteriorated so badly in later editions under other publishers that it qualified as sight-word material.)

The Alpha One program was one of the many fine American phonic programs developed by teachers in their own classrooms. It shared the charm of the French experience chart programs which I saw, because it was worked out by actual teachers to use with real children, and, as a result, it WORKED!

The program began as Alpha Time in kindergarten. Children may not have learned all the letters by the beginning of first grade, despite having been taught them in kindergarten, so letters must be reviewed in first grade. In the Alpha program, in kindergarten and first grade, the letters of the alphabet are presented as real people. The consonants are boys and the vowels girls. In kindergarten, these letter people appear as large, inflatable balloons, about two feet high. In first grade, they are shown as colorful posters. However, the letter people are not proper, dull personalities but, in the stories told about them to teach phonics, are, instead, difficult, comical, or sometimes even naughty ones whom the children find much more interesting than the "proper" kind.

Mr. F is Mr. Funny Feet, and he has enormous, colorful polka-dotted feet. Mr. B is Mr. Beautiful Buttons, and he is covered all over, naturally, with buttons. Mr. M, the first letter introduced, on which elaborate work is done for two weeks with auditory and visual discrimination activities, is Mr. Munching Mouth. He is treated as very real by the little ones. At snack time, they sometimes go over to "feed" their snack to Mr. Munching Mouth, and then rush to the teacher, complaining, "Mr. M ate all my snack!"

The letters are introduced very slowly at first in this program, to be sure that children are really developing the auditory and visual discrimination of letters on which real reading is based. Class games, many of them in small groups, and lessons take place on the M sound in beginning, medial and terminal position for about two weeks. This is followed by such work on other letters, the period of study for each letter gradually decreasing. Much art work is done on each letter. Button games and art collages of buttons are prescribed when Mr. B, Beautiful Buttons is being "studied." When Mr. H, Horrible Hair, is being covered, fanciful Easter hats are made by the children at the art table as independent work. When Mr. D, or Delicious Doughnuts is covered, it is time for the teacher to treat the class to doughnuts.

The children go home bursting to tell their parents of the letter people's activities. One father confided to his wife that he was delighted that their daughter was enjoying school, but was nevertheless so sick of Mr. Munching Mouth's stupid activities that if he could meet him, he "would like to punch him in the mouth." The program was meant to please the daughter, however, and not the father.

The program avoids the difficulty of teaching children which letters are "vowel" letters, because all the children have to remember is whether a letter is a "boy" (consonant) or a "girl"(vowel). All these letter people quickly become old friends to the children. Their names, of course, incorporate their letter sounds, and are used to "test" whether a spoken word begins with their sound: "Does "feel" begin with the same sound as Mr. F's name, Funny Feet?" This is auditory discrimination done with pleasure, zest, and most important of all, attention!

In November, "blending" of letter sounds begins. The children are taught "catching" (blending). If Miss A's sound is put with Mr. M's sound, the word "am" is made. At this point, a "word machine" appears in the program, to be "built" by the class, possibly from old boxes and tinfoil. If letters go through the word machine, they are supposed to make the "right" sound in the words they form. "Map," for instance, is a phonetically regular word. But, the children are told, sometimes letters run away from the machine and become "run-away" words (laugh, for instance) which words do not make the "right" sound. In the children's first book, such run-away words are shown circled, with legs on them!

This program also appears on a set of filmstrips with audio cassettes. I have used the filmstrips at the second- grade level to review phonics. The children love the characters, and the stories which are told to teach what are, actually, very dull rules from a child's point of view. But, when the child sees the phonic rule as growing from some argument between two colorful letter people, and the rules as the way they settled their differences, it is no longer dull!

At first grade, after much class practice, group lessons, and individualized games on blending, the first book, Alpha, begins about the end of November or early December, while the class still has to study many letters of the alphabet. No word is used in the book however, which is made of letters not studied to that point. The "stories" are geared to class introduction of new phonic elements.

After this first book is completed about January, the program rapidly picks up steam. The children rather quickly cover the second book and finish studying the more obscure of the phonic elements (ph, for instance) and rules of syllabication by about April. They are then free to work into any basal reading series.

The slow start of this program, however, intimidates many teachers, as, I suspect, does the individualized work and games. In other American phonic programs, for instance, the children are reading almost from the beginning week of school. In this program, they must wait almost until December before beginning the first reading book. The fact that Alpha One is eventually much faster than other programs does not lessen the reluctance of many teachers to try it because of its slow pace at the beginning. Recently, a woman told me of a first-grade teacher a few years ago (I do not know in what town) who was fired because parents felt she was not teaching reading quickly enough, and her class was "behind." Whether this story is true or not, this kind of parent pressure is felt by teachers and very few have the courage, unless they have strong administrative support, to try a slow-as-molasses program as Alpha One in the fall, even though they know it will pay off in the spring, and, obviously and more importantly, for the rest of the children's lives.

The Alpha One class which I tested at second grade had used the Houghton Mifflin primer and book one in the last part of first grade, but had continued all through first grade with a review of Alpha phonics. They had not used the Houghton Mifflin skill program at all, except for completing successfully most of the Houghton, Mifflin first-grade workbooks as independent work without teacher direction.

This Alpha One class was tested in September, and permission was obtained to retest again in January those children who scored below instructional level in September. This was useful to show the kind of reading improvement which might be expected from weaker readers in a phonics class. Improvement was marked. The statistics for the Alpha One class, U. S. 11, are shown in the appendix.

Initial Teaching Alphabet

One other program, the Initial Teaching Alphabet program, Code 7, was included in the phonics scores in this research. The Initial Teaching Alphabet is an expanded alphabet. Additional letters are added so that each of the 44 phonemes in English has a symbol of its own. This can put the learning of English on about the same footing as the learning of German, which uses an almost perfectly phonetic method of spelling.

However, just as in German, a "global" sight-word approach can be used, so that the emphasis is on whole words instead of phonemes. ITA children can be given whole words spelled in ITA letters without being taught the sounds of the ITA letters.

The ITA readers can therefore be taught as a phonic program or as a sight-word program. On a trip to England that some teachers from my school district, Wayne, New Jersey, made to visit English open classroom schools in 1971, at the time of Wayne's Open Classroom Project, an English first-grade teacher said to me, "The kindergarten teacher is using ITA to teach look-say!" That first-grade teacher was appalled, as she used the ITA edition printed in England to teach phonics. The point is, it is not the ITA system which teaches phonics but the teacher who is using that system!

The ITA American edition is arranged to be taught so that the sounds of the 44 ITA symbols are taught as letter sounds. The beginning text is very simple. The symbols introduced first are a, n, t, e, b, in that order. Available is an optional program to the standard Early to Read program, called the Easy to Read Sequence. Children who are having trouble for various reasons with the program after the first five letters are studied (for reasons such as lower intelligence or foreign language background) can be moved into the Easy to Read Sequence, which drills on sight words with special sight-word texts written in the 44 ITA characters. It continues to follow the ITA introduction of symbols in the Early to Read program. The 20 sight-word booklets in the Easy to Read Sequence are completed by the time the 23rd ITA symbol is studied and the children then go back into the regular Early to Read program for the remaining 21 symbols.

This regular program, Early to Read, although it systematically teaches letter-sound values, is not considered a blending synthetic phonics program. According to Jean Chall, in her book, Learning to Read, The Great Debate, page 354, the American ITA program uses visual analysis and substitution in decoding words, rather than sounding and blending. This, of course, is the jig-saw puzzle, whole-word phony phonics method of the sight-word basal readers. (If you know cup and bat, then the beginning sound of cup combined with the ending sound of bat make cat, so you can now read cat!)

Yet, even in the teacher's manual for Easy to Read, the sight-word slower-moving strand, there are on page 29 specific instructions for sounding and blending the new words, "Ann," and "Bess." The teacher is instructed to say to the children, "Who can sound out this word?" for both words. The teacher is also instructed, on page 11 of the teachers' guide of this short sight-word strand for slower children, to spend five or ten minutes, three to five times per week, to develop "auditory closure," in which she says a word, sound by sound, and the children must blend the sounds mentally to know what the word is, as in "Ben" or "desk."

The manual for Easy to Read does use visual analysis and substitution, however, as on page 38. (The known word "and" plus "st" makes "stand.") Yet most of the work in this "easy" sight-word strand is on straight sight-word recognition. However, it is evident that even in the temporary sight-word strand that sounding and blending is very much in use, so it is difficult to classify the total ITA program. The effect of the phonic spellings of the ITA words, plus the importance which the authors themselves attach to "auditory closure" (blending of sounds) and the specific instructions for blending certain words, even in the sight-word strand, identify it plainly as a phonics program, with both synthetic and analytic elements.

Each of the 44 symbols are introduced in My Alphabet Book, with each ITA character having a keyword (actually a sight word incorporating the sound).

Considering all these factors, I have coded ITA Code 7 on my global-phonics scale.

However, ITA's use of visual analysis and substitution removed the insurance against reversals in letters which is present in straight phonic blending programs. In analyzing and then substituting letters, the order of the letters can easily be reversed (i.e., spot, stop, sopt, pots, post, opts, ospt). I was to find when I tested an ITA class in October, 1977, which had 28 pupils, that 30% of the children made at least one reversal, which high percentage I attributed to ITA's visual analysis and substitution technique. In the United States from late September to mid October of 1977, 9% of phonically trained children tested made reversals, but 16% of sight-word trained children, despite the care that is usually taken in American sight-word programs to avoid the problem of reversals. In Europe in the last half of October and all of November, 1977, classes using predominantly phonics methods showed 6% reversals, but classes with considerably more global emphasis showed 19%.

One of the authors of the American ITA program, A. J. Mazurkiewicz, wrote a work on reading in which he discounted the values of the phonics rules which are normally taught in beginning reading in phonics programs. One of the rules, for instance, is that single vowels are short in most English words (as in cat) unless the vowel is followed by a single consonant and another vowel (as in local). Phonics proponents claim these rules work about 85% of the time, but with Mazurkiewicz's hair-splitting interpretation, he felt they work almost not at all. Phonics rules are not necessary in the beginning ITA readers since each symbol exactly matches the sound made in the word being spelled, but children transferring to books printed in regular letters in second grade are, I believe, faced with problems on vowel sounds without these rules. I have been teaching these rules to children for 16 years and have found them to be essential for children, unless children are going to be thrown back to guessing words from context and only some of the letters in the words.

The ITA program in America, Early to Read, should, however, be considered a phonics program. It is interesting that, on the USOE Gilmore oral test, the American ITA reader scored higher than the English Downing ITA reader. An exception was a program in which the American ITA reader was taught somewhat like a basal reader, with the class beginning with experience charts, and the lower part of the class using the English Downing readers. This mixed program was described as a "language arts approach," and this program scored quite low on the Gilmore compared to the phonics programs, which were the straight ITA and the Lippincott.

The ITA program which I visited was in a school building which was older, but extremely attractive. I was told that the children as a group were above average in ability. The first-grade room that I visited when I arrived was very cheerful. This was the only one of three United States first grades in which I saw the Unifix mathematics materials in use. The teacher had put out these varicolored interlocking plastic blocks, a grid to hold them, and the attachable caps giving numbers. She said she would put out more materials later. She also had a piece of equipment called a microfiche, on which she was running a class program under a grant, using films from which the children could read pictured stories on a screen (I assume with ITA print). It was obvious that talk was permitted in the room, and the children chatted freely among themselves, with a noise level which was very pleasant and in no way disagreeable.

On this date, October 14, the children had apparently covered some of the characters of the ITA expanded alphabet, which characters total 44. On one paper, I counted a child using six letters, the first six formally studied in the program: a, n, t, e, b, and s. The teacher had these characters read aloud in order, pointing to the pictures on the wall in ITA script as the children answered. Then she mixed them up, and they answered. Of course, in ITA script, when the children know these letter sounds, and the blending which the authors value, they ARE able to read anything printed in those letters!

In kindergarten, I was told that the children had cut out sound pictures, without reference to naming actual letters, but now they attached letters to these sounds. The children had little books in ITA script on their desks which they were trying to read by sounding out the words. The class was working on these activities as a whole group. The children also were working on lined papers, making three letter words, such as net, which would be synthetic phonics from these six letters written on their papers. For this work, the teacher said, "Stretch out the middle character," as in n e- e- e- t, in making words.

While I was there, the teacher showed a picture story on the microfiche to the children and discussed it with them while they sat on the rug. She was asking for language responses and thinking skills such as, "What is it?" and "How does the boy feel?"

Displayed in the room on this date, October 14, close to Halloween on October 30, was children's art work of ghosts made out of napkins and paper cups, with heads with painted features. Visible in the room were quite a few plants, a science table, a tape recorder, puzzle boards and several "activity centers," which she said the children could use when their written work was completed.

A substitute teacher was in the other first grade. It was a beautifully furnished room, with the children seated at tables instead of desks. On shelves for the use of the children were geometry materials such as the small parquetry wooden pieces and large parquetry pieces sold by Developmental Learning Materials, and a New York Times program by Dubnoff with materials such as spacial pattern board exercises and pattern cards. The room had a science center. Also in the room were the Scholastic company's story books and read-along records, and a record machine. In this room, like the other, were a microfiche, Unifix math materials, a filmstrip projector, and many plants. Also present was a Playschool magnet board with plastic alphabet letters, an aquarium, an easel used for display purposes, and an electrical practice machine with pegs in it which lit up for correct answers. This was, without a doubt, the best outfitted school that I had seen in the United States.

The ITA reading workbooks were in this room, so I assume they were in the other room, as well.

The second-grade teachers whose combined class that I tested (two teachers handled it in the morning with each half in separate rooms, and one teacher handled the whole class in one room in the afternoon) said that the ITA program gave children a love of reading and facility in writing.

This second-grade room which I saw in the afternoon was also a semi-open classroom type of atmosphere, with very interesting materials. The class scored well for the fall, comparable to other phonics programs, and higher than sight-word programs, as shown in the table for this ITA class.

Sight-Word Groups:

Houghton, Mifflin

In my visits to schools in the United States, I saw no schools which were running the old sight-word programs of the 1940's, 1950's and early 1960's, such as the "Dick and Jane" Scott, Foresman, or the Ginn readers of the period. Those two series had accounted for about eighty per cent of textbook sales as late as the early 1960's, according to Jean Chall in her 1967 book Learning to Read, The Great Debate. The aborted phonics revolution begun by Rudolf Flesch in 1955 had, at least, resulted in modifications in the old sight-word programs. At least in the case of the Houghton, Mifflin program, it had resulted in much more "incidental phonics."

My choices of schools in the United States were largely by chance (except that I was denied permission to test in two suburban New Jersey towns, Hasbrouck Heights and Clifton, which I believe may have been using sight-word programs at the time). Therefore, my encountering phonics or sight-word programs was largely by chance. As stated, the phonics programs I observed and tested were Lippincott, Open Court, Economy, Alpha, ITA and "teacher phonics". I think it is probable that these were the fairly widespread phonics programs since these were the ones which turned up by chance in my sampling, and they ranged from Code 7 to Code 10.

In the sight-word classes, I ran into Scott, Foresman Systems, Code 2, and Houghton, Mifflin's Reading for Meaning, Code 3. Again, I think this probably indicates that the use of these two phonics-assisted sight-word programs may have been fairly widespread. However, a school in which the first-grade teacher was using Economy by her own choice later had to change to Ginn, which I would also describe as a phonics-assisted sight-word program, Code 2. This change came about by - of all things! - a vote by the teachers from all grade levels, (not just the first-grade level) after reviewing many texts. Concerning that teacher-choice of Ginn, in 1986, for six months after I retired, I used a 1980's version of the newer Ginn in second and third grades in a private school. It had enormously time-consuming, exquisitely boring "workbooks", which could turn all but the most dedicated children against the idea of reading for pleasure. When I examined the first-grade materials, I found them to be sight-word materials with "incidental" phonics - about Code 2.

Houghton, Mifflin also published the Moffett Interaction Literacy Program, an elaborate phonics program using film cassettes, games, etc., suitable for individualized classrooms, where it meshed very well with the extraordinary Moffett Interaction task cards, books, tapes and games, a language arts program using art activities, the making of books, research, and many other approaches. Before I retired, I was fortunate enough to have the excellent Moffett Interaction language arts program (but not the phonics program) in my own public school classroom.

But publishing companies can market many different programs. While the Houghton, Mifflin Moffett literacy program reportedly has elaborate phonic blending materials (although I have not seen them myself and only know of them from its literature), the Moffett literacy program has no connection with the other Houghton, Mifflin reading program, a basal reader series, Reading for Meaning, with Paul McKee as senior author of the staff.

Dr. McKee was reported to have contacted the Reading Reform Foundation, which published in the 1970's a list of readers which were phonics-oriented. McKee was reported to have asked why his series was not included on the list, so, as an author, he presumably felt that he had a phonics series. Jean Chall, in her book, Learning to Read, The Great Debate, published in 1967, had a footnote to the effect that the series, Houghton, Mifflin Reading for Meaning, by McKee et al, published in 1963, did differ from other basals in that it had a stronger phonic emphasis at the beginning. A reading specialist, in the course of my research, referred to this series as "very phonic."

It was, of course, far more phonic than the books Jean Chall referred to in her study, but it was not a phonic series like Lippincott and Open Court (and most of the European phonic programs). The simplest test for any phonics series is whether or not it teaches, in the first half of first grade, the sounds of letters, with an emphasis on the vowels, and how to blend those sounds, and only those known sounds, into words.

Houghton, Mifflin's first grade program had three pre-primer pamphlets, a primer which was the Honeycomb hard-cover book, Level 1-1, and the Cloverleaf hard-cover book, Level 1-2. Cloverleaf was originally meant to be used in the last part of first grade, but was also supposed to be used at beginning second grade for slower children. (After the series had been in print for a while, the Cloverleaf book was officially moved to second grade, confirming that most sight-word trained first-graders could not handle it. Yet all but three or four of my phonically taught first graders would finish reading Cloverleaf, with ease, by about Easter of first grade.) The Houghton, Mifflin program specifically stated in its teacher's guide to Cloverleaf (page 1020) that it was NOT a sounding-and-blending program, by remarking:

> "We do not want to teach students to 'sound out' or 'puzzle out' the pronunciations of words in their reading matter."

There cannot be any doubt about the meaning of that statement! To emphasize that fact, the teachers' guide stated further that it wanted children to "decode" words by using three "clues:"

1. The meaning of the text.
2. The grammatical structure of the text.
3. Letter-to-sound association for the unknown word.

The first two items, of course, mean the use of context in what is being read, as in "Mary had a little ———." The guide went on to say, however, that "usually" one or more of the letter-sound associations were necessary to identify the word positively. Their use of the word, "usually," of course, meant that some words could be "decoded" without ANY reference to their phonic elements.

Vowels were not taught in the Houghton, Mifflin program until the Cloverleaf book, which book was often not covered by some children until the beginning of second grade. The omission of vowels was because the Houghton, Mifflin program guide claimed that vowels in English are too inconsistent to be dependable "clues". To support this extraordinary statement, the guide cited "o" words like no, to, gone, done, move, love, roll, doll, come, and home.

Yet the vast majority of English vowel spellings are completely regular and predictable, and surely the authors of the Houghton, Mifflin McKee program must have known that. For them to string rare "exceptions" together with regular spellings, as shown above, and then to claim there is therefore a massive problem, was inexcusably misleading. Some of the "o" words above are phonically completely regular and easily taught, but even the others fall into special vowel categories which can also be easily taught in any well organized phonic program. First graders learn to handle English vowel spellings with ease - both the regular vowels and the irregular ones - when they are taught to read by properly organized phonics programs, which the Houghton, Mifflin McKee program clearly was not.

In the course of first grade, the Houghton, Mifflin McKee basal series did teach so-called "phonograms" such as "et" in the word "get." This was really teaching jig-saw puzzle, whole-word phony phonics, in which whole words were pulled apart into pieces and then the piece from one whole word was put together with a piece from another whole word to form a third word. This so-called "phonogram" which was derived from the word, "get," did not teach the short letter sound for "e", and the consonant sound, "t." The detached segment, "et," remained in the child's mind as a part of a whole, meaning-bearing word and was not perceived as a blend of two isolated letter sounds. I found, when teaching second-grade, that children who had been taught the Houghton, Mifflin McKee way in first grade were incapable of giving in isolation the sounds of the short vowels, for the simple reason that children do not learn the short- vowel sounds from the so-called short-vowel "phonograms." When the Houghton, Mifflin McKee program finally made some attempt to teach short vowels in isolation at the Cloverleaf level at the end of first grade, it was too little, too late.

As proof for that statement, I tested 93 Houghton, Mifflin McKee children in one large school. Of these second graders, in January of second grade in 1978, one-third could not read the word "leg" in a story context, which context should at least have suggested the word's meaning. "Leg" is not a high frequency word, so it probably would not have been familiar to the children from the controlled vocabulary basal readers that they read. The fact that so many children missed the word, "leg,", despite the help that the context must have given others in guessing it, rather clearly shows that the pupils could not isolate the "e" sound from "et" that they had been taught at great length, and apply it to the new "phonogram," "eg."

The Houghton, Mifflin McKee program did, however, teach consonant sounds in the readiness book, Getting Reading to Read at kindergarten, and gave heavy drill on them, so the children by second grade must have known the sounds of "l" and "g" in "leg." The problem clearly was with the short vowel sound, "e."

It was, however, not only that Houghton, Mifflin did not teach the vowels in isolation until the end of first (and then inadequately). That would not have been so bad, since they did teach the consonants and sounding in left-to-right order, and children might therefore have eventually inferred the vowel sounds from context. What I believe the Houghton, Mifflin program was actually doing was to teach children to disregard vowels, which might explain the extraordinary fact that 1/3 of the January of 2nd grade class whom I tested could not read "leg". The children missed it, even though they had been drilled on the phonogram "et" containing the short "e" sound, and other such phonograms, and had eventually even been directly (but poorly) taught the short "e" sound in late first or early second grade.

Before I explain how the Houghton, Mifflin McKee program effectively taught children to disregard vowels, I will describe its beginning program.

As mentioned previously, the program depends primarily on context for decoding, plus some of the consonants, but, to use context in reading requires the use of words, so of course it must introduce sight words from the very beginning, and it does. In the beginning preprimers are 16 high-frequency words, which are used with rebuses (picture words) to tell stories, and to introduce the new words to be decoded.

When the initial sight words are introduced in the first preprimer, the children are taught to look for letter-sound associations in a right to left order, but with NO attention to vowels unless they are at the beginning of the word. These high-frequency words, which have been shown to constitute 28 per cent of words in children's present textbooks through fourth grade, are:

a	and	go	he
I	in	is	it
not	on	she	the
to	we	will	you

Of course, Houghton, Mifflin is not alone in this use of high-frequency words in basal readers. As long ago as 1921, the famous psychologist, Edward L. Thorndike, prepared the

Teacher's Word Book, which was revised in 1931 to include the 20,000 commonest words, and in 1944 to include the commonest 30,000 words. With his initial Word Book in 1921, it became possible to construct children's readers which used words of the highest frequency. It was the intent also to inform teachers of which words were "worth" spending time teaching because they were commonly met, and which words could be more casually passed over. For those teachers like me, who think words are best "taught" by children's sounding them out phonically, and figuring out their meaning from context, the book lacks any utility whatsoever in the teaching of beginning reading. (For those learning foreign languages, however, it has remarkable worth.)

The Ladybird reading series in England is based on research there which showed that some 250 words comprise more than 50 per cent of normally spoken and written material. The idea, and it is seductive, is that if children are "taught" to "read" these high frequency words primarily by sight, it enormously reduces the problems in beginning reading. This seductive idea has this failing: If children know most of the words in their books by sight initially, how much practice can they get in developing habits of systematic sounding-and-blending phonics so that they can eventually use these habits automatically?

This poses no problem for a reading program which has the philosophy of Houghton, Mifflin, however. They do not INTEND to teach sounding-and-blending phonics, but the use of context (known sight words) and only SOME phonic elements in words to guess at new words. They are also teaching for meaning at the beginning stages, necessary if context is to be used for word identification.

The Houghton, Mifflin McKee program, as mentioned, delayed the teaching of the five vowels, a, e, i, o, and u (both long and short) until the Cloverleaf book (end of first or beginning of second grade), and even at that level the vowels were poorly taught. However, in introducing the first 16 high-frequency words in the readiness book, they did mention the sounds of vowels in those of the 16 words which began with vowels: a, and, I, in, is, it, on. That means they are teaching a short "u" correspondence for the article, "'a", which is a totally irregular phonic usage for the vowel, "a", and a short "a" vowel sound for "and,", which is regular, but with no explanation for the different sounds for the same vowel. They simply say to the children that in the word, "a", the sound they hear is one of the sounds for "a", and in the word "and", that is another sound for "a".

For the words, I, in, is, and it, they say each time that the beginning sound is "one of the sounds for the letter 'i'" but again with no explanation on the reason for "I" having a long sound and the others a short sound. They are all just "sounds for 'i'".

The program introduce the word "on" by saying that it begins with one of the sounds for "o" but in the other sight words which have "o" but not at the beginning, they make no reference to the "o" vowels whatever or give any explanation, despite the fact that all but one of them have a very different sound of "o": not, to, go, and you.

The vowel "u" is not taught, though it occurs, in an irregular form, at the end of the sight word, you.

Neither is the letter "e" specifically taught. None of the first 16 high-frequency words begin with the letter "e", so "e" is not mentioned at this readiness level, but the children certainly see it in the words which are taught: we, he, she, and the.

Phonics-trained children, however, are systematically taught that single vowels in the middle of words are "short" as in "get," but single vowels, in isolation at the end of words, are "long" (say their names) as in we, he, and she. Phonics-trained children are also told that the "e" at the end of "the" is irregular (the word should be pronounced "thuh" and not "thee".) Yet these words containing "e" are introduced to the sight-word-trained children with no mention of the sound of the "e". In the very next preprimer book, the children are introduced to the "et" phonogram in "get", but again no mention is made on why the "e" sound is so different in "get" compared to the sight words they have already memorized (we, he, she and the).

The incredible mishandling of the teaching of the simple five vowels, a, e, i, o, and u, in the first 16 words in Houghton Mifflin is utterly ridiculous. The sounds of the five vowels, long and short, have been taught from time immemorial almost at the very beginning of reading instruction, right after the whole alphabet. It is true that some rare children in recorded history had trouble learning the whole alphabet. However, the vowels were covered since ancient times right after the alphabet had been memorized, and, apparently, in all of recorded history, no one has ever written that children had any trouble learning the sounds of the five vowels, once they knew the alphabet. Yet, with the mishandling of the vowels in these first 16 words in the Houghton, Mifflin reading program, future trouble with the vowels is absolutely guaranteed.

The program does make the claim that children will frequently infer vowel sounds from the common "phonograms" which are eventually taught, but its authors appear oblivious to something else they are doing, which is a potent, "reverse," form of teaching of this very claim.

This is their "checking" system, where, over and over, they are showing children to disregard vowels. This checking system is used in teacher lessons, and can also be used in introduction of new words (although they recommend that children themselves use the clues when reading the actual text to figure out the new words, which clues include context and some of the consonants, and that the teacher not just read the new words to the child).

The teacher writes two "context" sentences on the board, one containing the new word, which two sentences provide a little story with meaning. The children are asked to read the sentences, and, using letter-sound associations for consonants in a left-to-right order, to use the meaning of the sentences to "snap" into mind a word that would make sense. After the children have given the correct answer, the teacher always asks two checking questions, one of a phonic nature, and the other of a context nature, implying, in the latter, that the phonic elements are similar to the word just worked out. For instance, for the word "get," she asks how they knew "get" was not "jump," and they are to respond that "jump" did not begin and end with the right sounds. Then she asks how they knew that "get" was not "goat". The children are to respond that "It did not make sense." The former question is their method of checking by phonics, and the latter is their method of checking by context.

What is appalling in the latter is that the teacher is telling the child, inferentially, that the letters he sees in front of him in the word "get" COULD be read as the sound, "goat," and only the context is keeping him from making this error!

In a later checking lesson, again with the word, "get," the teacher is to ask the child how he knew "get" was not "gate," suggesting AGAIN that the printed word "get" might have been read as "gate" except for the context!

This total disregard of vowel sounds is done over and over and over with different pairs of checking words (and so is the disregard of some of the internal consonants, because the program claims that only enough consonant sounds should be used as are necessary to make a context guess). The wrong word, which is spoken by the teacher in her context checking as being a word the child might have considered initially from its letters alone, often differs from the right word by its vowel sounds only. Yet no first grade child in a phonic program, at the same period in first grade, would be confused on the vowel sounds in the two words being compared.

The second preprimer has a list of these context sentences and checking words for new words introduced. It is interesting, when they are tabulated, to see how sounding-and-blending phonics is ignored in presenting children with words which they are to reject by context alone, with no reference to phonic differences. (Not shown are the words rejected by phonics because they make sense but are phonically totally wrong, since these words are always completely different phonically. For instance, when the word "get" was being checked, "goat" was rejected because it was wrong by "context" but "jump" was rejected because it was wrong by phonics, not beginning or ending with the right sounds).

Word Being Decoded	Context Checking Word
cat	cut
truck	trick
can	corn
see	so
come	came
stop	step
here	her
tiger	tire
where	when
it's	itch
TV	temper
rocket	rainbow
are	art
bus	boss
have	heavy
this	those
me	mean
tigers	tease
want	went
can't	cart
real	roll
gang	going

    The fact that a teacher would suggest to a child that these choices should be rejected by CONTEXT alone instead of by sounds is totally antagonistic to the philosophy of any sounding-and-blending program. Further, for a teacher to point to a word like "truck" and suggest it might be confused with the sound of "trick," to point to "stop" and suggest it might be confused with the sound of "step," to point to "here" and suggest it might be confused with "her" and to have these words rejected solely by context instead of by reference to their vowels is to teach the children that vowels can have hopelessly variant sounds. This sort of thing in the second preprimer only confirms what the children learned intuitively from the 16 words in the first pre-primer: vowels do not mean anything much.

    When the "et" phonogram is introduced in <u>Rockets,</u> the second preprimer, the word "yet" is written on the board in a sentence saying that a girl looked at the clock and said it was not time to go home "yet." The children are asked to decode the word, and then the checking procedure is given. They are asked how they knew it was not "now", to which they are to reply that "now" had the wrong letter sounds. They then are asked how they knew it was not "yacht" and they are to reply it would not have made sense. Again, they are implicitly taught that the "e" in "yet" is to be disregarded, by being given a checking word with a different vowel sound (actually short "o" in this irregular word). Then comes the phonogram lesson. The teacher writes "get" on the board and tells the children that they already know the word. She asks what letters they see that are the same as in "yet." The children say the words aloud and listen for the sounds that the two letters stand for in those words. She then tells them that when "e" and "t" come together at the end of a word they usually stand for the sounds heard in "yet" and "get." They then practice decoding, in the context of sentences, the new words "pet," "jet," "let," and "net."

Teaching children these phonograms in occasional lessons in no way counteracts the teaching by example far, far, more often with "checking" lessons and the high frequency words that vowels do not amount to much, and the children therefore often do not infer the vowel sound from the phonogram.

The children are eventually taught the vowel sounds, (but inadequately), as mentioned, in Cloverleaf, the "swing" book between first and second grade, after the readiness book, three preprimers and the primer.

The fact that the program is not systematically teaching sounding-and-blending phonics, which would demand the use of vowels, is shown by its philosophy expressed in a third-grade lesson, a year or more after the vowel sounds have supposedly been "taught." In the Panorama third- grade book, in a skill lesson on figuring out new words, the children are told that they can figure out new words by thinking what the other words are saying (context) and by the sounds for the consonant letters in left to right order. They are actually told that they will usually need to think of a sound for a vowel only when that vowel comes at the beginning of the word! They are to decide what word has consonant sounds in that order which would make sense with the other words. They are specifically told, in the word "pleasant," to think of the consonants in left-to-right order and that they should not have to try different sounds for "ea" or worry about the sound for the "a".

No doubt can exist about where this program stands: It is almost back in 800 B. C., before the vowels were added to the alphabet. Children being "taught" by this program are placed in the position of trying to read, "The cow jumped over the moon," as if it were written, "Th cw jmpd ovr th mn"

The problem with using only those letters to "decode" the printed sentence (as is recommended by the Houghton, Mifflin McKee program) is that they might just as well prompt a child to read, "The crow jumped over the man." That latter sentence is something very, very different in meaning from the printed sentence. However, that incorrect reading is actually is a much more "rational" choice (if the Houghton, Mifflin checking advice is used, "Does it make sense?") than the actual, correct reading: "The cow jumped over the moon."

It is no wonder that one-third of the 93 second-grade children in a school using this program could not read the word "leg" in January of second grade when I tested them!

This program also does "substitution" phonics of the kind common to most basal readers. The teacher, for instance, in Honeycomb, the primer, is told to print on the board words that are familiar to pupils, and then to substitute beginning or ending consonant or consonant clusters. This consonant substitution form of word attack, building on known sight words, is certainly not phonics in the sounding-and-blending sense.

In the Honeycomb primer guide (to be used in spring of first grade in most classes), children are given a skill lesson on the new word, "everything" in a written sentence. The teacher uses the "checking" questions again. She asks how they knew the new word, "everything," was not "games" in the written sentence, and the children are to respond that "games" has the wrong sounds (but obviously would have been a possibly correct context meaning). Then she asks how they knew it was not "evening" in the written sentence (a word which has some of the same letters as "everything") and the children are supposed to respond that reading the printed word "everything" as "evening" would have made no sense in the printed sentence (the rest of which words they could read).

With this exercise meant for spring of first grade (or often later), the Houghton, Mifflin McKee program in effect was publicly admitting that it was not teaching children to read. Guessing the word "everything" in this exercise ("Does it make sense?") is certainly not reading. In contrast, phonically-trained first graders by spring of first grade not only can read these two words in word lists, completely independently of "guessing" contexts, but can spell them as well.

In addition to heavy reliance on context for word guessing, the Houghton, Mifflin program gives much straight sight-word drill on words once they are introduced. Of course, sight-word drill in Houghton, Mifflin means true sight- word drill, and not what Lippincott's program erroneously called sight-word drill. What I saw in the Lippincott classes was children systematically sounding out words, sound by sound, and with constant drill they were bringing their sounding-and-blending phonic skills to the automatic level. At their Code 10 end of the scale, this was a valuable activity. Yet, in the Houghton, Mifflin program, without the use of almost any vowels, and with the disregard of many consonants so that children can think the printed words "everything" and "evening" would be indistinguishable except for their meanings, sight word drill is true sight word drill.

The Houghton, Mifflin series also follows the basal reader philosophy of repeating "taught" sight words over and over in their "stories" so that the printed words are retained in visual memory. For instance, the first 16 words in the Houghton, Mifflin program are each repeated an average of 53 times in the second preprimer, Rockets, and in Levels B through F repetition continues to be made of new high frequency words.

Like all sight-word basal readers, this series attempts to teach numerous, obscure, so-called "skills" which are far above the mental age of the children, and which are frequently not skills at all but simply stages of language development that are reached automatically as children grow older. Yet, this program fails to teach children properly what is easily teachable and what should most emphatically be taught, such as how to use the sounds of the vowels. Little children have been taught the use of the vowels since shortly after the vowels were invented in Greece about 800 B. C.

Concerning so-called "skills" which are above the mental level of children, in the Houghton, Mifflin second-grade reader, children are taught the meaning of commas when seen in such sentences as, "Mark, the doctor is here," and "Mark, the doctor, is here," or "Do you want peanut butter, ice cream and cake?" or "Do you want peanut butter ice cream and cake?" Skill lessons on such fine points as this exhaust the children and "turn them off" on reading.

Almost no adults were ever "taught" such things, but instead learned them intuitively, just as we learned, at three years or four years of age, what the pauses meant in oral speech, the pauses for which these commas stand. Yet hours are spent in sight-word basal reader programs force-feeding children so-called "skills" like this that would come naturally with maturation. Should a program be teaching such a thing as the "puzzle" use of commas on an explicit, conscious level to little seven-year olds, when it has not taught them the proper use of even the simple vowels? Since one-third of the 93 Houghton, Mifflin second graders I tested in one middle class school could not even read the short "e" word, "leg" (and the word was used in a sentence context!) should their precious school time be wasted on such a "puzzle lesson" as this one?

Properly taught, children are simply told that commas stand for pauses in speech. I spent 23 years teaching primary grades, but never knew commas to cause children any trouble whatsoever in their reading.

"Skills" like this come with maturation and reading experience, IF the children have been taught to read. However, if a teacher who was forced to use the Houghton, Mifflin program decided sensibly to skip teaching her class such "skills," that unfortunately meant her class could not then pass the printed test forms, prepared by the publisher, (some eight or so enormously time-consuming tests a year) which tested whether children had "learned" the worthless "skills." The teacher may know that the tests are only showing that the children learned how to get right answers to such questions, by having worked pages like them in their noxious reading workbooks. If the teacher does not want her children to fail the printed test forms, which scores go into the children's permanent reading record and are carried with them all through school, she had better be careful to spend the necessary hours teaching these "skills" by drilling children on how to get correct answers in the workbooks on the same kinds of questions that will show up later on the tests. Those precious hours would have been far, far better spent teaching something worth while.

This program rated a Code 3 on the phonics scale, at all grades. The damage done in the first grade level was, in no sense, partially repaired at the upper levels. The program is actually a sight-word program with some attention to consonant sounds derived from whole sight words. It has the added emphasis of heavy reliance on context.

I asked a brilliant Catholic priest whom I know, who was born in Taiwan and raised there, if the use of context in reading helped in identifying Chinese symbols when reading, or if Chinese people just knew the meaning of the symbols immediately out of context. He looked startled, then amazed, and said, "Of course they know them. They just READ them!"

Then I told him that some reading methods claimed that people used context to identify English words. He said, disbelievingly, "Is this some new system?"

I said, "No, it's been around for about 50 years."

I was referring to the Scott, Foresman Dick and Jane readers of 1930, but actually the method had been around since the nineteenth century, being used heavily in the Farnham sentence method of 1870. However, the heavy spelling emphasis of the 1890's and the supplemental phonics of the period 1900-1930 made up for a lot of the potential damage.

Sight-words in our alphabetic system are almost impossible for beginners to memorize by sight in any numbers, as little Chinese children can memorize their symbols, so our beginners have to use context to help them identify words. When taught sight words, our beginners are put in the position of partially deaf people who decode words in conversation by the few sounds they can hear accurately, plus the context of the conversation. It must be exhausting for the hard of hearing, so they opt to use hearing aids. Yet there were no "hearing aids" for our poor little sight-word readers when the 1930 Dick and Jane readers arrived. Now those 1930 children have grown up and some of them are university professors. They wrongly think that reading is the "guessing" thing that they learned to do, the same thing that a partially deaf person does when he listens. So such "experts," possibly in all good faith, support the deaf-mute, psycholinguistic method of reading. That method is what is used in the Houghton Mifflin <u>Reading for Meaning</u> series by McKee et al, and in the great number of other basal reading series like it, which are so highly regarded by our reading "experts." Children are being taught to read as partially deaf people listen to conversations. Using only a few letter sounds to identify a word in context is NOT phonics, but psycholinguistic guessing - a psychological disability.

This sort of reading rates Code 3 on my scale, since it makes some use of sound, but Code 3 is a sick place on the scale, while Code 1 is not necessarily so, in another writing system like Chinese. Chinese characters may be hard to learn, but people have been learning them for well over two thousand years. Chinese characters are not read by context guessing. Context guessing is a sick use of an alphabetic writing system which was meant when it was created to be read solely by sound, at Code 10. When turned into a character "meaning" system by the use of sight words, the alphabetic system breaks down because it cannot function efficiently in that manner.

Most importantly, as I will discuss in my conclusion, sight-word trained children are being turned into readers who will forever be deaf to print, so badly conditioned that they will always have to use conscious guessing in decoding the words on the printed page. They can therefore never achieve the automaticity in reading which makes it possible to focus all conscious attention on the meaning being transmitted by the printed page. Their available functioning intelligence, when reading, is greatly decreased from what it might have been if they had achieved reading automaticity

To my surprise, I find myself impressed suddenly with the conclusions of Kenneth Goodman, after all. Dr. Goodman did analyze and describe what is actually happening when most present-day Americans, trained by the Dick and Jane deaf-mute method, are reading, and he did it very accurately - what he labeled, "psycholinguistic guessing." My contention is that this method of reading (guessing the words to come from the words that came before) is not the efficient, desirable, or easy method invented in 800 B. C. (the Phoenician alphabet plus the Greeks' newly invented vowels of about 800 B. C.) but something very, very different.

However, no one has formally suggested before my sabbatical research, to my knowledge, that there are two different habitual methods of reading for adults, one at a low Code and the other at a high Code, but I have become convinced there are two distinct types, or mixtures of those types. I will refer to that more fully in Chapter 8.

(Note: the above was written in 1978 and 1979. However, I learned in 1980 that Oskar Messmer in Germany in 1903 and Myrtle Sholty at the University of Chicago in 1912 had published material concerning the fact that there are two different and opposite types of readers, but they did not mention mixtures of types or that the types were the result of the method used to teach beginning reading.)

Dr. McKee's comment to the Reading Reform Foundation that his program should be on their list of phonic programs reveals that he believes it is a phonic program. Very surprisingly, he is joined in this curious delusion by Jean Chall. Dr. Chall has a footnoted reference in her <u>Learning to Read, The Great Debate</u> which reads:

> One series available during this period did differ from the others in that it has a stronger phonic emphasis at the beginning. The Reading for Meaning Series (McKee et al, 1963). published by Houghton, Mifflin. [Chall, page 102, footnote]

That it is generally accepted as a "phonic" program was brought home to me by the comment from a reading coordinator in a New Jersey town, who stated flatly that Houghton, Mifflin is a VERY phonic program!

When school systems buy this program, then, they are buying what they believe is a phonic system, but one which also includes the presumably very desirable work on so-called "reading comprehension," without which children cannot score on the standardized achievement tests by which the public judges an elementary school system. Some of the heavier phonic programs do NOT automatically raise a school system's so-called "reading comprehension" scores, which fact I will refer to in my conclusion, but for which I attach a totally different significance than that generally accepted. Therefore, when a school system buys this HM program, they are doing the best they know how for their children, getting a program which includes what is presumed to be heavy phonics in the beginning first grade, which heavy phonics is indicated by Jean Chall's summary of reading research, and HM does drill heavily on all consonant sounds in that period. The program simultaneously protects the children's so-called "comprehension" skills. After all, this program, as its name clearly states, is meant to teach "Reading for Meaning."

However, what is often passing for reading comprehension on standardized tests is only reading attention. If attention is voluntary (which it is if reading skill is automatic) that attention may wander. Yet attention cannot wander if it is forced by context guessing.

Therefore, context guessers have to pay attention or they cannot read at all, but they can never give the content of the material their undivided attention, as those who read automatically can.

The disabilities from the post-1930 deaf-mute method readers, like the Houghton, Mifflin, with their inadequate or missing phonics have been enormous. For instance, on the 1952 New Iowa Spelling Scale, 67% of American third graders could not even spell the word "pin."

On my sabbatical research from September, 1977, through January, 1978, I saw the Houghton, Mifflin program in use in three schools. In one, it was paired with a first grade which was using the Open Court program. In another school, for the second grade I tested, the first-grade teacher had begun the year with the straight Houghton, Mifflin program but found it too difficult for the bottom two-thirds of her class, so switched over to the Scott, Foresman readers, 1965 edition.

In the last school, it was the only reading program in use in this school which was, in my opinion, one of the finest schools I visited in the United States. In an apparent attempt to provide for the needs of the weaker students, the children were grouped by ability into five classes, instead of the four classes that the numbers in the grade normally would have indicated. The first three ability-grouped classes were of normal size, but the weakest children, who normally would have constituted one class, had been split into two classes with two separate teachers. This was obviously so that these slower students could get every possible kind of help. That alone indicated a fine school, but my impression of the administration and staff only served to underscore this reality. It was a warm, concerned, friendly and highly competent staff which I met, and, if I were not already happily employed in Wayne, I would consider myself privileged to teach there.

Because of the ability grouping in this school, however, it was necessary to observe in all first grades and to test in all second grades so that a meaningful score could be obtained by averaging classes. In this school, as in so many others, silence was generally enforced. However, I was wonderfully impressed with the warm and caring attitude of all the teachers, and the administrator with whom I talked. It was a happy building, and they were doing their very best for the children.

The first book of the Houghton, Mifflin series is meant to be handled either in kindergarten or first grade, Getting Ready to Read, and is followed by the first three preprimers, Rockets, Surprises, and Footprints. The hard covered primer, Honeycomb, is followed by the hard-covered first book, Cloverleaf, of which only 1/3 is to be completed by the average child in first grade, the rest being finished in second.

In the first grades that I visited, one was doing readiness work before the Getting Ready to Read text, two were working on Getting Ready to Read, and two were in the first preprimer, Rockets, on this date of October 7. Each level had word card sets, with the words introduced in the reading lessons, for developing instant recognition of new words. Also available were charts with context sentences for pre-introducing new words.

The first-grade class doing readiness work was obviously a special group, containing very few children. The teacher was working on auditory discrimination, using a text, Clues to Consonants, by Robert LaCosta. The work was concerned with auditory discrimination of consonant sounds, something which is very difficult for many children. She told the children who were looking at three pictures on a worksheet of a nut, a nail, and a book to circle the pictures of words that began with the same sound and to cross out the one which did not. She said, "That is the way we will do this page," and dictated the words nut, nail and book. The rest of the page had similar work.

The teacher's manner was pleasant and gentle, as was true all through this attractive school. I asked if the children were fairly successful with this activity, and she said that they were.

Many plants were in the room, and some games on shelves, but no learning centers. All first grade rooms in this school had on the board, "Today is Friday. It is October 7. It is sunny and cool." Most American schools I visited during the fall did this.

The next lowest ability class was doing far more complex work. They were on page 65 of Getting Ready to Read, and the class was working on the consonant Y (not its vowel sound). They had received so far five of the 16 sight words: is, to, go, a, I. Since school had opened on Wednesday, September 7, and it was now Friday, October 7, they had been in school 4 weeks and two days, to have covered this work, unless possibly it had been begun in kindergarten, which is sometimes the case in this program.

When I entered this room that had the next to the lowest of the ability levels, I was struck by its delightful, warm, accepting atmosphere. The children were cutting out Columbus ships when I came in, in preparation for Columbus Day, October 12. It was necessary for the teacher to correct a child, and she did it very pleasantly. The desks were arranged in groups of squares. There were no signs of learning centers, but I was told that some classes would have them later in the year "after the skills were taught."

When I came in, the children who were not at their desks working on the Columbus art work were in a reading group, working with cards on the letter "y." The teacher showed picture cards that had words beginning with "y" on them, and the children said the words and put the cards in the pocket chart in front of the group. They put the cards in positions to distinguish between capital and lower case "y". The teacher told me the group would later also do the Scott Foresman Talking Alphabet, which practices in Level One consonants in beginning and terminal positions, so presumably they would be working today on "y".

A rebus sentence appeared on page 65 of the Getting Reading to Read book, on which the children were working. Rebuses, of course, are pictures that stand for words. It read, "A (picture of a monkey) is in a (picture of a box). The previous page used the sight words is, I, and to. On this page, the children were to identify one of the words in the list, I, go, a. The teacher said she felt this work was too difficult except for the better students. As said previously, she was very warm, and thoroughly involved with her work. There was no waste time in her schedule, as I saw her at work. Her opinion underscored the decision of a veteran first-grade teacher in another school, who found Houghton, Mifflin too difficult for the bottom two-thirds of her class and who switched back to the 1965 Scott, Foresman first grade materials.

When I visited the middle class of the five classes, I found that it was also working on the Getting Ready to Read book. To go along with the pupil's text and workbook was a very large teacher's edition called Big Book, in two levels. This class was working with what must have been the second of these large books used in group instruction. The class had apparently covered 10 of the 16 sight words (we, you, and, I, will, go, in, a, the, is). The children were reading sight word rebus sentences from this Big Book, such as "I will go to the (picture of a lunch box)."

The children read the sentences together. This teacher's manner also was pleasant and warm, but obviously talk was not permitted in this classroom, either.

Other rebus sentences were:

> "The (picture of a lunch box) is in the (picture of something)."
> "It is on a (picture of a shelf)."

At the bottom of this Big Book page of rebus sentences was "th" - the "teeth sound," in the word thermos, so presumably the children were studying the "th" digraph.

I noticed when a child was reading the page aloud that he could not distinguish between "a" and "the."

Before the sentences were read aloud, the teacher asked that the children read the whole page to themselves and not move their lips. This is a classical recommendation of most sight-word oriented programs. LeRoy Boussion of France showed that children's oral reading is actually faster than their silent reading for the first few months, and that silent reading is temporarily the more demanding skill, but sight word programs do not recognize this.

These 16 high frequency sight words, of course, were introduced with no reference to vowel sounds unless they occurred at the beginning of the word.

The chairs in this room were in rows, and as yet there was no sign of learning centers. When the children were done with their written work, however, they were permitted to go to the library shelves in the room.

When I visited the class that was the next one to the top level, it was apparently working in the first pre-primer, Rockets, since the teacher said most of them remembered the 16 words if they were in sentences. She was not doing a reading lesson when I was there, however. She said she expected that her class would get to Honeycomb, the primer, by the end of January. She confirmed that Cloverleaf is intended as a swing book by the publisher, to be used at the end of the first grade and the beginning of second. She said that the average child finished Honeycomb, the primer, and most would also finish the first of three units ("magazines") of Cloverleaf. She said she liked the assessment tests in the Houghton, Mifflin program but felt the program was too difficult.

(I do think that, for purposes of comparison, I should record my personal reaction to the Houghton, Mifflin program at this point, since I was obliged to use it for years in the school system in which I taught. My school system did not group classes by ability, as was done in this school. In the fall, in whole-class lessons, not group lessons, I taught my first grades straight phonics (using various published materials). After the beginning of January, using three reading groups, the entire class read both Honeycomb and Cloverleaf. Except for perhaps three or so slower students in the bottom group, they were finished by about Easter. The children simply read through the books orally in class, with the greatest of ease and accuracy. I never permitted silent reading of these texts before the first oral reading in class.

(The Houghton, Mifflin program, if used after a true phonics program, is not at all difficult. I was forced to use the three Houghton, Mifflin preprimers in the fall, but started them very late, so that I could introduce all the words at the board, phonically, to the entire class, before having the very simple, very short, paper-backed pre-primers read orally in the class, at first sight, calling on pupils in turn to read portions, until the text was done. It was almost never re-read. The hard-cover book, Honeycomb was read at the beginning of January in groups. Concerning the assessment tests, I considered them a time-wasting abomination. As can be seen from my reporting on this excellently run school, a tragedy was taking place. With the most caring teachers, the most careful teaching, and the most responsible administration, the children were actually being coached to fail, as the appalling scores I received at this school testify. Those scores are shown in the appendix. I wish it were otherwise, because such fine professionals should not have been so terribly betrayed by a textbook series.)

The top class of the five classes was in the preprimer, Rockets, reading its last story, although some had started the second preprimer, Footprints. This class's teacher said she had the lowest ability class about two years ago. They had started with Getting Ready to Read but had only reached Rockets by June.

Some of the children in this class were doing seat work while the teacher was handling a reading group with other children. On the board, she was writing sentences with the phonograms "ot" and "op", substituting different beginnings. She said, "Take 'n' away from 'not,' and she added "tr." Then she said, "What is the sound of" tr? What is the sound of "ot?" Then she took "tr" away from the word on the chalk board and added "pl", having the children sound out "plot". She had the teacher's manual open in front of her. Then she substituted "sh" for "pl", producing "shot," and then "sl" for "sh," producing slot. She also did sentence work on the so-called phonogram "op", substituting different beginnings.

The teacher turned then to work in the preprimer, Rockets. This preprimer uses more actual words than the 16 in Getting Ready to Read, but continues to use rebus picture words. She said, "Find out what Elephant said they would do." She asked questions, and the children read parts in answer. She seemed to be following the manual exactly, and it seemed to be taking forever. The complaint made by a teacher handling the phonics series Open Court, that it was cut and dried, has to be made about ANY basal series, if it is handled straight from the guide, and yet that is the method most administrators prefer to have teachers use in teaching reading. The truth is that following ANY manual religiously is deadly, deadly dull for both teachers and children. Good teachers know the content of manuals, and can do a far better job if permitted to improvise in their own manner, covering essentially the same ground.

In the afternoon on this date of October 7, I tested a portion of a middle ability group second-grade class, U. S. 20, but had not finished testing the whole class. When I returned in January, I retested 16 of the 17 children I had tested in October. This second-grade teacher, who would, of course, have been using vowels in teaching the <u>Cloverleaf</u> swing book and the other second-grade books, nevertheless was also personally very convinced of the necessity of the vowel sounds for decoding. She said she really emphasized phonics, and had activities in the room with what she labeled her "short vowel friends," Eddie Elf, Octopus, Umbrella, Indian, and Apple. (I do not know if she bought these from a commercial house or invented them herself.) She had made classroom games using long and short vowels, such as "Go Fishing."

What I found most significant is that when a child could not read a word in a reading group, the teacher made him apply the vowel rules right then rather than to give him the word. This, of course, is applied phonics while reading, and while Houghton, Mifflin recommends it, as opposed to most basals, they do it without reference to the vowels. This teacher had these reading game activities set up attractively in the back of the room, and said she assigned them for basic skill work if needed, or permitted children to use them when they finished their seat work. They were told they must talk quietly to play the games, but in this room talking was permitted. She said that this very morning one boy had finally gotten the short vowels straight and was so very happy.

What I find sad is that this delay is unnecessary. In my first-grade class, children had no problem with short vowels, but in my third grade classes, if they had not been taught at first, they had great trouble with short vowels. It is when their teaching is delayed so long as in sight-word programs that the short vowels present problems. In the old sight-word programs, in the 1960's, most of my third graders had no knowledge whatsoever of the short vowels when they began third grade.

The improvement in the scores for the section of this class which I tested in October compared to the same section in January was amazing. (This teacher had kept a list of the children who had been tested.) It was an amazing victory for her dedicated teaching of vowels. Exact scores are shown in the appendix.

The Houghton, Mifflin classes in this building which I tested in January are reported in the appendix (U. S. Classes 18, 19, 20, 21, and 22). While their scores are far higher than might have been expected in January of second grade in the old sight word programs (as can be confirmed by the norms on the Gilmore oral reading test) they were sharply poorer than for the American phonic programs.

How does such an "improved" American program as the Houghton, Mifflin McKee program compare to the heavy phonics programs in France which were tested, where spelling is also difficult? For comparison, in all of France, of the 150 French children tested, only one child scored below 80% oral reading accuracy, or only 0.78% of the French sample. (A passing oral reading accuracy score is 90% accuracy or better, because, as previously discussed, 3/4 of any text (75%) is composed of the highest frequency words, which should be learned in first grade. A failing score below 80% accuracy on a test "story" composed almost completely of very high frequency words is a very severe failure.) Yet, in the Houghton, Mifflin program in this well-run school, 24 second grade children out of 93 scored below 80%, or 15% of the group, 20 times greater than in France. That strongly suggests they had not learned to read even the 300 highest frequency words after a year and a half in school. Scoring below 70% in January of second grade is obviously appalling, yet there were 11 children out of 93, or 12% of the group, scoring below 70% oral reading accuracy. In the 150 second grade children tested in France, NONE scored that low.

These horrible scores were obtained in a school where the weak classes had only about 10 children, so that they could receive extra help. Yet the far higher scoring French classes usually had about 30 children. The difference, of course, is that the French children had been taught true phonics, and the Houghton, Mifflin program used in this unfortunate school did not. Instead, the Houghton, Mifflin children had been trained to be psycholinguistic guessers with only a minimal use of phonics.

The kinds of errors made by the weaker children in this program were very meaningful because they frequently concerned vowels, such as the misreadings, "smile peppy" for "small puppy," "goat" for "got," "new" for "now, "has" for "his," and "he's book" for "his back" Some of the actual misreadings are recorded in the appendix.

What is so terribly sad is that for most of the children the confusions could have been avoided if simple vowels had been taught in the first three months of first grade. What should be emphasized is that these appalling problems occurred in a fine school which was using what it incorrectly thought was a phonics program!

Class 23, a second-grade in another school had also been taught by the Houghton, Mifflin program when in first grade. The other second grade in the building had used the Open Court program in first grade. The last week in September, 1977, I visited the first-grade class in that school which was currently using the Houghton, Mifflin program.

The classroom was extremely well outfitted, with a filmstrip projector for the children's personal use, blocks, and other interesting materials. The room had many books, and free talk was permitted. The teacher was pleasant and relaxed. The class was arranged with the seats in pairs, facing front. At this early stage of first grade (it was late September), the children were copying their names on their papers from the name tags on white paper attached to their desks. Some children called the Pink Group were in the back of the room listening with headphones to a story, The Emperor's New Clothes, obviously a language development and sequence development activity.

As the children were doing their seatwork, the teacher reminded them, "We must work neatly." The children were practicing the writing of digits 6, 7, 8, and 9, and making sets of objects: 6 stars, 7 flowers, 8 Christmas trees, and 9 balloons. Their papers were neatly folded lengthwise.

At this date in late September, the reading group with which the teacher was working was one-third through Getting Ready to Read, the readiness book. I believe the group was the top group. They were doing a workbook page with sounds, which the teacher called a "magic helper" lesson, for beginning sounds in words. The children could tell the sound of the illustrated W because it was super-imposed on a picture of something beginning with the W sound. That picture behind the W was the "magic helper."

Of the four pictures with words on the workbook page, two of them were of objects beginning with the W sound. The pictures were of a bird, a tent, a watch, and a waterfall. A sentence was read to the children. From the sense of the sentence and the pictures with identifying words, if they realized that "watch" and "waterfall" began with W but the other two did not, they would be able to pick the correct W word to complete the sentence. However, when making a choice of the correct W word, when the children "read" the words, two out of three of the children looked at the picture and not the printed word on it.

This, obviously, was supposed to be drill on the sounds of an initial consonant, plus the use of context or context guessing. It was obviously a very time-consuming exercise. So, even though the readiness book in Houghton, Mifflin did teach the sounds of the consonants, it had the children off to a great start in "reading with meaning" by developing context guessers from the very beginning.

The following January, 1978, I tested the second-grade class in this school which had been taught the Houghton, Mifflin program in first grade.

I found one incident particularly meaningful, which I mentioned earlier. One of the little girls was wearing a sweatshirt with a large word printed on it, over and over and over, as a design. I asked the child what the word was on the shirt that she was wearing. This superior second grader, who later scored at 99% accuracy and 80% comprehension on the oral test, said the word on her very own shirt was "Australia." It was actually the word, "outrageous". Although she could score very high on my oral test which really only covered very high frequency sight words, she was obviously totally unable to decode a long word phonically, even something so personal as the design emblazoned all over her own shirt. I doubt very much that most phonics-trained children would go so far off the mark in reading that word that they would read "Australia" for "outrageous."

The scores for this second grade Houghton, Mifflin class, Class 23, are shown in the appendix. Their January accuracy score was markedly lower than the Open Court second-grade class in this same school which I had tested the end of the previous September. The Open Court Class 4 scored at that early date with 70% at the instructional level and 100% above the frustrational level, which were the finest American fall scores. Based on my judgment as a teacher, both first-grade teachers were truly excellent. My research has shown, concerning oral accuracy, that good teaching is NOT the determining factor in achievement. A table comparing the over-all scores for Class 23 and Class 4 follows.

To support that statement were the scores on two Open Court first-grade classes in another school, one of which lost its teacher in January of first grade and the other in April of first grade. Despite change of teachers for first-grade classes, both second grade classes scored very high in oral accuracy and far above the sight-word classes!

It is interesting that this Houghton, Mifflin class, while scoring far lower than the Open Court class in the same school four months before, nevertheless was the high-scoring sight-word class in January, as the Open Court class in this school had been the high-scoring class in the fall (but of both phonic and sight-word classes). This very possibly indicated that the children in this school had a higher ability level than the children in the other schools tested.

The sharply higher score in "comprehension," however, of this January Houghton, Mifflin class 77%, compared to 44% for the Open Court class in the same school the previous September, underscores the real reason why sight-word programs are favored by administrators. Administrators must produce high standardized achievement class scores on tests like the Californias or Iowas, or those administrators risk enormous censure from parents, who read these achievement scores almost like the Bible. In my final chapter, in discussion of the "statistical profile" produced by all scores (on accuracy, rate, reversals and comprehension) I outline a totally different reason for the SEEMINGLY better scores on reading comprehension sometimes achieved by sight-word classes, showing conclusively, that what is being revealed by such "reading comprehension" scores is NOT higher achievement, but something else, something which is very undesirable.

Comparison of an Open Court Fall Class with a Houghton Mifflin January Class - Both from the Same School

In the September and October tests, the best scores were obtained by an Open Court Class. In the January tests, the second-best sight-word/global score, and the best Houghton Mifflin score, was obtained by a class in the same school as this Open Court class.

A comparison of the fall phonic Open Court score (Code 3) shows a clear superiority for the phonic approach, except in so-called "reading comprehension." The reading-comprehension-test fallacy is discussed elsewhere in this text. The cause for the sometimes-seeming superiority of sight-word classes is their forced attention to "meaning" because of crippled decoding. They must pay attention to meaning or they cannot "guess" words, but their attention is divided: part to guessing words and only what is left over to the text's meaning, reducing their potential comprehension. The cause for the sometimes lower reading comprehension scores for some phonics classes is their ability to read automatically, with or without attention to meaning. Children may let their attention wander. The best reading comprehension scores, however, are from the phonics classes since they do not read with the divided attention of the sight-word classes.

	Passing Accuracy		Failing Accuracy				% Passing	Estimated Speed	
	% Scoring at or above 95 on Test	% Scoring at or above 90 on Test	% Scoring Below 90	85	80	70	Comprehension	% Slow	% Fast
Class 4, Sept. Open Court	70	100	0	0	0	0	44	0	26
Class 23, Jan. Houghton Mifflin	50	82	18	5	0	0	77	18	9

A second-grade girl in the January Houghton Mifflin class was wearing a shirt with the word, "outrageous," printed over and over on it. When asked what the word was on her own shirt, she answered, "Australia." Although she read above 95% accuracy and passed "comprehension" she obviously had not yet learned how to read.

Scott, Foresman

Class 3, a Houghton, Mifflin/Scott, Foresman class in another school, I only had time to test in the fall on example 1, because of a conflict with other work scheduled at the school. Class 3 is therefore not averaged in with the other scores in the fall summary table.

It was taught by a combination of Houghton, Mifflin and the 1965 Scott, Foresman basal readers The first-grade teacher who had taught this second grade class was highly experienced and organized, and appeared to be a fine judge of children's abilities. The bottom two-thirds of her class the previous year, which I was testing in second grade, had found the Houghton, Mifflin Getting Ready to Read too difficult. After about a month, this teacher moved the bottom two-thirds of the class into the 1965 Scott, Foresman, which she used jointly with the Scott, Foresman Talking Alphabet in the fall. During the winter and spring, she also had a set of phonically regular supplemental readers for the children to use, which practiced the short vowel sounds. In the fall, therefore, one-third of the class had the standard Houghton, Mifflin program, and two-thirds of the class had the Scott, Foresman basal reader in the 1965 edition.

In Learning to Read, the Great Debate, Dr. Jean Chall referred to the Scott, Foresman reading program as the "best seller" in the early 1 960s. The Scott, Foresman series of course, is far less "phonic" than the Houghton, Mifflin Reading for Meaning. The 1965 edition was an "integrated" edition of the earlier 1962 edition, which Jean Chall described as having a looser control over vocabulary and with more phonics construction than early Scott, Foresman readers. What remained, nevertheless, was the sight vocabulary and emphasis on reading for meaning from the start. New words were still pretaught, but the child's attention was focused less on straight look-say and more on meaning. Teachers were told to call attention to the structure and phonics of a word more often, and all references to configuration clues (shape) were dropped. Also, during the guided reading, the teacher was still to pay no attention to phonics. In follow-up activities, the heaviest amount was on reading comprehension (3 2%) but phonics and structural analysis doubled from 13% in the 1956 edition to 25% in the 1962 edition. It cannot be emphasized too strongly, however, that "phonic and structural analysis" is in NO SENSE sounding-and-blending phonics.

Here, then, was a program which pretaught sight words, made no provision for the use of phonics during actual reading, and which used "analytic and structural phonics" which is a very different thing from total sounding-andblending phonics. That kind of "phonics" has usually been present in sight-word basal readers. If a child knows the word, "cake, and knows the word, "boy," he can substitute "b" from boy for "c" of "cake" and get "bake" (at least theoretically). Aside from being exhausting, Mary Johnson of Winnipeg, Canada, showed by her oral testing of primary school children that they do NOT use this substitution type of analytic phonics in "attacking" new words, even though they have been taught it. Also, what does a child do with a word like "picnic"? What "substitution, analytic phonics" can a child do with that word? I taught a third grader once who had been taught in the previous years to read by the Houghton, Mifflin method (in an earlier edition). For the word, "picnic," she spluttered "phazz..." and then something else and finally gave up altogether. Yet she WAS a bright child. But Houghton, Mifflin does not teach the so-called phonogram, "ic" and she did not know what to do with isolated vowel sounds and straight sounding and blending, which was the only way to read the word, "picnic".

One third of this class, then, had the straight Houghton, Mifflin program, plus use of some phonically regular readers, practicing short vowel sounds, and the bottom two-thirds had what amounted to the straight old sight-word basal readers (despite the changes in the Scott, Foresman, 1962 edition) plus extra practice on short vowel sounds given by these supplemental phonically regular readers at some time, apparently during the winter and spring. I regret that I did not question the teacher on how much emphasis she gave these linguistically regular readers, but my impression is that they were used only on a supplemental basis. All the class used the Scott, Foresman Talking Alphabet, Level I, which drilled on beginning and ending consonant sounds, the vowels being covered in its second level, Level II. Again, unfortunately, I very much regret that I did not ask her if she had used this second vowel level.

Since the most of the class used the Standard Scott Foresman basals, however, I coded the Class Code 2.

In this highly competent teacher's classrooom, quiet talk was permitted and considerable use made of games and manipulative materials, although the children had more than average amounts of academic work required of them and heavy practice in all skill areas.

It is interesting that these incomplete scores are almost identical to those of the other Scott, Foresman October class (which did not have the Letters and Sounds workbook, as one of the January Scott, Foresman classes did). The scores are identical, that is at the level above frustration, where, in this class, 43% passed, and in the straight Scott, Foresman October class, mentioned later, 42% passed. At the instructional level, however, 19% in this class passed compared to 37% in the straight Scott, Foresman class, possibly due to a somewhat lower ability level in this second grade class which their first-grade teacher felt was the case compared to her previous first-graders. Of course, it may also have been attributed to the fact that the top one-third of her class had the Houghton, Mifflin materials, while in the other Scott, Foresman fall school (although it was working with Systems, a completely different and later Scott, Foresman edition), the top one-third had Scott, Foresman materials. For comparison, the fall U. S. phonics classes averaged 78% passing above frustration and 58% passing at instructional, markedly higher than 43% and 19% for the mixed program class and 42% and 37% for the straight Scott, Foresman Systems class.

All the Scott, Foresman classes tested (except for the class just discussed which made a mixed use of Scott, Foresman's 1965 edition and Houghton, Mifflin) used the Scott, Foresman edition titled Systems. This can be described as a phonics-assisted, psycholinguistic, sight-word program, and it was published in the early 1970's.

Scott, Foresman have produced an un-interrupted series of sight-word programs since 1930. Dr. William Scott Gray, the college professor/sight-word "expert", was employed by Scott, Foresman as the principal author on their 1930 edition of the Elson readers. The 1930 edition was a true sight-word series, and the first (along with A. I. Gates' Macmillan series) to replace supplemental phonics teaching with so-called "intrinsic phonics." In "intrinsic phonics", unknown words are compared to known words to see similar and dissimilar parts, and then context is used in combination with that comparison to guess the unknown word.

In 1965, Kenneth Goodman published his study, Reading, A Psycholinguistic Guessing Game. He had presented third graders with a list of words to read. Some they did not know in isolation. When the same words occurred in a story, they could read more of them, so obviously he clearly demonstrated that they could read more easily when words were in context than isolation. Dr. S. Jay Samuels made the following comment in the October, 1978, issue of The Reading Reformer of the Reading Reform Foundation, Scottsdale, Arizona. He said that Goodman's study presupposed that the children already knew some words or they could not have read the context from which they inferred the new words. Samuels cited research at Texas Women's University which demonstrated that context did not help first graders in reading, apparently because first-graders did not know enough words to use as context! Samuels himself has done research that established that children learned new words best without context and without pictures, which tended to discount the utility of Dr. Goodman's findings.

(Note added in 2003: It is difficult to understand how this so-called "research" of Goodman's could have been viewed as real research except by those who were ignorant of history. Since the early nineteenth century, after learning a certain number of sight words by pictures, American deaf-mutes were taught to read new words by such context guessing. The "Dick and Jane" type of readers since 1930 were deliberately arranged on the deaf-mute pattern, depending on context guessing for word identification (Gates' "intrinsic phonics") after the basic sight-word vocabulary.

The "frustration" level on individual oral reading tests ("IRI's") since Emmet Betts' in the 1940's is the point that a reader is "frustrated" guessing the meaning of unknown words from the context, when the mix of known and unknown words has become too rich (more than about 10% of unknown words). Goodman's "research" was certainly in the "Born Yesterday" category.)

Dr. Goodman, in an interview quoted in a Scott, Foresman brochure, said in effect that when we read we are making constant predictions about what is to come next, and we anticipate words and phrases. He stated that children should be taught to read thoughtfully, anticipating the statements to come, and that this is a more economical way to get to meaning, rather than to focus on identifying letters or words. He felt that the key to efficiency is to minimize the quantity of graphic information needed to achieve meaning. In his opinion, probably the one really important thing in early reading material is its predictability. He felt that children should find what they expect in ideas and language, which is determined by the grammar of the language, hence the term psycholinguistic - the wedding of psychology to the structure of language.

Dr. Goodman, with his emphasis on meaning, became the senior author on the Scott, Foresman basal series entitled <u>Systems</u> which was published in the early 1970's, which rates a Code 2. He was also the senior author on a later series, in 1976, <u>Reading Unlimited.</u> It is essential to understand Goodman's concept that predictability is the most important thing in early reading material, which he feels is mandatory so that children can make psycholinguistic guesses to get meaning (and to identify words). To anyone who did not know of Goodman's "predictability" bias, his reading series would be incomprehensible in some of its directions to teachers, and in its story design. It is still, of course, a sight-word series with emphasis on context, but it is the newer, 1970's version, where many words are to be identified by context, and not the older, 1930 Gray version, where fewer "sight words" were to be identified by context, plus the possible use of some phonic clues.

Dr. Samuels said, in <u>The Reading Informer</u> (October, 1978), "What we're beginning to find is that Goodman has a good idea. We (adults) can use context. But... It doesn't make sense if you talk about beginning readers."

Unfortunately, I disagree with Dr. Samuels. It CAN make sense in teaching beginning readers, but only if we concede that "reading" can be done in different ways, and if we want the children to read in a particular one of these ways. "Reading" is NOT the same act for everyone. There are those people who can read "words" automatically (as Samuels said, and this can be whether the words are Chinese characters, sight words, or phonically decoded words) and who use context ONLY for the meaning of larger thought units. Then there are those who also use context for larger thought units but, IN ADDITION, use it for word identification, with some attention to letters. Obviously, in the latter group, attention must be divided, partly on meaning for word identification and partly on meaning for thought. The former group is reading at Code 10 and the latter at about Code 2.

What is disturbing is that the former group can achieve automaticity as defined by Samuels, to which I will refer next, but, by applying his definition, the latter group can NEVER achieve automaticity. Conscious dependence on context for word identification continues past the beginning reader stage (after the foundation sight vocabulary of some 150 words to permit context guessing has been established) and lasts all through life. Experimental data on types of oral reading errors from many studies which have been made show that readers at upper grades do differ in the kinds of errors they make, depending on whether they were taught by meaning or by phonics.

Samuels defined automatic as meaning that no attention is necessary for the behavior being done. He cited as examples driving a car, typing, and even tying shoe laces. At the beginning, or learning stage, the learner must devote all his attention to the task, since the mind is so constructed that it is incapable of devoting conscious attention to more than one thing at a time. Therefore, if you talk to a beginning driver, typist, or child learning to tie his shoe laces, he cannot listen to you without stopping what he is doing, as his conscious attention was on the task being learned. After the task is mastered, however it then becomes automatic, and he can perform it automatically, and carry on a conversation, which ALWAYS requires conscious attention. He cited comments by typists who have told him they daydream as they type. The fingers do what the eyes see, but the head goes elsewhere. I am writing this book while typing, and I am no more thinking of the structure or even spellings of the words or which keys to hit than I am thinking of what is on the back of a kitchen cabinet shelf. My typewriter has become my voice. My typing is now totally automatic, although, unfortunately, not totally accurate!

Samuels stated that the act of reading has two parts. One is decoding and the other is getting meaning. A beginner may have all his conscious attention on decoding, and because of the nature of the mind, it is not possible simultaneously to concentrate on anything else, including comprehension. However, as he said, we know beginning readers CAN comprehend, so it is supposedly that they are doing this by switching attention - first to decoding and then to comprehension, perhaps rereading the section. If a student is at the accurate level, which is decoding words correctly, it does not reveal whether he is also at the automatic level (doing so without conscious attention). Samuels said we should strive to go "Beyond Accuracy to Automaticity" in teaching reading. He said one of the best indicators of automaticity in decoding is speed. The other is accuracy. What should teachers do to bring children to the automatic level? Samuels said the trite but true answer is: practice. A good teacher can do two things: bring the student to the accuracy level and encourage the student to practice which means providing time and motivations.

If all beginning readers (those taught at Code 2 and those taught at Code 10) are doing the same thing, Samuels implied they should all pass through identical stages where attention is at first almost totally focused on word identification, and, finally, if lucky, reach the automatic level where attention is focused solely on thought. But, Goodman says children should instead be focusing more on thought from the beginning, as it is more economical and demands less attention, and NOT on the form of the symbol being learned. Since this kind of thoughtful focus, however, ALWAYS demands conscious attention, then, by definition, if the children never proceed beyond this context stage of identifying words they can NEVER read automatically. Goodman is saying, in effect, that is exactly what happens (though of course he makes no reference to automaticity, and he apparently has not thought of it) when he describes how adults are supposed to be reading, getting identification for words from the context with only some graphic information (in his description of the act of reading in the Scott, Fore sman brochure referred to elsewhere). Therefore, either Samuels is right, and readers eventually identify words automatically (which means, by definition, without conscious thought) or Goodman is right, and mature readers identify words through context, requiring conscious thought and making automaticity impossible, or they are both completely wrong, or they are both partly right.

I think the data I eventually got from the summary tables on my research support the contention that they are both partly right. I think the apparent conflict can be explained by the fact that "reading" is not the same for all people - and not just immature readers. Most people trained at Code 2 continue to read at Code 2 all their lives (Goodman's model for word identification) and people trained at Code 10 read at Code 10 all their lives (Samuel's model). Furthermore as was shown by F. Williams of England, some children master the phonic code (read at Code 10) despite being taught by sight words, so Samuels' "automatic" reading is done by a small minority of sight-trained people, muddying the research waters.

Like almost all popular errors, Goodman's psycholinguistic ideas on reading have a very large helping of truth. It is not that he is totally wrong. It is that he is wrong if you want to produce Code 10 automatic readers. It is not even that he is completely wrong there. At Code 10, his theories partially apply to comprehension. When decoding has become automatic, so-called "psycholinguistic" predictions are present in the mind of the reader, as for a listener, and assist comprehension. Samuels recognized that Goodman was partially right when he said that we use prediction in reading, and that the grammatical structure of language provides our clues, although he felt this had no place in beginning reading instruction.

As Goodman contends, it is true that we predict when we are listening. The only reason that many spoken jokes are funny is that their surprise ending is not what we would have predicted. But when we are listening, we should also clearly hear all phonemes spoken, and we should not be thrown on the context to identify sounds except rarely. People who lean too much on prediction when listening, however, frequently fail to understand a speaker's real meaning. The corollary of careful listening, which is careful reading, demands phonic mastery, as careful listening demands good hearing. Phonics mastery is NOT a luxury. Teaching children to read words without phonic mastery and by the use of context is equivalent to teaching children to listen to the radio with the volume so low that many words are inaudible. Both, of course, CAN be done, at least for some children, but should they be done?

If Goodman is right that reading is a "guessing game" for all readers - if we are ALL reading at Code 2 - then how did Rudolph Flesch read Czech so well, though he could not speak it, that a native assumed Flesch understood the language? How could little ITA kindergarten students, as cited by Betty Thompson of ITA, read German texts written in ITA script, though they knew not a word of German?

I believe decoding does become automatic for Code 10 readers, and then they can engage in so-called "psycholinguistic" predictions, as do listeners, and such predictions will aid comprehension. Yet Goodman's ideas on "predictions" have absolutely no place in the teaching of beginning reading.

What my research turned up, surprisingly, is data that prove not just that phonics-trained children read more accurately, but that there are two different kinds of readers. My research data showed that teaching sight words and context guessing produced readers whose attention was forced but divided, resulting in better comprehension for children who were still learning to read words (to decode) but poorer comprehension in advanced readers. (However, this obviously contradicted Samuels' thesis that all beginning readers, both sight-trained and phonic-trained, focus on word identification, but not comprehension.) My research data contradicted the theory that teaching reading "by" meaning produces advanced readers who read "for" meaning best. The reality is quite the opposite The comprehension of meaning-trained children is affected adversely by the habitual divided attention resulting from using context meaning for word identification. The end result is a lack of automaticity. I will refer to this more fully in my conclusions.

Goodman did his 1965 research with children who almost certainly learned by sight words, and it is highly probable that he learned that way himself. His "psycholinguistic" method of word identification, which uses the meaning of the context, is actually a very good match for reading as it has been done in the post 1930 Gray era. It undoubtedly rings true to most Americans under 50, because that is how they were trained themselves.

With this informational background on the theorizing behind Goodman's Systems reading texts, the following notes taken in classrooms using his material will be easier to understand.

The first time that I saw the Scott, Foresman Systems in use in a first grade was in early October, 1977. The class was one of several first grades in the building. Its teacher had taught for many years and loved both her work and the children. In this building's classrooms, however, as in so many other American schools, silence was enforced in the classroom except during recitations

The teacher had an interesting mathematics laboratory table in the back of the room for the children's use, and I had the impression that much of the material she had bought herself. It contained peg boards for counting and number relations, balancing equipment with blocks for counting activities or for developing a measuring sense by weighing, and parquetry pieces to complete design puzzles for beginning work in geometry. The children also had abacuses at their desks which they used while doing math workbook pages on simple number combinations.

This teacher said she liked the Scott Foresman <u>Systems</u> reading program and preferred it to earlier programs because she felt that the results were better. Since sight words are so difficult for little children to remember, training them to use systematic context guessing does give temporary - but in the long term harmful - assistance but she apparently did not realize that fact.

While I was present, the teacher was working with the second reading group on page 96 of the Level 2 book of "Systems". She was using the "Magneboard", which was a board with magnetic picture and word cards. She displayed them in sentences, such as, "The rooster has a rocket," which was Magnepiece picture 90, according to the guide. A child read the sentence by context guessing, with the aid of the picture and the initial consonant being practiced, which was "r". Next, she put up the sentence and matching pictures for "The fox is chasing the fireman," to practice initial "f". The teacher said that she had children practice the letter "f" in all positions, not just the initial position, but I did not see in glancing through the manual any indication that this was the case.

While the children were working with the "f" sound in words, they identified words on workbook page 23 beginning with that sound, and did the same thing for "r" sounds with the sentence, "The rooster has a rocket."

The teacher continued Magneboard work with "h" (horse on hill), "b" (boy in boat) and "g" (girl in garden). The children were to do written work on workbook page 23 and master page 19 later to practice only the "h", "f" and "r" sounds.

The teacher said that, to date, the children had received work on the sounds of "b", "f", "g", "h", and "r". They had learned the names of the letters of the alphabet in Level 1, but were now learning the sounds of the letters of the alphabet. Following the Magneboard practice geared to workbook page 23, the children worked on work book page 24. On this page were six questions, and under each question were three pictures, one of which was to be checked as the correct choice. The first question read, "Which one is a boat?" and underneath were pictures of a gate, a helicopter and a boat. The children either had been given the pattern before for the words ("Which one is a...") on the workbook page, which would seem to be in keeping with the so-called "psycholinguistic" philosophy, or the teacher had told them these words while I was glancing at the guide and did not therefore hear her, or those words were actually known beforehand as sight words. In any event, a child was able to read the first sentence on the page, "Which one is a boat?" without being asked.

The purpose of the page obviously was to practice initial consonant sounds "b" (boat), "f" (fish), "r" (rabbit), "h" (hammer), "g" (guitar) and "f" (feather. Under each sentence were three pictures, one of which was the object named. The children were to look at the initial consonant of the printed word (as "boat") and check the pictures to see which one began with that letter. Then they would be able to read the unknown word. The other words in each sentence remained the same, "Which one is a..." The guide told the teacher that, if no one volunteered to read the question as this child had done, then the teacher was to read it aloud. Even if the other children could not read the words, "Which one is a..." when they sat down with the workbook page, after the pattern had been set, they would all be able to "read" the words in the question, and, if they knew the initial consonant being tested, they could "read" the new word containing it by looking for a picture with that beginning sound.

This whole procedure, of course, is the total antithesis of sounding-and-blending phonics, but totally in keeping with the so-called "psycholinguistic" philosophy of Kenneth Goodman, "reading" by context with "some" attention to graphic clues. There was no reason to believe that any of these children had any knowledge of the phonic structure of any of the words other than that of the initial consonant being practiced. After all, to date, the children had only been taught the sounds for the letters "b", "f", "g", "h" and "r".

In the first sentence, "Which one is a boat?", the only phoneme the children had been taught was "b". They had been taught none of the sounds in the word, "which." The word "one" is almost totally unphonetic (sounding phonetically like "wun"), and its irregularity had not been pointed out to them. A word so irregular as "one" is never introduced this early in a phonics program. The children also had not been taught any of the sounds in the word, "is," which is irregular, anyway, since "s" says "z" in this word. On this workbook page, therefore, the children were reading almost completely for meaning from context and sight words, with very, very little graphic information. This pattern was to continue on the little story from a reader which they did later.

At the completion of this workbook page, the teacher had the children play a memory game, "Go to the store and buy..." Each child whose turn came had to repeat all items that had been given before. While the reading groups were working with the teacher, the rest of the children were doing number papers which had been folded carefully and on which examples had been copied from the board. The children also had workbook pages on simple number combinations.

The teacher then worked with a story in an individual book, "The Bus Ride." <u>Systems</u> has its separate stories in very attractive little individual story books. However, if you talked to a child when reading any other story as the teacher's guide requires the teacher to talk to the children when this story is initially introduced (today they were just rereading it), you would be assumed to be insane. It would be interesting to ask any parent if he or she could go through a conversation like this to teach his or her six-year-old child anything. The story itself was delightful enough for little children, but it had the "prediction" quality that Goodman recommends. However, the only phonic elements in this story for the children at this point in first grade (almost mid-October) was the use of the initial consonants covered to date: "b", "f", "g", "h" and "r", although nowhere in the reading of the story was the child asked to make the association between the initial consonants and the words containing them, as had been done in the skill lesson. It was not necessary, however. Each new word was accompanied with a large picture which "told" the child what that word was.

The story concerned, in sequence, a girl, a boy, and a series of animals. "Girl," of course, begins with "g", one sound studied, boy with "b", another sound studied, and the animals had names which began with one of the letter sounds already "studied." The word "girl" and "boy" and so on were easily read because "girl" occurred on a page with a picture of a girl, "boy" with a picture of a boy, and so on, page by page. I will repeat what was said on the first two pages, because the pattern was set for the rest of the book.

On the first page, the children are told that a girl got on a bus, with a picture illustrating it. The opposite page showed the bus under motion with the information, that the bus was going fast. As each new passenger got on the bus and the bus moved, the words remained the same except to insert the name of the new passenger: "___ gets on the bus," on one page, followed by the bus going fast on the opposite page. Obviously, this text has high predictability, particularly with the picture "clues."

In the middle of the story, a bee got on the bus. Each succeeding pair of pages after it had a passenger getting off the bus on one page and running fast on the opposite page. Again, the only change in the text for the get-off-and-run section was the name of the passenger doing it, who was shown by his picture on the page, so the word on the page for his name could be "read" by the picture!

Idiotic as this story is to adults, little children would find it charming. The complaint is not with the story, but with the lack of real phonic teaching in it (limited only to initial consonants on passengers' names) and to the ludicrous "questioning" required of the teacher.

The teacher's guide told the teacher to tell the children to look at each picture in turn, then to ask who got on the bus, and to confirm the answer each time by repeating who got on the bus, and then to have that particular sentence on that page read aloud. She was to ask, on each page facing the "getting-on" page, what the bus did then, and the children presumably would tell her, one way or another, that the bus went fast. The teacher was then to repeat what the children have just told her about the bus, but in the precise word pattern printed the book, and then they all read the patterned words in the book out loud.

The teaching for all pages in this little book was the same. After the teacher has (1) asked what happened, (2) after the children have told her, (3) after the teacher has repeated or paraphrased what the children told her, by using the printed words in the book (4) then the children read the printed page out loud. The teacher and children follow this procedure, page after page, ALL pages being "read" only after this so-called "teaching."

It should be an utterly exhausting process to go through this story this way. It is interesting that a teacher using the phonic Open Court method found it "cut and dried" (because of how she handled it). Nothing could be more cut and dried than the sight-word handling of this little story. Yet the teacher was instructed to handle the story precisely in this way.

On the day that I observed this class, they were only rereading the story, and were presumably to use the "cues" of pictures, past experience and so on to help them- plus, presumably, initial consonants, the only "phonics" in the whole Scott, Foresman <u>Systems</u> program at this point in first grade.

Later, in the Level 2 guide for <u>Systems,</u> is an assessment story (apparently to be covered, on the average, sometime before January). The decoding approach used by Scott, Foresman is shown by the directions to the teacher in how to handle this reading "assessment." This assessment is meant to be used with each child individually to help in diagnosing specific strengths and weaknesses. The child is to use picture cues, context cues and initial consonant clues in reading the story. The child is to read it first without help, and the teacher is to record omissions, spontaneous corrections and to show whether the child got the meaning, even if he "miscalled" a number of words. If the child had too much trouble the first time, then later the teacher is to give the "guidance" suggested below in reading each page. Each word the teacher is to help the child decode is underlined.

<u>new</u> - "Do you suppose Rudy got an old toy or a new one? With what letter and sound does this word begin? red -"What color was Rudy's new wagon? What word that names a color begins with the letter "r" and the "r" sound?

<u>wagon</u> - "Can you tell from the picture what Rudy got that was new and red? Think of the sound you hear at the beginning of wagon. With what letter does this word (point to wagon) begin?

<u>he</u> - "With what letter does this word begin? What word that begins with the "h" sound can we use instead of the name Rudy?"

<u>sit</u> - "What did Rudy like to do in his wagon? What is the first letter in this word?"

<u>ride</u> - "Look at the picture. Can you think of a word beginning with the "r" sound that tells what

Rudy liked to do in his wagon?

take - "Do you think Rudy liked to take anything for a ride in the wagon? Could this word be take?"

Of the 19 words which received this kind of "decoding" instruction on page 187, only three were phonically irregular (his, put, wagon). Some had special vowels that most phonics programs do not cover till midterm (ey, ew). Yet most were very simple to decode in any phonic program with the use of simple vowel rules, on which rules phonics programs normally give extensive drill so that their use becomes automatic. The word "get" for instance, has a short vowel sound, but "go" has a long vowel sound, because the rule is, "A single vowel at the end of a word is long," (me, my, so). First-graders learn such rules with ease and apply them just as easily, if the program and approach are kept simple.

The questioning above was meant to "help" a child having difficulty reading words. Yet absolutely no help was given to the child to sound out any of these words, even one as simple as "red," except for the initial consonant sound. Asking a child what the first letter's sound is does not constitute sounding-and-blending phonics or phonics in any real sense of the word. How a child can be helped by anything like the guesswork just quoted is a mystery, but makes sense if reading is presumed to be an activity taking place at Code 2 - sight words plus only SOME phonic attention, plus context guessing.

This very dedicated teacher told me that her class would begin Level 3 by January. Level 3 covered vowels, and she said the children would then spontaneously begin to read words. Level 4 had the special vowel sounds such as (ow) and dictionary work, and would be the level on which the class would complete the year. Nevertheless, this program did not provide at any level any systematic decoding practice on all phonic elements in a word, and even in the second half of the year relied on context plus use of only some phonic elements. The phonics was strictly analytic and never became synthetic sounding-and-blending phonics.

On page 165 of the Level 3 teacher's guide, where vowels are finally being "taught," the children are told to put their fingers under the last word in a sentence and to explain how they knew the word was "ring" and not "rake" or "rice." The guide told the teacher that the pupils may mention either the vowel or consonant sounds, or that they remember seeing the word before. She is to accept any reasonable response. Phonically, of course, the only "reasonable" response is that ALL of "ring" says ring, and ALL of "rake" says rake, and ALL of "rice" says rice. Any child who confused any part of these words as late as the end of Level 3, which apparently would be well into February of first grade or most probably later, simply has not been taught how to read. This, however, is what "reading" at Code 2 means. It means "any reasonable response," not reading what is on the page.

Despite the omission of vowels in the critical first half of first grade, this program did teach them in January (although only analytically, and without sounding-and-blending training). Even with the addition of the vowels, however, it was evident, so many years after Jean Chall's documented call for a code emphasis in the first half of first grade, that this program was not giving it.

The teacher in the first-grade class which I visited had, I understand, two or three children retained from the previous year. Three other first grades were in this school, and I understood that they were all using Scott, Foresman <u>Systems.</u>

I tested one second-grade class in this school in October, U. S. Class 1, and three more the following January, U. S. Classes 24, 25, and 26. I am deeply grateful to this school, which was doing its best for the children, to give me the opportunity to see the Scott, Foresman <u>Systems</u> program taught in first grade exactly as outlined in its guides, and then to test the results from the Scott, Foresman <u>Systems</u> program at the second-grade level.

I previously referred to the scores for the second-grade class in this school which I tested in the fall, and which had used Systems in first grade, when I compared it to the fall Scott, Foresman basal second-grade class which had used Houghton, Mifflin for the top third. As mentioned, the accuracy score for the second grade Scott, Foresman class in this school which I tested in the fall was well below the fall phonic second-grade classes' average.

The January accuracy scores for three other Scott, Foresman second-grade classes in this same school were also well below the phonic classes' January average. The three classes in this school tested in January scored above the accuracy frustration level with 75, 60, and 71% passing, compared to 92% of the phonics classes, and at the accuracy instructional level with 47, 33 and 47% compared to 77% of the phonics classes. On comprehension, 53, 73, and 77% passed, compared to the phonic classes' average of 64%. (The crucial significance of the comprehension scores is discussed later.) All scores are reported in the appendix.

Some of the comments made by the children in the Scott, Foresman classes in this school were meaningful. One child said, "I am not good at reading - only big words." Possibly those were words he could decipher from context and pictures, but he could not handle the small, high frequency words.

Another child decoded "catch" by reading "cat" and then adding the "ch" sound, saying, "catch." I asked how he knew how to do that. He said, "My mom taught me, not school. That's how I got it."

In January, a girl who scored a low 85% on accuracy but 100% on comprehension read, instead of "The dog has learned.... to do," "The dog has lemon to do...." I asked her to read the sentence again, and she repeated "lemon." Sight-word-trained children are drilled in reading whole sight words to such a degree that they cannot fall back on phonic skills in decoding, but instead must search their memories for similar whole sight words, and, to this little girl, "lemon" was apparently the closest she could get in her sight-word memory to "learned".

Another error made in January, a meaningless substitution of a known sight word without regard to context, was "It was a shell puppy," instead of "small puppy."

Another was, instead of "number of times, "name of times."

Another was the following: "When Peter got the dog" became "When Peter got on dog."

The children were being forced by training to substitute approximate whole sight words instead of approximate letter sounds for unknown words, and that training was leading them down blind alleys. If the little "lemon girl had read, instead of the incorrect whole word, "lemon" some incorrect but approximate letter sounds, such as "The dog has leerned to do" for "The dog has learned to do," she would have been on a road which could have led her to the correct pronunciation, but when she said "The dog has lemon to do," she was in a blind alley.

These errors were to be expected, however, because during the entire first half of first grade. these Scott,- Foresman-trained children had been systematically drilled in guessing whole, meaning-bearing words, using only the initial letter sound of the unknown word and the context, but ignoring all the other letters in the unknown word. The children making the errors I noted were only doing what they had been taught to do - although sometimes, as with "on" for "the," they ignored even the sound of that initial consonant in the unknown word.

The only other class that I visited which was using Scott, Foresman Systems was U. S. 27, in January. A small first grade and a small second grade class were operating as a unit, although for part of the day they were separated. One teacher was new, and, though she had a teaching degree, was in the position of assistant to the other teacher. This first and second grade class totaled perhaps 27 children in all. The first-grade class was using Scott, Foresman Systems and the Scott, Foresman phonics workbook, Letters and Sounds. The slower children used Scott, Foresman Open Highways instead of Systems, which is similar to that described in the first Scott, Foresman class, the early 1960's edition.

The room was very attractive. The children's seatwork assignments, to be done while the teachers were working with the reading groups, were written on the board. The desks were arranged in a square. The bulletin boards had as a display a colored paper bookworm in sections, for the second graders, with stars next to the children's names. Not too many manipulative games were on the shelves, but primarily books. Not too much children's work was displayed, but very nice paper snowmen were hanging on a string next to the windows. The children in this room were permitted to talk quietly.

When I arrived, the senior teacher was reading with the second graders in a reading group. She asked questions on comprehension and inference, such as, "Why is it a good cat?" She was obviously following the reading-formeaning approach of all sight-word basals. I saw the assistant teacher however, doing much drill on sounds as she worked with the first-grade children individually, who were coming to her for help on workbook pages which they were completing. They were working on the Scott, Foresman Letters and Sounds, a Phonics Workbook for Primary Grades, which I did not see in the other Scott, Foresman schools.

This workbook gives beginning first-graders a very, very different emphasis than the standard Scott, Foresman program, either the Open Highways earlier standard basal edition or the newer "psycholinguistic" Systems. It consists largely of three and four letter words, under colored pictures, arranged in 72 short lessons, which could easily be covered in a term, even though, as its "primary" title indicates, it is meant for use through grade three. Each lesson systematically practices a consonant or consonant blend in beginning or ending positions, and a few work on long and short vowels, but only "analytically."

Pictures of objects are shown, and the "studied" element is meant to be written in the blank space in the word shown under the picture. For instance, a picture of a cup is shown, and a child doing the review lesson on page 22 picks which of three letters (m, n, c) should be inserted under the picture of a cup and before the given letters "_up." In no sense is this a good phonic workbook, since it gives only passing attention to the long and short vowels, and no "teaching" at all of the critical special vowels, as in moon, took, boy, boil, law, fault, etc. But it DOES very specifically teach phonic elements, and is therefore vastly different from the Systems program.

If a child had ONLY this workbook in the first half of first grade, the program would rate a Code 7, despite its weakness, because if definitely emphasizes "sound". Used as it was, with the standard Scott, Foresman Systems or Open Highways, the overall classroom program rated a Code 5, because of the heavy emphasis the assistant teacher gave to the phonic work. The work was obviously being done under the tutelage of the regular teacher who was sitting within earshot. It was the early use of this workbook in first grade, inadequate as it was, which apparently accounted for the startling differences in scores between this Scott, Foresman school and the other Scott, Foresman classes tested.

Fifteen of the 17 second graders in this classroom were present. All passed the oral accuracy test above the frustration level, and 73% read at the instructional level. This compared to 92% passing above the frustration level in the phonics programs in January, and 77% of the phonics programs passing at the instructional level in January. A remarkable 100% of this January Scott, Foresman plus-heavy-phonics January class passed the comprehension test, and an equally remarkable 47% read quickly (compared to the phonics average of 35% reading quickly and the sight- word average of 14% reading quickly in January). None of the children read slowly (compared to 8% of the phonics January classes reading slowly and 15% of the January sight-word classes reading slowly).

This Scott, Foresman class with analytic phonics certainly did score well with 100% passing at the "frustration" level, but the alarm flag was up, nevertheless. The phonics classes had an average of 77% reading at the instructional level, but this class - remarkable in other scores - showed only 73%. It was not just that they might have had one weak student, because 100% did pass above the frustration level, while the phonics classes had only 92% pass above the frustration level. Therefore, the relationships between those scores was inconsistent. The SF class scored the best at the "frustration" level with 100% compared to 92% for the phonics groups. Yet the phonics classes outscored this SF class at the instructional level, 77% to 73%.

It is easy to explain. To score above "frustration" was less demanding than to score at "instructional." The oral test had been chosen for this study precisely because it was composed of the very highest frequency words - the words taught in sight-word programs - because it would have been impossible to test sight-word classes with low frequency words. This class handled the simple test very well - and actually scored better than the phonics classes at the "frustration" level. But they could not keep up their lead at the more demanding "instructional" level.

If a more realistic oral test had been used, not composed of the highest frequency words, but of lower frequency words which used the special vowels which this class had not been taught, the results would have been very different. The phonics-trained classes would read low frequency words with special vowels with ease. Yet this class would have had to fall back on context guessing, and then their seeming "lead" at the "frustration" level would disappear.

CHAPTER 6
On the Methods Used in This Research

This research study has <u>labeled materials differently, tested materials differently, and analyzed materials differently</u> than has been the case in the few comparisons made between phonic and sight-word programs in the past. It is necessary to explain why these different procedures were used.

<u>First, concerning labeling, there were excellent reasons for labeling programs on a continuous scale from 1 to 10, from sight-word to phonic emphasis.</u> Any meaningful discussion of reading history and reading instruction is impossible without a commonly-agreed upon numerical scale for reference, to rate reading programs on phonic or sight-word/ global emphasis. The alternative is to be lost in a swamp of words whose definitions vary with each user. A good part of the present reading problem has arisen because of the lack of such a scale by which to evaluate the nature of historical reading programs, and the nature and results of present reading programs.

For instance, Lippincott calls its method phonic linguistic when it has none of the failings of Bloomfield's linguistic method or the pure syllable method (neither of which teach isolated letter sounds). The Lippincott program talks of sight words when what I saw children actually doing in the first-half of first grade was intensive sounding-and-blending drill on phonically regular words, at which the children were achieving greater and greater speed.

Houghton Mifflin's <u>Reading for Meaning</u> is often called a phonic program, yet it drills children to focus on only some of the consonants plus the meaning of the context. Even someone as knowledgeable at Jean Chall was misled when she called it "more phonic" before it was published.

Scott, Foresman talks of "good, solid instruction in phonics skills" on page 8 of the 1977-1978 catalog for their new <u>Basics in Reading</u> program. However, the catalog shows an illustration of a page from the readiness level book of this series, working with the initial consonant "m", and it is the same kind of "phonics" I reported seeing in a Scott, Foresman <u>Systems</u> classroom. Children were to read whole words and sentences containing most of the letters in the alphabet when they only had been taught a few consonant sounds such as "m", and they were being drilled in psycholinguistic guessing of sight-words with the aid of that consonant. Yet any program which does not give systematic training in synthetic sounding-and-blending phonics, or analytic breaking down of ALL phonemes in all words being studied in the first-half of first grade, is not a true phonic program. It is as simple as that.

The confusion caused by all this mislabeling - phonics programs called linguistic (although almost everyone recognizes Lippincott's as highly phonic) and psycholinguistic programs called phonic, is revealed in a remark a made by Joseph J. Tremont, Director of the Massachusetts Right-To-Read program. He had worked with Jeanne Chall on her book, <u>Learning to Read: The Great Debate,</u> and was referred to in a Boston article by Samuel Blumenfeld, who is himself adamantly opposed to the basal sight-word approach, as "a congenial, level-headed Ph. D. from the Harvard Graduate School of Education... [who] knows the ins and outs of the reading problem pretty well."

Tremont felt teachers were the key to reading failure, but (THIS is absolutely shocking) he said, "Actually, kids are learning to decode pretty well these days in the elementary grades. But once they learn to read, there's no practice, no use."

Yet the oral reading accuracy tests in this study, which were composed almost completely of the highest frequency words, recorded THREE TIMES AS MANY FAILURES in American sight-word basal-reader second grades as in American phonic second grades. That was ONE OUT OF EVERY FOUR SIGHT-WORD TRAINED CHILDREN. Furthermore, NONE in those sight-word classes, even those passing, had been taught the simplest sounding-and-blending phonics, so that most will NEVER be able to decode new words automatically. In addition, 15% of a large Houghton Mifflin sample scored, not just below the frustration level (below 90% accuracy), but below 80% accuracy. (That school had 93 second-grade children in that school, and it was excellently run except for its unfortunate decision to use the Houghton Mifflin program). These very grave Houghton Mifflin failures were TWENTY TIMES greater than the percentage of second graders who scored below 80 in the 150 second-grade children that I tested in France.

It would appear that the kind of test information obtained by the oral reading accuracy testing in this study is simply not available to the Right to Read program and to Tremont. Tremont's conclusion that "Kids are learning to decode pretty well these days in the elementary grades," is at fault not just for his ignorance of the reality of such absolutely terrible failures, but because he lumps all first-grade programs together. Teachers are NOT the deciding factor as he implied, but the first-grade method most certainly is. That Houghton, Mifflin school with the horrible scores (15% second-graders below 80% accuracy, TWENTY TIMES greater than the percentage who scored blow 80% accuracy in the 150 second-grade children I tested in France) had some of the very best teachers - and perhaps the best administrator - that I met during my entire sabbatical. The failure was solely in their Houghton, Mifflin program, which I rated Code 3 on a scale going from Code 1 for pure sight words to Code 10 for pure sounding-and-blending phonics.

Tremont was very far off the mark for not distinguishing between programs. Yet, in the absence of a commonly agreed upon scale (such as Code 1 - pure sight to Code 10 pure sound), Tremont was undoubtedly unable to label programs adequately and so fell back on "teachers" as the "key to reading failure".

Sight words, of course, when used as hieroglyphs, are theoretically at Code 1, but they do not usually function at pure Code 1. More commonly, they are used with some degree of phonic information. At the beginning of the Scott, Foresman Systems, I saw that the only phonic information used was the initial consonant, but another factor was also used, that of context. It is probable that, between Code 1 (pure symbols for ideas, or meaning) and Code 10 (pure sounds for words), the reading of a single form makes use of both visual and auditory memory. As a result, the reader is forced to use the context as an additional aid to word identification. That is because, with two different sensory avenues being used at the very same time on the very same stimulus, the mind is forced to reason its way through the resulting conflict by the meaning of the context.

The use of different sensory avenues in reading is supported by studies by S. Sasanuma and O, Fujimura, "Selective Impairment of Phonetic and Non-Phonetic Transcriptions of Words in Japanese Aphasic Patients (Cortex, 7, 1971). Japanese characters are a mixture of symbols for sounds (Kana, or syllables), and picture writing (Kanji). What this remarkable study found was that there was a difference in people who had lost the power of speech, presumably through strokes. Some could read one part of Japanese script but not the other, which showed that the brain processes sound in different areas of the brain than it processes visual information. It has been reported elsewhere that most Japanese children come to school already knowing the Kana or syllable characters and so must only be instructed in the picture ideographs, the Kanji.

Presumably, reading Japanese would be like watching a movie, part of the information coming from the images and part from sound. It is reported by K. Makita (Journal of Orthopsychiatry 38 [1968]) that Japanese children have almost no reading disabilities. But, in

America, children are being asked to use visual and auditory faculties on the SIMULTANEOUSLY ON THE VERY SAME symbol, a printed word, instead of on different symbols, and that creates a real conflict. In contrast, Japanese children reserve visual faculties to read Kanji and auditory faculties to read Kana, and that does not create a conflict. Therefore, Japanese children are not forced into the conscious use of context to resolve a conflict, but can read automatically. Yet sight-word-taught American children certainly are forced into the conscious use of context, and their use of consciousness means they are not reading automatically

It is critically important, in labeling beginning reading programs, that use be made of a scale which shows the relative use of "meaning" or "sound" in word identification. For that reason, a scale from Code 1 for pure sight-word "meaning" to Code 10 for pure phonic "sound" has been used in this research.

Secondly, concerning testing materials differently, Tremont also ignored this second item, the proper use of testing materials, because he failed to define what he meant by children's doing "pretty well." Undoubtedly, his idea of what constituted "pretty well" was based on averaged group scores on the worthless standardized silent reading comprehension tests. Yet reliance on such silent reading comprehension tests is useless (and so are averaged group scores largely useless, as will be discussed). With the use of silent reading comprehension tests and their multiple choice answers, it is impossible to tell whether a child is silently guessing or whether he is really reading.

The only way to test reading, to find out whether a child (or an adult) can or cannot really read test material, is to hear the child (or adult) attempt to read that material aloud. No reading score means anything unless it is an oral reading score, concerned solely with word accuracy, and not with other such considerations as repetitions, pauses, accenting or omitted punctuation. (In France, "liaison" errors on the oral tests I gave were not counted either, as they are speaking errors, not decoding errors. I recorded them, however, on test sheets, but they were VERY infrequent.) Surely, one of the wonders of the age is that "silent reading comprehension tests" were EVER permitted to displace simple tests of oral reading accuracy.

It must be emphasized that the ONLY valid test of reading competency is an oral reading accuracy test. Yet there is scarcely ANY data on the oral reading accuracy of connected texts by sight-word vs. phonically-trained children, except from the Gilmore tests in the USOE first-grade 1967 studies. Those 1967 scores were averaged, so that large differences at the lowest and highest ends may have been hidden by that averaging. The Gilmore scores are reported by grade levels which were fixed extremely low when the Gilmore test was normed at the height of the pure sight-word basal reader era about 1950. Gilmore's original work, reported in his doctoral thesis at Harvard in 1950, was done in Massachusetts and presumably on a population of children who were trained in the old sight-word basal readers since almost nothing else was available at that time.

As I outlined at the very beginning of this book, in order to test for oral reading accuracy, I found it necessary to adapt a portion of an IEA silent reading test (with their permission) to use as an oral reading test for second graders because almost nothing else that was suitable was available. I needed just such exceedingly simple, very high-frequency vocabulary as on that selection, because otherwise I would have been unable to get any usable oral reading accuracy scores from sight-word trained second-grade children who can only handle high-frequency vocabulary.

Therefore, my data on reading competency was obtained in the only way that is valid, by the use of material which tested oral reading accuracy. However, the IEA test form also included five "reading comprehension" questions. These were scored separately from the accuracy scores, and it thus became possible to compare oral reading accuracy with so-called "reading comprehension." The results from this comparison will be discussed later.

Thirdly, besides LABELING materials differently (from Code 1 to Code 10), and TESTING differently, by a simple oral reading accuracy test, I have ANALYZED my materials differently than has been the case in previous comparative oral reading research. Instead of using an overall "average" or "mean," I have used the device of "ranking," which makes it possible to compute the percentage who "pass."

The use of a statistical "average," or "mean" to analyze raw data, such as my oral reading accuracy scores, often erases very meaningful differences. To avoid this, I have analyzed my raw data by "ranking" the individual scores above and below what is called the "frustrational" level, and then computing how many "passed" and how many "failed." Such statistics on "passing" and "failing" are of far greater utility than flat "averages."

Saying that an "average" child in a program reads at grade level does not reveal the percentages of children in that program who are reading above grade level, and how far above, or the percentages of children who are reading below grade level, and how far below. It would be entirely possible (though unlikely) for instance, to have a second-grade class in which every child scored at grade level. It would be equally possible to have a second grade class in which none scored at grade level, but half scored at fourth and half could not read at all. The average score for both these classes would still be about second grade. By the use of "means," or "averages," two totally dissimilar groups are therefore made to look alike. It is true that it is possible to treat such data further with the complex "analysis of variance" approach which is presumed to reveal any meaningful differences of "statistical significance". Yet such treatments do very little to clarify the real facts for most people.

I consider such elaborate methods of dealing with "means" or "averages" to reveal "statistical significance" to be opaque gobble-de-gook and so I rejected them. Instead, my test results were analyzed by the same very clear, very simple, easy-to-understand statistical method that is used in New Jersey's state assessment tests, the method of "ranking" of individual scores. Ranking of individual scores makes it possible to compute the percentage of children who manage to "pass" above the cut-off score.

My cut-off score was the "frustrational" level. The use of a "frustrational" level for oral reading accuracy tests has been in use by "reading experts" for a very long time, but only in what are called Individual Reading Inventories. These are given to individual children who are usually having trouble reading, in order to determine their actual "reading level" and to prescribe "remediation" treatments. According to the IRI standards that were reported by Emmet Betts (a foremost reading authority and author of a widely used basal reader series), the "independent" oral reading level is 99% word accuracy, the "instructional" oral reading level is 95% word accuracy, and the "frustrational" or "failing" oral reading level is below 90% word accuracy.

Betts then combined the IRI oral reading accuracy score with the IRI "comprehension" score. A child was expected to pass BOTH accuracy and comprehension in order to pass the IRI. Yet I contend, since accuracy and comprehension measure two totally different things, the two scores should NOT be combined for a "pass" mark. I can "read" (decode) German but do not understand it. I can understand a letter from my sister but cannot "read" (decode) it if I spill something on it.

As a result, my scores on accuracy are separate from my scores on comprehension. This made it possible to look for a relationship between accuracy and comprehension, either positive, negative, or equal. The nature of the relationship that I found, as I will discuss later, turned out to be very startling indeed. However, if looking for such a relationship, between large numbers of oral reading accuracy scores and oral comprehension scores, has been done before to any extent, I am not aware of it.

Yet the REAL meaning of Betts' "frustrational" level for connected text, set at below 90% word accuracy, should be explained. In actual fact, a score of 89% on the oral reading of connected text does NOT mean that a reader can read 89% of a list of completely different words, since so very many high-frequency words are constantly repeated in any selection of connected text. For instance, the Ladybird Publishing series in England quoted research done there showing that more than 50% of printed English consists of only 250 high-frequency words (although English has about half a million words!), constantly being repeated (such as "the," "when," etc.). (For instance, count the number of "the's" and "of's" in the previous two sentences.) Also, as mentioned previously, Leonard Porter Ayres found that 300 of the highest frequency words compose over 75% of most texts.

Almost all these 250 or 300 highest-frequency words are learned in the first and second year of school. When a child is taught these highest-frequency, constantly repeated, words as sight words, plus being taught the psycholinguistic context-guessing method for "new" words, which uses initial consonants to confirm guesses, it is possible for a child to reach third or fourth grade without any knowledge of "new" printed words beyond their initial consonants. Of course, depending on having memorized the highest-frequency words, and depending on initial consonants plus guessing from the meaning of the context for "new" words, can only be called "crippled decoding." It often leaves the child helpless when faced with really difficult words which he cannot guess from the context because these "new" words are not already in his spoken vocabulary, which had been the case with the easier words. Such a child cannot really decode at all, but is dependent on pure psycholinguistic guessing when reading material above the fourth-grade level.

However, the higher the child's native intelligence, and the larger the child's spoken vocabulary, the longer can such context "guessing" be successful. With the use of the highest-frequency words, plus psycholinguistic guessing, a child can sometimes score startlingly high on a test of connected oral reading when he cannot read most of a disconnected list of words at the same grade level where no context is given as an aid for guessing.

Someone might assume, therefore, that a child failing my 144-word test with a frustration score of 89% knows about 89% of the 144 words on the test. It means no such thing. If word identification were solely by sight (even without psycholinguistic guessing) on a test like mine, the fallacy can be seen. My test has 144 words, but of these only 64 are <u>different</u> words. Furthermore, if a child misses a word the first time on an oral test like mine, he is then told it, which means, in his short-term memory, he may retain that word at least for the rest of the test and not miss it the next time he sees it. However, even without allowing for the aid of short-term memory which greatly inflates the accuracy scores for poor readers, every error on my test is really not 1/144 of the total, as I did count it to get 89% as a frustration score, but only 1/64, so a score of 89% on my test, if converted to number of <u>different</u> words missed, becomes 75% (16 gross errors). A score of 85% on 144 words becomes a possible 66% on 64 words, and a score of 80% on 144 words becomes a possible 55% on 64 words. Taking only the first score, 89% as frustration, it could mean that the child does not know about one out of every four words on this very simple test composed almost completely of very high frequency words. (This is even without allowing for the aid of short-term memory, when a child can read a word correctly the second and third time, because he had been told it when he missed it the first time. Without the aid of short-term memory, the scores would be very much lower than about one out of four words at the 89% level.)

But it does not end there. With psycholinguistic guessing from the meaning of the sentences and the first letter of unknown words, it is highly possible for any child trained to read psycholinguistically to guess the words which he could not read if he saw them isolated on a word list. That this is expected to happen, according to "reading experts," is shown by the Informal Reading Inventory Recapitulation Record from the publication, <u>Informal Reading Inventories</u> by Marjorie Seddon Johnson and Roy A. Kress of The Reading Clinic, Temple University, published by the International Reading Association (1965). Informal reading inventories, as mentioned, have frustrational, instructional, and independent levels, based on connected oral reading, but they also give isolated word recognition tests, both "flash" (quickly) and untimed. Both the oral reading selection and the word recognition list are at the same grade level. A child is tested until he reaches a "frustration" level on the oral reading selection (below 90%) or until he misses all but three or four words on the word list (which runs about 20 words at all levels). So a failing score of 89% on connected oral reading might therefore be equated to a failing score of 20% (4 of 20 words) on a list of disconnected words.

However, a score of 90% accuracy or above on connected oral reading is counted as a passing grade, and it was marked as such on my tests. The individual scores for each class were ranked, from lowest to highest. With that ranking, it then became possible to compute the percentage of the class which "passed" above the frustrational level (and the percentage who scored at or above the "instructional" level).

The faulty use of averages or means, instead of ranking, can be seen in reading research data that is actually on record when no further "statistical treatment" to reveal meaningful differences was done, and when an appropriate "passing" or "failing" grade was completely ignored. For instance, the USOE first-grade Gilmore tests on oral reading in 1967 presented only averaged oral reading scores, and it treated variances by only giving the "high" and "low" boy and girl. Obviously, such a treatment was grossly unacceptable.

Some Tests Which Demonstrate How Misleading an Average Can Be

To demonstrate further how misleading the use of "averages" or "means" instead of "ranking" can be, even with the use of analysis for "statistical significance" on the "means," I cite a study that is available in the ERIC files by Kay Wedel McKnab. However, (and this is amazing since she had advice from her faculty advisors at the University of Kansas), she made no reference to the "frustrational" level. Yet that is standard on Individual Reading Inventory oral reading tests and I believe it should have been used on her small study.

The study by Kay Wedel McKnab is entitled <u>Speed and Accuracy in the Reading of Regularly Spelled and Irregularly Spelled Words for Students Instructed in Distar versus the Holt Reading Program</u> (University of Kansas, Ed. D., 1975). Her conclusions are examples of the distortion that can result from analyzing test data by the use of means instead of rankings, and without using the frustrational level on tests of oral reading.

At the end of her report, McKnab stated:

> "The statistical analysis employed by this investigation gives no greater support to one method of reading instruction than the other. General observation by this investigator, as well as a relevant literature review, supports the practice of supplying the teacher with the instructional program she believes she can get greater results from.
>
> "Perhaps the more effective teacher is the one who uses several approaches, always remaining cognizant of the effects of each approach on each individual learner."

She had said earlier, however:

> "An informal analysis of the raw data presented in Chapter 4 shows a trend for comparatively greater speed and accuracy in the Distar/Houghton Mifflin sample. The possibility that this could become statistically significant within a year or two bears some investigation."

McKnab's study concerned 20 first graders, 20 second graders, and 20 third graders. The Distar phonics class (which switched to Houghton Mifflin in third grade, NOT a true phonics program) was being compared to a Holt sight- word basal reader class. Oral reading tests were given at the first and second grade levels which were different for each group, the Distar group being tested with Distar materials and the Holt group with Holt materials. However, this obviously made the testing unequal. With this method, no significant differences were found.

At third-grade, however, the children in both the Holt and the Distar groups were tested with the same material, paragraphs from the <u>Durrell Analysis of Reading Difficulty</u> (1960). They were scored with an unusual method. Each child was given a percent accuracy score, but it was broken into two parts, one for regularly spelled words and one for what Distar children would consider irregularly spelled words. The mean scores for the groups were Distar 93% on regular words and 93% on irregular words, but Holt 87.6% on regular and 85.1% on irregular. When these means on connected oral reading, which were nowhere related to frustrational (or instructional) levels, were treated to "analysis of variance," it was concluded that they were not "statistically significant." The note was made, however, that an informal analysis of the raw data" shows a trend for comparatively greater speed and accuracy in the Distar/Houghton Mifflin sample, and that it was possible it could become statistically significant within a year or two.

The table on the following page presents this raw data, broken down, not by averages or means, but by the methods of ranking and the levels for frustrational and instructional, so that readers can decide for themselves if it is "statistically significant." This WAS a test of connected oral reading, and should obviously have had the same frustrational standards applied as it as an Individual Reading Inventory. Imagine parents being presented with the data, once it has been treated by ranking and the frustrational level, and asked:

> "Which class do you want your child to attend in first grade - a Distar phonics class or a Holt basal reader class? The researchers tell us this data has 'no statistical significance.' Is it significant to you, as a parent, that children are reading like this at third grade?"

When treated by "ranking," the Distar averaged phonic scores on the two tests of 93% and 93% are instead turned into <u>80% and 80% reading above "frustrational" level,</u> but the Holt averaged sight words scores of 87.% and 85.1% are turned into only <u>40% and 30% reading above "frustrational" level!</u>

What would a parent, who saw those "ranked" scores, conclude about the "correct" program for his little child about to begin school?

A great need exists for reform in scoring American oral accuracy group tests in the future so that they consistently show the frustrational and instructional levels, and that averaged scores on such tests (which were so misleading on the McKnab data) be totally replaced by ranked scores which can demonstrate the actual percentages who "pass". Without such information on accuracy tests of connected oral reading, the data is essentially meaningless. That was the case with the Kay Wedel McKnab study which found its way into the massively used ERIC computer files, with the manifestly false conclusion that Distar phonics showed no superiority to a sight-word program, based on oral reading accuracy tests at third grade.

To show further the misleading effect of "averages" in comparison to "rankings", shown next are the scores for two classes which I tested in the United States in January of second grade. One was a Scott, Foresman sight-word class which had an "average" oral accuracy of 91%. The other was an Open Court (heavy phonics) class with an "average" oral accuracy of 96%. Since both classes, by Betts' definition, are above the "frustrational" level (above 89%), the difference between these "averaged" scores (96% vs. 91%) does not appear very meaningful nor should it have great "statistical significance." Concerning the often-used "low" and "high" scores, the Scott, Foresman group had a "low" score of 81, and the Open Court group had a "low" score of 80. Using these statistics (Open Court oral accuracy 96, low score 80, Scott, Foresman oral accuracy 91, low score 81) no advantage appears for the Open Court phonics program in comparison to the Scott, Foresman sight-word program.

Yet, when the individual scores for each child are "ranked," instead of "averaged," so that it becomes possible to see how many "passed" above the frustrational level (and at or above the instructional level) a very large advantage appears for the Open Court phonics program, in comparison to the Scott, Foresman sight-word program. The ranked scores for both programs are shown on the following tables.

As the two tables demonstrate, what were small differences between the two classes when the "averaging" method was used became huge differences when the "ranking" method was used.

Ranking showed that 81% of the Open Court class was at or above the instructional level, but only 27% of the Scott, Foresman class was at or above the instructional level (95% accuracy)! The Open Court class had 87.5% above the frustrational level (90% accuracy), but the Scott, Foresman class had only 60% above that level. Only 12.5% of the Open Court class was at the frustrational level (below 90% accuracy), but 40% of the Scott, Foresman class was at that level.

Therefore, as ranking made clear, Open Court produced 87.5% passing above the frustrational level in comparison to only 60% from Scott, Foresman. Yet what is even more meaningful is that Open Court produced 81% at the instructional level (which is the manageable level for a classroom teacher), but Scott, Foresman produced only 27% at that level!

Furthermore, as the following table indicates, the 12.5% failing in the Open Court class (two children) had excellent reasons for failing. One child had hearing problems and was scheduled for an ear operation, and the other child showed massive problems in arithmetic as well, the teacher's conclusion being that he had very grave problems with visual reversals.

It should be emphasized, again and again, that this little oral test (144 words in the English form) which was used in my research at the second-grade level is very, very simple. It should have been read easily by any normal child at the second-grade level. To fail such a simple test was to demonstrate the inability to read. Therefore, the only conclusion that is possible from considering the above "ranked" scores, instead of the "averaged" scores, for the Scott, Foresman program, is that the Scott, Foresman program is a terrible failure.

The Effect of "Ranking" of Scores, Instead of "Averaging," When Applied to the Study, Speed and Accuracy in the Reading of Regularly Spelled and Irregularly Spelled Words for Students Instructed in Distar versus the Holt Reading Program, by Kay Wedel McKnab (University of Kansas, Ed. D., 1975).

Individual Children's Scores Regular Words Per Cent Accuracy				Individual Children's Scores Irregular Words Per Cent Accuracy			
Distar		Holt		Distar		Holt	
99.5		97.3		100.0		96.1	30%
97.7		96.0	40% Above	98.0		94.2	Above
94.2		94.2	Frustrational	96.1		92.3	Frustr.
93.7	80% Above	90.7	Level	96.1	80% Above	88.0	
93.7	Frustrational	89.7		96.0	Frustrational	84.6	Failing
93.7	Level	88.0	Failing	92.3	Level	82.6	70%
92.8		82.2	60%	92.3		82.6	
92.0		81.3		92.3		80.7	
88.4	Failing	80.0		86.5	Failing	78.8	
84.4	20%	76.8		82.6	20%	71.1	

The Effect of "Ranking," Instead of Averaging, When Applied to Class 25, Scott, Foresman - 15 Pupils

Accuracy, Per Cent	Number of Pupils Obtaining Score	
99	2	
96	1	4/15, or 27% Scored
95	1	at Instructional Level or Above
93	2	
92	2	9/15, or 60% Scored
90	1	Above Frustrational Level
89	1	
88	1	6/15, or 40% Scored Below 90,
87	1	At Frustrational Level
84	1	
82	1	3/15, or 20% Scored Below 85,
81	1	or Exceedingly Low

The Effect of "Ranking," Instead of Averaging, When Applied to Class 14, Open Court, 16 Pupils

Accuracy, Per Cent	Number of Pupils Obtaining Score	
100	3	
99	4	
98	1	13/16, or 81% Scored
97	1	at Instructional Level or Above
96	2	
95	2	
94	1	14/16, or 87.5% Scored Above Frustrational Level
89	1	Referred for testing for inability to learn number facts.
80	1	Hearing disabled, with operation scheduled. 2/16, or 12.5% Below 90, at frustrational level. 1/16, or 6% Below 85, or exceedingly low, but both children had severe physical problems to account for failures.

CHAPTER 7
On the Results

With the foregoing background that I have just given on why I <u>labeled materials differently, tested materials differently,</u> and <u>analyzed materials differently</u> than had been the case in the few comparisons made between phonic and sight-word programs in the past, I will present the results of my research.

Before doing so, however, I would like to point out that the results from American schools will differ to some extent from the results from European schools (independently from the issue of phonics vs. sight words) because the European schools moved far more slowly in the first half of first grade than the American schools. That may very well have given an advantage to the European schools. Furthermore, decoding English which has many irrational spelling patterns is obviously far more difficult than decoding Swedish, Dutch and German whose spelling patterns are quite regular. Even French, which has large numbers of silent letters and vowel sounds which are spelled in many different ways, is easier to learn than English, because at least its spellings are rather consistent

However, that the reading of French for beginning readers is a more complex task than the reading of Swedish, German and Dutch is shown by fewer French second-grade children at the "perfect" end in my scores, 100% accuracy, even though the French second-graders did score remarkably high otherwise. In the Swedish samples, the perfect scores in the three most heavily phonic schools totaled 16 of 30 children tested, indicating that perfect reading on a test of the difficulty of mine is only "average" performance for Swedish children using the heavily phonic <u>Nu Laser</u> program. (The Swedish children were, of course, a year older than the children in other second grades since Swedish children do not start first grade until they are seven years old.)

Nevertheless, despite these differences between languages (which differences are obviously separate from the question of phonics vs. sight-words), my test results showed a clear victory for the phonics method over the sight-word method in both American and European schools.

The summary table listing all the data is on the next page. (<u>CAUTION:</u> the most critical, unsuspected conclusion to be drawn from this raw summary data is not discussed until the next chapter.)

Concerning The Total Scores

Concerning the European scores, between October 17, 1977, and November 25, 1977, I tested 338 second- grade pupils in 19 different European classes, and gave a partial test to one other class of 16 children which is not included in the total. Of the 338 total pupils included in the score, 237 were from 13 heavily phonic programs (average Code 8.6) and 101 pupils were from six classes in programs which used the sight-word, or global approach, plus phonics (average Code 6). On my test which is at grade level 2.3, at a time of the year in Europe which was roughly grade 2.3, 90% of the phonic-trained children were at instructional level, and 96% passed above the frustration level.

The more global European classes showed a marked inferiority. Only 74% were at instructional level and 86.5% passed above the frustrational level. What was notable was the degree of extreme failure of a few children in the global groups. Of the total global sample, 2.5% scored below 70% accuracy, but none of the European phonic group scored that low.

For comparison, in the American group, and despite the fact that learning to read English is a more demanding task for beginners, only 1.4% of the phonics children read below 70% in January.

The summary table on the next page presents the total scores, European Late Fall and American Early Fall and American January. The American Early Fall group was tested from early September to October 15. At this early point in the school year, that group was not comparable to the European Late Fall and American January group. However, even so, it showed at that early point in second grade that the phonics classes were notably better than the two sight-word classes I was able to test for comparison. On one of those two sight-word classes, I was only given the opportunity to test Example 1 on my 144 word test of 5 examples. Yet both these sight word classes, the one reading all 5 examples of the 144 word test and the other reading only example 1, showed approximately the same number of second-grade children reading below the frustrational level on this easy, easy test, 58% in the class which was tested through Example 5, or all 144 words, and 57% in the class tested only on Example 1. Yet, even at that early point in second grade, only 22% of the phonics classes were reading below the frustrational level.

The American January scores showed an overwhelming victory for the phonic method. Only 8% of the American phonics classes read below the frustrational level, but TWENTY-FIVE PER CENT of the sight-word global group, or ONE OUT OF EVERY FOUR CHILDREN IN THOSE CLASSES! Yet it should be pointed out emphatically, once again, that the test only concerns very high frequency words and in no way shows how children could perform when sounding out unfamiliar words. Therefore, even though some sight-word children "passed" this test, in no way did that indicate that they could sound out unknown words as phonics-trained children can. The USOE 1967 first-grade studies did settle quite conclusively the fact that phonics-trained children were superior to sight-word trained children when reading disconnected lists of words. The phonics-trained children on my tests had been given word attack skills, which is shown by the fact that only 1.4% of the phonics group read below the terrible score of 70% accuracy, but 6.5% of the American sight-word group read that badly, ore MORE THAN FOUR TIMES AS MANY AS THE PHONICS CHILDREN.

At the instructional level of 95% word accuracy, 77% of the phonics classes passed this test in January, but only 53% of the global classes. Again, in terms of actual class impact, that means that in the phonics second-grade classes the teachers can give grade level work to three out of four children, but in the sight-word classes to only half the class.

Concerning Certain Individual Scores

Phonics teaching had shown a clear superiority in my tests results in the U. S. early fall sample, in the European late fall sample, and in the U. S. January sample. Where individual groups were compared, when one group had more phonic background than another (a higher Code number), the same superiority was demonstrated.

For instance, the Scott, Foresman Code 2 groups which did not use the Scott, Foresman workbook, "Letters and Sounds," did markedly worse than Class U. S. 27, the Code 5 Scott, Foresman group which did use the phonics workbook (a relatively weak analytic approach which

Notes for

Summary Table - Oral Reading Test Results - Second Grades - 1977-1978

On a scale from 1 to 10, a total sight-word/global program would be Code 1, and a totally synthetic-phonics program would be Code 10.

It should be remembered, when comparing these scores, that the test only concerned very high frequency words and in no way showed how phonics children and global/sight-word children would perform on sounding out unfamiliar, low-frequency words. However, the only way it was possible to compare sight-word achievement to phonic achievement was on such a test as this, which is composed almost completely of very high frequency words, the kind of words on which sight-word children are drilled. Word-frequency is of no concern at all when testing phonically taught children.

Summary Table - Oral Reading Test Results - Second Grades - 1977-1978

	Passing Accuracy		Failing Accuracy				% Passing	Estimated Speed		
	% Scoring at or above 95 on Test	% Scoring at or above 90 on Test	% Scoring Below				Comprehension	% Slow	% Fast	Reversals
			90	85	80	70				
Sept. and Early Oct. **American Tests** Phonic programs - 7 classes, 166 pupils Average Code 9.4	58	78	22	14.1	11	6.1	58	15	10	10
Sight-word/Global 1 class, 19 pupils Scott, Foresman Code 2	37	42	58	36.8	36.8	5.3	63	26	0	16
Late Oct. and Nov. **European Tests** Heavily phonic programs, avg. Code 8.6, 13 classes, 237 pupils	90	96	4	2.2	0.4	0.0	44	17	26	6
Sight-word/Global programs, avg. Code 6, 6 classes, 101 pupils	74	86.5	13.5	3.3	2.5	2.5	57	37	10	18.5
January, 1978, **American Tests** Phonic programs, 8 classes, 133 pupils, Code 10	77	92	8	6	4.3	1.4	64	8	35	6
Sight-word/Global 10 classes, 177 pupils, avg code 3	53	75	25	14.5	8.8	6.5	68	15	14	11

See attached notes

did, however teach short vowels).

In Class U. S. 24, one of the Scott Foresman Code 2 classes which did not use the phonics workbook, the teacher used sight-word drill to fix the sight words in children's minds. Her class (despite the fact that I considered her, in my professional opinion, to be a truly fine teacher) did not do so well as the other Scott Foresman Code 2 classes.

In another school, where one second-grade class, U. S. 4, had used Open Court in first-grade, and the other second-grade class, Class 23, had used Houghton Mifflin, the Open Court Code 10 class noticeably outscored the Houghton, Mifflin Code 3 class, even though the Open Court class was tested in September and the Houghton Mifflin class was tested the following January.

In another school using the Houghton Mifflin materials, the second-grade teacher (U. S. 20) who gave heavy emphasis to teaching short vowels and sounding out words scored better in January than a similar class in the school which made no mention of using this approach.

Consistently, from any angle, the scores I obtained showed the superiority of the phonics approach in comparison to the sight-word approach.

The Pattern of Scores Was the Result of the Teaching Method Used

One result of this research, contrary to what is commonly reported, was that the test results seemed to be dependent solely on the reading method used, and independent of the quality of the school or the mode of teaching. Some schools were modified open classrooms, and most were highly structured, but these facts also seemed to have no effect on the results.

The same pattern appeared here and abroad: Where the first half of first grade stressed heavy phonics and vowel sounds, the children scored far better at the beginning of second grade on oral reading accuracy and speed. In those phonics programs which stressed reading comprehension, the children generally scored higher on reading comprehension, but in phonics programs where reading comprehension was not stressed, they scored far lower. In contrast to the wildly swinging phonics program scores on so-called "reading comprehension," from terrible to marvelous, the sight- word class reading comprehension scores fell into a very narrow band, far higher than the worst phonics scores but somewhat lower than the best. Yet the seeming stability of "reading comprehension scores" from the sight-word method, which is the probable reason that so many school superintendents have chosen the method ever since the 1920's, turned out on analysis to be its Achilles Heel. This is explained in the next chapter.

The pattern of differences between the two groups is demonstrated by the differences in the percentages of errors on three particular words on the oral test. On these three words on the test, #10 (leg), #125 (fed) and #143 (less), a comparison was made on the errors for the January U. S. phonics and sight-word classes.

Since the children who were obviously failing were stopped before the last selection, which included words #125 and #143, it was only on #10 that every child tried the word. For those who were "incomplete fails" before the last selection, however, they were counted as missing the two words, #125 and #143.

On Word #10, "leg," which is on the Thorndike word list from 500 to 1,000 frequency, but which all children should have been able to figure out, phonics classes averaged only 4.6% missing in January. American sight-word classes averaged 20.2% missing, or more than four times as many.

Word #135, "fed" is one of the 11 words out of the 64 different words on the 144-word test which were above the 500-most-frequently-used-words-group. It is also among the 5 words out of the 64 different words on the test which were above the 1,000 frequency. However, because it is so phonically regular, it is suitable to test decoding skills on unfamiliar words. Children in phonics groups should handle it easily by phonic sounding and blending. Sight-word groups should get it easily by visual analysis and substitution (from a known word, "red," substituting the initial consonant, "f") or by context and guessing from the initial and possibly terminal consonants. This is how the two different approaches succeeded on this easy word (including "incomplete fails" as missing the word): Phonic classes averaged 15.4% missing it and sight-word classes 37.9% missing it, or more than one out of every three children.

The next to the last word on the test was #143, "less." It was one of three choices to complete the last sentence: "The number of times is now.... Often, Less, Many." Yet I believe this kind of language structure or syntax is not at the child's level. Therefore, this is one of the more difficult sentences. Combined with the fatigue resulting from having read to the end of the test, "less" becomes one of the most difficult words on the test, even though it is on the list of the 500 most frequently used words (because it is not normally used by children in such syntax). In the January phonics classes, 14.1% of the children missed this word (including the "incomplete fails") and 31.6% of the sight-word groups. Again, it was evident that the sight-word groups were at a great disadvantage.

The one Scott, Foresman group, U. S. 27, which had used the Scott, Foresman phonics workbook in first grade which covered short vowels, and which group, as a result, I labeled Code 5, showed the results of that work on short vowels. On the first word, "leg," only 7% missed it. On the second word, "fed," only 7% missed it, and, on the last word, "less," only 13% missed it. The data is shown on the following table. What is obvious, however, is that there were some phonic failures on each word. What these failing children now require is not a DIFFERENT course than phonics. They need to take the same course again. Although the data showed that many more of the sight-word trained children needed phonic help, it also showed that some of the phonically trained children require additional phonics instruction. A teacher in France said to me that she felt it was normal to have three children out of twenty-five fail the first-grade course and have to repeat it, because such children were just not ready. The phonics course must be repeated with certain children, but one more year should suffice for almost all of them. Even if they do not repeat the first grade, the phonic material can always be reviewed in second grade.

Concerning the Speed of Reading

Because of interruptions, it was not possible to "stop-watch" the time spent reading. I anticipated, however, based on previous studies in the literature, that the children in phonics programs would read more slowly. I noted on the test forms, intending to use the data only for my own information, when a particular child's reading was noticeably slower or faster than the reading of the other children. I made no note if the reading rate was merely satisfactory. It was not until my research was over and I had averaged all the other statistics (accuracy, reversals, and comprehension) and was "done" with them that I turned in curiosity to the supposedly unimportant scores on relative speed, which I had no intention of using. Yet, when I averaged these scores, I uncovered a startling fact. Twice as many sight-word trained children were "slow" readers in comparison to the phonics children, both here and abroad! When I looked at the "fast" scores, I found that only half as many sight-word-trained children read quickly in comparison to the phonics children. Again, the ratio held with the European scores and with the American fall and January scores.

It is interesting that S. J. Samuels ties speed to automaticity, saying that automatic readers are both more accurate and faster. Sure enough, when I compared my U. S. fall phonics scores to my U. S. January phonic scores, the results showed that the phonics-trained children were improving in

<u>Error Analysis, U. S. Classes
January, 1978</u>

	<u>Word #10 - leg</u>	<u>Word #125 - fed</u>	<u>Word #143 - less</u>
Phonic Average Code 10	4.6%	15.4%	14.1%
Sight Average Codes 2 and 3	20.2%	37.9%	31.6%
Scott, Foresman Plus SF Phonics Workbook Teaching Short Vowels Code 5	7%	7%	13%

possible automaticity because they had higher accuracy scores and greater speed in January.

Therefore, concerning published reports that sight-word trained children read faster at second grade than phonics- trained children, it seems evident that the sight-word-trained children's better rate of speed, at least at the second grade level, in finishing silent reading comprehension tests, has been a result of skimming for contextual meaning. Yet their phonics-trained counterparts were generally really reading, not skimming, and that obviously takes more time.

On Outside Factors Which Can Affect Achievement

On my second-grade oral tests in America, in programs where the phonics emphasis was heavy and the failures therefore slight (a total of only 8%), a pattern emerged. The failures occurred with startling regularity in tandem with some other severe disability reported by their teachers. One child had severe ear problems and was actually scheduled for an ear operation. Another had visual problems, wore thick glasses, and was also scheduled for an operation the following week. One almost total non-reader in the fall (read only 10% of the first 30 words, probably from context, as I had given him previous words he missed) had been diagnosed as having severe emotional problems, and he was receiving psychological counseling.

It has been said for many years that the cause for reading failures is often outside the reading situation itself. With the phonics failures on this test, only 8% compared to 25% for the sight-word groups in the United States, there appears to be truth in the statement. Yet, obviously, it would not apply to the many failing children in the sight-word groups. That far greater number in the sight word groups can be attributed to poor teaching methods.

The following table shows all the phonics failures for U. S. January classes, and the comments that were made casually by teachers concerning some of these children. These comments reveal a startling pattern of explanations for these phonic reading failures, a pattern of real disabilities unrelated to reading instruction. It is possible that a failure on an oral reading test given to phonically-trained children at the second-grade level might reveal that certain children have unsuspected handicaps which need treatment, unrelated to reading. An oral accuracy reading test might be used as a rough screening device for follow-up by the school health department.

Notes That Were Made on Children in U. S. Phonics Programs Who Failed the Accuracy Test in January, 1978

Below 90% word accuracy was failing: 11 phonic-trained pupils failed, 8% of the total.

Note
Emotional problems per teacher. Receiving counseling.

Parents from India. Foreign language at home

Read exceedingly slowly and did not complete test. He read words easily where there was less chance of reversals (little, white, color, mostly) but had great trouble with b - d words (dog, back). The teacher said he has trouble also even with the most simple addition facts. From this child's performance, it was evident that he had mastered decoding skills and his trouble lay elsewhere. He has been referred for psychological testing by his teacher.

Hearing disabled. Operation scheduled.

Diagnosed in spring term of first grade as having severe chronic illness, which is responding well to treatment.

According to teacher, severe reversal problems, particularly in dictation. He can perform silent reading tasks with fair success (70% on simple workbook pages). Kept losing his place when reading orally.

* Eye operation scheduled. Thick glasses.

* Heavy glasses

* Made saw/was reversal.

* No comment.

* No comment.

*The teachers in these phonic second-grade classes used Scott Foresman sight-word books for the slowest children. These two classes, with 41% of the total phonic pupils tested, account for five of the 11 failures below 90%, but four of the six very worst scores, below 79%. For the six children from the other phonic classes who failed, sufficient reasons were suggested for their failures, as shown above. Yet, for three of the five children from these two classes who failed the test, no reason at all was offered. However, it seems probable that there is a very good reason for their failure. It is the fact that sight-word materials were given to these failing children instead of the phonic materials that were given to failing children in the other phonic second grades

CHAPTER 8
The Test Results Show Not Just One Kind of Reader, But Two Different and Opposite Kinds, or Mixtures of Those Kinds

The test figures just cited are meaningful only if it is conceded that they describe DIFFERENT kinds of readers. One-quarter of a class failing (or 25%) as happened in the January U. S. sight-word classes, cannot really be compared to the 8% failing in the U. S. phonics classes, as if both groups are traveling toward a solitary goal called "Reading." The two groups have been taught to do different and opposite things, and so they ultimately become different and opposite kinds of readers. Sight-word-trained children at Code 1 are taught to decode by the MEANING of print, but phonics children at Code 10 are taught to decode by the SOUND of print (and mixed methods from Code 2 to Code 9 produce readers using different mixtures of SOUND and MEANING).

The 8% of the phonics children still having trouble in mid-second-grade can anticipate ultimate success, even those who have some degree of real dyslexia, because they will most probably continue to be taught sounding-andblending phonics, and that is the ONLY way that such children have ever been taught to read. (I cite the Orton- Gillingham phonic methods, among many others)

But the 25% who failed in the sight-word classes have been taught to read psycholinguistically, by the meaning of the print. Yet they are NOT considered severe failures, because few people think it is terribly wrong when one-quarter of the children in our schools cannot really read. Most of these children will not even qualify for reading remediation (probably only the 6.5% who read below 70% accuracy, which NONE of the European phonics children did). They will continue to get more of what got them into trouble in the first place, psycholinguistic "teaching", and they will NEVER really be able to read. Of this 25%, based on statistics from the recent <u>Functional Literacy</u> study, 13% can expect to be functionally illiterate all their lives.

It is not even possible to equate the successful readers in both programs. The American phonics group did overwhelmingly better, producing 77% in the classes reading at instructional level (95% or above on this test), while the American sight-word classes had only 53%. But this American phonic group, reading at or above 95% word accuracy, is really an independent group of readers, despite the "independent" level of 98 or 99% word accuracy that is set by the sight-word "experts." The American phonic readers at or above the 95% oral accuracy level may need some further instruction to assure "automatic" decoding, but they can nevertheless immediately be turned loose in any library and can work out and read the material in any books which interest them. They can anticipate becoming, very soon, automatic decoders in the true sense of the word, with all of their attention available to concentrate on the meaning of what they are reading, without being "hung up" on word identification.

Yet the 53% of the sight-word readers who scored at or above the "instructional" level of 95% word accuracy have demonstrated only that they can read Grade 2.3 material as on this oral test. They probably have only been taught sight-words to about that level! They have no sounding-and-blending word attack skills to sound out words for themselves that they have not been "taught," and they probably never WILL have such skills. (Consider the Houghton, Mifflin trained second-grade girl in Class U. S. 23, in January of second grade, who scored at the "independent" level on this oral test composed of high-frequency sight words, but was unable to read the word printed over and over on her own blouse, "outrageous," reading it as "Australia.")

Unless the sight-word-trained children are fortunate enough to have a teacher who will teach them the simple, synthetic phonics that they should have learned in first grade, those sight-word-trained children will be locked into the dreary, exquisitely boring basal reader sequence. They will only get what passes in those basal readers as analytic phonics instruction. Yet that so-called analytic phonics instruction is actually only a cut-and-paste, jig-saw puzzle operation with meaning-bearing sight-words. The sight-words are pulled apart into pieces and the pieces are then reassembled in new combinations to form different words. Sounding-and-blending of isolated letter sounds blissfully devoid of "meaning" (true, synthetic phonics) is no where to be found in the sight-word basal reader approach.

Yet the most critical difference between the phonic and the sight-word groups is not the result on oral reading accuracy, striking as that difference is in favor of the phonics groups. It is the tell-tale profile of scores that demonstrate that sight-word readers are crippled in decoding, and so are forced to focus part of their conscious attention on the context for word identification. That means they have to read with a divided attention. Part is on word identification, and only that part of the attention that is left over is available to concentrate on the meaning of the text. Obviously, with only part of their conscious attention free to focus on ultimate meaning, their "reading comprehension" has to be lessened. Yet they are almost certain to get a score well above zero on "reading comprehension", because their attention to the "meaning" is forced. They cannot fail to pay attention to "meaning" when reading because, if they did not, they would be unable to read at all, since they are decoding consciously from the text's meaning. But the phonics child, who does not use the context to decode, may or may not pay attention because his attention is free, and not forced.

The following table compares the relative scores on accuracy, reversals, speed, and comprehension of the phonics and the sight word groups in the early fall, 1977, in America, in the late fall, 1977, in Europe, and in January, 1978, in America. Greater-than and less-than arrows have been inserted after each comparison. The startling and almost perfect consistency in the direction of those arrows, when comparing a more phonic group to a more sight-word group, confirms the fact that there are two different and opposite kinds of readers. The lower codes show poorer oral reading accuracy, slower speed, higher reversals and - a point to which I will return - slightly higher averaged scores on comprehension. (Yet that latter seemingly strong point turned out to be the Achilles heel of the sight-word method, when analyzed - as I will do when I discuss reading comprehension.)

This amazingly consistent profile of scores, when comparing higher phonics codes to lower sight-word codes, even turned up when comparing the very slightly more phonic Houghton Mifflin (Code 3) to the less phonic Scott, Foresman (Code 2).

The consistent direction of these arrows indicates the presence of a force in action, and I conclude that the force is conscious context-guessing, which constantly switches the attention of sight-word readers back and forth between word-identification and the ultimate meaning of the text.

S. J. Samuels discussed his idea of automatic decoding in his article, "Automatic Decoding and Reading Comprehension," in the magazine, Language Arts. Samuels said that research has established that the brain acts as a single channel processor. At any given moment, attention can only be on one thing at a time. If two sources of information are presented simultaneously to a person, each of which demands attention for its processing, the individual will find that both cannot be processed at the same time. He contrasted this conscious attention to the case with automatic processes, which can work without the use of conscious attention, which he said is "tantamount to putting a plane on automatic pilot."

However, even though certain activities required the use of conscious attention while they were being learned, he said that, once learned, they can function without the use of conscious attention, such as the tying of shoe laces or the riding of a bicycle. Samuels commented further:

> "...the one important area of human behavior which, regardless of the amount of practice one gets, cannot be performed automatically is that of comprehending language. To comprehend either visually or auditorily presented language requires the services of attention.
>
> "At this point, a definition of 'automaticity' is clear: behavior is automatic when it can be performed without attention....
>
> "At the beginning stages of learning to read, the student's attention is focused upon the decoding aspects of the task. Since processing information for meaning also requires attention, as long as the reader's attention is on decoding, what has been read cannot be comprehended.
>
> "The fluent reader, unlike the beginning reader, is able to decode automatically without the services of attention and thus is able to attend to processing meaning at the same time as decoding...."

Samuels' view of reading is obviously in stark contrast to the view presented by Kenneth Goodman in "Reading: A Psycholinguistic Guessing Game." Goodman claims that readers should use semantics in part to decode. Yet semantics - or the meaning of language - requires conscious attention, and its use therefore makes automatic decoding impossible. The psycholinguistic reader, by definition, since he uses not just graphic-phonic (sound) cues and syntax (language structure) cues, both of which can be handled automatically, also uses semantic cues - but they CANNOT be used automatically. The psycholinguistic reader is therefore permanently unable to read automatically and must therefore permanently suffer from divided attention while reading, part to word identification largely from the context, and only the part of attention that is left over to concentrate on the meaning of the text.

Yet Samuels had said further that a fluent reader might say he had read every word on a page but be unable to recall what he read. Such a reader, according to Samuels, was decoding automatically but, instead of focusing his attention on the meaning of the text, had permitted his attention to wander.

Samuels has obviously provided the explanation for the sometimes lower "comprehension" scores from phonics classes, who have nevertheless demonstrated that they can decode very well. They have simply failed to pay voluntary attention to the test material which they were reading.

In an article in the <u>Reading Informer</u> of the Reading Reform Foundation, Samuels commented that two of the best signs of automaticity in reading are speed and accuracy. However, obviously, another sign of automaticity, from what has just been said, is the ability to read WITHOUT paying attention to the meaning of what is being read! Yet psycholinguistic sight-word readers, unlike phonics-trained readers, MUST pay attention to the context, since they use it to decode, or they will be unable to read at all.

These three factors, then, should serve to distinguish psycholinguistic sight word readers from phonic, automatically- decoding readers: lower accuracy, lower speed and generally passing

On the Consistent Profile of Arrows When Comparing Phonics Scores to Sight-Word Scores - Totals for the second-grade level on oral accuracy reading tests given to 495 American children in English and 338 European children in German, Dutch, Swedish, and French.

On the 1-to-10 Code scale, 1 is total sight-word teaching and 10 total phonic teaching, with mixtures ranging from Code 2 to Code 9. Ratings were based on observations in first grades in schools where second graders were tested. The near-perfect consistency in the arrows' directions on this table of oral reading research results, when comparing higher codes to lower codes, shows the presence of a force. It is concluded that the force is the conflict between mutually exclusive conditioned reflexes for processing print, to the left angular gyrus or to the right angular gyrus (or between mixtures of these reflexes).

	Per Cent Passing Accuracy		Per Cent Passing Comprehension	Estimated Speed		Per Cent Reversals
	At or above 95% on Test	At or above 90% on Test		% Slow	% Fast	
U. S. Fall 1977 Phonic Code 9.4 Compared to U. S. Sight-Word Code 2 Sept. to Mid-Oct.	58>37	78>42	58<63	15<26	10>0	9<16
Europe Fall 1977 Phonic Code 8.6 Compared to Europe Sight-Word Code 6 Mid-Oct to End of Nov.	90>74	96>86.5	44<57	17<37	26>10	6<18.5
U. S. January 1978 Phonic Code 10 Compared to U. S. Sight-Word Code 2.9	77>53	92>75	*51<68	8<15	35>14	6<11
U. S. January 1978 Phonic Code 10 Compared to Europe Fall 1977 Sight-Word Code 6	77>74	92>86.5	*51<57	8<37	35>10	6<18.5
Europe Fall 1977 Phonic Code 8.6 Compared to U. S. January 1978 Sight-Word Code 2.9	90>53	96>75	44<68	**17>15	26>14	6<11
U. S. Jan. 1978 Code 3 Houghton Mifflin Compared to Code 2 Scott Foresman	55>42	74>68	62<68	16<17	8<13	11<13

**Note that this European phonics speed score is two months earlier than the American sight-word score. The arrow would probably have been reversed if classes had been tested at the same time.

*This score excludes three U.S. January sight-word classes which emphasized "comprehension" where 82% passed, in comparison to the 68% in the U. S. January sight-word group. The phonic average shown on this table of 51% is from the four other phonics classes, where presumably teachers had not drilled on so-called "reading comprehension" exercises which are nothing more nor less for phonics-trained children than inducements to pay voluntary attention while reading.

All of the above scores are averages for all classes in a category. However, when individual class "comprehension" scores are ranked, the U.S. phonics classes had scores that went all over the scale, from poor to excellent (showing the presence - or lack - of voluntary attention while reading the exercise). The U. S. sight-word class "comprehension" scores, however, fell into a narrow band: better than the worst U. S. phonics scores, but worse than the best U. S. phonic scores. Most sight-word trained children cannot read at all without paying attention, because they have to use conscious attention to guess so many of the words. (The 1985 U. S. Government report, Becoming a Nation of Readers, reported that most adult Americans today actually still guess words as soon as they see the first few letters. Trained in the sight-word method, they cannot read automatically as phonically trained people - and computers - can.)

Since the sight-word "comprehension" scores fell into a narrow band, it showed they were controlled by the method used, and that the narrow band was actually a function of the forced attention in the sight-word method, occuring in tandem with the sight-word group's lower accuracy and speed, and increased reversals. The sight-word group's stable, narrow comprehension scores were actually a FUNCTION of their crippled decoding. However, for the phonic classes, the very wide range of scores showed the presence of voluntary attention, and demonstrated that the phonic method had NO effect on comprehension, either good or bad. The fact that the best comprehension scores came from the phonics group shows that, with their ability to read automatically, phonics-trained readers have all of their attention potentially free to concentrate on "meaning," when they voluntarily choose to do so. Sight-word-trained readers never have all of their attention free to concentrate on meaning, since they must constantly use part of it to "guess" words, and the result is lowered "comprehension."

It should be noted that these oral reading accuracy scores, which are misleadingly high for most sight-word trained children, were based on a test composed almost exclusively of very high frequency words. That is the only kind of oral reading accuracy test that most sight-word trained children can handle. It would not have been possible to compare sight-word trained children with phonically trained children if an oral reading accuracy test had been given that was composed of low frequency words, because almost all sight-word trained children would have failed it. For corroboration of that fact, the word "fed" on this oral reading accuracy test was frequently missed by sight-word classes (but not phonic classes) because "fed" is a low frequency word. Even the use of context, which made the meaning of "fed" almost self-evident, did not help many of these children to guess the word. Since sight-word trained children cannot deal with isolated vowel sounds (the short "e" of fed), they are usually incapable of sounding out even the simplest of words, like "fed." "Intrinsic phonics" did not help these children, either (the meaning of the context plus the "known" "f-ed" and beginning sound, "f," to work out "f-ed").

scores on "comprehension" since they do read with a certain amount (but divided) of forced attention to "meaning." Also, since phonic readers are forced to work in a left-to-right direction in decoding by sounding and blending (but since psycholinguistic readers are not forced to read in that direction), this adds a fourth factor to distinguish between the two groups: more reversals for the psycholinguistic group.

This is the profile that psycholinguistic context reading produces when it is compared to potential or actual automatic decoders. Children who have been trained in automatic decoding do not necessarily pay voluntary attention when reading test forms. In the absence of specific training to focus on their test material, they often will not. When large samples of this kind of phonic reader are compared on accuracy, reversals, speed, and comprehension to large samples of psycholinguistic readers who must pay attention to context in order to read at all, the above profile should appear. The profile confirms the over-dependence of sight-word readers on context for decoding as a result of inadequate decoding skills. Their divided attention, part to context to figure out the words, and only what is left over to focus on the ultimate meaning of the text, ultimately reduces their ability to comprehend.

However, it is an error to conclude that we are testing true reading comprehension at such low grades as the second grade with such simple reading materials as this test. Since the material contained in my test and in most comprehension tests at this level is so simple that it can be easily comprehended by second-grade children if it is read to them, what we are really testing is something other than "comprehension" We are actually testing attention.

A child who has been taught in a heavy phonics program has no trouble decoding such simple print as in comprehension tests at this level. He can read mindlessly (word-calling!), and not know that he is not paying attention, as a distracted adult sometimes reads the newspaper when he has something heavy on his mind.

But the child who has been taught in a sight-word program with insufficient phonics practice has only one major clue to decode the print - and that is the meaning of the context. If he is going to read at all, he has to pay very close attention - forced attention. So he may score higher in comprehending something that actually requires no great powers of comprehension.

However, on my tests, it is interesting that the heavily phonics-trained children, when encouraged to pay attention, scored higher than the predominantly sight-word groups. For years, it has been stated in the United States that phonics- trained children cannot read with comprehension. Yet the U.S. test data I gathered on comprehension emphatically disagrees with this conclusion. Despite the fact that phonics averages from the phonic classes were slightly lower than the sight-word class average, the highest individual class comprehension scores were made by the phonics groups (and so were the lowest, to which I refer again later).

It is interesting that it was only in Europe where the phonics/global controversy has not been so prominent that comprehension scores showed sight-word classes consistently outstripping phonics classes. I believe this shows, instead of a strength in the global programs, a real weakness. The sight-word /global group was forced by its relative phonics weakness into relatively greater dependence on the meaning of the context, in order to guess unknown words on the test, and this forced attention to the meaning of the context was the cause for the resultant higher so-called "comprehension" scores.

The phonics group, in the absence of encouragement to pay attention, were more ready to read mindlessly as they read automatically. That does not mean that they CANNOT pay attention, as is proven by the U. S. phonics classes who scored far higher than the sight-word average, and, notably, by the Swedish 10-year-olds on the IEA 15-nation study, who outscored all others on comprehension, and Swedish children are taught by a straight sounding-and-blending phonics approach.

Attributing higher averaged comprehension test scores of sight-word groups to truly higher comprehension is the fallacy of false cause (non causa pro causa) when that which is not the cause of a phenomenon is taken to be its cause. My data showed in the United States and in Europe that the so-called higher averaged class comprehension scores of sight-word/global programs occurred uniformly in tandem with other scores which showed decoding weakness: lower accuracy in oral reading, slower speed, and greater reversals. Therefore, the cause of the higher comprehension scores was the poorer decoding, resulting in forced attention to context, which produced the higher scores. It was not the result of better understanding in comparison to phonics classes.

When I examined my reading comprehension scores in phonics groups and in sight word groups for those readers who read at 97% accuracy and above, which I am considering "independent" for the purposes of this analysis (lower than Betts' 99%), I found a difference between the phonics and sight-word groups in America (and in Europe but to a lesser degree, since all the programs there had a far heavier phonic element, even the global ones).

At this high accuracy level, 97% or above, what was most noticeable about the American phonics classes was the extreme spread of the averaged comprehension scores of those classes. The class averages went from 36% passing to 100% passing in January. The only certain thing that these classes had in common was heavy phonic emphasis, but, since the average class comprehension scores emerged as TOTALLY RANDOM, from dreadful (the bottom phonic class having only 36% passing) to marvelous (with 3 of the 7 phonic classes scoring with 100% passing) it is evident that phonics teaching had no effect whatsoever on comprehension, either positive or negative. The following table gives those statistics and a short analysis

Further confirmation of the complete lack of either a positive or negative influence from phonics first-grade instruction on comprehension came from comparing two second-grade classes in an Open Court school. This school had both original first-grade teachers leave during the first-grade year, one in January and one in April. The replacement teachers were concerned about the children's achievement and had considered retaining up to eight children at the first-grade level, but they eventually retained only one from one class and none from the other. The classes were then shuffled and promoted to second grade. (It should be evident that in these classes the influence from teachers on achievement should be far less than usual, the greater influence coming from the standard Open Court phonic program that had been used by all four teachers of these two first grades.)

I tested one of these shuffled second-grade classes, U. S. 6, in October, 1977 (a mixture from both first-grade Open Court classes). In the entire October class, 82% passed comprehension. However, I found that the high- accuracy group in the class (the 50% of the 22 children scoring at or above 97% oral reading accuracy) had an average of 91% pass the comprehension test! (The second-grade class actually had 23 children, but one, a badly failing student who scored only 75% word accuracy, had not been in the school in first grade and so was not included in the scores.) The second-grade teacher obviously did not have a "top" group, however, as 18% (four children from last year's classes) failed the accuracy test in the fall, and three of those failures had a foreign-language background (as did at least one of the children who passed the accuracy test). This second-grade teacher must have been doing something to produce the high comprehension scores for the best readers, 91% passing in the 50% of the class who read at 97% word accuracy or higher. My guess is that she was giving the class reading comprehension worksheets, which encourage children to pay attention in order to avoid the unpleasantness of getting back a paper to take home which has a "bad grade". (The test results for U. S. 6 are in Appendix 3.)

The other half of the shuffled first-grade Open Court classes, U. S. 13, in a different second-grade room, was tested in January, 1978. If the first-grade Open Court phonics program had been the cause of the high reading comprehension scores I had received from the first half of the shuffled class in October, it should have also produced high scores in this other room, no matter what this other second-grade teacher did or did not do. Instead, I found appallingly LOW reading comprehension scores! The total January class had only 44% pass reading comprehension, compared to 82% passing reading comprehension in the total October twin class. The top group in this January class, scoring at or above 97% on the accuracy test, had only 36% pass the reading comprehension test, in dismal comparison to the 91% passing the reading comprehension test in the top group in its twin second-grade class in October! It should be evident that it was NOT the first-grade Open Court phonics program which produced the huge difference in results between the top groups in the two classes, 36% passing reading comprehension in the top group in one class compared to 91% passing reading comprehension in the top group in the other class. Nor was it even the time of the year in which they were tested, since, in another school using Open Court which I tested in January, U. S. 14, the group at or above 97% word accuracy had 78% pass the comprehension test. (The test results for Classes U. S. 13 and U. S. 14 are also in Appendix 3.)

I certainly do not consider the 36% passing score for the top group on so-called "reading comprehension" to mean anything terribly important, or to reflect unfavorably against the second-grade teacher of that class. It simply revealed that the children in that room had not been drilled in getting "right answers" on the sort of format of my little "reading comprehension" test, and so did not have proper habits of attention on that kind of thing. It certainly did NOT mean that the children could not understand and learn class work covered in a normal classroom teaching and testing manner. But it is this kind of silly, narrow "reading comprehension" which is used to test so-called "reading" programs, which are not really reading programs, because they certainly are NOT teaching reading. Yet, on the meaningless results from "silent reading comprehension tests," good phonic programs are being thrown out of schools all over America.

Three phonics classes which scored very high on so-called reading comprehension did give much drill on this sort of "reading comprehension". One was U. S. 11, the <u>Alpha One</u> group which used Houghton Mifflin workbook pages that drill on "reading comprehension". However, the class did not use the Houghton Mifflin so-called "phonic" program which relies massively on context guessing from only some of the letters in unknown words.

Another was U. S. 17, the "teacher-phonics" group in which the teacher, in effect, threw the Harcourt Brace teacher's guide out the window and taught the children in her own way, with sounding-and-blending phonics from the very beginning after first having taught the children the sounds and letters of the alphabet. She did, however, eventually use the Harcourt Brace materials which, like the Houghton, Mifflin materials, would have given drill in paying attention to workbook sheets in order to get "right" answers.

The third phonics group was a Lippincott group, U. S. 15, whose second-grade teacher seemed very concerned with reading comprehension work (admittedly my subjective judgment). Her group above 97% word accuracy had 100% pass comprehension, but another Lippincott second grade in the same building had only 67% of those above 97% word accuracy pass the comprehension test. Since the proportion of children who read as accurately as 97% is far higher in phonics classes than in sight-word classes, that means that a far higher percentage of children passed both word accuracy and comprehension in these classes. (An average of 52% of the children in the Code 10 phonics classes scored in January, 1978, at or above 97% on oral reading accuracy, while only 37% of the children in the averaged Code 3 sight-word classes scored at or above 97% oral reading accuracy). (The test results from Classes U. S. 11, U. S. 17, and U. S. 15 are in Appendix 3.)

The range of reading comprehension class scores from the American sight-word groups (averaged Code 3) in comparison to the American phonics classes was a completely different story. The range of class scores did not run from near hopeless to perfect, which was the case with the phonics group. Instead, the sight-word class scores in January, 1978, all fell in a narrow band, startlingly close together, and well below "perfect". Under 97% oral accuracy, nine sight-word classes had average class reading comprehension scores from 58% to 75%, a range of only 17 points and well below 100%. At the 97% accuracy or above in eight of those nine classes, 74 to 89% of the children passed the comprehension test, a range of only 15 points but still well below 100%.

It is true that the ninth sight-word class was not included in the above range of comprehension scores for the best readers. That ninth class, U. S. 25, a Scott, Foresman class, was not included because its comprehension score is not at all comparable to the comprehension scores from the other eight sight-word classes. Three children in this class read at or above 97% word accuracy (representing only 20% of that class, not 52% as in the phonics classes and 37% as in all the Code 3 sight-word classes). It is true that all three of those children did pass comprehension, which is technically a 100% class score. But if even one of that unrepresentative tiny group had not passed, the class score would have dropped to 67%. Therefore, to change the sight-word range of 74 to 89%, based on the scores from 61 sight-word children, by adding in these other three sight-word children for a total of 64 children and then raising the range to 74 to 100% based on a test from that one child out of 64 children, would be very misleading.

The U. S. 25 class score of 100% on comprehension in January, 1978, was, however, counted in the average for all averaged Code 3 sight-word classes at the 97% or above accuracy level, resulting in 80% passing comprehension, in comparison to 79% of the readers at that accuracy level passing in the phonics group.

It is the range, of course, which is most informative, and not the average. The phonics Code 10 range in January for those reading below 97% accuracy ran from 33 to 78% passing comprehension, a 45 point spread. Yet the sight- word Code 3 range ran from 58 to 75, a far smaller 17 point range. At the level of 97% accuracy or above, the phonics Code 10 range in January ran from 36 to 100, a 64 point range, almost totally random. The sight-word Code 3 range for 8 of 9 classes of 61 children ran from 74 to 89, an astonishingly narrow range of only 15 points.

However, one Scott Foresman class, U. S. 27, was not included in the above listings because it had made heavy use of a Scott, Foresman phonics workbook in the first half of first-grade, and I therefore had coded that class Code 5. As a result, it is not comparable to the other nine sight-word classes which had an average of Code 3. That Code 5 class did very well, with 100% passing comprehension, and with 53% at the 97% accuracy level or better.

The table follows which contains the statistics on reading comprehension for those who scored below 97% word accuracy and those who scored at or above 97% word accuracy.

The reading comprehension scores in the phonics groups were almost random, from not very far above zero to 100% passing in three of the seven phonics classes. Yet the averaged Code 3 sight-word reading comprehension scores fell into a very narrow band, far higher than the worst phonic reading comprehension scores but noticeably lower than the best phonic reading comprehension scores. That non-random variability in the sight-word/global comprehension scores indicated that a control was acting, particularly since the phonic comprehension scores were almost totally random, which demonstrated that no control was acting. What was controlling the sight-word comprehension scores was the forced, conscious attention of its context-guessing method, in which conscious attention cannot wander from a text's meaning, because, if it does, reading stops, by definition. Yet guessing, also by definition, has to result in reduced word accuracy. That the context-guessing decoding method did reduce word accuracy, and that the reduction was a function of the context-guessing method, is proved by the fact that use of the method occurred in tandem with lower accuracy scores, slower reading speeds and greater numbers of letter reversals.

However, it is evident that the huge spread in phonic comprehension scores, from terrible to marvelous, CANNOT be caused by the phonic initial teaching method, since the phonic method's accuracy scores show no correlation at all with the phonic method's comprehension scores. Those widespread phonic comprehension scores resulted from free attention, and that free attention could either freely choose to focus on the content of the selection or freely choose to wander.

Undue attention to decoding isolated words phonically has always been blamed as the cause for the lower comprehension scores sometimes observed in phonics programs. Before phonics children have reached the "independent" level (which is possibly also the automatic decoding level), this is undoubtedly often true, but it is not true for phonics children who are able to decode automatically and can therefore give all their attention (if they freely choose to do so) to the meaning of a text. What has never been suggested, however, is the reverse, the existence of a very real "reading comprehension" problem for sight-word trained readers. Sight-word readers, taught to decode by the meaning of the context, have to be permanently hampered in reading comprehension because they can never have all of their conscious attention free to focus on the meaning of a text. By definition, they must permanently use part of their conscious attention to identify words from the meaning of the context ("psycholinguistically"), which means they can never have their total attention free to focus on a text's meaning, as a phonic-trained reader can do. The conscious attention of sight-word-trained, context-guessing readers when reading has to be permanently divided, part to identifying words, and only the part that is left over to deal with the ultimate meaning of the text. Yet independent phonic readers, decoding totally automatically, and so not needing any consciousness to do so, have all of their consciousness free to focus totally on meaning (IF they freely choose to do so.).

The selling point for sight-word programs has been that teaching initial reading for sight-word "meaning" instead of for phonic "sound" improves ultimate comprehension. Obviously, it does not. Permanently damaged ability to concentrate totally on the content of a message is the Achilles Heel of the "meaning" method.

The crutch of context decoding for many of these Code 2 or 3 readers becomes permanent and is crippling in itself. These children are not free to read automatically as they are free to listen automatically but will ever afterwards have the strained attention when reading of the partially deaf when they are listening, never fully relaxed and free to read for meaning, but instead caught at the word identification level all of their lives, becoming permanent Code 2 or 3 readers.

Sight-word programs give a short-term, shot-in-the-arm for reading comprehension tests, raising scores through the primary grades or so, but the cost is divided attention forever after in reading, the reader focusing not just on context for meaning but on context for actual word identification. This divided attention, when the reading becomes difficult, results in dropped comprehension scores and, I believe, along with lack of experience in reading difficult material, probably accounts for the appalling drop in college entrance test scores and in student quality in general.

This divided attention in sight-word groups can be demonstrated by the fact that the Houghton Mifflin and Scott, Foresman children that I tested had 20% of their BEST readers fail comprehension. Yet the phonics classes that had apparently stressed comprehension (three of the seven phonic classes) had NONE of their best readers fail. These three phonic classes had a total of 55 children, and 28 of them scored at 97 per cent accuracy or above. Every single one of those 28 children reading at that high accuracy level passed the comprehension test, unlike the sight-word group, which had 20% of their readers at or above 97% word accuracy fail the comprehension test.

Phonics programs in Europe and here develop students who rapidly reach the automatic decoding stage, where they simply blend sounds into words so that they are literally hearing the written page. English-speaking phonically- trained students can "read" German as readily as they do English, but only in the sense that they hear but do not understand German, as when a German person speaks. However, when reading English, which they do understand, they can always alter the occasional irrational spellings, by context of the selection, just as we adjust partially heard English words. Except for that, the attention of phonically-trained children, who read at Code 10, is totally focused on the heard message and on its meaning, just as when they are listening to oral speech. Their attention is not divided as with Code 2 and 3 students who must use the context to decode words and so NEVER can reach the automatically decoding stage. Phonics children will focus on the message, that, is, IF it interests them. Here is where the teacher comes in and interests them, if necessary, to PAY ATTENTION!

The phonics programs in Europe had comprehension scores on these tests, for those children who scored above the 97% oral reading accuracy level, which were often low, like those of the American phonics classes which did not stress so-called "reading comprehension." That there is ultimately nothing wrong with their "reading comprehension" is shown by the reportedly higher academic levels in European universities and, most meaningfully, by the reportedly greater difficulty in their school texts. Concretely, to show that phonics produces extremely high comprehension, in international tests, Sweden scored the highest of 15 participating countries in reading comprehension for ten year olds, and Sweden has a mandated sounding-and-blending first-grade program.

The results of this study showed that reading comprehension scores are spuriously "higher" for psycholinguistic readers whose crippled decoding results in forced attention, while reading comprehension scores for phonically trained children, who really can read, go all over the scale, from marvelous (if they have been trained to pay attention) to terrible (if they have not been trained to pay attention). This is also what happens with standardized silent reading tests, on which the reputations of school administrators often hinge. Those administrators who have phonic classes "drilled" in attention habits when reading are ecstatic over their "high" scores.

These children, of course, really CAN read. Those with sight-word basal readers, however, produce fairly constant scores, but lower than the best phonics classes. But those with phonics classes which did NOT receive training in paying attention score low, and self-preservation often dictates that the administrators adopt a sight-word basal program which will produce fairly high averaged scores for a school district instead of the low comprehension scores they are getting.

After all, an administrator can hardly tell a group of outraged parents with test scores in their hands (and we have constant groups of outraged parents these days) that he has a "gut" feeling that the phonic program is better, even though Billy and Mary and Johnny scored so low on reading comprehension compared to their sight-word-trained cousins in the next town. And he himself has no rational reason to believe it is better, because he believes in the silent reading comprehension tests.

These standardized silent reading vocabulary and comprehension tests are utterly fallacious in design and score interpretation (grade 2.3 does NOT mean grade 2.3 in any real sense). They are the unholy offspring of their basal reader parent, representing, like it, a multi-million dollar vested interest industry, and they are currently the probable cause of resistance to phonics in the schools, and the dropping of phonics programs where they have been adopted.

The most important contribution that this research has been able to develop is that such higher scores, attributed to comprehension achievement in sight-word students, are being so attributed because of the fallacy of false cause. This research debunks the spuriously higher class averaged comprehension scores of the sight-word trained students and makes it possible to take the "standardized reading test"monkey off the backs of school administrators so that they can feel free to use phonics programs.

The startling truth my data uncovered is that phonics instruction has NO effect on reading comprehension at this low second grade level. After all, why should it? Phonics class averages on comprehension scored all over the scale, from very low class averages to very high class averages, which proved there was no statistical force controlling them. But with sight-word class averages, they scored consistently quite high at the bottom of the scale but lower at the top of the scale. This narrow band of class scores demonstrated conclusively that something was controlling the comprehension scores in the basal programs, which obviously was the forced attention from context reading.

This crippled decoding was confirmed by comparing the profile of all scores (accuracy, comprehension, reversals and speed) of sight-word groups to phonic groups. As accuracy and speed went down in sight word groups compared to phonics groups, comprehension and reversals went up. It was apparent that the weak decoding skills resulting in poor accuracy, poor speed and high reversals were also resulting in apparently higher averaged comprehension scores through the forced attention to the context which was necessary to decode the words in print.

Of course, a theoretical explanation might have predicted exactly this. Goodman's model of reading (psycholinguistics, which I rate Code 2) has word identification, even for mature readers, partially dependent on the meaning of the context. But processing context mentally always requires conscious attention. So, the psycholinguistic Code 2 reader has a permanently divided attention, part to context for word identification and part to context for meaning. As discussed previously, S. J. Samuels has stated that phonic decoding of words can be done automatically, which means with no conscious attention, as we tie shoe laces automatically. All conscious attention, therefore, is free potentially to use context to process meaning. Therefore, phonic Code 10 readers should have the potential to read with greater comprehension than psycholinguistic readers because they can have all of their attention to devote to the task, not just part of it. The test data from this research study confirms that this is exactly what is happening.

A COMPARISON OF READING COMPREHENSION SCORES FOR THE BEST READERS IN SIGHT WORD (CODE 3 AND CODE 2) AND PHONICS (CODE 10) GROUPS

Code 3 and Code 2 Classes	Percent of Class at 97% Oral Reading Accuracy Level Who Passed Comprehension	Number at 97% Accuracy Level	Percent of Class	Total Number in Class
HM - U.S. 18)	74			
U.S. 19) Ability	74			
U.S. 20) Grouped	74	39	42	93
U.S. 21) School -	74			
U.S. 22) Averaged	74			
HM - U.S. 23	89**	9	41	22
SF - U.S. 24	80	5	33	15
SF - U.S. 25	100*	3	20	15
SF - U.S. 26	80	5	29	17
AVERAGE	80		37	

*This group of 3 children, which was only 20% of Scott, Foresman Code 2 Class U.S. 25, is too unrepresentative to equate with the other scores. For instance, if only one of the three children had failed, U.S. 25's 100% comprehension score at 97% word accuracy level would drop to 67%.

Code 10 Classes	Percent of Class at 97% Oral Reading Accuracy Level Who Passed Comprehension	Number at 97% Accuracy Level	Percent of Class	Total Number in Class
Open Court U.S. 13	36	10	44	23
Open Court U.S. 12	55	11	69	16
Open Court U.S. 14	78	9	56	16
Lippincott U.S. 16	67	7	32	22
Lippincott U.S. 15	100	11	48	23
*Alpha One Plus HM Workbook, U.S. 11	100	11	65	17
*Teacher Phonics Plus Harcourt Brace Workbook, U.S. 17	100	8	53	15
AVERAGE	78		52	

**This January sight-word Code 3 Houghton Mifflin class was in the same school as the Fall Code 10 Open Court class which made the highest U.S. fall oral reading accuracy score. This suggests a higher ability level in this school. Correspondingly, the somewhat lower scores in the ability-grouped Code 3 Houghton Mifflin school suggest a somewhat lower ability level.

Analysis

The Code 2 and Code 3 January classes had an average of 80% passing reading comprehension at the 97% word accuracy level, but the most meaningful fact is that there was such a small spread in the percentages passing in these classes at the 97% word accuracy level, from 74% passing to 89% passing, or only FIFTEEN POINTS (after excluding the unrepresentative figure from the 3 children in SF 25). That small spread in the percentages of passing scores compares very strangely to the Code 10 January phonics spread of percentages of passing scores at the 97% word accuracy level. The phonics spread was SIXTY-FOUR POINTS. In addition three of the Code 10 January phonic classes had 100% of their students at the 97% or above accuracy level passing comprehension, which was more than half of the children in those classes, but nothing comparable appeared with the Code 2 and Code 3 scores.

It appears evident that the context-guessing and therefore divided-attention of the sight-word method does raise the scores at the bottom end (as demonstrated by the other tabulation showing scores below 97% accuracy). At below 97% word accuracy, more at the bottom end of the phonics group, its weaker readers, are still focused on "sound." However, as the spread of the passing class comprehension scores for the best readers indicates, the context-guessing method lowered the scores for the best sight-word readers because their attention continued to be divided by the permanent context-guessing of the sight-word method, where only part of conscious attention can be focused on "meaning" since the other part of conscious attention has been forced permanently to focus on for word identification.

Yet, the scores from the Code 10 phonic group at the 97% word accuracy level, (fairly "independent") were obviously totally random, from terrible to marvelous, indicating that the phonic method had no effect on reading comprehension, either positive or negative. Since the conscious attention of these best readers who could decode automatically was not divided, with part of that conscious attention being given to word identification as was the case with the sight-word group, that left their conscious attention potentially free to concentrate totally on meaning, if they chose to do that. Obviously, the three classes with 100% passing comprehension did do exactly that.

The Percentages in the Various Classes Who Passed the Reading Comprehension Test

	Fall Range of Class Scores on Comprehension	January Range of Class Scores on Comprehension	Fall Average	January Average	Difference Between Fall and January Averages
Under 97% Word Accuracy U.S. Phonics Classes, Code 10	17 to 75% (58 point range)	33 to 78 (45 point range)	45	54	+9
U.S. Sight Word Classes, Code 3	Only one class, 62% passed	58 to 75 (17 point range)	62	61	-1
European Phonics Classes, Code 8.6	0 to 100 (100 point range)		30		
European Global Classes, Code 6	20 to 100 (80 point range)		50		
Over 97% Accuracy U.S. Phonics Classes, Code 10	67 to 91 (24 point range)	36 to 100 (64 point range)	78	77	-1
U.S. Sight Word Classes, Code 3	Only one class, 80% passed.	74 to 89 (15 point range, excluding faulty U.S. 25)	80	80, Including U.S. 25	0
European Phonics Classes, Code 8.6	22 to 83 (61 point range)		47		
European Global Classes, Code 6	40 to 82 (42 point range)		64		

Analysis: When a group of lower code programs were compared to a group of higher code programs, the lower code programs consistently showed a narrower range of class comprehension scores. That narrower range, higher at the bottom but lower at the top in comparison to the higher code programs, demonstrated that a force acted to narrow the range.

CHAPTER 9
The Data Suggests That Black Children Become the Best Readers When They Are Taught by Phonics

My test results suggest that Black children suffer the most from the faulty sight-word "meaning" method.

In Europe, I found very few children from Black families. Nevertheless, there were a few, and, in most cases, it was evident that they were from immigrant families and correspondingly not "privileged" children who are always expected to achieve better than average. The startling thing about this tiny sample of Black children, however, was that they DID achieve far better than the European averages I recorded!

My cousin's wife grew up in Jersey City, New Jersey, years ago, when it had many stable residential neighborhoods. She said, in the neighborhood elementary school she attended as a child in the 1920's, "The Black kids were always the smart ones." She did not mean just in the first grade. She meant the whole of the elementary years. It is true that her school was in a stable and respectable neighborhood, and that therefore the Black children she remembered would have come from solid home backgrounds. But the European Black children I tested had to be a recent immigrant class for the most part, and yet they achieved in the same superior way that my cousin's wife reported for the Black children that she personally knew in her classes in the 1920's.

Among the 428 European second-grade children that I tested (not counting children given the partial test in the third Hamburg class), I tested five Black children. One child was new to her French school from French-speaking Martinique, so I could not include her with the European samples since she had not learned to read in Europe.

Another was new to her Swedish school from Russia, although her family came from Africa, and she could not yet speak Swedish. However, since she had learned to read in a European country, Russia, I included her accuracy score (100%) but obviously could not include her comprehension score (25%) since she could not, according to her teacher, understand Swedish yet. (The child's perfect accuracy score indicated success in the Latin alphabet, although she had presumably learned in Russia which uses a different alphabet. Yet she may have been taught both alphabets. Since Russian schools uniformly teach by phonics, she presumably would have been taught even the Latin alphabet in Russia by "sound" and not by "meaning," whether she learned it at home while living in Russia or in a Russian school.)

The other three Black children had all learned to read in European programs which were heavier on global/sight words, but, as mentioned, these programs are still heavily phonic by American sight-word standards. The testing results are given in the table on the next page.

The little second grader who learned to read in Martinique, and whose score I have therefore excluded in the European sample, was obviously very nervous when reading with me, which may have contributed to her low score. I suspect this low score of 65% accuracy reflected poor training in her Martinique first grade, because her sister, only a year younger, whom I saw in the first-grade class, was answering questions and reading the materials on the blackboard with ease. The first-grade teacher said she found that surprising because of the dialect difference between Martinique French and Continental French. Children from the same family do tend to achieve in the same manner in school (although, of course there are many exceptions) so it seems very possible that the second-grade girl who learned to read in Martinique might also have been as successful as her first-grade sister if she had spent her first-grade year in the European school.

Concerning the other three Black children, however, who had no language problem (two in France and one in the Netherlands), all passed both the comprehension test and the accuracy test. In addition, two of the three were reading at the instructional level for second grade. Two of the three were also reading at a "fast" rate. The little Amsterdam boy who was reading at a slow rate with an accuracy at 92%, above the frustrational level but below the instructional level, and who was receiving supplementary reading instruction in the Amsterdam school, passed the comprehension test, even though only 37% of his class did so. Also, he was the only one out of the 10 children in that class who were reading below 95% accuracy who passed the comprehension test!

If I include the first grader whom I saw perform very successfully indeed, but whom I could not test, that means that of the six Black children I saw in Europe, all but one were performing at a very high level compared to the total American sight-word test results, and, except at the instructional level, were also above the European average levels. The one child who was having trouble (and whom I did not include in my statistical sample) did not learn to read in Europe! Overall, only 50% of the total European children passed the comprehension test, but of the three Black European children that I tested on comprehension, all passed it, and the little Black first-grader I saw was also obviously having no trouble at all either with comprehension or decoding, despite her different dialect, as she readily answered questions on the experience chart story on the blackboard. (It seems highly likely that the little Black girl new to her Swedish school, who orally read Swedish at 100% accuracy, could also have passed the comprehension test when she learned to speak Swedish.)

This is a very small sample, admittedly, and a large sample in all probability would closely approach the European norm, rather than exceed it. However, what is interesting is that it is the total opposite of what our American Black children are scoring with the sight-word basal readers. The European Black children that I tested were apparently not from rich homes, and yet the European schools had taught them to read - and to comprehend - very well indeed, just as the schools in Jersey City did in the 1920's when supplementary phonics was used.

I believe that our Black children who are not scoring adequately on reading tests are just another burnt offering to the sight-word basal reader money makers. Black children used to learn to read very well in America before 1930, before the deaf-mute sight-word method had invaded American schools with William Scott Gray's "Dick and Jane" published by Scott, Foresman, and the comparable deaf-mute method series, Macmillan's, written by Arthur I. Gates. Real phonics went out the window after 1930 with that installation in American schools of the deaf-mute, sight-word context guessing method, and Black achievement plummeted. So, of course, did achievement for all the other students, but the Black students lost their leading edge over those others.

Talents are inherited, and history certainly seems to indicate that many Black people are heavily gifted in processing and dealing with sound in all its aspects, even to the point where they were able to translate speech by voice into speech by drums. But the lunacy of the sight-word, context-guessing method (a defective approach used to teach deaf-mutes) tries to make little children into aphasics (or deaf-mutes), going directly from print to "meaning" without concentrating on actual speech, so that "accuracy" errors at the word level are not important. (It is incredible, but "pony" is as acceptable as "horse" to the sight-word experts!) The child who is forced to pay undue attention to context to decode the meaning of words is therefore often bypassing the sound of words, and instead is forced to think in images as dogs and cats do. Little children are drilled in getting "main ideas" and "meaning" while simultaneously correct word identification is trivialized. Here is where the ultimate confusion must come for a child who is heavily endowed with auditory skills as many Black children apparently are. The child knows that he cannot identify the words on the page, and it is natural for such a child to think of words as sounds. But he is told not to identify words by sounds and is almost encouraged to look out of the window and guess what soundless "idea" might come next!

I suspect that for children who are higher than average in auditory abilities, as many Black children apparently are, it is more difficult to function with the divided attention in reading that results from the use of the sight-word context guessing method (a defective deaf-mute method), in which word identification is largely from the "meaning" of print and not its sound. Yet, the precise sounds of words may be more important for many Black children than for other children so that the defective deaf-mute method may be even more harmful to them than to other children. I also suggest that children who are endowed with higher than average auditory abilities (as many Black children apparently are) will achieve higher than other children when they are promptly taught word identification skills by phonics upon entering school. They should also learn phonics skills faster than other children, all other factors being equal, and be well on their way to a real education even before they leave first grade.

Perhaps my cousin's wife's memory was correct. The Black children in her school in her day, when phonics was the norm, having gotten the business of "learning to read" out of the way faster than the other children, were able sooner to begin to "read to learn," as Dr. Dykstra puts it.

Tony Tselentis of the <u>Tucson Citizen</u> on January 13, 1978, reported on articles by Dick Dougherty of the Rochester (N. Y.) <u>Times-Union.</u> Dougherty's front-page headline read, "Oh, oh! Look, Spot, Look,... Dick and Jane Are Dead!" He was reporting on the fact that sight words had been thrown out of the Rochester schools and replaced by the phonic programs, Distar, Open Court and Lippincott. Many people were responsible for the happy event, but the moving force was apparently a man named Archie Curry, who was described in this article as an angry Black parent in 1972, and in 1978 an education specialist for the Urban League and member of the Rochester school board.

It was reported that some years before, a principal in Rochester "gave the school administration fits by using a phonetic system and working miracles with the Black pupils. His name was Fred Parker. When he retired in 1965, the program he used was shut down by the director of elementary education."

Tselentis went on to report that a seventh-grade Rochester teacher named Marian Hinds told reporter Dougherty of the <u>Times-Union</u> that later:

> "...so many bright kids were failing because they couldn't read. That's how I got into all this.... I went up against the Board of Education... and got some terribly rough treatment. I tried to get on the textbook selection committee, but there was no way. They wouldn't let 'outsiders' on. Only teachers and administrators who liked things the way they were."

Dougherty continued his story in Curry's words:

> "What happened was that we in the black community discovered our kids couldn't read.... Then Bernie Gifford said, okay, if you're not going to go for real integration, we want to control our own schools.... We heard about a

The Superior Scores from European Second-Grade Black Children
Who Had Been Enrolled in European First-Grade Programs at Code 6 or Higher

Country	Sex	Accuracy	Comprehension	Speed	Reversals
France A1	Girl	99%	100%	Fast	None
France A 1	Girl	97%	75%	Fast	Nomme, not monne
Holland, Amsterdam 4	Boy	92%	75%	Slow	None
Stockholm 3	Girl	100%	Did not speak Swedish yet.*	Normal	None

In addition, a Black girl in first grade, whom I did not test, and who had arrived in France from Martinique just a few months earlier, was performing excellently at both reading orally and answering oral questions from lesson material on the blackboard in a Code 6 class, despite having what the teacher considered a strong accent that was different from Continental French. Yet, in contrast to that little girl's success, her second-grade sister, who had been taught reading in Martinique and so had been in the European school only about two months, failed the test. Because the second-grade child had not been taught reading in Europe, her failing score is not shown above.

*The Black girl in the second-grade Stockholm class, who did not yet speak Swedish but who read it flawlessly, had recently arrived from Russia (her family having gone there from Africa some time earlier). Russia uses a heavy phonic emphasis but on its own alphabet. Yet the child obviously had a total command of the Latin alphabet. The assumption is made that, whether she learned to read the Latin alphabet while at home in Russia or in a Russian school, the probability is that she was given a phonic approach since it is the only one in use in Russia.

> program called BRL in New Orleans. It was a strong phonetics program.... We went down with some parents and looked at it. We were really impressed. So we came back here and put the pressure on the school board to try the program at Schools 4 and 19.... It worked. It really worked. The reading scores started going up... and those in the white schools were still going down. People in the white schools started saying, hey, let's look at this. When the white community was affected, things started happening."

The result was a unanimous Board of Education vote for a strong phonetic approach in Rochester, and to limit its schools to a choice of three such programs, Distar, Open Court, or Lippincott.

So Rochester's Black pupils had such fantastic success with a phonics program that ALL of Rochester went phonic!

The story is repeated in so many places. The Reading Reform Foundation sent me results of Mary Johnson's spelling test administered to first-grade classes, one in a Harlem first grade class at P. S. 57A, Madison Avenue at 114th Street, May 31, 1972, and one in a first grade at Arizona State University Laboratory School in April, 1961. The list included phonetic words like jot, spun, lump yelp, quilt and frog - 26 words in all. The Harlem group spelled 80% of the new words correctly and 84% of the "basic words." The more privileged children at the Arizona University Laboratory School, who had used Scott, Foresman, spelled only 16% of the new words and 47% of the "basic words." Their performance using Scott, Foresman in relation to children in the Harlem school which had used Spalding's Writing Road to Reading (a phonic method) can only be described as indefensible. Nevertheless, it should be obvious that the Harlem children (mostly Black and Puerto Rican) with their phonics program did exceedingly well.

A very remarkable woman, Marva Collins, is Director-Teacher of Westside Preparatory School, Chicago, Illinois. She spoke at the Reading Reform Foundation meeting at Princeton in 1979 and I had the privilege to talk to her later. The very impressive-sounding school is one she founded herself, after she had become disenchanted with the public schools in Chicago. Her success in her school in a poor urban Black area has been so unbelievable and noteworthy that she has been asked to permit television programs to be filmed in her school and, I believe, she has been on the nationwide program, Sixty Minutes.

It is impossible, of course, to ignore the effect that this remarkable personality would have on children, and it is unlikely that more average teachers could achieve her amazing results, even using her methods, (which obviously include real phonics). Nevertheless, in what is apparently a slum area, she has third-grade children reading so well that they read - AND DISCUSS - Chaucer and many other literary giants! Marva Collins read aloud many of the essays that her children, of all ages, wrote. What was so notable that it almost struck one in the face was the facility that these children had with language structure and vocabulary. The language of great books will never be a foreign language to them because it has become their own language.

It is beside the point to argue whether third or fourth or fifth graders could understand the deeper meanings in these literary works. That is totally irrelevant at this point. The purpose of the elementary school is to turn out a LITERATE population, with the potential to understand the complex speech and arguments in great books, when the students reach the age to weigh them properly. Marva Collins, in her own little Chicago private school, because of the use of real phonics which made it possible for her students to "hear" these great works, has turned out Black children for whom Horatio Alger's books are as easy as comic books, who write more beautifully than most college students today, and who are ready now to deal with great literature for the rest of their lives.

And what do our sight-word basal reader authors have to show as their contribution to our

American Black community? Just read the results of the National Assessment of Educational Progress to find out what those sight-word basal readers accomplished - or did not accomplish. Because of the sight-word basal reader materials, our Black children are frequently being deprived of literacy, not just while they are in school, but often for the rest of their lives.

A thought occurred to me. The International Reading Association, judging from remarks at the New Jersey Teachers Convention by Ralph C. Staiger in 1978, wishes to publicize good news about reading. In what issue, if any, of which of their widely read publications, have they reported on the good news of the phonics programs in Rochester, New York?

CHAPTER 10
On the Superior Reading of Phonics-Taught Swedish and Dutch Sixth-Grade Students

The second-grade oral reading selection that I used had been appropriate for second grades in America and Europe because it had already been part of a cross-national silent reading comprehension study that had been carried out by IEA. IEA had tested 10-year-olds in many countries on silent reading (not 7-year-olds on oral reading, as had been done on my test). Yet the IEA silent reading comprehension test for 10-year-olds had been constructed so that it started with an extremely simple section of 144 words in English (which rated a Grade 2.3 level) and then only gradually became more and more difficult until the end of the test. IEA's intent had been to see how much of the progressively-more-difficult material each child could read in the time allotted, and then how accurately the child responded to the questions for that portion he had succeeded in reading. Since the beginning 144-word portion of the IEA silent reading test at Grade 2.3 level had already been used in a cross-national study, I felt it was appropriate for my own cross-national study of oral reading accuracy (and comprehension, since the 144 words in English included five comprehension examples). I then had a commercial translating firm translate the 144-word test in English into Icelandic, Dutch, Swedish, German, and French

However, it was also my desire to see how well European sixth-graders could read adult-level material orally, and I would need that material in all of the above languages. (As it turned out, however, I was not able to test at all in Iceland.) The logical choice for adult material which is available in all languages was the Bible. I chose the 104th Psalm (103rd in Catholic Bibles) since I am particularly fond of it, but I used only a portion of the Psalm so that the selection lacked the continuity which is of help in context-guessing, and I wanted a difficult test for oral reading which would be as free as possible of context-guessing help. The American Bible Society provided me with translations in Icelandic, Dutch, Swedish, German and French, for which I am wonderfully appreciative. (The English version and the translations are in Appendix 3.)

A grade-level study was not done on this selection, but its structure is at an adult level and the vocabulary is not simple. Its level is certainly well above the sixth-grade level at which I tested. In Sweden, at least, the structure and vocabulary of the selection were archaic, since the translation was apparently from hundreds of years ago, to judge from comments I heard about its difficulty. The Swedish children, most of whom read with amazing fluency, often went back to say to their teachers, "What was THAT all about?"

One Swedish word, in particular, was so archaic that a fascinated sixth-grade Swedish teacher and others in his school looked up the word in an unabridged Swedish dictionary, since they had never heard the word before in their lives.

Time did not permit, however, the testing of sixth-graders anywhere but in Sweden and Holland, so the following reports concern only the results in the Swedish and Dutch sixth grades.

On this obviously difficult oral reading test, 27 of the 56 Swedish sixth-graders read at 100%

accuracy, 73% of the 56 Swedish sixth graders read at 99% or 100% accuracy (independent level on Individual Reading Inventories), 93% read at 97% accuracy or above, and 3 of 56 read at 94%. Of the 56, 55 were apparently native Swedes, and ALL of these read at 94% or above, or almost at Instructional Level on something of the difficulty of an archaic translation of the Bible! One child read at 91% (still above the frustrational level), but he was a foreign child from Finland, so a test in Swedish presented a language problem. Nevertheless, EVERY SINGLE ONE OF THESE CHILDREN READ ABOVE THE FRUSTRATION LEVEL, INCLUDING THE IMMIGRANT CHILD, AND ON AN ARCHAIC VERSION OF THE BIBLE!

A kind of norm exists for American oral reading, not because anyone has tested children to see how well they do between phonics and sight words, but because norms had to be worked up for the few oral tests in existence which are used almost exclusively by reading remediation specialists. One of the few available is the Gilmore, which was the one used on the USOE studies referred to earlier. It was normed about 1950 by being administered to 1,620 pupils in 12 communities in 5 states in the Northeastern United States. At grade 6.5 level, a total of 164 children were tested. The oral reading selection for grade 6.5 and those below it may, I feel, be considered far easier than the portion of the Bible Psalm that I used in my test. According to the norms set up by Gilmore on this carefully measured test sample, at grade level 6.5 (a few months older than the Swedish sample I tested), 7% of the children read below a grade 3.9 level on the oral test, 34% read below the grade 5.5 level on the test, and 69% read below the grade 7.7 level. Very significantly, all but 5% of all words used at grade level were checked against E. L. Thorndike's The Teacher's Word Book of 30,000 Words and were rated as suitable to be "taught for permanent knowledge" at the corresponding grade level.

The Gilmore children, of course, had all their school readers "practicing" these grade-level words, so they "knew" them, but these Swedish children had apparently never seen some of the words they were reading on this Psalm! Even with this great handicap in favor of the American sixth-graders that Dr. John V. Gilmore tested, where they had been "taught" most of the words, 69% of them read below a grade 7.7 level. I think it can be safely assumed that the Psalm in question is above the grade 7.7 level. Yet EVERY SINGLE ONE OF THESE SWEDISH SIXTH GRADERS, AND THE FINNISH CHILD, READ THE PSALM ABOVE THE FRUSTRATIONAL LEVEL. Leaving out the foreign child, the class came very close (within one percentage point) of reading the Psalm, EVERY SINGLE CHILD, at the instructional level of 95% accuracy.

That means that Swedish sixth-grade teachers can give almost all of their children to study - by themselves - materials in which the decoding is at the level of the Bible, and 93% of them read it at close to the independent level. It is no wonder that Swedish schools are teaching all the children physics, chemistry, and biology, besides history, geography, etc.

It might be very tempting to conclude that perhaps these Swedish children are just a lot smarter than most, but, in one of his articles, Malmquist quoted very clear data on IQ. Entering 7-year-olds in Swedish schools score very much like children everywhere, from low intelligence to high intelligence. But the Swedish schools ARE doing something we are not, and that is mandating the use of a very delightful reader in first grade, Nu Laser, which practices simple, uncomplicated, sounding-and-blending phonics. Teachers adapt it, of course, to their own programs, but every child in Sweden must be given this phonic "sound"-emphasis reader in first grade.

The Dutch sixth-graders also did remarkably well on the oral reading test of the 104th Psalm in the Dutch language. I tested a total of 59 students in three sixth-grade classes. Of the 59 students, 61% scored at 99% or 100% accuracy (the independent level), 93% scored at 95% or higher accuracy (the instructional level), and 97% scored at 94% accuracy or above, very close to the instructional level. None scored below 91% accuracy (the lowest scores being one at 93%

accuracy and one at 91% accuracy).

The results for the Swedish and Dutch sixth-graders are shown on the following pages.

Every Swedish and Dutch sixth-grader scored above the passing level on this rather difficult oral test with low- frequency vocabulary, and the vast majority scored very high. Yet, if this same demanding test were given to an average sample of American sixth graders, most of whom were taught in first-grade by sight-word "meaning" and "highfrequency-word vocabulary" instead of by phonic "sound" like the Swedish and Dutch students, we can be quite certain the comparative results would be very disturbing.

The Netherlands - October, 1977 - Oral Reading Accuracy Test
Oral Reading of Verses 10 to 18, Psalm 104, in the
Dutch Bible, By Sixth-Grade Students
Total of 59 Students Tested

School A-1 % Accuracy	School A-2 Accuracy (Read with 18 of 24)	School A-4 Accuracy	By Individuals
100	100	99	100-24
98	100	100	99 -12
94	99	98	98 -15
99	100	100	97 -1
100	100	98	96 -2
100	100	98	95 -1
98	98	99	94 -2
99	100	98	93 -1
98	98 Foreign -	99	92 -0
100	Pakistani?	100	91 -1
98	Speaks English and	99	None Below
93	Dutch	98	91%
100	100	97 Fast	
91	100	98	At 99 or 100
99	94	100	61%
98 Australian here 1 year	96 Fairly slow	96 Fast	
100	98	99	At 95 or
99	95 Slow	99	Above
100	99	100 Fast	93%
100	100		
100	98		At 94 or
100			Above
			97%

% Accuracy A-1	% Accuracy A-2	% Accuracy A-3
At 99 or above 64%	At 99 or above 61%	At 99 or above 58%
At 95 or above 86%	At 95 or above 94%	At 95 or above 100%
At 90 or above 100%	At 90 or above 100%	

Sweden, November, 1977 - Oral Reading Accuracy Test
Oral Reading of Verses 10 to 18, Psalm 104, in the
Swedish Bible, By Sixth-Grade Students

Total of 56 Students Tested

School S-1

Teacher considered this class to be better readers than some of her earlier classes.

% Accuracy
100
97
100
100
100
99
98
98

At 99 or 100 - 63%
At 95 or above - 100%

School S-2

The children were chosen by chance because they were near the door. The bell rang to to home at 2:30. Teacher said that I had an average mix of children.

% Accuracy
100-Fast
100-Fast
99-Fast
100
100
100 Fast
100 Fast
99 Halting but fast
99 Slower

At 99 or 100 - 100%

School S-3

% Accuracy
99
97
98
99 Slow
100 Quick, fast
100
100 Fast
99
91 Finnish
99
99
94 Slow, uncertain
98 Fast
97 Foreign
98 Foreign
98

At 99 or 100 - 50%
At 95 or above - 88%
At 91 or above - 100%

School S-4
Front rows from 26 students
% Accuracy
99
100
100
100
100
100

At 99 or 100 - 100%

School S-5
% Accuracy
97
100
99 Fast
98
100
100
100

At 99 or 100 - 71%
At 95 or above - 100%

School S-6
% Accuracy
94
99
100
94
99
100 Fast
99
100
100
100

At 99 or 100 - 80%
At 95 or above - 80%
At 90 or above - 100%

Individually Ranked Scores for 56 Swedish Sixth-Graders Tested

% Accuracy	Number of Children Obtaining Score
100	27
99	14
98	7
97	4
96	0
95	0
94	3
93	0
92	0
91	1 (Finnish boy - whose native language is unrelated to Swedish)

At 99 or 100 accuracy
73%

At 97 accuracy or above
93%

At 94 accuracy or above
100%, if foreign Finnish boy at score of 91% accuracy is excluded

Note made at time of Swedish sixth-grade testing:

> "It is harder to distinguish the Swedish sounds on the Bible verses than the Dutch. With the Dutch, I was sure of what I was hearing. Here, many words are said differently than written: manniskans, kallor."

I rapidly became familiar with the proper pronunciations, however, and asked the child to repeat if I had doubt

CHAPTER 11
Further Supporting Data Confirming the Existence of Different and Opposite Kinds of Readers

Children are taught beginning reading at different ends of a scale, from Code 1 for sight words to Code 10 for phonics, but programs are certainly not clearly labeled to demonstrate that difference. Nor have studies of oral reading errors by phonics children in comparison to sight-word trained children acknowledged their very obvious finding, that the two different ways of teaching reading (or mixtures of the methods) had developed two different KINDS of readers (or mixtures of the kinds).

Those oral reading error studies only implied the existence of different subskills in what they conceived of as a single, unitary product, the ability to read. Yet even I, myself, did not know, until I had completed my research, that the fundamental problem in the Great Debate, phonics vs. sight-words, is not just that each side is in the position of the blind men examining a single elephant named Reading, so that each side comes up with different descriptions, depending on which part of the elephant they touch. Rather, the problem is that the phonics people and the sight-word people have actually been examining TWO DIFFERENT ELEPHANTS, BECAUSE THERE ARE TWO DIFFERENT KINDS OF READING.

What the sight-word people say about their "Reading" elephant is perfectly true for them. They DO read by depending on context for word identification, and on structural clues, and on dictionary meanings and on "sight words" (although I hope, by the time they become college professors, they have ceased using the "picture clues"). That is how they were taught to read, so that is how they read today, making frequent misreadings, just as Frank Smith claims. But the phonics people, when they read, are making an immediate correspondence between the written word and its spoken form and so read as they speak, automatically, and without straining at context.

Proof of the existence of different kinds of reading can be found in articles which are appearing in educational journals (though they do not acknowledge that there are two different kinds of readers). A whole cult has grown up around what has been labeled "psycholinguistics." However, the cult's remarks made about "reading" confirm that its idea of what reading is and how reading should be taught are very different that has been the case for almost 3,000 years.

That the two methods, teaching by phonic "sound" or teaching by sight-word "meaning," are mutually exclusive can be demonstrated from comments made by Kenneth Goodman in his article, "The Psycholinguistic Nature of the Reading Process," 1968. In this article, Goodman published a nonsense story followed by comprehension questions, of which I will give the first two sentences and the first question:

> "A marlup was poving his kump. Parmily a narg horped some whev in his kump.

"1. What did the narg horp in the marlup's kump?"

The questions were asked:

"What cue systems were available? Which cue system is missing?"

Goodman concluded that this story, whose question given above CAN be answered, provided the cue systems of graphophonic cues (sounds) and syntactic cues (word order used) but that the third cue, semantic or word meaning, is missing. He concluded further, that native speakers have mastered the word order cues or syntactic cues and can use them in a <u>non-conscious</u> way, but that reading for children can be much easier if they use all three cue systems in reading, graphophonic, syntactic and semantic.

Goodman's error is in the omission of the concept of automaticity. Syntactic cues (word order) are used unconsciously, as Goodman said. Phonic cues also can be used unconsciously. But meaning cues, or semantics, can ONLY be used consciously. To make word identification (whether in reading, or in listening by the hard of hearing) dependent on semantics brings word identification to the conscious level, and that makes automaticity impossible, by definition. Furthermore, to divide the conscious attention between the identification of words in a text and the ultimate meaning of that text certainly has to lower the comprehension of that text, since obviously less conscious attention will be available to concentrate on the meaning of the text.

Yet this fact, that conscious attention is divided by "psycholinguistic guessing" words in a text, has apparently not occurred to the psycholinguistics proponents. The resultant situation is utterly ridiculous, since the stated goal of the psycholinguistics movement is to increase "reading comprehension," but the reality is that "psycholinguistics" lowers "reading comprehension" since it leaves only a part of conscious attention free to focus on a text's meaning. Therefore, instead of "reading comprehension" being the prize exhibit of the psycholinguistic movement, it turns out that "reading comprehension" is its Achilles heel.

Nor do the psycholinguistic proponents mention the fact that, even if we could tolerate lowered reading comprehension, their method of word identification is exceedingly awkward and totally unusable for large numbers of below average children. By contrast even mentally retarded children can be taught phonics.

Goodman went on in his article to tell teachers how to teach reading psycholinguistically. He included suggesting that they tell children to skip unknown words in a paragraph and to read the rest of it as a help in guessing the unknown words, or to start again at the beginning of a paragraph to try to "predict" an unknown word by guessing, or for a teacher to cover a word a child cannot read, forcing the child to guess from syntactic and semantic information. The specific suggestion was given:

"For example, if a child does not recognize the word 'slowly' in the sentence, 'The turtle walked slowly,' cover the word and ask the child how turtles walk. Soon children will realize the effectiveness of such a strategy. That is, <u>they will learn to recognize words using nonvisual information from the text.</u>" (Emphasis mine)

Therefore, from the writings of the psycholinguists themselves, such as Kenneth Goodman, it can be clearly seen that they are developing different KINDS of readers.

Of course, we have had psycholinguistic guessers ever since the tragic advent of the so-called "intrinsic phonics" sight-word basal readers in 1930, and even before when sight words were taught without real supplemental phonics. "Psycholingistics" is only a new label for an old failure.

The ultimate cost of teaching children to read at Code 2 or 3, the "psycholinguistic" way, and long before Kenneth Goodman popularized that label, can be seen in an article by Helen R. Lowe, "Solomon or Salami," published in the early 1960's and referred to in The Reading Reporter of the Reading Reform Foundation, April, 1978. Mrs. Lowe (a Smith College graduate) had worked with nearly 1,000 students of all ages who were having trouble in school. She had recorded 10,000 of their appalling oral reading errors, such as in the title of the above article, and as in her 1951 paper, "How They Read." The errors cited in her 1951 paper included Switzerland for Massachusetts, noodles for mill bells, twelve onions for the travelworn paper bag, and even worse.

Mrs. Lowe gave a very fine description of psycholinguistic reading, and it is certainly unhealthy reading. Nevertheless even Mrs. Lowe did not clearly state that there are two different kinds of readers, but only that "reading" was not taught and, instead, something that was not reading was taught.

Yet the most important result of my research certainly was my discovery that different teaching methods do, indeed, produce different and opposite kinds of reading, and different and opposite kinds of readers. The end product of reading instruction is not a single goal carrying the label, "a reader," because there are two kinds of readers - those who read by the "meaning" of print and those who read by its "sound" (or mixtures of those two kinds).

Some earlier research, and certainly Mrs. Lowe's analysis of errors, should certainly have suggested that there are different and opposite kinds of readers. Instead, the interpretation of such research has been that it only showed different paths (some dead-ends) on the way to a single, final destination, the ability to read. Guy T. Buswell had come to the conclusion that there is a single destination, the ability to read, as discussed in his 1922 paper at the University of Chicago, Fundamental Reading Habits: A Study of Their Development. Buswell implied that there is just that one ultimate goal to be reached in whole or in part: the goal of "reading ability," even though the paths to that goal may differ. Since Buswell's 1922 conclusion became more or less the official, "expert," conclusion, that fact may explain why the following, quite arresting, research studies which clearly show opposite kinds of reading were not interpreted as they should have been.

That different kinds of readers are developed by different teaching methods can be confirmed by studies in the ERIC computer file. One was by Donna E. Norton and Patty Hubert of Texas A. and M. University. They made a study in 1977 of differences in errors of first-grade children who were taught by sight-word basal readers in comparison to first-grade children who were taught by phonic readers. Their study showed that the sight-word pupils made more errors that "did not change meaning" while the phonics pupils made more errors that "had high phonic or graphic proximity"

To demonstrate the meaning of the Norton-Hubert results by an old analogy, it is as if both sight-word and phonics children both misread the word "battle" in the sentence, "My father was in a battle." The sight-word children, who decode by "meaning," might misread "war" for "battle." The phonics children, however, decoding by "sound" and not by "meaning," might misread "bottle" for battle. Yet the phonics children reading, "My father was in a bottle," will know they made a mistake and can correct themselves, but the children reading, "My father was in a war," may not even know they made an error.

The Norton-Hubert study also confirmed that the first-grade phonics children read words more accurately but with lower comprehension scores on the total selection. The sight-word first-grade children read words less accurately but with higher comprehension scores. Yet, as I establish elsewhere from my oral reading statistics, the highly touted and seeming "strength" of the sight-word method, its seemingly slightly higher averaged comprehension scores, turns out when analyzed to be its appalling Achilles heel.

A doctoral study by Marion Edelson Dank of the University of Massachusetts in 1976 on second-grade pupils showed, among other conclusions, that children using McGraw-Hill "Programmed Reading" (very phonically regular) made more mistakes (called miscues in these studies to which I am referring) that had "high graphic and sound similarity" but the children with the Ginn 360 sight-word basal reader approach "generated more miscues which were semantically acceptable and showed better understanding of what they had read, reflected in their retelling of the story."

Concerning the last statement on "comprehension," I consider this kind of story-retelling "test" to be very unreliable because the two groups being tested had very different training on "comprehension". McGraw-Hill programmed reading is an individualized program which provides little teacher-pupil discussion on its materials. Basal reader series like Ginn 360 have "retelling" of stories done almost daily in the "reading groups," from the level of the first pre-primers. Ginn children would have had overwhelmingly more practice in "retelling stories."

Perhaps we should conduct a guided tour for the public of these "reading groups" for those adults who may have forgotten what they were like. Children remember, years later, how much they HATED reading groups. But we teachers, if we follow the basal reader suggestions, have to plague the little ones with the basal reader "comprehension" questions such as story-telling day after noxious day.

The point is, however, that this study confirms that at second grade, as in the first-grade study just mentioned, children were making different kinds of errors: phonics children make errors that approach the unknown word in sound, and sight-word basal reader children make errors that approach the unknown word in meaning.

Before her 1977 study with Patty Hubert discussed above, Donna Elithe Norton did a doctoral study at the University of Wisconsin-Madison in 1976 on forty first and third grade students concerning their "oral reading strategies" showed that the "reading miscue inventory" (that means reading mistakes) for the phonics children were mistakes that showed "graphic, phonic and syntactic reading strategies, with small numbers of self corrections," but the analytic-eclectic program (which means sight-word basal reader type without sounding-and-blending phonics) produced "syntactic reading strategies and self-correction strategies and produced readers who relied heavily on the semantic acceptability of the passage." It was concluded that "miscue patterns are directly related to reading approaches," according to the ERIC print-out on this study.

However, it should be noted that the phonics group used strategies which can be done at the automatic level - phonic and syntactic (sentence order) but the sight-word basal group added "semantic" strategies which can only be done at the conscious level. Therefore, the sight-word basal group cannot be "automatic decoders", according to the definition given elsewhere by S. J. Samuels.

These studies confirm the presence of two different kinds of readers, either context guessers or phonic decoders. Another study by Warren S. Hayes in 1974, "Types of Word Recognition Errors Made by Second and Fifth Grade Students," confirms the existence of context guessing to the fifth-grade level. Hayes was not, however, comparing phonics to sight-word groups as in the studies just mentioned, but was just talking about readers in general. It is evident, however, from his description of these readers (and from the information just provided in those previous studies) that his subjects HAD to have been sight-word students or they could not read as he described.

A random sample of 25 second graders and 25 fifth graders was taken from three middle-class metropolitan schools. Hayes concluded, according to the ERIC print-out:

> "The results indicated that second and fifth graders made similar types of word recognition errors during oral reading, with the following exceptions: (1) second graders had more words given by the examiner, (2) fifth graders confused the initial consonant more frequently, and (4) fifth graders made more

> meaningless guesses. Both groups tended to use initial clues combined with syntax and semantics as a primary aid to word recognition."

In other words, they were guessing at words from the initial consonant and the meaning of the sentence, just as I have observed in my 13 years of teaching children at third grade who had been taught by sight-word basal readers in first and second grade. At fifth grade, the children that Hayes tested were still unable to decode phonically, but they did use the psycholinguistic bag of tricks.

In her 1967 book, <u>Learning to Read: The Great Debate,</u> Jean Chall quoted a reading specialist in a school in the 1960's who said that fifth and sixth grade teachers in her school felt that a stronger phonics program was in order because at those levels the children could not phonically decode words that had not been in their "high frequency word" school books. That, of course, confirms the thrust of the previous studies.

I have a friend, a fellow teacher, who had great interest in reading disabilities. She had read widely and was familiar with the approaches of Dr. Samuel Orton and others for dealing with the problem. Yet, she said it was not until she worked with first-grade children, teaching phonic word-attack all year, that she realized she had to modify a life-long habit she had in reading of skipping over unfamiliar words! The horror of this is that she is a highly educated, intelligent woman whose field of interest is reading disabilities, and who is a phonics supporter.

Yet such almost unconscious habits as hers, acquired through learning to read with sight-word methods, may last all through life, except for the fortunate few who figure out the phonics principle for themselves very early in school, or those who meet a teacher of real phonics somewhere along the way.

I took evening and Saturday courses at Fairleigh Dickinson University in Rutherford, New Jersey, in 1958. In an English class, where many young ex-servicemen were enrolled, working towards a college degree, the instructor asked some of the young men to read aloud from some of the texts being used. In my lifetime, I have seldom heard anything sadder than these young men stumbling and tripping on simple language as they were forced to reveal to all who were listening that they were unable to read their native tongue. A terrible, terrible wrong had been done to them! Yet when I asked sixth-grade Netherlanders and Swedes to read a difficult verse from the Psalms in their own languages, most sped through it with close to perfect scores. But in this American college-level class were grown men who were unable to handle the printed page. I find it very difficult to be patient and understanding about the American reading theorists whose undocumented, unscientific but highly profitable theories brought about this tragedy.

To make a very sad and probably very unpopular statement, I think it is probable that the majority of America adults today under 50 years of age are somewhat crippled in their phonic decoding, many actually skipping all "difficult" words when reading silently, or at least mispronouncing them to themselves. It is asinine to claim that this is a necessary result when the average healthy child can be taught all the phonics he needs to know for the rest of his life from September to March of first grade. The child's facility in using the phonics he has been taught will, of course, come with practice.

Now, however, some men who grew up learning to read "psycholinguistically" are telling us that reading "psycholinguistically" is the "normal" way to read because that is what "reading" is for them - guessing from the context, and constantly going back to previously read print in order to check and recheck for meaning so as to read the next words as they come up. Such "regressions", going back to reread material that has already been read, are the norm when reading psycholinguistically, but such regressions are virtually unknown when reading phonically. However, I used to get angry when I read the things that the famous psycholinguists, Kenneth Goodman and Frank Smith, said about the phonics method and in favor of the psycholinguistic method, because their statements were so manifestly rank lunacy. Yet, ultimately, I realized they may be speaking objectively and validly about what reading is for them. They may truly have to read in that appalling crippled fashion because they may very well have been taught to read by sight words.

Unfortunately, the bulk of American and Canadian readers under 50 may accept the madhouse conclusions of Goodman and Smith since such conclusions may "ring true" to most of those readers. That is because they learned to read by the sight-word method, too, and so can only read with the unpleasant strain of conscious, context guessing.

They have not the faintest idea that there is another, far better, far more comfortable and far quicker way to read, the automatic phonic way. So they reject true phonics, which they do not understand, just as native tribes living near the Equator reportedly once laughed uproariously when they were told that water could turn into stone in far away lands.

CHAPTER 12
Conclusion

It is we, the American general public, who are at fault for permitting the appalling American reading situation to have developed in the first place. We are at fault any time that we grant almost total control in any intellectual area to "experts" and fail to have some kind of a brake on their power. Yet, appallingly, in the area of reading instruction, we have granted almost total control to an inter-locking group of American reading "experts," and they are vested interest "experts," at that, who profit from their power. We certainly did not need an investigation by a detective agency to uncover the self- evident fact that the American reading "experts" have vested interests in the highly profitable sight- word basal-reader series, and in the college teachers' texts and in the college graduate courses which promote the "meaning" method and condemn the "sound" method. Yet we have blindly given almost absolute power over American reading instruction to just such a group of "experts." We are emphatically at fault for forgetting that such absolute power always corrupts.

The primary cause for this appalling shuffling off of personal responsibility in primary reading instruction is that, to paraphrase a fifth-grade teacher whom I respect, Patrick Liloia (who also suggested the title for this book!), most people have always found beginning reading instruction to be so very, very boring. Yet teaching the fundamental skill of accurate reading puts the plug in the bathtub of learning. If that plug is not there, little or nothing can accumulate.

While mentally mulling over the unpleasant thrust of my final argument, and wishing to temper it out of simple charity to those vested-interest "experts" and authors of sight-word materials who have such a stranglehold on American reading instruction, (the phonics methods having made very small inroads on the "experts'" status quo), I walked into a camera store to have copies made of part of my manuscript. A pleasant young girl, who said she was in tenth grade, and a nice young man, perhaps 25 or 30 years old, were behind the counter. When I mentioned that I was writing a book and received the expected surprised laugh, in which I always have to join, I told them the book was about first- grade reading. I was then given the response that I receive more commonly than not when I talk about reading to American young people - a recital of their reading troubles in school. The pretty young girl complained that she had not learned the alphabet until second grade and still had trouble reading today. The young man said he always thought he was a good reader until he reached ninth grade and a teacher put him in the remedial reading class. He said he guessed he always thought he was a good reader because he was "so much better than the other kids!"

I told him that most Dutch and Swedish sixth graders had read a section of the Psalms almost like the wind, and most with almost no errors. He replied that, in his sixth grade, when children tried to read aloud, some missed so many words that the others had to call them out to them, and the "readers" broke right down and cried out loud in class.

Cried out loud in class! But no one tested their oral reading - only their so-called "silent reading comprehension" at which they could guess the "right" answers, even if they could not read many of the words on the test. With the fakery of the "silent reading comprehension tests", and with almost no oral reading accuracy tests in the literature except for "remediation" work, the sight-word "experts" have protected their flanks very nicely indeed, so that the hosts of reports like this young man's can be labeled only "hear-say."

Where are the spokesmen for these sixth-graders who "cried out loud in class" only a few years ago, and for the others like them? What does charity require - that we ignore the errors of the vested-interest group of "reading experts" and sight-word basal-reader authors who have brought this disaster upon us and who have profited personally by doing so? (Both the college "expert" and the "basal reader author" hats are often worn by the same person.) Or, should we do everything within our abilities to remove these people from power over the reading curriculum?

We can change this appalling situation if we really try. If a real, continuing and concerted effort is made by many private citizens and parents, the happy day will finally arrive when we have chased the ghosts of Horace Mann and the ghosts of all his benighted sight-word "expert" followers - E. B. Huey, William Scott Gray, and the lot of them - out the front door of the last school in America.

APPENDIX 1
American Sight-Word Programs Have Been Exported Around the World Because W. S. Gray Seeded UNESCO With His Errors

American sight word errors have been sown on the four winds of the earth, through the UNESCO publications of William Scott Gray's works, <u>Preliminary Survey on Methods of Teaching Reading and Writing</u> (UNESCO, Paris, 1953), and <u>The Teaching of Reading and Writing</u> (Paris, UNESCO, 1956, reprinted in 1969).

According to Jean Chall in <u>The Great Debate</u> (1967, McGraw Hill, New York, page 96) William Scott Gray was "the acknowledged leader of, and spokesman for, reading experts for four decades [in America]; major summarizer and interpreter of reading research, and author of America's leading basal reader series, the Scott, Foresman & Company series."

Gray's 1930 Scott, Foresman basal reader series and Arthur Irving Gates' 1930 1931 Macmillan basal reader series were based on a method used to teach reading to deaf mutes. The method was the silent use of sight words and context guessing ("meaning") to decode print instead of the use of phonics ("sound") to decode print. Arthur I. Gates was the other major "expert" of the period and, like Gray, was a former student and associate of Columbia Teachers College psychologist Edward L. Thorndike. Gates said in a personal note to Jean Chall (quoted on page 133 of The Great Debate):

> "...almost everything I wrote and said during the 1920-30 decade was based on the assumption that most teachers were committed to a very heavy program of phonics."

There is, of course, no reliable data on the "success" of Gray's 1930 basal readers and Gates's 1930 1931 basal readers in teaching children to read words, compared to earlier readers, as there is NO oral research data whatever comparing those new series to the older ones. This is a really striking omission, to put it mildly, since W. S. Gray had constructed an oral reading test as early as 1914, a revised edition of which is STILL in use today, and Gates also constructed oral tests in 1923-1924 on the reading of lists of progressively more difficult words, portions of which are also still in use today.

Gray's 1930 deaf mute method series turned America around, and almost all American reading instruction went down the sight word drain after that. Gray must have been well aware, however, of the greater success of children in learning to decode words (read) with the older phonic methods, as he had personally tested oral reading as early as the academic year 1913 1914. In addition and most meaningfully, he had been a visitor to a Chicago parochial school using an adaptation of Leonard Bloomfield's phonic method with great success (apparently about 1940). Dr. Mitford Mathews, the philologist from the University of Chicago, knew Gray of the University of Chicago personally and mentioned conversations there with Gray. It was in <u>Teaching to Read: Historically Considered</u> (University of Chicago Press, Chicago, Illinois: 1961, pages 158-159) that Mathews reported that Gray had discounted such superior oral reading as in the Bloomfield adaptation phonic classes. Gray had said there was nothing difficult or remarkable about getting children to read correctly with phonics, since the really important thing was their comprehension. Of course, the general public was unaware of the superior oral reading possible when children learned to read by phonics and at that time probably did not give a "hoot" about comprehension. However, the general public knew nothing about the Bloomfield method phonic classrooms about 1940. The general public also knew nothing of the highly successful phonic classes in the Argo Summit Bedford Park school district near Chicago visited by Rudolf Flesch, until Rudolf Flesch "took" the public there in his 1955 best seller, Why Johnny Can't Read.

Gray's unfounded bias was that teaching children sight words taught them to "read for meaning" but teaching phonics did not. Yet he had no really valid data to support this contention, despite his citing of much so called "research" in The Teaching of Reading and Writing (UNESCO 1956). (See Jean Chall's review of much of this research in her 1967 book, The Great Debate.) It would be difficult to find more unfounded statements than the following collection of "facts" presented by Gray in his second UNESCO book, The Teaching of Reading and Writing (page 82):

> "Methods Which Emphasize Meaning at the Beginning
>
> "...At least two groups of arguments have been advanced in support of this [global] approach. Since reading is a thought getting process, use should be made from the beginning of meaningful material, with emphasis on the development of ...thoughtful reading.... Learning to read thus becomes an interesting, enjoyable and rewarding process and progress is greatly hastened.
>
> "Then, again, as psychologists* have demonstrated that children recognize things and ideas as wholes, more or less vaguely at first, proceeding gradually to the recognition of details, this procedure follows the natural mode of perception.
>
> "*Decroly, O. Le role du phenomene de
> globalisation dans l'enseignement,
> Bulletin annuel de la societe royale des
> sciences medicales et naturelles.
> Brussels, 1927, pp. 65-79.
>
> "Dottrens, Robert and Margairaz, Emilie.
> L'apprentissage de la lecture par la methode globale.
> Paris. Neuchatel,
> Delachaux et Niestle S. A. 1947, p. 9 41 (Actualites
> pedagogiques et psychologiques)
>
> "Seegers, J. E. Psychologie de l'enfant
> normal et anormal d'apres le Dr. O.
> Decroly. Brussels,
> D. Stoops, 1948, p. 271."

This reference to Decroly, famed in reference to the European global method, is the only reference I have ever seen to him in any American reading publications. The Seegers reference Gray gave refers back to Decroly in 1927. The Dottrens reference he gave may or may not have added anything of moment, but dates from as late as 1947. It is highly unlikely, however, that Decroly's 1927 article, published in Brussels in French, had much influence on Gray's views, which were already well formulated and known long before 1927 (since well before 1920).

Gates' use and Gray's use of high frequency words instead of phonics in their readers was presumably supported by Thorndike's work with animals which purported to show that there was no such thing as "transfer of training" so teaching children phonics to decode words while actually reading was supposedly of no use in such actual reading. Children supposedly could not "transfer the training" to work out new words phonically as they were reading connected texts for meaning. They had to learn words only for (and by) meaning, so that they would be of use in the act of reading for meaning. Teaching children to read by "sound" or phonics, the method used before 1930, was supposed to have lowered reading comprehension, as the children would supposedly just be pronouncing unknown new words by their sound, with no thought of their meaning.

In 1920, Thorndike published his list of the 10,000 commonest words, which were supposed to help teachers to teach the most important words for "meaning" first. Thorndike's 1920 word frequency lists were the basic materials used to prepare the word lists for the 1930 deaf mute method readers. The Gates and Gray deaf mute method readers were constructed to be read solely by meaning, with no use whatsoever of isolated sounds. The only so called phonics used was the comparison of an unknown whole word to known whole meaning bearing words. The comparison was to see like parts to use in guessing the unknown word's identity, along with the help in "guessing" that was given by the meaning of the context.

Since the American emphasis on sight words dated from before 1920, to cite Decroly as an historical "reason" for the use of sight words by an American was silly. This is particularly so since Decroly is not even referred to in the encyclopedic manuals, Harris and Sipay's How to Increase Reading Ability, or Bond and Tinker's Reading Difficulties, Their Diagnosis and Correction, or even Chall's The Great Debate, or any others I can recall seeing, except the Englishman John Downing's collection of papers from around the world. In Downing's Comparative Reading, an Argentinian, Berta Perelstein de Braslavsky, refers to Decroly. Gray's reference to Decroly occurred, significantly, after he had been in touch with reading publishers and authorities from around the world in connection with his book for UNESCO.

Decroly's "global" ideas presumably deal with gestalt (field) psychology. As Walcutt, Lamport and McCracken state in a footnote on page 36 of Teaching Reading:

> "Earlier commentators on the teaching of reading frequently cited Gestalt (field) psychology as a theoretical basis for look say instruction. It should be noted, however, that look say theory was completely formulated long before the 1920s when Gestalt psychology appeared on the American scene. The Gestaltist views of the primacy of the whole object over its parts and emphasis on the learner's organization of the perceptual field were interpreted as supportive of whole word and meaning first learning to read. Gestalt psychology no longer exists as an identifiable school of thought. Its theories have been absorbed and transmuted into the frameworks of motivational theory, associative learning, and cognitive processes. For a short review, see... E. R. Hilgard, in Theories of Learning and Instruction (Chicago: University of Chicago Press, 1964) pp. 54-77."

Gestalt psychology was used by the "experts" to support the use of whole words, which were supposed to be seen "globally." Whole words, of course, need not have ANY meaning, but, even so, gestalt psychology had been largely supplanted by 1964 at the University of Chicago (Gray's school) according to the source just quoted. Gray's 1956 book which I have quoted was reprinted in 1969, long after Gray's death in 1960. It is the 1969 reprint which I used, but it carried no hint of the conclusions concerning Gestalt's demise which were published by Gray's university five years earlier, in 1964.

What other evidence, then, besides the reference to a 1927 psychological basis for "global" words (which do not need to have anything to do with meaning) did Gray have for teaching beginning reading for "meaning?" Gray started with the statement, "Since reading is a thought getting process...." but is it, necessarily? Or can thought enter the act AFTER reading? Can YOU read this: jarfle spunk nosh? What "thought" does it contain? (And it should be remembered that each "word" is global!)

Let's allow the unfounded argument in his dependent clause, though, "Since reading is a thought getting process," so that we can continue to the independent clause: (therefore) "use should be made from the beginning of meaningful material, with emphasis on the development of thoughtful reading." Even if you allow the argument that "Reading is a thought getting process," which means NO ONE can READ "jarfle spunk nosh," does it follow, then, that use should NECESSARILY be made from the beginning of meaningful material? What kind of reasoning is that? What evidence, since the conclusion is not contained in the statement itself, like two plus two equals four, did he produce to show that meaningful material is necessary from the beginning?

Gray's most marvelous statement, however, was his next one: "Learning to read thus becomes an interesting, enjoyable and rewarding process and progress is greatly hastened."

What EVIDENCE did he have for this? The studies like that of Currier and Duguid in 1916 had subjective conclusions, and no real data. To accept Gray's conclusion, I would have to disregard my own evidence from 13 years of working at third grade with children who had the "privilege" to learn to "read with meaning," most of them with Gray's 1950's Scott, Foresman materials or with their successors, the 1960's Scott, Foresman materials published after Gray's death. The LAST thing in the world most of those little third graders found to be "interesting, enjoyable and rewarding" was reading! Their progress, besides, was so "greatly hastened" that many could not read at third grade the words which my little phonics trained children could read with ease and pleasure at the end of three months in first grade. Gray presented NO evidence, only his opinion that reading for meaning at the start is better than phonics. However, since he was an "expert," his opinion became FACT!

However, W. S. Gray was THERE when UNESCO started to talk about the world literacy problem, and he was "important" and "expert," so it is a tragedy that he was chosen to write a book on reading for the U.N. which is still today sowing the seeds of confusion and trouble in beginning reading all over the world. Gray's "expertise" was not to be limited to America, so that only we can exclaim in the late 1970's that our Army and Navy recruits often cannot read well enough to understand their manuals, and that Harvard, which accepts only top quality students, complains about literacy problems in its undergraduates. Sight word "expertise," like a virulent form of flu, has now been exported all over the world to "developing" countries who are trying to rid themselves of illiteracy, and Gray's "methods" are being used in many places besides America.

UNESCO's book, Literacy Primers. Construction, Evaluation and Use, by Karel Neijs (Paris, 1961) does, it is true, present a far more balanced discussion of methods to teach beginning reading (phonics or sight word global) than can be found in most American teacher college reference works. Yet, though it quotes from many kinds of references, it also quotes very greatly from Gray's UNESCO book. Specifically, I found, when glancing through this 111 page book, FIFTEEN references to W. S. Gray and his works! The influence of Gray's ideas can be seen in the flat statements that reading for meaning is retarded by the phonic approach and that interest is stimulated by the global approach. The chapter outlining these "conclusions" begins with a reference to Gray's 1956 book!

Some of the foreign language primers referred to in this work, Literacy Primers...., were phonic, but examples of the sight word or global approach were primers for Mysore, India, in 1954 55. The following quotation concerning these Mysore books is from page 37 of <u>Literacy Primers</u> :

> "The approach followed is a story continued through two books. This method was selected in accordance with the aim of teaching from the start reading with comprehension based on interest in village development. The style is 'rhythmic' and the unit of thought is the sentence. Word recognition through flash card drill takes place from the start and letter teaching practice is given after Primer I has been taught. Each lesson consists of an illustration page and a text page. The first book contains 19 lessons and the second 16 lessons.... Sentences increase in length and complexity.... The two primers and their teaching aids were thoroughly tested and on the whole this purely global approach was found to be successful. The experience gained pointed, however, to the necessity of considerable simplification of this essentially 'difficult' method and the original and revised editions of the primers showed the following differences...."

What were the differences in the revised edition? Would you believe the same kinds of revisions as happened with the sight word primers in America in the 1930's and 1940's? They cut the number of new words in the first primer from 196 to 80, and in the second primer from 213 to 65! Those "lucky" adult residents of Mysore had trouble "learning" the sight words!

A later book is UNESCO's <u>Practical Guide to Functional Literacy</u> (Paris, 1973). This book says (page 104):

> "Deferred word breakdown
>
> "Adult illiterates acquire, initially by the global method, a certain number of words which they find in contexts of increasing variety. As they progress, they are shown how to make comparisons and draw parallels leading them on to identify like elements (syllables, letters) which will be used for training in the reading of syllables or words containing identical elements."

This same page has a section titled, "Teaching Methods and Techniques," with a footnote referring to... guess who?

> "For a detailed treatment of teaching methods and techniques, the reader is referred to: William S. Gray, <u>The Teaching of Reading and Writing. An International Survey,</u> 2nd ed. Paris, UNESCO, 1969."

Gray's errors, his opinions masking as "scientific facts," have been exported to those areas of the world which can least afford them, the undeveloped nations.

This last 1973 UNESCO publication, <u>Practical Guide to Functional Literacy,</u> makes an amazing time warp reference to the 1927 idea of "gestalt" theory, saying on page 102:

> "Studies and research on the development of the reading capacity of persons able to read have highlighted the following facts:
>
> "The reader's eye perceives only the shape of each word. In other words, according to gestalt theory, which teaches that the 'whole' is perceived before the 'parts,' the word is recognized in its global form without letter by letter identification by the reader."

With due respect to Walcutt, Lamport and McCracken's statement in <u>Teaching Reading</u> (based on E. R. Hilgard's University of Chicago book), gestalt psychology DOES still exist as an identifiable school of thought at UNESCO! And gestalt is still working hand in glove with W. S. Gray's ideas there, too.

In 1977 in Amsterdam, Holland, I observed Dr. Kooreman's beginning reading program which he had adapted from a very heavy phonics program he saw in Russia. Teaching reading by such heavy phonics is the norm in Russia. In his 1975 book (University of Texas Press), Winfred Lehman told of his seeing seven year old first graders in China being taught to read with the pinyin alphabet and phonics. The first graders learned Chinese characters later. The Chinese and Russians who teach beginning reading with such heavy phonics are apparently not faced with numbers of Army and Navy recruits who cannot read their manuals.

However, in the free world, where beginning reading is usually taught by "meaning" instead of phonics, large numbers of Army and Navy recruits CANNOT read their manuals. Can we in the free world afford that state of things?

APPENDIX 2
French Language Primers - Belgium and France

In the second school I visited in Avignon, I was told by a first-grade teacher that the commonest method for teaching beginning reading in France was a book she showed me, using what was called a mixed method. It introduced sight words on the first page and by about the sixth page had about 20 sight words. It introduced the vowel sounds from the beginning, but she said it was a syllabic method, not a phonetic method. She said, in her opinion, if you asked children several years later, some would not know the sight words on the first pages of the first book. She said she and a first-grade teacher were working jointly on the method which I described under Avignon 2.

In the third Avignon school I visited, I was shown a copy of the book, Remi et Colette, Premier Livret, Editions Magnard, 122, Bld. Saint-Germain, Paris 6, by J. Juredieu and E. Mourlevat. Unfortunately, I did not write the title of the book shown me in Avignon school 2, but it sounded very similar to this one, and was probably the same. (Edition date - 1975 - Imprime en France IME, 25 Besancon No. - D'editeur: 3773 - Depot Legal: 2e trimestre 1975.)

Its preface read:

> "Remi and Colette is a mixed method. It commences by global acquisition but the work of analysis begins much quicker than in global methods. Some very precise teaching notes and varied apparatus facilitates considerably the task of the teachers and permits them to give to the apprenticeship of reading the most educational value and effectiveness."

Under a heading on page 2, "The Learning of Sight Words," it says, "They are the object of five lessons. We admit they are limited to a small number of words, 20 in all. These lessons are very interesting. They furnish the key words for the study of the elements. Thanks to them, the children discover immediately in writing the means to express a thought and in reading the means to understand this thought. On one hand, as they learn to recognize words according to their total appearance, they express them in a natural way. Later, when they try to decode a word, they know that this word forms a whole and that it is necessary to read it as one pronounces it in ordinary language."

Of course, the above means that children were supposed to read all the words that they learned later as sight- word wholes, and that the presentation of these original 20 sight words was intended to produce just that effect. Happily, from my testing of children who had this text, the results indicated otherwise.

The preface continued:

> "The directions in the book and the supplementary information given in guides to the teacher permit all instructors to conduct effectively the exercises devoted to the global attainments. The first book, Remi et Colette, simplifies

very much the laying out of the words studied."

Under the heading, "The Study of the Elements", this appeared:

"The succession of the exercises is always the same. The first work of analysis one starts with a sentence of which the words are known. A methodical analysis follows from the sentence to the words, from the syllables to the element that one wishes to study. The
second work - one reconstitutes the key words. One forms new syllables and new words. Then one composes some sentences and, as soon as possible, one reads some little books. Reading, writing and spelling are strongly associated. The pupils write frequently in the course of the lessons. In particular, we ask them as soon as possible to write under dictation, not only from words already studied, but also, after they can distinguish the syllables, new words formed from known elements when these words do not contain any complicated spelling."

The beginning of that last paragraph reads as though it could have been written by Jacotot himself in Belgium back about 1820!

The program includes elaborate teaching aids. Available are 54 engravings in four colors. Also available are "Sentences for group work" which sentences "serve as a point of departure... [and] are printed in very big letters on three sheets of paper 120 cm x 140 cm, two for the first book and one for the last book."

Also included are sentences to be separated into their parts for individual work, in two sets for the first book and one for the second. Another item contains movable "elements" which are letters or groups of letters corresponding to the different sounds to be studied in the two books. Fifty-eight "elements" are printed on cardboard in big letters. Key words are included, with a picture in color of the thing, the written word itself, and the sound that has been separated from the word. The key words are meant to simplify the learning of letters and sounds. Syllable material is included for individual work. It is called "a very practical tool" with movable plastic letters, its own file and a holder in which a child can place letters as he builds words. Also available are wall charts of reading lessons to help in review. The publisher offers rubber stamps in boxes, one for the words studied at first globally in the beginning book and written in manuscript characters, and one for the same words in printed characters, as well as one for the silhouettes of the principal people and objects of the first book. The stamps are intended to permit teachers rapidly to duplicate written exercises.

The table of contents for the first primer (first half of first grade) is very revealing. Although this program is called a mixed global program, and, although, as has been demonstrated by the material quoted, the authors intend it to have a strong global (sight-word) emphasis, I believe it nevertheless has an enormously heavier phonic emphasis than the "phonics-assisted" Scott, Foresman or Houghton Miflin or similar American basal reader programs. This shows the pointlessness of comparing reading programs simply by the description provided by the programs' publishers. Just as this European so-called heavily "global" program turns out to be heavily phonic, so do many American so-called heavily "phonic" programs turn out to be heavily sight-word oriented.

<u>Table of Contents</u>

Sight words - pages 4, 6, 8, 14

Page 10 - o
12 - u
16 - a
18 - i
20 - e
22 - e e e [each with a different accent mark]
24 - l
26 - n
28 - p
30 - t
32 - r
34 - c
36 - m
38 - ou
40 - d
42 - Review 44 - s
46 - es et er [same sound in French]
48 - j
50 - v
52 - b
54 - on [nasalized sound in French, almost a vowel]
56 – Review

Three books are supposed to be read along with the first book, and six with the second book. The letters not covered in the table of contents in the first book are f, g, h, k, q, w, x, y, z, and many variant vowel spellings in French. Therefore, by mid-first grade, this partly global program will already have covered 17 of 26 letters of the alphabet. This is not too different from other European phonics programs such as the Austrian Kommt, Wir Wollen Lesen und Schreiben, which was one of the most heavily phonic (and successful) of the programs I saw. Besides the introduction of the letters, the preface to this book makes it very evident that it is a heavily phonic method in the analytic phonics fashion, breaking words down into all their parts ("much quicker than in global methods"). Apparently, from the "preface" to this book, the introduction of sight words is almost immediately followed by synthetic phonics, building words from known "sounds". The "sounds" listed in their table of contents indicate that this is pure, synthetic phonics and not "syllable" work in the Bloomfield sense, in which the syllable is not broken down into the sounds of individual letters or built from the known sounds of individual letters.

A teacher in the third Avignon school I visited said, concerning this book, that it was too difficult for children and that they could not handle the beginning at all. (She meant the 20 sight words, presumably.) I observed a first grade in that school using another method, but the second grade I tested had been taught previously by two different teachers and I understood the children had learned to read with this book. The principal said that their ability level would be about average for France. The teacher who made the above comment also said that, of 25 who had this book, on the average three would be retained, but she said this was not the fault of the book but because the child was "not ready". However, I consider that a retention rate of 3/25 for first-grade children indicates a weakness in the phonics of this text, which would not be there if the text rated Code 10 instead of Code 7.

All of the foregoing points up the difficulty in labeling reading programs by ill-defined labels and then comparing those programs to others in cross-country research. By American standards,

Remi et Colette, despite its introduction of 20 words in about the first eight pages, would never be called a mixed sight-word/phonic program but a very, very heavy analytic/synthetic phonic program, something which we have had little of in America but which was common in the 19th century in Germany. Instead of calling this a mixed sight-word method, I consider it largely phonic. I would give it at least a Code 7 on the global-phonics scale. It is interesting that the "average" children in the second grade I tested who had Remi et Colette scored very, very well indeed on my reading test!

The approach of this program, from the sentence to the word, from the word to the letter, is not too dissimilar in practice from the linguistic method I saw in Quimper except that the letters in Quimper were not specifically named early in the linguistic program.

I heard reference - negatively- by some teachers in France to the use of the syllable method, which apparently had been common in the past. While in Brussels, I bought three sets of beginning readers for Belgian schools. I do not know if they are actually in use in their schools, but they were all that was available in the textbook store I visited, if I understood the clerk correctly. Two of the three used what was called the "syllable" method. This syllable method, however, is not at all the syllables of the American linguist, Bloomfield, who did not introduce letters in isolation. In all three books, the vowels were introduced first, and then on successive pages new consonants to be blended to the vowels, which consonants were obviously being introduced in isolation.

One of the two approaches which called themselves "syllable" methods was Syllabaire Illustre, by Francis Martin, published in two little books, parts 1 and 2. Part 1 first gave vowels and pictures of words using the vowels (page 3 - i, u; page 4 - o, a) and then on page 5, one page of syllables with "n" in the end position. This was the only page where the new letter was not shown in isolation, but written in syllables - apparently because "n" used after vowels produces the peculiar nasalized "n" sounds in French. On page 6, "n" was combined with the four vowels already given, but in beginning and middle position (ni, uni, etc.). On that page, all the vowels were given and the letter "n" was written in isolation, separated from syllables. Page 7 blended the letters already given with the new letter, "m" and used "m" in middle and beginning position. On this page, "m" was written in isolation once. Page 8 introduced "r" and wrote it in isolation three times, combined it in syllables with the four vowels given to date, and formed words from the letters given (rame marie, ranime, morue, etc.) Page 9 was a review page with sentences of many blended words to be matched to the pictures with the meanings of the sentences, straight comprehension exercises. Pages 10 and 11 were reviews on syllable blending, and page 11 had comprehension exercises matching sentences to pictures. Page 12 introduced "v" in isolation, and wrote it five times, and used it in syllables and words. Page 13 contained sentences and matching pictures. Sixteen fairly complex pictures were on this page, and 11 of the sentences were in print and 5 in cursive writing. (Cursive writing and print had been introduced simultaneously on the first page.)

The first book continued in this fashion, introducing new phonic elements in isolation, after practicing them in syllables and words, all on the same page, and following this with reading texts, in which every word could be decoded phonically from sounds already given. This book was followed by a second book arranged in the same fashion. The organization and content of both appeared to me (who admittedly had never been faced with teaching children to read in the French language) to be highly satisfactory texts. What is notable compared to American primers is that these two little books are hardly more than pamphlets, yet contain tremendous lesson material. By contrast, American first-grade basal reading programs sometimes weigh up like sets of encyclopedias and ALL of them are bulky, yet they do not even pretend to begin to do the job that is done by this French language primer by the 1 3th page, which is also only about 6 1/2 by 8 1/2 inches, and written in large print. By page 13, the children are to read complex sentences made from sounds they had learned by analytic phonics, and were obviously expected to know THE SOUND OF EVERY LETTER IN EVERY WORD.

The name of the program is Syllabaire Illustre 1 and 2, and yet the syllables are used (except in the case of the first letter, "n", to illustrate the sound of every new consonant letter, which is then immediately written in isolation after the introduced new syllables and words. Children in this program would therefore be made acutely aware of the sounds of the letters. Also, all vowel sounds were given in isolation before they were blended into syllables (except for "e", which has different values in French depending on the accent mark, and they should be demonstrated in sample words).

Therefore, in my opinion, this should be called a heavy analytic phonic program which uses syllables to demonstrate letter sounds in isolation, and not a pure syllable method where letters are never used in isolation (as in Bloomfield's). It is, emphatically, at least Code 9 and probably Code 10.

Another Belgian primer De La Syllabe A La Phrase Pensee by E. A. M. Hebetter, J. Lambiotte, and E. Watelet, published by Wesmael-Charlier (S. A.), Namur (1975), proceeds in very much the same fashion. It moves from isolated study of simple vowels (a, i, o, u, e, e, e) to isolated study of "r" and "r" in syllables (page 12). By page 13 the first blending of "r" plus the given vowels is in these words: rue, rare, riri, rire, rira (in both print and cursive). "M" is introduced on page 14, and the European cat, "Mimi," appears again. Page 14 practices isolated "m"'s and syllables made with "m" and the simple vowels. Page 15 practices words from the two consonants already given ("m" and "r") and the simple vowels, resulting in the first sentences: "Marie a remue. Mere rira." Both are written in script and in print, but no capitals are used. On these two facing pages, 14 and 15, are ten little colored drawings to illustrate the use of syllables in words. New consonants are introduced on every second page. By page 19, the sentences composed only of phonic elements introduced so far have become surprisingly complex:

"emilie a merite la tarte. (Emily has earned the tart.)

"emile a ma moto. (Emile has my motorcycle.)

"la tortue tire la tirelire." (The turtle pulls the piggybank.)

By page 21, the pupils are practicing verbs in the present, past and future tenses, and substituting different objects. This work starts with the cat Mimi again, "Mimi porte la tulipe," (Mimi carries the tulip) and a picture of Mimi, a bow around her neck, carrying a wilted tulip. Following the first sentence is, "mimi a porte... and mimi portera..." (Mimi has carried, and Mimi will carry...) With a footnote to the teacher: "Replace the words by others. Orally, very numerous substitutions are possible."

As each new consonant is introduced, the sentences become more and more complex. By page 37 (obviously about the feast of St. Nicholas in early December), the children are given a REAL STORY to read, without ANY controlled vocabulary! All they have to do is to sound it out. It reads, as I translate it roughly, as:

"Cocorico, the rooster is there. [This must mean "time to rise"] Quickly, Luke gets up and cries, 'Mother, has Saint Nicolas come?' He flies to the little table. 'Oh, a piano, a motorcycle, a bike and a desk!' Luke is delighted: 'Long live Saint Nicolas!'"

A picture is shown of a toy piano and motorcycle, and a real bike and desk. Following the little story are exercises based on the content of the story.

A Christmas tree is introduced on page 53, with a more elaborate story, and this first book ends three pages later, on page 56, obviously to be covered right after the New Year. On this last page, "x" is introduced, the last letter of the alphabet, and the children fortunate enough to have had this program will have learned the entire alphabet and how to blend it into words to write complex sentences. This work will all have been covered in the first six months of first grade, as Jean Chall recommended, while their American "basal reader" counterparts will still be struggling with initial consonants and identifying the word, "red," by the fact it begins with "r" and the teacher gives them the "hint" that it is a word meaning a color!

The second book in this series, to be given after Christmas, covers the more complex French vowels and consonant blends, but only the first forty pages of the 83-page Book Two cover phonics. The last part of the book almost totally abandons the study of phonics, so the program is DONE with teaching phonics by about March of first grade! It then concentrates on reading stories and doing comprehension and spelling exercises based on the content of the stories. Phonics is where it belongs in this program, in the first part of first grade. Of course, some few children will have failed to learn the material and would therefore have to repeat the program in the following year. The vast majority, however (my European statistics showed 96%) can pass such a course. Nevertheless, it is desirable for the phonic material to be reviewed in the second-grade year by all children, as review of any kind of learned material serves to reinforce it.

Another Belgian primer, with an earlier edition date (1959) is <u>Methode Boscher ou La Journee des Tout Petits (The Day of All the Little Ones)</u> by M. Boscher, V. Boscher, J. Chapron, Teachers, and M. J. Carre. No publisher is given, but the information is given on the cover, "Address all orders to Mme. J. Chapron, Editor, at Loudeac (Cotesdu-Nord), and "Pay by postal check - 2859 at Rennes." The preface states that the book received the Bronze Medal at the International Exposition at Brussels in 1958. It is a combination reading, spelling and arithmetic book, about six by nine inches, and only 72 pages long. The preface states:

> "The Boscher Method is a syllabic method, complete, not avoiding any difficulty. It presents, among other advantages, that of learning to read quickly."

The text states later that the learning of reading should take three or four months. Concerning spelling and writing, it states that every lesson should be followed by dictation, from the beginning of the Course Preparatoire (beginning of first grade). While I cannot endorse such a rapid method of "learning to read" by phonics, it is the opposite of what the sight-word American basal reader publishers usually claim is the appropriate time to spend on "phonics," not three months but more than three years!

This book introduces the vowels first in isolation (3 pages) and then the letter "p" in isolation and in syllables, with a sample sentence written on top of the page, the p's being underlined. Words built from the phonic elements given are on the page: pipe, epi. Each page also has a picture illustrating the sample sentence, and on the bottom, a third of a page on simple arithmetic.

Each succeeding page introduces a new letter, with a sample sentence in which the new letter is underlined, and a picture of the sentence. The words after this built from the phonic elements already studied become more and more complex. By only page 9, the first sentence is given from known phonic elements: "pere a repare ta petite ratiere." (Father has fixed your little rat cage.) From this point on, every page has syllables, words, and simple sentences built from known phonic elements. After all phonic elements have been introduced, the book ends with 13 pages of stories, in small print, with totally uncontrolled vocabulary!

Another Belgian reader, <u>Mes Premiers Pas en Lecture (My First Steps in Reading)</u> by A. Pierret and R. Basiaux, published by Wesmael-Charlier at Namur (1975) does not use the syllable method but introduces vowels and consonants to form three-letter words. The preface states, "We have abandoned the systematic syllabication of the traditional method which begins ba, bo, bi, be. At the beginning we study two consonants and two vowels, r, c, a. o. That is all! Then we pass immediately to true reading... little words of three letters like car, rat, roc, cor, arc..."

The book is described as a kind of renewed syllabaire, "which could be used equally by the gesture method or the mixed method (which starts with global but has immediate phonic analysis)."

This method, like the previous one, supplied separate letters to each pupil so that he could use them to build words.

The book has elaborate tables, as I saw on the blackboard in Paris, where consonants are connected to vowels for children to make blends. This is of course, a syllable approach.

The little textbook contains much work that resembles American workbook exercises, unscrambling of letters, and filling in of blanks.

I find it interesting that page 43 of the first of the two first-grade books includes the following sentences, expected to be dictated to the children sometime apparently before Christmas, which the children are obviously expected to spell:

"Pol a vu une ile. (Paul has seen as island.)

"La tortue porte une tulipe." (The turtle carries a tulip.)

Also included are 12 other sentences just as hard. A reasonable proportion of first-graders must be expected to be able to spell these words. That expectation makes the dismal American Iowa spelling norms of 1952 even more dismal, since they showed that 26% of American children beginning THIRD grade, not in the middle of FIRST grade, could not even spell "tan"!

APPENDIX 3
Test Forms, Statistical Summaries, and Tables of Research Data for Individual Classes

Test Forms, at Second Grade and Sixth Grade, in Various Languages.........................252

Individual Summary Tables for Early Fall American, Late Fall European, and January American...265

Graphs on Accuracy Scores and Comprehension Scores for American Phonic vs. Sight-Words And European Phonic vs. Sight-Words 272

Individual Class Scores, Comments and Graphs...276

TEST IN ENGLISH

1. Peter has a little dog. The dog is black with a white spot on
   1   2   3 4   5   6 7   8   9   10 11 12 13 14
   his back and one white leg. The color of Peter's dog is most
   15 16   17 18   19   20   21   22 23   24   25 26 27
         black   brown   gray
          28   29   30

2. When Peter got the dog it was a small puppy. Now the dog
   31   32   33 34 35 36 37 38 39   40   41 42 43
   a little more than two years old. How many years has
   45 46   47   48   49   50   51   52   53   54   55
   Peter had the dog?
   56   57 58 59
        one   two   three
         60   61   62

3. Peter's dog has a spot on his back. That is why Peter named
   63   64 65 66 67 68 69   70   71 72 73 74   75
   the dog Spot. The dog was named after the spot on his
   76 77 78   79 80 81   82   83   84 85 86 87
       back   ear   leg
        88   89   90

4. The dog has learned to do two tricks. One trick is to catch
   91 92   93   94   95 96 97   98   99 100 101 102 103
   a ball. To stand on its hind leg is the second
   104 105 106 107 108 109 110 111 112 113   114
      story   trick   way
       115   116   117

5. When he was a puppy Spot was fed three times a day. Now
   118 119 120 121 122   123 124 125 126   127 128 129 130
   he is fed only once. The number of times is now
   131 132 133 134 135   136   137   138 139 140 141
      often   less   many
       142   143   144

Analysis of Second-Grade Oral Reading Test

This five-item oral reading test in English for second grade was translated into Dutch, Swedish, Icelandic, German and French by a commercial translating firm for Geraldine E. Rodgers.
The five items were a portion of the 40-item copyrighted test from IEA, International Association for the Evaluation of Educational Achievement, Stockholm, Sweden. The 40-item test had been used as a speed reading test for 10 and 14 year olds, reported in <u>Reading Comprehension Education in Fifteen Countries</u> (by IEA, Stockholm). Permission was granted to Geraldine E. Rodgers to use these items if IEA were acknowledged in any written material and if, when possible, a copy were sent to IEA.
The Harris-Jacobsen Readability Formula 1 yields a grade level of low second grade (about November) on these items. Classes were tested in the 1977-1978 first-half term in September, October, and January in the United States, and in October and November of second grade in Europe.
The test totals 144 words in English, using 64 different words. Of these 64 different words, 40 are among the 250 most commonly used words in English, according to <u>Key Words to Literacy</u>, The Schoolmaster Publishing Co., Ltd., London, England. Most of the rest are among the 500 most commonly used words listed in the section "Original Thorndike Words 1 to 500" of The <u>Teacher's Word Book of 30,000 Words</u> (Thorndike and Lorge, Teachers College Press, Teachers College, Columbia University, New York, New York, 1944). Only 11 of the 64 words are above the 500 frequency. Six of them are on the list from 500 to 1000 (born, catch, dog, gray, leg and spot). Five are above the 1000 frequency (Peter, trick, fed, hind and puppy). Concerning word frequency, it should be mentioned that the English language contains in the neighborhood of 500,000 words. Estimates of the vocabularies of beginning school children range from the low figure of Dr. Jean Chall (4,000) to that of Dr. R. H. Seashore (24,000 words). (These figures are discussed by Dr. Rudolf Flesch on pages 100 to 106 of <u>Why Johnny STILL Can't Read</u> (1981). Besides the half million or so words in the English language, names in the telephone books, directories and atlases must total hundreds of thousands more. Yet, since this oral test is limited almost totally to very high frequency words, in no sense does it test anything but the ability to read very high frequency words with the help of context to confirm guesses.
This second-grade oral reading test of very high-frequency words gives an advantage to children trained in programs which stress sight words (which are usually the high-frequency words) rather than phonics. This test does not attempt at all to determine which children are better at decoding unfamiliar words.
In accordance with standard practice in testing oral reading, if the child could not read a word when he saw it for the first time, it was pronounced for him. That meant, in his short-term memory, he would probably recognize the word when he saw it later in the test. Each error was counted (as is normal on oral reading tests) as 1/144 off, since the test totals 144 words. However, since unknown words were given to children the first time, it might be reasonable to consider each error as 1/64 off, because there are only 64 DIFFERENT words. Nevertheless, the standard marking procedure was used. and each error accounted for a 1/144 loss

GERMAN

1. Peter hat einen kleinen Hund. Der Hund ist schwarz und hat einen weißen Fleck auf dem Rücken und ein weißes Bein. Peters Hund ist größtenteils

            schwarz   braun   grau

2. Als Peter den Hund bekam, war dieser noch ganz, ganz jung. Jetzt ist der Hund etwas über zwei Jahre alt. Wie viele Jahre hat Peter den Hund schon?

            eins   zwei   drei

3. Peters Hund hat einen Fleck auf dem Rücken. Darum hat Peter dem Hund den Namen Fleck gegeben. Der Hund bekam seinen Namen wegen des Fleckes auf seinem

            Rücken   Ohr   Bein

4. Der Hund hat zwei Tricks gelernt. Der eine Trick ist, einen Ball zu fangen. Männchenmachen ist der zweite

            Akt   Trick   Fall

5. Als Fleck noch ganz klein war, wurde er dreimal am Tag gefüttert. Jetzt wird er nur noch einmal gefüttert. Die Fütterungen sind jetzt

            oft   seltener   viel

(DUTCH

1. Piet heeft een kleine hond. De hond is zwart, met een witte plek op z'n rug en een witte
   _{1   2   3   4   5   6   7   8   9   10   11   12   13 14 15   16 17 18   19}
   poot. De kleur van de hond van Piet is vooral
   _{20   21   22   23 24   25   26   27 28   29}

           zwart   bruin   grijs
            30   31   32

2. Toen Piet de hond kreeg, was hij nog heel jong. Nu is de hond iets meer dan twee jaar oud.
   _{33   34 35   36   37   38   39 40   41   42   43 44 45   46   47   48   49   50   51   52}
   Hoeveel jaren heeft Piet de hond?
   _{53   54   55   56 57 58}

           een   twee   drie
            59   60   61

3. De hond van Piet heeft een plek op z'n rug. Daarom noemt Piet de hond: Plek. De hond
   _{62   63   64   65   66   67   68   69 70 71   72   73   74 75 76   77   78   79}
   wordt zo genoemd naar de plek op z'n
   _{80   81   82   83   84   85   86 87}

           rug   oor   poot
            88   89   90

4. De hond heeft twee kunstjes geleerd. Een kunstje is de bal te pakken. Op z'n achterpoten
   _{91   92   93   94   95   96   97   98   99 100 101 102 103 104 105   106}
   staan is het tweede
   _{107 108 109 110}

         sprookje   kunstje   padje
           111   112   113

5. Toen hij nog een jonge hond was, werd Plek drie keer per dag gevoed. Nu wordt hij maar
   _{114 115 116 117 118   119 120   121 122 123   124 125 126   127   128 129 130 131}
   een keer gevoed. Het aantal keren is nu
   _{132 133   134   135   136   137 138 139}

           vaak   minder   veel
           140   141   142

SWEDISH

1. Peter har en liten hund. Hunden är svart med en vit fläck på ryggen och ett vitt ben. Färgen på Peters hund är huvudsakligen

      svart   brun   grå

2. När Peter fick hunden var den en liten valp. Nu är hunden lite mer än två år gammal. Hur många år har Peter haft hunden?

      ett   två   tre

3. Peters hund har en fläck på ryggen. Det är därför Peter kallar hunden Fläck. Hunden uppkallades efter fläcken på sin

      rygg   öra   ben

4. Hunden har lärt sig göra två konster. En konst är att fånga en boll. Att stå på bakbenen är den andra

      berättelsen   konsten   sättet

5. När han var valp fick Fläck mat tre gånger om dagen. Nu får han mat bara en gång. Antalet gånger är nu

      oftare   mindre ofta   flera

FRENCH

1. Pierrot a un petit chien. Le chien est noir avec une tache blanche sur le
   1   2 3   4   5   6   7   8   9   10   11   12   13   14 15

   dos et une patte blanche. Le chien de Pierrot est surtout
   16 17 18 19   20   21   22   23   24   25   26

         noir   brun   gris
         27   28   29

2. Quand Pierrot l'a reçu, c'était un très jeune chien. Maintenant le chien
   30   31   32 33   34   35 36   37   38   39   40 41

   a un peu plus de deux ans. Depuis combien d'années Pierrot a-t-il le chien?
   42 43 44 45 46 47   48   49   50   51   52   53   54 55

         un an   deux ans   trois ans
         56 57   58   59   60   61

3. Le chien de Pierrot a une tache sur le dos. Voilà pourquoi Pierrot l'a
   62 63   64 65   66 67 68   69 70 71   72   73   74   75

   nommé Tacheté. Le chien a été nommé en raison de la tache qu'il a sur
   76   77   78 79   80 81 82   83 84   85 86 87   88   89 90

         le dos   l'oreille   la patte
         91 92   93   94 95

4. Le chien a appris deux tours. Un de ces tours consiste à attraper une balle.
   96 97   98 99   100 101   102 103 104 105 106   107 108   109 110

   Marche sur les pattes de derrière c'est le deuxième
   111   112 113 114   115 116   117   118 119

         ~~étage~~   tour   chemin
         120   121   122
         histoire

5. Quand il était petit, Tacheté mangeait trois fois par jour. Maintenant, il ne
   123   124 125 126   127   128   129   130 131 132   133   134 135

   mange qu'une fois par jour, c'est-à-dire que maintenant, il mange
   136   137   138 139 140   141 142   143 144   145 146

         souvent   moins   plus
         147   148   149

1. Pétur á lítinn hund. Hundurinn er svartur með hvítan blett á
   bakinu og einn hvítan fót. Liturinn á hund Péturs er aðallega

   Svartur   Brúnn   Grár

2. Þegar Pétur fékk hundinn, þá var hann lítill hvolpur. Nú er
   hundurinn aðeins meira en tveggja ára. Í hvað mörg ár hefur
   Pétur átt hundinn ?

   Eitt   Tvö   Þrjú

3. Hundurinn hans Péturs er með blett á bakinu. Þess vegna skýrði
   Pétur hundinn Blettur. Hundurinn heitir eftir blettinum á

   Bakinu   Eyranu   Fætinum

4. Hundurinn hefur lært að gera tvær þrautir. Ein þrautin er að
   grýpa bolta. Að standa á afturfótunum er önnur

   Sagan   Þrautin   Aðferðin

5. Þegar hann var hvolpur var Bletti gefið gefið þrisvar á dag.
   Nú er honum gefið aðeins einu sinni á dag. Hversu oft núna

   Oftar   Sjaldnar   Mörgum sinnum

103rd Psalm in Catholic Bible
Which Is 104th Psalm in
Protestant Bibles

10 You send forth springs into the watercourses that wind among the mountains,

11 And give drink to every beast of the field, till the wild asses quench their thirst.

12 Beside them the birds of heaven dwell; from among the branches they send forth their song.

13 You water the mountains from your palace; the earth is replete with the fruit of your works.

14 You raise grass for the cattle, and vegetation for men's use,

Producing bread from the earth, 15 and wine to gladden men's hearts,

So that their faces gleam with oil, and bread fortifies the hearts of men.

16 Well watered are the trees of the LORD, the cedars of Lebanon, which he planted;

17 In them the birds build their nests; fir trees are the home of the stork.

18 The high mountains are for wild goats; the cliffs are a refuge for rock-badgers.

104th Psalm – German Bible
From American Bible Society
Reference Library, New York, N. Y.

¢ Du lässest Wasser in den Tälern quellen,
 daß sie zwischen den Bergen dahinfließen,
daß alle Tiere des Feldes trinken
 und das Wild seinen Durst lösche.
Darüber sitzen die Vögel des Himmels
 und singen unter den Zweigen.
Du feuchtest die Berge von oben her,
 du machst das Land voll Früchte, die du schaffest.
Du lässest Gras wachsen für das Vieh
 und Saat zu Nutz den Menschen,
daß du Brot aus der Erde hervorbringst,
 daß der Wein erfreue des Menschen Herz
und sein Antlitz schön werde vom Öl
 und das Brot des Menschen Herz stärke.
Die Bäume des HERRN stehen voll Saft,
 die Zedern des Libanon, die er gepflanzt hat.
Dort nisten die Vögel,
 und die Reiher wohnen in den Wipfeln.
Die hohen Berge geben dem Steinbock Zuflucht
 und die Felsklüfte dem Klippdachs.

```
                104th Psalm - Dutch Bible
                From American Bible Society
                Reference Library, New York, N. Y.
```

10 Hij zendt de bronnen naar de beken,
   tussen de bergen vloeien zij daarheen;
11 zij drenken alle dieren des velds,
   de wilde ezels lessen hun dorst.
12 Daarbij woont het gevogelte des hemels,
   van tussen de takken laat het zijn lied horen.
13 Hij drenkt de bergen uit zijn opperzalen,
   van de vrucht uwer werken wordt de aarde verzadigd.

14 Hij doet het gras ontspruiten voor het vee,
   het groene kruid ter bewerking door de mens,
   brood uit de aarde voortbrengende
15 en wijn, die het hart des mensen verheugt,
   het aangezicht doende glanzen van olie;
   ja, brood, dat het hart des mensen versterkt.
16 De bomen des HEREN worden verzadigd,
   de ceders van de Libanon, die Hij heeft geplant,
17   waar de vogels nestelen.
   Des ooievaars huis zijn de cypressen,
18   de hoge bergen zijn voor de steenbokken,
   de rotsen een schuilplaats voor de klipdassen.

104th Psalm - Swedish Bible
From American Bible Society
Reference Library, New York, N. Y.

10. Du lät källor flyta fram i dalarna, mellan bergen togo de sin väg.
11. De vattna alla markens djur, vildåsnorna släcka i dem sin törst.
12. Vid dem bo himmelens fåglar, från trädens grenar höja de sin röst.

13. Du vattnar bergen från dina salar, jorden mättas av den frukt du skapar.
14. Du låter gräs skjuta upp för djuren och örter till människans tjänst. Så framalstrar du bröd ur jorden
15. och vin, som gläder människans hjärta; så gör du hennes ansikte glänsande av olja, och brödet styrker människans hjärta.
16. Herrens träd varda ock mättade, Libanons cedrar, som han har planterat;
17. fåglarna bygga där sina nästen, hägern gör sitt bo i cypresserna.
18. Stenbockarna hava fått de höga bergen, klyftorna äro klippdassarnas tillflykt.

104th Psalm - French Bible
From American Bible Society
Reference Library, New York, N. Y.

Il conduit les sources dans des torrents,
Qui coulent entre les montagnes.
Elles abreuvent tous les animaux des champs.
Les ânes sauvages y étanchent leur soif.
Les oiseaux du ciel habitent sur leurs bords,
Et font résonner leur voix parmi les rameaux.
De sa haute demeure, il arrose les montagnes:
La terre est rassasiée du fruit de tes œuvres.
Il fait germer l'herbe pour le bétail,
Et les plantes pour les besoins de l'homme,
Afin que la terre produise de la nourriture,
Le vin qui réjouit le cœur de l'homme,
Et fait plus que l'huile resplendir son visage,
Et le pain qui soutient le cœur de l'homme.
Les arbres de l'Éternel se rassasient,
Les cèdres du Liban, qu'il a plantés.
C'est là que les oiseaux font leurs nids;
La cigogne a sa demeure dans les cyprès,
Les montagnes élevées sont pour les boucs sauvages,
Les rochers servent de retraite aux damans.

104th Psalm - Icelandic Bible
From American Bible Society
Reference Library, New York, N. Y.

Hann sendir lindir í dalina,
    þær renna milli fjallanna ;
þær drykkja öll dýr merkurinnar,
    villiasnarnir slökkva þorsta sinn ;
yfir þeim byggja fuglar himins,
    láta kvak sitt heyrast milli greinanna.
Hann vökvar fjöllin frá hásal sínum,
    jörðin mettast af ávexti verka þinna.
Hann lætur gras spretta handa fénaðinum
    og jurtir, sem maðurinn ræktar,
til þess að framleiða brauð af jörðunni
    og vín, sem gleður hjarta mannsins,
olíu, sem gjörir andlitið gljáandi,
    og brauð, sem hressir hjarta mannsins.
Tré Drottins mettast,
    sedrustrén á Libanon, er hann hefir gróðursett.
þar sem fuglarnir byggja hreiður,
    storkarnir, er hafa kýprestrén að húsi.
Hin háu fjöll eru handa steingeitunum,
    klettarnir eru hæli fyrir stökkhérana.

Sight-word 2nd Grade U.S. Oral Reading Tests for Last Week of September and First Two Weeks of October, 1977

Sight-word Text in First Grade	Passing Accuracy		Failing Accuracy			% Passing Comprehension	Estimated Speed		Reversals
	% Scoring at or above 95 on Test	% Scoring at or above 90 on Test	% Scoring Below 90	85	80	70		% Slow	% Fast	
Class 1, 19 pupils Scott, Foresman Code 2	37	42	58	36.8	36.8	5.0	63	26	0	16
Class 3, 21 pupils Scott, Foresman for bottom 2/3, Houghton Mifflin for top 1/3 Code 2	19	43	57	47.5	28.6	19.1	-	-	-	10

Only Class 1 appears on the final summary sheet, because only one child from Class 3 had time to read the whole oral reading test. The rest of Class 3 only had time to read the first example, to word 32 of the total 144 words.

The bottom 2/3 of Class 3, the critical portion, had Scott, Foresman (Code 2). The top third had Houghton Mifflin (Code 3). Since it is the bottom 2/3 which most determines a class score, Class 3 is given the Scott, Foresman Code 2 classification used in this research, not the Houghton Mifflin Code 3.

Since Class 11, an Alpha One phonic class, used Houghton Mifflin reading books and workbook sheets only for the practice of reading skills already taught, it remained a straight Code 10 class and was not affected by Houghton Mifflin's instructional methods.

Phonic 2nd Grade U.S. Oral Reading Tests for Last Week of September and First Two Weeks of October, 1977*

Phonic Method in First Grade	Passing Accuracy % Scoring at or above 95 on Test	Passing Accuracy % Scoring at or above 90 on Test	Failing Accuracy % Scoring Below 90				% Passing Comprehension	Estimated Speed % Slow	Estimated Speed % Fast	Reversals
			90	85	80	70				
Class 2, 18 pupils Economy - Code 7	56	83	17	6	6	6	83	11	17	0
Class 4, 23 pupils Open Court - Code 10	70	100	0	0	0	0	45	0	17	4
Class 5, 16 pupils Open Court - Code 10	44	63	37	31	25	19	31	31	0	13
Class 6, 22 pupils Open Court - Code 10	68	82	18	14	5	0	82	5	9	14
Class 7, 21 pupils Lippincott - Code 10	57	76	24	5	5	5	48	14	10	10
Class 8, 27 pupils ITA - Code 8	52	70	30	15	15	4	52	22	0	30
Class 9, 22 pupils Lippincott - Code 10	55	73	27	18	14	9	55	23	18	0
Class 11, 17 pupils* Alpha One Plus Partial Houghton Mifflin in Spring - Code 10	65	76	24	24	18	6	65	Not recorded, but noted, "Most read at a good rate."		12
Fall average for 8 phonic classes, 166 pupils	58	78	22	14.1	11	6.1	58	15	10	10

*Class 11 was tested 3rd and 5th day of 2nd grade fall term

Sight-word 2nd Grade U.S. Oral Reading Tests for January, 1978

Sight-word Text in First Grade	Passing Accuracy % Scoring at or above 95 on Test	% Scoring at or above 90 on Test	Failing Accuracy % Scoring Below 90	85	80	70	% Passing Comprehension	Estimated Speed % Slow	% Fast	Reversals
Classes 18, 19, 20,# 21, 22 - 93 pupils Houghton Mifflin Code 3 - Classes were ability grouped, so scores are averaged	55) 55) 55) 55) 55)	73) 73) 73) 73) 73)	27) 27) 27) 27) 27)	20) 20) 20) 20) 20)	15) 15) 15) 15) 15)	13 13 13 13 13	59) 59) 59) 59) 59)	16) 16) 16) 16) 16)	8) 8) 8) 8) 8)	12) 12) 12) 12) 12)
Class 23 - 22 pupils Houghton Mifflin Code 3#	55	82	18	5	0	0	77	18	9	5
Class 24 - 15 pupils Scott, Foresman, Code 2	47	73	27	20	13	0	53	13	27	0
Class 25 - 15 pupils Scott, Foresman, Code 2	33	60	40	20	0	0	73	13	0	33
Class 26 - 17 pupils Sott, Foresman, Code 2	47	71	29	0	0	0	77	24	12	6
Class 27 - 15 pupils Scott, Foresman Code 5**	73	100	0	0	0	0	100	0	47	7
January averages for 10 sight-word classes, 177 pupils	53	75	25	14.5	8.8	6.5	68	15	14	11

#See additional tables on these classes.
**This class had extra phonics training using Scott, Foresman's Letters and Sounds, A Phonics Work book for Primary Grades. Despite the generally excellent results, the achievement above 95 (73% of the class), is below the average achievement in this category of 77% for all phonic classes.

Phonic 2nd Grade U.S. Oral Reading Tests for January, 1978

Phonic program in First Grade	Passing Accuracy % Scoring at or above 95 on Test	% Scoring at or above 90 on Test	Failing Accuracy % Scoring Below			% Passing Comprehension	Estimated Speed		Reversals
			90	85	80	70		% Slow	% Fast	
Class 11 - 17 pupils Alpha One - Code 10	82	88	12	6	6	6	82	See note*		12
Class 12, 16 pupils Open Court - Code 10	81	88	12	12	6	0	50	6	38	6
Class 13, 24 pupils Open Court - Code 10	78	100	0	0	0	0	44	0	26	0
Class 14, 16 pupils Open Court - Code 10	81	88	12	6	0	0	56	13	44	6
Class 15, 23 pupils Lippincott - Code 10**	74	91	9	9	9	4	83	9	52	4
Class 16, 22 pupils Lippincott - Code 10**	61	87	13	9	9	0	55	17	30	17
Class 17, 15 pupils Heavy phonic emphasis by teacher - Code 10	80	100	0	0	0	0	80	0	20	0
January averages for seven phonic classes, 133 pupils	77	92	8	6	4.3	1.4	64	8	35	6

*This class was tested first on the 3rd and 5th days of school in September. Only those scoring in September under 95% on accuracy or 80% on comprehension were retested in January. No speed score was recorded in September, except for the note, "Most read at a good rate." In the January retest group, all but one read at a good rate. January averages were computed from the 7 January retest scores and the 10 satisfactory but not re-tested scores from September..
**These second-grade teachers used Scott, Foresman for their slowest pupils.
Note: This table omits students new to the schools in second grade only if they failed the test.

Partial Sight-Word/Global 2nd Grade European Oral Reading Tests for Last Two Weeks of October and Month of November, 1977

Heavy Emphasis on Sight-Word/Global Approach But Including Phonics	Passing Accuracy % Scoring at or above 95 on Test	Passing Accuracy % Scoring at or above 90 on Test	Failing Accuracy % Scoring Below 90		85	80	70	% Passing Comprehension	Estimated Speed % Slow	% Fast	Reversals
Stockholm 4, 10 pupils LTG + Nu Laser, Code 6	80	100	0	0	0	0		80	30	20	30
Stockholm 5, 21 pupils LTG + Nu Laser Code 6	67	86	14	5	5	5 (1 pupil at 64)		62	38	19	38
Amsterdam 4, 21 pupils Caesar, Code 6	67	86	14	5	0	0 (1 pupil)		37	43	0	5
Amsterdam 2, 14 pupils Caesar, Code 6	86	93	7	0	0	0		71	29	7	14
Amsterdam 1, 10 pupils Caesar, Code 6	70	70	30	10	10	10 (1 pupil at 64)		33	60	0	20
Avignon 2, 25 pupils Experience Charts - Code 6	76	84	16	0	0	0		56	24	12	4
Averages for 6 classes, 191 pupils, sight-word/global plus phonics	74	86.5	13.5	3.3	2.5	2.5#		57	37	10	18.5

#Actual number of pupils scoring below 85 was 3 of 101, and below 80 and 70 was 2 of 101. This table omits students new to classes only if they failed the tests.

(Page 1) Phonic 2nd Grade European Oral Reading Tests for Last Two Weeks of October and Month of November, 1977

Dominantly Phonic Method	Passing Accuracy		Failing Accuracy % Scoring Below				% Passing Comprehension	Estimated Speed		Reversals
	% Scoring at or above 95 on Test	% Scoring at or above 90 on Test	90	85	80	70		% Slow	% Fast	
Luxembourg, 12 pupils Code 8	92	100	0	0	0	0	30	33	0	8
Hamburg 1, 9 pupils Code 10	78	78	22	0	0	0	44	22	44	11
Hamburg 2, 14 pupils Code 10	93	100	0	0	0	0	50	0	29	7
Innsbruck, 28 pupils Code 10	93	100	0	0	0	0	42	4	46	4
Stockholm 1, 7 pupils Code 9	100	100	0	0	0	0	43	29	71	0
Stockholm 2, 15 pupils Code 8	87	100	0	0	0	0	80	27	20	20
Stockholm 3, 8 pupils Code 9	88	88	12	12	0	0	71**	13	63	0
			(1 pupil)							
Amsterdam 3, 19 pupils Code 8	95	100	0	0	0	0	42	5	11	11
Avignon 4, 27 pupils Code 9	85	93	7	7	4	0	30	11	26	4
			(2 and 1 pupils)							
Avignon 3, 31 pupils Code 7	90	97	3	3	0	0	33	13	13	0
			(1 pupil)							

(Page 2) Phonic 2nd Grade European Oral Reading Tests for Last Two Weeks of October and Month of November, 1977

Dominantly Phonic Method	Passing Accuracy % Scoring at or above 95 on Test	Passing Accuracy % Scoring at or above 90 on Test	Failing Accuracy % Scoring Below 90	85	80	70	% Passing Comprehension	Estimated Speed % Slow	% Fast	Reversals
Avignon 2, 23 pupils Code 8	83	96	4 (1 pupil)	0	0	0	30	35	0	4
Quimper, France 16 pupils, Code 8	100	100	0	0	0	0	47	13	0	0
Paris, 23 pupils - approx. bottom 2/3 of grade - Code 8	86*	93*	7 (2 pupils)	5	0	0	29	18	18	11
Averages, 13 Phonic Classes 237 pupils in all	90	96	4	2.2#	0.3#	0	44	17	26	6

This table omits Hamburg 3 where time permitted only a partial test. 16 children were tested, but 10 tests were incomplete. For general information (not included in the final averages) those Hamburg 3 averages are given below.

| Hamburg 3, 16 pupils Code 10 | 63 | 94 | 6 (1 pupil = 6%) | 6 | 6 | 6 | - | 44 | 0 | 31 |

#Actual number of phonically-trained pupils scoring below 85 was 6 of 237, and below 80 was 1 of 237.

**This table omits students new to classes only if they failed the tests. Therefore, the marked "comprehension: score (**) omits the score for a black child, new to Swedent, who was unable to speak Swedish. Howver, she passed the oral accuracy test at 100% accuracy, and that score is included in the class "accuracy" average.

*Adjusted to include the probable top 1/3 of the class (assumed to be about 14 pupils), who were in a separate top-ability first and second grade. Time did not permit their testing. As superior students, it is assumed all 14 would have passed at 95% accuracy, since 79% of the approximately bottom 23 did, and 89% of that bottom 1/3 also passed at 90% accuracy,

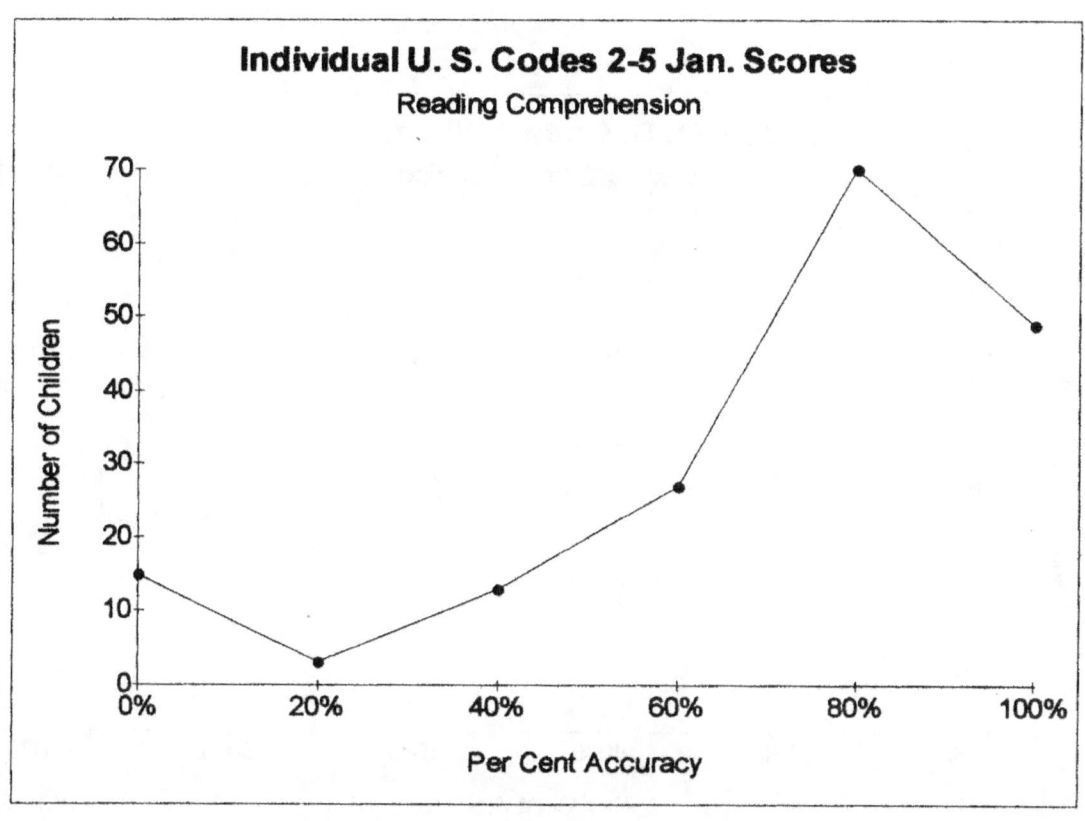

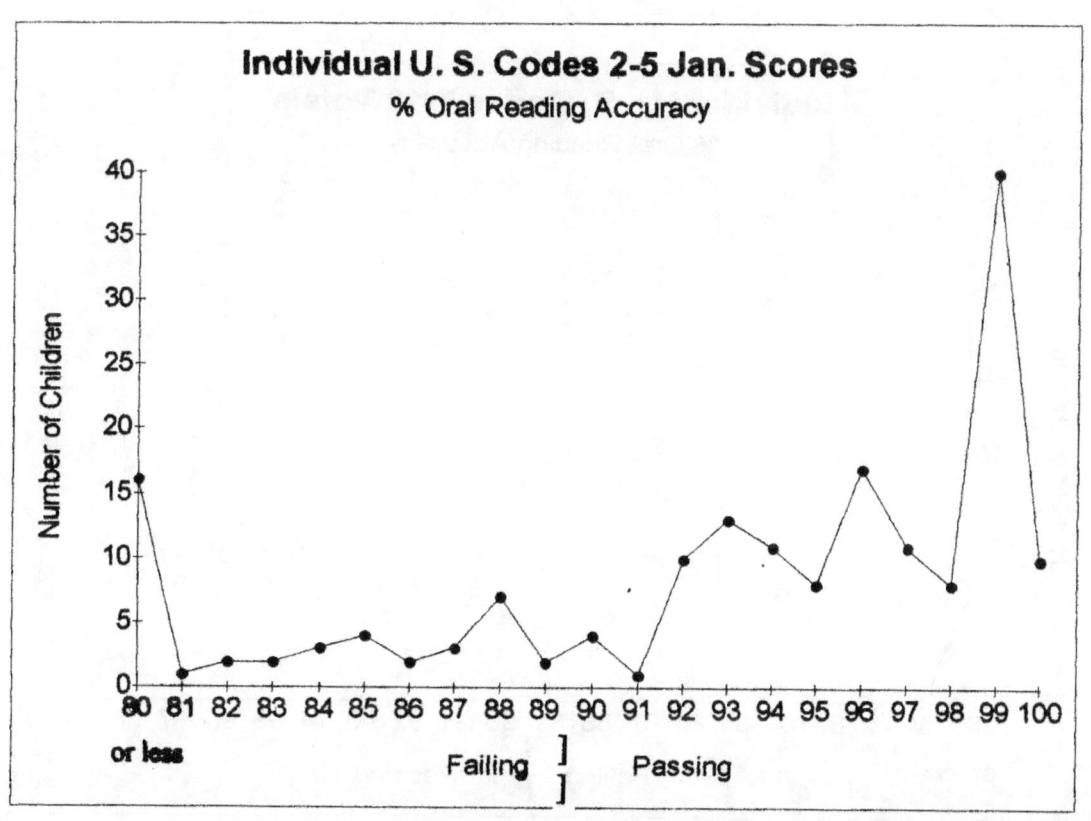

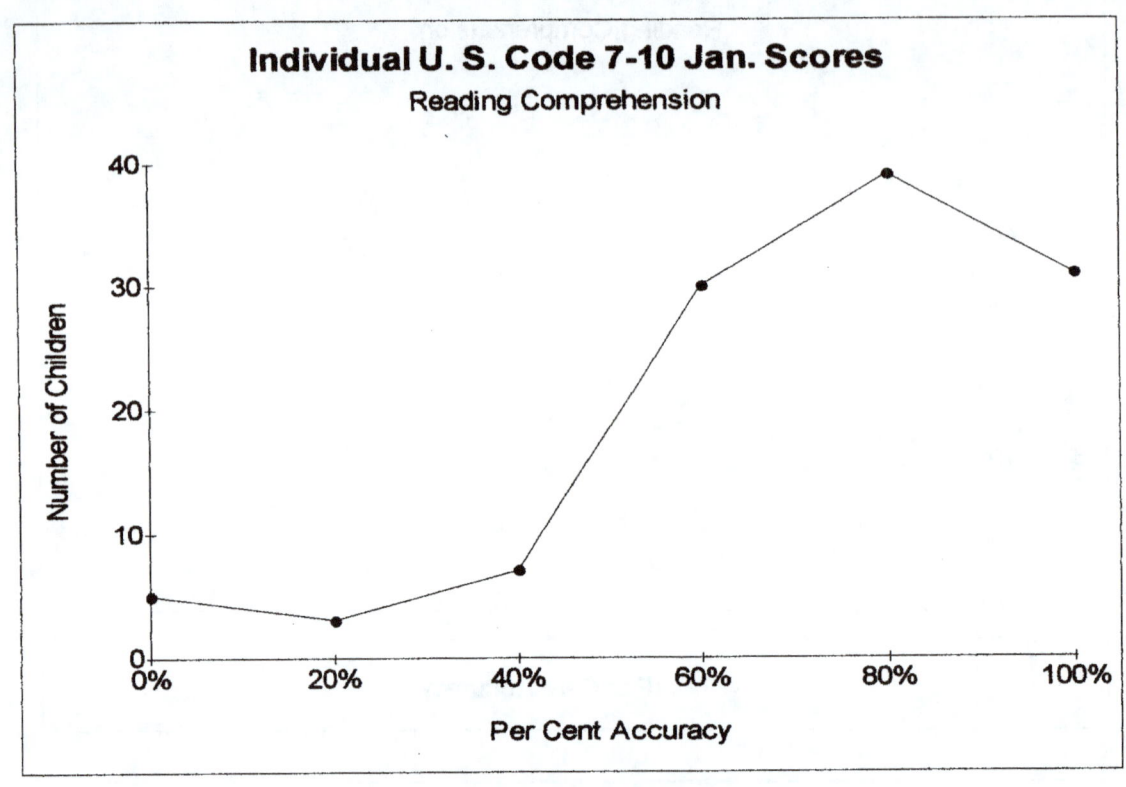

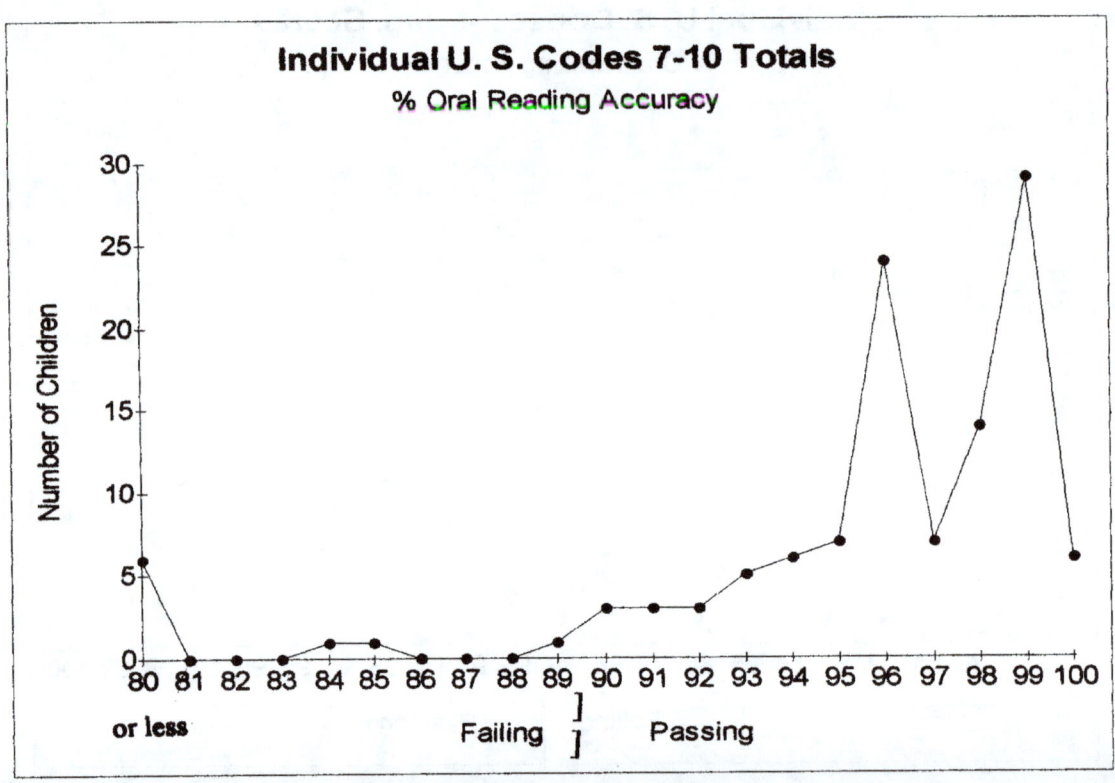

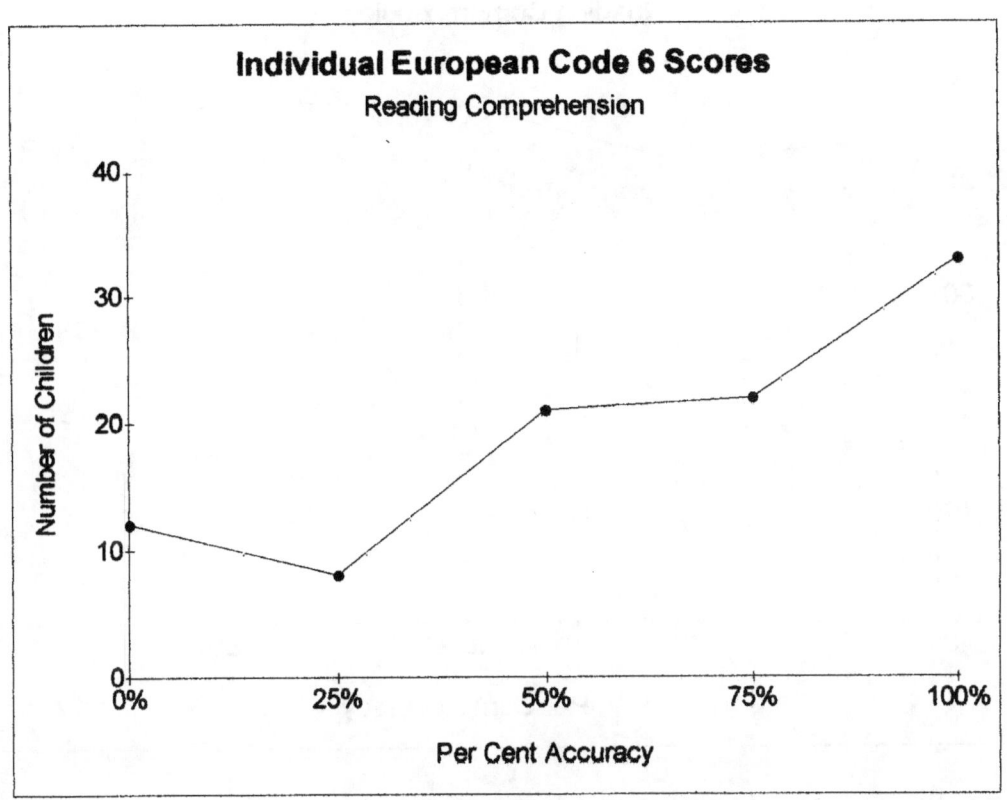

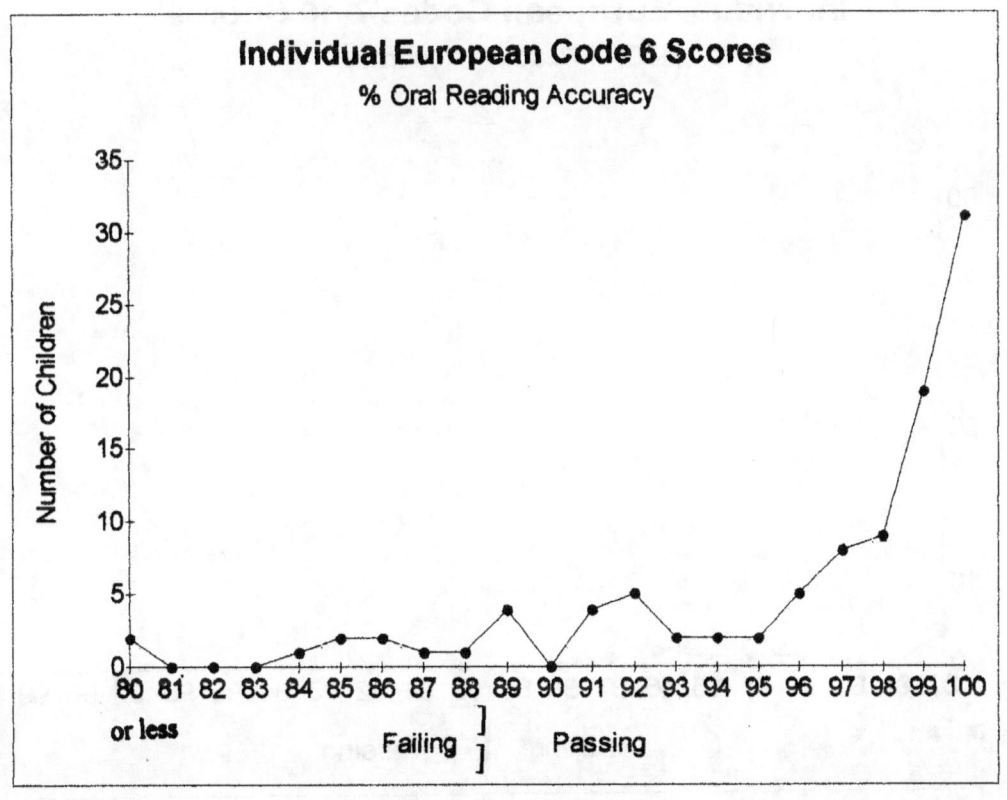

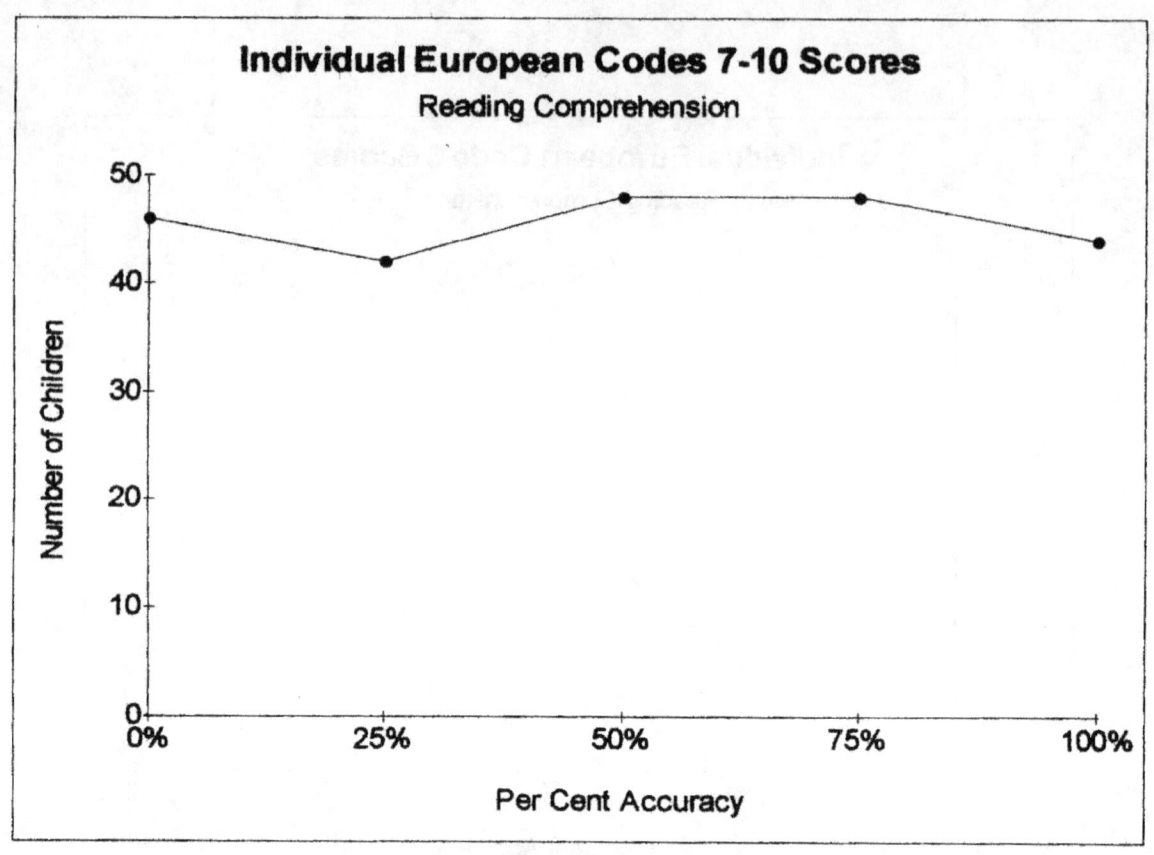

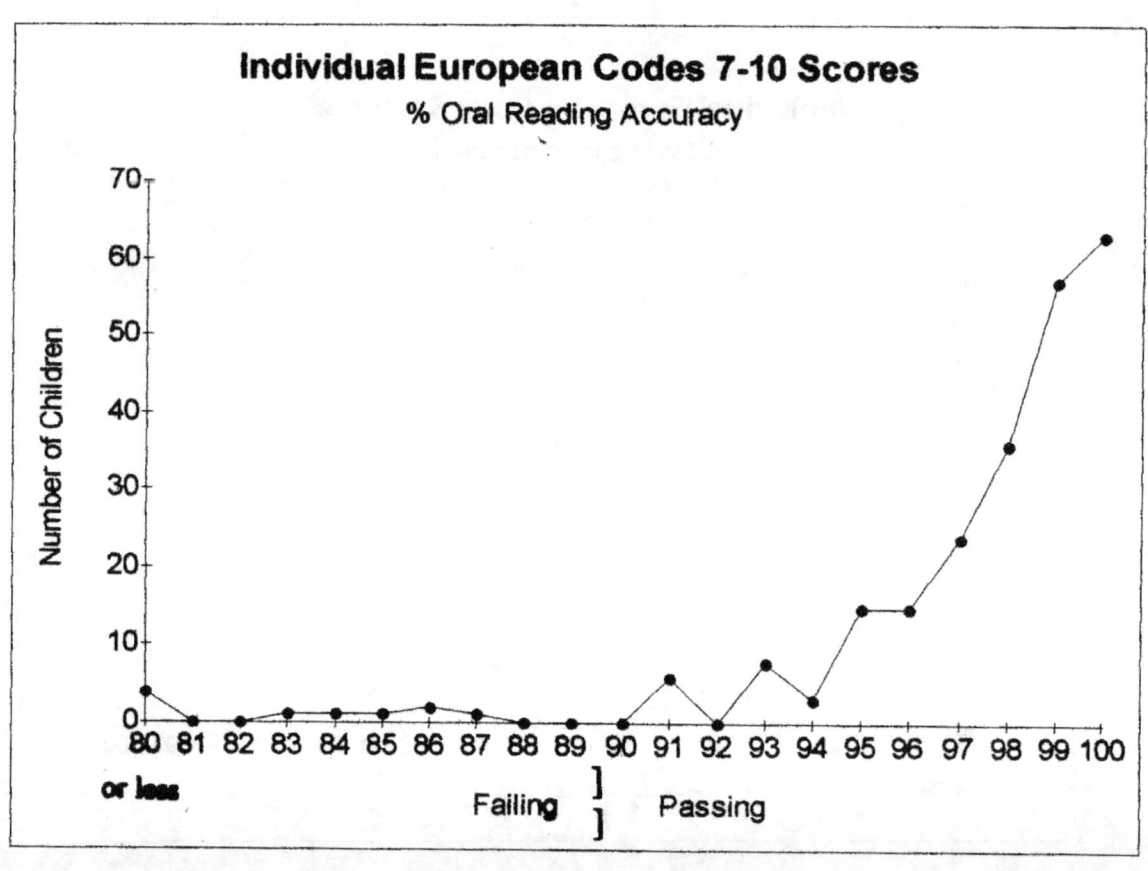

<u>U. S. 1 - Code 2 - 19 Pupils Present - Scott, Foresman - October, 1977</u>

Oral Accuracy Per Cent	Number of Pupils Obtaining Score	
		Pupils Scoring
99	2	<u>95 or Better</u>
98	3	7 of 19 or 37%
96	2	
92	1	**Pupils Scoring** <u>90 or Better</u> <u>8 of 19 or 42%</u>
88	1	
87	1	
85	2	
76	1	
74	1	
73	2	
72	1	
71	1	
60	1 (Incomplete)	

<u>Comprehension of Five Questions</u>

Per Cent Correct	Number of Pupils Obtaining Score	
100	3	**Pupils Scoring 80 or Better**
80	9	<u>12 of 19 or 63 %</u>
60	5	
40	1	
20	0	
0 (Incomplete)	1	

Rate: 4 slow of 19, plus 1 incomplete counted slow, or 5 of 19, or 26%. None fast.

Reversals: 3 of 19, or 16%.

As a group, children read very slowly and haltingly. Started at 12:45, finished at 2:50 - 19 children.

Retentions: One first grade teacher (of three or four first grades last year) reported she held two back last year.

U. S. 1, Code 2 - 19 Pupils Present - Scott, Foresman - October, 1977

Individual Scores in Order Tested
Accuracy/Comprehension

    87-100
    85-80
    98-60
    85-80 Tries to sound out, but takes wild guesses.
           Reversal: tricks~tircks
    92-80 Fairly slow. Possibly Indian or Pakistani.
    74-80
    72-60 Reversal: dog~bug
    73-60 Slow. Word-by-word. Labored.
    88-80 Slow
    71-80
    98-60
    73-80 Very slow. Word by word.
    99-80 Good rate.
    96-40
    76-60 Slow. Word by word.
    99-100 Good rate. Phrasing.
    60 Incomplete to Word 62. Reversal: now~on.
    98-100 Good rate. Fluent.
    96-60. Reads fairly rapidly, but word by word.

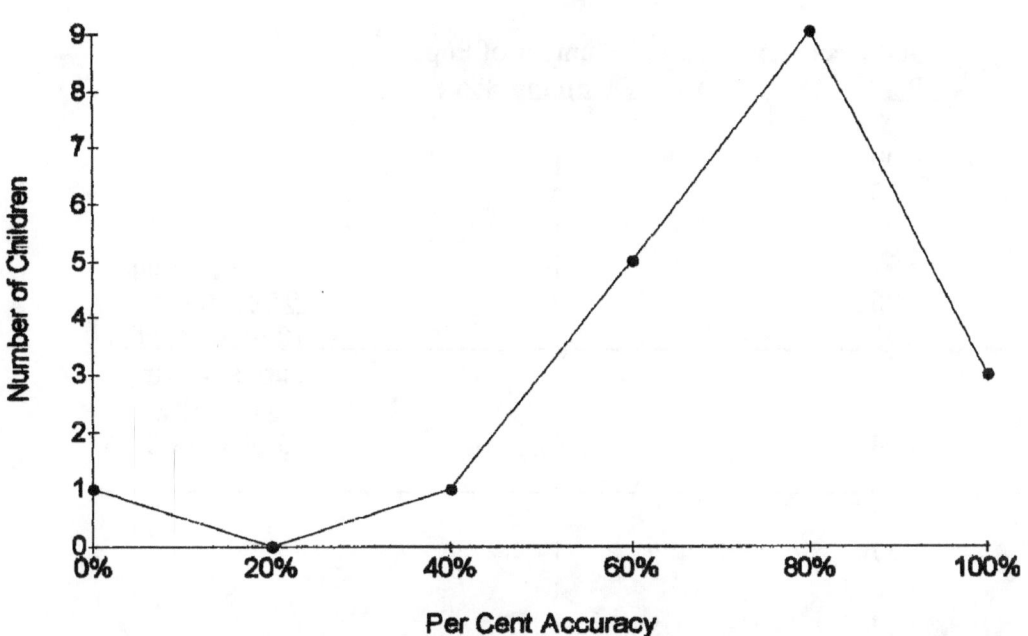

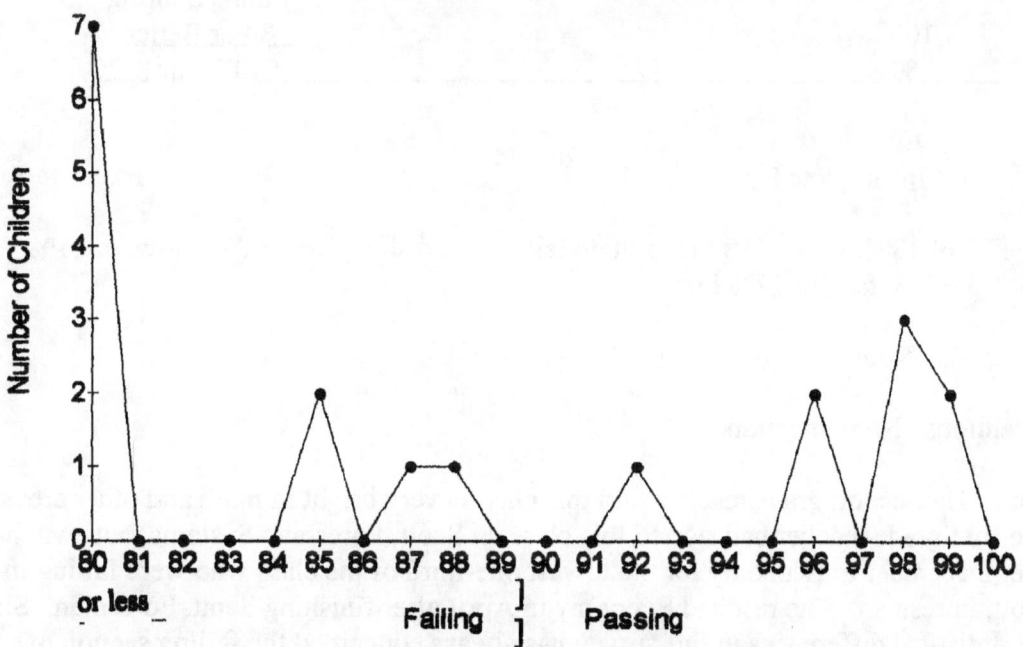

U. S. 2, Code 7 - Text: Economy, 18 Pupils Present, All Tested, October, 1977

Oral Accuracy Per Cent	Number of Pupils Obtaining Score	
100	1	
99	4	
98	1	
97	1	Pupils Scoring
96	2	95 or Better
95	1	10 of 18 or 56%
		Pupils Scoring 90 or Better
94	4	15 of 18 or 83%
92	1	
87	1	
85	1	
64	1	

Comprehension of Five Questions

Per Cent Correct	Number of Pupils Obtaining Score	
		Pupils Scoring 80 or Better
100	8	80 or Better
80	7	15 of 18 or 83%
40	2	
Incomplete Fail	1	

Rate: 1 of 18 slow, 1 of 18 incomplete fail counted slow, for 2 of 18 slow, or 11%
    3 of 18 fast, or 17% fast

Reversals: None.

Retentions: None mentioned.

Note: The second-grade teacher said this class is very bright in math and other areas. The first-grade teacher had started this class on Scott, Foresman Systems, but switched after December to Economy for the lowest one-third of the class who were failing in Scott, Foresman. The rest had Economy in April after finishing Scott, Foresman. Since the statistical differences in this survey has always concerned the failing section of classes, this class is counted as an Economy class.

U. S. 2, Code 7 - Text: Economy, 18 Pupils Present, All Tested, October, 1977

Individual Scores in Order Tested

Accuracy/Comprehension

92-100
100-80
98-80 Rapid
94-100 Rapid
96-100
99-100
87-80
85-80
94-40
99-100
97-100
96-40
99-100
94-80 Slow
99-100
95-80
94-80 Quick
64-Incomplete to 90.

U. S. 2, Code 7 - Oct. 1977
Reading Comprehension

U. S. 2, Code 7 - Oct. 1977
% Oral Reading Accuracy

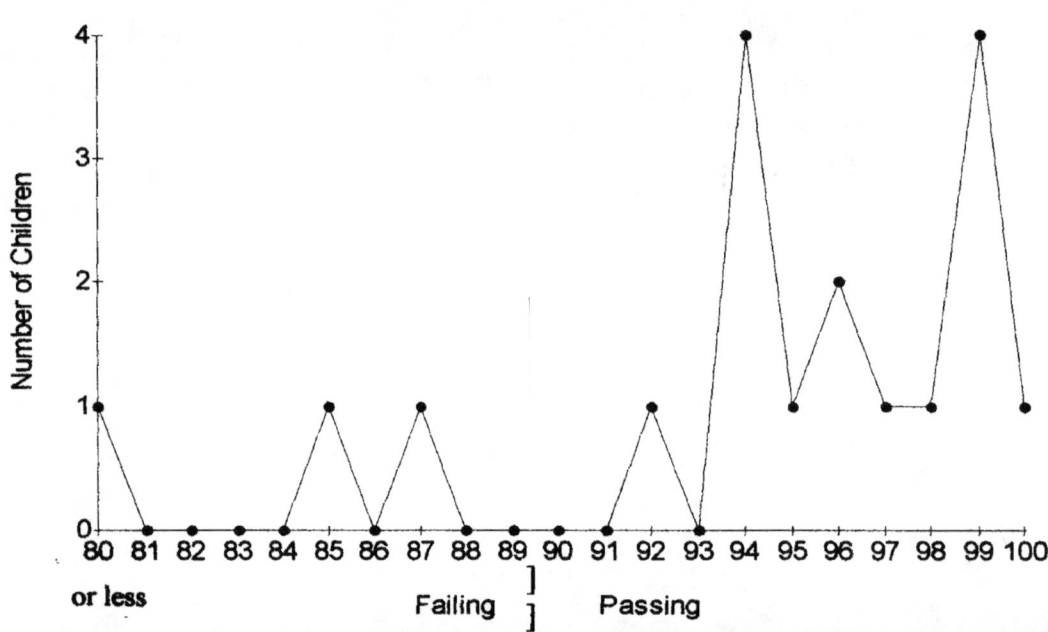

U. S. 3, Code 2 - Texts: Scott, Foresman/Houghton Mifflin - 21 Children in Class, October, 1977

This American fall sight-word class is omitted from the fall summary table because because only one child had time to read the whole test, and the rest of the class only had time to read the first example, to word 32 of the total 144 words.

The bottom 2/3 of this class, the critical portion, had Scott, Foresman (Code 2). The top third had Houghton Mifflin (Code 3). Since it is the bottom 2/3 which most determines a class score, this class is given the Scott, Foresman Code 2 classification used in this research, not the Houghton Mifflin Code 3.

One Hamburg class, Hamburg 3, is also omitted from the summary tables because there was insufficient time to test the children, but its partial scores are also shown, as are the partial scores below for U. S. 3.

The results from only one school, U. S. 10, had to be completely omitted from the statistics for this research because of the great number of non-English speaking children in its first grades. They had the insurmountable problem of trying to learn to read in irregularly-spelled English in the Economy reading series which has heavy sight-word lists and only partial phonics. As a result, such "reading" scores are largely meaningless.

The results for U. S. 3, Scott, Foresman/Houghton Mifflin, on the first example only, are:

Oral Accuracy Per Cent	Number of Pupils Obtaining Score	
97	4	Pupils Scoring 95 or Better: 4 of 21, or 19%
93	3	Pupils Scoring 90 or Better:
90	2	9 of 21, or 43%
87	2	
83	3	
80	1	
77*	1	
70	1	
60	1	
50	2	Reversal: spot~stop
47	1	Reversal: brown!down. Slow.

Reversals: 2 of 21, or 10%.

Retentions: None.

*This girl scored 77% on the first example, the first 32 words. She then read the entire 144 words and scored 74% accuracy and 80% on comprehension.

U. S. 4, Code 10 - Text: Open Court, 23 Pupils Present, All Tested, September, 1977

Oral Accuracy Per Cent	Number of Pupils Obtaining Score	
99	4	
98	1	
97	5	Pupils Scoring
96	5	95 or Better
95	1	16 of 23 or 70%
94	2	Pupils Scoring
93	1	90 or Better
92	1	23 of 23 or 100%
90	3	

Comprehension of Five Questions

Per Cent Correct	Number of Pupils Obtaining Score	
		Pupils Scoring
100	5	80 or Better
80	5	10 of 22 or 45%
60	7	
40	4	
20	1	
Incomplete	1	Not possible to finish testing since child had to leave. Omitted from Comprehension Average.

Rate: None slow, or 0% slow.
    4 of 23 fast, or 17% fast

Reversals: 1 of 23, or 4%

Retentions: One child from this class was held back at first.

U. S. 4, Code 10 - Text: Open Court, 23 Pupils Present All Tested, September, 1977

Individual Scores in Order Tested

Accuracy/Comprehension

96-100 Fluent
99-40
99-100
94-20
90-60 Fluent.
96-40 Word by word.
90-60
97-80 Very fluent
96-60
96-60 Very fluent.
95-40
99-100
92-60
94-100 Fast
97-80
97-80 Fast
98-60
97-40
99-100
97-80 90-80 Reversal: spot—stop
93-Incomplete to word 60. Child had to leave.
96-60

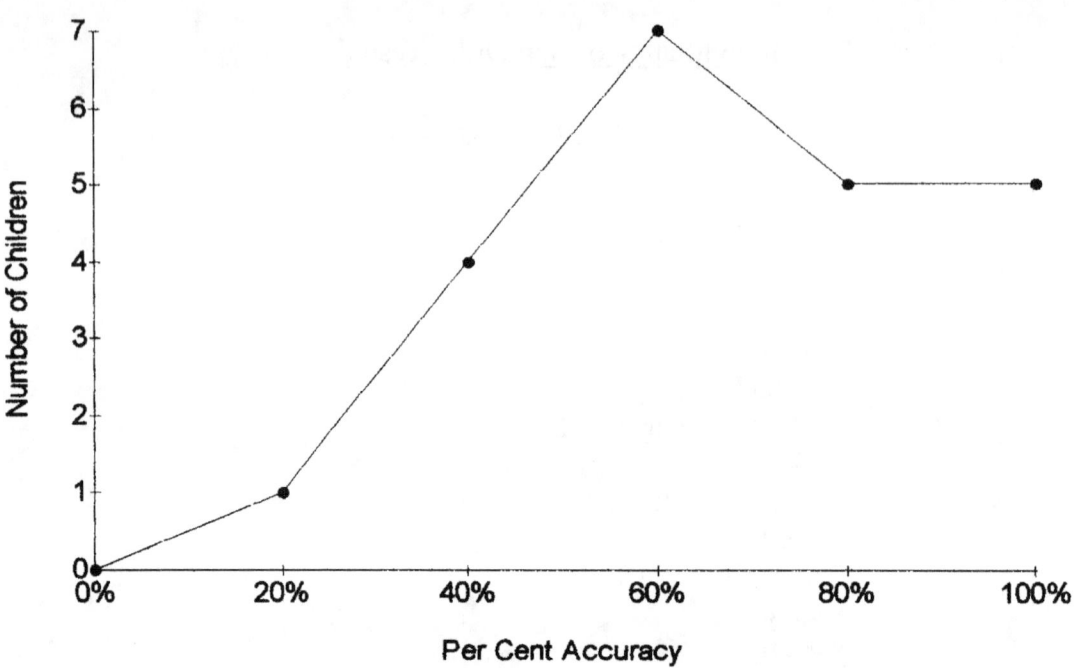

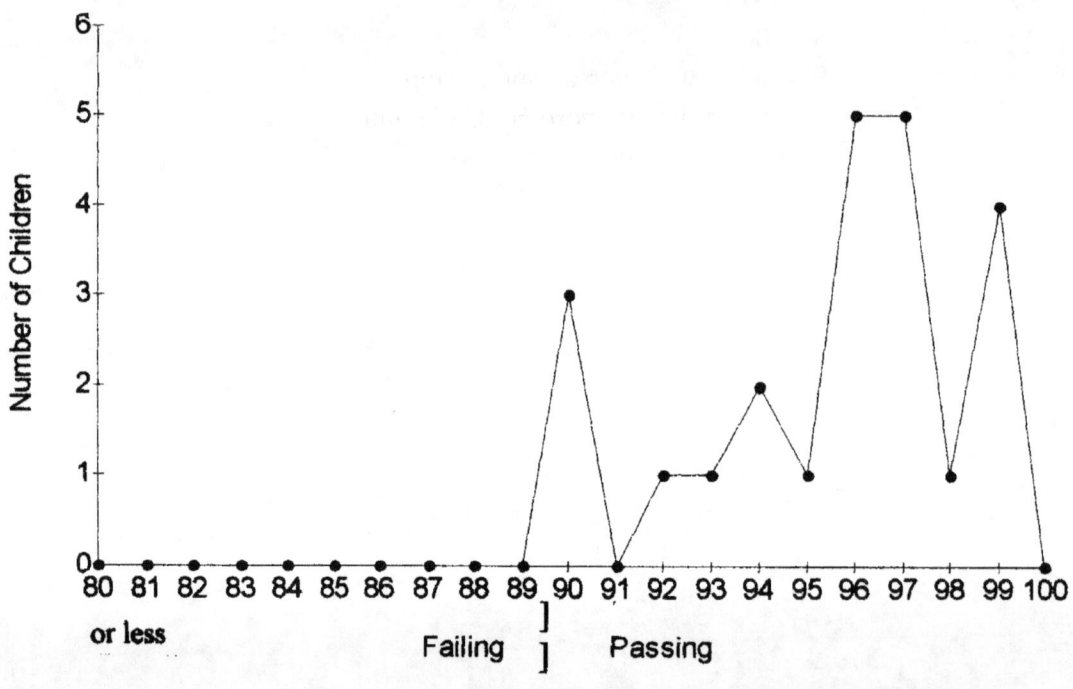

U. S. 5, Code 10 - Text: Open Court, 16 Pupils in Class, All Tested, September, 1977

Oral Accuracy	Number of Pupils Obtaining	
100	2	
99	1	
98	2	Pupils Scoring
97	1	95 or Better
95	1	7 of 16 or 44%
93	1	90 or Better
91	1	10 of 16 or 63%
90		1
87	1	
80	1	
70	1 Incomplete	
63	1 Incomplete	
53	1 Incomplete, Very slow	
33	1 Incomplete	

Comprehension of Five Questions

Per Cent Correct	Number of Pupils Obtaining Score	
		Pupils Scoring
100	2	80 or Better
80	3	HA)
60	4	
40	2	
20	1	
Incomplete fail	4	

Rate: 2 of 16 marked slow, and 3 other incomplete were slow, so 5 of 16 slow, or 31%
  None fast

Reversals: 2 of 16, or 13% (One with foreign language background)

Retentions: None mentioned.

U. S. 5, Code 10 - Text: Open Court, 16 Pupils in Class, All Tested, September, 1977

Individual Scores in Order Tested

Accuracy/Comprehension

87-40 Slow
53-Incomplete to word 30. Very slow.
91-60
80-60 Reversals: was~saw, got~took
90-20
63-Incomplete to word 62. Oriental. Reversals: spot~stop, on~no.
70-Incomplete to word 30
95-40
98-80
98-60
33-Incomplete to word 30
100-80
99-60
97-100
100-100
93-80

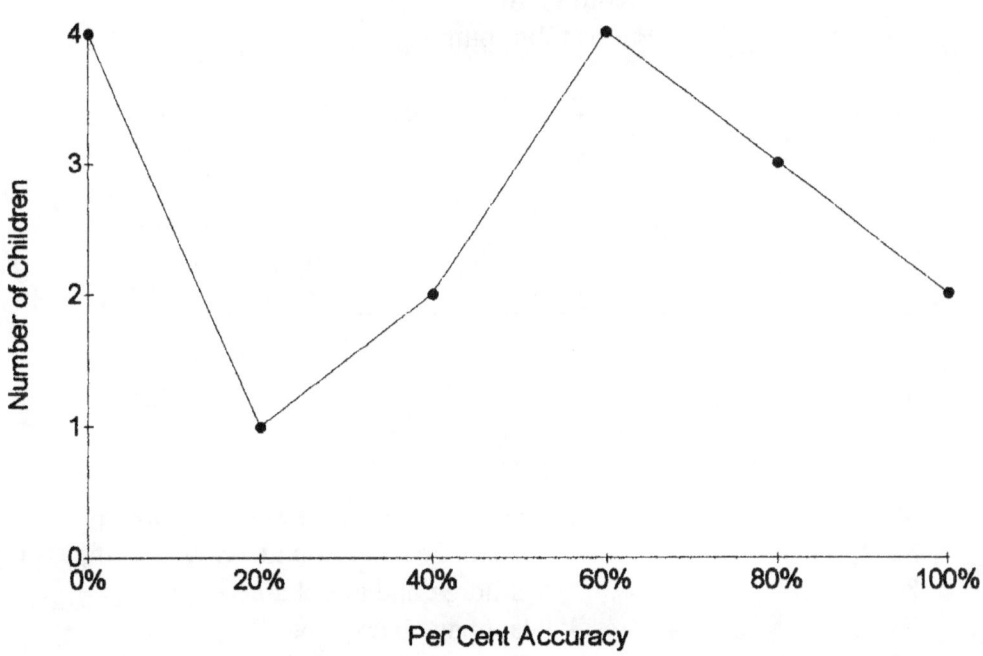

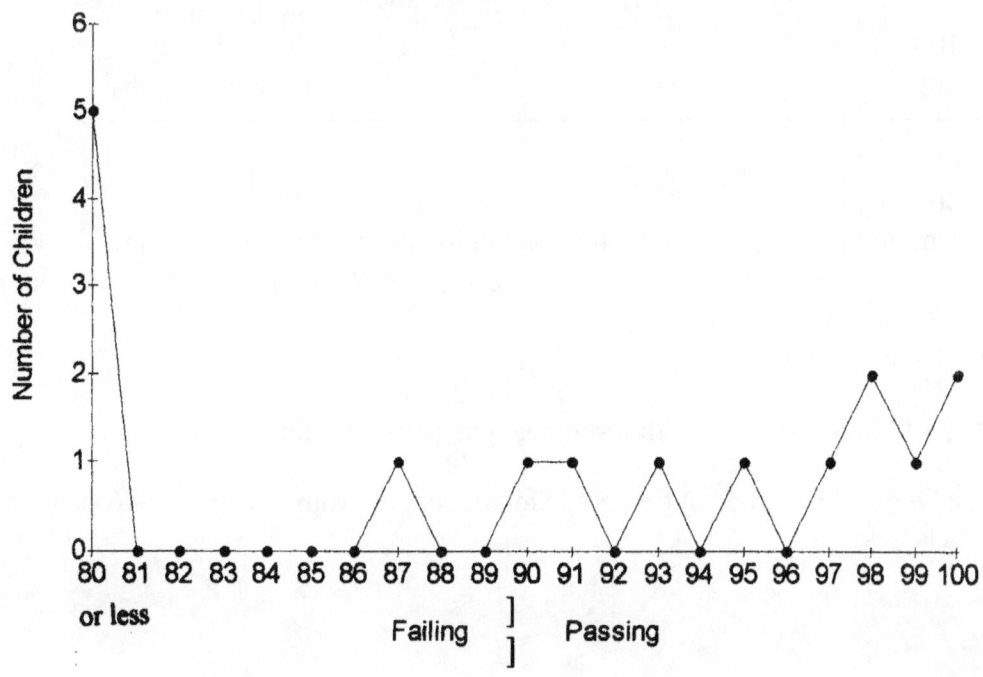

U. S. 6, Code 10 - Text: Open Court, 23 Children Present, All Tested, October, 1977

Oral Accuracy	Number of Pupils Obtaining	
100	1	
99	4	
98	5	
97	1	Pupils Scoring
96	3	95 or Better
95	1	15 of 22, or 68%
94	1	90 or Better
93	1	18 of 22 or 82%
92	1	
85	1	Three of four failures had a foreign
82	1	language background. Only one of passing
80	1	children had a probable foreign
73	1	language background.
75	1	Omitted. Not in building last year.

Comprehension of Five Questions

Per Cent Correct	Number of Pupils Obtaining Score	
100	9	Pupils Scoring 80 or Better
80	9	18 of 22 or 82%
60	3	
40	1	
Omitted	1. Child was not in this building last year, and failed accuracy at 75%. He scored 80% on comprehension	

Rate: 1 of 22 slow, or 5% slow
    2 of 22 fast, or 9% fast.

Reversals: 3 of 22, or 14% (All with foreign language background)

Retentions: One child retained in first grade in this school, from one of the two first grade classes.

U. S. 6, Code 10 - Text: Open Court, 23 Children Present, All Tested, October, 1977

    Individual Scores in Order Tested

        Accuracy/Comprehension

98-80	
96-100	
80-60	Repeating second grade. Came from Near-Eastern country as a baby. Reversal: spot—stop
100-100	Said he read before he came to school, Sesame Street. Doubtful.
96-80	
98-40	
99-100	
99-80	
75-80	Omit. Not in building last year. Reversal: trick—tirk
82-100	
85-60	Parents from Near-Eastern country. Reversal: spot—stop
92-80	
99-100	
99-100	Fast
94-80	Mother Finish. English spoken at home.
98-80	Very fast.
98-100	
97-80	
73-80	Parents Near-Eastern. Very slow. Reversal: got—dog
93-100	Moslem first name, possibly Near-Eastern.
96-60	
98-100	
95-80	

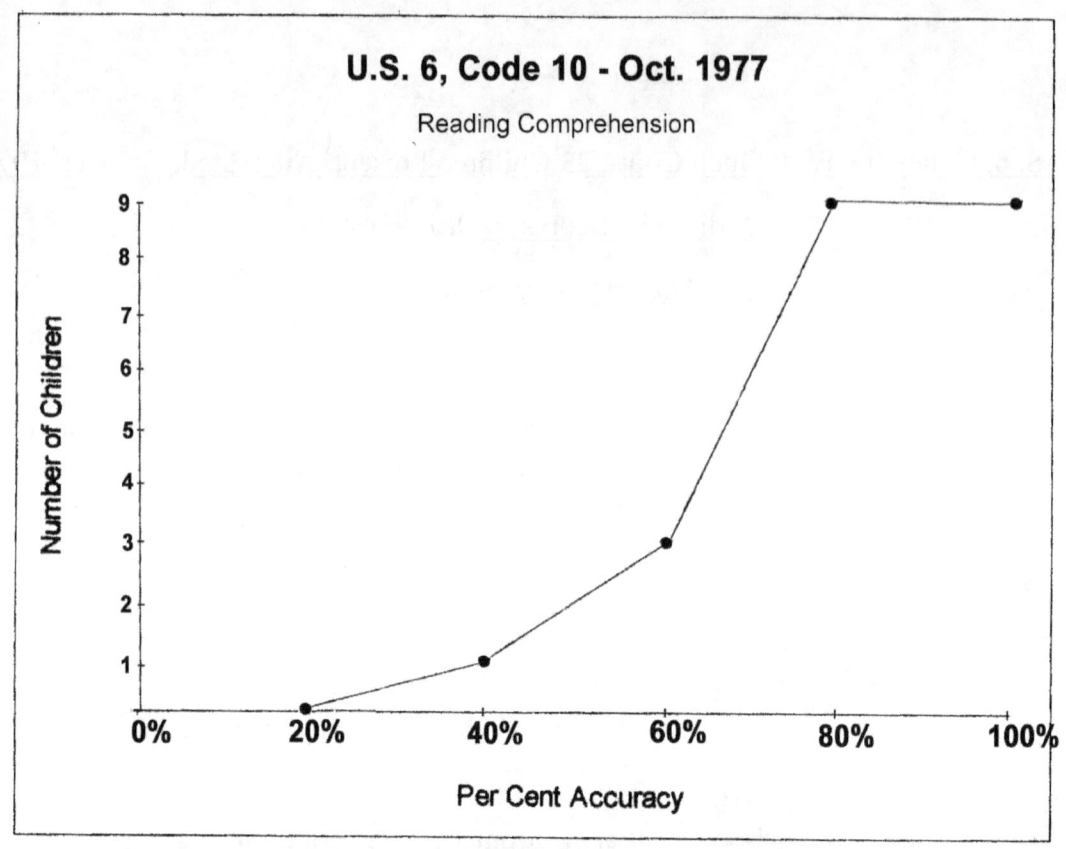

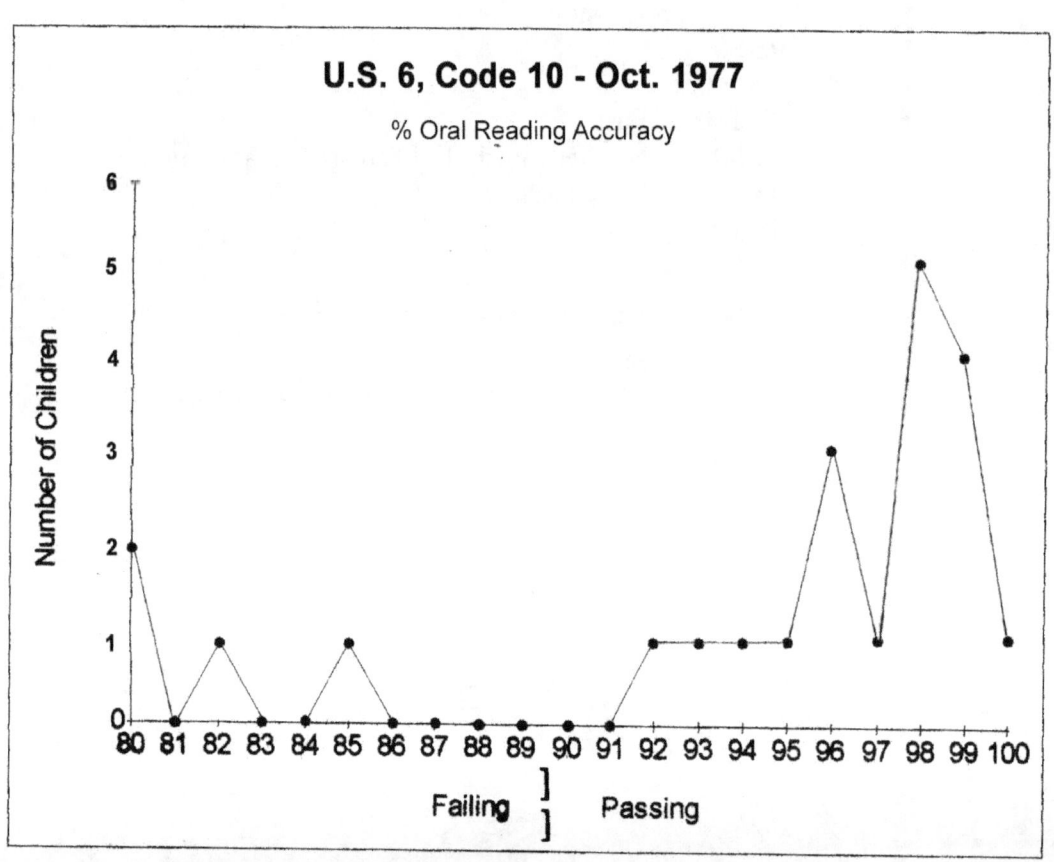

U. S. 7, Code 10 - Text: Lippincott, 21 Children Present, All Tested, October, 1977

Oral Accuracy Per Cent	Number of Pupils Obtaining Score	
100	2	
99	6	Pupils Scoring
97	3	95 or Better
96	1	12 of 21 or 57%
93	1	90 or Better
92	2	16 of 21 or 76%
90	1	
87	3	
85	1	
68	1	

Comprehension of Five Questions

Per Cent Correct	Number of Pupils Obtaining Score	
		Pupils Scoring
100	4	80 or Better
80	6	10 of 21 or 48%
60	7	
40	3	
Incomplete Fail	1	

Rate: 2 of 21 marked slow plus 1 "incomplete fail", for 14% slow
   2 of 21 fast, or 10% fast.

Reversals: 2 of 21, or 10%

Retentions: None mentioned.

In this class, none of those passing comprehension failed accuracy.

U. S. 7 _ Code 10 - Text: Lippincott, 21 Children Present, All Tested, October, 1977

Individual Scores in Order Tested

Accuracy/Comprehension

96-100
93-60 Slow
92-80 Speed okay.
87-40 Rapid. This child did not appear bright.
87-60 Reversal: own—now. Child did not appear bright. 92-80
85-40 Very slow, decoding slowly. Reversal: day—bay.
68-Incomplete. Slow
87-60 Reversal: do—go
99-60 Quick
99-60
99-100
99-100
100-80
97-60 Rapid
100-80
99-100
97-80
99-40
97-80
90-60

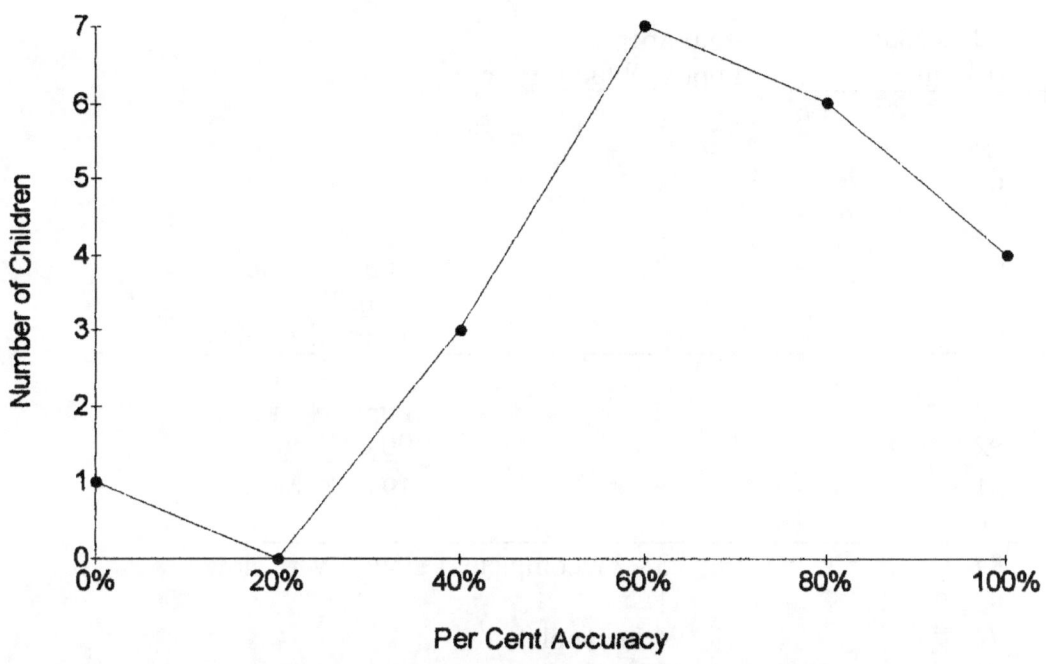

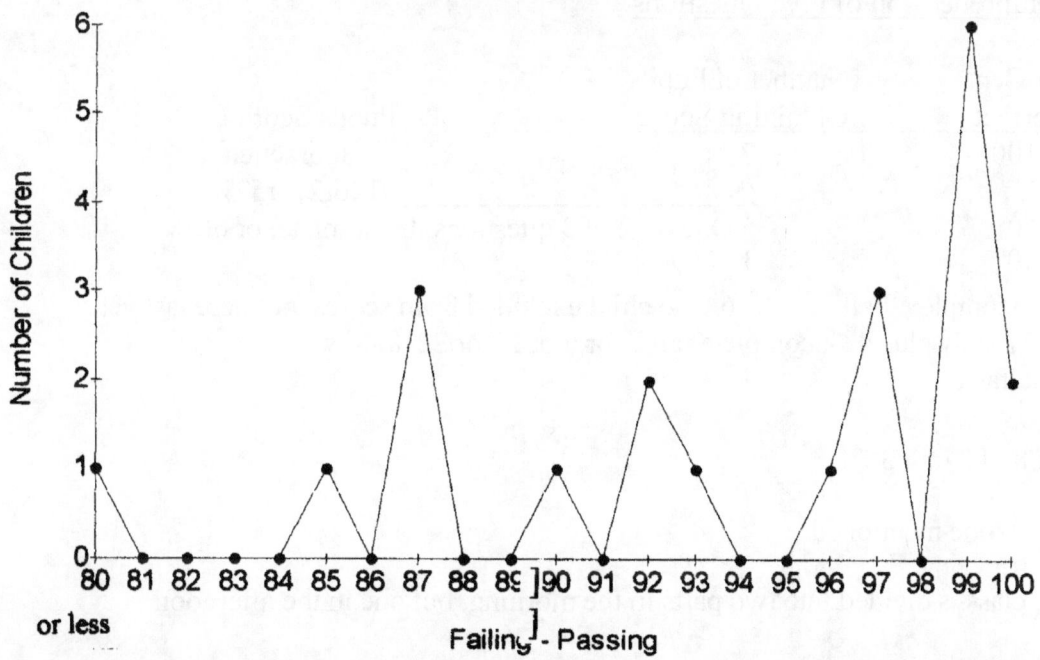

U.S. 8. Code 8 – Text: Initial Teaching Alphabet
28 Pupils Present, All Tested October, 1977

Oral Accuracy Per Cent	Number of Pupils Obtaining	
100	3	
99	3	
98	3	
97	3	Pupils Scoring
96	1	95 or Better
95	1	14 of 27 or 52%
93	1	Pupils Scoring
92	2	90 or Better
91	1	19 of 27 or 70%
90	1	
87	3 - 2 incomplete, 1 slow, 1 very slow	
85	1	
74	1 Incomplete	
73	1 Incomplete	
70	1 Incomplete	
63	1 Incomplete	
53	1 Incomplete - not in school last year	

Comprehension of Five Questions

Per Cent Correct	Number of Pupils Obtaining Score	Pupils Scoring
100	7	80 or Better
	7	14 of 27 or 52%
60	5	One on 2 of 3 questions, Incomplete, or 66%
40	3	
Incomplete Fail	6	One child excluded from scores, not here last year

Rate: 2 of 27 slow plus 4 "incomplete fail", for 6 or 27 or 22% slow
None fast.

Reversals: 8 of 27, or 30%

Retentions: None mentioned.

Note: This class is divided into two parts in the morning, but one in the afternoon

<u>U. S. 8. Code 8 - Text: Initial Teaching Alphabet
28 Pupils Present, All Tested, October, 1977</u>

<u>Individual Scores in Order Tested</u>

<u>Accuracy/Comprehension</u>

100-100
92-80   Reversal: After—fatter
87-40   Reversals: spot—stripe,, spot—stop
74-66   Incomplete (ex. 1, 2, 3) Reversals: back—dogs, of—for
91-40   Reversals: dog—big, spot—stop
97-80
85-60
97-80
90-40 Reversal: spot—stop
99-80
99-100
100-100
98-100
53-Incomplete. Very slow. Reversal: spot—stop. Not here last year.
92-60
98-100
93-80
95-100
98-80
100-60
97-60
96-80
87-Incomplete. Very slow. Reversal: spot—stop
87-Incomplete. Slow
70-Incomplete
73-Incomplete
99-100
63-Incomplete. Reversal: spot—stop

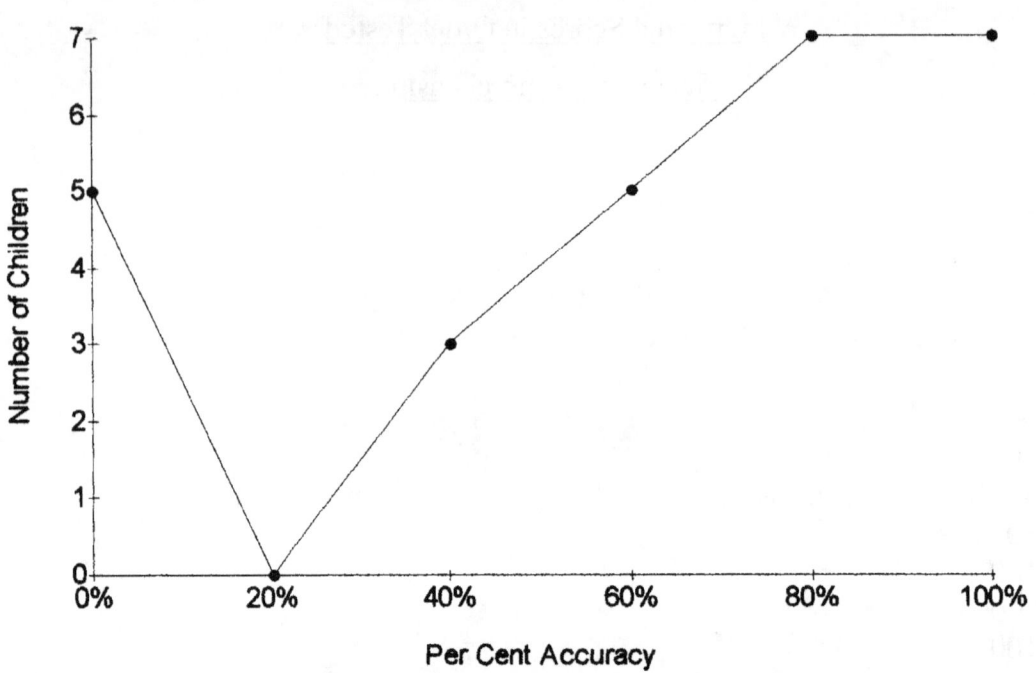

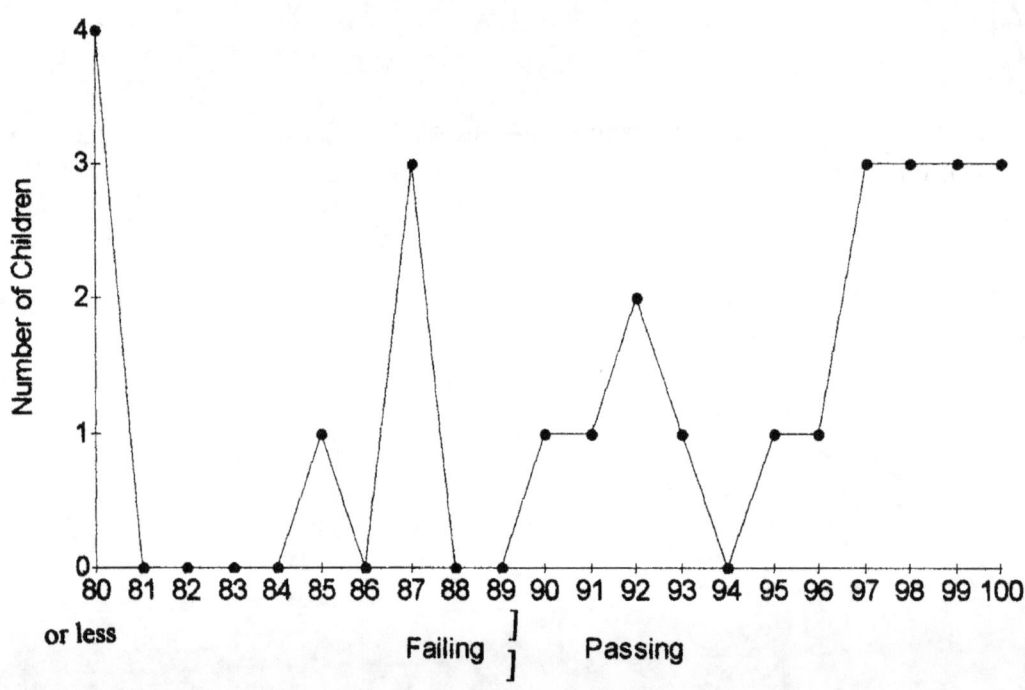

U. S. 9, Code 10 - Text: Lippincott, 22 Children Present, All Tested, October, 1977

Oral Accuracy Per Cent	Number of Pupils Obtaining Score	
99	7	
98	2	Pupils Scoring
96	2	95 or Better
95	1	12 of 22 or 55%
94	1	90 or Better
93	2	16 of 22 or 73%
90	1	
86	1	
85	1	
80	1	
76	1	
68	1	
13	1	

Comprehension of Five Questions

Per Cent Correct	Number of Pupils Obtaining Score	
100	6	Pupils Scoring 80 or Better
80	6	12 of 22 or 55%
60	5	
40	2	
Incomplete Fail	3	

Rate: 4 of 22 marked slow plus 1 "incomplete fail", for 23% slow
4 of 22 fast, or 18% fast.

Reversals: None

Retentions: None mentioned.

U. S. 9, Code 10 - Text: Lippincott, 22 Children Present, All Tested, October, 1977

Individual Scores in Order Tested

Accuracy/Comprehension

99-80
86-80   Slow
99-80   Quick
13-Incomplete. Slow. Had been referred for psychological help.
76-Incomplete to word 90. Slow
95-60
99-100   Rapid. Fluent.
93-100   Slow
96-60
96-60   Rapid
99-100
98-100
99-100
93-60
90-80
94-80
99-40   Rapid. Fluent.
99-100
85-60
98-40
68-Incomplete to word 62
80-80

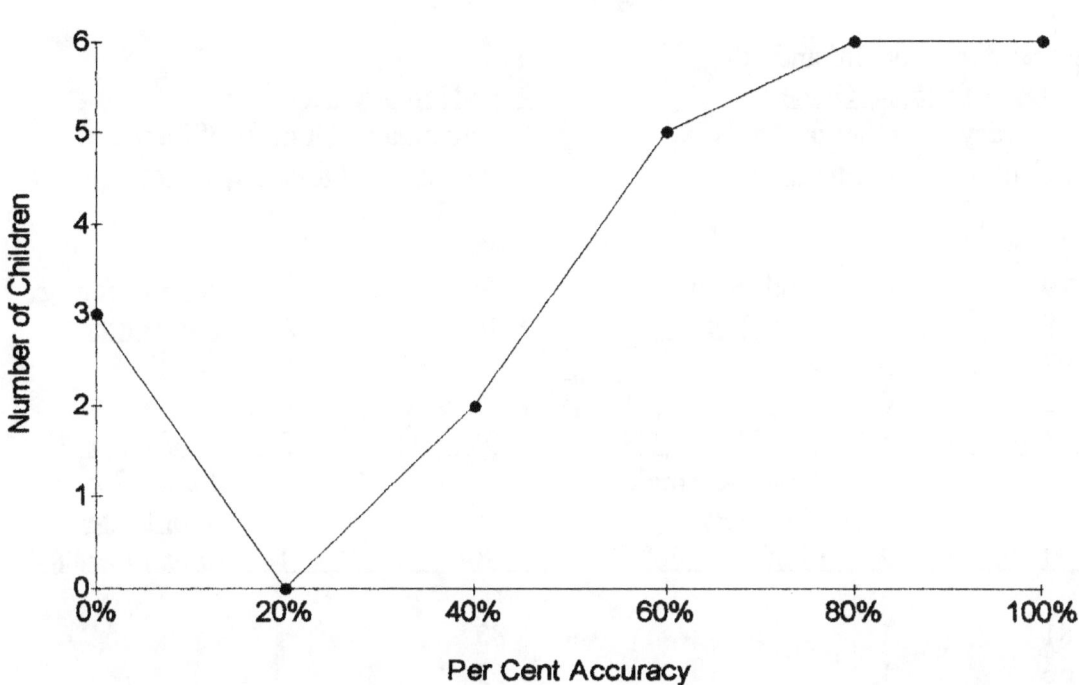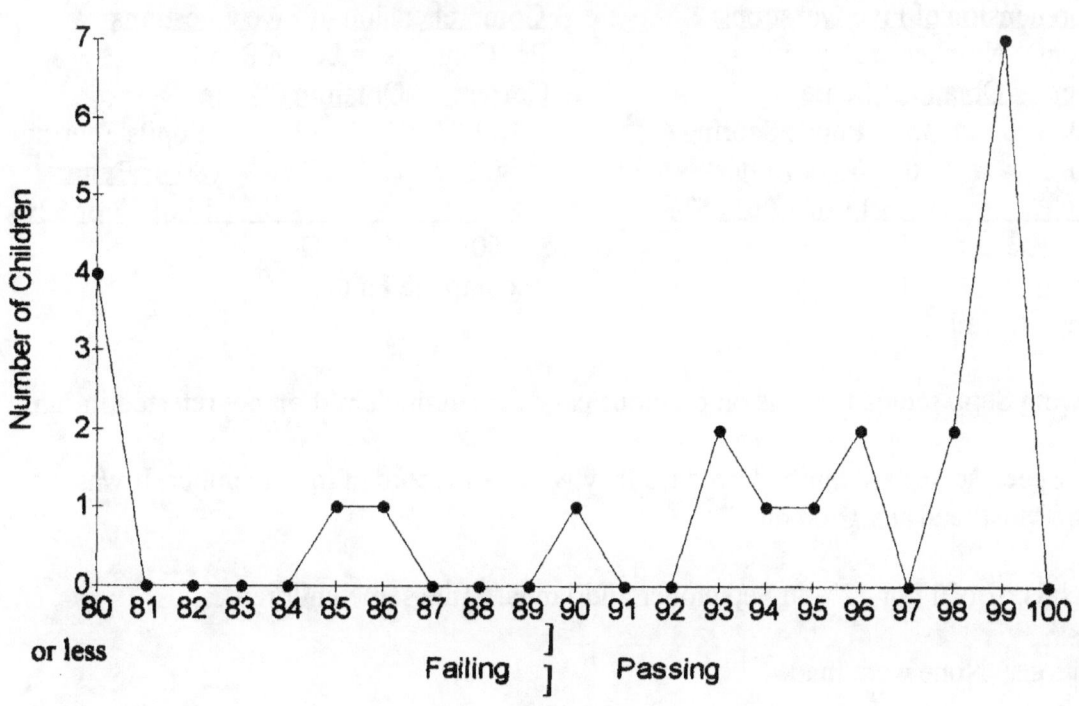

U. S. 11, Alpha One Plus Partial Houghton Mifflin in Spring of First Grade, Code 10, 17 Children, Sept., 1977 and Jan., 1978

September Scores on 3rd and 5th Day of Second Grade			*January Scores		
Oral Accuracy Per Cent	Number of Pupils Obtaining Score		Oral Accuracy Per Cent	Number of Pupils Obtaining Score	
100	1		100	2	
99	4	Pupils Scoring	99	3	Pupils Scoring
98	2	95 or Better	98	2	95 or Better
97	3		97	4	
96	0		96	1	
95	1	11 of 17 or 65%	95	2	14 of 17 or 82%
		Pupils Scoring 90 or Better			Pupils Scoring 90 or Better
90	2	13 of 17 or 76%	90	1	15 of 17 or 88%
81	1		85	1	
66	1		63	1	
62	1				
33	1				

September Scores on 3rd and 5th Day of Second Grade Comprehension of Five Questions			*January Scores Comprehension of Five Questions		
Per Cent Correct	Number of Pupils Obtaining Score		Per Cent Correct	Number of Pupils Obtaining Score	
100	5	Pupils Scoring	100	7	Pupils Scoring
80	6	80 or Better	80	7	80 or Better
		11 of 17 or 65%			14 of 17 or 82%
60	1		60	2	
40	1		Incomplete Fail	1	
Incomplete Fail	4				

*Showing Sept. scores for tests on previous page for passing children not retested in Jan.

Rate: Speed scores are omitted because they were not recorded in September It was noted, "Most read at a good rate."

Reversals: 2 of 17 or 12% in September and January (the same children).

Retentions: None were made.

U. S. 11, Alpha One Plus Partial Houghton Mifflin in Spring of First Grade, Code 10, 17 Children, Sept. 1977 and Jan., 1978#

September Scores on 3rd and 5th Day of Second Grade	January Second Grade Scores (Asterisks Show Passing Sept. Scores for Children Not Retested in Jan.)
Accuracy/Comprehension	Accuracy/Comprehension
97-80	*97-80
97-100	*97-100
99-80	*99-80
98-100	*98-100
95-80	*95-80
98-100	*98-100
100-100	*100-100
97-80	*97-80
99-100	*99-100
99-80	*99-80

September/January Retest Group:

99-40	100-100 (Retest in Feb.)
90-80	97-100
90-60	96-80
81-Incomplete to ex. 4. Reversal: d for b.	90-60 Reversal: number~under
66-Incomplete to ex. 3. Reversal: on~no	85-80 Reversal: saw~was
62-Incomplete to ex. 3	95-60
33-Incomplete to ex. 2	63-Incomplete to ex. 2.

#January retests were necessary on this class because it was tested so early in the term, in the first five days of second grade. Therefore, the scores were not comparable to other fall U. S. scores taken after the fall term was really under way, during the third to the sixth week.

U. S. 12, Code 10 - Text: Open Court, 17 Children Present, All Tested, January, 1978

Oral Accuracy Per Cent	Number of Pupils Obtaining Score	
99	7	
98	3	Pupils Scoring
97	1	95 or Better
96	2	13 of 16 or 81%
		Pupils Scoring
		90 or Better
94	1	14 of 16 or 88%
84	2	One incomplete, not here last year. Omitted from averages.
77	1	Incomplete. Child from India.

Comprehension of Five Questions

Per Cent Correct	Number of Pupils Obtaining Score	
		Pupils Scoring
100	2	80 or Better
80	6	8 of 16 or 50%
60	5	
20	2	
Incomplete Fail	2	Omit one from scores. Not here last year.

Rate: 1 of 16 slow, or 6% slow
6 of 16 fast, or 38% fast.

Reversals: 1 of 16, or 6%

Retentions: None mentioned.

<u>U. S. 12, Code 10 - Text: Open Court, 17 Children Present, All Tested, January, 1978</u>

<u>Individual Scores in Order Tested</u>

<u>Accuracy/Comprehension</u>

- 99-60   Fast
- 99-80   Good rate.
- 99-60   Fair rate
- 99-60   Fast
- 99-80   Good rate
- 99-80   Fast
- 98-100 Fast
- 99-100 Fast
- 98-60   Good rate
- 97-80   Fast
- 94-60   Fair rate
- 84-80   Fairly slow. Reported to be under counseling for emotional problems. Reversals: spot~post, one~now.
- 98-20   Fair rate
- 77-Incomplete. From India. Slow.
- 84-Incomplete. Very slow. Not here last year. Reversals: back~dock, got~dog, white~with.
- 96-20
- 96-80   Good rate.

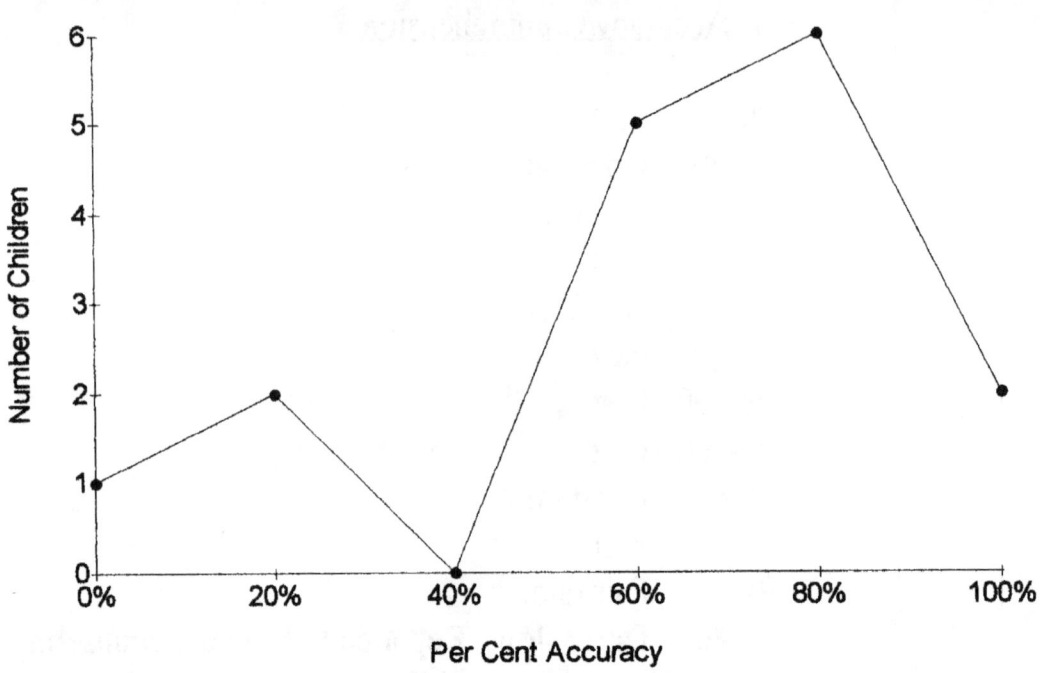

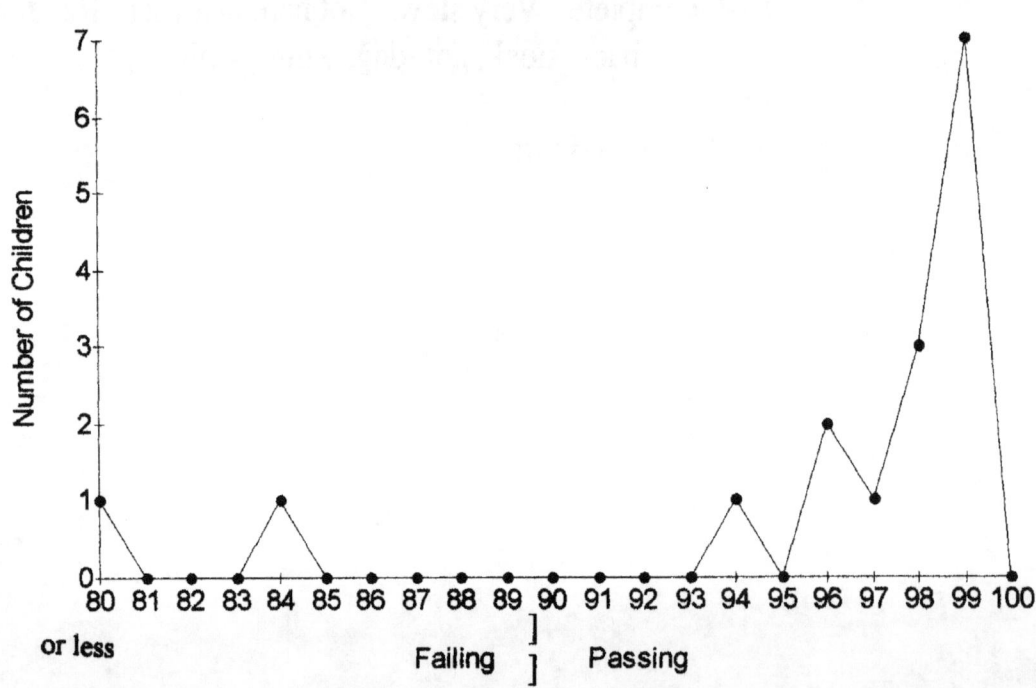

U. S. 13, Code 10 - Text: Open Court, 24 Children Present, All Tested, January, 1978

Oral Accuracy Per Cent	Number of Pupils Obtaining Score	
100	1	
99	5	
98	2	
97	2	Pupils Scoring
96	6	95 or Better
95	2	18 of 23 or 78%
94	2	Pupils Scoring
91	1	90 or Better
90	2	23 of 23 or 100%
67	1	Incomplete, not here last year. Omitted from averages.

Comprehension of Five Questions

Per Cent Correct	Number of Pupils Obtaining Score	
		Pupils Scoring
100	3	80 or Better
80	7	10 of 23 or 44%
60	8	
40	5	
Incomplete Fail	1	Omitted from scores. Not here last year.

Rate: None slow
    6 of 23 fast, or 26% fast.

Reversals: None, except new child

Retentions: This school considered making 8 to 9 retentions from the total children in the two first grade classes because of the effect of the teachers leaving from those two classes. One teacher left in February of first grade, and the other in April. Yet, finally, <u>only one first-grader was retained from all the children in the two first-grade classes.</u> The two first-grade classes were shuffled when promoted, and this January second-grade class is composed of about one half of the former first-graders. The other half of the former first-graders are in U. S. 6 which was tested in October.

U. S. 13, Code 10 - Text: Open Court, 24 Children Present, All Tested, January, 1978

Individual Scores in Order Tested

Accuracy/Comprehension

96-100 Good rate
97-60   Fairly slow
100-100 Good rate
99-100 Fast
96-60   Fairly slow
90-80   Good rate. Staccato.
96-80   Good rate
98-60   Good rate
97-60   Good rate. Adenoidal, hard to understand.
94-80   Fairly slow
67-Incomplete. Slow. Not here last year. Reversals: spot~stop, with~white.
96-40   Good rate
98-80   Fast. Lisp.
99-60. Fast. Black
99-60   Good rate
96-40   Good rate
99-60   Fast
90-40   Halting. Fair rate.
91-80   Fast
95-40   Fair rate
94-80   Good rate
95-80   Good rate
96-60   Fast
99-40   Fair rate. Lisp: ch~s

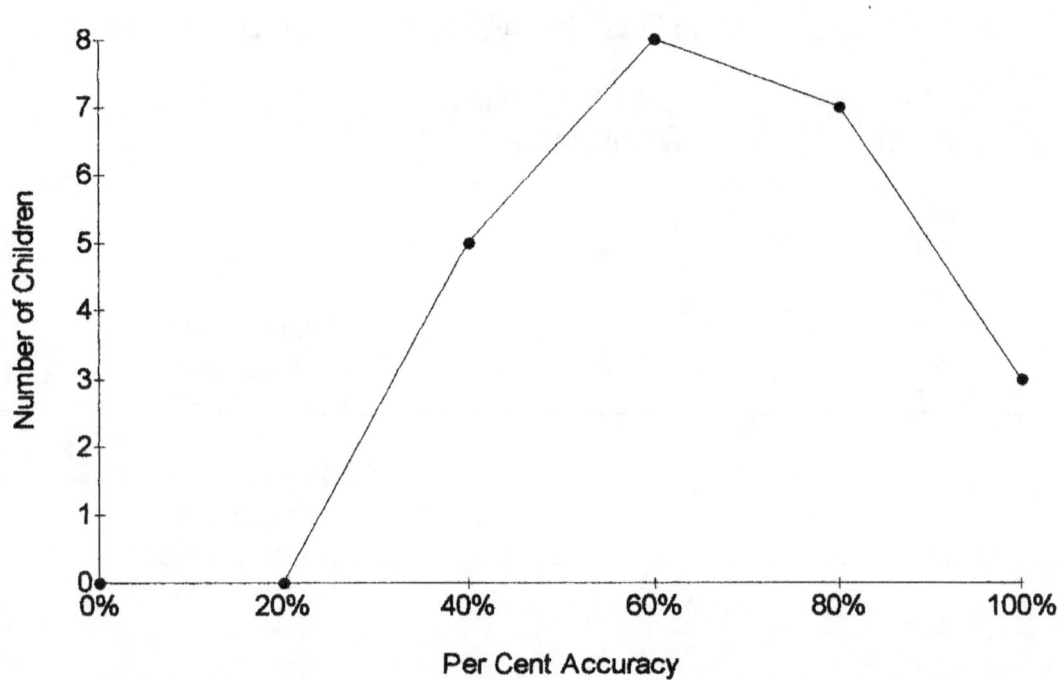

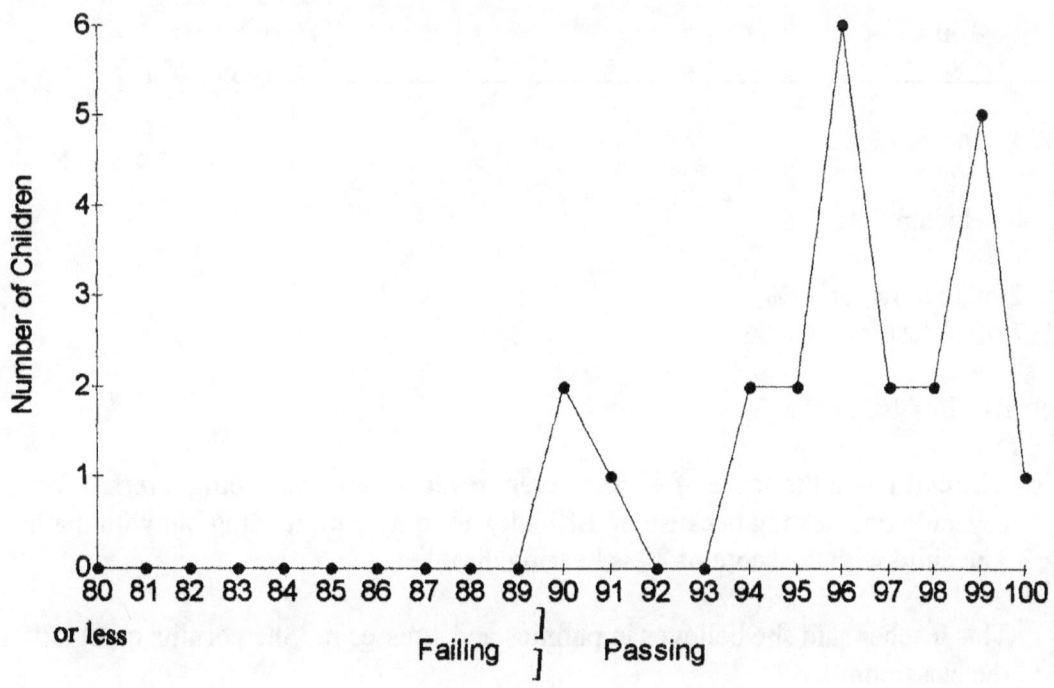

U. S. 14, Code 10 - Text: Open Court, 16 Children Present, All Tested, January, 1978

Oral Accuracy Per Cent	Number of Pupils Obtaining Score	
100	3	
99	4	
98	1	
97	1	Pupils Scoring
96	2	95 or Better
95	2	13 of 16 or 81%
		Pupils Scoring 90 or Better
94	1	14 of 16 or 88%
89*	1	
80*	1	

Comprehension of Five Questions

Per Cent Correct	Number of Pupils Obtaining Score	
		Pupils Scoring 80 or Better
100	5	80 or Better
80	4	4 of 16 or 56%
60	4	
40	2	
Incomplete Fail	1	

Rate: 2 of 16 slow, or 13%
7 of 16 fast, or 44% fast.

Reversals: 1 of 16, or 6%

Notes: The child with the score of 89 had severe reversals and was being referred for psychological testing because of difficulty not only with reading but with math. The child with the score of 80 is hearing disabled.

This teacher said she believes in phonics and stresses it. She permits quiet talk in the classroom.

<u>U. S. 14, Code 10 - Text: Open Court, 16 Children Present, All Tested, January, 1978</u>

<u>Individual Scores in Order Tested</u>

<u>Accuracy/Comprehension</u>

99-60   Fast
99-60   Fast
80-60   Slow. Hearing problem. Scheduled to have operation. Reversals, 3 times: spot~stop
96-40
100-80   Fast
98-100   Fast
94-100   Slow
99-100
95-60   Slow
97-80   Good rate
96-80   Fast
89-Incomplete. Very slow with severe reversals Being referred for testing. Also has trouble with math.
100-100 Fast
99-100   Good rate
95-40   Fair rate
100-80   Fast

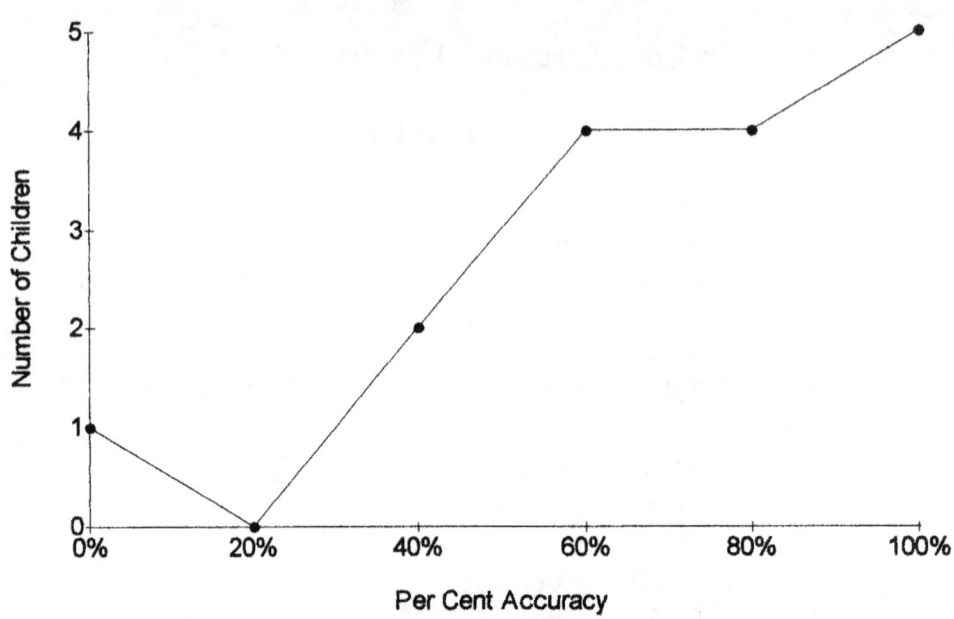

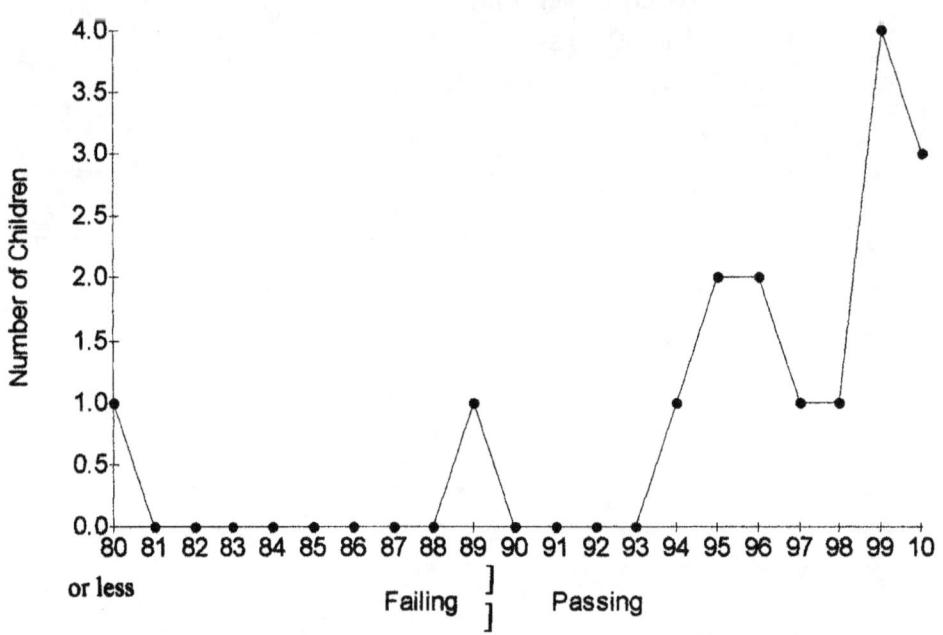

U. S. 15, Code 10 - Text: Lippincott, 23 Children Present, All Tested, January, 1978

Oral Accuracy Per Cent	Number of Pupils Obtaining Score	
100	1	
99	6	
98	3	Pupils Scoring
97	1	95 or Better
96	6	17 of 23 or 74%
94	1	Pupils Scoring
93	1	90 or Better
92	2	21 of 23 or 91%
70*	1	
57*	1	

*Note: The second-grade teachers in this school liked Lippincott (Code 10) but used Scott, Foresman (Code 2) for the lowest group. That should be considered in reviewing their scores.

Comprehension of Five Questions

Per Cent Correct	Number of Pupils Obtaining Score	
		Pupils Scoring
100	8	80 or Better
80	11	19 of 23 or 83%
60	2	
Incomplete Fail	2	

Rate: 2 of 23 slow, or 9% slow
 12 of 23 fast, or 52% fast.

Reversals: 1 of 23, or 4%

Retentions: None mentioned.

<u>U. S. 15, Code 10 - Text: Lippincott, 23 Children Present, All Tested, January, 1978</u>

<u>Individual Scores in Order Tested</u>

<u>Accuracy/Comprehension</u>

    96-80   Fast
    99-80   Fast
    98-100 Fast
    96-80   Good rate
    92-60   Fair rate. Lost his place.
    99-100 Fast
    99-80   Fair rate
    98-80   Very fast
    100-100 Fast
    98-100 Fast
    99-80   Good rate
    92-60   Emotional problems, per teacher.
    96-80   Good rate
    99-100 Fast
    96-80   Fast
    57-Incomplete to word 30. Slow, heavy glasses. Receives supplemental help. Said, "I am only on A book," so apparently he is reading Lippincott with the supplemental teacher, not Scott, Foresman as with classroom teacher. See earlier note on her use of Scott, Foresman for bottom group.
    94-80   Fair rate
    96-100 Fast
    96-80   Fast
    99-80   Fair rate
    97-100 Fast
    70-Incomplete to word 30. Slow. Eye problem, thick glasses, operation scheduled. Reversal: of~for.
    93-100 Not here last year.

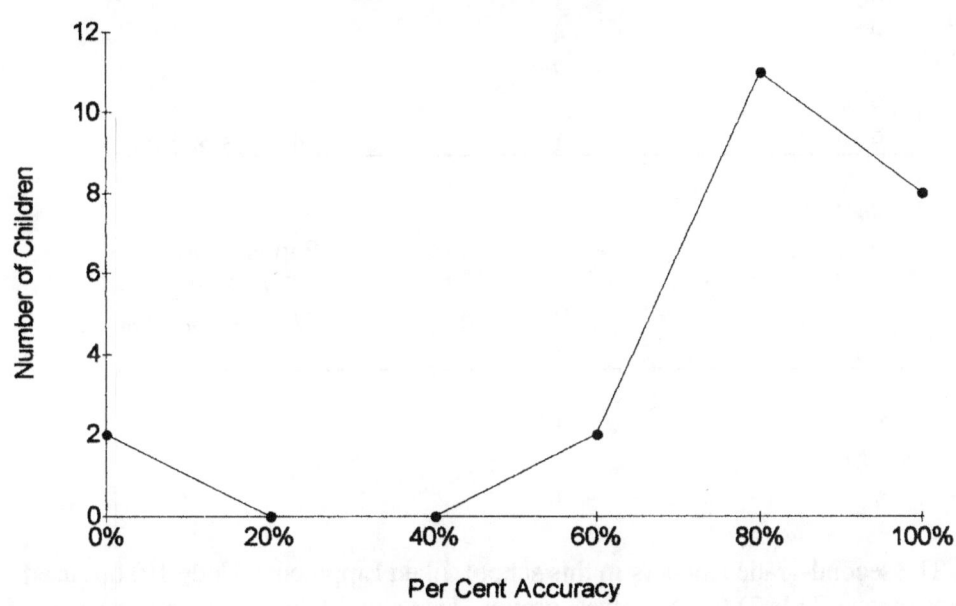

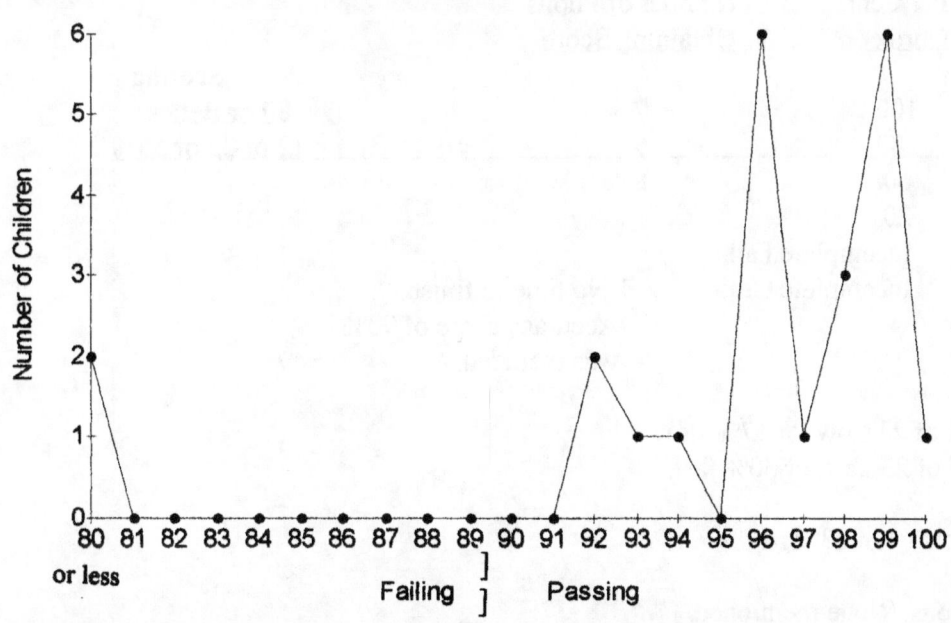

U. S. 16, Code 10 - Text: Lippincott, 23 Children Present, All Tested, January, 1978

Oral Accuracy Per Cent	Number of Pupils Obtaining Score	
100	1	
99	4	
97	2	Pupils Scoring
96	6	95 or Better
95	1	14 of 23 or 61%
94	1	
93	1	Pupils Scoring
92	1	90 or Better
91	2	20 of 23 or 87%
90	1	
85*	1	
78*	1	
73*	1	

*Note: The second-grade teachers in this school liked Lippincott (Code 10) but used Scott, Foresman (Code 2) for the lowest groups. That should be considered in reviewing their scores.

Comprehension of Five Questions

Per Cent Correct	Number of Pupils Obtaining Score	
		Pupils Scoring
100	7	80 or Better
80	5	12 of 22 or 55%
60	8	
20	1	
Incomplete Fail	1	
Incomplete Omit	1	No time to finish. Accuracy score of 90% was included.

Rate: 4 of 23 slow, or 17% slow
7 of 23 fast, or 30% fast.

Reversals: 4 of 23, or 17%

Retentions: None mentioned.

<u>U. S. 16, Code 10 - Text: Lippincott, 23 Children Present, All Tested, January, 1978</u>

<u>Individual Scores in Order Tested</u>

<u>Accuracy/Comprehension</u>

- 99-60   Fast
- 95-60   Slow. Lisp, severe speech problem.
- 96-80   Fast. Chinese
- 99-100   Fair rate
- 93-80   Slow
- 92-80   Fast
- 100-60   Good rate
- 97-100   Fast
- 96-100   Good rate
- 85-20   Reversal: saw~was, with~white.
- 90-Incomplete. No time. Was not present on my second day of testing. Reversal: white~with.
- 96-100   Fair rate. Reversal: was~saw
- 96-80   Good rate.
- 99-80   Fast
- 94-60   Good rate. Slight speech problem
- 96-100   Good rate
- 73-Incomplete. Slow
- 96-60
- 91-60   Fair rate
- 99-60   Fast
- 91-100   Fast
- 78-60   Slow. Reversals: Number~nameder, was~saw, day~bay (This was a boy.)
- 97-100

U. S. 16, Code 10 - Jan. 1978
Reading Comprehension

U. S. 16, Code 10 - Jan. 1978
% Oral Reading Accuracy

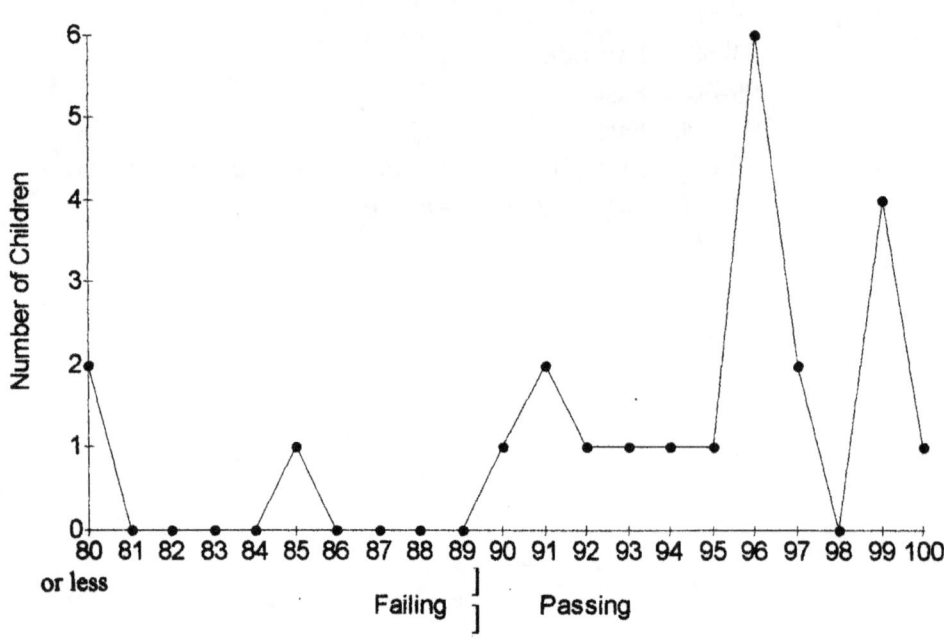

U. S. 17, Code 10 - Text: Teacher Phonics*, 15 Pupils Present, All Tested, January, 1978

Oral Accuracy Per Cent	Number of Pupils Obtaining Score	
99	3	
98	5	Pupils Scoring
96	2	95 or Better
95	2	12 of 15 or 80%
		Pupils Scoring
		90 or Better
94	3	15 of 15 or 100%

Comprehension of Five Questions

Per Cent Correct	Number of Pupils Obtaining Score	
		Pupils Scoring
100	6	80 or Better
80	6	12 of 15 or 80%
60	3	

Rate: None slow
    3 of 15 fast, or 20% fast.

Reversals: None

Retentions: None mentioned.

*Note: The teacher who taught this second-grade class in first grade said she never gave sight words and made children decode phonically from the beginning. She said the children had all letter sounds before she gave them any words. In sounding the words, she worked from the sounds to the words, synthetic phonics, and not analytic,. For reading material, she had used the Harcourt Brace texts, but not their word introduction material. The same teacher had this class in second grade, so she was able to follow through on her method. Even allowing for the fact that this teacher obviously could not have had any real learning disabilities in her group, it should be noted that this January class is one of the most successful classes in this survey, with 100% passing accuracy, 80% passing comprehension, none slow, no reversals, and 20% reading "fast." Her Code 10 self-devised phonic method was obviously very superior.

U. S. 17, Code 10 - Text: Teacher Phonics, 15 Pupils Present, All Tested, January, 1978

Individual Scores in Order Tested

Accuracy/Comprehension

96-100 Fast
95-80   Fair rate
99-100 Fast
98-80
99-100 Good rate
95-80   Fair rate
99-80   Good rate
98-100
96-60   Fast
98-80
98-80   Fairly sloiw
98-100 Good rate
94-60   Good rate
94-60   Fair rate, halting
94-100

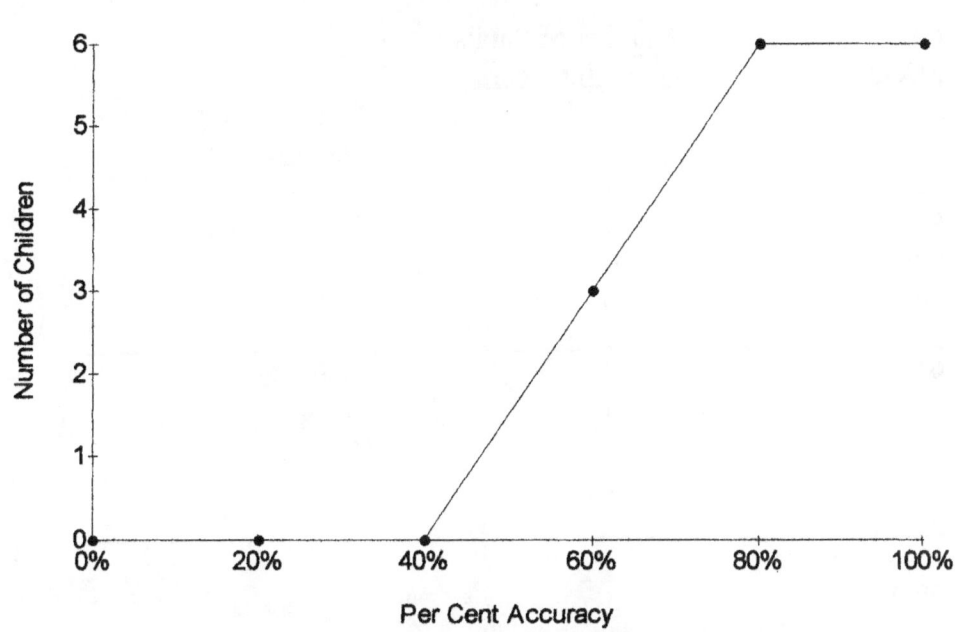

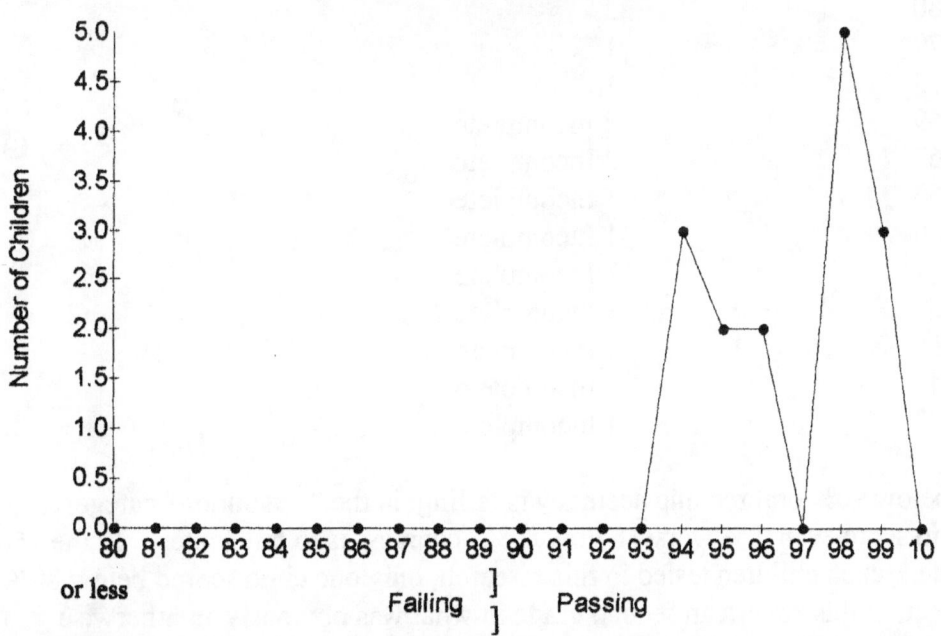

Averages for U. S. 18, 19, 20, 21, 22, Ability-Grouped Second-Grade Classes in a Single School, Total of 93 Pupils - Code 3, Text: Houghton Mifflin - January, 1978

Oral Accuracy Per Cent	Number of Pupils Obtaining Score	
		Pupils Scoring
100	5	95 or Better
99	24	
98	4	51 of 93, or 55%
97	6	
96	6	
95	6	
94	5	Pupils Scoring
93	4	90 or Better
92	6	68 or 22, or 73%
91	1	
90	1	
88	3	
87	1	
86	1	
85	1	
84	1 Incomplete	
83	2 Incomplete	
80	2	
79	1	
73	1	
69	2 Incomplete	
67	2 Incomplete	
63	1 Incomplete	
60	1 Incomplete	
57	1 Incomplete	
53	1 Incomplete	
50	1 Incomplete	
43	2 Incomplete	
23	1 Incomplete	

Any score below 90% oral reading accuracy is failing, in the "frustration" category. Obviously, to score even10% worse, below 80% accuracy, is to fail acutely. In the 150 second-grade French children tested in this research, only one child scored below 80% accuracy. Yet, in this American second grade in what was obviously an otherwise well-run and organized school, but which was using the Houghton Mifflin series, 14 of the 93 children tested scored below 80. That was15% of the total group and was 20 times greater than for the comparable group of children tested in France.

Averages for U. S. 18, 19, 20, 21, 22, Ability-Grouped Second-Grade Classes in a Single School, Total of 93 Pupils - Code 3, Text: Houghton Mifflin - January, 1978

Comprehension of Five Questions

Per Cent Correct	Number of Pupils Obtaining Score	Pupils Scoring 80 or Better
100	24	
80	31	55 of 93 or 59%
60	16	
40	6	
20	1	
0 or Incomplete Fail	15	

Rate: 2 slow and 13 incomplete counted as slow, for 15 of 93, or 16%
7 of 93 fast, or 7%.

Reversals: 11 of 93 or 12%

The best "comprehension" scores for this school were in one of the two middle-ability second-grade groups, whose teacher said she had stressed heavy synthetic phonics since the beginning of the second-grade. Her individual scores are shown in the summary sheet for her class, U. S. 20. A portion of her class (17 children) had been tested in October. Those October group scores can be compared to the scores for 16 of the same children who were re-tested in January (although scores for individual children in that group cannot be compared). The great improvement in that class is obvious.

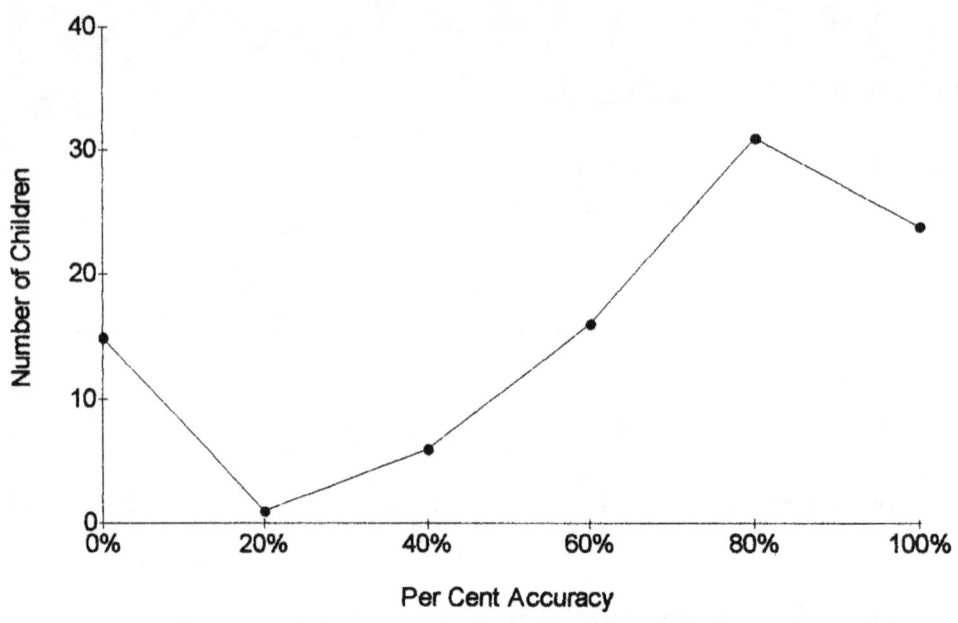

U.S. 18-22, Code 3 - Jan. 1978
Reading Comprehension

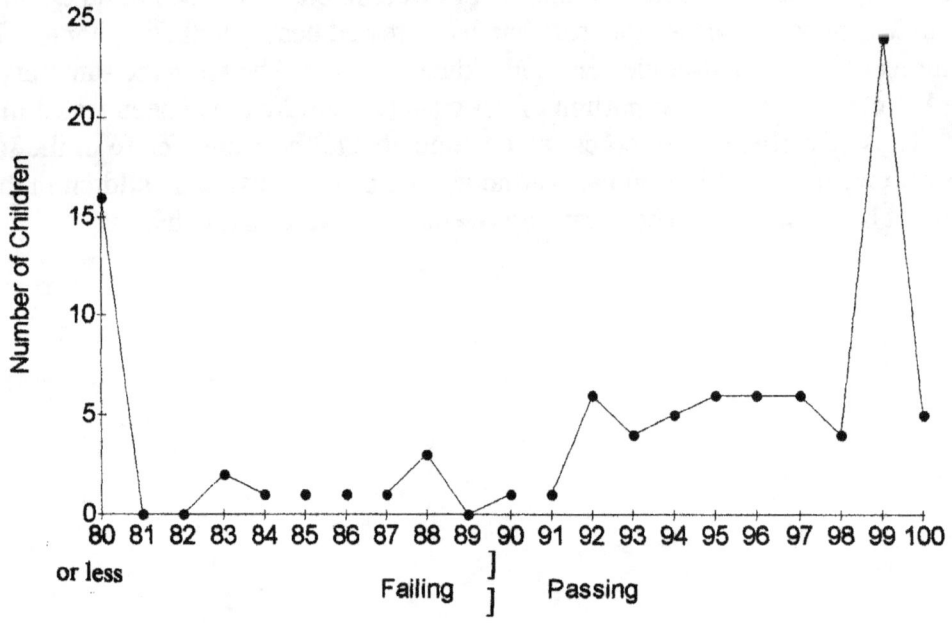

U. S. 18-22, Code 3 - Jan. 1978
% Oral Reading Accuracy

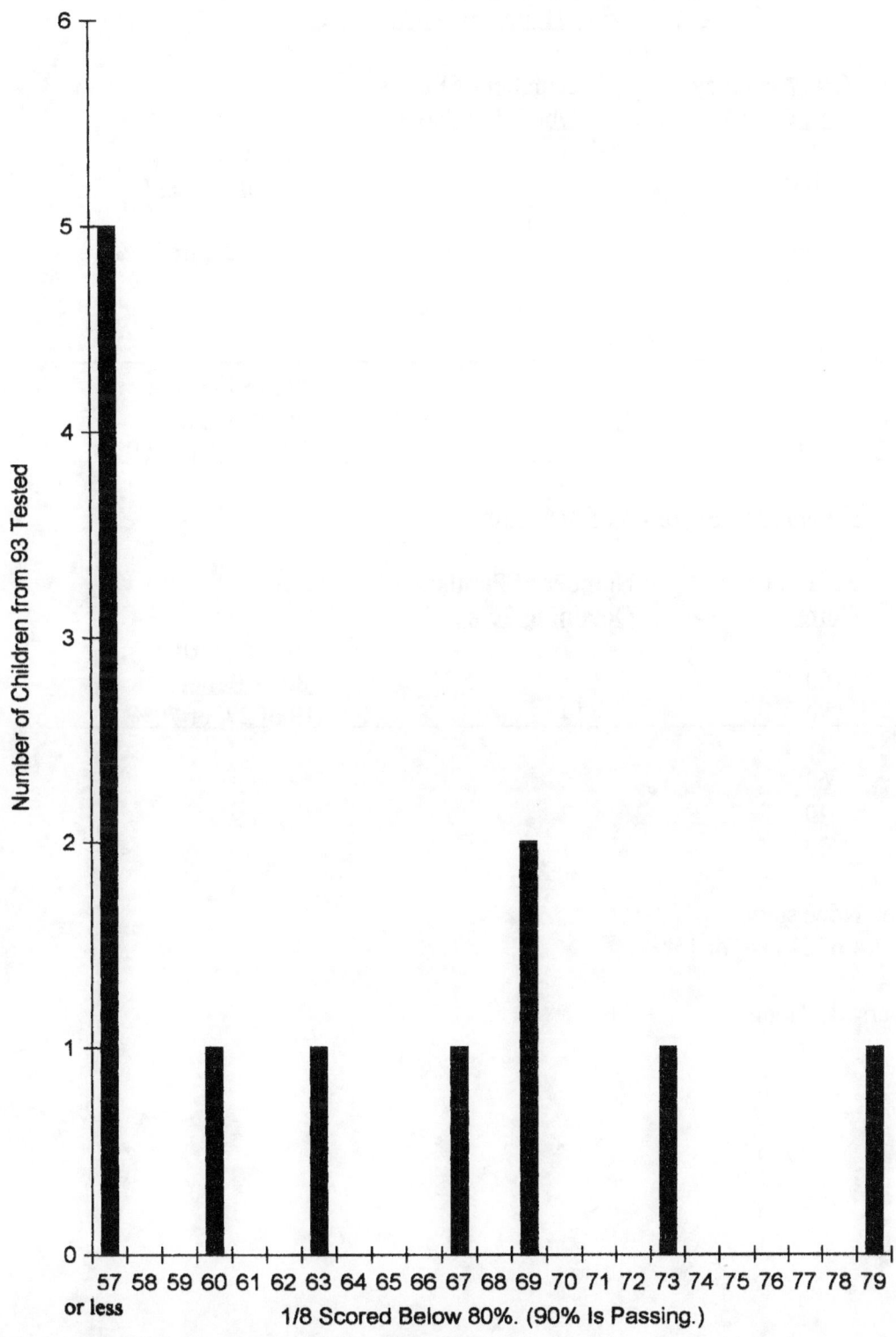

U. S. 18, A Top-Ability-Grouped Second-Grade Class, 27 Pupils - Code 3, Text: Houghton Mifflin - January, 1978

Oral Accuracy Per Cent	Number of Pupils Obtaining Score	
		Pupils Scoring 95 or Better
100	5	
99	13	
98	1	26 of 27, or 55%
97	3	
96	1	
95	3	
		Pupils Scoring 90 or Better
94		27 of 27, or 100%

Comprehension of Five Questions

Per Cent Correct	Number of Pupils Obtaining Score	
		Pupils Scoring 80 or Better
100	5	
80	14	19 of 27, or 70%
60	5	
40	2	
20	1	

Rate: None slow.
    4 of 27 fast, or 15%.

Reversals: None

U. S. 18, A Top-Ability-Grouped Second-Grade Class, 27 Pupils - Code 3, Text: Houghton Mifflin - January, 1978

Individual Scores, In Order Tested

Accuracy/Comprehension

95-60	Average rate
100-60	Good rate
97-60	Fair rate. Bad phrasing, possibly because of omissions.
99-80	
99-100	Good rate
96-100	Repeats. Halting.
99-80	Good rate
99-80	
98-80	Good rate
99-80	
100-60	
100-80	
99-100	
95-40	Fair rate
99-100	Fast
94-80	
97-40	
99-80	Halting. Good rate. Long pause reading "back."
99-20	Good rate
100-100	Good rate
97-60	Good rate
99-80	Good rate
99-80	Fast
99-80	Fast
99-80	Good rate
100-80	Fast
95-80	

U. S. 19, A Middle-Ability-Grouped Second-Grade Class, 24 Pupils - Code 3, Text: Houghton Mifflin - January, 1978

Oral Accuracy Per Cent	Number of Pupils Obtaining Score	
		Pupils Scoring 95 or Better
99	4	10 of 24 or 41%
98	3	
96	3	
		Pupils Scoring 90 or Better
94	3	20 of 24, or 83%
93	3	
92	4	
88	1	
87	1	
69	1	

Comprehension of Five Questions

Per Cent Correct	Number of Pupils Obtaining Score	
		Pupils Scoring 80 or Better
100	6	14 of 24, or 58%
80	8	
60	5	

Rate: None slow.
     1 of 24 fast, or 4%.

Reversals: None

U. S. 19. A Middle-Ability-Grouped Second-Grade Class, 24 Pupils - Code 3, Text: Houghton Mifflin - January, 1978

Individual Scores, In Order Tested

Accuracy/Comprehension

- 98-60   Good rate
- 88-60
- 92-80   Read "back" as "black" twice. Inserted "little" before second "dog." For "leg," said, "I do not know this."
- 96-40   Black child
- 93-80   Fair rate
- 93-100
- 94-80
- 87-60   Fair rate
- 94-80
- 94-80
- 98-60
- 93-60   Fair rate
- 99-60
- 96-80
- 99-100   Fairly fast
- 92-100   Fair rate. Reversal: spot~stripe
- 99-80
- 96-100
- 92-60   Lisp
- 69-Incomplete to word 62. Answered two of two questions correctly.
- 92-100   Fair rate
- 99-100   Fast
- 88-60
- 98-80   Fairly slow

U. S. 20. A Middle-Ability-Grouped Second-Grade Class, 22 Pupils - Code 3, Text: Houghton Mifflin - October, 1977 and January, 1978

October Scores			January Scores		
Oral Accuracy Per Cent	Number of Pupils Obtaining Score		Oral Accuracy Per Cent	Number of Pupils Obtaining Score	
99	1	Pupils Scoring	99	7	Pupils Scoring
98	2	95 or Better	97	3	95 or Better
97	1		96	2	
96	1	5 of 17 or 29%	95	3	15 of 22 or 68%
		Pupils Scoring			Pupils Scoring
94	3	90 or Better	93	1	90 or Better
90	1	9 of 17 or 53%	92	2	20 of 22 or 91%
86	1		85	1	
85	2		79	1	
82	1				
80	1				
77	1				
71	1				
64	1				

Comprehension of Five Questions			Comprehension of Five Questions		
Per Cent Correct	Number of Pupils Obtaining Score		Per Cent Correct	Number of Pupils Obtaining Score	
100	7	Pupils Scoring	100	13	Pupils Scoring
80	3	80 or Better	80	7	80 or Better
		10 of 17 or 59%			20 of 22 or 91%
60	5		60	2	
40	1				
Incomplete	1				
Fail					

For the October portion retested in January, 56% read at 95 accuracy or above, 87.5% read at 90 or above, (above the frustration level) and 94% passed comprehension.

October Notes

Rate: 3 of 17 slow, or 18% slow.
    None fast

Reversals: 4 of 17 or 24%.

January Notes

Rate: None slow.
    2 of 22 fast, or 9% fast.

Reversals: None.

Comparative Scores <u>FOR THAT PORTION ONLY</u> of U. S. 20,
Which Was Tested Both In October, 1977, and in January, 1978,
<u>A Middle-Ability-Grouped Second-Grade Class, Code 3, Houghton Mifflin Text</u>

This second-grade class had received the standard Houghton Mifflin program in first grade. It was a middle-ability-group class in a homogeneously-grouped school. The second-grade teacher stressed synthetic phonics strongly, spending much time on short-vowel sounds and blending, making children use these skills to identify unknown words. The rate of growth from this approach is shown by the following scores from October in comparison to the following January for those 16 of the 17 children who were tested in October who were still in the class.

OCTOBER, 1977

Oral Accuracy Score	Number of Pupils Obtaining Score		Comprehension Score	Number of Pupils Obtaining Score	
99	1		100	7	10/17 or 59%
98	2	5/17 or 29%	80	3	passed
97	1	above 95	60	5	
96	1		40	1	
94	3	9/17 or 53%	Incomplete	1	
90	1	above 90			
86	1				
85	2	Below 90 - 47%	SLOW: 18%		
82	1	Below 85 - 29%	FAST: 0%		
80	1		REVERSALS: 4 of 17, or 24%		
77	1	Below 80 - 18%			
71	1				
64	1	Below 70 - 6%			

JANUARY, 1978

Oral Accuracy Score	Number of Pupils Obtaining Score		Comprehension Score	Number of Pupils Obtaining Score	
99	4		100	12	15/16 or 94%
97	2	9/16 or 56%	80	3	passed
96	2	above 95	60	1	
95	1				
94	1				
93	1	14/16 or 88%			
92	2	above 90			
90	1		SLOW: 0%		
85	1	Below 90 - 12.5%	FAST: 2/16 or 12.5%		
79	1	Below 80 - 6%	REVERSALS: None		

The October sample totaled 17 children. One moved by January, but the other 16 were retested.

U. S. 20, A Middle-Ability-Grouped Second-Grade Class, 22 Pupils - Code 3, Text: Houghton Mifflin - October, 1977 and January, 1978

The principal said U. S. 20 was a little worse than U. S. 19 in October. Another teacher said they are now about the same. However, the January test scores show U. S. 20 is now superior. The teacher for U. S. 20 made great use of phonics and was using and drilling with phonics charts. She said that just that morning a boy had finally gotten the short vowels straight and was "so happy." She was giving great emphasis to vowel sounds which is not done in the Houghton Mifflin program.

October Scores, In Order Tested

A mixed group of 17 were tested in October. One child moved, but the other 16 were retested in January, along with another six from Class 20.

Accuracy/Comprehension

- 97-100
- 85-80 Reversal: spot~sept, also, spot~spet
- 98-100
- 71-80 Very slow and halting
- 85-40 Slow, halting
- 86-100 Slow
- 82-60
- 98-60
- 90-60 Reversal: spot~top
- 94-80 Reversal: spot~strip
- 77-60
- 94-100
- 96-100
- 80-60 Reversal: spot~straight, then "corrected" to spot~stripe, and I told him it was "spot." Then read spot as stripe in two more places.
- 94-100
- 99-100
- 64-Incomplete to word 66.

January Scores, In Order Tested
(Asterisks for Children Tested in Oct.)
Accuracy/Comprehension

- *97-100 Fair rate
- *96-80 Fairly slow
- *92-100 Fair rate
- *99-100 Fair rate
- *95-100 Good rate
- *90-100
- *93-80 Fair rate, halting.
- *94-100 Good rate
- *96-60 Good rate
- *85-100 Good rate
- *97-100 Good rate
- *99-100 Good rate
- *92-80 Good rate
- *99-100 Fast
- *79-100 Fast
- *99-100 Fair rate
- 99-60
- 95-80
- 95-100 Rate okay
- 99-80 Rate okay
- 99-80 Fair rate
- 97-80 Rate okay

U. S. 21, One of Two Bottom Classes in an Ability-Grouped Second-Grade
10 Pupils - Code 3, Text: Houghton Mifflin - January, 1978

Oral Accuracy Per Cent	Number of Pupils Obtaining Score	Pupils Scoring 90 or Better
90	0	None
84	1 Incomplete	
83	1 Incomplete	
80	1	
69	1 Incomplete	
67	1 Incomplete	
63	1 Incomplete	
60	1 Incomplete	
53	1 Incomplete	
50	1 Incomplete	
23	1 Incompletre	

Comprehension of Five Questions

Per Cent Correct	Number of Pupils Obtaining Score	Pupils Scoring 80 or Better
100	0	
80	0	None
60	1	
Incomplete fail	9	

Rate: 9 incomplete counted slow, or 90% slow
None fast

Reversals: 4 of 10, or 40%

U. S. 21. One of Two Bottom Classes in an Ability-Grouped Second-Grade
10 Pupils - Code 3, Text: Houghton Mifflin - January, 1978

Individual Scores, In Order Tested

Accuracy/Comprehension

- 69-Incomplete through example 2, word 62. Both questions answered correctly. Reversals: spot~stop, white~with.
- 80-60, so three of total of five questions (ending at ex. 5, word 144) were answered correctly.
- 67-Incomplete through example 1, word 30. Question answered incorrectly.
- 53-Incomplete through example 1, word 30. Question answered incorrectly.
- 83-Incomplete through example 1, word 30. Question answered correctly. Reversal: white~with.
- 63-Incomplete through example 1, word 30. Question answered correctly. Reversal: spot~stop
- 60-Incomplete through example 1, word 30. Question answered correctly.
- 50-Incomplete through example 1, word 30. Question answered incorrectly. Reversal: white~with.
- 23-Incomplete. Could not read opening words, which I gave her slowly, one at a time. When I had gotten as far as, "Peter has a little...." and waited for her to try to read the next word, "dog," she said, "cottontail," which I then corrected to "dog." Later, she read "spot" as "tail" and "leg" as "tail," which I corrected. Stopped at word 30, end of example 1. She missed the answer to that question. She did read a few of the first 30 words correctly, for a percentage score of 23.
- 84-Incomplete through example 2, word 62. Both questions answsered correctly. Vowel confusions: his~has, got~goat, small~smile, puppy~peppy, now~new.

These children had great difficulty decoding. When it became evident that a child was going to have a failing score, I stopped him at the end of example 1, word 30, or example 2, word 62, and marked him "incomplete." These incompletes are also counted as "slow."

U. S. 22. One of Two Bottom Classes in an Ability-Grouped Second-Grade, Recorded as "Non-Circulating" 10 Pupils Present, 1 Absent - Code 3, Text: Houghton Mifflin - January, 1978

Oral Accuracy Per Cent	Number of Pupils Obtaining Score	Pupils Scoring 90 or Better
91	1	1 of 10 or 10%
88	1	
86	1	
83	1 Incomplete	
80	1	
73	1	
67	1 Incomplete	
57	1 Incomplete	
43	2 Incomplete	

Comprehension of Five Questions

Per Cent Correct	Number of Pupils Obtaining Score	Pupils Scoring 80 or Better
100	0	
80	2	2 of 10, or 20%
40	3	
Incomplete fail	5	

Rate: 2 slow and 5 incomplete counted slow, or 70% slow
None fast

Reversals: 6 of 10, or 60%

U. S. 22. One of Two Bottom Classes in an Ability-Grouped Second-Grade, Recorded as "Non-Circulating" 10 Pupils Present, 1 Absent - Code 3. Text: Houghton Mifflin - January, 1978

Individual Scores, In Order Tested

Accuracy/Comprehension

- 73-40   Slow. Heavy glasses. Loses his place. Commented on the numbered words in the story. Seemed delighted that he was reading 144 words. Reversal: of~for.
- 80-80   Slow. Reversal: often~father.
- 86-40   Fair rate. Reversal: white~with
- 57-Incomplete to word 40. She did not understand that she had to pick an answer to the first example ending at word 30. Reversals: of~for, with~white.
- 43-Incomplete through example 1, word 30. Question answered incorrectly. Reversal: with~white. After pointing to "has," said, "I don't know that word." Said, for "of," "I forget that word." Read "mostly" as "big," "black" as "blue," and "brown" as "blue," but read "back" as "black." Read "with" as "white" but said, for "white" I don't know that one." For "on" read "in." She said she was in this class last year.
- 91-80   Good rate. Reversal: with~white. Pointed to "fed" and said, "What is that word?"
- 83-Incomplete through example 3, word 90. All three questions answered incorrectly to word 90.
- 67-Incomplete through example 1, word 30. Question answered incorrectly.
- 88-40   Fair rate. Very soft voice. Started to read "was fed" as "has" which I corrected to "was" and then stared at "fed" a long time before I told her.
- 43-Incomplete through example 1, word 30, for a total of three sentences. Question answered incorrectly. Snapped his fingers when he missed a word. After I gave him the word, he went back and read the whole sentence with assurance. He could not read the first word, "Peter." He said, when I gave it to him, "I know him. He was in my first-grade class."

U. S. 23 - Code 3 - Houghton, Mifflin - 22 Students Present, All Tested - January, 1978

Oral Accuracy Per Cent	Number of Pupils Obtaining Score	
		Pupils Scoring 95 or Better
100	2	
99	3	
98	2	12 of 22, or 55%
97	2	
96	2	
95	1	
94	2	Pupils Scoring 90 or Better
93	1	
92	2	18 of 22, or 82%
90	1	
89	1	
88	1	
85	1	
84	1	

Comprehension of Five Questions

Per Cent Correct	Number of Pupils Obtaining Score	
		Pupils Scoring 80 or Better
100	7	
80	10	17 or 22, or 77%
60	2	
40	3	

Rate: 4 of 22 slow, or 18%.
     2 of 22 fast, or 9%.

Reversals: 5%.

One child absent, per teacher, a poor student. Of children not here last year, one (95 acc., 80 comp., slow) had Macmillan Land of Pleasure last year. One (92 acc., 80 comp.) from Florida, unknown program last year.

U. S. 23, Code 3 - Houghton, Mifflin - 22 Students Present, All Tested - January, 1978

Individual Scores, In Order Tested

Accuracy/Comprehension

    99-100 Good rate, not fast.
    94-100 Good rate
    94-80   Fast
    97-80
    99-80
    100-100
    96-100 Slower rate, adequate
    98-40 Good rate
    99-80 Fair rate
    98-80
    95-80
    92-80 Foreign, in Florida last year
    89-40
    100-100
    97-100 Fast
    96-80
    92-80 Slow
    90-60
    84-80 Very slow
    88-100 Slow
    93-40 Slow
    85-60

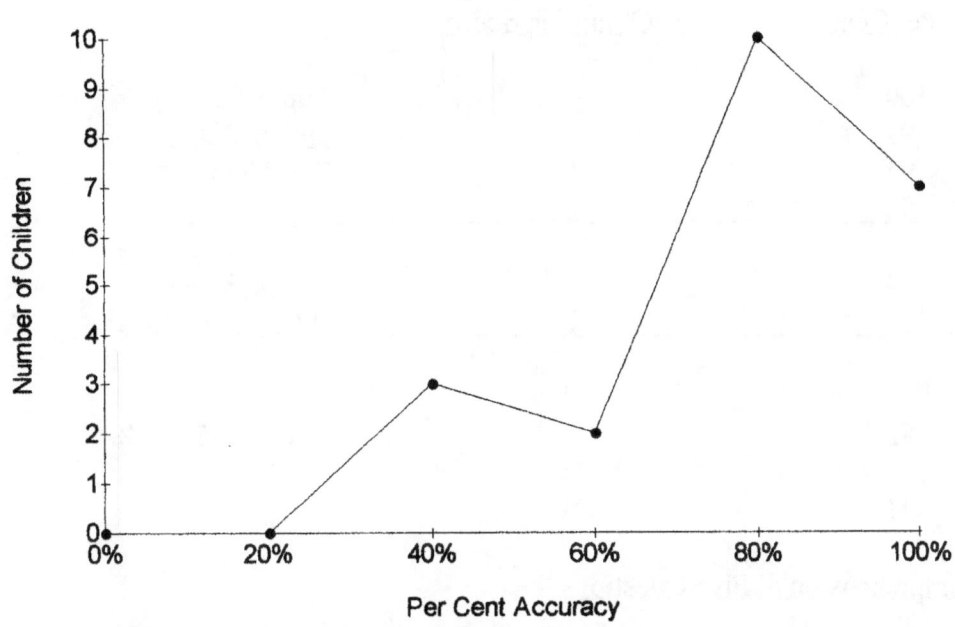

U. S. 23, Code 3 - Jan. 1978
Reading Comprehension

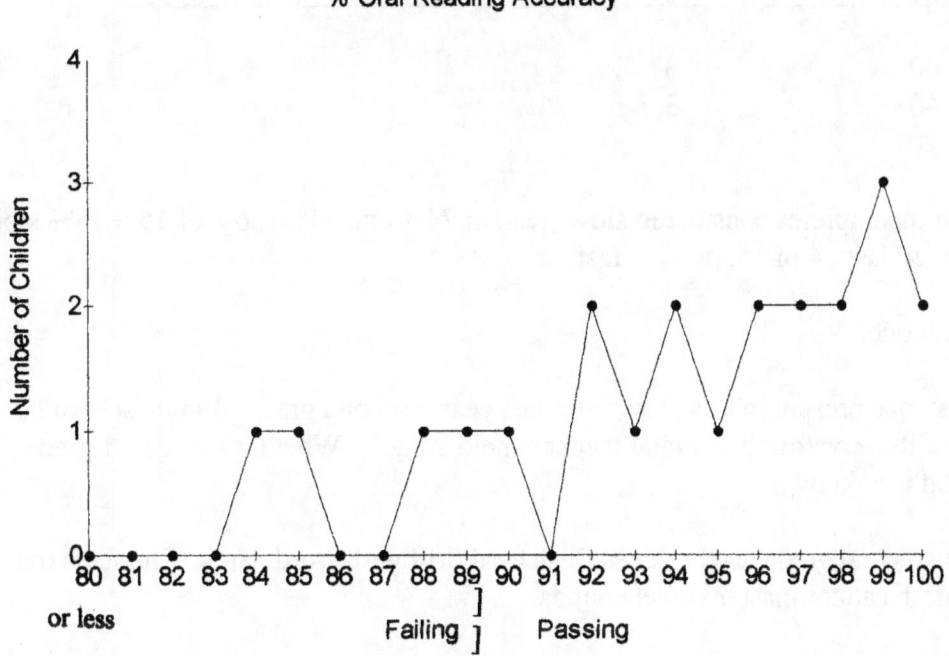

U. S. 23, Code 3 - Jan. 1978
% Oral Reading Accuracy

U. S. 24 - Code 2 - Scott, Foresman - 15 Pupils Present, All Tested, January, 1978

Oral Accuracy Per Cent	Number of Pupils Obtaining Score	
100	1	Pupils Scoring
99	3	95 or Better
97	1	7 of 15 or 47%
96	2	
94	3	Pupils Scoring 90 or Better
93	1	11 or 15 or 73%
87	1	
82	1	Below 85 - 20%
74	1	
71	1	

Comprehension of Five Questions

Per Cent Correct	Number of Pupils Obtaining Score	
100	2	Pupils Scoring 80 or Better
80	6	8 of 15 or 53%
60	3	
40	3	
20	1	

Rate: Two incompletes considered slow (read at 74% and 71%) so 2 of 15 = 13% slow. Marked fast: 4 of 15, or 27% fast.

Reversals: none.

Retentions: one present in this class from last year's second grade. In this school last year, one of three or four first grade teachers held 2 back. Whether other first-grade teachers did is unknown.

Note: This second grade teacher does flash card drill with word cards. She feels that some children cannot master vowel sounds.

U. S. 24 - Code 2 - Scott, Foresman - 15 Pupils Present, All Tested - January, 1978

Individual Scores in Order Tested

Accuracy/Comprehension

- 94-80 Good rate. Read "less" as "lettuce."
- 99-80 Fast
- 99-100 Fast
- 96-60
- 94-60
- 71-40 Incomplete to Word 90. Black. Read "named" as "might." Two of three questions read were correct. Counted as 40% comprehension, (correct on two of five total questions).
- 93-40 Read "second" as "sound."
- 87-60 Fair rate. Read "learned" as "little."
- 94-80 Fast
- 97-40 Fast
- 96-80 Good rate
- 82-80 Fair rate. Read "number" as "month" and "stand as "start."
- 99-80
- 100-100
- 74-20 Incomplete to Word 62. "Years" read as "young." One of two questions read was correct. Counted as 20% comprehension (correct on one of five total questions.)

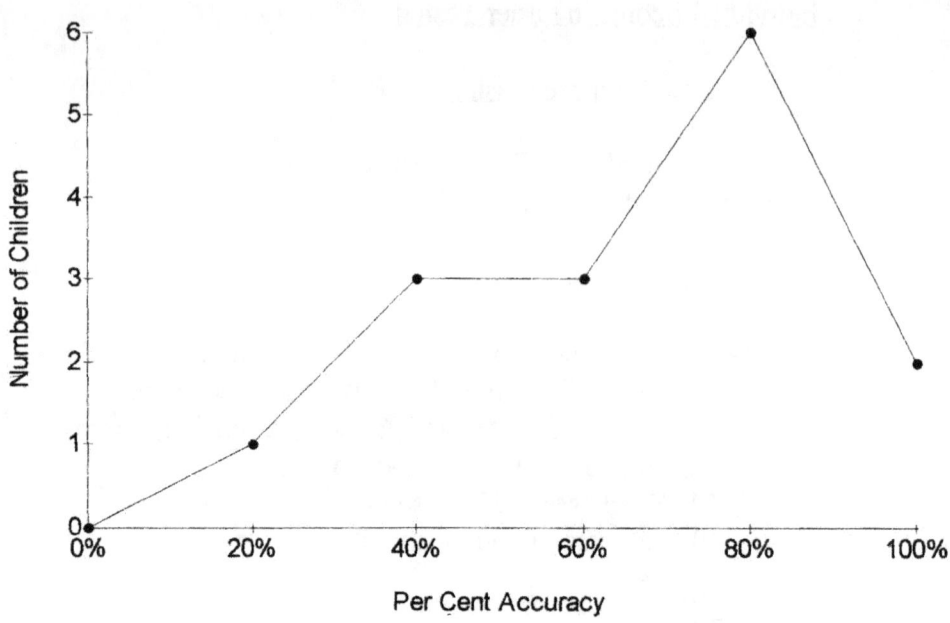

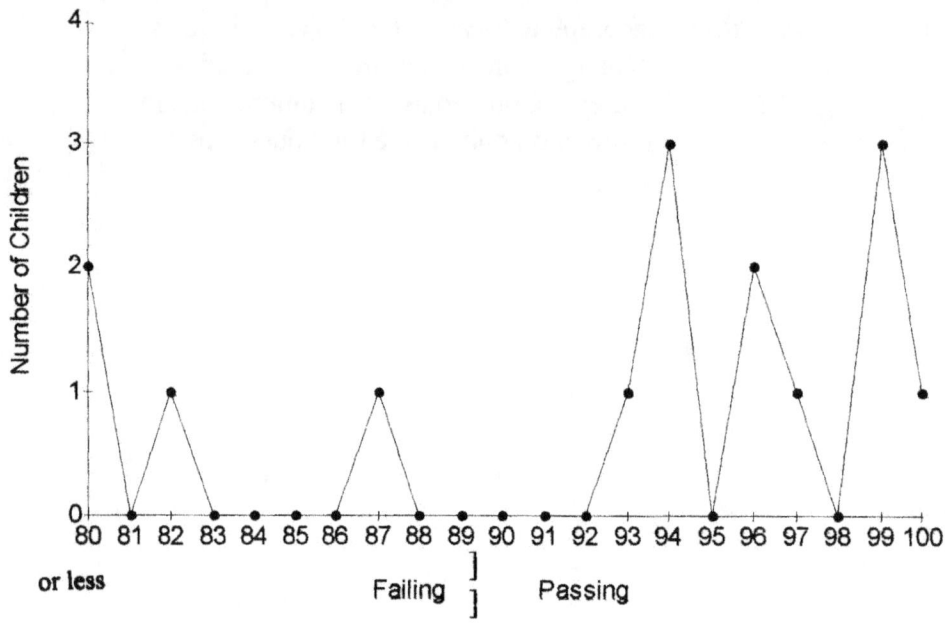

U. S. 25 - Code 2 - Scott, Foresman - 15 Pupils Present, All Tested, January, 1978

Oral Accuracy Per Cent	Number of Pupils Obtaining Score	
		Pupils Scoring 95 or Better
99	3	
96	1	5 of 15 or 33%
95	1	
		Pupils Scoring 90 or Better
93	2	
92	1	9 of 15 or 60%
90	1	
89	1	
88	1	
87	1	
84	1	Below 85
82	1	3 of 15 or 20%
81	1	

Comprehension of Five Questions

Per Cent Correct	Number of Pupils Obtaining Score	
		Pupils Scoring
100	5	80 or Better
80	6 (one 75% on 4 questions)	11 of 15 or 73%
60	4	

Rate: 2 of 15 slow, or 13%. None fast.

Reversals: 5 of 15 or 33%

Retentions: one present in this class from last year's second grade. In this school last year, one of three or four first grade teachers held 2 back. Whether other first-grade teachers did is unknown.

U. S. 25 - Code 2 - Scott, Foresman - 15 Pupils Present, All Tested - January, 1978

Individual Scores in Order Tested

Accuracy/Comprehension

82-75 Incomplete. Black child. He was in second grade last year. Reversals: stop~spot. Many phonic misreadings. Read "years" as "yellow," "more" as "mother," "stand" as "star."
99-100
93-60
99-80
87-80 Read "second" as "smallest."
95-100 Fair rate. Reversal: do~go
88-60 Read "little" as "small," "years" as "young," "catch" as "clean," "number" as "next."
92-80 Reversal: dog~big.
93-100
99-80 Good rate, even. Most in class to this point read at a satisfactory rate.
96-60
81-100
90-60 Very slow
89-100 Slow. Reversal: white~with
84-80 Reversal: spot~stripe. Read "number" as "neighbor."

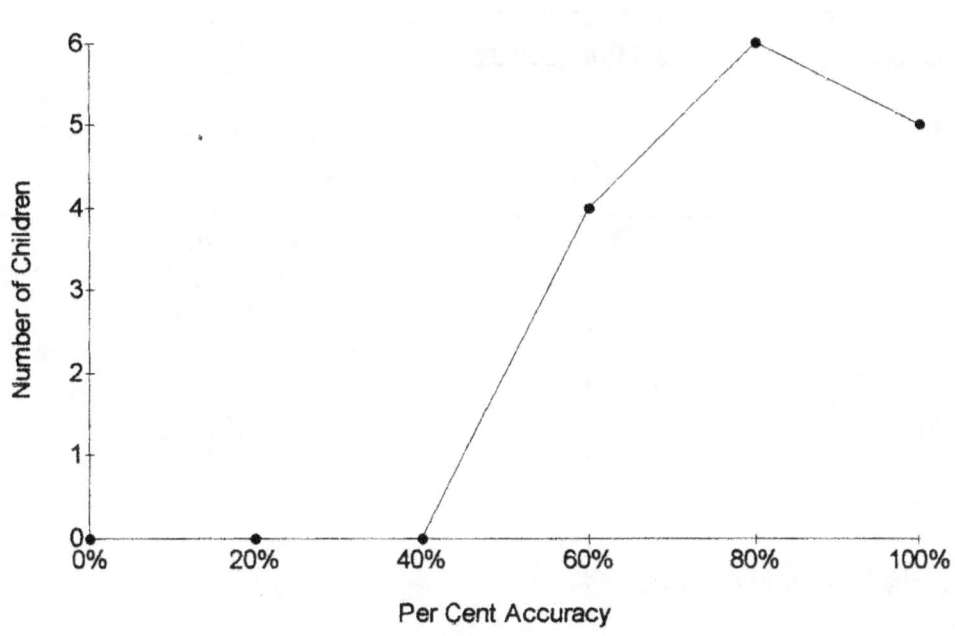

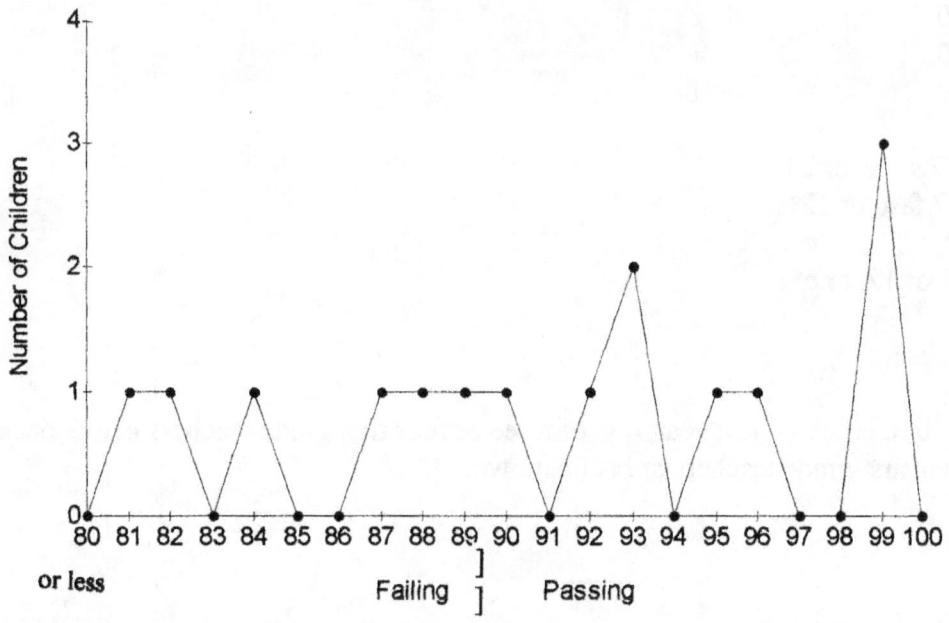

U. S. 26 - Code 2 - Scott, Foresman - 17 Pupils Present, All Tested, January, 1978

Oral Accuracy Per Cent	Number of Pupils Obtaining Score	
100	1	Pupils Scoring
99	4	95 or Better
96	3	8 of 17 or 47%
		Pupils Scoring
		90 or Better
93	4	12 or 17 or 71%
88	2	
86	1	Below 85 - None
85	2	

Comprehension of Five Questions

Per Cent Correct	Number of Pupils Obtaining Score	Pupils Scoring
100	5	80 or Better
80	8	13 of 17 or 77%
60	2	
40	1	
20	1	

Rate: 4 of 17 slow, or 24%
2 of 17 fast, or 12%.

Reversals: 1 of 17, or 6%.

Two pupils absent.

Retentions: In this school last year, one of three or four first grade teachers held 2 back. Whether other first-grade teachers did is unknown.

U. S. 26 - Code 2 - Scott, Foresman - 17 Pupils Present, All Tested - January, 1978

Individual Scores in Order Tested

Accuracy/Comprehension

99-80
96-100
93-80   Fairly slow
99-80   Fast
96-100
100-80 Points with finger, constantly losing her place.
99-80   Good rate
96-100 Fast
85-80   Substitution, non-phonic: many~middle
86-60   Slow
99-60   Black (In contrast to this Code 2 program, NO European Black student tested, who were all from Code 6 or higher programs, failed comprehension.)
88-80   Very non-phonic substitution: learned~listened
93-20   Fairly slow
88-40   Slow. Very non-phonic substitution: second~shoulder.
85-100 Fair rate. Very non-phonic substitutions: small~shell, learned~lemon.
93-80   Slow, reversal: number~under.
93-100 Slow

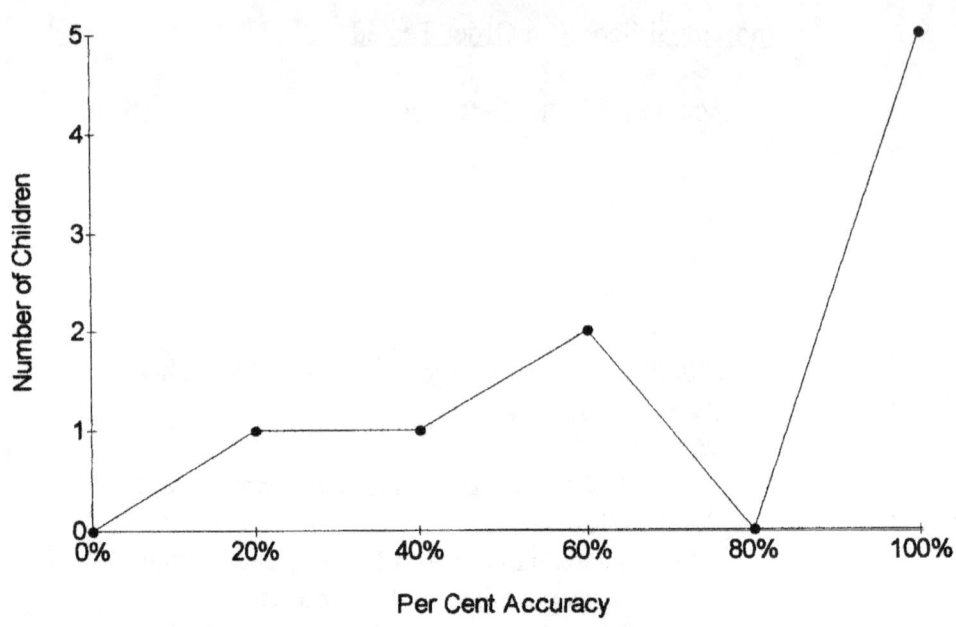

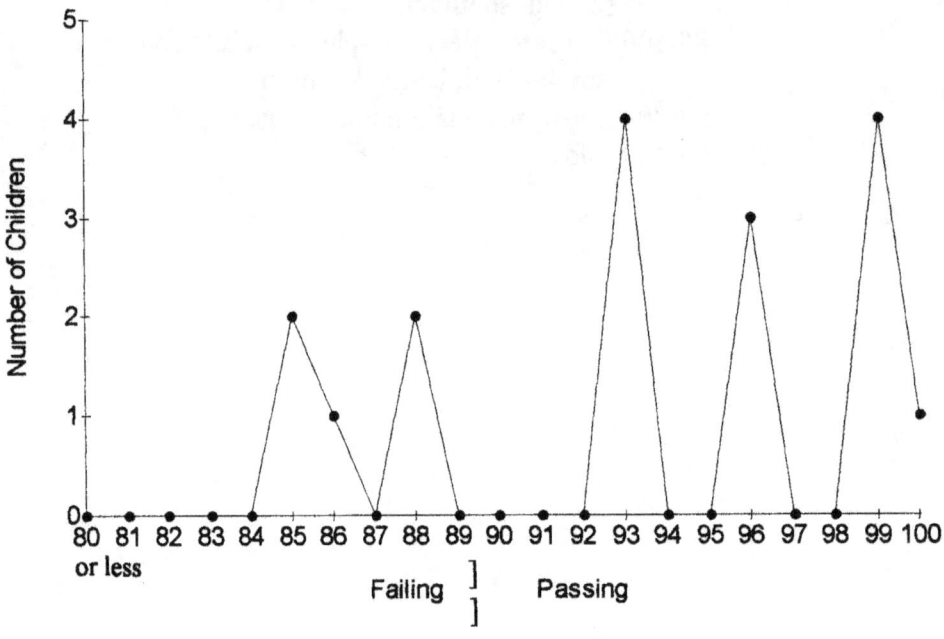

<u>U. S. 27 - Code 5 - Scott, Foresman plus Scott, Foresman Phonics Workbook, "Letters and Sounds," 15 Pupils Present, All Tested, January, 1978</u>

Oral Accuracy Per Cent	Number of Pupils Obtaining Score	
		Pupils Scoring
100	1	<u>95 or Better</u>
99	3	11 of 15 or 73%
98	2	
97	2	
96	3	
94	1	Pupils Scoring
93	1	<u>90 or Better</u>
92	1	15 of 15 or 100%
90	1	

<u>Comprehension of Five Questions</u>

Per Cent Correct	Number of Pupils Obtaining Score	
		Pupils Scoring
100	6	<u>80 or Better</u>
80	9	15 of 15 or 100%

Rate: None slow.
7 of 15 or 47% fast.

Reversals: 1 of 15 or 7%.

Note: Teacher reported two children were absent.

<ins>U. S. 27 - Code 5 - Scott, Foresman plus Scott, Foresman Phonics Workbook, "Letters and Sounds," 15 Pupils Present, All Tested - January, 1978</ins>

<ins>Individual Scores in Order Tested</ins>

<ins>Accuracy/Comprehension</ins>

92-80 Good rate
90-80
99-80 Fast
99-80 Fast
96-80 Good rate
97-100 Good rate
96-80
97-80 Fast
96-100 Fast
98-80
93-100 Good rate
94-100 Fast
99-100 Fast
98-80
100-100 Fast

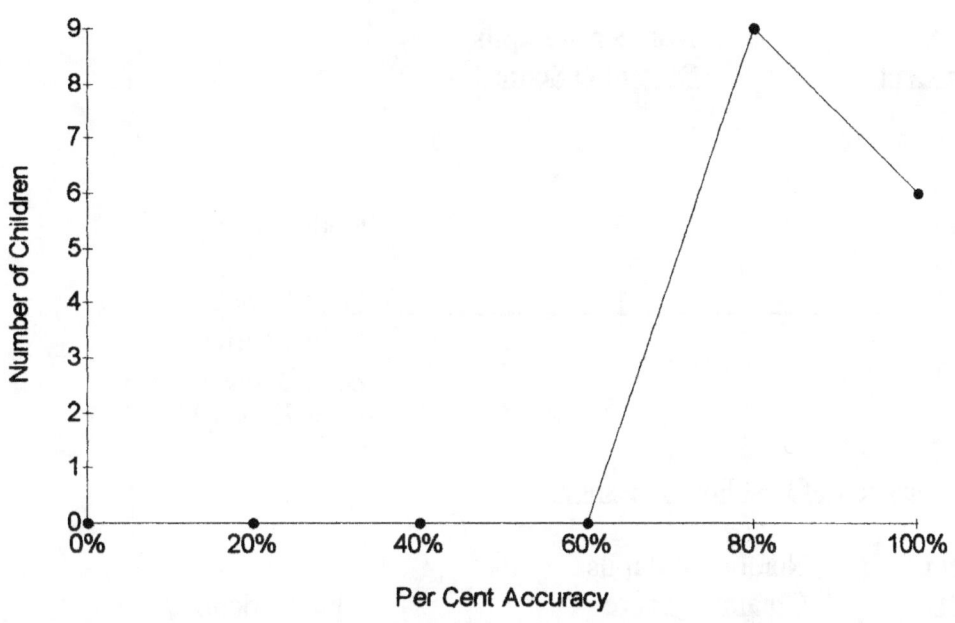

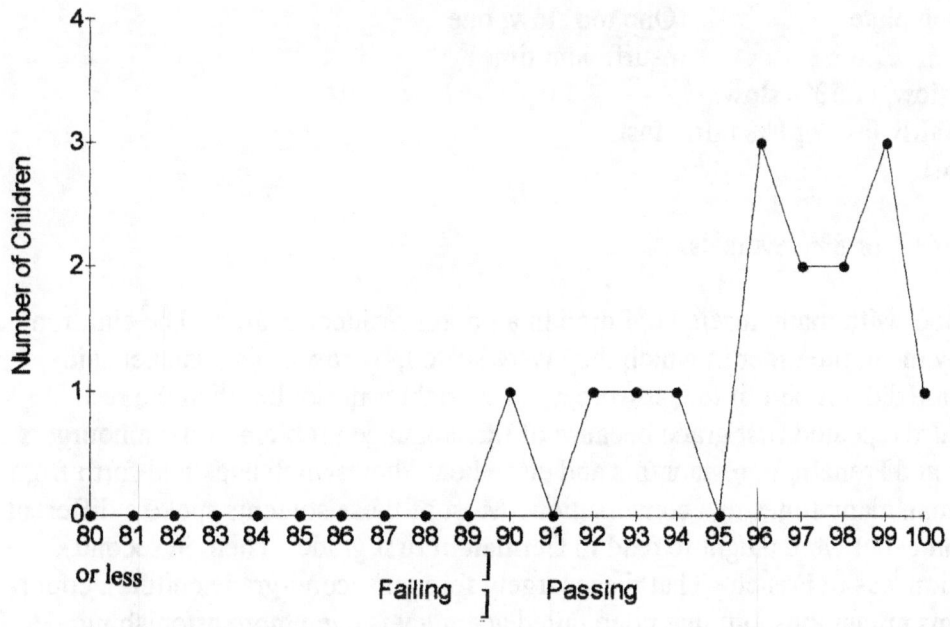

Luxembourg - Code 8, Text: Toni, Bim, Lee, Karin, Ann - Tested 12 of 18 Pupils Present, October, 1977

Oral Accuracy Per Cent	Number of Pupils Obtaining Score	
100	3	
99	3	
98	3	Pupils Scoring
97	1	95 or Better
96	1	11 of 12 or 92%
91	1	Pupils Scoring 90 or Better 12 of 12 or 100%

Comprehension of Last Four Questions

Per Cent Correct	Number of Pupils Obtaining Score	
		Pupils Scoring
100	1	75 or Better
75	2	3 of 10 or 30%
50	4	
25	3	
Incomplete	2 (One too slow, one insufficient time)	

Rate: 4 of 12 slow, or 33% slow.
       1 of 12 fairly fast, or 8% fairly fast.
       None fast.

Reversals: 1 of 12, or 8% reversals.

This was a school with many foreign children in a poorer residential area. The children were chosen by me in the order in which they were seated, by rows. The teacher said those whom time did not permit to test were neither brighter nor duller than the rest. Perhaps one-third repeated first grade because of the language problem. Luxembourgers speak German and French. In restaurants and elsewhere, they switch back and forth from French to German many times in a conversation. Most of these students spoke a different language at home, but were taught to read in German in first grade. Then, in second grade, instruction was in French. That these largely foreign second-grade children could read at all seems miraculous, but that none failed accuracy is even more astonishing. However, their slow speed in reading German in second grade is certainly understandable.

Luxembourg - Code 8, Text: Toni, Bim, Lee, Karin, Ann - Tested 12 of 18 Pupils Present, October, 1977

Individual Scores in Order Tested

Accuracy/Comprehension

99-100
96-75 Slow
97-25 Slow
100-50
99-50
100-75 Fairly fast
98-66 Incomplete, only through item 3, because too slow.
98-50
91-25 Slow
98-50 Reversal: Fleck~felck.
99-25
100-Incomplete through item 1, no time.

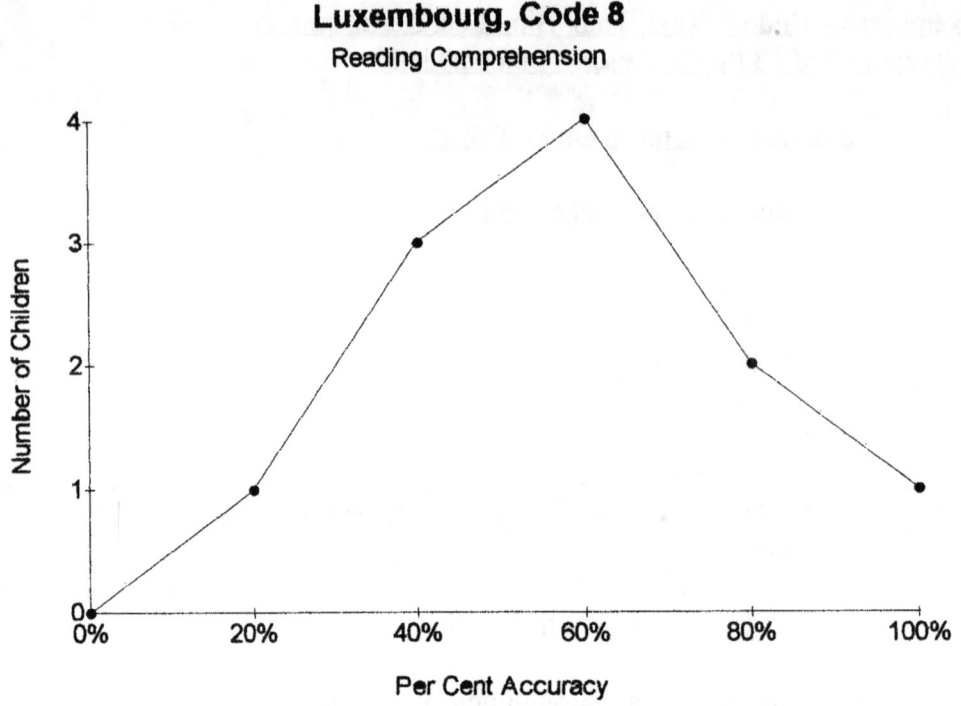
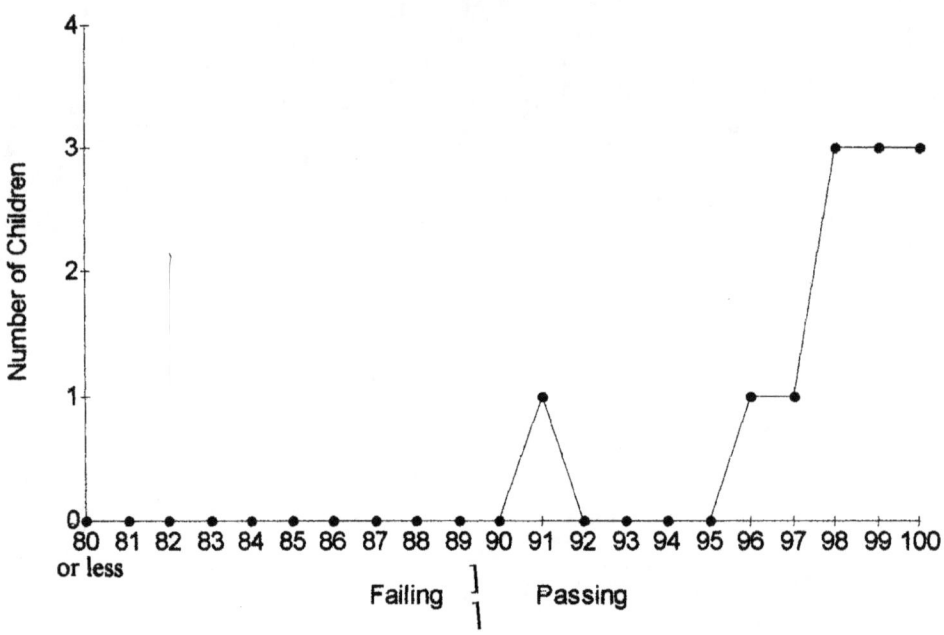

Amsterdam 1 - Code 6, Text: Caesar - 10 Pupils Tested from Class, October, 1977

Oral Accuracy Per Cent	Number of Pupils Obtaining Score	
100	3	Pupils Scoring
99	2	95 or Better
98	1	
95	1	7 or 10 or 70%
89	1	
87	1	
64	1	

Comprehension of Last Four Questions

Per Cent Correct	Number of Pupils Obtaining Score	
		Pupils Scoring 75 or Better
75	3	3 of 9 or 33% (Not counting one at 99% who read too slowly to finish past example 2.)
50	3	
25	1	
0 Incomplete	2	

Rate: 6 of 10 slow, or 60% slow.
     1 of 10 fast, or 10% fast.

Reversals: 2 of 10, or 20% reversals.

Retentions: General impression that there were no retentions.

Amsterdam 1 - Code 6, Text: Caesar - 10 Pupils Tested from Class, October, 1977

Individual Scores in Order Tested

Accuracy/Comprehension

95-50 Slow. Indonesian.
100-75 Fast
100-75
89-75 Very slow. Reversal-like errors: nu~un, oor~roat, op~peet. Receives help from reading specialist.
100-50
99-50 Slow
98-25 Reversal-like errors: plek~bloc. Do not count as reversal because of doubt.
64-Incomplete (ex. 1 and 2). Exceedingly slow. Reversals: bruin~druin, iets~iest.
87-Incomplete (ex. 1 and 2). Very slow. About 5 minutes to read this much. Word-by-word, incredibly.
99-Incomplete (ex. 1 and 2). Very slow. Waited 20 seconds for him to read "plek," 10 seconds for "vooral," 10 seconds for "dan."

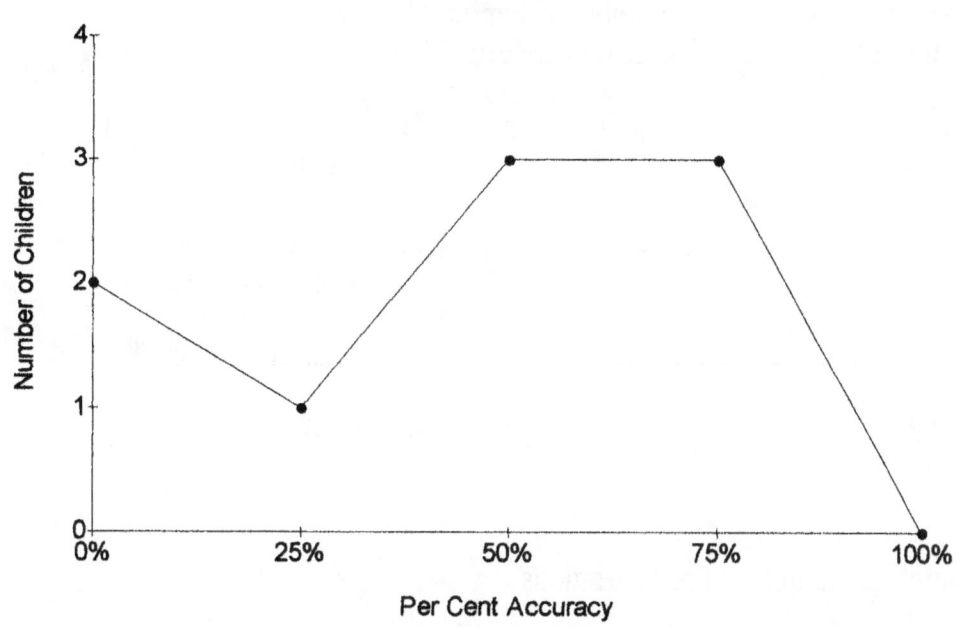

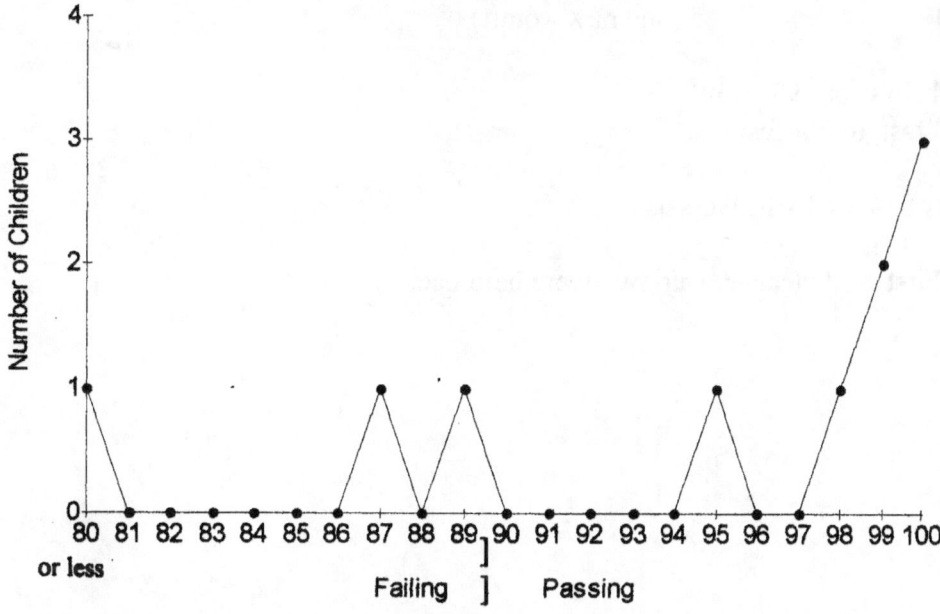

Amsterdam 2 - Code 6, Text: Caesar - 15 in Class Present, All Tested, October, 1977

Oral Accuracy Per Cent	Number of Pupils Obtaining Score	
100	4	
99	6	Pupils Scoring
98	1	95 or Better
97	1	12 of 14 or 86%
		Pupils Scoring
		90 or Better
92	1	13 or 14 or 93%
89	1 (new to school - omit)	
86	1	

Comprehension of Last Four Questions

Per Cent Correct	Number of Pupils Obtaining Score	
100	5	Pupils Scoring
75	5	75 or Better
		10 or 14 or 71%
50	5 (one new - omit)	

Rate: 4 of 14 slow, or 29% slow.
  1 of 14 fast, or 7% fast.

Reversals: 2 of 14, or 14% reversals.

Retentions: First grade teacher said two were held back.

<u>Amsterdam 2 - Code 6, Text: Caesar - 15 in Class Present, All Tested, October, 1977</u>

<u>Individual Scores in Order Tested</u>

<u>Accuracy/Comprehension</u>

99-75
100-75
89-50   Very slow. New to school
100-75
98-50   Slow
92-100 Slow. Pauses to sound out many words. Syllable reversal: keren~kreihen.
99-100
99-100
100-75 Fast
97-100 Slow. Heavy glasses.
99-50
86-50   Very slow. Sounds out. Reversal: nu~un
99-75
100-50
99-100 Confused on "m" and "n" in two words.

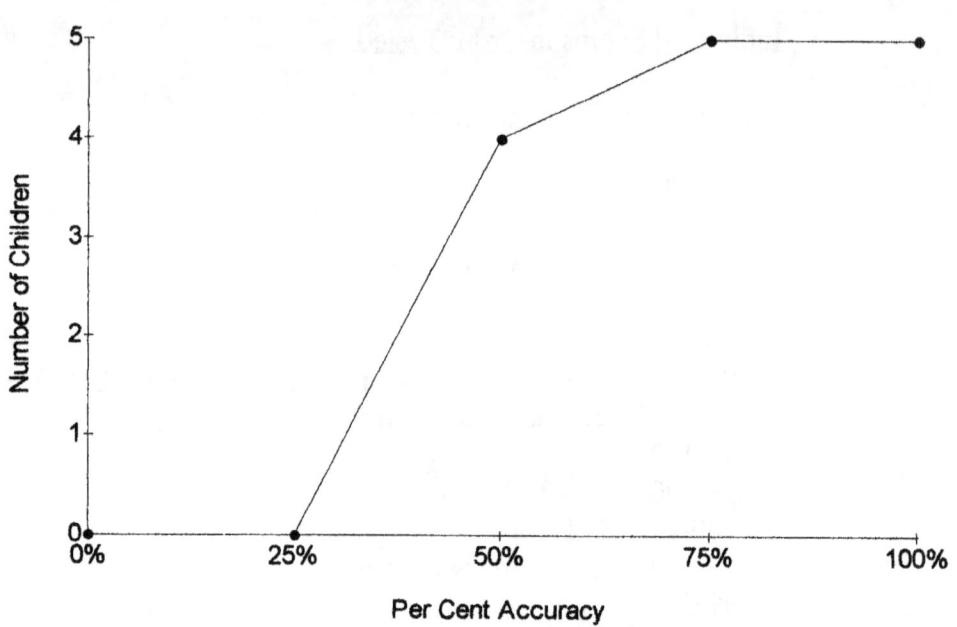
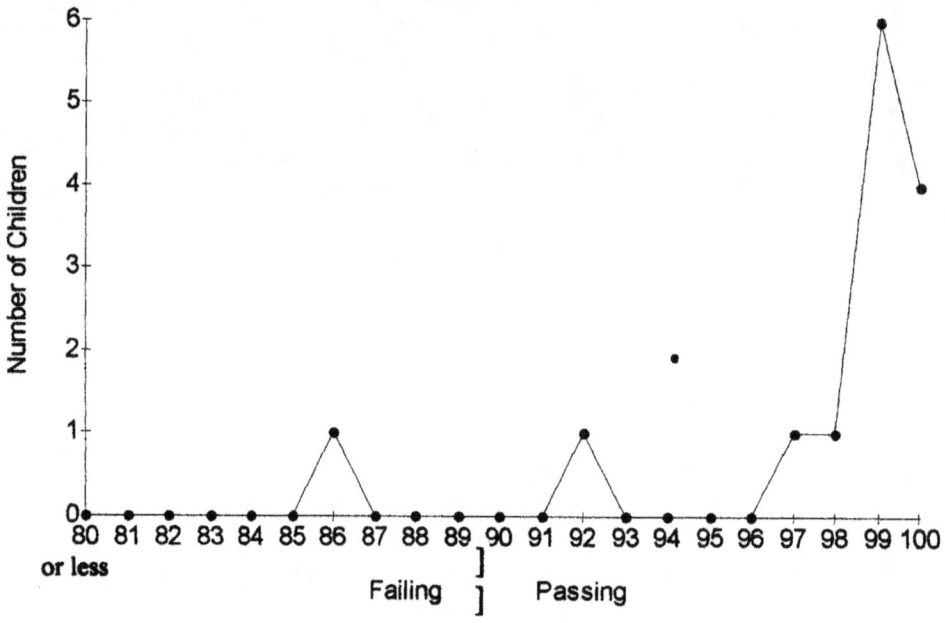

Amsterdam 3 - Code 8, Text: Leesfeest - Tested 19 of 30 Pupils Present, October, 1977

Oral Accuracy Per Cent	Number of Pupils Obtaining Score	
100	8	
99	7	
98	1	Pupils Scoring
96	1	95 or Better
95	1	18 of 19 or 95%
94	1	Pupils Scoring 90 or Better 19 of 19 or 100%

Comprehension of Last Four Questions

Per Cent Correct	Number of Pupils Obtaining Score	
100	5	Pupils Scoring
75	3	75 or Better 8 or 19 or 42%
50	5	
25	3	
0	3	

Rate: 1 of 19 slow, or 5% slow.
2 of 19 fast, or 11% fast.

Reversals: 2 of 19, or 11% reversals.

Note: Pupils chosen by seating arrangement. Teacher said I missed 3 of the very best but got the worst. The principal said there were usually about 3% retentions. Most read at a good rate - steady. Two had been held back at first this year.

Amsterdam 3 - Code 8, Text: Leesfeest - Tested 19 of 30 Pupils Present, October, 1977

Individual Scores in Order Tested

Accuracy/Comprehension

100-100
99-75   Slow
100-100
99-75
100-0
99-50
99-75
98-0
99-100 Teacher said boy was epileptic.
           One reversal: vooral~ovarl.
100-100 Indonesian.
100-25
99-25   Very fast
100-50
100-50
96-0   Slower. Pauses on words.
94-50   Slower.
99-100 Fast
100-50 Slower - adequate.
95-25   Slower. One reversal: keren~krei-an.

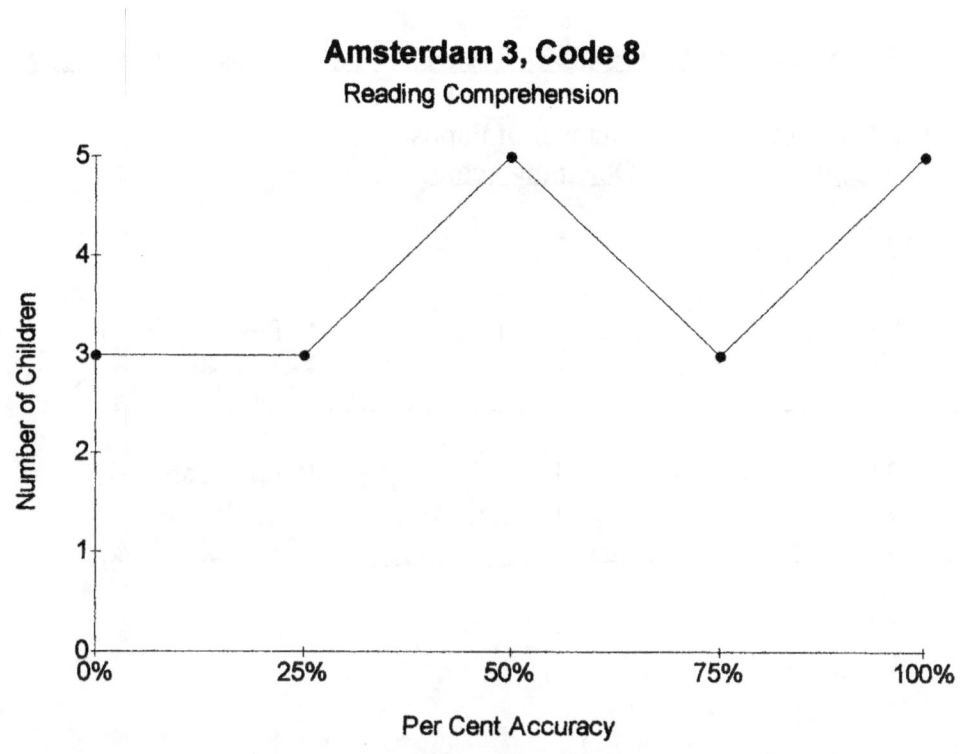

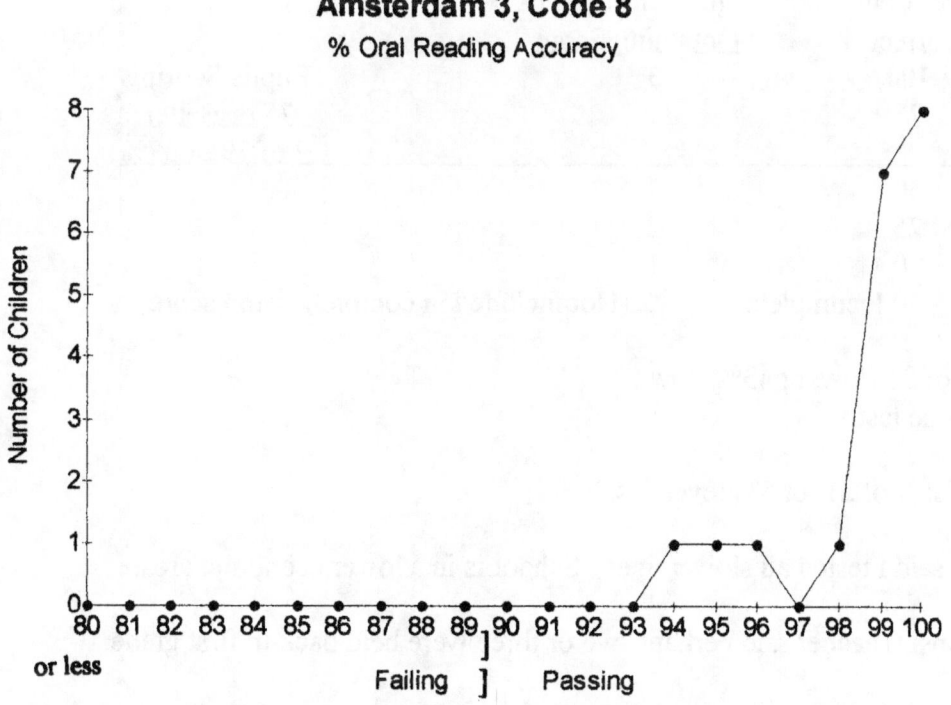

Amsterdam 4 - Code 6, Text: Caesar - Tested 21 of 25 in Class, October, 1977

Oral Accuracy Per Cent	Number of Pupils Obtaining Score	
100	7	
99	3	
98	1	Pupils Scoring
97	2	95 or Better
95	1	14 of 21 or 67%
93	1	Pupils Scoring
92	1	90 or Better
91	2	18 or 21 or 86%
89	2	
84	1	

Comprehension of Last Four Questions

Per Cent Correct	Number of Pupils Obtaining Score	
100	3	Pupils Scoring
75	4	75 or Better
		7 of 19 or 37%
50	7	
25	2	
0	1	
0 Incomplete	2 (Not included in comprehension score)	

Rate: 9 of 21 slow, or 43% slow.
    None fast.

Reversals: 1 of 21, or 5% reversals.

Teacher said I tested all slower ones. School is in a lower economic area.

Retentions: Teacher said perhaps two or three were held back in first grade.

Amsterdam 4 - Code 6, Text: Caesar - Tested 21 of 25 in Class, October, 1977

Individual Scores in Order Tested

Accuracy/Comprehension

100-50
91-Incomplete (ex. 1 and 2). Stopped because he had a sty making it difficult to read.
92-75 Slow. Black. Getting reading remediation.
99-50
100-100
95-50 Slow
84-Incomplete (ex. 1, 2 and 3). Very slow. Reversals: bruin~druin, twee~weet. Diagnosed as retarded. Spent two years in first grade. Receives supplemental help.
93-Incomplete (ex. 1 and 2). Slow. Left for gym class with other boys.

Tested girls returning from gym:

100-100
100-75
100-50
89-25   Very slow.
97-50
99-75
89-0   Very slow.
100-75 Turkish.
100-100
99-50 Slow
98-50
97-50 Slow. Pakistani or Indian.
91-Incomplete (ex. 1, 2 and 3). Slow. Missed 3 of 3 comprehension questions. Errors included reading "plek as "speck."

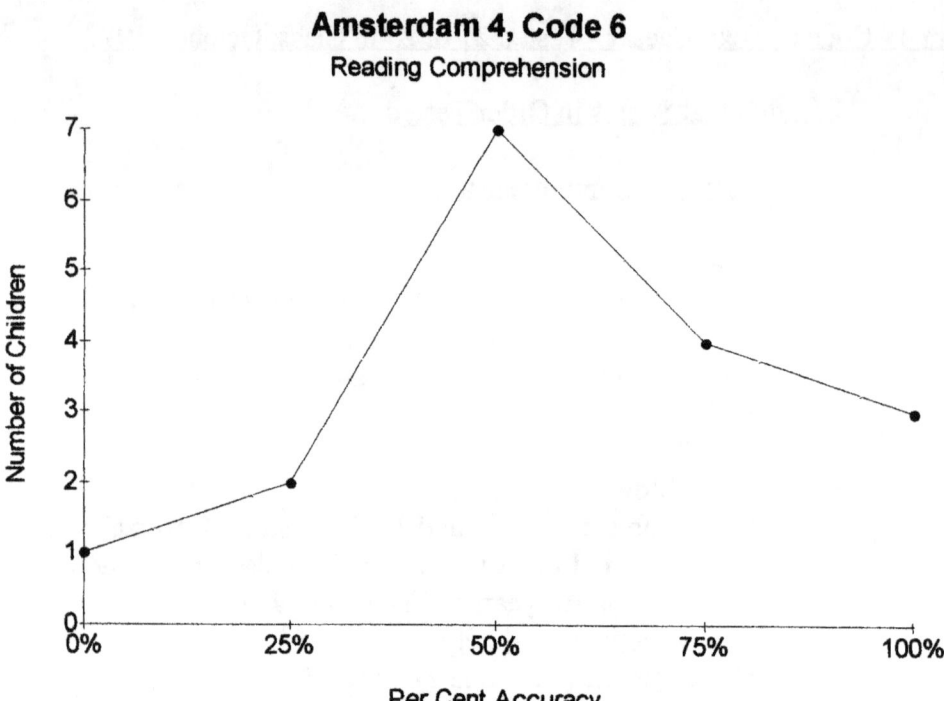

Stockholm 1 - Code 9, Text: Nu Laser and "Some LTG"
Tested 7 of 12 Children in P.M. Half of Class, October, 1977

Oral Accuracy Per Cent	Number of Pupils Obtaining Score	
		Pupils Scoring
100	6	95 or Better
97	1	7 of 7 or 100%

Comprehension of Last Four Questions

Per Cent Correct	Number of Pupils Obtaining Score	
100	2	
75	1	Pupils Scoring
		75 or Better
		3 of 7 or 43%
50	3	
25	1	

Rate: 2 of 7 slow, or 29% slow.
      5 of 7 fast, or 71% fast..

Reversals: None.

This class dismissed at 1:20 p. m. so there was insufficient time to test all 12. This sample was chosen by chance on the basis of the seating arrangement of the 12 children present.

Retentions: None mentioned.

Stockholm 1 - Code 9, Text: Nu Laser and "Some LTG"
Tested 7 of 12 Children in P.M. Half of Class, October, 1977

Individual Scores in Order Tested

Accuracy/Comprehension

100-75   Fast
100-100 Fast
100-50   Fast
100-25   Fast
100-50   Slow. Sounds out.
97-50   Very slow. Sounds syllable by syllable. Nu~du.
100-100 Fast

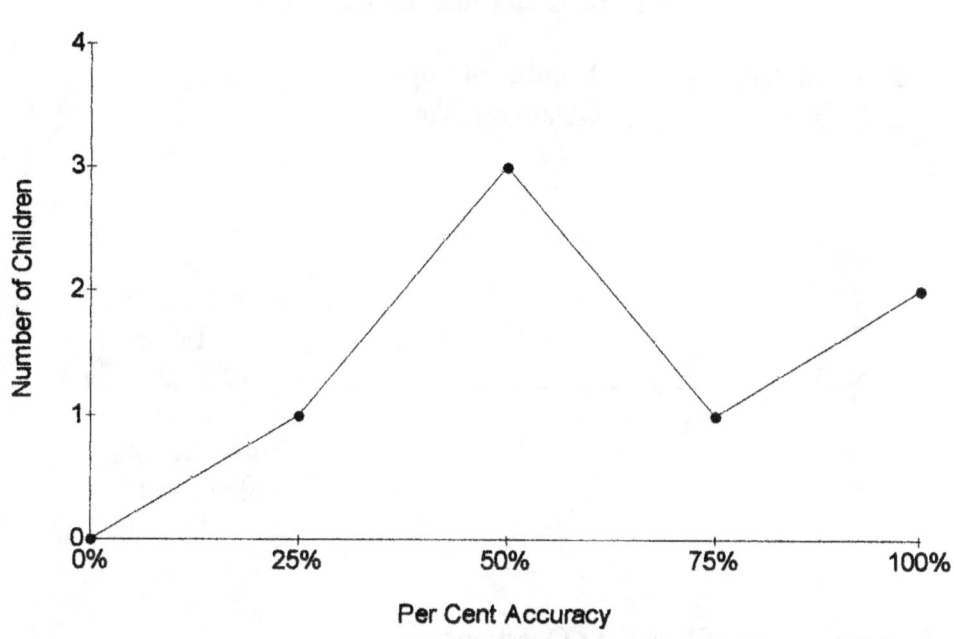

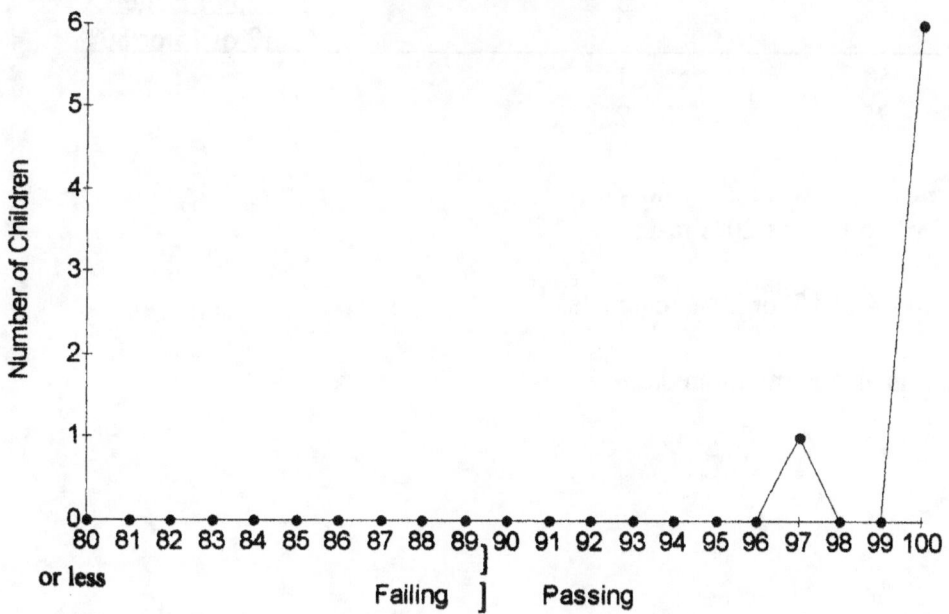

Stockholm 2 - Code 8, Text: Nu Laser and Language Experience
Tested All 15 in Class, November, 1977

Oral Accuracy Per Cent	Number of Pupils Obtaining Score	
100	6	
99	1	
98	3	
97	1	Pupils Scoring
96	1	95 or Better
95	1	13 of 15 or 87%
94	1	Pupils Scoring
91	1	90 or Better
		15 or 15 or 100%

Comprehension of Last Four Questions

Per Cent Correct	Number of Pupils Obtaining Score	
100	7	Pupils Scoring
75	5	75 or Better
		12 of 15 or 80%
50	1	
25	2	

Rate: 4 of 15 slow, or 27% slow.
        3 of 15 fast, or 20% fast..

Reversals: 4 of 15, or 20% reversals.

Retentions: None mentioned.

Stockholm 2 - Code 8, Text: Nu Laser and Language Experience
Tested All 15 in Class, November, 1977

Individual Scores in Order Tested

Accuracy/Comprehension

99-50
96-25 Slow
100-100
98-100 A little slow
100-75 Fast
100-75 Fast
91-100 Reverses syllables, boll~blau
100-100
94-100 Very slow. Reversals: 5 on b-d.
98-100 Faster
95-75   Slow. Two reversals: kallar~klaller, berattelsen~berattlesen (pronounced "lee").
97-25   Slow. Omitted "st" in "konster." For "bakbenen," read "bakstassen." For "konsten," read "bonsten."
100-75
98-75
100-100

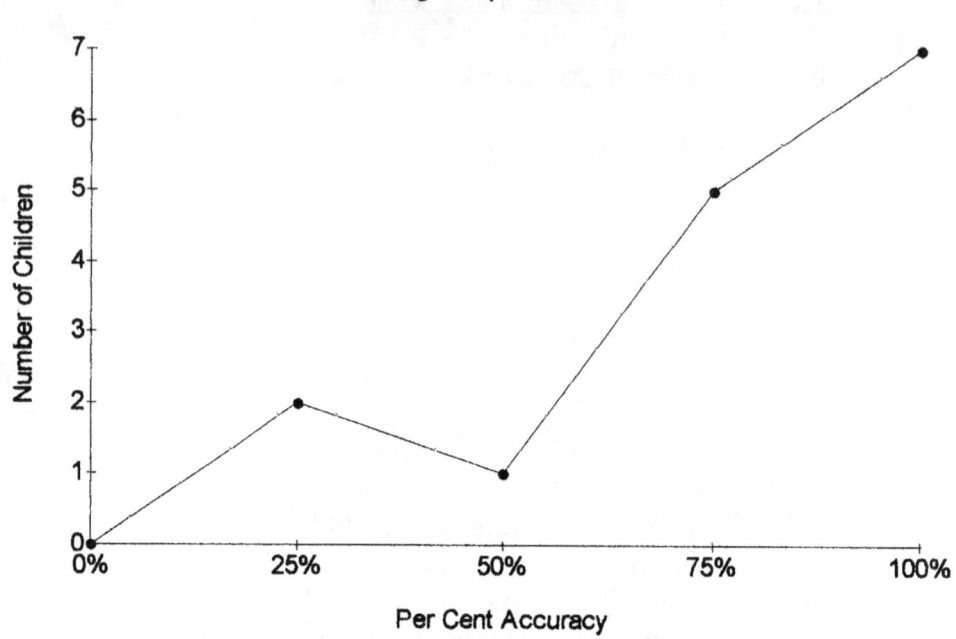

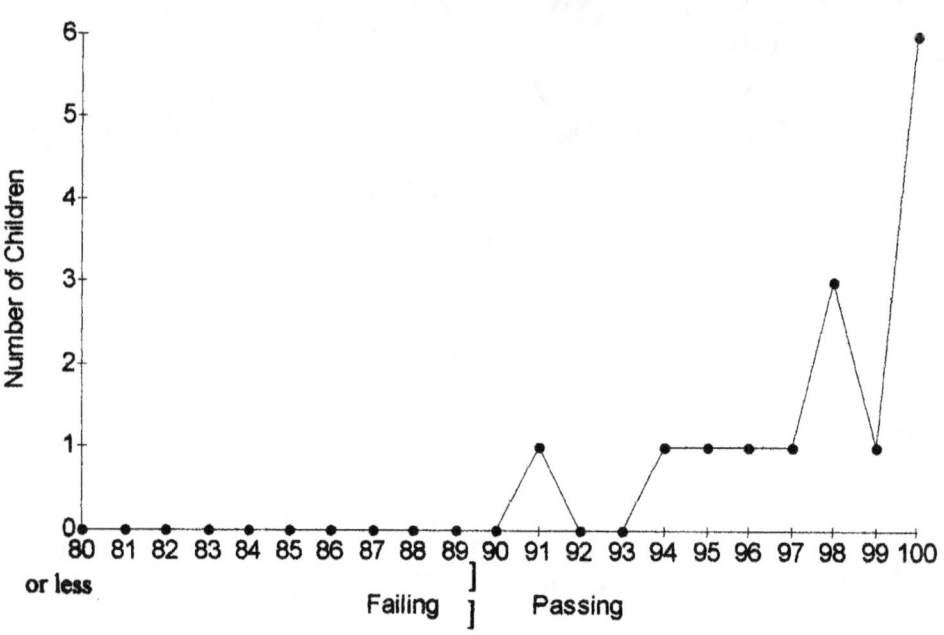

Stockholm 3 - Code 9, Text: Nu Laser, Tested All 9 in Afternoon Session (Total Class Was 19), November, 1977

Oral Accuracy Per Cent	Number of Pupils Obtaining Score	
100	4	Pupils Scoring
99	2	95 or Better
98	1	7 of 8 included, or 88%
84	1	
72	1*	

*Omitted from both accuracy and comprehension scores this brain-damaged boy who was "mainstreamed." Such children are not in the other classes tested.

Comprehension of Last Four Questions

Per Cent Correct	Number of Pupils Obtaining Score	
100	2	Pupils Scoring
75	3	75 or Better
		5 of 7 included or 71%
50	1	
Incomplete	1 (This new immigrant child spoke no Swedish but read it with 100% accuracy. She and the brain-damaged child are not included in the "comprehension" scores.)	

Rate: 1 of 8 included slow, or 13% slow.
      5 of 8 included fast, or 63% fast..

Reversals: None.

Retentions: One brain-damaged boy held back one year.

Stockholm 3 - Code 9, Text: Nu Laser, Tested All 9 in Afternoon Session (Total Class Was 19), November, 1977

Individual Scores in Order Tested

Accuracy/Comprehension

- 100-75   Fast
- 99-75   Fast
- 100-50   Fast
- 98-75
- 100-100
- 99-100 Fast
- 100-25 African Black girl new to Sweden from another European country. Did not speak Swedish.
- 72-Incomplete. Did only example 1. Very, very slow reader. Had been diagnosed as brain-damaged. School policy is to include such children in classes wherever possible. He received individual tutoring also from a supplemental teacher. Had unusual behavior. Refused seat offered. Drooled, and sucked on fingers. Had already repeated one year.
- 84-Incomplete. Did only examples 1 and 2. Very slow. Received supplemental teaching help.

These last two children returned from working with supplemental teachers just as I finished testing the others.

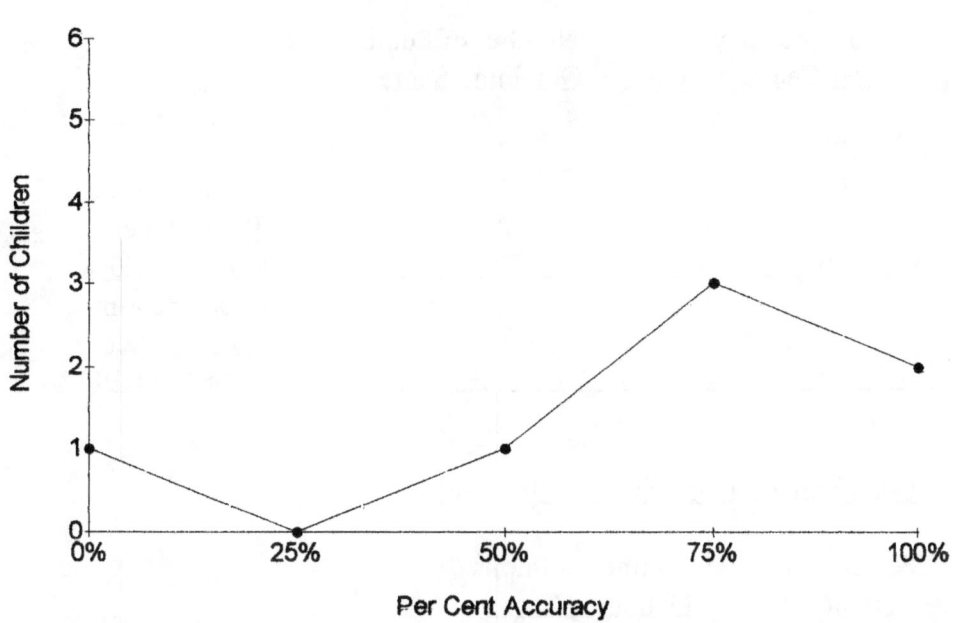

Stockholm 3, Code 9
Reading Comprehension

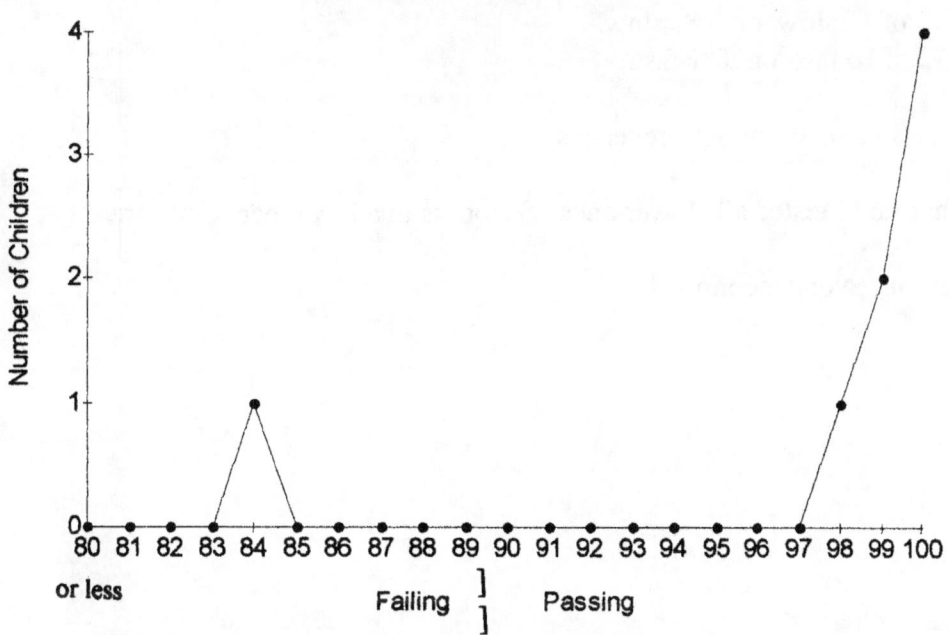

Stockholm 3, Code 9
% Oral Reading Accuracy

Stockholm 4 - Code 6, Text: LTG Plus Nu Laser - Tested P.M. Half of Class, 10 Pupils, November, 1977

Oral Accuracy Per Cent	Number of Pupils Obtaining Score	
100	3	
99	2	Pupils Scoring
98	2	95 or Better
96	1	8 of 10 or 80%
92	2	Pupils Scoring
		90 or Better
		10 or 10 or 100%

Comprehension of Last Four Questions

Per Cent Correct	Number of Pupils Obtaining Score	
100	6	Pupils Scoring
75	2	75 or Better
		8 of 10 or 80%
50	2	

Rate: 3 of 10 slow, or 30% slow.
2 of 10 fast, or 20% fast..

Reversals: 3 of 10, or 30% reversals.

Teacher said I tested all slower ones. School is in a lower economic area.

Retentions: None mentioned.

Stockholm 4 - Code 6, Text: LTG Plus Nu Laser -
Tested P.M. Half of Class, 10 Pupils, November, 1977

Individual Scores in Order Tested

Accuracy/Comprehension

100-50
99-100
100-100 Fast. Chinese.
98-50
92-100. Very slow. Possible reversal: fargen~flecken, fanga~franga. Little phonic sense. Nu~du. For "bakbenen," said "cawk" and stopped. Read multisyllable word like "uppkallades" at same speed as short words, but had trouble in the second syllable of "berattelsen."
100-100 Fast
98-100
99-100 Good rate.
92-75 Very slow. Reversal: den~ben.
96-75 Slow. Reversal: boll~blau

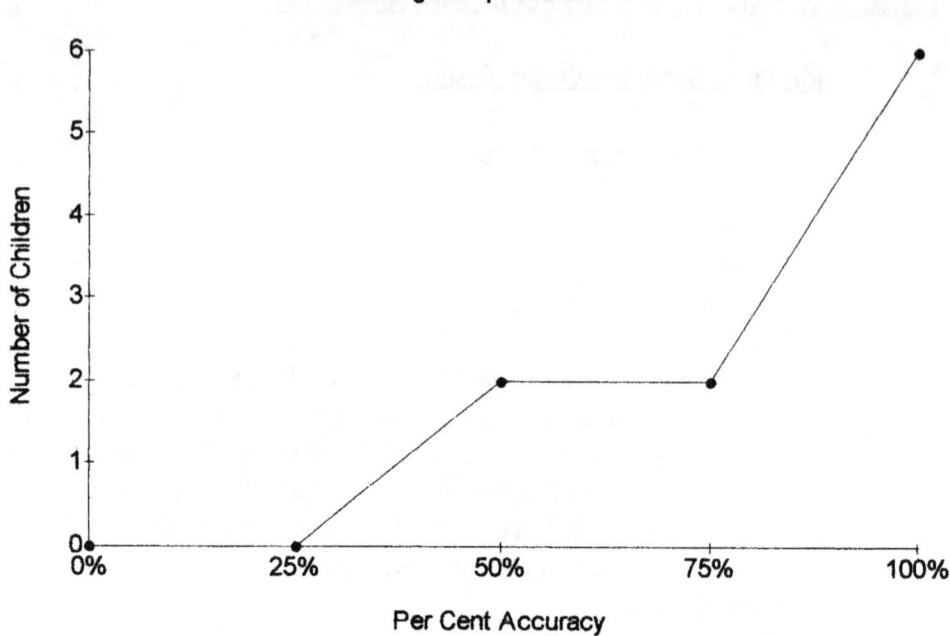

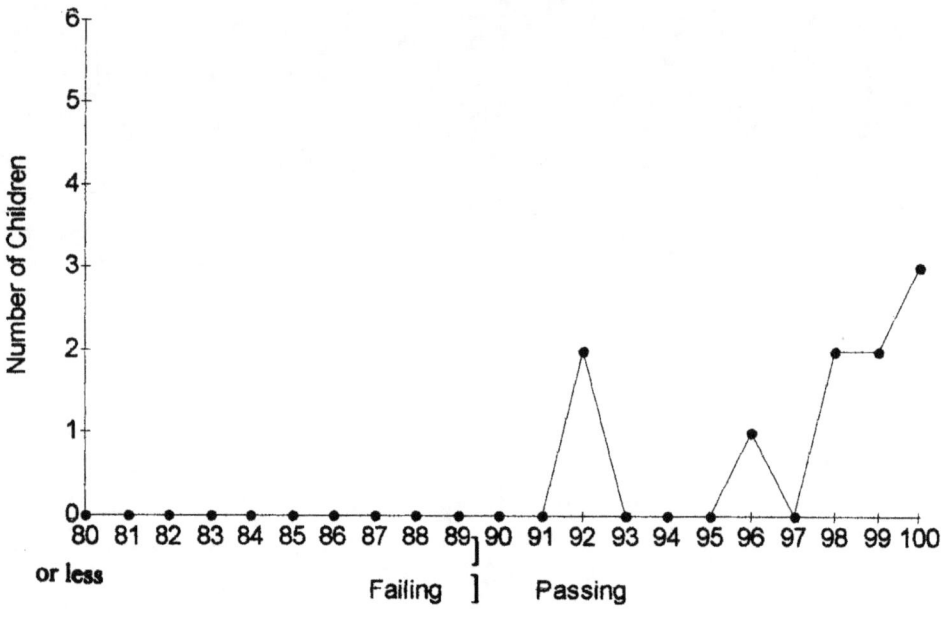

Stockholm 5 - Code 6, Text: LTG Plus Nu Laser - Tested 21 Pupils, Whole Class, November, 1977

Oral Accuracy Per Cent	Number of Pupils Obtaining Score	
100	7	
99	1	Pupils Scoring
98	3	95 or Better
96	3	14 of 21 or 67%
94	1	Pupils Scoring
92	1	90 or Better
91	2	18 of 21 or 86%
86	1	
85	1	
64	1	

Comprehension of Last Four Questions

Per Cent Correct	Number of Pupils Obtaining Score	
100	10	Pupils Scoring
75	3	75 or Better
		13 of 21 or 62%
50	1	
25	2	
0	5	

Rate: 8 of 21 slow, or 38% slow.
     4 of 21 fast, or 19% fast..

Reversals: 8 of 21, or 38% reversals.

Retentions: None mentioned.

Stockholm 5 - Code 6, Text: LTG Plus Nu Laser -
Tested 21 Pupils, Whole Class, November, 1977

Individual Scores in Order Tested

Accuracy/Comprehension

94-75   Very, very slow. Reversals: 3 d's for b's.
98-0
98-100 Slow. Syllable reversal in "hu<u>vud</u>sakligen,"
         "daf" for "vud."
91-0   Very, very slow. Reversals: 4 d's for b's.
96-100 Fairly fast.
64-25   Very slow. Reversals: 5 d's for b's. No physical
         problems, so far as teacher knows.
100-100
100-100
100-75
98-100
91-100 Very slow. Word-by-word agonizing
         sounding-out. Reversals: 4 d's for b's.
96-0   Fairly fast
100-75 Fast
99-100
100-100 Fast
96-50   East Indian or Oriental.
100-100 Fast
100-25 Fast
92-0   Very slow. Word-by-word. Reversals: 3 d's for
         b's. Agonizing sounding-out.
85-Incomplete to word 27. Very slow. Agonizing
         sounding-out. Reversals: b for d.
86-100 Incomplete, through item number 4. Reversals: 2
         d's for b's. Very slow. Word-by-word.
         Agonizing sounding-out, letter by letter. It took
         seconds to say each word.

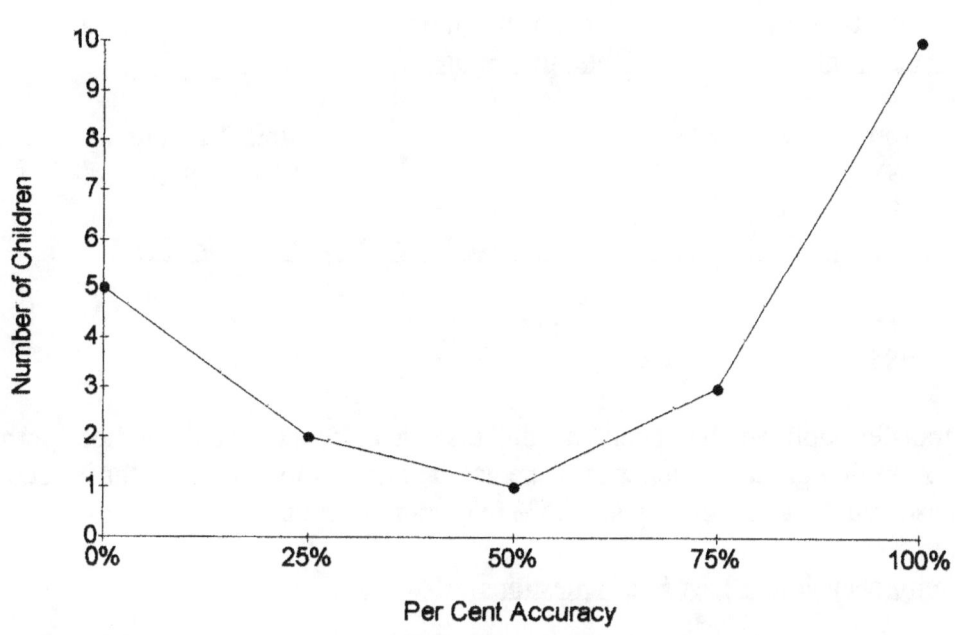

Stockholm 5, Code 6
Reading Comprehension

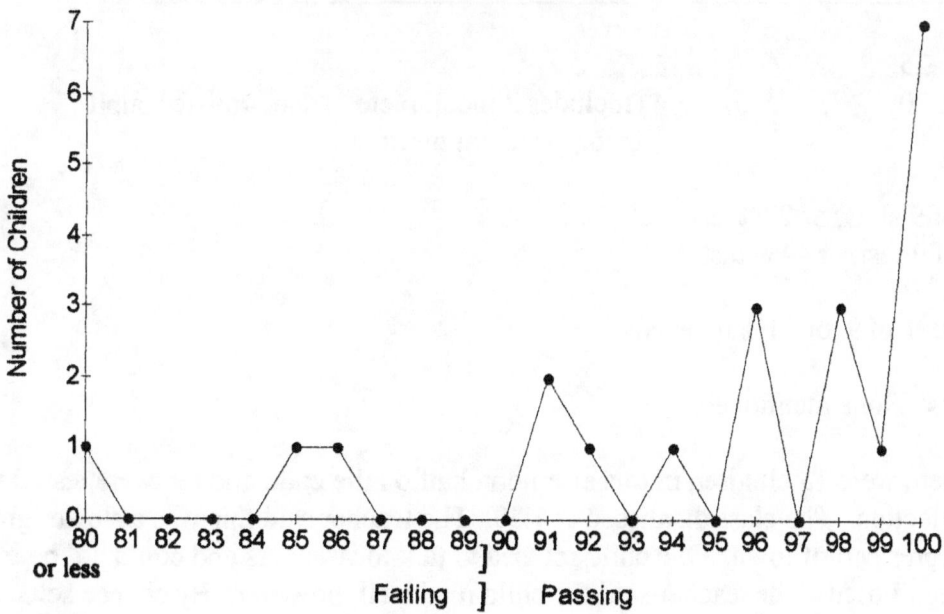

Stockholm 5, Code 6
% Oral Reading Accuracy

Hamburg 1 - Code 10, Text: Bunte Welt - 10 Pupils of 15 Tested, November, 1977

Oral Accuracy Per Cent	Number of Pupils Obtaining Score	
100	1	Pupils Scoring
99	3	95 or Better
98	2	
97	1	7 or 9 or 78%
86	1	
85	1	

Omitted transfer pupil who had been "taught" elsewhere by the global method (perhaps Code 1 to 3) in first grade. Teacher said she had taught him to read this year in second grade. He scored 75% in accuracy and 25% in comprehension.

Comprehension of Last Four Questions

Per Cent Correct	Number of Pupils Obtaining Score	
		Pupils Scoring
100	3	75 or Better
75	1	4 of 9 or 44%
25	1	
0	4 (Includes 2 incomplete. Also, transfer pupil incomplete but omitted.)	

Rate: 2 of 9 slow, or 22% slow.
4 of 9 fast, or 44% fast.

Reversals: 1 of 9, or 11% reversals.

Retentions: None mentioned..

Note: There were 15 children in this afternoon half o Fthe class and ten were tested by chance selection. The class dismissed at 1:20. The teacher said this was a slower group from a poorer part of town. One child refused to talk to strangers and could not be tested even though I tried. The teacher said the child read well, however. By chance selection, four others were not tested bcause of lack of time

Hamburg 1 - Code 10, Text: Bunte Welt - 10 Pupils of 15 Tested, November, 1977

Tested 10 of 15 afternoon pupils. One was omitted from the total because he was a new pupil and failing.

Individual Scores in Order Tested

Accuracy/Comprehension

99-25   Good rate
100-0   Fast
75-Incomplete. Slow. Reversal: braun~draun. (Omit - transfer pupil.)
85-Incomplete. Very slow. Reversal: Fleck~felck.
98-100   Fast
98-100   Fast
99-100   Fast
86-Incomplete. Slow.
99-0.
97-75

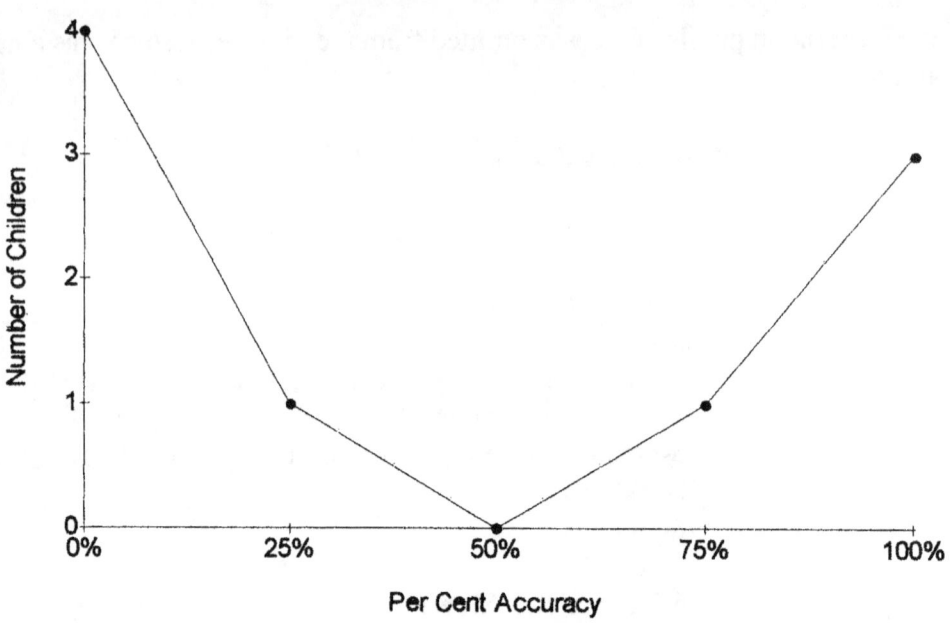

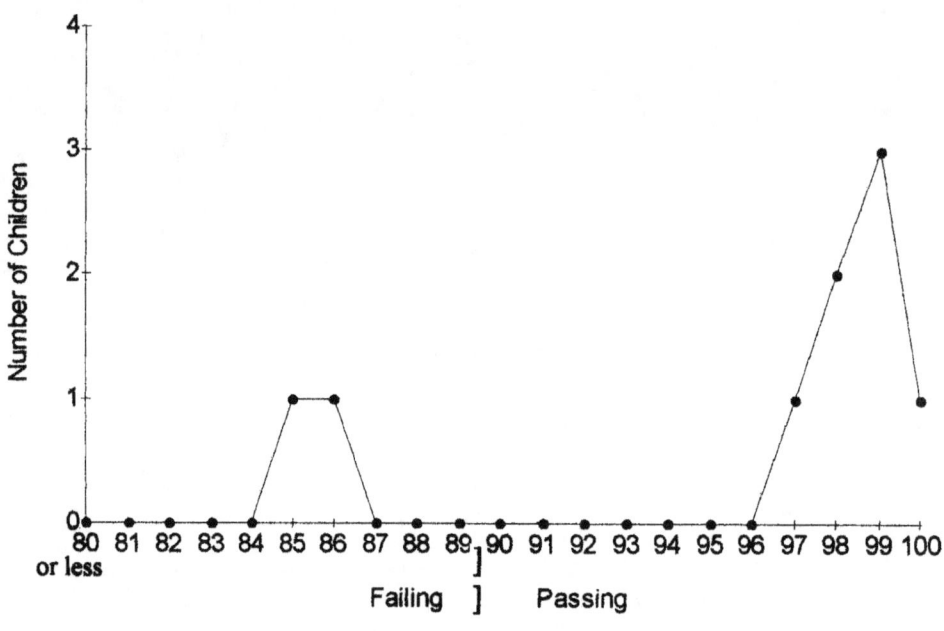

Hamburg 2 - Code 10, Text: Bunte Welt - 14 of 16 Children Present Tested, November, 1977

Oral Accuracy Per Cent	Number of Pupils Obtaining Score	
100	3	
99	1	
98	6*	Pupils Scoring
97	1	95 or Better
96	2	13 or 14 or 93%
91	1	Pupils Scoring 90 or Better 14 of 14 or 100%

*One incomplete. Read 2/5 because of lack of time.

Comprehension of Last Four Questions

Per Cent Correct	Number of Pupils Obtaining Score	
100	6*	Pupils Scoring
75	1	75 or Better 7 of 14 or 50%
50	2	
25	2	
0	3	

One incomplete. Read 2/5 because of lack of time.

Notes: 14 of 16 children in this afternoon half of the class were chosen by chance selection. All these children read at a good rate - no dragging except on occasional long words. This was a poor residential neighborhood.

Rate: None slow.
    4 of 14 fast, or 29% fast.

Reversals: 1 of 14, or 7% reversals.

Retentions: None mentioned..

Hamburg 2 - Code 10, Text: Bunte Welt - 14 of 16 Children Present Tested, November, 1977

Individual Scores in Order Tested

Accuracy/Comprehension

*100-75   Fast
*97-100   Fast
*98-50   Fast
*98-0
*91-0   Added "en" to many words, to the amusement of the Rector and myself. Without these, the score would be 98%.
*96-100
100-0
99-50
98-25
98-100   Appeared to be Indian or Pakistani. Reversals: bekam~dekam, twice.
100-25   Fast. Appeared to be foreign.
98-100
96-100
98-100   Read only 2/5. No time.

*Woman Rector observed as these first children were tested.

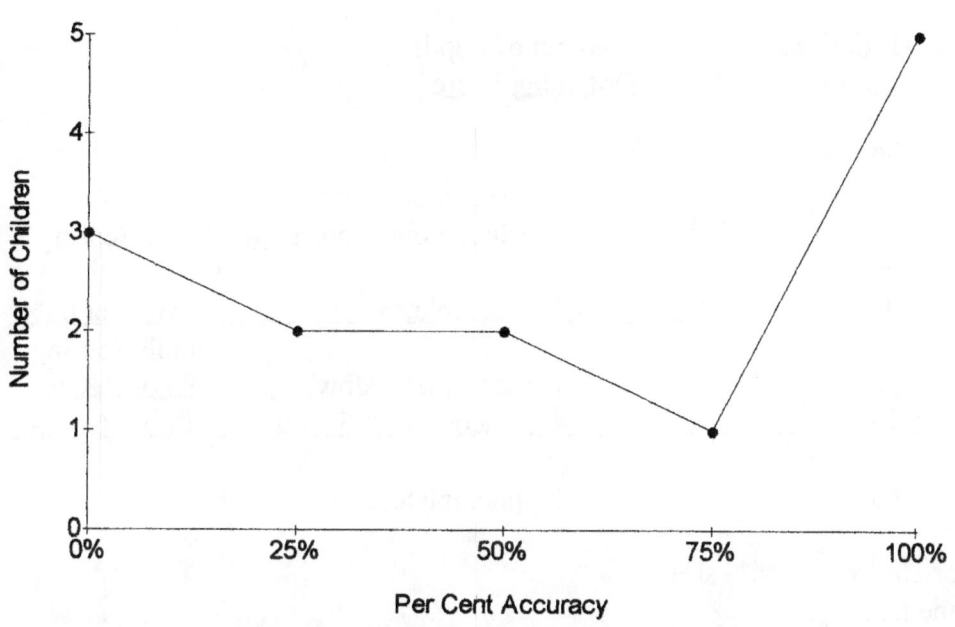

Hamburg 2, Code 10
Reading Comprehension

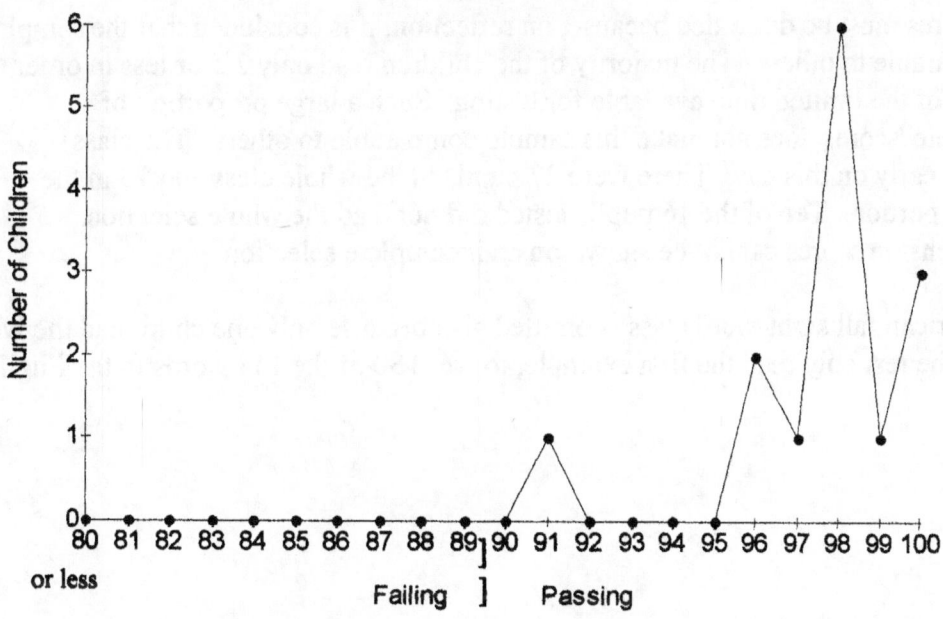

Hamburg 2, Code 10
% Oral Reading Accuracy

Hamburg 3 - Code 10, Text: Bunte Welt - 16 of 27 in Class Tested, November, 1977

Oral Accuracy Per Cent	Number of Pupils Obtaining Score	
99	1	
98	4 (2 incomplete, one slow)	
97	3 (3 incomplete, one slow)	Pupils Scoring
96	1	95 or Better
95	1 (Incomplete)	10 of 16 or 63%
		Pupils Scoring
93	1 (Incomplete, slow)	90 or Better
90	4 (2 incomplete, 3 slow)	15 of 16 or 94%
60	1 (Incomplete, slow)	

Rate: 7 of 16 slow, or 44% slow.
   None fast.

Reversals: 5 of 16, or 31% reversals.

Retentions: None mentioned..

These scores must be discarded because, on reflection, it is concluded that the sample is not comparable to others. The majority of the children read only 2/5 or less in order to make use of the limited time available for testing. Such a large proportion of "incomplete" scores does not make this sample comparable to others. The class dismissed early on this day. There were 27 pupils in the whole class and 13 in the afternoon portion. Ten of the 16 pupils tested did not read the whole selection. Comprehension scores cannot be shown on an incomplete selection.

One American fall sight-word class is omitted also because only one child read the whole test, and the rest only read the first example, to word 30 of the 144 words in the English form.

Hamburg 3 - Code 10, Text: Bunte Welt - 16 of 27 in Class Tested, November, 1977

Concerning the five comprehension questions, after the child read the first example and its three possible answers, the tester demonstrated to each child how to choose the correct answer from the three choices given. That was to ensure that the child understood what he was expected to do on the remaining four questions. Therefore, the European scores are computed on only four of the five questions, not on all five, as was done for American children who are very familiar with this kind of "reading comprehension" exercise and who do not need such a demonstration.

Individual Scores in Order Tested

Accuracy/Comprehension

90-0   Very slow
90-Incomplete to word 59. Very, very slow.
       Reversals: braun~draun, bekam~dekam
98-100
97-Incomplete to word 59. Very slow.
       Reversal: Jetzt~yet is.
97-Incomplete to word 89. Good speed. Had to leave.
       Missed two comprehension questions asked.
       Reversal: bekam~de-k (stopped)
99-100
90-25   Very slow. Reversals: Fleck~felck, Fall~fla
98-75
97-Incomplete to word 89. Missed two comprehension
       questions asked.
95-Incomplete to word 89. Missed two comprehension
       questions asked.
96-75
93-Incomplete to word 28. Slow. Reversal: braun~draun.
98-Incomplete to word 89. Missed one of two
       comprehension questions asked.
98-Incomplete to word 59. Slow, halting, word by word.
       Missed one comprehension question asked.
90-Incomplete to word 59. No time.
60-Incomplete to word 25.

10 of 16 tests were "incomplete."

Innsbruck - Code 10, Text: Kommt, Wir Wollen Lesen und Schreiben - 28 in Class, All Tested, November, 1977

Oral Accuracy Per Cent	Number of Pupils Obtaining Score	
100	2	
99	4	
98	6	
97	5	Pupils Scoring
96	7*	95 or Better
95	2	26 of 28 or 93%
		Pupils Scoring
93	2	90 or Better
		28 of 28 or 100%

*Two of the seven took only part of the test because time ran out.

Comprehension of Last Four Questions

Per Cent Correct	Number of Pupils Obtaining Score	
		Pupils Scoring
100	4	75 or Better
75	7	11 of 26 or 42%
50	7	
25	7	
0	1	
Incomplete	2 (not enough time)	

This class dismissed at 11:00 a. m. this day, so there was no time to complete testing on all children, despite the remarkably rapid rate at which they read: 13 of 28, or 46%, read either fast, very fast, or very, very fast. Only one read slowly (4%) but tested at 96% accuracy. The teacher considered this to be an average income neighborhood.

Rate: 1 of 28 slow, or 4%.
      13 of 28 fast, or 46% fast.

Reversals: 1 of 28, or 4% reversals.

Retentions: None mentioned..

Innsbruck - Code 10, Text: Kommt, Wir Wollen Lesen und Schreiben - 28 in Class, All Tested, November, 1977

Individual Scores in Order Tested

Accuracy/Comprehension

100-50 Fast
97-25 Fairly fast
93-25 Average
93-100 Very fast
96-50 Good rate
97-25 Fast
100-25 Good rate
95-75 Reversal: Fleck~felck
97-100 Good rate.
98-75 Good rate
97-50 Fast
96-25 Good rate
95-75 Good rate
99-100 Fast
98-75 Fast
98-50 Fast
96-50 Very fast
99-75 Fast
96-50 Fast
96-25 Slow
99-100 Very fast
98-75 Very fast
98-50 Very, very fast
98-75
99-25 Satisfactory
97-0 (First 3 questions only)
96-Incomplete (One question - no time)
96-Incomplete (One question - no time

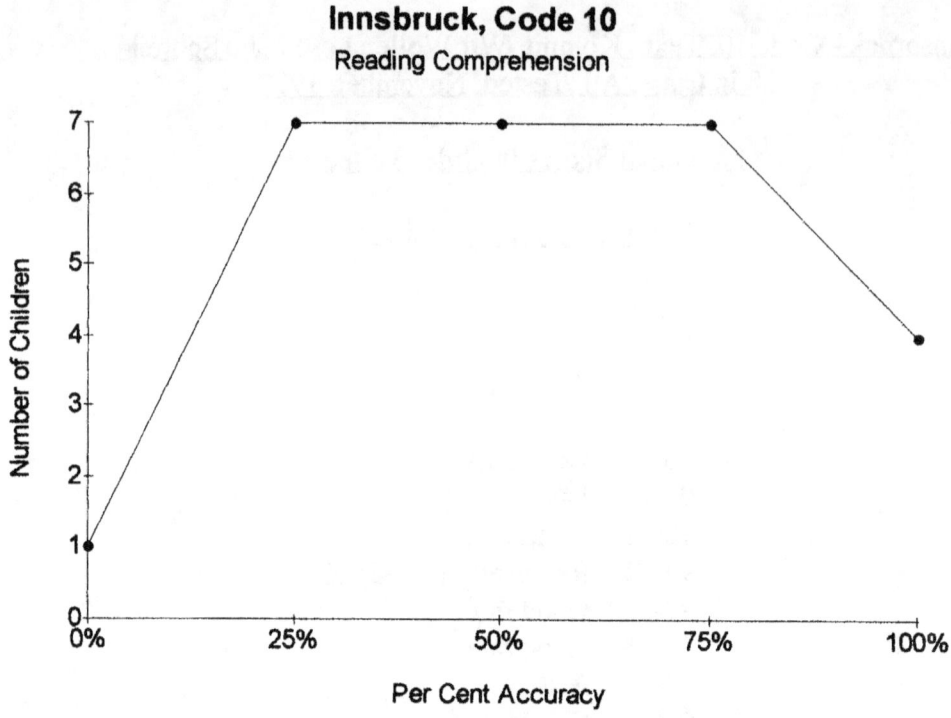

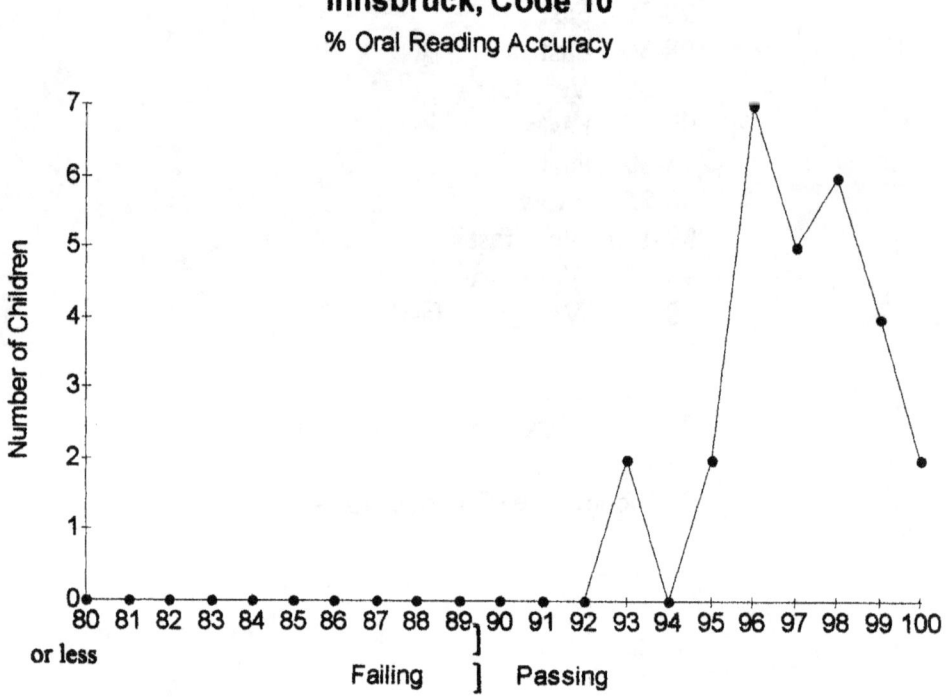

<u>Paris - Code 8, Text: Experience Charts to Teach Phonics Heavily -
28 in Approximate Bottom 2/3 of Grade, All Tested, November, 1977</u>

Oral Accuracy Per Cent	Number of Pupils Obtaining Score	
100	6	
99	7	
98	3	Pupils Scoring
97	2	<u>95 or Better</u>
96	1	22 of 28 = 79%, or
95	3	36 of 42 = 86%, if adjusted*
		Pupils Scoring
		<u>90 or Better</u>
93	2	25 of 28 = 89%, or
91	1	29 of 42 = 93% if adjusted*.
86	1	
80	2	

*If adjusted to include the top pupils (presumably about 1/3 of the total second-grade age group) who were in the vertically-grouped first and second grade class. Those top pupils were not tested because of lack of time. See the next sheet for the figures supporting this adjustment.

<u>Comprehension of Last Four Questions</u>

Per Cent Correct	Number of Pupils Obtaining Score	
		Pupils Scoring
100	2	<u>75 or Better</u>
75	6	8 of 27, or 29%**
50	8	
25	2	
0 and Incomplete Fail	9	
Incomplete	1	(because not enough time)

**This score is for the approximate bottom 2/3 of the second-grade level only.

Rate: 5 of 28 slow, or 18% slow for approximate bottom 2/3 of grade..
     5 of 28 fast, or 18% fast for approximate bottom 2/3 of grade.

Reversals: 3 of 28, or 11% reversals for approximate bottom 2/3 of grade.

Retentions: None mentioned..

Paris - Code 8, Text: Experience Charts to Teach Phonics Heavily - 28 in Approximate Bottom 2/3 of Grade, All Tested, November, 1977

Individual Scores in Order Tested

Accuracy/Comprehension

99-50   Fair rate
91-25   Fair rate. Reversal: nomme~monne.
97-50   Good rate.
100-25 Fast
98-0   Very fast
95-100 OK rate, no pauses.
97-50   Fair rate, even
99-75   Good rate, fast
95-50   Good rate, fairly slow, even.
99-75   Good rate
100-50
100-100 Good rate
100-0   Good rate
93-0   Good rate
99-50   Fast
93-75   Slower, but even rate.
80-Incomplete. Very slow, syllable by syllable. Reversal: dos~bo.
100-75 Fast
99-75
99-25   Fair rate, even
96-75   Fair rate, slow on a few words.
99-0
100-0   Good rate
86-Incomplete. Very slow.
98-Incomplete. Too slow.
98-50   Good rate
80-Incomplete. Count as slow.
95-Incomplete, because of no time. Reversal: tache~chat

Note: This school had the top second-grade pupils in a vertically-grouped first and second grade class, which time did not permit testing. The logical assumption must be made that this top portion would account for perhaps 1/3 of the total second grade (or 14 pupils) and that these top 14 pupils would have passed at 95%, since 79% of the bottom 2/3 did pass at that level. The accuracy of such an adjusted score is confirmed by the fact that it is very close to the other French Code 8 scores, though on the low side. However, the probability is that there were more than 14 second grades in the vertically grouped class, and relatively fewer first graders. That would raise the score to conform to the other French Code 8 scores.

Some Code 8 scores were later given to classes in France using experience-charts-with-heavy-phonics plus the Remi et Colette partially global series (which series was probably a French-government standard). The extraordinarily competent first-grade teacher whom I observed in this Parisian school on Tuesday morning was teaching heavy phonics with experience charts, but I saw no sign of the Remi et Colette reader. However, since I sometimes saw that reader elsewhere in French schools in use along with the experience-chart-with-heavy-phonics approach, it is possible that reader plus the phonic experience charts had been used at first grade with these Parisian second-graders. Unfortunately, there was no time available to check this background with the school principal (who had also been very courteous and helpful when I met her earlier in the day) because the school day was over by the time I finished my testing on Tuesday afternoon, and the school was to be closed the following day, which was to be my last day in Paris.

My allotted three days to test in Parisian schools (Monday, Tuesday and Wednesday) had been badly disrupted because of a very discourteous official in the Parisian central office. I had been assured by mail that I would have no problem testing in Parisian schools and had only to call the official (whose name was on my confirming letter) upon my arrival for the particulars concerning my appointments. After the extraordinary courtesy that had been shown to me in arranging ahead of time such school appointments in Amsterdam, Stockholm, Hamburg, and Innsbruck, I did not anticipate any real difficulty. However, when I called the official about nine a. m. Monday morning, whose name had been on my confirming letter, he was extremely discourteous. He had absolutely no patience with my broken French and just slammed the phone down after about 15 or 30 seconds. Later in the day, after I had gone to the Parisian education office, I did find a very couteous lower-level offiicial who managed to arrange a single appointment for me, apparently on the spur of the moment, for Tuesday, since by then it was too late to do anything on Monday. I had not been told ahead of time that schools are closed on Wednesday in France. Since I had to leave Wednesday night to keep my arranged appointment in Quimper (where I also found the same kind of extraordinary coutesy that I had found elsewhere in Europe and later found in Avignon), it was impossible for me to test the remaining second graders in that Parisian school.

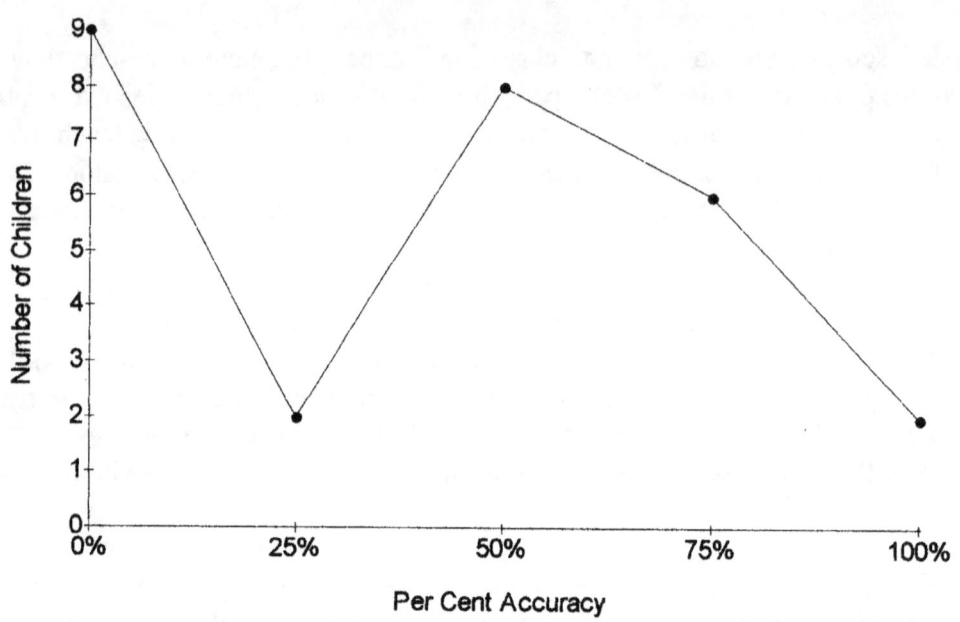

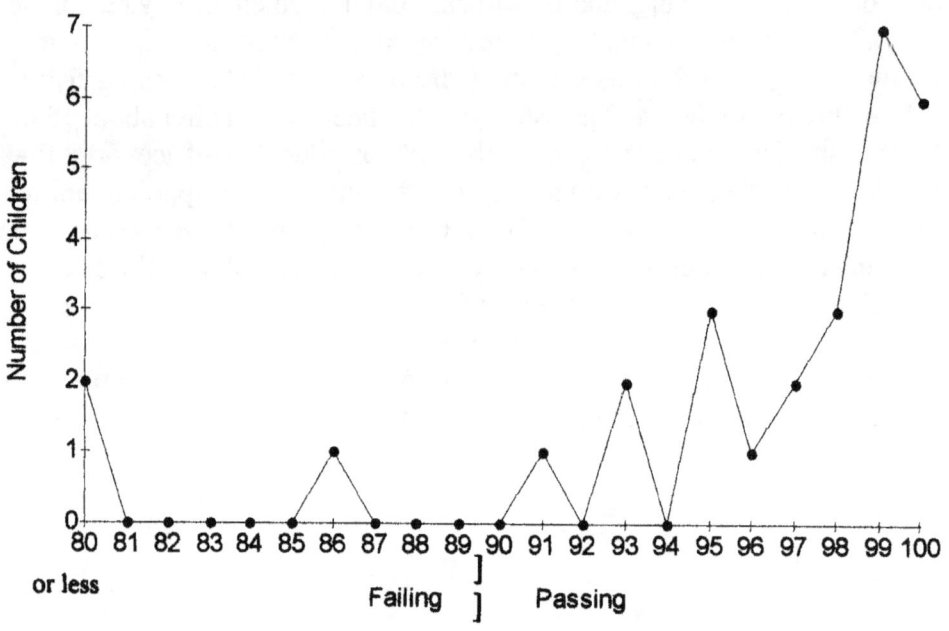

Quimper - Code 8, Text: Pas a Pas Sur Le Chemin a Lire with Experience Charts Teaching Phonic Letter Sounds Very Heavily - 17 Pupils Present, All Tested - November, 1977

Oral Accuracy Per Cent	Number of Pupils Obtaining Score	
100	5	
99	5	
98	3	Pupils Scoring
97	2	95 or Better
95	1	16 or 16 or 100%
62	1 Omit. New to school this year.	

Comprehension of Last Four Questions

Per Cent Correct	Number of Pupils Obtaining Score	
		Pupils Scoring
100	4	75 or Better
75	3	7 of 15 or 47%
50	3	
25	1	
0	5 Omit one new to school.	
Incomplete	1 Omit. New to school this year.	

Rate: 2 of 16 slow, or 13% slow
    None fast.

Reversals: None except in foreign child new to program
Retentions: None mentioned.

Quimper - Code 8, Text: Pas a Pas Sur Le Chemin a Lire with Experience Charts Teaching Phonic Letter Sounds Very Heavily - 17 Pupils Present, All Tested - November, 1977

Individual Scores in Order Tested

Accuracy/Comprehension

99-100
95-75   Good rate
99-0
100-50
100-100
98-0
100-25
99-100 Fairly slow
100-0
100-75
97-75
60-Incomplete. Slow. Excluded score from totals because child was new this year from outside Europe. Black girl. Was told she had difficulty understanding French because of her dialect. Very timid. Possibly could do better if not so shy. Her sister, a year younger, is doing very well in first grade despite the language problem. Reversal: dos~bo. Read only first example.
98-100
97-0   Slow
99-50   Slow
99-0   Good rate. Not in this school last year. Included in accuracy scores only because of high phonic emphasis seen in all French schools. Omitted from comprehension because new child and failing comprehension
98-50   Fairly slow

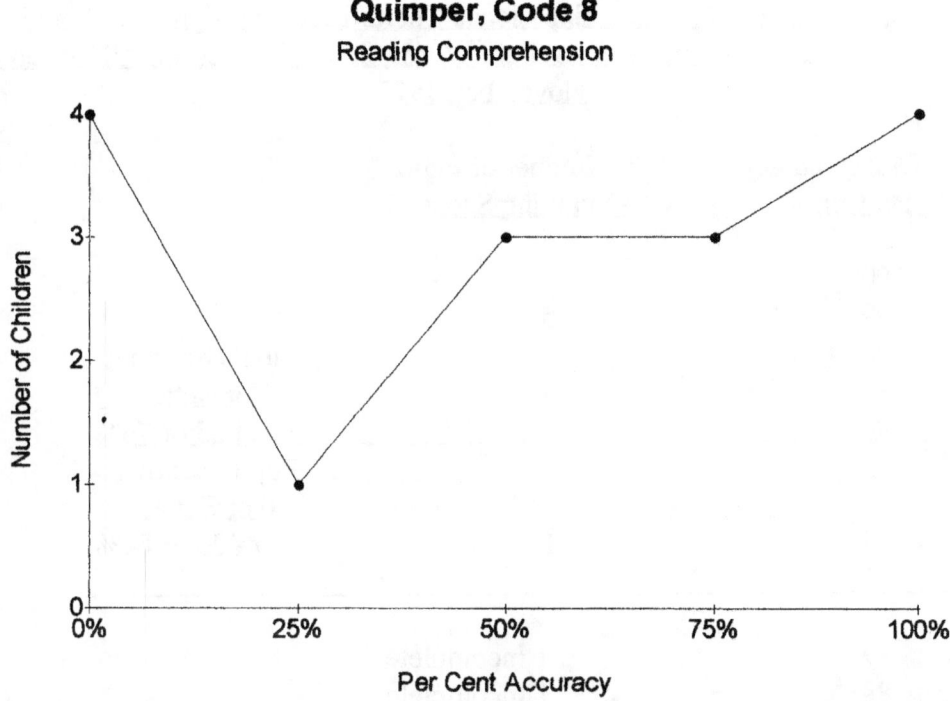

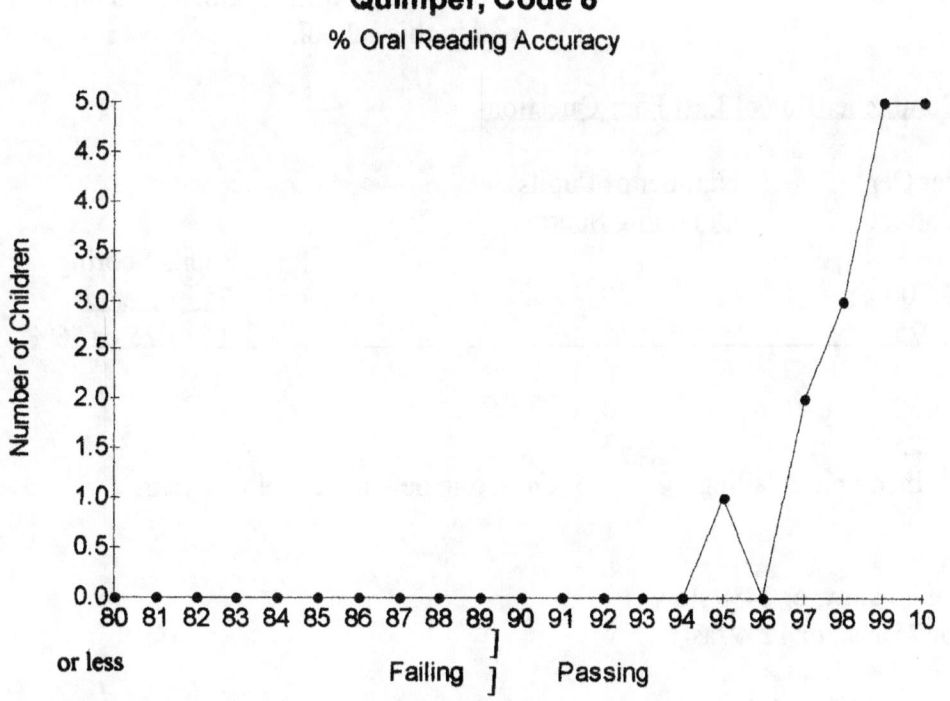

Avignon 1 - Code 6. Text: Experience Charts Teaching Sight Words and Phonics, But With Emphasis on Sight Words. 26 Pupils Present, All Tested - November, 1977

Oral Accuracy Per Cent	Number of Pupils Obtaining Score	
100	7	
99	5	
98	1	Pupils Scoring
97	5	95 or Better
96	1	19 of 25 or 76%
		Pupils Scoring
		90 or Better
94	1	21 of 25 or 84%
93	1	
89	1 Incomplete	
88	1 Incomplete	
87	1 Incomplete	
85	1 Incomplete	
80	1 Incomplete. Omit: Spani;sh, did not learn to read in this school.	

Comprehension of Last Four Questions

Per Cent Correct	Number of Pupils Obtaining Score	
		Pupils Scoring
100	9	75 or Better
75	5	14 of 25 or 56%
50	4	
25	3.	
Incomplete failing.	5 Omit one new to school this year.	

Rate: 6 of 25 slow, or 24% slow
       3 of 25 fast, or 12% fast

Reversals: 1 of 25 or 4%

Retentions: None mentioned.

Avignon 1 - Code 6, Text: Experience Charts Teaching Sight Words and Phonics, But With Emphasis on Sight Words, 26 Pupils Present, All Tested - November, 1977

The director of the school helped me administer most of these tests.

Individual Scores in Order Tested

Accuracy/Comprehension

100-75
100-100
99-50
96-25   Fairly slow.
100-100 Fast
100-75   Fast
99-100   Black girl. Good speed.
98-75.   Fairly slow. Substitution: balle~table.
97-100   Fair
89-Incomplete
94-100
99-50   Fairly slow
87-Incomplete. Slow.
80-Incomplete. Slow. Spanish - did not learn to read in this school Omit.
97-75   Fast. Black girl. Reversal: nomme~monne. Substitution: balle~table.
85-Incomplete. Slow
88-Incomplete.
100-25 Good rate
99-100   Fair
99-100
100-50
97-50   Boy, 4 insertions of "qui."
93-25   Very slow
97-100   Very slow
100-100
97-75   Fairly slow.

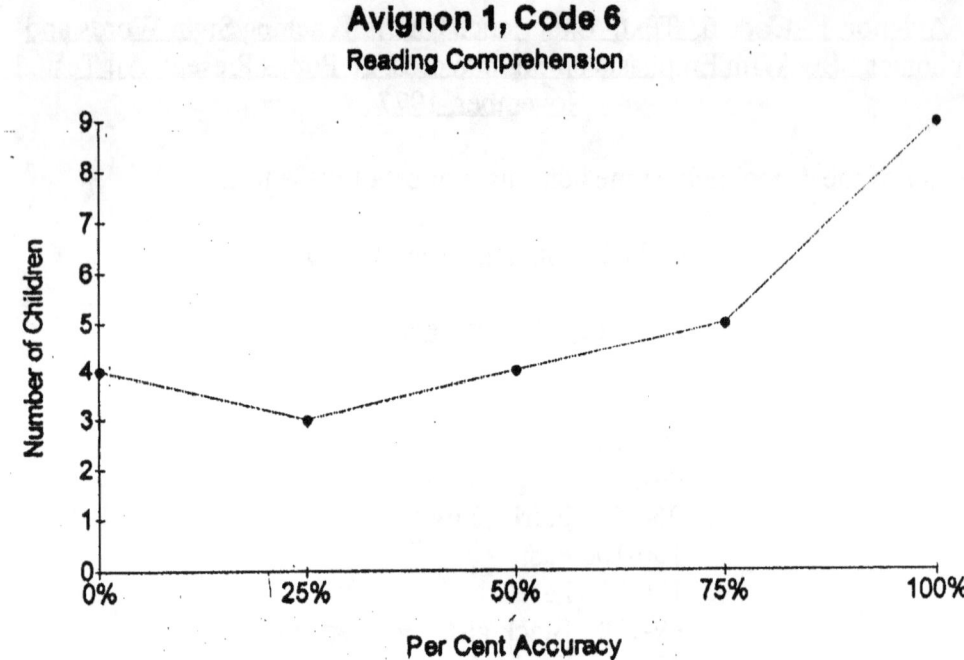

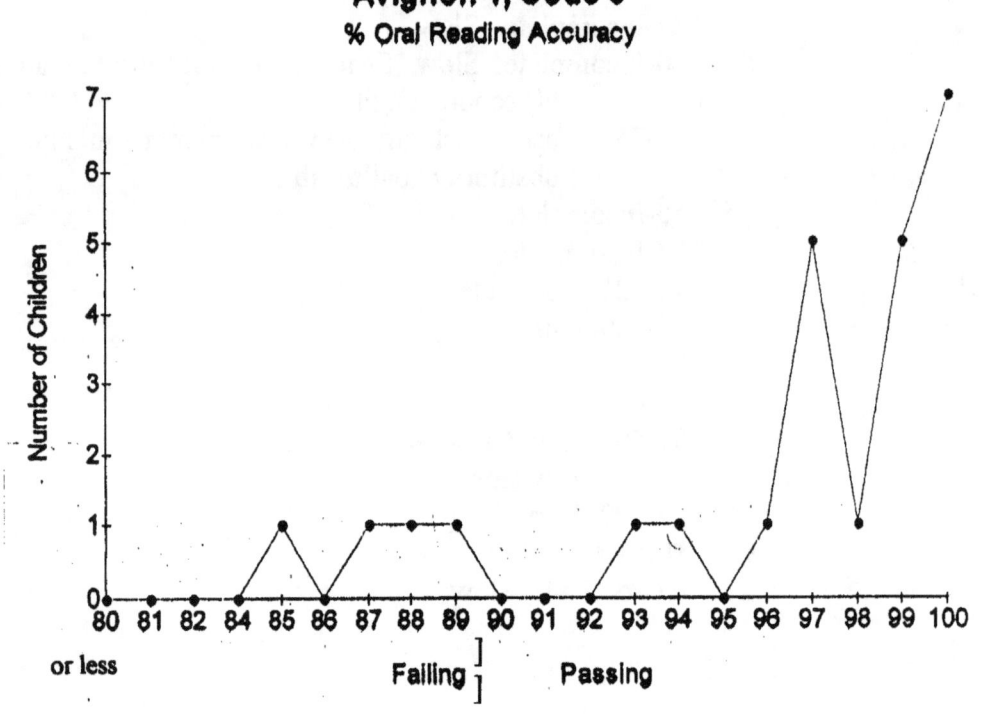

Avignon 2 - Code 8. Text: Experience Charts Teaching Phonics Very Heavily. 23 Pupils Present, All Tested - November, 1977

Oral Accuracy Per Cent	Number of Pupils Obtaining Score	
100	3	
99	9	
97	3	Pupils Scoring
96	1	95 or Better
95	3	19 of 23 or 83%
		Pupils Scoring
		90 or Better
93	2	22 of 23 or 96%
91	1	
87	1	

Comprehension of Last Four Questions

Per Cent Correct	Number of Pupils Obtaining Score	
		Pupils Scoring
100	3	75 or Better
75	4	7 of 23 or 30%
50	3	
25	8.	
0	5	

Rate: 8 of 23 slow, or 35% slow
    None fast

Reversals: 1 of 23 or 4%

Retentions: None mentioned.

Avignon 2 - Code 8, Text: Experience Charts Teaching Phonics Very Heavily, 23 Pupils Present, All Tested - November, 1977

Individual Scores in Order Tested

Accuracy/Comprehension

99-0	Good rate, smooth
100-0	Good rate
99-25	Substitution: balle~table
97-100	
99-75	Good rate
99-0	
93-0	Fairly slow
99-25	Good rate
100-100	Good rate
99-25	Good rate
99-25	
97-25	Slow
96-50	Slow
99-50	Fair rate
99-75	Fair rate
91-100	Reversals: nomme ~ monne, pattes~ tatappe. Slow
100-75	
93-25	Very slow
87-25	Very, very slow
95-0	Very slow
95-25	Very, very slow
95-75	Very slow
95-50	Fairly slow

This teacher said she seated her slower pupils in one area by the window for instructional purposes. This was the only school in which I was told of seating by ability grouping. This can be confirmed by comparing this sample, obviously grouped for the last six children with my scores from elsewhere.

French orthography is every bit as difficult to learn as English. Therefore, it is interesting that, in this BOTTOM Avignon sample of six children in November, 83% passed oral reading accuracy at 90, and 67% were at the 95 level or better, the so-called "instructional" level on American "individual reading inventories." Yet, later in January, American TOTAL CLASS SCORES for the "sight-word" groups (Scott Foresman, and Houghton Mifflin) were only 75% at the 90 level and only 53% at the 95 level, far lower than these "bottom:" French score two months earlier!

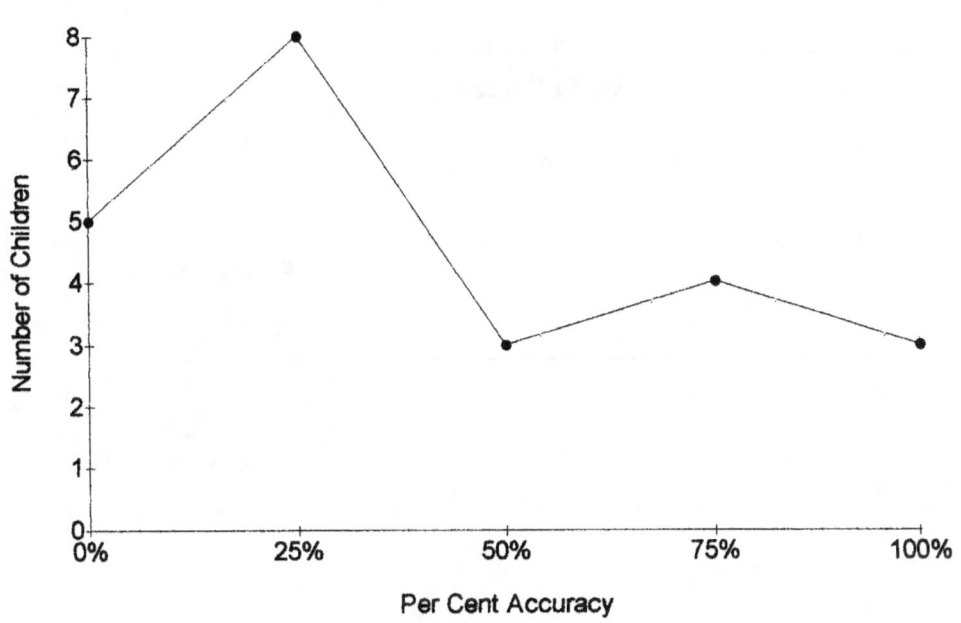

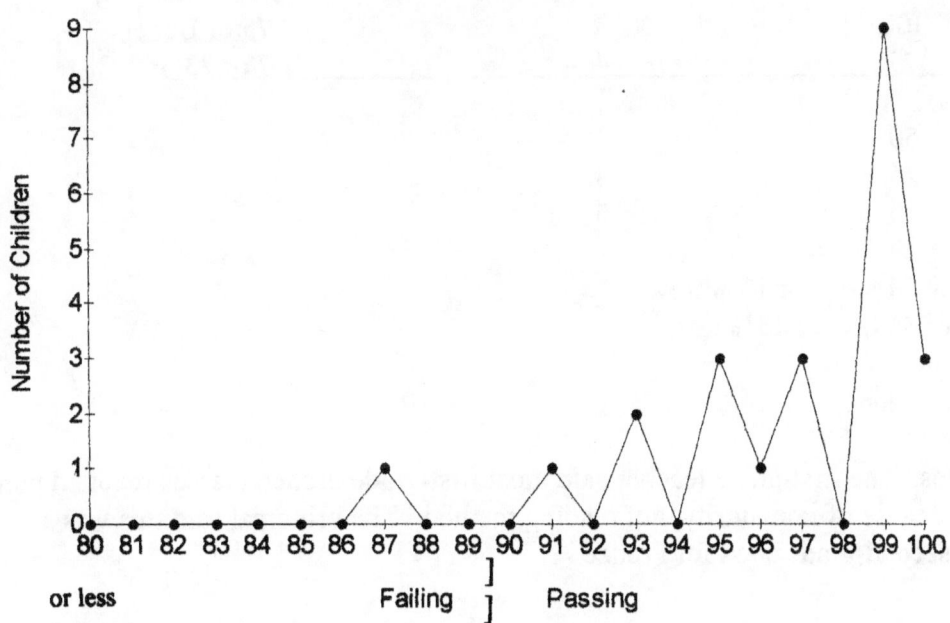

Avignon 3 - Code 7, Text: Remi et Collette, Mixte Method - 31 Pupils Present, Whole Class, All Tested - November, 1977

Oral Accuracy Per Cent	Number of Pupils Obtaining Score	
100	8	
99	9	
98	4	
97	3	Pupils Scoring
96	1	95 or Better
95	3	28 of 31 or 90%
		Pupils Scoring 90 or Better
94	1	30 of 30 or 97%
93	1	
83	1	

Comprehension of Last Four Questions

Per Cent Correct	Number of Pupils Obtaining Score	
		Pupils Scoring
100	3	75 or Better
75	4	7 of 23 or 30%
50	3	
25	8.	
0	5	

Rate: 4 of 31 slow, or 13% slow
4 of 31 fast, or 13% fast

Reversals: None

Retentions: The first-grade teacher said most first-grade French classes retained perhaps 3 of 25 because of immaturity, not reading method. The principal said this was an average second-grade class for France. .

Avignon 3 - Code 7, Text: Remi et Collette, Mixte Method - 31 Pupils Present, Whole Class, All Tested - November, 1977

Individual Scores in Order Tested

Accuracy/Comprehension

98-75	Good rate
100-75	Good rate
99-50	Slow
100-50	
100-75	
97-50	
100-50	
99-25	Fairly slow
94-25	
99-75	
99-25	Fairly slow, OK.
97-0	
100-100	Fair rate.
99-100	Good speed
100-75	Fast
100-100	Fast
95-25	Fairly slow, immature appearance and manner. Does not seem to understand.
96-0	Fairly slow. Does not seem to undestand anything.
93-0	Slow. Appeared dull.
99-25	Good rate
100-75	Fast
98-100	Good rate
98-0	Fair rate, even.
99-50	Fast
99-0	
98-50	Good rate
95-25	Fair rate
97-25	Fair rate
95-0	Very, very slow
99-0	Fair rate
83-0	Very slow. Had him read all, but there was no time to ask him the questions. Halting reading. He was omitted from the class comprehension scores.

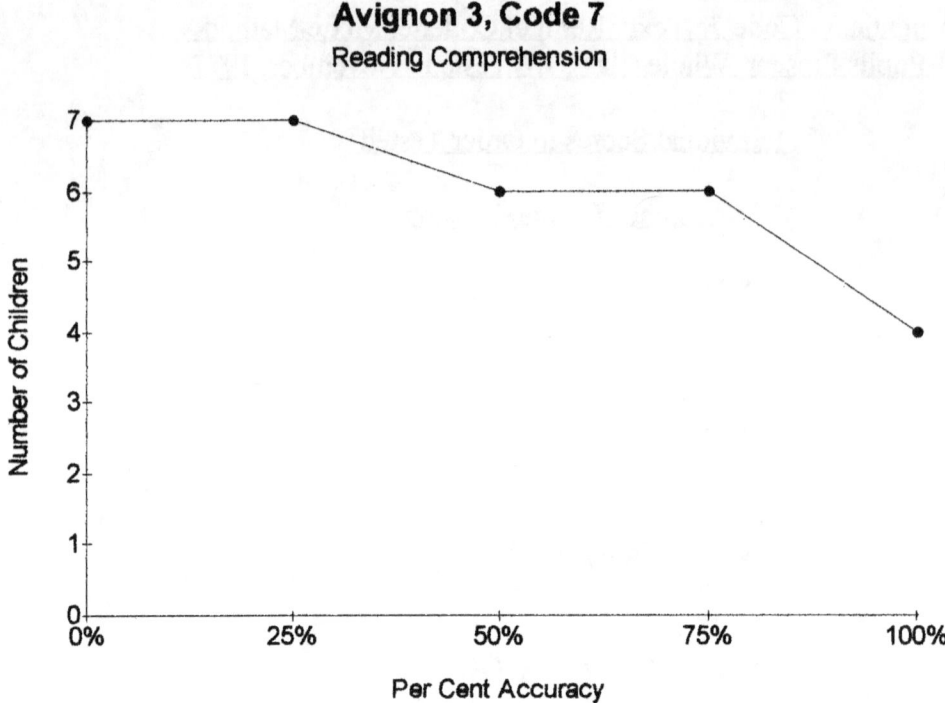

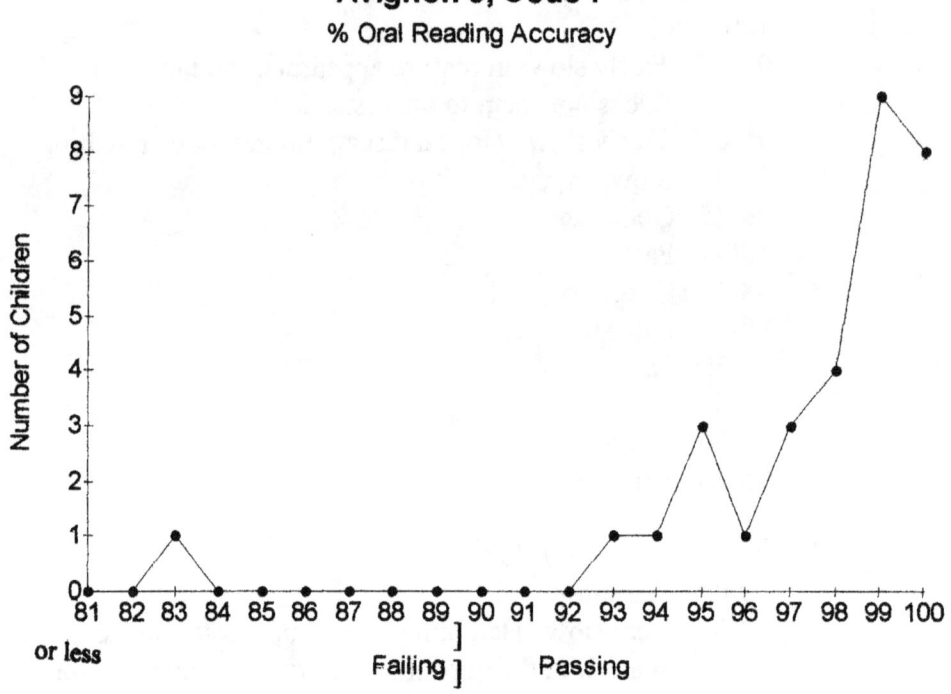

Avignon 4 - Code 9. Text: Experience Charts Teaching Heavy Phonics, With Syllable Emphasis - 27 Children in Class, All Tested - November, 1977

Oral Accuracy Per Cent	Number of Pupils Obtaining Score	
100	8	
99	6	
98	4	Pupils Scoring
97	4	95 or Better
95	1	23 of 27 or 85%
		Pupils Scoring
		90 or Better
93	1	25 of 27 or 93%
91	1	
80	1	
70	1	

Comprehension of Last Four Questions

Per Cent Correct	Number of Pupils Obtaining Score	
		Pupils Scoring
100	2	75 or Better
75	6	8 of 27 or 30%
50	5	
25	6.	
0	8 (One incomplete)	

Rate: 3 of 27 slow, or 11% slow
7 of 27 fast, or 26% fast

Reversals: 1 of 27 or 4%

The teacher considered that the children who scored 70 and 80 "could only read a word here and there." She said she would send me the slow ones first.

Retentions: One mentioned, the girl who scored 80, who had repeated two years.

<u>Avignon 4 - Code 9, Text: Experience Charts Teaching Heavy Phonics,
With Syllable Emphasis - 27 Children in Class, All Tested - November, 1977</u>

<u>Individual Scores in Order Tested</u>

<u>Accuracy/Comprehension</u>

93-0	Very slow	
80-25	Slow. Girl, retained twice.	
91-25		
95-0	Good rate.	
97-25	Good rate	
98-50	Fair rate	
97-25	Fair rate	
97-25	Fair rate	
70-Incomplete. Read 61 words. Boy. Read very, very slowly. Reversal: d'annees~de-na.		
100-100	Fast	
98-75	Good rate	
99-75		
100-50		Common French Errors
100-75	Fast	<u>Observed in Most Programs</u>
98-50		
100-25	Fast	chemin~chien
97-0	Good rate	recu~reku
100-75	Fast	balle~table (a few)
98-0		
99-50	Fast	Most make liaisons
100-75	Fast	correctly. Almost never do they
99-0	Fair rate	read silent consonants. One
99-100	Good rate	did, who read perfectly
100-0	Fast	otherwise but said the "t" in
99-0	Good rate	"est" and "c'est."
99-50	Good rate	
100-75		

In the "slow ones" that this Avignon teacher sent me first, none passed comprehension or read fast. Yet 7 of the 9 (78%) passed the accuracy test, scoring above the "frustration" level at 90 or higher. Also, 5 of the 9 (55%) read at the "instructional level" of 95 or higher. This teacher really knew her second-grade class, as every one one of the remaining 18 not only read above the frustration level (at 90 or above) but read at the "instructional level" of 95 or above. Also, 7 of the remaining 18 read fast (or 39% of the 18), and 8 of the remaining 18 (or 44%) passed comprehension.

Her "slow" second-grade group in November, with 7 of the 9 (78%) scoring above frustration (90 or above) and 5 of 9 (55%) scoring at the "instructional level" of 95 or above, was almost identical but slightly higher than U. S. sight-word classes two months later in January (75% above the "frustrational" level and 53% at the "instructional" level). This is despite the fact that this teacher's "slow" group included two of the three worst readers I tested in France, and two of the six worst readers I tested in Europe (excluding a brain-damaged child and two children who had not learned the language in which I tested them.) If these two highly unrepresentative children are omitted from this Avignon teacher's scores, then 100% of the remaining 7 children in her second-grade "slow" group scored above the frustration level (at 90 or above) and 59% of her "slow" group scored at the "instructional" level (95 or above). That would make her second-grade "slow" group in November superior to ALL of the U. S. second-grade Scott, Foresman and Houghton Mifflin sight-word classes that I tested about two months later, in January.

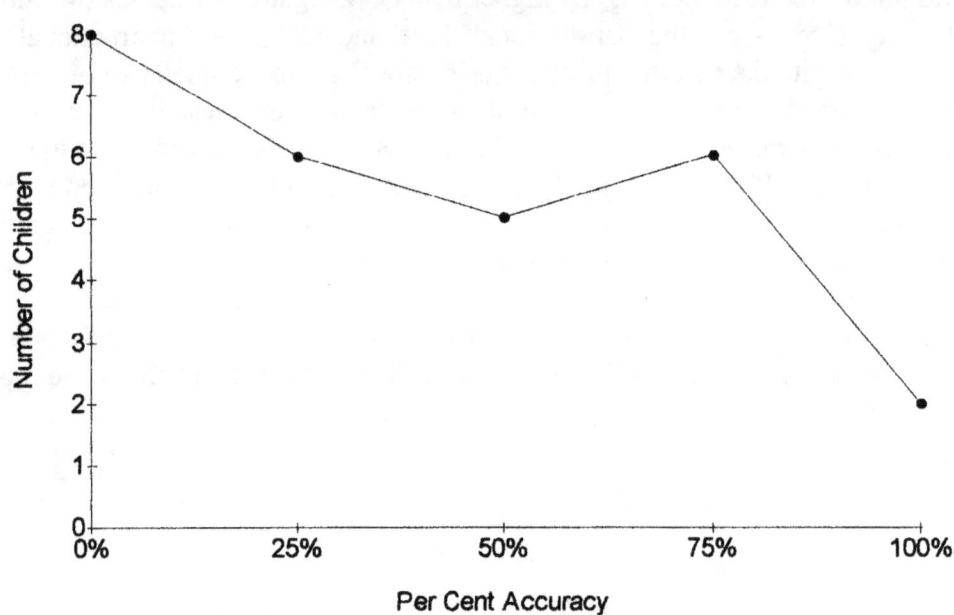

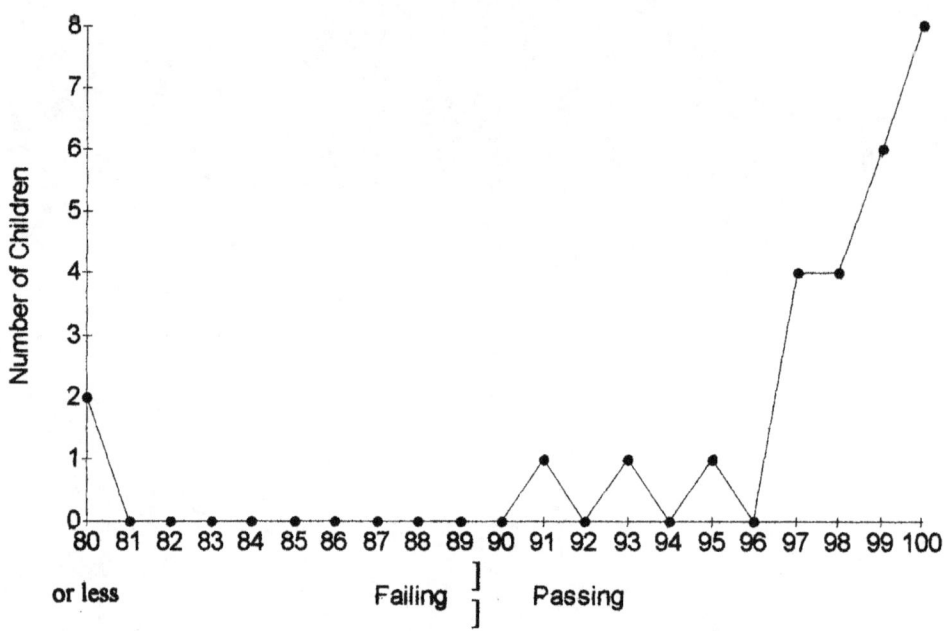